DATE DUE

FEB 1 8 2006		
MAR 0 9 2006		
MAR 2 9 2006		
AUG 2 4 2006		
JAN 2 2007		
JUL 1 7 2007		
APR 0 4 2008		
JAN 0 4 2010		
AUG 8 3 2016		

home
enlightenment

home
enlightenment

practical, earth-friendly advice for creating
a nurturing, healthy, and toxin-free home and lifestyle

annie b. bond

RODALE

Illustrations © by Dara Goldman

Interior design by Joanna Williams

Cover design by Christopher Rhoads

Library of Congress Cataloging-in-Publication Data

Berthold-Bond, Annie.
    Home enlightenment : practical, earth-friendly advice for creating a nurturing, healthy, and toxin-free
home and lifestyle / Annie B. Bond.
        p.   cm.
    Includes index.
    ISBN-13 978–1–57954–811–7 hardcover
    ISBN-10 1–57954–811–3 hardcover
    I. Title.
RA770.5.B475   2005   2005018868
615.9'02—dc22

Distributed to the trade by Holtzbrinck Publishers

2   4   6   8   10   9   7   5   3   1   hardcover

We inspire and enable people to improve their lives and the world around them
For more of our products visit rodalestore.com or call 800-848-4735

To my daughter, Lily.
What a gift!

contents

introduction

The essence of the Navajo worldview is to "walk in beauty," to achieve balance and harmony together with beauty and order. To find healing is to "return to beauty."

Returning to beauty as a way to find healing is an insight offering profound guidance. I see now that to walk in natural beauty is to walk in health. When I really listen to my senses, they clearly tell me what feels life enhancing, and what doesn't. When I really weave into my life the elements Earth, Water, Fire, and Air in their purest, most natural state in balance with each other, I see how much they nourish my whole being and how I thrive.

All you have to do to return to

beauty is to start somewhere. I begin Chapter 1 by saying, "It starts with the little things"—like appreciating marigolds in the sun, moonlight on ocean waves, or tasting wild blackberries warmed in the sun. But I am getting ahead of myself. I need to address where we need to return to beauty from, and why. Most of us do, after all, resonate with moonlight on ocean waves on a balmy summer night.

Today I read in *Scientific American* the article "Doubt Is Their Product," about a 3-decade-long disinformation campaign by industry groups to cast doubt and vilify scientific studies when they implicate their products as being harmful to humans, pets, and the environment. I've known this tactic has been used since 1980 because I became very sick from the same toxic products that industry groups were trying to shield. I had classic organophosphate pesticide poisoning, caused by a pesticide taken off the market years later because it is so neurotoxic. But it wasn't taken off the market early enough for me, and I have permanent central nervous system damage. It is doubly hard to be poisoned and vilified: Central nervous system damage can manifest as depression and lack of concentration—both symptoms of pesticide poisoning and an easy target for "It is all in her head."

I read elsewhere today that members of Congress are shielding MTBE polluters from liability. MTBE, or Methyl Tertiary Butyl Ether, is a gas additive and a suspected carcinogen. It can be toxic to kidneys, liver, skin, and respiratory and gastrointestinal systems and can affect sense organs. A few drops can render entire water supplies and well water undrinkable, and that is when the person is lucky enough to know MTBE is in their water (and can stay away from it).

These two media pieces were just part of a normal, regular day in the news in 2005.

Yesterday I was talking to a friend about writing this introduction, and I said to her that it makes me weep when I see pregnant women having their nails done with toxic finishes when I know the ingredients may cause testicular harm and reproductive damage if the fetus is a boy. Yet I confided that I'm unsure how to find the right voice so people will listen and not feel threatened by the information. My friend said she didn't know about the nail polish problem and would certainly want to inform others, including her daughters.

My self-doubt about speaking the truth as I know it shows that even I have been intimidated by the disinformation campaign by industries, and I also know that people are not fond of the person carrying bad news! I've realized how shy I have become with others as a result of its touchy nature. But what do I do when I see a child sprayed with a neurotoxic pesticide for mosquitoes and then reprimanded later in the day for bad behavior, when hyperactivity is one of the effects of having pesticides applied to the skin? I've watched as our society poisons itself and the planet, and I've seen children become as sick as I was. Children are poisoned out of ignorance by well-meaning parents trying to keep bugs or dirt away, because parents never imagine that the products they bought in the hardware store could harm their children. My grief about the situation is bottomless.

Who wants to believe that the chemical industry and even Congress have become so cynical and driven by greed that they are the enemy of healthy children and families?

The harm of synthetic chemicals on health and the earth is backed up by science. Don't let anybody tell you it isn't true. I am so convinced of the harm done by many synthetic chemicals that I have already written three books on healthier alternatives.

I would love to spread the word far and wide that there is a way to approach every product in the marketplace. It's called the Precautionary Principle, and it means that you should choose products and industries should make products that will cause the least amount of harm. I believe wholeheartedly in this. Products shouldn't be put on the market until they have been proven safe, not the other way around. This is the path of conscious harmlessness.

We've come a long way from the time when I had to make the majority of my household products from scratch since healthy ones didn't exist on the market to fill all my needs. Now there is a healthy alternative for most everything. But we are seeing the terrible harm to children and others from toxics. Just today (again, a normal day) I read in the prestigious magazine *Nature* that mouse breast tissue density grew when exposed to even minute amounts of the plasticizer bisphenol-A. Breast density is a marker for breast cancer. I am far from alone in knowing many who are dying of breast cancer (or the equivalent in men—prostate cancer).

What a heartbreaking rift our industrial society has caused. It's disconnected us from the earth and from the source of our food. We've allowed corporations to turn a blind eye toward their employees' health and welfare. What a terrible price we pay when our world is split between those who intentionally promote harm to babies, fetuses, and the environment through harmful products, and those who are working frantically to stem the terrible tide.

A Call

Heed the call of your truest nature.

Know the call of your senses.
Smell the sweet scent of summer's honeysuckle.
See the newborn foal struggling to stand upright on gangly legs.
Taste the nectar of a tree-ripened peach.
Touch the velvety, bright green moss that grows on forest-shaded rocks.
Hear the wood thrush mark July's dusk.
Intuit how to make others feel welcome in your home.

Know the call of the elements.
Eat food infused with the vibrancy of life, the essence of Earth.
Quench your thirst with Water, clean and fresh.
Warm winter on your face with the Fire of the sun.
Breathe deeply of the rain-cleared Air.
Know that you are one with the planet.

The rifts between the earth, corporations, and each other have to be healed. It is time. All we can do is start somewhere. So, where? A friend of mine offered some insight. He was visiting some friends whose land abutted 60 acres that had been clear-cut. The destruction was awesome and the grief of the land and neighbors palpable at the harm that had been done. My friend said that in the midst of so much grief for the loss of such beauty, he realized that his grief wouldn't do anything but bring more despair, so he walked into the wreckage and slash and found the beauty that was there—in the new tree shoots and in the sun on the horizon. Where there was harm, he found healing by celebrating the beauty that was left.

We have to start somewhere. I can say it starts with the little things such as sleeping under a natural fiber comforter or eating organic food. Returning to beauty holds so many unexpected gifts.

Here I will teach you what I have learned about how to walk in beauty—even in our modern culture. I will show you how to surround yourself with healthier choices. And I'll share with you what wisdom I can about leaving the earth better than you found it. This is a timeless way of living and one that can bring you into harmony with nature. I wish you joy as you discover the wonders of the journey.

Annie B. Bond

Annie B. Bond

the spirit of home

It starts with little things. You bite into an ear of corn grown by an heirloom seed, and a symphony of sweetness and flavor bursts forth in your mouth. The taste is new to you, but you realize it used to be commonplace. While visiting a friend, you sleep in an all-wool, nothing-synthetic bed, and you wake up more fully refreshed and rested than you've felt in months. You switch to nontoxic cleaning products, and your chronic headache disappears.

Bit by bit, the experiences add up, and you realize that you thrive when you are surrounded by nature—natural materials, nature's sounds, and naturally produced food. You *can* have more of this healthy and balanced lifestyle.

We are a society craving the real elements. Real earth. Real water. Real fire. Real air. The real elements bring us

healing, abundance, and vibrant energy. Awareness of the positive impact of the real elements is increasing (even while their use in our society is diminishing), and now decorators and retailers are selling candles, aromatherapy essential oils, rose quartz pendants, and feng shui. Even though the celebration of the elements is creeping into the mainstream consciousness, often synthetic elements, such as petroleum-based candles with synthetic scents, are used, and they are dead substitutes for the real thing.

Our intuition knows nature is where we belong and who we are. I feel that you always know when you are in the presence of the highly vibrant essence of nature. The Cherokee say that there is no name for this energy because it is so beyond our imagination that there aren't any words in the language to describe it. But all of us know it. We know it when there is a sparkling day by the ocean and we see a whale breach or when a full dozen goldfinches swarm the birdfeeders, bright yellow against the early spring landscape of bright leaf green. We know it when a hummingbird comes to drink the nectar of bee balm. We know it when meeting our baby for the first time. Or when we see a dazzling moonlight reflected off the winter snow, and we hear the restless animals in the woods.

The city is as full of the life force as anyplace else. I have rarely been as moved by a film as I was by the 16-minute black-and-white documentary *New York Portrait: Chapter One* by Peter Hutton. The film sweeps the New York City landscape of rooftops and clouds—the world of the birds—without a human presence or sound. The images

are of flocks of birds and their complex worlds atop buildings, the sun filtering through the clouds to break through at dawn, and the wind blowing through the pathways between buildings. As noted by *Millennium Film Journal,* the film depicts "the primal force of a universal presence . . . the natural elements that retain their grace in spite of the city's artificial environment." The film will inspire any city dweller to seek the true elements there.

The contrasts between nature in its full radiance and nature in a polluted state are endless. The ways in which these differences affect our own daily lives are endless as well. A tomato grown on an industrial farm is often flavorless and almost colorless, and it has a mealy texture with skin that can barely be cut. It doesn't hold a candle to a locally grown organic variety that is deep red and vine-ripened in the full

A photo method called biocrystallization allows scientists to record the vitality, or life force, in plants. The carrot with the most feathering—the organic carrot—is on the right. The industrially raised carrot is on the left.

Photo granted by permission of Kimberley Paterson, www.lodestarmedia.co.nz.

sun. Organic tomatoes are succulent and sweet, and they sing out with wholesome goodness. You may also be pleasantly surprised when you switch from a synthetically perfumed skin cream (made of petroleum oil and wafting neurotoxins to you all day long) to an organic and nutrient-rich skin-care lotion, scented gently with a pure essential oil. When you notice that the birds are not at your feeders because of neighborhood pesticide spraying, it's a desolate feeling and in complete contrast to the pure joy of having feeders swarming with songbirds.

The contrasts are so stark that at times, you may wonder why most of the world chooses to live surrounded by pollution and synthetics. Who would consciously choose a life with dull food, sallow skin, and few songbirds? How especially tragic if children don't even know what they are missing, having never experienced truly mouthwatering real food or what it feels like to sleep in an unpolluted bed or live in a home without neurotoxic pesticides.

There are benefits to living without synthetic chemicals that are not so obvious unless you know to look. A child who uses solvent-based gel pens or markers for his artwork on a Saturday morning may exhibit neurotoxic exposure later in the day with hyperactive behavior—with no link being drawn to the markers as a cause. A woman may take an antidepressant when, in fact, her symptoms of depression are classic symptoms of organophosphate pesticide poisoning from the pesticides used by the lawn care company. A man may feel exhausted after work every day and attribute it to job stress, when the true cause may be the formaldehyde in the pressed-wood desk he sits at all day. These common, everyday chemical exposures have a subtle but profound impact on a person's well-being and quality of life.

Rediscovering Home

Finding your way to a home of healing energy and natural sanctuary is a path of discovery and reward. One thing is for sure—once you start living in a healthier home, you never look back. Some people like to start by removing all of their toxic household products and replacing them with safe and natural alternatives virtually overnight. Others prefer the step-by-step approach. Whatever works the best for you is the path to travel.

Here's a good rule of thumb to follow to make an easy transition to a natural lifestyle: *Simply choose the least toxic, most natural alternative every time you buy anything, be it a couch, peach, shampoo, furniture polish, or three-ring binder.*

A general rule is to practice the timeless way of living. This lifestyle is one that is in harmony with the earth, and it honors us as human beings living on a beautiful planet. Humans survived for a few million years without destroying the earth or destroying its resources by living in a timeless way. As stated in the Great Law of the Iroquois Confederacy, "In our every deliberation, we must consider the impact of our decisions on the next seven generations."

Another good starting point is to be guided in your purchases by what you need, not what you want. The purpose of this book is to help you find a healthier, more natural lifestyle and to think things through whenever you act, buy, or do.

A natural lifestyle is not more expensive in the long run. While it may cost more to choose an organic apple, choosing not to put a toxic stain-repellant on your couch will save you money. Natural cleaning costs about a sixth of what it would to buy comparable commercial products; you can mix and match effective homemade formulas with a few well-chosen commercial brands. The numbers aren't an exaggeration: I was asked to work out the dollars and cents once. When I started living this way, I had very little money, and I have learned that wealth is not a prerequisite for natural health. I found a path to a lifestyle of nature and health, and I'm thrilled to teach you what I've learned.

I grew up in rural New England, and I certainly experienced the vibrancy of nature all around me in the 1950s and '60s. As a child, I grew up on skis and spent hours in the pine forests of my neighborhood. I learned to fish, and we could swim in any river we chose because they were all clean. Our milk came from a dairy down the road (I still remember the smell of the cows inside that dairy barn), and we would pick our own tender sweet corn in August and sugar snap peas in July. The summers were never too hot.

I didn't realize what it was about the natural lifestyle of my childhood that was slipping away until it had fully slipped away! It has taken years for me to really isolate the crucial component that was the centerpiece of that lifestyle and why it was so important. I think that what I lost, and what I expect almost all of us on earth are now losing, is being in the presence of the highly vibrant essence of nature in healthy balance.

I came to the natural lifestyle, literally, by accident. My personal story begins to unfold almost 25 years ago, when I was 27. I was severely poisoned, first by a gas leak in a restaurant and then by pesticides that were used in an apartment building where we lived (pesticides that have since been taken off the market because they were so neurotoxic). I have permanent central nervous system damage as a result of these back-to-back exposures. It is important for me to live in clean air, drink clean water, use clean heat, and have a clean earth around me, or I experience neurological symptoms.

My story is one of recovery, renewal, and transformation. By healing the immediate world around me, I went from being poisoned to being healthy. I also became healthy enough to lead a normal life, albeit within a few carefully maintained parameters.

In order to get well, I had to learn where pesticides might lurk, regardless of whether they were pesticides sprayed long ago that would contaminate a house well past my lifetime or a more recent contamination that would supposedly dissipate. I had to learn more than most people would ever care to know about

From Other Voices

The song of the waters is audible to every ear, but there is other music in these hills, by no means audible to all. To hear even a few notes of it, you must first live here for a long time, and you must know the speech of hills and rivers. Then, on a still night, when the campfire is low and the Pleiades have climbed over rimrocks, sit quietly and listen for a wolf to howl and think hard of everything you have seen and tried to understand. Then you may hear it—a vast pulsing harmony—its score inscribed on a thousand hills, its notes the lives and deaths of plants and animals, its rhythms spanning the seconds and centuries.

—Aldo Leopold, *A Sand County Almanac*

materials and chemicals and how they affect the home environment.

For example, I learned about formaldehyde and how it outgasses at higher levels when it heats up (such as when the heaters turn on next to a particle board–based cabinet containing formaldehyde-based glue). The list of things I needed to learn went on and on. My husband and I moved 10 times in 4 years in a desperate escape from pesticide drift and chemical hazards lurking in unexpected places. We learned our lessons as we moved, getting clearer and clearer about what constituted a safe home along the way.

Who could have imagined that products for managing life's chores, such as weeding, pest control, cleaning, and washing, could change the course of existence on earth? Who could have imagined that household products could so profoundly change the health and harmony of everyday life? It seems ironic that the problems of DDT were discovered in the town where I grew up. Robins were dying in our town, Hanover, New Hampshire, but not across the river in the neighboring town in Vermont, just 3 miles away. The difference between the two towns was determined to be the spraying of DDT.

All those years when I was really sick and hanging on by my fingernails made me realize the importance of a lifestyle that is in full balance and harmony with the ecosystems of the earth. Healing the natural world around you offers a life of transformation and renewal in many more ways than just having a healthier body. The healing works deeply for body, mind, and spirit. You feel fully at home. And once a larger community of people starts living by honoring the environment and themselves, then communities are renewed, revived, and transformed. Your own path will transform the environment for you and your family, and it will expand outward and upward from there.

Rediscovering the Experience of the Senses

Our sixth sense, or intuition, is keenly aware of when we are in balance with our surroundings. We know when we are breathing wonderfully clean air, when we drink water that is as sweet as sugar, and when our surroundings feel healing. We know deep down inside what feels right and true—something sings inside of us.

In the years since I became so sick, it has been my intuitive weathervane that has helped me to understand how to heal myself and my environment. Even as I was learning and researching the chemical basis of materials, my intuition was an everyday guide. You can't see most poisons, so I was dealing with

the invisible most of the time. If the air in a room didn't feel just right, I knew to leave to protect my health; eventually, I would find out that there was a toxic chemical present. So I became very acutely attuned to the feeling of places and honed all of my senses, especially my sixth sense, so that I knew when my body was reacting to something, even when I couldn't identify the offending chemical at the time.

I have a unique vantage point because of my fine-tuned awareness of my surroundings. Over time, I've realized that there are always markers present in a polluted environment and home. Your senses will react—you hear something different, you smell an off-putting odor, you taste metal in your mouth, or you're repelled by what you touch. Conversely, your spirits are lifted when you hear the cacophony of songbirds at dawn, your heart opens when you smell a gently sweet and sensual gardenia, and you feel refreshed and alive when your sixth sense recognizes that you are smelling wonderful air.

Hearing Rain on the Roof

The senses teach us so much and give our lives so much richness that it is ironic that we have to relearn how to pay attention to them. The latest findings in physiology, according to Diane Ackerman writing in *A Natural History of the Senses,* suggest that the mind doesn't really dwell in the brain but travels the whole body. It is our senses that catalog the world for our mind.

Who knows how we got to a place where we clean the oven with a toxic product even if it gives us headaches, smells horrible, and leaves a bad taste in our mouths, and our sixth sense tells us that it is bad for our kids. It is so easy instead to use something that makes you feel great because it doesn't cause harm to anything.

The senses also teach us luscious things about the world. Waking up to the meditative sound of rain on the roof or outside the window reminds us of where we are. The sound places us on earth. The sound of rain orchestrates a story of nature on a deep level—a story of belonging and of being part of the grass, trees, sun, and dirt. It is no accident that one of the fastest-selling meditation CDs is of a gentle falling rain. The sound is centering and meditative. I believe that this is nature speaking to us and reminding us that we *are* nature, and we *are* part of the biosphere called earth. Rain teaches us about the cycles of life—water falls to earth, the sun turns it to vapor, and it returns to the sky to fall again.

Rediscovering the Experience of the Elements

There are deep, overarching markers that can clarify the whole picture of pollution in our environments, if we only know to look. The central markers are the eternal elements earth, water, fire, and air. An imbalance of an element tells us to pay attention. It is these elements that we, as an industrial society, have tried to transform into synthetic materials, and the result has been disastrous.

Work with the elements rather than against them. The real elements recharge and balance you rather than deplete you. I have learned to avoid having the synthetic elements in my life because they make me sick. I believe they drag almost everyone down, not just those who are very sensitive like me.

When the elements are true, it is most likely that the environment is in harmony and balance. For example, a house heated entirely with solar energy is significantly less polluting to the outside environment than one heated with nonrenewable oil. The benefits don't stop there though. The indoor air quality is completely different and hugely healthier in a solar-heated home because there aren't combustion appliances in the house spewing out harmful carbon emissions. (Only if you have electric or solar heat can you avoid the dangers of carbon monoxide; however, electric heat comes at an environmental price.) If you have chosen solar power, you have voted with your dollars and supported sustainable businesses. And you can have peace of mind because you are being a good caretaker of the earth's resources and your family's health.

Of course, there are aspects of the pure elements that can be exploited and consumed in a way that's harmful or detrimental to the earth. For example, while wood is a natural earth element, wood smoke can cause indoor air-quality problems. In that case, the air element is not in balance if it is polluted with wood smoke. It is key that all four elements—earth, water, fire, and air—are in balance with each other too.

NATURAL FIBERS COMPARED WITH SYNTHETIC FIBERS

The pure elements in natural fiber clothing make us feel better and more comfortable. Synthetic clothing becomes a hindrance and burden because the synthetic elements don't function in a healthy way like the pure elements.

ELEMENT	NATURAL FIBERS	SYNTHETIC FIBERS
Earth	The material used is grown from or on the soil of the earth and can be returned to the soil when no longer usable.	Synthetics are made from non-renewable resources and are not biodegradable.
Water	They wick moisture from our bodies and keep us dry.	Some synthetics also wick moisture, but the fabric often retains odors such as perspiration.
Fire	They moderate our body temperature.	Most are not versatile in extreme swings of temperature.
Air	They allow our bodies to breathe through our clothing.	Certain types of fabrics made of synthetic materials don't breathe, so there is no air circulation between our bodies and the outside air. They also attract positive ions.

NATURAL ESSENTIAL OILS COMPARED WITH SYNTHETIC PERFUMES

Choose a perfume oil made from an essential oil, such as jasmine, gardenia, or sandalwood. Assume any perfume or fragrance is synthetic unless it's specified otherwise on the label.

ELEMENT	NATURAL ESSENTIAL OILS	SYNTHETIC PERFUMES
Earth	They are extracted from plants. Many essential oils offer therapeutic benefits called aromatherapy, alleviating tension, stress, fatigue, and pain and giving healing energy to the whole self.	Perfumes contain 95 percent synthetic ingredients. Up to 600 chemicals are used as ingredients in a single fragrance, and they can include toxins, such as toluene and petroleum solvents.
Water	The plants that produced the oils drank up water while growing, without polluting it.	Water is used in the manufacturing process, often contaminating it.
Fire	The energy of the sun is in the essential oil.	Labs making perfumes use nonrenewable petroleum fuel.
Air	Plants thrive on the humidity and breezes.	Some perfumes contain chemicals that can cause respiratory reactions in sensitive people.

Rediscovering the Timeless Way of Living

This is a book about everyday life. Developing a natural and nontoxic lifestyle based on what rings true to your senses isn't hard once you get started. Nor is it hard to learn to work with—and not against—the eternal elements. Simply remember to connect with your body, and pay attention to what it is telling you. We need to rediscover how to cooperate with and listen to our intuition.

There are simple skills involved in living the way I suggest, but you don't need to look at every task and weigh in your mind how the elements are balanced or which of the senses isn't quite singing yet. Mostly, you just need to choose the nontoxic choice at every turn.

If you do this in the kitchen, in the bathroom, and in your furnishings, you

ORGANIC PRODUCE COMPARED WITH CONVENTIONALLY GROWN PRODUCE

Conventional farms upset the ecological balance of the environs and attempt to control nature instead of working with it. These farms deplete the soil with intensive chemical use rather than enriching the soil with compost and soil amendments.

ELEMENT	ORGANIC CARROTS AND PRODUCE	CONVENTIONALLY RAISED CARROTS AND PRODUCE
Earth	Organic produce is grown without synthetic fertilizers, pesticides, and herbicides, and the growing practices are healthy for the environment, animals, and humans.	Large industrial farms that grow carrots and other produce have contaminated ecosystems with pesticides and fertilizers. Topsoil loss is greater on an industrial farm because more soil is lost to erosion, and organic matter is not replenished regularly as it is on organic farms.
Water	Water is managed in a sustainable way, and plants are grown in a way that doesn't pollute the groundwater.	The methods used by industrial farms can contaminate groundwater.
Fire	Organic farms use 60 percent less nonrenewable fossil fuel than industrial farms.	Industrial farms rely heavily on nonrenewable fossil fuels to drive production.
Air	Organic farms don't add synthetic pollution to the air.	The air is polluted with pesticide drift. There is no place on earth that doesn't have pesticide residue contaminating air, water, and soil.

will transform your home to a sanctuary of health and well-being.

I received an e-mail from a woman who had started to clean her bathtub with my soft scrubber recipe, and she wanted me to know how the experience transformed her. First, she didn't get the usual cleaning headache from the commercial cleaner she had used previously, and second, she felt she could invite her young children to be in the room with her when she was cleaning. She felt so relaxed about them joining her that she could even teach them how to help. She then became aware while soaking in the tub that she wasn't worrying about absorbing cleaning chemicals into her skin.

As she unplugged the drain and watched the water flow out into the waste stream, she thought of how much safer the septic and leach field would be from using the simple, less-toxic tub cleaner. This was an epiphany for her, and she became aware that she wanted to be an active caretaker of the earth. She set up a compost pile outdoors, and she cancelled the lawn care service (and its chemical lawn applications). She saw the interdependence she and her

NATURAL FIBER HAMMOCK COMPARED WITH A PLASTIC LAWN CHAIR

It is a hot summer day, and you decide to get on a rope hammock in the backyard under the shade of the trees, swaying while you have a nap or read a book. Or imagine, instead, spending time in a molded plastic chair made of petroleum products.

ELEMENT	NATURAL FIBER HAMMOCK	PLASTIC LAWN CHAIR
Earth	Many hammock frames are made of wood, and many hammock fibers are cotton or hemp.	The materials in a plastic lawn chair are nonrenewable, synthetic, and developed in a factory.
Water	Water helped to grow the raw materials naturally, without adding any pollution.	Some of the water used to make the chair is locked into the materials, not to be released and taking its precious contents out of the ecosystem probably forever. Groundwater may have been polluted from the factory discharge pipe.
Fire	The sun was the "fire" used to grow the wood and the rope materials.	The factory that made the chair most likely runs on nonrenewable fossil fuel.
Air	When on a hammock, the breeze cools you and dries your perspiration.	As the sun shines on the chair, the plastic may outgas and release toxic and hormone-disrupting fumes into the air you breathe. The production methods used to create the chair can cause air pollution.

family had with the world around them, and she made changes to live more lightly on the earth. What she found, essentially, was healing and restoration.

Another friend started on this lifestyle another way. A stray dog emerged, abused and abandoned, out of the mists one night. By walking her newfound friend, she discovered land that needed work, trash to pick up, and pollution that needed to be removed. Like others who have found healing in nature, she credits the moment the dog turned up in her life as the beginning of her recovery from chronic fatigue syndrome, and it led her to her work on improving the land. The process, however it starts and wherever it leads, will be rewarding for you and will be a generous legacy for future generations.

Transformation can begin at any age. My teenage daughter came home the other day telling me that a boy in her high school class was going on and on at lunch about how horrible hydrogenated oils were for you and that if you started reading labels, you'd find them everywhere. She was very impressed that concern about health and safety was reaching the mainstream in her own public school's lunchroom. Everyone at that lunch table is now thinking it is actually okay to read food labels!

We all start on the journey to a healthy home somewhere, and I did too. Now I look out at my bird feeders, and there is such a range of visitors: woodpeckers, a virtual flock of goldfinches, and this week, I've even had peregrine falcons visit the feeders. I've also been thrilled by visits from barred owls. The silver lining for me in having been poisoned is that it led me to establish a home with clean air. How joyful and uplifting a place it is for me to be. My houseguests light up and feel rejuvenated and open in response to being here, and the wildlife that flourishes here (not to speak of family and pets) is safe and protected. The rewards of having a home with clean air are bountiful beyond words—rosy-cheeked babies, deep and restful sleeps, complete relaxation, and rejuvenation of the body and soul.

The Heart of the Home

Most of us dream of having homes that are centers of love and harmony— places where we and those we love can flourish and be truly nourished and healthy, where our relationships can grow in intimacy and connectedness, and where our hearts can be open wide to acceptance, forgiveness, and unconditional love.

I truly believe that human wounds and environmental wounds mirror each other. By recognizing and honoring the interdependency of the rhythms of the natural world with the rhythm of our own lives, I believe that we can emerge into a place that fosters care, love, and harmony. The shift is one of the heart. We drop judgment against others and ourselves and work instead to heal the physical and emotional wounds to humans and to the earth.

We are all connected through the elements—the vibrant essence of nature. If these interwoven fields of energy connecting us all together hold a current of balance and vitality instead of pollution and despair, we can heal ourselves and our planet. With all my heart, I hope that we *can* change the world.

2

homescape

The front of our homes—the interface between the community and the interior lives of our families—always reflects who we are and how we relate to the world around us. Our landscape tells a complex story about our lives, and I believe that our homes speak volumes about how we live. My friends Pat and Svend welcome friends and family to their home with colorful pottery plant pots on the front porch steps that are always full of well-tended flowers in interesting color combinations. In the winter, the pots hold pine boughs or bittersweet. There is invariably a cat curled up on the windowsill and a couple of wicker rockers sitting on the porch to welcome homeowners and guests alike. The wreath on the door is always linked to the season, and the curtains showing through the front door's window are clean, white, and edged in pretty lace. Pat and Svend are two of the kindest, most accepting people in the world, and their front door reflects their open hearts.

Contrast this to a house down the street from them that has a sullen and glowering dog chained to a doghouse out front, with the grass worn down to barren dirt from his pacing in the hot sun. The entranceway to that home is forbidding and dark. Other people's entranceways are simply closed to the world with no windows around the front door, and they project a generally walled-off feeling.

Whatever the specifics, all entranceways tell a real story. What we see as we approach the front door can give us clues to the theme of this story: a chemically perfect lawn and plastic-looking flowers, a house with lots of kids and bikes and sports equipment overflowing onto the front lawn, a long tree-lined driveway and an electronic gate, or a relaxed, comfortable entrance with a porch swing and overflowing window boxes.

When helping my mother sort through her belongings before she downsized considerably to move into a retirement home, I came across a wreath of sorts that she had hung over her front door. She had used the wreath during a very complicated time in her life when she was trying to make a new marriage work with a combined family of stepchildren. The "wreath" was heart shaped with a wooden 2-inch-thick rim about 10 inches high; a bell hung inside the heart's center. Every time you opened the door, the bell jingled. I was touched by this door wreath because it told me and others what she was trying to do—make a home of love despite a stressful situation. I am still touched by the sentiment; I couldn't let the wreath go off to the junk dealer, so I kept it.

Making Your Homescape Feel Good to You

Most people want their homes to offer a sense of well-being, hospitality, safety, and presence. Integrating the building with natural surroundings is one way of presenting balance. How do you present nature and the earth at your front door? Seasonal touches are always a good starting point because they show an intention of welcome and attention to the earth. American bittersweet, pine boughs, crocuses, and stones all present a sense of place. Light is welcoming too—both artificial light at night and sunlight during the day. A big step toward a balanced and peaceful home is to take out the imprint of poisons and environmentally harmful materials and to make it a healthy place to be. There is little as off-putting as the smell of herbicides wafting through the air.

Pleasing the Senses

How does your entranceway speak to your senses and others' senses? The four seasons are great anchors for creative entranceway decisions that please the senses. Can you plant a fragrant-smelling bush near the front door so friends are met by its scent when they visit in the summer? A eucalyptus wreath in the winter adds a pleasantly unexpected air that welcomes guests. Wind chimes can enhance a front door at any season. Use your creativity for more ways of pleasing the senses at the entranceway to your home.

Sight: Providing a well-lit path to your front door is welcoming and important for the safety of those entering the area at night. There is also quite a tradition of stringing lights by the front door, a tradition that originated for the winter holiday season, but which is now a year-round tradition for many. Although they use energy, lights can be beacons of welcome.

Solar garden lights can line pathways without any electrical use or wiring. Solar lights absorb the sun during the daylight hours and turn on automatically at dusk. The price of solar lighting has come down considerably over the past decade, and the lights using LED (light-emitting diode) lightbulbs are 50 to 100 percent brighter than non-LED varieties. LED bulbs never need to be replaced, and they have no filaments.

The front door often sets the mood for the whole house. How welcoming is your front door? Is it quite clear that this is where you want people to enter? If you didn't know who lived there, would you feel comfortable going and knocking on the door? A front door welcomes and protects. This is a complicated dual function! Many entranceways to homes are very unexpressive. Is this what you want? Just a few hours of effort can yield an impressive sense of welcome. Add potted plants, planters, hanging plants, well-tended gardens, wreaths, statuary, lights, Tibetan prayer flags and flags of any kind, bird feeders, and a welcome mat!

An old Irish tradition is to paint the front door red so that spirits won't enter the house. Many cultures place "house guardians" at the front door. A special stone can serve this purpose. A cement gargoyle guards a friend's house. An image of a heron is thought to bring luck. Others place a horseshoe to bring good luck, a custom originating in Poland.

Besides beauty, it's important to have a front door that gives a sense of safety. Is the door sturdy? Can those inside see who is at the door? Is the front stoop lit? Signs announcing security alarm systems can be off-putting unless they are juxtaposed with an indication of welcome to those invited.

A Sense of Welcome: Door wreaths are an age-old tradition, and they have been used to symbolize welcome, protection, and a connection to nature. The round shape of most wreaths, with no beginning and no end, represents eternity and the circle of life. Trees are symbolic of life, and wreaths made of tree boughs or leaves represent the cycle of nature and the life-giving nature of forests. Evergreen wreaths have been hung since the earliest times and are symbolic of the survival of life against the odds—the lack of light and the cold of deep winter. The green-colored boughs represent hope and new life. In Europe, pine trees are thought to be the favorite dwelling places of the forest spirits. Holly wreaths, with their shiny leaves and berries, are popular substitutes for evergreen wreaths.

Harvested, dried plants made into a wreath and hung on the door are a gesture of gratitude. A Polish tradition celebrates the end of the harvest by saving the last clump of a crop and transforming it into a wreath to hang on the door. A Latvian tradition is to make a bonfire in midsummer, where last year's wreath is burned to get rid of that year's troubles. They then start anew with a new wreath made of the summer's bloom.

A tradition of hanging a wreath on the front door to bless the house has been passed down through time, but using specific plants for this purpose has been lost along the way for most. These are among the old-time traditional house-blessing plants (note that most of them are culinary herbs): basil, bay laurel, cinquefoil, cowslip, elderflower, figwort, garlic, juniper, mandrake, meliot, pine, plantain, rosemary, rowan, and rue.

Hanging wreaths for protection on a front door is a tradition that has almost disappeared. The sentiment of making a wreath of protection for your loved ones is a nice one and worth resurrecting as a tradition in your home. It is a simple gesture and can be simply cre-

MAKE IT YOURSELF
HERB, BRANCH, AND FLOWER WREATHS

Making your own wreaths is a really fun project, and kids enjoy it too. We provided all the materials and the directions to make wreaths at my daughter's fifth-grade birthday party, and the eight girls just loved the project. I still see the wreaths they made when I visit these girls' homes. I went to the farm of a local flower grower and bought a car's worth of stunning dried flowers. Wreaths are so easy to make that I now make a new door wreath for every new season.

   Heavy-gauge wire wreath armature
   Herbs, branches, stems, and dried flowers
   Green or brown florist's wire
   Decorative ribbon or found materials, such as a bird's nest, dried mushrooms, or seedpods

Either use the armature as is, or bend it into the shape of your choice. Determine the size of the floral bunches you'll need (big wreaths look balanced with longer bunches, about 12 inches long; small wreaths may look best with shorter bunches, about 6 inches long).

Assemble about 8 to 15 herbs, branches, stems, and dried flowers in bunches; wire the bunches together at the base of the stems with florist's wire. Wire each bunch to the wreath's armature, holding the stem end to the armature and covering the stems of the previous bunch, so you have a continuous presentation of flowers and petals. (A good way to gauge where to start adding the next bunch is to wire it about 1 inch past the ends of the previous stems.) Keep going until you have covered all of the stems and the armature. Trim and neaten the wreath, then add a ribbon or found materials as desired. ❖

ated by stringing hazelnuts along the door or weaving them into a wreath. You can place antibacterial flowers and plant materials in wreaths too. Antibacterial plants include birch, cinnamon, clove, eucalyptus, lavender, lemongrass, rose, rosemary, thyme, and more. Plants that have traditionally been used for protection against harm and evil spirits include agrimony, anise, basil, betony, birch, blackberry, carnation, fennel, frankincense, mullein, myrrh, parsley, sage, and sandalwood.

Placing stones at the entrance of one's home is age-old and intuitive. Stones are markers of welcome, and they also mark boundaries. I was driving through my town the other day and was really impressed at how many stones are placed along the sides of walkways, mark the entrance to a driveway, or decorate a porch step or two. One friend of mine has rose quartz on both sides of his front door. Rose quartz is traditionally known as a stone of unconditional love and represents the heart chakra (see page 416 for more on chakras). By placing rose quartz stones by his door, he is subtly telling those who come in that his is a heart-centered home.

Welcome mats can also make powerful and thought-provoking statements. My daughter's voice teacher, Jill, has a welcome mat that I find simply charming. *The Wizard of Oz's* "Wicked Witch of the West's" feet are shown with witch's shoes and knitted striped socks, with the words "ding dong." I appreciate the mat because it perfectly reflects the charming, lively woman who lives in the house!

Welcome mats serve a very useful purpose too—removing mud and dirt from shoes and boots. By doing this, you reduce the amount of water and cleaning materials you need to clean floors. Another very important purpose of a mat, and a good reason to suggest that everybody brushes off their shoes, is to remove the toxic chemicals that cling to the bottoms of shoes, such as pesticides from lawns, lead residue from chipping or peeling paint, and oil and petroleum products from driveways and roadways.

Hearing: Does your front door have a doorbell or a door knocker? If it has a doorbell, does it have a nice sound? A good door knocker can be a family treasure. I grew up with a great cast-iron one; it was distinctive, clear, and announcing. It didn't depend on electricity like today's doorbells. If you don't have either a doorbell or a door knocker at your front door, consider putting a bell on a little table outside there for people to ring until you can find something that you like. Be sure to do a sound check before buying a doorbell or door chime—some sound cavernous, high strung, or tinny.

Smell: One of the cardinal rules for judging the health of a house is to make sure that you pay attention to the first thing that you smell when you walk in the door. The first smell inside is always a critical and important clue to environmental problems. Do you smell mold? Is the chemical smell of a new carpet present, or do you smell other chemicals? Do you smell oil-based paint? Do you smell the sap being released from fresh pine? The smell of cleaning products may mean the home has been recently cleaned, but it doesn't mean that that kind of chemical-clean is good for you. Artificial scents, such as vanilla or flowers, can be a mixed bag too, since potpourri and candles are usually scented with synthetic fragrances and often create indoor air pollution. It's hard to define what a clean, natural home smells like, but I can assure you that you'll recognize one when you first walk in.

Your Sixth Sense: To get to know the energy that we don't see—called prana, hado, or chi in different parts of the world—is to start to identify and acknowledge the sense of a place, the feel of a place, and the story that is told in all but words. You learn volumes about a home by sensing it from the outside, standing on the front steps and feeling how it feels, and walking in the front door to experience the "vibe" from within the house. To learn to iden-tify the energies that make up the whole story of a home is to pull open a curtain into a world that has many wonders. You learn to train and listen to your sixth sense, or intuition.

The energy of a room changes with a pet, the color of the sofa has a vibration (what does it say?), and the introduction of a water fountain shifts one's feelings about a place. Everything has an imprint, and it is for you to discover what is influencing the energy in your own home. The goal is to work toward making a life-enhancing and harmonious environment.

Geomancy

Geomancy is the holistic science of living in harmony with the earth's energy centers. Geomancy is more complex than this, but for this book I've focused on the earth's life force energy and its aspects of geomancy.

Life force energy makes up the interwoven energy waves of the vast universe. We are all part of it, and we are all connected. I call the energy "interwoven fields of being" because the energy carries information. Each wave is made up of particles; these consist of sacred, geometrical forms that represent the exact moments in time and space of where they are, and each particle adds up to become a wave. All the waves interconnect to the whole. It is through these interwoven fields of being that we are all connected. The interwoven fields of being aren't rarefied; every aspect of life is part of this, from the toaster oven and the pesticides in a basement to love and harmony. Geomancy helps human beings in their interface with the earth's energy system.

The basic principles of geomancy ask that you:

❖ Sense and pay attention to the energy of a place on earth.

❖ Work within such energy parameters to create energetically healthy places for human and all life forms.

❖ Heal the energy that is out of balance, such as removing geopathic stress.

The goal of geomancy is to maintain the web of life and to ensure that the elements are balanced in human habitats. In the home, geomancy is about consciously participating in the energy of your home: sensing it, correcting it, working with it. Chinese geomancy is called feng shui. I am not a feng shui practitioner, and I would recommend hiring a consultant if you are interested in learning more about the feng shui principles. I have spent 25 years studying the energetic health of homes, and I know that there is always more to a healthy home than an absence of synthetic chemicals.

The key to thinking about the energy of your home is that you want to reduce the negative energy and increase the positive energy. Your internal sixth sense will tell you what works and what doesn't work energetically in your home. You can also use your sixth sense to tell you if there is poison somewhere that needs to be removed.

One pearl of wisdom that I would like to pass on is that your own instincts should take precedence over what you read in a book. I took a walk with a friend of mine who said, "My bedroom is a feng shui disaster!" I asked her why, and she said that there is only one way for her to sleep where she feels safe, and it is always facing the door. She had read that the direction in which she places her bed is not right, and she was genuinely worried! My advice to her was to sleep where she felt safe. It would upset her life to do anything but that.

It is more important to meet our own deepest needs than to obey formal feng shui rules. In looking at a cluttered bookshelf the other day, my "should" mind said (as does the feng shui dictum), "I need to clean that up!" But my intuitive mind said that the reason I put so much on that bookshelf is that I need all the colors I see there. And I need those books askew to have a movement of energy. If that part of the room had been too still, it would feel stagnant to me.

A Sense of Place

Anything you can do to enhance your home's connection to the land and the bioregion in which you live will enrich your life. Does the land of the region where you live run in your veins? Do you sing in resonance with it when the season's change? Do the crops that grow locally make your mouth water as you anticipate the harvest season? If not, ask yourself why. Although energy is at the core of geomancy, it's also about bioregionalism, deep ecology, being "green," organic agriculture, and bonding with the local environment.

Where is the beautiful energy in your community or on your land or nearby? We all have beautiful places where we can commune with nature, even in a city. Is there a beautiful tree on your land that you like to sit under on a hot day? Do you have a glade that is full of wildflowers in early spring? Find these spots and go to them as often as you can. A wicker couch on my porch is one of my favorite places. I have looked out at the day, the garden, and the sun from this place more times than I can count. Invariably, I see something I have never seen before or a wildlife event of some sort.

Establishing Good Energy

In Western culture, we are often denigrated if we rely on our feelings, but let your feelings rule the day. As a dowser (traditionally known as a person who finds water by the use of a divining rod), I have found that my gut and intuitive feelings before dowsing are always confirmed when I (or others) dowse. If only we could learn to trust ourselves! If a corner in your living room feels dark and forbidding, trust that it is. If the porch just doesn't feel right, something is off there and needs to be corrected. Would some flowerpots help? Another chair? Fewer chairs? If you and your family members are always arguing about who gets to sit on one specific spot on a couch, you know something is just perfect there and worth emulating elsewhere. Puzzling out the answers to these questions is really fun, and the whole family can get involved.

Feng Shui's Bagua Map Associations

Feng shui practitioners use a Bagua map to analyze the layout of a home to promote the well-being of the residents; according to the Bagua map, each part of your home has a symbolic meaning for a different aspect of your life. I have found an eerie truth to the health or lack of health in different parts of a house and family relationships, as identified on this map. If nothing else, it is fascinating to see how you can harmonize your life and home with feng shui. The health and family section of the Bagua map is in my kitchen, and that feels right, for example. There are other places in my home that need work when I look at the symbolism! Contact a qualified feng shui expert for a consultation if you are interested in learning more.

Space Clearing

There are many times when you will want to change the energy of a place— if you move into a home and the house has lingering emotions from previous owners; if you had a very bad argument and you want to change the mood; or if you had house guests and you'd like to reclaim the energy of a room quickly. There are also serious negative energies that you may want to change—if someone died in the building, if you think you might have ghosts, or if you think the home has geopathic stress (the potentially harmful effect on your health and well-being from radiation or electromagnetic fields). If someone died peacefully, just smudging a home can be all that is necessary to cleanse the house of that person's energetic death imprint. For possible ghosts or geopathic stress, consult a professional (see page 106 for more on geopathic stress).

Smudging

Many Native American tribes have used smudge bundles for millennia. They help to purify an area of negativity and induce a feeling of serenity and calm. You can purchase smudge sticks made of cedar, juniper, sage, and sweet grass, or you can make your own. Always gather and use smudge bundles ceremonially.

Any action engaged in with conscious intent can become a ceremony. You can use dried plants to create your own sacred ceremony to purify and bless your home. Make a small fire in a heat-proof bowl, large ashtray, or abalone shell. (As with any indoor flame, please be cautious when burning smudge

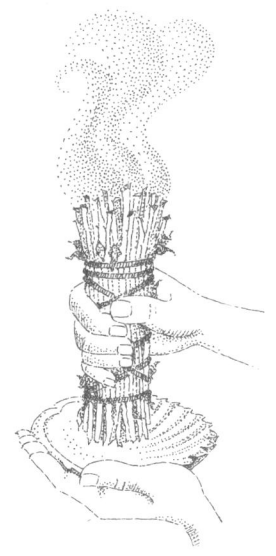

The ritual of smudging can cleanse and purify you and your environment. Make a smudge bundle of cedar, juniper, white sage, and sweet grass, and allow the smoke to ceremoniously clear away negative energy.

sticks.) Then place a small amount of dried material on the charcoal or in the fire, and hold your ceremony.

Look for downed cedar or juniper branches. If you cut cedar or juniper branches, pick them from the east side of the tree where the sun rises. Or gather white sage or sweet grass. White sage is native to Southern California, but you can grow it as a houseplant. Sweet grass grows in northern latitudes, such as Maine, upstate New York, and the Dakotas.

Healing Your Neighborhood

There is no whole-house air filter that can fully protect you from the pollution from outdoors. I know people who have tried desperately to do this with every means at their disposal, and they've been unable to do it. One chemically sensitive friend of mine died because she wasn't able to screen out all the neighborhood herbicides that were so deadly to her. Yet full protection comes at a price too; there is an unhealthy quality to houses that have been so sealed up that the air lacks life even with a fresh air exchange.

Make your neighborhood an oasis for birds and wildlife, a fresh air sanctuary for kids, and a compelling place to take a walk or plant a garden. You simply start somewhere. You can participate in the protection of local flyways, rivers, and parks and in the protection of nesting birds, bees, but-

MAKE IT YOURSELF
SMUDGE BUNDLES

Keep your bundles 8 inches or shorter to avoid creating a long torch. To smudge, untie the bundle and take out a branch or two. Light a leaf on one or two of the branches and then blow it out. It will glow and smoke. Hold the bundle over a traditional abalone shell, bowl, or large ashtray to catch the ashes. When you've burned enough of your smudge, tamp out the end.

Cedar or juniper branches
White sage leaves (*Artemesia*), sweet grass blades, or lavender stems (optional)
Cotton thread and colorful cotton yarn

Cut branches into 8-inch lengths. Holding the branches together, make a bundle about 2 inches in diameter at its thickest part. Add sage leaves, sweet grass blades, or lavender stems, if you'd like. Secure the bundle with cotton thread. If you'd like a decorative smudge bundle, use colorful yarn to create a crisscross pattern up and down the stems. Hang the bundle upside down in a cool, dry, dark place, and allow the plant material to dry thoroughly for a month or two.

From Other Voices

"Something there is that doesn't love a wall . . . "

—Robert Frost, Mending Wall

terflies, foxes, pigeons, and more. You can also work to make sure that local farms and industry don't pollute the ecosystems you share. The process, however it starts and wherever it leads, will be rewarding for you and a generous legacy for future generations. Connecting to your surroundings can be more fun if you start a neighborhood group to join you in the endeavor or find a friend to help.

Sharing the Work with Friends and Neighbors

Neighborhood groups can make very big changes as well as provide a great deal of political clout. Even though "everyone" said we couldn't win a battle with a cell tower company where I live, about 15 families banded together to successfully keep a 150-foot cell tower from being built in our "backyard." Each family had a special skill to offer or made a contribution of value; by combining our efforts, we protected our neighborhood from radio waves, declining property values, and a significant eyesore. We became friendlier

with each other, stopping to chat more, and we're now welcomed into each other's homes, feeling more a part of a community.

Make a Neighborhood Map

You can make the most educated decisions about where environmental problems may be found in your neighborhood, as well as prioritizing the areas to focus your attention for change, if you make a map of the area that notes all potential environmental concerns. If you live in suburbia or in the country, make a map that covers a 2-mile radius around your home, but be sure to include, say, a smokestack 5 miles away if you smell emissions. If you live in the city, make a map of a 5-block radius, also making sure to include emissions that reach your home, even if from a farther distance than 5 blocks.

When I made a neighborhood map for myself, I was genuinely surprised at how close a high-tension power line was to my house, for example, when analyzed according to the way the crow flies. My concern wasn't with electromagnetic fields (because they drop off very fast and don't pose a problem at a relatively small distance from the lines) but with the herbicides used to keep the swatch of land under the lines free of underbrush. I was concerned because of the possibilities of the herbicides contaminating my well and my neighbors' wells and the potential for herbicide drift onto my property when the wind is blowing in my direction.

Each neighborhood has its own unique issues. When you make your neighborhood map, be aware of all potential sources of environmental pollution, and be sure to include anything you think could be of concern. Your yard and neighborhood features may help pinpoint trouble hot spots, so include as many of the following features as possible on your map.

Natural Light, Wind, Weather, Natural Habitat

❖ Note how the sun hits your house. Does it get adequate sun year-round? Is it shaded during some seasons and not during others? Shade provided by leafy trees in the summer can cut down on air-conditioning bills, and sun streaming in the windows in the winter can reduce heating costs.

❖ From which direction does the prevailing wind blow?

❖ Are there wetlands, rivers, streams, and wildlife in your neighborhood that require attention and care? For example, the Hudson River is near where I live, and it's one of the biggest flyways in the world; maintaining pesticide-free areas is very important for the migrating birds.

Herbicide and Pesticide Drift

❖ Record all the lawns within 1 to 2 miles of your home, depending on what is realistic (if you live in the middle of suburbia, a 2-mile radius covers a large number of lawns!). If you know that neighbors use chemical lawn treatments or commercial lawn services, note it on the map.

❖ Identify all of the commercial farms within 2 miles of your home.

❖ Are there swamplands or low-lying wet areas (these may be sprayed for mosquitoes)? Are there streams that flood often or are eroding stream banks or berms, sending excess amounts of topsoil into the water and watershed? Are there golf courses or recreation parks in your area?

❖ List all schools, camps, and college campuses.

❖ Mark the location of all roads.

Industrial and Corporate Pollution

❖ Are you downwind of an industry, home-based business, highway, or other notable commercial venture? Are there any smokestacks that you can smell? Is there heavy truck traffic from any business?

THE HEALTH OF YOUR NEIGHBORHOOD

Using authoritative scientific and government data, Environmental Defense's Scorecard Web site provides up-to-date and extensive environmental information online. To learn about environmental issues in your community, type your zip code in the search box. Or learn about specific hazardous chemicals that you find on product labels or that are identified as emissions in your community by using Scorecard's profiles of 6,800 chemicals. Scorecard is available at www.scorecard.org.

❖ Is there an industrial production or business park near your home?

❖ Are there businesses that use chemicals that could enter the neighborhood air space (dry cleaners, auto body shops, and gas stations, for example)?

❖ Is there a quarry nearby?

Electrical Pollution, Radio Waves

❖ Is there an electrical power station in the area?

❖ Are there high-tension wires or transformer substations nearby?

❖ Any cell phone or communications towers?

Other Environmental Concerns

❖ Are there any other features that, intuitively, you feel you should add to your list?

❖ Are there unique businesses or qualities in your neighborhood, such as a firing range, a rainy weather retention pond, or abandoned buildings?

❖ If you live in a city, note electrical power stations, sources of chemical odors, and water-supply systems.

Once you have included all landmarks on your map, discuss and analyze the map and its implications with family members and interested neighbors. Identify potential issues and problems, and start making an effort to investigate the situations you've noted. Once you've gathered the facts, you can start problem solving, step-by-step, season by season, person by person, and lawn by lawn. It may be that you institute a "pesticide-free neighborhood," or you raise money for a park bench (once people begin to enjoy sitting in that place, people might litter less and want to plant flowers). Every change starts with a single effort. Start on your better-the-neighborhood campaign with an issue that's deeply meaningful to you. Once you've reached your goal, choose the next issue on your list and get started!

It Takes a Village to Raise a Child

Each one of us has something we can offer to our communities. It may be coaching softball, helping at a church, or volunteering once a month with an environmental group. I agree with Hillary Clinton—it takes a village to raise a child. Think of all the people a child meets and the impact they have on the child. If those people are caring, supportive, helpful, and committed to the people and community in which they live, it is likely that the child will develop into a person with a community-minded soul.

Community Spirit

Both my mother and I have done volunteer work for different organizations that suit our talents and goals individually. My mother helped to set up a conservation easement for the community of Hanover, New Hampshire. She loves open fields, wildlife habitats, wetlands, and scenic locations, so she learned how to protect them in her town.

A conservation easement on a parcel of property will preserve it as a special place forever. A legally binding document, the easement places restrictions on development that will remain no matter who owns the land in the future.

Landowners can grant conservation easements to protect their land from inappropriate development while re-

From Other Voices

My mother, Nancy Prosser, shares her story in her own words:

"I learned how to set up a conservation easement when a 26-acre farm in my town was at risk of being turned into a subdivision. If it was possible to restrict the chance of a subdivision and commercial use of these fields with easements, then these 26 acres could be saved from development forever.

We needed to raise well over $100,000 and apply for extra-large sums in grants from a state land protection agency in order to buy easements for this farmland. A private conservation council footed a tremendous fund drive. The town itself contributed funds from their land-protection fund, and many people from nearby towns who know the fields contributed to the funding of the easement as well. We succeeded! The town now owns the easements and will monitor the lands to ensure that there are no violations of the agreement, no matter who the owners may be in the future!

You can be a catalyst for conservation in your own community by working to set up a conservation easement. In addition to the long-range goal of preserving land in perpetuity, landowners can expect tax benefits as well. If the easement is a gift, it might qualify as a charitable deduction. If the easement qualifies for Current Use Assessment, the landowner's property tax could be reduced. Land protected by a conservation easement may be sold or transferred, but the restrictions of the easement go with the transaction."

taining private ownership. A conservation easement assures the landowner that the value of the resources of his property will be protected forever, no matter who the future owners are. Any property of value for agriculture, forestry, recreation, water resources, and wildlife habitat or for its scenic or historic qualities may be protected by means of a conservation easement.

One skill that I could offer my community was to participate on the school's Health and Safety Committee. I was particularly interested in this because I had a daughter in the school system. I was helped in the effort by other concerned parents (one mother in particular, Gail Lee, who started the initiative) and a very receptive school administration, especially the superintendent. To this day, I continue to send him e-mails about studies regarding children's health and toxins, and he always replies and implements change in the school when he can.

The way that we successfully established a healthy school in our community was to proceed with a straightforward plan that prioritized the environmental health concerns that would most affect the children. (Every school has safety issues, but let's put environmental issues at the forefront.) These were, in order of concern: pesticides; ventilation; renovating; cleaning products; the science, shop, and art rooms; and art supplies.

The committee successfully switched the school to a system of integrated pest management. Next, we solved a serious indoor air problem that was the result of shutting down the air-to-air exchange ventilation system during the '70s energy crunch. No steps had been put in place to recirculate fresh air, and the result was high levels of carbon dioxide and germs in the school. We identified safer approaches to renovations, ensuring that any polyurethanes would be water-based and used in the summer months when the school was empty, and new carpet would be added during that time too. We instituted new procurement procedures for safer cleaning products. Vents were added to the shop room because there weren't any before, and solvent-based whiteboard pens were retired in favor of water-based.

One person can really make an extraordinary difference in any community, in any neighborhood, and in the world. Because our hearts are usually connected to our neighborhoods, we are more invested in protecting them and in bettering our surroundings. You will enjoy the fruits of your efforts firsthand.

The Porch and Patio

My favorite place in the summer is the wicker couch on the front porch. Its colorful cushions welcome anybody to sit there in the cool shade and look out at the beauty of the day. I have passed many a tranquil hour sitting there, drinking iced tea, and just looking at the garden or listening to the birds. If you don't have such a place, make one for yourself. Even if you live in the city, find a park or public garden where you can go sit on a bench and just rest.

Cooking Outdoors

Most of us love an outdoor barbecue or picnic. Traditional grills, however, do have an environmental impact because of having to use lighter fluid to light charcoal briquettes. But you can be eco-conscious when you barbecue. Buy a metal charcoal chimney, and you can virtually avoid petroleum, a nonrenew-able resource that causes toxic air pollution. Charcoal chimneys are available at most hardware stores and can be reused for years. All you need to light the charcoal are some old newspapers and matches. Fill the cylinder with charcoal (try real wood chip charcoal), scrunch newspaper under the charcoal in the special housing for this purpose, and then light the newspaper to heat up the coals. Once the coals are red hot, you turn over the cylinder and pour the coals into the bed of the grill.

No need to use petroleum-based lighter fluid to get your charcoal grill lit! Try a charcoal chimney instead. Place real wood chip charcoal in the chimney, then crumble newspapers and place them in the bottom of the chimney. Light the newspapers, and in just a few minutes, you'll have blazing hot coals.

Outdoor Furniture

There's an amazing and beautiful variety of outdoor furniture available today. Most of what you'll see in the home centers is made of plastic or metal, but you can still find outdoor furniture made with natural fibers. Wicker furniture and baskets are made from a lot of different materials that are woven to create a structure that's strong. Here's a quick rundown on some of the most common natural materials.

Rattan: Rattan palm vine can grow 600 feet long. What a wonderful gift from nature! From Asia, rattan cane and reed are both processed from this vine and are used in the making of the oldest and most traditional wicker furniture.

The rattan vine isn't used as the wicker per se, but as the framework because the vines themselves can grow to 3 inches in diameter. "Stick Wicker" was popular in the 1930s. Records of rattan vine go as far back as 2500 BC.

After the thorns and outer layer of the rattan vine have been removed, the outer bark is sliced into the cane found on chair seats and backs and as the wrapping used at the joints of wicker furniture.

Commonly used in basketry as well as furniture, rattan reed can be cut to many different sizes to accommodate different projects. Rattan reed is cut from the inside of the rattan vine and is woody in appearance.

Willow: Commonly available in many northern climates such as North America, willow holds its own moisture very well; it is very flexible and long lasting.

Bamboo Furniture: Bamboo is a large tropical grass that grows straight from the ground to heights of 100 feet in wooden pipelike hollow reeds. Bamboo furniture has a very distinctive look due to the nodular marks on the wood, the hollow reeds, and the yellowish, honey color. Although it is sometimes called bamboo wicker, it doesn't look the same as traditional wicker furniture; the slats tend to be wider and the designs more indicative of the less-flexible, straight bamboo reed.

Paper Fibre Rush: Paper fibre rush is ropelike with a "barber-pole" diagonal twist. This manmade cord was invented in 1904. These paper cords were made stronger around 1930 by the addition of a thin metal wire running along the inside of the cord.

Caring For and Cleaning Wicker

In making your decision about the best way to clean wicker furniture, it is important that you determine whether your wicker is vine- and wood-based or paper fibre rush. Wood-based wicker can handle water. I've even heard of unpainted rattan wicker cleaned in car washes! But fibre rush definitely cannot be soaked to that extent. Painted wicker is sensitive to water no matter what kind of wicker furniture it is, so use water sparingly.

Vacuuming is recommended to get into the nooks and crannies. You can also scrub lightly with a touch of detergent or soap and a damp toothbrush, and then rinse. Use a small bristle brush to dust closed areas; for really small crevices, use a toothbrush.

Wicker needs to be completely dry after washing before being put into use again, and this usually takes a few days. Put wicker in the sun on a dry day, bringing it onto a covered porch or inside at night to help the drying process.

Cleaning Rattan

Use a mild detergent with a wet cloth or even a garden hose to clean unpainted rattan. One tablespoon of detergent to 1 gallon of water is a good ratio unless it's really dirty.

Cleaning Paper Fibre Wicker

Water can break apart the paper cord of paper fibre wicker. Clean only with a damp cloth and vacuum cleaner.

Wicker Restoration and Repair

The best way to find an expert to help you repair old wicker is to look in your local Yellow Pages. Basket weavers can sometimes help repair wicker because the weaving techniques are often the same, and their suppliers provide rattan and fibre rush. Antique wicker is quite valuable, so repairing it professionally may help it retain its value.

The best way of "finishing" wicker is the timeless way—by doing nothing. This is called natural wicker. If you decide to paint wicker, you will have to keep the wicker in good repair, and you'll need to repaint every few years (oil-based paints will last longer, of course, but these paints are very disharmonious with life because they are full of toxic solvents that will outgas for

months). In my opinion, it is best to just let wicker weather to a natural patina.

If the furniture is already painted and it needs to be maintained, paint it with a water-based safe paint (see page 51) or a shellac. Many recommend coating the wicker with liquid furniture wax, but this process will cover the furniture with solvents and synthetic fragrances, so I do not recommend it.

Placing Wicker Outdoors

Vine- and wood-based wicker needs some humidity, but it shouldn't be considered "outdoor" furniture. It's best to use it on a covered porch or patio. Wicker should not be exposed completely to the elements (rain, sun, or dew) because it may start to decompose. On the other hand, dry indoor heat will cause wicker to crack and creak.

Other Outdoor Furniture Options

You may have seen hemp hammocks in some of the natural products catalogs. Hemp is the strongest plant fiber on earth, and it has been used for centuries to make rope and cloth for sailing. It is naturally ultraviolet (UV)-,

mold-, and mildew-resistant, making it ideal for outdoor furniture such as hammocks. Why not splurge on a hemp hammock?

Aluminum is a good choice for outdoor furniture because it won't rust, is very light, and will last for decades with little maintenance. If the outdoor furniture has hardware, choose models with stainless steel components, so you won't have to deal with rust. There are two types of aluminum: One type, hollow tube aluminum, is very light and is often used for lawn chairs. The second type is cast from hand-carved wooden molds, and it is heavy enough that this type of furniture won't blow over in gusts or windy situations.

You can also look for sustainably harvested woods when shopping for outdoor furniture. Western red cedar is naturally resistant to bacteria, fungus, and insects and makes wonderful and attractive furniture. Eucalyptus is also a hardwood timber that can be harvested from renewable plantations. The key is choosing wood that has been labeled as having been grown through sustainable means.

The Trouble with Chromated Copper Arsenate (CCA) Treated Wood

Do you have any green-tinted wood in your backyard? On your porch? Your kid's jungle gym? Often referred to as pressure-treated wood, CCA wood is no longer used for manufacturing decks, playground equipment, walkways and boardwalks, landscaping, and fencing due to its release of arsenic, a known carcinogen and contributor to nervous system damage and birth defects. This voluntary agreement between the EPA and the wood-preserving industry went into effect in January 2004. Pressure-treated lumber is treated with highly toxic chemicals that leach into the soil, groundwater, and our bodies. Much like lead, however, even though CCA wood isn't allowed in new buildings or construction of the outdoor features listed above, it still exists in millions of backyards because it was purchased or installed prior to the ban.

Limit Contact with CCA Wood

According to the Environmental Working Group (EWG), the United States wood products industry is the world's largest consumer of arsenic, using half of all the arsenic produced worldwide. EWG researchers found that CCA-treated wood leaches unsafe amounts of arsenic for years, an especially dangerous scenario for children playing on and around pressure-treated lumber.

If you can't replace or remove the CCA wood, here's how to reduce your exposure.

❖ Change your vegetable garden over to a flower or ornamental garden if you have CCA wood in or near your vegetable garden. Test your soil for arsenic, and plant only nonedible plants near existing or removed CCA wood structures.

❖ Have your well tested for arsenic if you currently have or have had a lot of CCA wood in your yard.

❖ Wash your hands after handling or touching CCA-treated wood.

❖ Use a tablecloth to cover the top of a pressure-treated table and benches, especially when using the table for serving food or dining. Consider getting rid of the table altogether.

❖ Seal CCA wood to prevent arsenic leaching into the environment. The safest way to do so is with a water-based latex paint that you reapply every year. Make sure you avoid sealants with volatile organic chemicals (VOCs), formaldehyde, fungicides, heavy metals, and mildewcides.

Disposal of CCA

Absolutely do not burn pressure-treated wood because this releases arsenic into the air. Contact local or state agencies to locate disposal facilities in your area. Do not put CCA wood out for the trash; if pressure-treated wood goes to the landfill, it will leach arsenic into groundwater.

Plastic Lumber as an Alternative

Plastic lumber is an environmentally friendly and economically viable alternative to CCA wood. It is made from recycled-content plastic. It will not rot, warp, splinter, or crack; and it is resistant to moisture, corrosive substances, insects, and other environmental stresses. It does not absorb paint or marker graffiti, and it requires no waterproofing, staining, or similar maintenance when used outdoors. It also offers a way to conserve our forests. Note, however, that plastic can offgas and leach some chemicals, especially when heated. Know these guidelines for selecting and using plastic lumber.

❖ Be sure your plastic lumber contains UV stabilizers to protect its color and prevent it from deteriorating.

❖ Higher-end plastic lumber is made from a single polymer, usually HPDE (the #2 on the bottom of a plastic bottle). Commingled-plastic lumber will be darker and is more suitable for applications such as landscape ties and car stops where strength isn't as important.

❖ Purified plastic lumber is cleaned and free from contaminants, with no foreign materials or colored flakes. Nonpurified plastic lumber will contain contaminants that will mar the finish.

❖ Composite lumber can be quite heavy, so shop locally in order to keep shipping costs down.

❖ Some plastic lumber can get wavy if it is not very dense or made with UV stabilizers to prevent sun damage.

❖ Plastic lumber is not recommended for load-bearing projects.

Conquering Trash Mountain

It's not an impossible mission to reduce trash, reuse more, and recycle. From buying products that are packaged simply, to reusing and revamping old furniture, to recycling cardboard and paper, you can greatly reduce the amount of trash going to the landfill with just a little time and effort.

The first step to less trash is to live a healthy life by eating pure food that's had very little processing. Fresh fruits and vegetables require minimal packaging, and all the wastes (such as peels) can be composted. Whole beans and grains are available in bulk and require only a bag, not sealed metallic or plastic bags and cardboard boxes like those you'll find in processed foods. When you bring fewer food cartons and packages into the house, you'll have less to dispose of.

Second, reuse items whenever you can. If you have a broken-down dresser, for example, can you spruce it up and put on a marble top instead of sending it off to the landfill? Or, set the piece in your driveway with a "Free" sign, and you'll probably find an interested party in just a few hours. One community in Pennsylvania has a recycling store for building products. Building contractors and homeowners can donate their castoffs, such as old sinks, doors, appliances, windows, flooring, staircases, and architectural features as well as tiles, glass panes, and moldings left from new construction or remodeling projects. The recycling store sells the items to interested do-it-yourselfers, with the proceeds from the sales going to a local nonprofit physical rehabilitation center. My friend has donated many items from her old home, including a porcelain sink and wooden table legs. When she was remodeling her kitchen, she was able to find solid wood doors to match her existing doors for just $5 each. It's a unique idea that benefits everyone—the contractors get a tax deduction for donating brand-new and reusable extras from their building jobs, homeowners get interesting and usable architectural furnishings for bargain-basement prices, and fewer items end up in a landfill or dump!

And, of course, there's recycling. We've made great strides, but we can still do more. Find out about recycling facilities in your community; if your community doesn't recycle some items, perhaps a neighboring community will accept your materials. It takes a little time to get used to recycling and to work it into your schedule, but it's rewarding. Enlist the help of your kids! With a small up-front investment of properly labeled bins, recycling becomes a habit and takes us one step closer to a cleaner planet.

The Nitty-Gritty on Plastics

In 2000, the United States disposed of almost 25 million tons of plastic. As of 2001, 1,591 million pounds of plastic were recycled annually. That leaves roughly 24 million tons of plastic that's not recycled. Do your part; every little bit helps.

There are seven recycling codes that indicate the type of resin base for the particular plastic. Be aware, though, that just because there's a recycling number, it doesn't mean that the plastic is recyclable! The codes are as follows:

#1—polyethylene terephthalate (PET or PETE)

#2—high-density polyethylene (HDPE)

#3—polyvinyl chloride (V or PVC)

#4—low-density polyethylene (LDPE)

#5—polypropylene (PP)

#6—polystyrene (PS)

#7—Other (This covers everything else, although it usually refers to a polycarbonate of one sort or another.)

#1 and #2 plastics are commonly recycled. Number 2 plastics are good choices for consumers because they are often recycled into multiple-use containers. Number 2 plastics can be reused by the consumer if they are thoroughly cleaned. Beyond #1 and #2, look for #4 and #5 plastics because they are also recyclable, although you may not find facilities willing to accept these plastics. Be continually on the lookout for biodegradable plastic; it's becoming much more available due to its low production cost and environmental benefits. Look for the biodegradable notation on the label. Avoid #3, #6, and #7 plastics because these are the worst polluters during production and the least likely to find a home in your local recycling center.

Piles and Piles of Paper

There's no reason not to recycle paper—it's easy, paper recycling facilities are almost everywhere, and all you need is a bin instead of a wastebasket! Recycling paper is easier than emptying the trash.

For the environment's sake, know what type of paper products you are buying, and try to buy products that have as much postconsumer paper as possible (see page 376). A label that says recycled these days could mean anything from 100 percent recycled paper to just 1 percent, so check the percentages on the label.

Office Paper: White sheets of office paper are acceptable for recycling everywhere. The wrappers from reams of paper are usually of a lower grade, as are colored or lower-quality paper, so do not mix these. Staples are generally okay to recycle if they're still attached to paper or cardboard, so don't worry about them.

WORDS TO THE WISE

WHY REUSE BEATS RECYCLING

Reuse is often confused with recycling, but they are really quite different. Examples of reuse include cutting a wool skirt into strips to reuse in a braided rug, refinishing an upholstered chair instead of throwing it away, keeping pins and needles in an empty cookie tin instead of tossing the tin, or reclaiming a rusted metal outdoor table by painting it instead of buying new patio furniture.

Why is reuse so important? According to the book *Choose to Reuse:*

❖ Reuse keeps goods and materials out of the waste stream.
❖ Reuse doesn't deplete the earth's resources.
❖ Reuse means energy won't be used to recycle the item or to create a brand-new replacement.
❖ Reuse creates less air and water pollution than would be created when making a new item or recycling.
❖ Reuse results in less hazardous waste because you don't have manufacturing by-products.
❖ Reuse saves money in purchases and disposal costs because you're not buying new, and you're not tossing out the old.
❖ Reuse generates new business and employment opportunities for both small entrepreneurs and large enterprises. Think about all the antique stores in your local area!
❖ Reuse creates an affordable supply of goods that are often of excellent quality, which is especially important for those with tight budgets or those trying to live sustainably. Reuse means bringing resources to individuals and organizations that might otherwise be unable to acquire them.

The best case for reuse is made by the more than 2,000 examples of individual, business, government, and charitable reuse that are included in *Choose to Reuse: An Encyclopedia of Services, Products, Programs, and Charitable Organizations That Foster Reuse,* by Nikki and David Goldbeck.

Newspapers: The entire newspaper, inserts, ads, and flyers can all be thrown in together, but remove any plastic bags, free samples, or rubber bands that might be included. Just toss all of your old newspapers into a brown paper bag and throw the whole thing in your recycling bin.

Telephone Books: Check inside the phone book to see what it is made from (often phone books are made from virgin forests!) and also where it can be locally recycled. All this information should be printed somewhere in the book.

Cardboard: Check with your local recycling facilities. If your neighborhood facility can't accept cardboard, ask your local supermarket if they recycle their cardboard and will allow you to pass yours along.

Milk Cartons: Some recycling facilities take waxed milk cartons (and waxed juice containers). Be aware that any plastic spouts must be removed and put in the trash because they usually aren't recyclable.

Aseptic Packaging: These are complex containers made from plastic, metal, and paper; if you're not familiar with their name, you'd recognize them when you saw them. Think kid-style sippy boxes of juice with the little plastic straw. All square boxes for juice, soymilk, chai, or any other liquid generally cannot be recycled because the container wall layers are bonded together. Coca-Cola has a list of aseptic recyclers available at 800-888-6488. If there's a recycler near you, that's wonderful news. Otherwise, buy products with this packaging as infrequently as possible.

Mixed Paper: This is essentially all types of paper not mentioned before. As long as it is dry, clean, and free of food and wax, it's considered mixed paper. Most junk mail goes in this category. Plastic window envelopes are fine. See if your local recycler accepts mixed paper.

Unrecyclable Paper: It is impossible to recycle anything with food, wax (milk cartons are an exception), oil, carbon, stickers, or plastic lamination or any sanitary products and tissues. These will have to head to the landfill until new technologies are developed.

Glass

Broken glass cannot be recycled, but everything else should be easily recycled. Clear glass is most valuable for recycling purposes. Do not mix glass bottles with other types of glass, such as mirrors, Pyrex, auto glass, and lightbulbs. Remove caps and lids from glass jars and bottles, and recycle them with metals or plastics, if possible.

Metals

Aluminum cans are almost always recyclable. It is no longer necessary to remove labels, and you need to clean them only enough to prevent odors. Scrap aluminum is sometimes accepted at recycling facilities; other metals are generally not accepted. Steel containers should be separated from other metals when they're recycled.

Printer Cartridges

Ask for postage-paid mailers from the store where you buy your printer cartridge. Many companies are now including such mailers with each new cartridge so that the cartridges can be easily recycled by the company for little cost.

Household Toxics

Paint, oils, pesticides, mercury thermometers, and other toxics should be disposed of as household hazardous waste. They should not be thrown into the garbage, where they can leach dangerous chemicals into landfills and, ultimately, the water supply, nor should

they be incinerated because that can release mercury and other metals into the air. Hazardous materials include automobile fluids, antifreeze, charcoal lighter fluid, mineral spirits, many art supplies such as turpentine and photographic chemicals, lawn and garden chemicals, old paint cans, and more. When in doubt, assume the product is household hazardous waste.

Every community has different facilities and guidelines, so call your town's recycling service to find out the best way to dispose of the toxic chemicals you have in your possession. Never pour anything down a storm drain because water entering roadside drains goes directly into streams and rivers untreated.

Batteries

Start a box in your house where you can place batteries that are past their prime. Store them until your community has a household hazardous waste pickup.

WORDS TO THE WISE

STATE-SPECIFIC UNIVERSAL WASTE REGULATIONS

There are universal waste regulations that have streamlined and standardized collection requirements for certain hazardous wastes, such as batteries, pesticides, mercury thermostats, and mercury lamps (mercury-containing lamp guidelines are still under development). Check out the Environmental Protection Agency's Web site on waste regulations for your home at www.epa.gov/epaoswer/ hazwaste/id/univwast/uwsum.htm.

This site lists every state in the United States with a link to that particular state's waste regulations as well as links to recycling facilities and answers to technical questions.

Alkaline and Heavy-Duty Batteries: These types of batteries are generally not recyclable. Since these batteries generally do not deteriorate, some municipalities consider them safe for landfills. Check out the Environmental Protection Agency's (EPA) Web site www.epa. state.oh.us/opp/recyc/battery.html for current information.

Nickel-Cadmium and Sealed Lead-Acid Batteries: These batteries contain heavy metals that will leach out in a landfill. Collect these batteries year-round for hazardous waste disposal; do not throw them out! Nickel-cadmium (Ni-Cd) and small sealed lead-acid batteries, which are found in many common items including electronic equipment, mobile telephones, portable computers, and emergency backup lighting, are classified as Federal Universal Wastes and need to be handed over to a household hazardous waste facility.

Rechargeable Batteries: If the rechargeable battery is no longer usable, type your zip code into the search box at www.rbrc.org/consumer/index.html to find information about how to dispose of it. A local Radio Shack may have a collection box for rechargeable batteries.

Thermostats

Thermostats can contain as much as 3 grams of liquid mercury and are located in many households. These are classified as Federal Universal Wastes and need to be disposed of at a household hazardous waste facility.

Motor Oil

Call your local garbage company or hauler, local quick-lube business, or 800-TEAM-VAL (832-6825) to learn how to properly dispose of motor oil in your area. Do not try to dispose of motor oil yourself. Every year, more oil is improperly dumped than was spilled by the *Exxon Valdez*.

Lamps

Some electric lamps have a hazardous component and are categorized as Universal Waste because they may contain mercury and other toxic materials. Fluorescent lights, high-intensity discharge, neon, mercury vapor, high-pressure sodium, and metal halide lamps may all contain hazardous or toxic materials.

Paints, Pesticides, and Other Toxic Materials

I don't buy the "use it up" recommendation for old cans of paints and pesticides (those that haven't been taken off the market). In my opinion, the potential risk to health from many of these products is too high. Instead, safely store them for a household hazardous waste pickup day.

Refrigerators, Heat Pumps, Air Conditioners, and More

You can't just throw them away! Many appliances contain chemicals that destroy the ozone layer—our planet's natural protection against the sun's harmful ultraviolet radiation. Refrigerators, window and car air conditioners, and dehumidifiers rely on refrigerants that contain ozone-depleting chlorofluorocarbons (CFCs) and hydrochlorofluorocarbons (HCFCs) (often known by the trade name Freon).

Anybody who throws out appliances with CFCs or HCFCs can be fined up to $25,000 for each day the refrigerant is escaping into the atmosphere. Contact the public works department in your town or county and ask for information about home appliance recycling or CFC/HCFC–recovery programs.

Still Don't Know?

Check with your local garbage hauler or your municipal public works department. It's always better to ask than to dump something that could potentially damage the environment for generations to come.

Burning Trash

Research now suggests that trash incineration leaves behind prodigious quantities of dioxins and related compounds, which other studies have shown can cause cancer and damage the liver and immune system. In poor urban areas of underdeveloped countries, people frequently set fire to refuse that accumulates along streets and in unofficial dumps, creating additional health hazards for poverty-stricken residents.

The Ultimate in Recycling—Composting!

When you make compost, you recycle wastes—kitchen scraps, grass clippings, fallen leaves, and dead or pruned garden plants—that otherwise would end up being dumped in a landfill. Composting saves not only landfill space but also the precious nutrients contained in the organic matter. In fact, composting is the only form of waste disposal that conserves these nutrients, so they can, eventually, be returned to the soil. Composting also helps the environment by eliminating the need for chemical fertilizers.

Worm Composting

I worm-sat for a friend's worm composting bin over one summer, and I can tell you firsthand that this system of composting really works, and it doesn't smell. If you live in a city, you can compost your garbage in a worm composting bin without any problem, and you'll reap the benefits of rich compost for your container plants, window boxes, or outdoor pots. Just put the composting bin somewhere dark, like under your kitchen sink.

You generally buy your worms from a local gardening shop, through mail order, or online. Little worms are the most adaptive to under-the-sink compost bins; avoid bait-shop worms because they tend to be too large. Red worms or manure worms work best. These worms process large quantities of kitchen scraps, they reproduce well, and they tolerate a range of household temperatures.

Backyard Composting

The amount of vegetable peels, coffee grounds, fruit, and eggshells that one family throws out in a day can be really impressive. If you have a yard, it is perfectly safe to take one small corner for a simple composting bin. I don't always find composting easy or convenient, but I continue doing it year after year

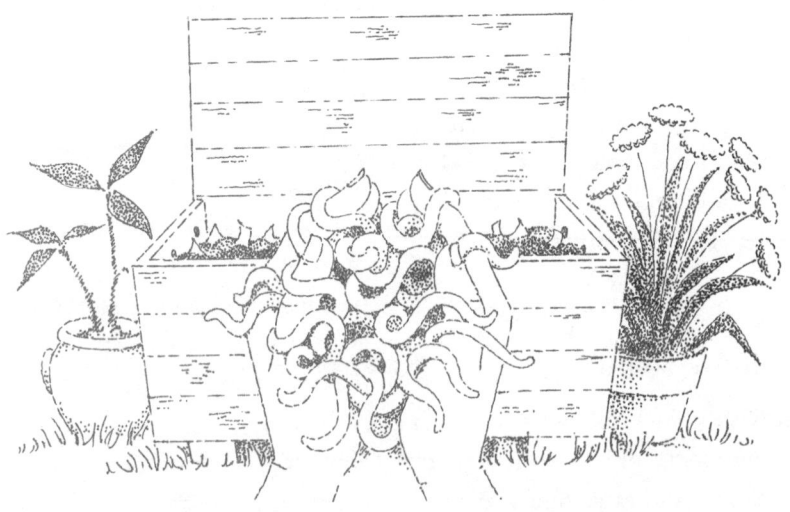

Worm composting starts with a ventilated bin, newspaper, water, garden soil, and red worms. Feed the worms your kitchen scraps, and watch them turn your garbage into rich, black humusy soil. With minimal effort, composting kitchen waste with worms is virtually odor free!

MAKE IT YOURSELF
MAKE IT YOURSELF
A SUCCESSFUL WORM COMPOSTING BIN

Just put "worm bins" into an Internet search and up will pop worm composting newsletters, directions for making your own worm bins, reviews of worm bins, mail-order worms, and where to buy ready-made worm bins!

Worm bin with holes in the sides
Newspaper
Water
Garden soil (a few handfuls)
Red worms (½ pound of worms is best for one person; 2 pounds will handle the compost
   of a family of four)

Cover the bottom of the bin with newspapers and saturate the newspapers with water. Add in the garden soil. You must have enough water in the bin, or the worms will die. The rule of thumb is to use 8 pounds of newspaper to 1 gallon of water.

Place the worms in the bin with the wet newspapers. Two pounds of worms will eat 1 pound of garbage a day. To start with, weigh your garbage so that you don't overfeed the worms. If there is too much garbage for the worms to eat, the compost will smell.

Check to make sure there is enough water in the bin every few weeks. Every 2 to 3 months, you will need to "harvest" the bin. The bin will be full of dirt (which is really vermicompost or worm excrement), and you'll need to gently separate the worms from the dirt. The dirt can be used as a fertilizer and added right to a garden bed or yard. (If your goal is only to compost kitchen scraps, and you have no use for the vermicompost, find a friend willing to use it on their garden rather than discarding it.)

Start with fresh newspaper and water, return the worms to the bin, and start again. ❖

because I hate to think of all those vegetable peels going into the landfill.

To be fair, if I weren't so sensitive to mold, I would consider the process easier than I do. But one has to be careful not to have food rot in the kitchen, which is unhealthy, so you need to continually take the compost to the outdoor bin. Once there, you need to maintain the bin if you want to have good compost for your garden. Make sure you place the bins downwind from the house and the neighbors.

Compost results from mixing household vegetable matter with brown material from the yard (such as twigs and leaves) in a big bin and giving the mixture regular air circulation using a pitchfork or other method until it decomposes. Compost makes a rich, dark, and highly nutritious soil amendment that helps your garden grow. There are many styles and varieties of compost bins available, so do some research into the model that will best serve your needs. I finally settled on one that is easy to use and that doesn't attract animals; it's a large plastic barrel that you can turn with your foot to increase air circulation. Even someone as sensitive to mold as I am can use this bin.

Ideally, a compost pile should be a blend of 75 percent brown materials and 25 percent green materials. Brown materials include leaves, twigs, dried weeds, straw, and hay. Green materials include kitchen vegetable and fruit scraps and green grass clippings. Note that this ratio is 75 percent *brown* materials to 25 percent green; many beginners mix this up. For the first 4 to 5 years that I composted, I reversed these numbers, which is why I had such trouble with a mold smell coming from my composting bin. It isn't easy keeping up with all the brown material when you are a family that eats a lot of fruits and vegetables. Needing that many leaves inspires you to keep up with your yard work. Never include meat, fish, dairy products, fats, or treated or synthetic materials in your compost bin. Build your pile at least 3- by 3- by 3-feet so materials heat up and decompose quickly.

Stepping Inside Your Home

Your house has a number of features that need to be understood and analyzed if you want to assess how healthy

it is and how changes can improve your indoor environment and your indoor air quality. Inside your front door is the perfect place to begin taking stock.

Color in the Home

Choose the colors in your home with awareness of how different colors affect your emotional and physical states. Every color has a unique vibration all its own, and this can significantly affect how you feel in a room. You want to choose colors that are in balance and harmony with the role you'd like a room to have in your and your family's life.

Room Colors

In general, light, cool colors such as blue, green, and violet recede and make a room appear larger. Darker cool colors help make a room feel more intimate. Warm colors, by contrast, such as red and yellow, help make a room feel cheerful.

Red: Red is a call to action. A room that is painted red will energize, inspire activity and movement, heighten passion, and be powerful and stimulating. A red room can also be exhausting and overpowering and stressful for those who are anxious. Pink is less demanding. Choosing a red bedroom would not be restful, although some red can be used to enhance sensuality. A red exercise room would be energizing! In feng shui, red means luck.

Orange: Orange rooms encourage happy, joyful social gatherings. Since an orange dining room or family room can stimulate the appetite, it is an ideal choice for such gathering places. Orange enhances parties, communication, positive feelings, and general good cheer.

Yellow: Yellow rooms can inspire intellectual clarity, organization, clear-headed, articulate thinking, and happy energy. Yellow is considered a color for the logical left side of the brain. Yellow is also very bright and somewhat energizing, so you need to choose its placement with care. A yellow office might be intellectually beneficial, but it will not allow restful downtime; you might want to choose yellow accents instead of painting each wall yellow.

Green: Green rooms are very restful but combine with an energizing quality. Green is the color of the outdoors—calm and active at the same time. Green brings balance and harmony, healing, and rejuvenation to a room and can be used for a calming place for people who are troubled or in need of refreshment.

Blue: Blue is often chosen for bedrooms and meditation rooms because its cool energy is very calming, restful, peaceful, and spiritual. Blue also helps inspire a quiet meditative quality, and color therapy with blue has been found to reduce blood pressure. Blue is useful to soothe one to sleep.

Purple and Indigo: Purple is very comforting, protective, spiritual, and calming. It is a rich color that inspires faith, intuition, and trust. Entire rooms painted purple could be overpowering, but a light violet could provide a very healing and calming atmosphere.

White: White rooms work anywhere combined with accent colors. White is very purifying, uplifting, and cleansing, although too much white can reflect a sterile, isolating quality. White ceilings are recommended because they reflect light and brighten any room.

Earth Pigment Colors

Natural pigments are wonderful, complex colors that are deeply resonant to the eye. If I could, I would redo each and every room in my house to have plaster walls with a natural earth-pigment-colored paint. Natural pigments from the earth provide a broad range of colors. They are usually made of clay combined with different iron oxides, and it is the way these minerals have been exposed to the weather and their ratios that determine the resulting colors. Lapis lazuli—an ultramarine rich, dark blue—is made from minerals, as are the blue-greens of azurite and mala-

(continued on page 50)

Healthy Home Checklist and Questionnaire

If you answer "yes" to any of these questions, read more about how to solve the issues surrounding that topic in this book and through credible sources online or in magazines and books.

❑ Does your house have a noticeable smell, which is particularly evident on your return after you've been away for a day or two? Isolate the smell and work to remove or seal in the cause. See pages 179 and 383.

❑ Is your house or apartment building less than 5 years old? Have you done any renovating in the past 3 years? Unless building or renovating was done with nontoxic materials, the more time that has passed between renovating or building and your occupation of the house, the better, or you might have high levels of VOCs, including formaldehyde. Try to avoid living in a house that has been substantially renovated in the past year. See pages 51, 78, and 85.

❑ Do you live in an apartment or duplex? Be aware that your neighbors' use of toxins will affect you—for example, if they use kerosene space heaters. See pages 6 and 425.

❑ Does your home have a history of pesticide applications? If so, test it for chlordane. Chlordane is a long-lasting contaminant that is one of the most dangerous pesticides used in homes (it is now off the market for home pesticide application). If you have chlordane residue, contact a professional pesticide remediation company. Consult the Yellow Pages of your phone book.

❑ Are you exposed to unsafe levels of electromagnetic fields (EMFs)? If you don't know much about EMFs and haven't tested for them with a gaussmeter, see pages 280 and 370.

❑ Has your foundation been damp-proofed with asphalt-based sealants, or is it wood that has been treated with pesticides or is pressure-treated? Does it smell? If so, contact www.needs.com and inquire about a product to seal in the asphalt-based sealant. See page 35.

❑ Does your basement smell moldy or is it damp? Work on removing the mold. See page 383.

❑ Are some of your kitchen countertops, bookshelves, desks, cupboards, and other furniture made of particleboard or unsealed chipboard or fiberboard? You might have quite a formaldehyde problem. Contact AFM Safecoat & Safechoice for safe sealants that can help reduce formaldehyde. See pages 487 and 488.

❑ Are cabinet doors or interior doors made of particleboard or plastic laminates? See page 367.

❑ Is your garage attached to the house and used for cars? Fumes from the car exhaust and chemicals stored in the garage can waft into the house. See pages 426 and 427.

❑ Do you use kerosene space heaters? Is your gas or oil furnace part of the living space? Do you use an unventilated petroleum-based heating system? These are very unhealthy situations and should be rectified. Remove kerosene space heaters and rehouse furnaces to be outside of the living space. See pages 425 and 426.

❑ Does the home have a forced hot-air heating system with or without a filter? Dusts, molds, and pollutants can waft throughout the house. See page 425.

❑ Do you heat with an older woodstove that isn't well sealed? It is important to update the stove with one that is environmentally safe and doesn't pollute both the inside and outside of the home. See page 310.

❑ Is the insulation in your house expanded polystyrene, polyurethane, polyisocyanurate, phenolic rigid boards, asbestos, urea-formaldehyde, or fiberglass that is exposed to the living space? Contact an indoor air quality expert to determine how to solve the situation. See page 307.

❏ Does the house have vinyl or plastic wallpaper, or is there wallpaper attached with toxic glue (containing fungicides or mildewcides)? Put its removal on your list of chores.

❏ Does your roofing material smell when the sun shines on it? Keep your upstairs windows closed to avoid the smell.

❏ Are the subfloors of your house made of particleboard? This will contribute a great deal of formaldehyde to your home and really should be removed. If that isn't possible, seal it in using an AFM sealant. See page 487.

❏ Do you have asbestos-wrapped pipes? Contact experts to remove this. See pages 397 and 399.

❏ Do you have a gas stove? Studies show that a house with an unvented gas stove can have significant air-quality problems. If it isn't possible to replace the gas with electric, make sure you upgrade to a gas stove with an electronic pilot. See page 179.

❏ Is there sufficient ability to get "fresh" air? Adequate ventilation is mandatory for good health, both to maintain sufficient oxygen levels and to reduce buildup of any pollutants that might be present in the house. Make sure there is adequate ventilation through open windows, exhaust fans, or air-to-air heat exchangers. If the house needs more ventilation, plan where additional ventilation can be installed. See pages 179, 425, and 426.

❏ Does the house have sufficient natural light? The healthiest light source is the natural light of the sun. Look at the windows, the path of the sun, and any obstacles to determine if you can go through the day inside the house with minimal use of artificial light. If necessary, more sunlight can be brought into the house with the installation of windows and skylights. If natural light isn't available, look into buying full-spectrum lighting. See pages 299 and 302.

❏ Have oil-based paints and insecticide-treated stains been used? Choosing either of these options from the start isn't recommended because the fumes are neurotoxic, and many are carcinogenic. If you already have these finishes in the house and lead has been eliminated as a problem (see later in this chapter), dry the oil-based paint as quickly as possible using fans and ventilation. Seal in the treated stains by contacting www.needs.com or AFM Safecoat & Safechoice for sealants designed to eliminate toxins. See pages 52 and 487.

❏ Is there paint in the house that was applied before 1978? If so, you most likely will find lead in the paint, and you'll need to be concerned about lead contamination. See page 53.

❏ Is there wall-to-wall carpeting or laminated flooring? See pages 78 and 85.

❏ Are the supply pipes of the house lead? The pipes that feed into your house will probably need to be changed. See pages 53 and 213.

❏ Is there a water-filtering system for drinking and bathing? See page 211.

❏ Do you have carbon monoxide, smoke, and fire alarms? See page 397.

❏ Have you tested your home for radon? See pages 399 and 400.

It is important not to become overwhelmed when trying to create a healthy home. If you choose environmentally friendly products and have an awareness of the issues, you're making good health a high priority.

It's important to prioritize the environmental concerns in your home. Work on the top of the list as soon as you can; and if your budget allows it, consult with air-quality or natural products experts to solve those, and whittle away the rest of the issues as time and money allow. Every effort you make will reduce your chemical overload.

chite. Red colors can be made from the mineral composition cinnabar. For more suggestions for natural dyes and pigments, including recipes for how to use them, see my book *Better Basics for the Home*. Always wear a protective dust mask approved by the National Institute for Occupational Safety and Health (NIOSH) when working with any powdered pigment.

Iron Oxides: These hematite pigments range from violet-purple to red to orange. Limonite ranges from yellow to brown. Rubefield earth pigments are reds produced when iron is exposed to rain. Ochers are mixtures of quartz, clay, and iron oxide and range from brown to violet.

Terre Verte: Green earth is abundant in nature and makes hues of blues and greens, but terra verte pigments tend to be weak because the color is diluted with so much clay.

Insect Colors: Cochineal dye is made from the bodies of dead scale insects; the resulting color is a rich purple-red.

Plant Colors: The earth provides an abundant supply of plants for dyes. Alkanet is a plant root that provides a deep, rich red, and it is often used as a natural cosmetic as well as an art pigment. Saffron provides a yellow color, and mulberry juice contains red and purple pigments. Tannins, like those found in black tea and walnuts, pro-

duce browns. Indigo, that gorgeous deep blue of the night sky, is produced by tropical plants, but beware that most indigo available is synthetic, so verify your sources.

Walls and Their Impact on Your Indoor Environment

Once, when I was very sick with chemical sensitivity, I had to cover the walls of an apartment we were living in with foil because the fumes from the walls were so strong. The paint had dried, but it was the spackle that was the biggest environmental health problem, followed by the outgassing drywall.

My respect for healthy, natural walls began at that time. While I don't live with natural walls now, all the spackle and drywall has long since outgassed, and the paint we used to paint the walls is free of biocides. By now, the walls are quite inert. The goal for most building materials should be "the more inert, the better."

Plaster Walls

True, old-fashioned plaster walls are made of the mineral gypsum. These are wonderful walls full of character. Clay-based and lime-based plasters are also natural. Gypsum is the strongest and

Safe and Sound

THE SAFEST WALLS

The most ecofriendly walls are made of plaster and painted with a low-biocide paint, such as milk paint. Second for environmental friendliness is ceramic tile (using Portland thinset and Portland cement grout) if it doesn't require a finish. Gypsum board, sheet rock, drywall with a nontoxic joint compound, or solid wood paneling would be a good third choice.

Avoid wallpaper altogether if you can because most is adhered to walls with glues that contain fungicide. Some kinds of wallpaper, such as natural-fiber fabric wallpaper, collect dust. Avoid wallpaper made of vinyl and other plastics or any wallpaper applied with a toxic glue high in VOCs and fungicides.

hardest, although the lime and clay-based plasters breathe more. Plaster walls are very ecofriendly because they are so natural. The clays can retain a lot of moisture, however, so they can become moldy more quickly than drywall.

Traditional gypsum plaster is worth the effort and expense; there is very little maintenance when finished because it is so durable. Clay-based plaster is the easiest for beginners to apply, though. Clay is an earthy dirt that hardens when dry and is used in a wide range of building materials. The earth tones of various clays are truly beautiful. Lime (mason's lime, specifically) is a highly alkaline mineral used famously for white wash and milk paint.

More recently, plasterboard (with a gypsum core) or gypsum board has been substituted for traditional plaster walls. Most walls built today are made from drywall, which also has a gypsum core with a paper facing. The joint compound and finishing tape in these plas-

ter substitutes can be irritating to sensitive individuals.

Painted Walls

A new paint job can brighten up any room, and the array of colors available in paints today can add to one's enjoyment of life. What you don't want to do is to bring a new set of pollutants into your home. Fortunately, due to some proactive paint manufacturing companies, there is a wide array of safer paints on the market today, so do your homework before you buy.

Latex Paint: Water is the principal solvent, substantially reducing the level of harmful VOCs, although not eliminating them. Search for low-VOC or zero-VOC paints. Quite a number of the largest brand-name paint manufacturers offer versions of low- and no-VOC paint—an excellent choice for everyone. Some national brands and a number of special niche brands offer paint that is designed to be healthier by reducing VOCs; they're also low odor. Glidden is a large national brand that has produced a zero-VOC paint. There are no petroleum-based solvents, such as ethylene glycol, in these paints.

Oil-Based Paint: Because of their environmental impact, avoid oil-based paints if you can. These contain petroleum-based solvents, and the paints are high in VOCs. Aerosol spray paints are particularly dangerous. Avoid oil-based paint on the exterior of your house too, because VOCs can linger for months and could enter through exterior walls.

Plant-Oil Paint: Sounds like a good idea, but there are pros and cons to plant-oil paints. They are petroleum free, but they can be high in VOCs, and the smell of the solvents can last for months, even years. Terpenes from natural plants, such as citrus and balsam, are used as the solvents in these paints, and they can be highly problematic for those sensitive to terpenes.

Milk Paint and Whitewash: Both milk paint and whitewash allow the underlying material—be it plaster or wood—to breathe, thereby reducing mold and rot. Milk paint is made of the milk protein casein, lime, and natural earth pigments. Whitewash is made of lime and water and sometimes casein. Both milk paint and whitewash have a high alkaline content that makes them a natural insect repellent and disinfectant.

Low-VOC, Low-Biocide, and No-Fungicide Paints: Unless designated otherwise, paints contain fungicides to prevent mildew growth and biocides to extend the shelf life of the paint. By far, the safest interior paint (aside from milk paint, for those not allergic to milk) is paint that is described as having no fungicides or biocides in the product.

Exterior Paints: All exterior paints have fungicides, and exterior stains are even more laden with them than paints. The best choice for an exterior paint is one that has zinc oxide as the fungicide.

Recycled Paints: I don't recommend so-called green paints made by recycling old paint because the paints con-

SHOPPING SOLUTIONS
THE NATURAL PAINT BOOK

Here is a gem of a book: *The Natural Paint Book: A Complete Guide to Natural Paints, Recipes, and Finishes*, by Lynn Edwards and Julia Lawless. In this book, there are more than 50 recipes and techniques for natural paints and finishes, and they use readily available ingredients. The book provides in-depth information about how to make your own beautiful, luminous, natural paints using earth pigments.

tain VOCs and possibly heavy metals. The exception to my rule would be if you had no choice but to buy a regular latex paint and could buy a recycled version instead, assuming that none of the original paint going into the mix contained lead or mercury.

Lead in the Home

Every new study that comes out seems to have more bad news about the impact of lead on our lives and, especially, the lives of our children. Lead is neurotoxic and can reduce IQ points, delay puberty, and affect cognitive development. About 900,000 children ages 1 to 5 have a blood lead level above the level of concern, according to the EPA. Studies in 2003 showed that concentrations of 1 microgram per deciliter negatively impacted children's IQ levels, suggesting that there may, in fact, be no safe level for lead exposure.

Lead is found in far more places than you may realize. Lead is most likely to come from lead-based paint. Houses built before 1978, the date when lead was taken out of paint, should be tested. Powdery white paint is usually a sign of lead. Even household dust may be a source of lead, if the dust is from deteriorating paint. (Lead-testing kits are available at a reasonable price from your county health department or a local hardware store.)

Lead can be found in soil around the house, especially near siding or wooden molding that's been painted in the past. You may also find lead in your drinking water from lead pipes or lead solder used on copper water pipes.

Old painted toys (such as tin soldiers) or furniture can have remnants of lead paint. Food kept in old lead-glazed pottery, lead crystal, or dishes from foreign countries can become contaminated with lead. While newer pottery made in the United States should be lead free, you can also test with a lead swab kit if you're unsure. Some hobbies, such as stained glass or antique toy trains, can bring lead into your home. Telephone cords can contain lead compounds that are still commonly used as plasticizers for vinyl plastics. As a rule, the older the cord, the more surface lead is found.

And be wary of home remedies that could contain lead, such as "greta" or "azarcon," which are used for upset stomach or indigestion, and "pay-loo-ah" used for rash or fever.

Solutions to Lead Contamination

If you have any concern about the paint in your house, make sure that you take care of chipping or peeling paint, dust and wet-mop frequently, and have your home tested in one of two ways. The first way is to have a paint inspection that will tell you the lead content of every type of paint in your house. The second is a risk assessment that will tell you if there are any sources of lead exposure (peeling paint or dust); the assessment will also tell you how to address these issues.

If you have lead-based paint, it is best to allow a professional to take care of remodeling or repainting. They will be required by federal law to give you a pamphlet informing you about the risks of lead. Contact the National Lead Information Center for a list of professionals in your area. Don't try to remedy lead paint in your home by yourself. Don't use or allow removal methods that increase the amount of dust and fumes in your home, such as heat guns, dry scrapers and sandpaper, belt sanders, or propane torches. And temporarily move your family, especially children and pregnant women, until abatement work is done and the area is thoroughly cleaned.

Clean play areas regularly, wash your children's hands frequently, and make sure they eat a nutritious diet high in iron and calcium, because these will lead to less lead absorption. Children absorb lead at the highest rates between 6 and 24 months of age, peaking between 18 and 24 months, so have lead levels tested regularly, especially during these years.

Lead Testing Kits

Did you know that the Centers for Disease Control and Prevention (CDC) has patented a "Handwipe Disclosing Method for the Presence of Lead?" Released in fall 2002, this handwipe can quickly detect lead on the skin, a steering wheel, windowsills, tables, or anywhere else lead might be suspected of lurking. It was developed by the CDC's NIOSH. For more information on CDC technologies, look on the Internet at www.cdc.gov/od/ads/techtran/tech.htm. Professional x-ray fluorescence lead testing of paint and laboratory testing of lead (check the Yellow Pages) are also recommended.

Talk to the local health department if your home or apartment was built before 1978. If you are concerned that your children have been exposed to lead, have your pediatrician do a simple blood test.

If you are concerned about lead in your plumbing, have your water tested by a professional, and contact your local health department or water supplier to analyze the lead content of your pipes or pipe solder. You can flush your pipes for 2 to 3 minutes every morning before you use any water for drinking or cooking.

I remember drawing my finger along the windowsill of my childhood bedroom and seeing the white powdery dust that would come onto my finger.

What a dead giveaway that there was lead in that paint, if only we had known it at the time. I hate to think of how much IQ I must have lost because of my early childhood lead exposure! My daughter was on the high end of normal for lead in her blood, and I was quite scrupulous about her childhood surroundings from an environmental health exposure; her doctor and I have concluded that her lead exposure came from me in utero. What a tragedy lead exposure is, but thanks to the law of 1978 regarding lead paint, we can keep exposure to a minimum. If you live in an old house, be assured that lead paint remediation is done all the time and done successfully. Just make sure to work with experts. All it takes to get started is an inexpensive lead-testing kit. If you discover lead in your home, you can start working toward remediation.

3

dining, living, and family rooms

When I asked my daughter how she would describe a successful dining, living, or family room, she answered: "It is a place you want to be." What a great answer. Defining what makes a room "a place you want to be" is one of the joys of homekeeping. While we may differ in decorating style or details, we all yearn to create an atmosphere that promotes welcome, sharing, acceptance, unconditional love, trust, stability, and friendliness—attributes that most of us want and need in the communal spaces of our homes. We all like to belong, to be part of a place, and to feel welcomed and well received. I have found that "professional decorator" beauty that doesn't also promote a sense of welcome and connection doesn't hold up in the communal rooms of a home. A living room

may have exquisite furniture and paintings, but if the room is designed for show, and you don't feel welcome to sit there or don't feel a connection to yourself, nature, or others, you don't feel welcome to open your heart there, either.

Create a Welcoming Place

Ironically, some of the most welcoming homes I have been in reflect that the owners obviously cherish spending time alone. There is space for reading, relaxing, listening to music, or just watching the wildlife outside of a window. Rest, renewal, and contemplation are essential to being a healthy person, and they all have a place in a healing home. You should make room in your home for quiet places—for yourself and for you *and* others in the family to share. Once you're rested and renewed, you'll find that you have more to give to others.

An important part of rest, renewal, and contemplation is feeling a sense of balance and connection to your surroundings. Turn to the four elements—earth, water, fire, and air—to bring harmony to the shared rooms in your home. Bring plants, natural fibers, and rich, earthy colors into a room to embrace the earth element. Introduce the water element in a room by using a bubbling tabletop fountain and windows that allow you to see the rain and the snow as they fall. A fireplace and lots of natural light streaming into a room will welcome the fire element. The air element can be enhanced with beautiful music and clean indoor air quality.

The changes needed to connect you to nature can be small or large. Making even the smallest connection to the elements will bring you harmony—think what a major shift in lifestyle and surroundings could do to change your family's life.

Please the Senses

No matter what our preference or style, when we see real beauty, most of us are uplifted. I've seen beauty in a number of homes—each of them was beautiful in a different way. It was subtly obvious that care and thought had gone into the aesthetic choices when the owners were building, decorating, and just plain thriving in their homes.

Homes with a view of nature are particularly beautiful, I think, and help to minimize our separation from the rhythms of the world. Fish tanks, bird feeders outside the windows, stones (inside and outside), and a view of a garden can visually enhance your life. Do you have an indoor/outdoor thermometer within view to connect you to the weather? Do you have a barometer? How about a book on backyard birds or identifying clouds?

Remember how much fun it was when you were a kid and you turned on the porch light every hour to see how much snow was falling? It was a connection to nature that you reveled in, even if you were shut inside a toasty, warm home. There's no reason not to enjoy that same connection as an adult. Outdoor lights are a treat in a snowstorm—turn off all the inside lights, then throw the switch for your outdoor light, and watch the snow fall. You'll be amazed at how calm and peaceful you'll feel after just an hour of watching the snowflakes—if you allow yourself to connect to nature in a setting this peaceful.

Decorating with nature often brings with it a sense of harmony. One of my friend's homes is decorated almost exclusively with stones, feathers, and dried plant materials found nearby on the land. She has exquisite taste and what appears to be a spiritually guided sense of design; while the objects are sparsely placed, the overall aesthetic is one of spiritual beauty, tranquility, and abundance.

Houseplants bring cleaner air and living companionship, in a way. Watching a plant grow, change, and develop can be an enrichment for one's life. They can also be a helpful addition: My sister has a huge aloe vera plant in her living room, and every time someone gets a burn or other skin problem, she cuts off an aloe leaf to help the person heal. For more about houseplants, see page 77.

nal spaces, especially the dining room, where the harvest can be shared and enjoyed. Many of the earthen colors also radiate calmness and serenity, so these work well in areas where you want to be more self-reflective and spiritual. Blue is a tranquil color, too. Who doesn't appreciate the vast expanse of a blue sky? We're used to being surrounded by blue, so blue décor, whether it's a wall, furniture, or accessories, brings calm and restfulness to any room.

Soothing with Sound

The sounds of nature and music make the senses sing. Water fountains can be very soothing and grounding; the continuous gurgling, splashing, and

Choosing Colors

To create a look that welcomes and nurtures, choose browns, oranges, and greens for the communal rooms of your home. The greens give the restful and rejuvenating feeling found in nature; and when grounded by the browns of dirt, tree trunks, and wood, you feel secure and safe. Orange is a very social, joyful color, and it supports fun, lively social gatherings. Orange is also a color of the harvest, so it fits well in commu-

A cascading tabletop fountain provides a tranquil respite from a nonstop day. As water tumbles over rocks and pebbles, you'll tune out household noise and lose yourself in the moment.

movement actually lull you into a more passive mood whether you're outside enjoying a rushing stream and a waterfall or you're inside gazing at a tabletop fountain. Water isn't static in sound, though; as it moves over rocks or down its courseway, it provides nuances of drips and splashes to keep your ear tuned.

Not all sound is so peaceful. You already know that horns beeping, trucks shifting gears, and the drone of airplanes can disturb your quiet time, but you may not realize how small noises can overstimulate your senses. I've never liked a room where a clock ticks loudly. Such methodical ticking is even worse when you are alone. A constant television sound in the background of a room is a huge drain on energy if you aren't the one watching. Even the noises that household heaters or furnaces make when they turn on and off can be disruptive on a day when you're easily distracted.

The human voice is one of the most comforting sounds you'll hear. Listening, really listening, to what others have to say involves more than just having good hearing. Are your ears open or closed? Do you judge what you hear? Do you just listen? Do you offer feedback? So many people are afraid to speak the truth—what's in their hearts—because they haven't had an opportunity to speak so that others listen.

How can you improve this scenario in your own home? If you are married or have a partner, perhaps you can connect while you're preparing dinner or right before bedtime to discuss issues before you go to sleep. If you have a family, dinnertime might be the best time to get everyone's undivided attention. One family I know has established that dinnertime is "together time," and each family member is encouraged to share something about their day. No matter what kind of day the family members have had, sharing means everyone connects, everyone stays informed about day-to-day experiences, and most important, everyone listens.

Tactile Touch

Natural materials offer us their life force energy. Wood, stone, and natural fiber enhance our lives, and we respond positively to touching them and living with them. Clean furnishings feel much better than those that are dirty, so keeping upholstery and furniture clean is important to your enjoyment of a room. I've seen wooden chairs with the finish worn down on the arms; it's the smoothness of the wood that makes people caress the rounded edges whenever they sit in the chair.

Your feet and toes can be as receptive as your hands when it comes to touch. Do you like the way old wooden floor-

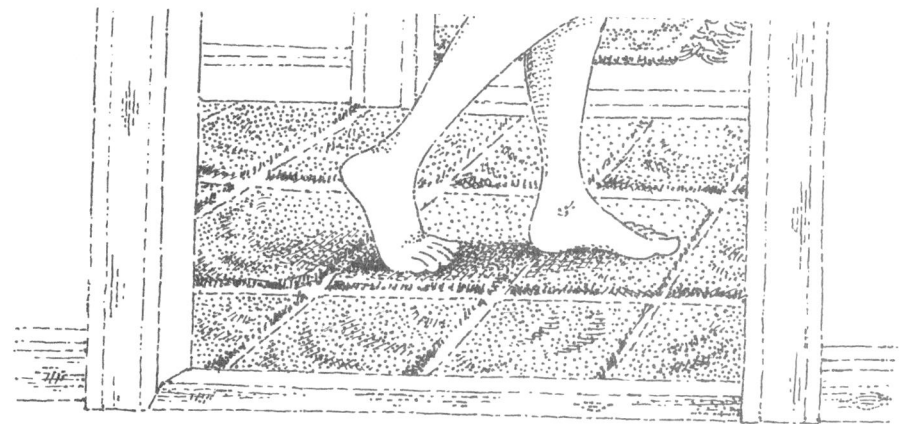

Stroll across a slate floor and feel its refreshing coolness and naturally irregular surface underfoot. The texture of natural materials can convince you that simple choices are often the best choices.

boards "give" as you walk across them? They're absorbing your energy as you take in their tactile nature underfoot. Walking barefoot through a slate entryway or across a flagstone patio allows you to connect with eons-old stone. Even glass, with its subtle beginnings as sand, can offer a mesmerizing array of textures and colors that attract your hand as well as your eye. We take touch for granted in our everyday lives, but decorating with natural things keeps you subtly connected to the world just outside the door.

The Pleasure of Smell

Clean air is essential to a healthy home. The less you smell of that which isn't natural, the better, because it means that your furnishings are not outgassing synthetic chemicals. There are smells that you'll welcome in your home—the smell of freshly baked bread wafting from the kitchen, the scent of lily of the valley stems on your windowsill, or the freshness of sun-dried pillowcases. The scents of nature and natural things make you feel grounded. Plants, flowers, and dried botanicals should be a part of your environment, and prudent use of aromatherapy can enhance the communal rooms of your home.

Honoring Your Sixth Sense

The family fireplace used to be the year-round gathering place for families, where chairs were set for a place to sit and talk. Watching flames seems to put people in touch with themselves and helps them feel at ease. Design or rearrange rooms to create centers that let you connect to others or provide downtime for yourself. If you don't have a fireplace, you can still provide

SYNTHETIC SMELLS

Synthetic materials can emit toxic fumes that are bad for our health. They can also put an imbalance of ions in the air. Air contains billions of electrically charged particles called ions. Ions act upon our capacity to absorb and utilize oxygen and therefore can have powerful effects on our lives and well-being. The ions in the air can affect our mood, energy, and health. Too many positive ions make us feel bad; they are loaded down with pollution and allergens that are drawn to them and are suspended in the air. Negative ions actually feel good; they remove the pollution and allergens from positive ions.

Polyester and plastic attract positive ions so that the healthful and uplifting negative ions are in a less auspicious balance, and the resulting atmosphere is one where it is harder to thrive. Many synthetics are also toxic, neurotoxic, and carcinogenic. Neurotoxic chemicals are chemicals that affect the central nervous system and brain specifically. Toxic chemicals can affect any of the body's systems and organs, including the brain and central nervous system.

It's difficult to locate natural products for many of the items in your home, but don't be discouraged. Even mainstream retailers are recognizing trends and are stocking more products that cater to those who prefer real wood, natural fibers, and nontoxic formulas for cleaning. Catalogs, Web sites, and natural and health food stores are your best bets for finding products to support your natural lifestyle.

Do your homework and be especially careful before buying any of these products if they're made with synthetic materials: art and craft supplies, inks and pens, renovating or building materials, cleaning and pest control products, and candles and aromatherapy.

that same atmosphere in your room arrangement.

Comfortable couches and chairs gathered together are a welcoming way to encourage conversation and sharing time together. I have round coffee tables in two different such spots in my home because I find the round shape is so inclusive that everybody feels like they belong. Natural candles on the tables bring in some of the fire element.

A cozy area for television- and movie-watching is another place that is central now to most homes. Who doesn't love sharing the experience of watching a good movie with a family member and being able to fully stretch

out and be comfortable? Turning the television off is important, too, so that friends and family can participate in activities, such as playing games or cards or having tea or hot chocolate, in these cozy nooks.

Even cluttered spaces can be lovely if there is a sense that you are welcome in them. Rate your comfort in a room on a scale of 1 to 10, with 10 being perfect. If you don't have a perfect score, figure out what it is that doesn't feel perfect, and try to correct the issues, one at a time. Only *you* know what is and isn't right. Ask other family members to rate their feelings in a room, too, so that you can help them feel more comfortable.

Listen to your sixth sense, and you'll be able to figure out what needs to be changed or improved.

It is a place where daily patterns have been repeated so much that the energy around it is of an intense vibration full of stories.

The Dining Room

Most dining rooms are used for multiple purposes: for homework, projects, meetings, formal entertaining, birthday parties, and casual family dinners. The homes I've lived in have always had a combined kitchen/dining room. I still have the dining room table I grew up with, and it has carried the emotional life of my family in its essence. If someone had been taking notes at this table over the years, our life story and daily patterns would have been revealed in all of their rich detail, from what we ate, to how we communicated, to laundry that was folded, to how news of the world was digested. I literally made my wedding dress on the table and fed my daughter her first meals on the table. All of us have laughed and cried there.

Sharing Meals and Giving Thanks Together

Sharing meals together is one of the oldest forms of communion. Giving thanks for the blessing of the food and the people present at a meal is a tradition that harkens back to pagan times.

Centerpieces of Life

Before a recent holiday meal at our dinner table, a friend of mine inquired about the blessing I was planning to use. I thought about this for a while because asking for a blessing isn't a ritual that comes easily to me and isn't something that was part of our family's holiday meals. Then I realized that I already had a ritual: I've always honored special meals and holidays by

WORDS TO THE WISE

WOOD FINISHES

You'd be surprised at how many homes I have visited that have a toxic dining room table! In each case, the problem is in the wood finishes used—either stains, oil-based polyurethanes, or petroleum-based wax and polish—and the fumes waft up to anyone sitting there. While the finish is drying and curing, the fumes can be irritating, especially for those with asthma or other respiratory problems. You can seal in most wood finishes using an AFM Safecoat & Safechoice product (see page 487). If you have the opportunity, you may want to purchase unfinished solid wood furniture and finish it yourself with nontoxic wood-finishing products.

working hard to make the table look beautiful. This is how I show my gratitude for being on earth, for my family, for the beauty of the seasons. My mother always set a beautiful table for dinner parties, so I realized that our table settings and centerpieces were, in fact, a tradition of giving thanks for the blessings bestowed upon us.

I always want my guests to feel comfortable and tended to when they're dining in my home, and I think it's important that they feel a connection to the earth when sharing earth's bounty at my table. For my table centerpieces, I like to use potted blooming plants, dried flowers, or fresh flowers that I have cut myself or that come from an organic nursery.

Forced bulbs, such as narcissus, are lovely to have on the table in the spring. Potted tulips and hyacinths are practically a dime a dozen in spring, and they make a wonderful living centerpiece. Looking at them uplifts you

because you know that winter will soon end, and blooms will soon be in the garden. Cyclamen is another blooming potted plant well suited to the dining room table, and it blooms over a long period. Heather is a colorful potted plant that I love to have in my kitchen. It can be quite large in the pot, sometimes too large for a table centerpiece, but it looks great in the kitchen when I'm preparing a meal. I often can find heather around Thanksgiving. Naturally, you can find mums during the fall and poinsettias in the winter (both have miniature varieties available) to bring the outdoors in.

Tables set with dried plants, pods, seeds, and pinecones continue the natural theme. Most of us have seedpods and cones outside our back doors, or you can scoop up a pinecone or dried leaves on a city street to decorate a dining or buffet table. From gum tree pods and rose hips to grapevine and boxwood sprigs, you'll discover that nature

SHOPPING SOLUTIONS
REALLY FRESH FLOWERS

It is hard to find organic cut flowers, but if you can, support the growers by buying these. Commercially grown cut flowers are grown with pesticides, causing harm to farm workers, soil, and water. Organic Bouquet is one company that offers cut flowers just like any other cut-flower business, except that theirs are organic (see page 476). You may also be lucky enough to find organic flowers at your local farmer's market. Just follow the pollinators and bees, and you'll quickly find the organic blooms.

is made of beautiful patterns and designs. Each of nature's gifts is beautiful in its own right, and together these collected and living centerpieces remind us to be grateful for the feast before us.

Keeping Fresh Flowers Fresh

I've included fresh flowers on my dining tables and in my home for as long as I can remember, and I've learned a few tips over the years to minimize the fuss of keeping cut blooms looking their best. These six ideas make it easy to incorporate nature into your day-to-day living without making more work for yourself.

1. Place freshly cut flowers in cold water, not warm water. Warm water dehydrates flowers.
2. Place cut flowers in the refrigerator for 6 hours before arranging them—it triples their lifespan.
3. Use hot water (between 110°F and 200°F) to restore very wilted flowers (the more wilted the stems are, the hotter the water should be).
4. Flower stems should be in about 6 inches of water. If you're cooling flowers, you'll want the water to cover the entire flower stem.
5. Recut flower stems every few days.
6. Remove all leaves and foliage below the water line.

Harmonize the Space with Crystals

Crystals are a beautiful addition to any table; they are like butterflies of light. If I'm hosting a dinner party that includes people with complicated relationships (stepfamilies, for example), I will make a small crystal grid in the center of the table to help hold the energy of the group at a stable level. The best approach is to find crystals of about the same size and power (judge this aspect using your intuition and experience), then place them in an appropriate place on the grid. Different traditions mention different crystals for these grids, but here is what has worked for me: citrine and amber on the east side of the table, amethyst on the south, smoky quartz on the west, and quartz crystal on the north.

For my family, I usually keep a heart-shaped stone on the table and a collection of rocks that one or the other of us has recently picked up on walks or from our driveway if they are interesting. My mother always said that a rock with a ring that goes all the way around the stone meant good luck. We have lots of those stones in our house! Rocks picked up on walks by a family member tend to anchor us in the moment of their discovery in the natural world, like a rune might, and I love having them on our table.

Rose quartz is a perfect stone to have on a table at any time because it is a stone for the heart chakra, and it radiates unconditional love. Another good heart-centering stone is green tourmaline. If you need to have a good conversation with lots of communication, try including a blue stone, such as aquamarine or lapis lazuli to support the throat chakra. For a romantic dinner, place rhodochrosite, pink tourmaline, or rose quartz in the center between place settings.

Candles Light the Soul

Lit candles at the dinner table profoundly and positively affect the mood of the meal. Flickering candlelight can set a peaceful, relaxing, and romantic mood. Candles make a heartfelt statement if you use them on an "average" weeknight, instead of saving them just for special occasions. Family members around the table will take notice, and I'll bet that the mood of the meal will be very pleasant.

Pure beeswax candles are the best

WORDS TO THE WISE

CANDLE SOOT

Many are finding that some aromatherapy candles produce very tenacious black soot, an emerging air-quality problem. The major culprits are scented and aromatherapy candles. Experts report that computers have been ruined by the soot. In some instances, there is so much soot generated from burning candles that it is causing severe damage to many homes and furnishings, and homeowners are mistakenly suing their builders and furnace and HVAC companies for improper installation of the systems.

Unfortunately, soot from candles can also be toxic. The soot particles can travel deep into the lungs, and those with asthma or lung or heart disease are particularly vulnerable. To make matters worse, many scented and aromatherapy candles are made with paraffin and synthetic fragrance oils. Paraffin is a petroleum product—a by-product of oil refining—and most fragrance oils used for candle making are petroleum-based synthetics. The soot from these materials can contain carcinogens, neurotoxins, and reproductive toxins. Testing and air chamber analysis by the Environmental Protection Agency has found a toxic soup of chemicals including benzene, lead, toluene, and carbon tetrachloride. Some metal wire wicks can contain lead.

Scented and aromatherapy candles often contain synthetic fragrance oils. Buy unscented candles made without petroleum and with wire-free wicks. Or use essential oil diffusers to practice aromatherapy; options include lamp rings or clay pot, fan, or electric heat diffusers that disperse scents throughout the room. Diffusers are available in most health food stores and from many online sources. Be sure your essential oils are pure.

MAKE IT YOURSELF
FLOATING HALLOWEEN CANDLES

One of my favorite projects for Halloween is to make floating pumpkin candles. We put them on our harvest dinner table in nice blue glass bowls filled with water.

Buy six to eight miniature pumpkins, 3 to 4 inches in diameter (and locally grown if possible), and the same number of votive candles (pure beeswax votives, if you can find them). Place a votive candle on top of the pumpkin, and trace a circle around it. Using a sharp knife, carefully cut out the circle so that a votive candle will fit snugly into the hole. Repeat for all the candles.

Fill bowls or pails with water, place the votives in the pumpkins, light the candles, and float the pumpkins in the water.

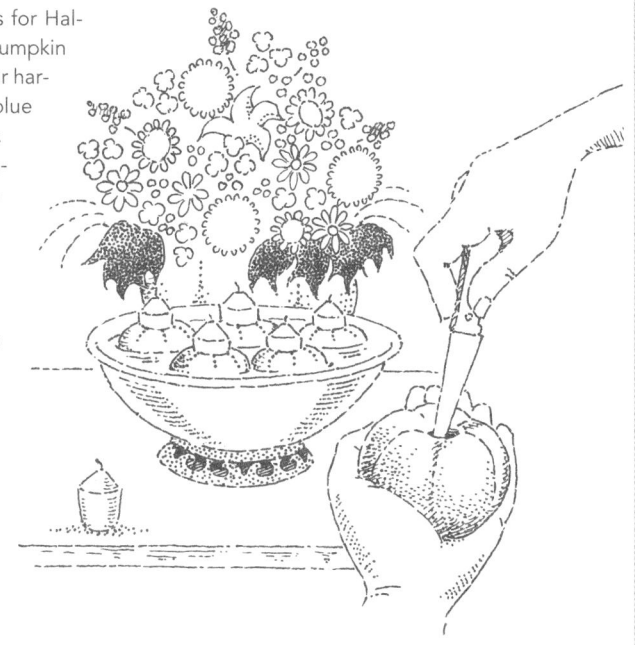

Make low-stress decorating part of your harvest celebration. It's easy to insert beeswax votives into the tops of miniature pumpkins and float them in a pretty bowl as part of your fall centerpiece.

choice for a table because they are the least polluting. Beeswax candles are a golden amber color, and they're just beautiful; you even get the wafting scent of honey when you burn them. Beeswax candles last longer than paraffin candles and smoke very little as they burn. Natural beeswax candles can develop what looks like a bit of a frost on the sides, but this is normal.

If you live in a rural location, chances are that you might be able to find a local beekeeper making and selling beeswax candles. This option is usually the cheapest way to buy beeswax candles and worth researching if you burn a lot of candles. There are bound to be beekeepers or candle makers selling beeswax items at local art shows and craft fairs too. The next cheapest way to keep beeswax candles in supply is to search the Internet for a good source.

Unscented beeswax, bayberry, and vegetable oil–based candles (such as soy and palm) are the healthiest choices for us and for the environment because they burn cleaner than heavily scented candles made from synthetic ingredients. As easy and as inexpensive as it is to buy scented paraffin candles, resist the temptation!

If you decide to make your own candles, borrow a book on candle making from the library or from a friend for basic how-to instructions. During a rainy day on our beach vacation, my daughter and I made stunningly beautiful candles using sustainable, low-toxicity supplies, and we had a great time. Here are a few tips that will help make your handmade, natural candles a success.

❖ Buy vegetable wax (usually soy) in craft stores. Look for microwavable soy wax for convenience, or use a double boiler for regular soy wax.

❖ Beeswax is another pure wax choice, although it's expensive. I personally love the smell of pure beeswax candles, and we make 100 percent beeswax candles for special occasions. Beeswax needs to be melted in a double boiler.

❖ Avoid petroleum products such as paraffin wax and synthetic fragrance when making your candles.

❖ Choose pure essential oils from natural food stores. You'll need only about 5 drops for every 2 cups of dried wax flakes. Add the essential oils after the wax has melted and has been removed from the heat source. Stir thoroughly to disperse the oils.

❖ Use lead-free wicks. If the packages aren't labeled "lead free," buy metal-free wicks to be on the safe side.

Setting the Table

I haven't bought a paper napkin in a decade or more, although I risk sounding self-satisfied by saying this. I am mentioning it because the practice of using cloth napkins is so gratifying that I highly recommend it for all families. We love our day-to-day napkins, our festive Thanksgiving napkins, and our dinner party napkins. Each napkin will last for years and years. I just toss them in the wash with our clothing; they take up so little room in a laundry load that I'm not using any extra resources (soap, water, or electricity) to wash them. The only time I iron them is when we are having a party.

I've been given a lot of cloth napkins over the years—organic ones, handwoven ones, and colorful ones—and I am always grateful. I've also made my own cloth napkins, and I am especially inspired to do this when I find really beautiful natural fabric. It's easy—simply copy the pattern of your favorite existing napkins. It is so nice to step outside

REDUCING LEAD RISK

Be cautious about serving food in colorful dishes if you don't know the provenance of the dish or if the dish shows signs of wear, such as hairline cracks, chips, crazing (overall spidery cracks under or in the glazing), or overall heavy usage. This is true whether it's ceramic, pottery, enamel, china, or glazed. Follow these guidelines when cooking, serving, or storing food in pitchers, bowls, pots, pans, and dinnerware to reduce the chance of lead leaching into or contaminating food.

❖ It's best to store food and leftovers in clear glass storage containers.

❖ Avoid storing food, especially acidic food such as tomato sauces, fruit juices, and vinegar-based recipes, in glazed china dishes. The acidity can break down the glazing even further, and lead can leach into the food.

❖ Tea and coffee are also acidic. Be sure your coffee cups and mugs are lead free and in good shape (without cracks, crazing, or chips), or choose glass coffee cups with no glazing.

❖ Do not store brandy or other liquors in lead crystal decanters.

❖ Avoid heating or microwaving food in questionable dishes or dinnerware. Heat can leach lead from china and dinnerware.

---

of the throwaway commercial paper industry and find other systems that work instead. And this is a perfect example of how you can make small changes in your everyday life; all the small changes add up to a smaller footprint on the earth.

The Dinnerware Decision

Setting a table with old family china or snapping up a bargain set of beautiful dishes from a garage sale may seem like a great way to recycle or reuse, but many older dishes have unacceptably high levels of lead and should not be used. Lead is a heavy metal that causes such a wide range of damage to the human body and mind that it should be avoided (see page 53 for more about lead). Lead can damage the brain and nervous system, and very small amounts can significantly affect learning and behavior in children.

Glazed china, most made prior to 1970 or newly imported, is a big source of lead in diets. The glazing that's applied to the dinnerware is the true culprit. Glazing creates a glossy finish or is a finish coat that is colored, clear, or white. China, stoneware, ceramic, and terra cotta dishes can all contain lead, especially if the pieces are old or if they're imported from countries that have few standards about lead content.

You need to be especially vigilant about dinnerware if the pieces are highly decorated, handcrafted, or old, or if there are raised, hand-painted areas, because the decorative paint can

contain lead. If the colors are bright and vibrant, chances are the paint is lead based. Avoid using dinnerware or serving bowls or pitchers that have multicolored decorations that will touch food, decorations painted over the glazing, or decorations that are fading, dusty, or chalky looking.

If you have doubts about any dinnerware or serving piece, buy a lead-testing kit at your local hardware store or through your local department of health. The kits are very inexpensive (less than $5), and they usually contain a swab or tester strip that you rub across the dinnerware in question.

Your best bets in china or dinnerware are plain white dishes, stoneware (plain, undecorated, and labeled lead free), bone china if it's labeled lead free, and glaze-free glass.

Maintaining the Dining Room

If you're making your dining room part of your living space and not keeping it as a showplace, you're bound to meet a few stains and blemishes from time to time. I'm happy to share a few tricks with you about keeping the dining room in good shape.

Weathering Wine Stains: My friend Susan, the hostess of a dinner party I once attended, astonished us all by her actions when one of the guests spilled a glass of red wine on the white tablecloth.

She jumped up and first put a full kettle of water on the stove, then removed everything from the table, took up the tablecloth, and stretched the fabric over a pan in the sink. Once the water was boiling, she pulled a chair up to the sink, stood on it with the kettle, and poured the boiling water over the stain from a height of 3 to 4 feet. This stain-removing technique worked like magic!

It isn't everyone who would be willing to disrupt their dinner party by removing all the food, plates, and utensils, but I've since learned that Susan's tip works most successfully when the stain is fresh. If the stain is dry, try soaking the red wine in white wine to

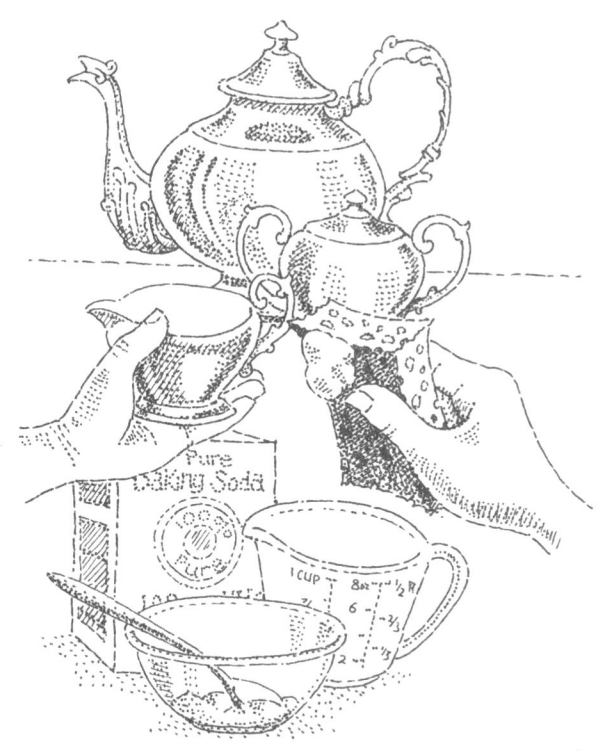

No need to give yourself a headache with toxic silver polish fumes. Mix up a baking soda and water paste, then gently rub it on your silver pieces to remove tarnish. Rinse the silver with hot water, and dry with a soft cloth.

bleach it out. Finally, cover the stain with a thick baking soda paste and leave it for a few hours, keeping it moist by spraying it with water from a spray bottle. Wash as normal.

Keeping the Shimmer on Silver: Silver can be lovely on a table because it dresses up any occasion. You can clean silver very successfully using kitchen cupboard ingredients instead of products with synthetic chemicals. The secrets of silver cleaning using household basics may surprise you, but the techniques are easy, tried, and true!

If you have a small job, the best silver polish is traditional white toothpaste. Dab some on your finger, and rub it into the tarnish. For bigger pieces, use baking soda and a clean, damp sponge: First, make a paste of baking soda and water. Scoop the paste onto the sponge, and rub the paste onto the silver. Rinse the silver with hot water, and polish it dry with a soft, clean cloth. For badly tarnished silver, leave the baking soda paste on the silver for an hour or so before cleaning it off with a sponge and hot water.

Beautiful Brass: There are good, easy ways to clean brass without using a synthetic commercial cleaner that may have toxic ingredients. Commonly used kitchen cupboard or refrigerator ingredients such as vinegar, Tabasco sauce, ketchup, tomatoes, milk, and lemons or lemon juice contain a natural acid that will remove tarnish. An acid rub or soak will wash away tarnish. If your brass piece is new, you may have to remove the lacquer sealer in order to polish the brass. Do this by submerging the brass in boiling water with a few teaspoons each of baking soda and washing soda (available in the laundry section of the supermarket). Once the lacquer has peeled off, polish the piece dry.

Waning and Waxing on Candle Drips: One of the best ways to remove candle wax from hard surfaces is to melt it with a hair dryer. Wipe up the wax as it melts with an absorbent towel or cloth. Or, if possible, put the item with the drippy wax in the freezer for a few minutes. It will chip right off. A straight edge, such as a ruler or credit card, may also come in handy as a scraper for wax stains.

Candle wax on fabrics, tablecloths, and carpets poses more of a challenge. An iron may be your best bet. For darker fabrics, place newspaper on both sides of the fabric (or on top of the carpet). Iron over the newspaper with a medium-hot iron; the newspaper will blot up the wax once it starts to melt. Replace newspaper as needed. For lighter fabrics, try using plain craft paper so you don't have to worry about newspaper ink adding to your stain. And remember, don't use a hair dryer or an iron on any fabrics or surfaces that are flammable.

The Living and Family Rooms

Unconditional love is one gift you can bestow on your family members at any and all times. I was told about a wise person who said, "What other kind of love is there, but unconditional love?" If your home exudes unconditional love, every person who lives there will find a place where they belong.

A Place for Your Family

I believe that it's important for families to spend time together, and the living and family rooms can be the hub of every house. Whether you flop down together after dinner for homework,

EVERYDAY HOUSEHOLD PRODUCTS AND THEIR LASTING EFFECTS

Most people don't realize that many household products, from a felt-tipped marker to furniture polish, can affect the central nervous system and the brain. Brain fog, inability to relax, lack of concentration, and even aggression can result from such exposure.

A number of doctors now suspect that environmental toxins may be responsible for the large number of children diagnosed with attention, learning, behavioral, and emotional disorders. Children are particularly sensitive to neurotoxic chemicals because their brains and central nervous systems are still developing. The fetus is the most sensitive to such exposures. For the fetus, even small exposures are damaging if they happen at the wrong time in development.

While you may not be able to control pollution outside of your home, you can cut down on toxins indoors by avoiding plastic and by using "green" products. Petroleum-based products often offgas respiratory irritants, so a rule of thumb is to buy water-based pens, inks, paints, polishes, cleaners, and more. Freshly painted walls or floors and tables with oil-based polyurethane can be highly neurotoxic. The more natural the material, the safer your home.

games, or a video, showing an interest in and interacting with spouses, partners, and children can encourage discussion and closeness.

Create a space that allows family members to interact and participate in activities rather than focusing on passive participation, such as watching television. Include a game table in your family room, and store games, puzzles, coloring books, and art supplies on nearby shelves or in a cabinet so they're always within reach. One of my friend's friends managed to squeeze a small table behind her couch; she keeps a 1,000-piece puzzle-in-progress on the table all winter long. Her kids and husband often rush over during television commercials and add a few pieces, or they get on their knees and lean over the couch every few minutes to help

out. It's a subtle and fun way to engage the whole family.

Did you ever consider designating one night a month as craft night or movie night? How about choosing a theme each month and changing your activities to match the theme? I'll admit that it might take some planning and time to dream up new ideas and activities to keep your family interacting, but it's something that will repay you many times over. Friday nights are movie and make-your-own pizza night in my home and have been great for us.

Many parents are concerned about the impact of television on their children's lives. My daughter looks at me in utter horror when she hears me talk about growing up without a TV! I was 16 before my parents bought one. Although I don't regret my TV-free days, I realize that it would be extremely isolating in today's times if a child grew up without a TV. Television is a part of our lives, and it does involve us in community activities, especially if you tune in to local broadcasting.

But there's a little more to the television debate than just whether or not you should have one. Televisions give off electromagnetic fields (EMFs), and while the EMFs are very strong right in front of the television, they drop off quickly within a few feet of the set. I suggest that viewers sit at least 6 feet away from a television set. For more on EMFs, see page 370.

A Place for Your Friends

Entertaining means different things to all of us, but the best gifts a generous host can offer are time, attention, and acceptance.

My friend Barbara has moved three times in the 30 years that I have known her, and each of her new homes has been as welcoming as the previous one. As soon as you arrive, you realize that this is a home where you can take the time to sit down and have a cup of tea, eat a scone, chat, and even flip through an interesting magazine about food or gardening. The temperature is always somehow perfect, and the natural fibers on her comfortable furniture are color-

ful and compelling in their designs and prints. A sense of "rush" is absent, replaced with calm comfort.

Making your children's friends feel comfortable is a knack, especially when it comes to teenagers. I've noticed that it always helps when the parents have made an area of the house teen-friendly and private so that they have a gathering place where they can be themselves. Can you transform an attic or a basement into a teen hangout? An overstuffed couch, beanbag chairs, and music or TV can be the start of a safe retreat for older kids. If you have a dining room that gets little use, consider changing it over to a computer room, TV room, or a playroom especially during a child's impressionable years when the neighborhood friends are in and out of the house on an hourly basis. The kids will be close at hand, but they'll have some sense of a room of their own.

One local family with three kids (ages 10, 14, and 16) decided that it was so important to keep track of the comings and goings of their children and their numerous neighborhood friends that they invested in setting up their family room and the backyard, which is just a step outside the family room. Buying a big-screen TV and kid-friendly den furniture was the first step, followed by adding sliding doors leading to a new covered porch. The parents reasoned that being able to supervise the children and provide entertainment right at home was well worth the cost of the improvements. The multipurpose family room and backyard suits all age groups and gives each child and his or her friends their own space, and it gives parents peace of mind knowing that they can keep an eye on what's happening after school and during the summer months.

Even if making such substantial changes to your home isn't practical, you can do small things to make your home welcoming to friends near and far. A simple porch rocker, a plate of cookies always at the ready, or pretty potted flowers on the steps lets friends, both young and old, know that they'll always feel at home in your home.

A Place for Yourself

Virginia Woolf once said, "In solitude, we give passionate attention to our lives, to our memories, to the details around us." Set up a place in your home where you feel completely and tranquilly at home, where you can let the world go, where you can do and think whatever you want, where you can renew and replenish yourself. Having such a place is a wonderful thing. Each of us is unique, so find what works for you, puts you at peace, allows you to sing inside, or whatever it is that brings calm. A cozy and comfortable place to read is high on my list of priorities when I'm by myself, since reading is one of my favorite pastimes. "Extra" time isn't something many of us have much of, but when we do, what a treasure.

Making a place just for you in your home is really more about "you" than it is about the "place" you make. You need to take time to nurture your authentic self, and often that's possible only if you create a sacred or quiet place in your home that allows you to focus on your own needs. There's a particularly interesting aspect of spiritual healing that shows that, once people's pain and trauma are revealed and begin to heal, they begin to have compassion for themselves. They drop the usually crushing self-judgment they are burdened with, and they begin to parent their wounded inner self. They become more compassionate toward others and less judgmental, too. This has huge ramifications for family dynamics. One thing leads to another, and the next thing you know, they are kinder, softer people, and their relationships with their loved ones improve.

Pay attention to how rested or stressed you feel in different areas of your home and during various activi-

Find a place in your home just for you—a quiet place, a comfortable chair, a bathroom spa, or a whole studio. Whether your passion is reading, bird watching, yoga, or knitting, you'll feel comforted and embraced when you create a sanctuary that feeds your spirit.

ties. Over the course of a few weeks or months, pinpoint what really, truly, and completely relaxes you. Is it rocking in a chair in the family room or curling up in a window seat in the bedroom, or is it baking cookies or surfing the Web?

MAKE IT YOURSELF
HEALTHY HOUSEPLANT HELPERS

HOUSEPLANT POLISH

The best way to polish the leaves on houseplants is to put them out in the rain and let the rain-drops wash away dust. If you live in a cold climate, you'll need a different plan for the winter months, though. Try this easy formula to restore luster to your houseplants.

> 1 tablespoon vegetable oil
> ¼ teaspoon liquid castile soap
> 3 cups warm water

Combine the ingredients in a jar. Shake to blend. Using a soft cloth, rub some of the mixture onto the plant's leaves, polishing as you go. Rinse the leaves after you polish them. Discard any remaining polish. ❖

MILDEW AND MOLD CONTROL FOR PLANTS

Even where indoor conditions and humidity are good, houseplants can develop mildew and mold. Tea tree oil is a broad-spectrum fungicide that will help control the problem.

> 1 teaspoon tea tree essential oil
> 1 teaspoon liquid castile soap
> 1 gallon water

Mix well and spray on plants and topsoil. ❖

Cleaning the Air with Houseplants

There are several reasons why house-plants can help clean pollution from indoor air. One is that plants give off negative ions, which attract positive ions to them, thereby taking pollution out of the ambient air because positive ions are often loaded with plastic, petroleum, and other pollutants. The plants themselves also absorb pollu-tants, and the biodynamic cycle of plant growth can help to balance a room's humidity, particularly in dry climates and during the winter.

Using plants to counteract indoor air pollution gained attention after NASA researchers found that plants signifi-cantly reduced pollution in the closed rooms of spacecraft. A spider plant, for example, did a good job of removing formaldehyde. Certainly our homes aren't airtight capsules like a spaceship, but placing two or three plants per room seems to help the quality of indoor air.

The researchers found that any plant will help clean the air, but 'there are 10 plants that may be effective in reduc-ing pollutants: areca palm, Australian sword fern, Boston fern, dwarf date palm, English ivy, peace lily, reed palm, rubber plant, spider plant, and weeping fig.

Carpets

In a way, I wish I could approve of wall-to-wall carpeting. Homes with carpeting can feel very cozy—the floors are warm and soft to someone like me who is usually barefoot. Wall-to-wall carpet also muffles and absorbs sound, and it's a soft surface for toddlers to play on. Carpeting is less expensive than hardwood floors, so it's appealing for that reason too.

At a glance, wall-to-wall carpets seem like a wonderful choice for bedrooms, family rooms, hallways, and living rooms. Unfortunately, carpets can be a sinkhole of allergens and toxins, providing the underpinnings for an unhealthy home. Mold and mildew grow on carpets from water that drips off wet boots and shoes, bathing suits, water leaks, and spilled drinks. Inde-

pendent of water spills, carpets pose a particularly conducive environment to mold growth—the cool floor underneath warm carpet produces a high relative humidity that forms condensation. For more on relative humidity, see page 384.

Carpeting is a factor in many cases of indoor air pollution and irritants. The pile can harbor fine particulates as well as dust mites, which thrive in carpet fibers. Dust mites live on human skin cells and moisture, and carpets provide a reservoir for both. The resulting dust mite excretory antigens are very hard to remove from carpets and are a big cause of allergies. Cat and animal dander also get lodged in carpets, as do cockroach antigens. I have two dogs, and more than one parent has told me that their pet-allergic child has fared better at my house because we have hardwood floors and only a few cotton area rugs that can be easily washed.

Toxic materials found in carpets can range from glues used to attach the carpet to the floor, antimicrobial/fungicidal

WORDS TO THE WISE
REDUCING FUMES IN EXISTING CARPETING

A colleague moved into an apartment, and the smell of new carpeting was overwhelming. He found the smell repulsive and suffered from headaches when he was there. He was desperate to improve the air quality, so he used a carpet-sealing product from AFM Safecoat & Safechoice (see page 487), which substantially reduced the smell. The closets still smelled of new carpet after the first application, so he put on a second coat there, and the outgassing fumes became tolerable.

CARPET LABELING

The Carpet and Rug Institute (CRI) has established a voluntary "Green Label" testing program; see the chart on page 80 for the types of tests performed. If a carpet sample passes the established safety criteria tests, the manufacturer is allowed to use the CRI Indoor Air Quality (IAQ) Carpet Testing Program label. Carpets and their components are tested for various chemicals, and if they fall at or below the CRI's acceptable levels, they are certified.

Be aware that the testing isn't comprehensive, nor do many experts believe it is stringent enough, but it is a start. A representative sample of the product is tested by an independent laboratory as part of the testing program.

pesticides, and 4-phenylcyclohexene (4-PC) from latex binders, to volatile organic compounds (VOCs) from a chemical soup of dozens and dozens of chemicals used in carpet manufacturing. We know little about many of these toxins. Another proven source of carpet contamination can be found right at your feet. Family members track in lead and pesticides from the street, yard, and workplace. Some indoor/outdoor carpet is treated with powerful, long-lasting pesticides and should be avoided at all costs. Remove it if it's used in or around your home. At this time, there are no federal guidelines regarding hazardous ingredients in carpets.

Most of the chemicals in carpets, carpet adhesives, and pads are neurotoxic; symptoms of exposure include difficulty concentrating, headaches, and nervousness. Some carpets emit particularly harmful chemicals, and some don't. VOCs can outgas from any of the 40 to 50 chemicals found in carpets, although the fumes typically drop off

dramatically a few months after the rug is installed. If you are buying synthetic carpeting, find a low-VOC brand. Install the carpet in the summer when the house can be aired out frequently, and ask the carpet installer to air the carpet out in the warehouse for at least 3 days (the longer the better) before installing it in your house. You may pay a fee to have the carpet aired out, but in my opinion, it's certainly worth the price.

Many carpets are tacked or glued onto pressed wood or particleboard subflooring, and the subflooring emits high levels of formaldehyde. Formaldehyde is a sensitizer and recognized carcinogen. It outgasses more when it is heated, so any part of the flooring near a heating system or hot water pipe will consistently give off fumes. If you plan to install wall-to-wall carpet, go with fully natural, untreated material, and tack it down rather than gluing it.

Before moving into my house, I had to take out all the subflooring (along with the wall-to-wall carpet) to make it healthier for me. The subflooring in the house was particleboard; to avoid outgassing formaldehyde, I replaced the subfloor with exterior-grade plywood and put down third-grade maple floors. It was a big job to replace the subfloor, but it wasn't that expensive. If you plan to replace your subflooring, the safest choice under wall-to-wall carpet is wood. The next best choice is exterior-grade plywood, which is typically constructed using a safer kind of glue than the types used to make particleboard.

Carpet backing can be the most toxic component of synthetic carpets. Avoid styrene-butadiene-rubber latex combinations and polyurethane. Carpet adhesives can contain formaldehyde, VOCs, and more, causing strong outgassing odors while the glues are drying. Some of the odors, such as the odor from formaldehyde, may never fully outgas.

Besides the toxic burden of carpeting, another downside is that carpeting is hard to clean. Stains can cause expensive damage. Replacing a stained carpet is very expensive, so most manufacturers added stain repellents over the years. Many of these stain repellents have been taken off the market because they damage the ozone layer and release dangerous VOCs. Even 100-percent wool carpets are suspect for toxic ingredients because they are often mothproofed. An attractive substitute for wall-to-wall carpet is an area rug made of natural materials that can easily be washed or cleaned.

The safest flooring solution is to have floors of wood, slate, marble, brick, or ceramic tile. This being said, you can easily pollute your home by using toxic stains and sealants on the flooring material. Choose floor-finishing products very carefully, going for low-VOC products at

CARPET AND RUG INSTITUTE CARPET TESTING PROGRAM

CRI has established a labeling program to identify carpet products that are low in VOCs. Tests are performed by an independent laboratory. Products with low emissions can display a CRI green label; look for the green and white logo on showroom samples.

	Butylated hydroxytoluene (BHT)	Formaldehyde	Styrene	Total VOCs	2Ethyl-1	4-PC-Hexanol
Carpets			X	X	X	X
Carpet cushions	X	X		X		X
Carpet adhesives		X		X	X	

MAKE IT YOURSELF
NEEM OIL MOTH CONTROL

Neem oil is an excellent repellent if you have a wool carpet, such as an Oriental rug, that you suspect has moths or moth eggs.

2½ ounces neem oil
1 gallon water
¼ ounce liquid detergent (unscented)

Combine the ingredients in a spray bottle. Spray the solution on the rug (make sure to spot test first to check for fading or staining). Let the solution set in the rug for a few hours before steam cleaning. ❖

every turn and even avoiding wood stains when possible due to the fungicides and wood preservatives included. (For more on paint, stains, and healthier alternatives, see pages 51 and 63.)

Natural Fiber Carpets

Natural fiber wall-to-wall carpet is the best choice if you feel you must use wall-to-wall carpet in a particular space. It may take some effort to locate a retailer in your area who sells natural fiber carpets, or you may end up ordering your carpeting from a Web source, but I firmly believe that it's worth your time.

Wool Carpet: If you find a source of wool carpet that hasn't been treated with pesticides, and you can afford it, such a pure carpet would be the very best choice if you needed to go with something from wall to wall. Wool is very durable and resilient, will not mat or crush, naturally evaporates moisture, is naturally antistatic and dust repelling,

and is also flame resistant. A note of caution, though, that some wool carpeting has been treated with moth-killing pesticides; make sure to inquire before you buy.

Even though wool is expensive to start with, its ability to wear so well makes up the difference and more. If well cared for, it can last for more than 50 years! The higher the pieces of wool per inch of fabric, the more crush and mat resistant. New Zealand wool has long fibers, and it makes for particularly durable carpets.

Wool is heralded as an air purifier because it absorbs pollutants, according to studies by the Wool Research Institute of New Zealand. The wool absorbs the pollutants but does not release them back into the atmosphere because gas particles become bonded to the wool molecules. Scientists speculate that wool carpets can continue to purify the air for 30 years without releasing the pollutants.

Last but not least, wool carpets are completely biodegradable and can be used as mulch, if they haven't been treated with pesticides.

Plant Fiber Carpets

Tight-weave plant-fiber carpets are strong, fully biodegradable, and made from renewable resources. They also don't create static electricity.

Sisal: The yarn for sisal carpets is made from the stems and leaves of a subtropical plant called the agave. Sisal makes a durable carpet. It has a smooth pile that doesn't trap dust; and like other plant fibers, it is antistatic. No pesticides are needed in the production of sisal. The downside of sisal carpets is that they are susceptible to mildew and need to be kept in a dry location.

Coir: Coir fiber is derived from the husk of the coconut, and the fibrous yarn is then woven into a number of different designs such as bouclé, panama, herringbone, and brush matting.

As opposed to sisal, coir can be used in damp places. Coir has a casual look to it, and it is the strongest of the plant fibers. The fibers are pale yellow and look hairy (yes, they're a bit scratchy). If you have a fibrous doormat, it's most likely coir. Coir is often made into carpets and runners for halls, stairs, and entranceways.

Jute: Jute is a soft fiber derived from the stalk of a woody herb found in India. The stalk is soaked in water, then beaten to open to the fiber, which can then be spun to make yarn. Like sisal, it is prone to mildew, so keep it in dry locations.

Seagrass: Seagrass is soaked in seawater, which softens the grass enough for it to be spun into yarn. Seagrass carpets repel stains well and are antistatic. It is a mellow green color.

Paper: Paper carpets are made of yarns fabricated from the pulp of coniferous softwoods. The yarn is then woven into soft, durable, versatile carpets. Resin is added to help the paper resist water. Those with pine allergies need to test this product carefully.

Cotton: Cotton is a great choice for carpets, especially throw rugs, because it makes a very durable floor cover. Cotton is a soft fiber that can be spun and woven into complex textures and designs. Cotton dyes beautifully, and natural dyes look rich and even on cotton rugs and carpets. Be sure to choose 100 percent cotton (organic cotton, if you can find it).

Carpet Pads

These are carpet underlayments that will extend the life of the carpet. They also act as a shock absorber and a spring. The three basic types of padding are foam, rubber, and fiber.

The quality of carpet padding is measured by density, not thickness or softness. Carpet padding is rated by pounds per cubic foot; the carpet industry recommends a pad of 5 pounds for light traffic areas and 6.5 pounds for heavy traffic areas. Pads should be around ⅜ inch thick, but no thicker than ⁷/₁₆ inch.

Cotton Carpet Pads: There are many styles and thicknesses of cotton carpet pads available. They can be 100 percent recycled and can offer reduced noise. You should also be able to find cotton carpet pads that aren't treated with chemicals.

Other Natural Carpet Pads: Wool, jute, true natural rubber, horsehair, and felt padding are also good substitutes for plastic or synthetic rubber or foam padding. Natural sponge rubber or foam padding is molded into a waffled pad (as is synthetic). Camel hair and wool needled (not glued) carpet pads are safe and hold up very well.

Some carpet pads advertise that they are environmentally friendly because they are made from recycled rubber tires, but I would never recommend this choice because tires are full of petroleum-based materials and are not healthy for any home.

Natural Fiber Backings

Look for those made of jute, hemp, cotton, or natural latex (avoid synthetic latex). Hemp is a good choice because it doesn't mildew.

Carpet Adhesives

Look for natural adhesives derived from the rubber tree, which are completely biodegradable and nontoxic, or use tacks.

Carpet Cleaning and Care

If you have carpets, you are going to need to vacuum them frequently to keep them clean. You will also undoubtedly face challenging washing and stain removal problems. Vacuum carpets thoroughly with a brush and beater bar. However, make sure not to overbrush wool and cotton because the fibers can fuzz. If spot- or steam-cleaning, clean carpets with the least amount of moisture possible. Natural fiber carpets, including plant fiber carpets and rugs, are very absorbent and stain easily. Scoop up any spills or stains carefully, then blot. Keep blotting until the stain has been absorbed. Plant fiber carpets should be cleaned by a dry extraction method instead of using water, steam cleaners, or carpet shampoo.

My Steam-Cleaning Technique

I have successfully steam-cleaned carpets (including an Oriental rug) using a fragrance-free, all-purpose detergent. I've rented steam-cleaning equipment and just used my own health food store–type detergent, all with great success. (Very old or delicate carpets should probably be cleaned by a professional. Be sure to ask about the cleaning method to verify that strong and harmful chemicals are not used.) You need to rinse out the rental machine thoroughly before using it because some people use flea killers in their shampoo, and there may be residue left on the cleaner.

I've reduced the amount of detergent asked for in the rental machines because most health food store brands of all-purpose cleaners are concentrated. I have also added a teaspoon or two of tea tree oil to the detergent to kill mold and bacteria. (Tea tree oil is a great broad-spectrum fungicide and bactericide.) You can also kill mold by rinsing the carpet with diluted vinegar: Add about 2 cups vinegar to a gallon of water. Use white distilled vinegar from a major brand-name manufacturer (major brands are usually made from plant material and not petroleum).

Fortunately, more and more carpet cleaning companies now offer fragrance-free carpet cleaning. A decade ago, it was not possible to find a carpet cleaner who would come to your house offering this service.

It is critical to thoroughly dry any carpet that you clean, otherwise you invite mold and mildew to contaminate the carpet. Once these microbes take hold, they are hard to remove. Extract as much water as you can with the steam-cleaning machine. If weather permits, keep windows open to help dry carpeting and rugs. It may be possible to dry movable area rugs by draping them over a picnic table or porch swing or by fashioning a sturdy clothesline.

Eliminating Carpet Odors

Ah, the wonders of baking soda! Baking soda adsorbs odors because the baking soda particles draw odors in. When you sprinkle baking soda onto a damp carpet

CARPET DISPOSAL

The Environmental Protection Agency notes that 2.5 million tons of carpet and rugs were deposited in landfills in just 1 year in the United States.

Some carpet manufacturers offer carpet take-back programs. Call around to find one or go online for a source if you are disposing of wall-to-wall carpet. The carpets are recycled or reclaimed and kept out of landfills.

SHOPPING SOLUTIONS
DURABILITY AND HARDNESS OF WOOD

There are many natural wood floors available, and it can be confusing to sort out which is best for your home and situation. The most important thing to remember when shopping for hardwood flooring is that the harder the wood, the longer the floor will last. The Janka Hardness Test for wood assigns a number to each variety of wood—the higher the number, the harder and more durable the wood. The soft wood of Douglas fir has a number of 660, for example, while southern yellow pine has a number of 690. Red oak is designated 1,290, black cherry is 950, ash is 1,320, and hard maple is 1,450. Durable mahogany is rated 2,200.

and then clean it up, the baking soda takes the odor with it. But baking soda odor removal can be a challenge if you're in a hurry. It's hard to remove baking soda while it's still damp because it can cake and cling onto the carpet fibers.

Sprinkle baking soda onto the carpet where the spill or mess was, and let it set overnight. Be generous—the more baking soda you use, the more odors you'll remove. Let the carpet and baking soda dry thoroughly. Sweep up as much baking soda as you can, then vacuum up the remainder. For an herbal carpet freshener, add a dozen or so drops of pure essential oil (scent of your choice) to the baking soda. Mix well. Sprinkle the mixture on your carpet and then vacuum. You could substitute borax for the baking soda if you'd prefer because borax is also a very good deodorizer.

Flea Control for Carpets

A hearty session with the vacuum cleaner is your best line of defense for bringing flea problems under control. If you need additional control, citrus solvents that contain d-limonene, now widely available in health food stores and many supermarkets, kill all stages of the flea. I can personally attest that this is a fabulous find. There are some caveats for its safety, however, because citrus solvents are volatile organic compounds (VOCs), even if natural, and can irritate the lungs of chemically sensitive folks and those with asthma. Cats are very sensitive to d-limonene, so you should not use citrus-based solvents to treat a flea infestation if you have cats. For more about fleas, see page 94.

Flooring

Natural flooring can be wonderful, but it can quickly become toxic with the finishing products recommended by many manufacturers. What a shame! And more durable finishes mean more dangerous solvents were used to formulate the product. Fortunately, natural flooring has huge advantages over carpeting and is very much in vogue right now, so homeowners have more options than they did just a decade ago.

Wood Flooring

Allergists recommend hardwood flooring (without carpets) if there is a family member with allergies to animal dander, dust, mites, mold, or pollen. You'll find more about hardwood and forest stewardship on page 132.

We have two dogs, and my daughter's friend wanted to come for a sleepover. The girl is so allergic to dogs that she needs to travel with special bedding and even a cot; her mother came by to check out the house and possible allergens. She immediately relaxed when she saw the hardwood floors without carpets and gave her daughter permission to come to the party. The next day, the mother told me on pickup that she had never seen her daughter feel so well after being in a house with dogs!

Bamboo Floors

Bamboo is a woody *grass* and not a wood, and it is increasingly being chosen as a rapidly renewable alternative to wood. It grows one-third faster than the

MAKE IT YOURSELF
WOODEN FLOOR CLEANER

The smell of true vegetable oil soap on wooden floors is as wholesome as the smell of bread baking in the oven. Rich and nutty smelling because they contain linseed oil, all-purpose vegetable oil soaps are ideal for cleaning wooden floors if you are lucky enough to have soft water in your tap. When sloshed in a bucket with soft water, true vegetable soap makes a terrific wooden floor cleaner.

If you have hard water as I do, however, you'll have to depend on a commercial detergent soap to avoid the soap scum residue associated with hard water. I rely on Murphy's Oil Soap, Ecover's All Purpose Soap, or Life Tree's Home Soap for the all-purpose detergent in my favorite homemade floor cleaning formula. I also add some fragrant herbal antibacterial tea, such as peppermint or lavender. The mixture has worked wonders on my floors.

⅛ cup all-purpose pure vegetable soap or commercial soap detergent (such as Murphy's Oil Soap, Ecover's All Purpose Soap, or Life Tree's Home Soap)
¼ to ½ cup vinegar or lemon juice
½ cup fragrant herbal tea
2 gallons warm water

Combine ingredients in a pail or bucket. Swirl the water around until it is sudsy, then apply to the floor with a mop, recycled cloth, or sponge. Rinse the floor with clean water. ❖

fastest-growing tree and can grow from 60 to 150 feet in a few months (compared with 100 years for a Douglas fir). It takes only 3 to 6 years for a fully mature grass to grow to harvest. There are about 1,200 species in the world, with some species growing up to 3.3 feet a day. The root system sends up new shoots after the grass is harvested, so it doesn't need to be replanted.

Bamboo's strength-to-weight ratio is so good that it is used for structural roof applications. It is a very strong fiber and is 27 percent harder than red oak. It is also very flexible, making it a popular choice in earthquake zones. Because bamboo is not very flammable, it can be used in all types of buildings. Aesthetically pleasing carbonized bamboo has been pressure heated so that its sugar compounds become brownish in color. The longer it is heated, the darker the bamboo becomes.

If you have a bamboo floor, invest in a natural fiber cloth dust mop, and use it frequently on the floor. Avoid alkaline cleaners, such as baking soda and soap, and water-based solutions because the water can dull the finish. As a rule, wax should never be used on bamboo.

Natural Linoleum

Natural linoleum floors are often called 40-year floors because they are so durable. Real linoleum floors are a composite material made from rapidly renewable resources including linseed oil (from flaxseeds), pine rosin, dust "flour," cork, limestone dust, and jute. You need to be on your toes when you shop for a linoleum floor—most so-called linoleum floors are actually vinyl! And most salespeople think vinyl is what you're asking for if you don't specify "natural" linoleum floors. Some of the oils in natural linoleum floors outgas, which could bother some sensitive people. Natural linoleum is durable and can be used not only on floors but on countertops and desktops as well. It is available in tiles and sheets and is cost effective because it lasts so long. It is soft to walk on and provides acoustic dampening. Compared with vinyl, it has two times the resistance to dents. To care for a natural linoleum floor, wet-mop with a mild detergent, and avoid highly alkaline materials such as baking soda, washing soda, and borax.

Natural Cork

Cork oak trees grow in Spain and Portugal. The outermost bark can be sustainably harvested every 9 years without harm to the tree, which can live for more than 500 years. The bark is first stripped when the tree is around 20 to 25 years old. The best of the bark is used for wine bottle corks; the residue is put into presses and heated to a temperature high enough to fuse the cork granules together into blocks and other shapes for flooring.

The cork floors in the New York Public Library are in excellent shape after 50 years of hard use, showing great durability. The flooring is resilient and very resistant to abrasion, making it well suited for high traffic areas. Because cork is 50 percent air, it is very buoyant and is preferred by many chefs for their kitchens. In addition, cork flooring doesn't rot because it contains a natural, waxy substance that makes it impervious to moisture. It is also fire resistant and low maintenance. Cork flooring is available in tiles, slabs, blocks, rolls, granules, and floating tongue-and-groove planks. It is less expensive per square foot than some hardwood floors.

Synthetic chemicals are often added to cork, such as the polyurethane commonly used as a coating for keeping the floor clean. (Some manufacturers recommend recoating cork floors with polyurethane every 6 months to a year, which would bring unwanted chemi-cals into the home.) Contact natural cork flooring companies to find alternative methods of keeping the cork clean.

Decorative Concrete

Decorative concrete seems to be the new floor of choice for modern spaces. Concrete can be stained, dyed, and stenciled. Strong acids and urethanes are sometimes recommended by the manufacturer when mixing or decorating the concrete, but these substances could cause indoor air pollution. Additives in concrete floors can be very strong smelling, and they persist throughout the life of the concrete. Concrete floors can be cold and damp unless a heating system is installed under the flooring, so make sure they're appropriate for your home and your family's needs before including a concrete floor in your plan. It's certainly not as easy to remove as carpeting or wood flooring.

SHOPPING SOLUTIONS
SEALING IN FORMALDEHYDE

If you have furniture that has been made of pressed wood, particleboard, or laminated materials, seal it with a sealant made by AFM Safecoat & Safechoice to reduce, if not eliminate, formaldehyde from outgassing. The sealants have been designed for those with chemical sensitivity, so the product won't add any new VOCs into the air. See page 487 for more information.

Furnishings

As you discover the health benefits of choosing more natural furnishings—less outgassing, fewer toxics, and materials that please the senses—you'll also discover how grounded you feel when you're surrounded by chemical-free fibers, wooden furniture, and natural flooring.

Wooden Furniture Care

Real wood with minimal or completely dried stains and sealants are the best choices for furniture frames. Pressed wood, particleboard, and laminated woods should be avoided because most of these products outgas formaldehyde. As an added benefit of real wood furniture, you'll find it's easier to clean, too, because you don't have to contend with paper or wooden veneers or rough composite surfaces while you're polishing or dusting.

We all know the smell that we identify as commercial furniture cleaners and polishes—lemon with a touch of engine oil. What we may not identify with the smell is the irritability, depression, and other bad moods that can be the response to its use.

How many people clean, polish, or wax their furniture before a dinner party, only to wonder why they are so cranky before the guests arrive? Even worse, the smell can linger on furniture for weeks and months after use, causing a low level of air pollution that puts a strain on the central nervous systems of everyone living there. The petroleum distillates and solvents in commercial furniture products are highly neurotoxic.

Replacing commercial and brand-name furniture cleaner, polish, and wax with a homemade formula is at the top of the list of priorities for establishing a healthier home.

Upholstery

Nestled deep into our periwinkle blue couch, cushioned by pillows, surrounded by books and newspapers, covered by a blanket, and quenched by my favorite beverage, I'm at the height of comfort. Add enough light in the right places to see what I need to see, keep the phone handy so I don't have to get up if it rings, and place the dog beds nearby, and watch me really settle in to replenish and fully relax.

Teenagers love couches. They lead busy lives, so any time that they have to relax and unwind while stretched out and comfortable on the couch is time well spent, it seems to me.

Cushions

Modern upholstery practices most often rely on cotton, Dacron polyester,

FURNITURE CLEANING HELPERS

Our homes may not be the showplaces featured in magazines, but these simple recipes make it easy to care for and clean furniture, from prized heirlooms to everyday casual styles.

LEMONY FURNITURE-CLEANING CLOTH

This simple-to-make formula will give your home a lovely lemon fragrance. The acid in lemon juice works particularly well to pull dirt right out of the wood, leaving your furniture sparkling clean.

> 2 or 3 tablespoons lemon juice
> Few drops food-grade linseed oil or jojoba oil
> Recycled, clean flannel or cotton cloth

Place the lemon juice in a bowl, add a few drops of the oil, and saturate the cloth with the liquid. Use the cloth for cleaning wooden furniture. ❖

LEMON OIL DUSTER

This lemon oil dusting cloth is perfect for weekly dusting passes. Traditionally, lemon oil has been used for furniture because it is so lubricating and antiseptic. Contact herbalists for sources of pure lemon oil. Most commercial lemon oil is not all natural and may contain petroleum distillates, so it's best to seek out pure lemon oil.

> 10 drops lemon oil
> 2 tablespoons lemon juice
> Few drops olive oil or jojoba oil
> Recycled, clean flannel or cotton cloth

Mix the lemon oil, lemon juice, and olive or jojoba oil in a small bowl. Dip the cloth into the mixture, and wipe furniture. ❖

---

and polyurethane foam for padding. Cotton or wool is the best choice.

Fire Retardants in Cushions

Fire-retardant chemicals that are found in foam and other synthetic cushioning material have been found to be highly problematic for health because they are endocrine disrupters. The chemicals, polybrominated diphenyl ethers, called PBDEs, are also linked to impaired brain development in the very young and dysfunction of the central nervous system. They are also long lasting in the environment. This may be particularly important for families with daughters and for women of childbearing age, because these toxic, fire-retardant chemicals have been detected in breast milk.

What can you do about it? Unfortunately, not much—unless you are buying new furnishings. Before you start shopping for upholstered furniture, do some

HOMEMADE FURNITURE POLISH

Most of the old folk formulas for furniture polish leave the furniture too oily, and in hot weather, the oil can go rancid. My formula uses vinegar to pull the dirt out of the wood and just a very small amount of oil to keep furniture from drying out.

    ¼ cup distilled white vinegar
    Few drops of olive oil or liquid jojoba wax

Mix the vinegar and oil together in a small bowl. Dip a soft rag into the mixture and work the polish into the wood, moving along the grain line. Store leftover polish in a glass jar indefinitely. ❖

Notes: Distilled white vinegar won't stain wood, so that's what I usually recommend. You could substitute lemon juice or organic apple cider vinegar, but the apple cider vinegar could stain. You can find liquid jojoba wax, which never goes rancid, in most health food stores. You can also use food-grade boiled linseed oil, which is rich and nutty, instead of olive oil or liquid jojoba wax. Do not use boiled linseed oil from a hardware store or home center because that form has synthetic drying chemicals added.

CREAMY POLISHING WAX

This more-elaborate polish includes a wax, but it isn't much harder to make than frosting for a cake.

    2½ ounces olive oil or jojoba oil
    1½ ounces coconut oil
    1 ounce beeswax
    1 ounce carnauba wax
    4 ounces distilled water

Melt the oils and waxes in a double boiler over medium heat. Remove from heat, pour in water, and mix with a hand mixer until thick and creamy. Dab some cream onto a soft flannel or cotton cloth and rub into furniture. Buff and polish until the oils are well worked into the wood. Store in an airtight container indefinitely. ❖

research to find progressive companies that make cushions without PBDEs.

Natural Upholstery Fibers

Furniture covered in natural upholstery fabrics presents an atmosphere of beauty and relationship with the outside world. Natural fibers are also often richly textured, adding an interesting look to any décor. There are natural fibers available through some upholstery shops.

Natural fibers suitable for upholstery include the following:

Cotton is very durable, absorbent, easy to care for, and economical. It is a popular covering for all kinds of upholstered furniture. It does burn and wrinkle easily, though.

Linen is a strong upholstery fabric, but it can be scratchy on bare skin.

Wool is a resilient and naturally absorbent fabric that is moderately strong. It attracts dust but is not hard to clean. It can be uncomfortable in hot, humid climates, however.

Silk is very strong and slinky and may be most suitable for decorator pieces that get light use.

Stain Protectors

One thing you don't want is a couch emitting toxic stain protectors from its upholstery. Fortunately, when ordering a custom-covered couch with the upholstery of your choice, you often have to pay extra for the stain protection—giving you an ideal opportunity to decline adding the stain protection to the fabric.

Sealants and stain repellants are long lasting in the environment, harmful to the ozone layer, and toxic to pets and humans. The EPA announced in 2004 that it has "intensified and accelerated" its review of investigating whether Teflon-coated products (including cookware, water- and stain-resistant clothing and furnishings, cosmetics, and more) could be a serious health risk to young girls and women of childbearing age. The concern is an increase in birth defects and reproductive problems.

Teflon is a member of a family of chemicals called perfluorochemicals (PFCs). According to the nonprofit advocacy organization Environmental Working Group, "PFCs virtually never break down in the environment and have been found to contaminate most of the US population, including 92 percent of children tested to date."

Upholstery Fabric Care and Cleaning

Real life isn't perfect, and our couches get a very hard workout as a relaxation destination for kids, dogs, and snack-eating movie watchers. The upholstery-cleaning techniques below are a good part of any weekly cleaning routine.

❖ Vacuum the cushions.

❖ Dust nonwoven fabrics, such as leather or suede, with a soft cloth.

❖ Softly brush woven fabrics with a soft-bristled brush.

❖ Fluff up loose-filled cushions and pillows to preserve their original softness.

❖ Rotate removable cushions and pillows to spread wear and reduce exposure to direct sunlight.

Living with Companion Animals

Our two dogs are never far from each other or my feet. Their companionship is a treasure in my life. Who else but my dogs would turn inside out with excitement to see me every morning? Our family spends many happy hours

MAKE IT YOURSELF
UPHOLSTERY CLEANERS

These homemade upholstery cleansers make it easy to keep toxic commercial cleansers out of your home.

WHIPPED DETERGENT
I like the foamy aspect of this formula so much, it is always my first choice for cleaning spots and stains from upholstery. The whipped detergent disperses the cleaning agent around so that no part of the upholstery gets a thick coating. This mixture works best when you use a mild soap. I like to dip a soft brush into this formula, scrub the upholstery, and then rinse using the brush.

> 1 part water
> 1 part liquid detergent

Mix with a hand mixer until frothy. Scoop the froth onto a sponge, brush, or recycled cloth, and scrub into the stains. Rinse until the soap residue is removed. ❖

STRICTLY WATER CLEANER

Use cool water. Warm or hot water may set most stains, but you may need warm or hot water to remove greasy stains. Just use sparingly. ❖

SHAMPOO GREASE CLEANER
Shampoo removes oil from hair, so why not from upholstery? It works wonders! Just be sure to use fragrance-free natural shampoo.

> 1 part natural shampoo
> 1 part water

Mix shampoo and water, and agitate. Dab mixture onto a sponge or brush, then gently work the suds into greasy stains. Rinse with water until the suds are removed. ❖

3% HYDROGEN PEROXIDE CLEANER
Hydrogen peroxide kills bacteria and is helpful for removing odors.

> 3% hydrogen peroxide

Dab 3% hydrogen peroxide on the stain, but don't rinse. Repeat until stain is gone. Because hydrogen peroxide can remove color, be sure to spot test first. ❖

SADDLE SOAP LEATHER CLEANER
Leather needs special conditioning to keep it from cracking. This polish cleans and shines and works best on smooth leather. It can be stored in an airtight container for 1 year.

> 4 ounces vegetable, jojoba, grapeseed, olive, or peanut oil
> 1 ounce beeswax
> 1 ounce grated soap or liquid castile soap
> 1 ounce rum or vodka

Place the oil, beeswax, and soap in a double boiler and melt over low heat. Remove from heat and blend with an electric blender (preferably an old machine that is no longer used for preparing food). Add the rum or vodka. Rub the mixture into the leather, let it sit for a few hours, then buff with a clean, lint-free cloth. ❖

observing and laughing about their attempts to manipulate each other and us. Being a pet owner is rewarding and enriching, so consider making room in your home for an animal if you have the time and resources to care for a pet properly.

Pets need healthy food and healthy environments just as much as humans do. Read food labels. The first few ingredients should be animal protein (beef, chicken, or lamb). Other good signs on a pet food label are listings for whole grains, vegetables, and fruit. Avoid pet foods that list meat by-products, meat and bone meal, and artificial colors on their labels. Be aware that pet food labeling is unregulated, so terms such as "gourmet" or "premium" don't guarantee that the ingredients are of a higher quality than low-priced brands.

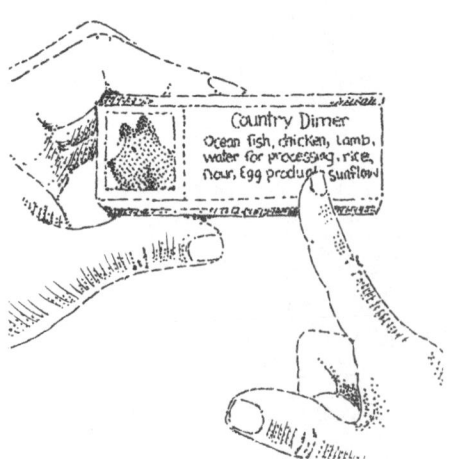

Your pet's diet should be just as healthy as yours. A well-balanced pet food includes animal protein, grains, vegetables, and even fruit, without a meat by-product or chemical additive in sight.

When it comes to pest control products for pets, it's equally important to be vigilant, so read those labels, too. Pet pest control can pose serious health hazards to you and your pet.

For example, the label of a very popular method of tick and flea control says that a common side effect of the product is severe depression for the pet! Discuss a healthy pest control plan with your veterinarian or consult one of the many books available that discuss natural healing and nontoxic remedies for eliminating pests on pets.

Even products that you thought were benign can be cause for concern. Cat box litter is a perfect example: You buy the brand you've always bought, dump it into the litter box, and give it nary a thought. Unfortunately, cat box litter made with clay can cause intestinal problems for pets if ingested (because it contains sodium bentonite, a material that turns to an expandable cement). Other litters contain silica (a known human carcinogen) and synthetic chemicals, such as perfumes. The best bet may be the new plant-based cat box litters, such as those made from pine, wheat, corn, and kenaf.

Those Pesky Fleas

A flea infestation can make everybody miserable—the infested pet, anybody in the house who is allergic to fleas, and the person trying to rid the house of

PAMPERING PET CARE

ALOE VERA PET SHAMPOO
About as pure a shampoo as you can get, this recipe is detergent free. The healing properties of aloe vera gel help to soothe skin irritations.

> 2 cups water
> 2 teaspoons liquid castile soap
> 2 tablespoons pure aloe vera gel
> Up to 1 teaspoon vegetable glycerin or vegetable oil

Combine all ingredients in a jar. Shake thoroughly to blend. Get the pet's coat wet, then pour on the shampoo a few tablespoons at a time, lathering as you go. Work the shampoo in with your hands. Rinse the pet thoroughly. Towel the pet dry or allow the pet to shake itself dry. ❖

VINEGAR RINSE
A final vinegar rinse can help the pet's coat shine and return the acid mantle to the skin.

> ¼ cup organic apple cider vinegar
> 3 cups warm water

Combine the vinegar and water. Pour the rinse over the pet's coat, being sure to avoid the eyes and nose. ❖

---

fleas in a safe way. Fleas can carry intestinal dog tapeworms that are transferable to humans and can be picked up easily by children. Female fleas can lay up to 25 eggs a day, and they thrive in 65° to 80°F conditions (which is why there are so often flea infestations during heat waves).

It is my belief that pesticides of all sorts should be avoided in the home at all costs, and this includes any synthetic pesticide for fleas, whether it's a collar, a pesticide swab, pesticide baths, or pesticide bombs or sprays. There simply isn't enough research available on the long- and short-term effects of the pesticides and the inert ingredients to consider them safe for humans or pets. Period.

I know too many people who have developed permanent disabilities from pesticides—and from flea pesticides in particular. You can get rid of fleas without poisons. I have succeeded, and so can you.

Simple Flea Control

Avoiding fleas is part luck and part common sense. Wash dogs (and cooperative cats) frequently to stay on top of any possible flea exposure. There's no need for a special natural flea shampoo; regular natural shampoo is enough to do the trick. Use a flea comb to groom pets a few times a week; you may even be able to isolate a single flea before she lays eggs. Vacuum often and dispose of vacuum bags in an airtight container (or you can freeze the sealed vacuum bag to kill flea eggs and larvae). You can also find natural flea collars at health food stores and progressive grocery stores or shop online.

Flea-Free Cats

Washing cats, cat bedding, and area rugs frequently is your best defense against fleas, but sometimes it's just not enough to spoil a flea infestation. If your cat has fleas, bathe her with a mild shampoo once a week to remove adult fleas, larvae, and eggs. Groom her with a flea comb between baths. Beneficial nematodes may be used to dust your lawn. These creatures will infest and kill fleas but are harmless to pets and humans.

You need to be careful when it comes to treating fleas on cats. Some natural remedies that work on dogs may be dangerous to cats. Avoid flea powders containing pyrethrins (derived from chrysanthemums). Avoid giving raw garlic to your feline because it can cause a dangerous form of anemia. While citrus peel extract (d-limonene) kills all stages of fleas, cats should not be exposed to it. And stay away from essential oil and herbal remedies on cats as well.

Flea-Free Dogs

Citrus peel extract is an excellent choice for treating fleas on floors because its components, d-limonene and linalool, kill all stages of the flea's life cycle. I have completely eradicated our home of fleas using citrus peel extract—I don't think anything else works as well. Still, you must use caution: While it is a natural material and much safer for health and the environment than toxic synthetic pesticides, it is not without problems. Asthmatics should not be exposed to citrus peel extract because citrus solvents are VOCs. And, as noted above, citrus peel extract shouldn't be used around cats.

Tick Attack

In the United States, deer and dog ticks are becoming a chronic, dangerous, expensive, and upsetting problem. Our two dogs (Sammy and Clayo) now have ticks most of the year. We aren't even tick-free here in upstate New York in the middle of January after an ice storm! Because the whole family has suffered from Lyme disease, and the dogs get it, too, I have made an all-out effort to find natural repellents.

MAKE IT YOURSELF
FLEA-FREE FLOOR CARE

CITRUS PEEL EXTRACT FLOOR CLEANER

You can get rid of fleas in your home by washing floors twice a week with a citrus peel extract cleaning solution (assuming, of course, that you don't own a cat). Keep your windows open when using citrus peel extract products because of their strong smell.

> ¼ cup citrus peel extract (available in health food stores)
> 1–2 gallons water

Mix the citrus peel extract and water in a bucket and use it for mopping floors.

Note: You can spray dog bedding with a mixture of 2 teaspoons citrus peel extract and 2 cups water mixed in a spray bottle. ❖

FLEA REPELLENT FLOOR SOAP

Washing the floors with essential oil repellent scents can help repel fleas from dogs.

> 10 drops rosemary, lavender, or other essential oil
> ¼ cup unscented liquid detergent
> 1 gallon hot water

Combine all ingredients in a bucket. Wash the floor with a mop or sponge. Do not rinse. ❖

My easy and effective strategies keep ticks away without resorting to toxic chemicals. The essential oil rose geranium is an excellent tick repellent. I put just a drop or two—no more—of rose geranium essential oil on each dog's cloth collar every week, and it really keeps the ticks away. Essential oils are very concentrated, so be sure not to use more than a few drops. Palmerosa is a good (and less expensive) substitute for rose geranium. You could also try essential oil of rosemary.

I check the pets daily for ticks. Deer tick nymphs are the size of poppy seeds and are incredibly hard to spot at the nymph stage so common in the spring. You can find ticks by feeling your pet all over with your hands (just make sure to check your hands for ticks afterward), or you can use a flea comb to easily pick up even the smallest ticks from your pet's coat.

Neutralize Pet Odors

Pets can smell the residue from a prior mess, so they tend to feel comfortable soiling that same spot again. After I clean up a pet mess and wipe up any

Place a drop or two of the essential oil rose geranium on your dog's collar to keep ticks away naturally.

liquid, I always sprinkle the area with baking soda and leave it overnight. In the morning, I sweep or vacuum up the baking soda. Because pet urine often has both acidic and alkaline components, the next step is to neutralize the alkaline baking soda and residual alkaline odor using a strong vinegar wash. I add 2 cups of white distilled vinegar to 1 gallon of water, and I wash the area with a sponge or cloth. Then I do another rinse with plain warm water. The strong vinegar smell will dissipate in a few hours.

While all pet odors can be difficult to remove, cat urine is probably one of the most challenging smells to combat. I receive e-mails from people requesting solutions to this odor problem all the time. Author and *Care2* editor Cait Johnson has come up with this four-step solution that really works.

❖ Use water with soap or detergent to dilute and remove as much of the urine as possible.

❖ Apply straight white vinegar to the area (spot test first to make sure you don't discolor carpets or furniture). Rub the vinegar into the spot, and allow the area to dry until it is just damp.

❖ Sprinkle baking soda liberally on

SHOPPING SOLUTIONS
PURE ESSENTIAL OILS

Aura Cacia is an essential oil company that offers pure rose geranium; their product line is available through Frontier Natural Products. If you'd prefer a ready-made product, Quantum Herbal Products sells a tick and flea spray for pets with pure rose geranium as its main active ingredient. Both products are available in health food stores. *Note:* If you are pregnant or nursing, you should discuss the safety of using essential oils in your home with your doctor.

the damp area, and allow it to dry completely. (If the baking soda is sprinkled on while the carpet is still too wet, it will stick to the fabric of the carpet and will be hard to vacuum.)

❖ When the spot and baking soda are completely dry, vacuum thoroughly.

Dander

All warm-blooded animals slough off tiny flakes from their skin, fur, or feathers called dander (much like dandruff on humans). The flakes contain protein that can cause severe allergic reactions in susceptible people. The dander easily becomes airborne when it is dry. Dander can remain in the home for up to 20 months after the animal is no longer present. While furry animals cause the most allergic reactions, birds can also cause reactions. Fish, reptiles, and amphibians are usually not a problem.

Try significantly reducing the amount of fiber in the home environment because carpets, upholstery, and curtains all collect dander. Bedding does, too, of course, so it should be washed frequently in hot water (140°F). Clean animal beds frequently, and replace them every 6 to 12 months if your pet sheds heavily. Run an air cleaner that has a HEPA filter 24 hours a day if there is someone in the home who is sensitive. Steam cleaners are also helpful for cleaning.

Tannic acid is frequently used to neutralize dander. Make a strong black tea (4 tea bags to 4 cups of water), and spray dog beds and environs. A note of caution: Tea tannin causes brown stains, so spot test areas first. Or search the Internet to find a supplier of pure tannic acid powders.

Poison Prevention for Pets

You should always be on the lookout for potential poisoning hazards in and around your home. According to Steve Hansen, DVM, senior vice-president of the ASPCA Animal Poison Control Center, medications and flea control products are some of the most frequent commercial products that poison pets because flea control products often contain powerful pesticides. Make sure all

SAFETY CONCERNS ABOUT PET CHEWS

Pet chews are made of animal hides. The book *Why Is Cancer Killing Our Pets?* by Deborah Straw notes that lead, arsenic, mercury, chromium salts, and formaldehyde residues have been found in poorly processed animal hides. The worst offenders are the animal chews imported from Asia. The US Department of Agriculture (USDA) has jurisdiction over animal products imported into this country but requires only an import license and a certificate of origin. While US rawhides are safer, chemical processes are used to manufacture all of these products. It is safest to avoid the chews altogether.

medications are kept in inaccessible medicine cabinets.

Some surprising pet poisonings happen from these seemingly innocuous ingredients in your household: yeast dough, coffee grounds, chocolate, tomato leaves and stems, and onions. Each of these contains compounds that can poison pets.

Many popular house and garden plants are poisonous to animals. Seemingly innocent avocado leaves, bittersweet, and daffodils can sicken or kill a pet. Do your research before bringing plants into the home, especially if your pet has a tendency to eat plants or be curious. Check the Toxic Plant Database at the Veterinary Medicine Library at University of Illinois online at www.library.uiuc.edu/vex/toxic/intro.htm.

If you suspect your pet has ingested something poisonous, call your vet and the ASPCA's Animal Poison Control Center's 24-hour hotline at 888-426-4435. The center is staffed by veterinarians and is affiliated with the University of Illinois; it's the only animal-oriented poison control center in North America.

Annie's Insight

There's nothing like a beloved pet to give you unconditional love when you need it most. If spending time with a companion animal does wonders for you, you won't be surprised to learn that it may work for others in need, too. At therapeutic and caregiving centers across the country, pet volunteers—dogs, cats, and even birds—are more and more in demand to help people achieve physical goals, such as lowering high blood pressure, and psychological ones, like regaining their emotional balance and relieving stress.

Pets make people feel good and may help break down barriers when human-to-human contact isn't working. Just 5 minutes of petting a dog or cat can start the release of feel-good hormones, and that chemical shift can have physiological benefits. One example: University of Missouri–Columbia researchers recently found that regularly stroking an animal lowered blood levels of the stress hormone cortisol in people. Other studies have shown that spending time with a pet also relieves pain and reduces anxiety.

Dogs are the most common candidates for therapy volunteers, and any breed can qualify. Lap cats also make great therapy pets. The only prerequisites are that the pet has to love people and has had basic obedience training. For example, a dog must know how to walk on a leash and be quick to respond to rudimentary voice commands, such as "stay," "sit," and "down."

Volunteering your pet requires a commitment in terms of time and money, even beyond the actual visits to care facilities. You have to keep your pet well groomed, take her for regular professional teeth cleanings and vet checkups, and consistently reinforce her training. Once you've decided that both you and your pet are up for it, consider getting certified through a national organization. Each organization has its own set of guidelines and training standards. If you have a dog, for example, many organizations recommend that potential therapy dogs pass the American Kennel Club's Canine Good Citizen Test. The 10-part exam evaluates skills like sitting politely for petting, walking through a crowd without being distracted, and welcoming the attention of a friendly stranger.

After your pet is certified, you'll need to decide where to volunteer. It's smart to visit several facilities to see where you and your pet are most comfortable. If Fido or Fluffy is relatively laid-back and responds well to older adults, you might consider a nursing home or hospice. If he is active and enjoys being stimulated, working with children or in a rehabilitation center may be a better choice.

4

earth

As a child, I used to lie awake in a sleeping bag on the front lawn of my house, where my sisters and I would sleep out, and I'd look up at the Milky Way and wonder about the night sky. I'd attempt to process the vastness of it and try to understand something that is too big to grasp and beyond human comprehension. I think that stargazing, more than anything else, helped me to realize that I was a speck and nothing more. But I had an inkling that I was connected to something much bigger—the universe—and that gave me comfort.

As I observed in my childhood, the immeasurable universe also appears in small form—the fireflies we tried to catch on our sleepouts, the earthworms in our garden, the conch shell we held to our ears, the nightingale, the rose-scented evening, the salt and tomato for cooking, and the perfect nautilus. These small things are no less awe-inspiring than the vast galaxies or the solar system. I see Earth as a place of beauty and complexity, where humans share the same air as the tree frog and feel the same rain as slime in a pool down in the darkest swamp. The same minerals, sun, and air that bring life to the swamp nourish me too. The web of life sustains us all.

Who could disagree with what I saw through the clear eyes of a child, that all life on Earth—the gardenia, the hummingbird, and the Tibetan monk—is woven together and interconnected, that our cells absorb the same infusion of energy? We can easily open our hearts to the song of the earth by participating in it, enhancing our lives with it, and acknowledging the sacredness in it. Air provides essential oxygen to feed our hearts, and the sun beams to us our circadian rhythm.

Philosophers, ecologists, and many thoughtful people try to understand what it is about connecting to nature that is so healing and why instead we are in such a state of discordance with the earth and nature. Why do we want to conquer and exploit nature instead of cooperating and connecting with it? Consciousness is an incredible gift, but it is hard to shoulder. It is my hope that one day we will be able to use our consciousness to reconnect on a higher level to all that is. Being connected is fundamental if all species, including humans, are to flourish; and we need to learn more about how deep the connections are.

It is hard for many of us to deal with our sense of grief over the loss of species and ecosystems at the hands of man. We can now see how perfect nature was and how we have exploited many life forms to extinction. It is humbling; and as the losses mount, we are bereft. We are endangering our own home. In the past, my grief about the environment has focused on the earth itself, but now I realize that my mourning is for humans and other species.

The earth will endure, but humans and other species might not. Many species aren't enduring. Nature is nurtur-ing, but it is also very harsh. My daughter's children will be born to a planet not nearly as hospitable and glorious as the one where I spent my childhood, due entirely to human behavior. Their children may not have a chance to drink maple tree sap because of global warming, see a whale, or jump in a small stream to cool off. Too much is being lost. My hope is that there are enough of us who want to see change in the world and who can band together in small and large ways to change the course we are now on.

The Planet

Earth is 4.5 billion years old, born from rocks, ice, and other debris colliding in the solar system. Everything on our planet is part of what biologists call the web of life—we are all dependent and interconnected. Human beings exhale carbon dioxide, which plants need to live. Plants give off oxygen, which humans need. Think of how bees and flowers are interdependent. Bees help flowers to reproduce by gathering nectar and pollen from them, and flowers help bees by providing ingredients to make honey. Bees also carry pollen from flower to flower, allowing fertilization—and life—to go on. If you consider how the loss of even one species can affect an ecosystem, you begin to realize how fragile our earth is.

The Gaia Hypothesis

Could it be that the earth is alive and is not just a planet formed of rock? The Gaia Hypothesis, conjectured by James Lovelock and others, suggests this. Lovelock was invited to work for NASA in the early 1960s to discover if there was life on Mars. It was Lovelock's hypothesis that, if there was life on Mars's surface, it would leave some sort of mark on the atmosphere, just like on Earth. He found that the composition of the atmosphere of Mars, with a small amount of oxygen and no methane, was completely inhospitable to life at 95 percent carbon dioxide.

Lovelock found it odd that Earth, by comparison, was full of gases that react violently with each other. Yet Earth had no reactions and functioned in a chemical equilibrium. Earth, a place teeming with life, had around 77 percent nitrogen, 21 percent oxygen, and a comparatively large amount of methane. How could life survive here when there was no chemical explanation for the coexistence of these various gases? Lovelock concluded that the gases must be constantly circulating and finding equilibrium and that it was life on Earth itself that caused the circulation.

Lovelock considered the ways in which the countless organisms on Earth reacted to and controlled their environment. He began to see the earth as a self-regulating system of checks and balances involving both living and nonliving systems, organisms and gases, and biological and chemical processes. Lovelock sought the advice of his friend, novelist William Golding, on a name for the hypothesis. Golding suggested Gaia after the Greek earth goddess, thus the Gaia Theory was born.

The Gaia Theory developed into its full form when Lovelock collaborated with microbiologist Lynn Margulis. They defined numerous cycles by which chemicals were removed and returned to the environment and how life regulated the chemical content of the earth and was, in return, regulated. Perhaps the simplest example of this is the way in which solar energy and carbon dioxide are converted into chemical energy in plants, creating simple sugars and oxygen, which are consumed by other organisms, then returned to the earth in waste and carbon dioxide.

Perhaps the most important thing to glean from Lovelock's and Margulis's studies is that the earth is in a constant interdependent flux. It is a collection of self-regulating ecosystems, and unless human beings can *fit* into the larger picture rather than *dominating* it, we are going to destroy the very system we depend on for life. This is a very sad but probable truth.

GEOMANCY FOR YOUR HOME

If you decide to identify sources of geopathic stress in your home, I'd like to suggest that you find dowsers who work in teams. Two heads are always better than one, and there is a margin of error in intuitive work and dowsing because in both disciplines, the practitioner is open to influence. Double-checking results with another is always a good barometer. The team doesn't need to visit your house or be local; they can provide a distance "healing." Just like map dowsing for water, those who practice geomancy or energy healing frequently work from a distance. Contact the American Society for Dowsers or go to www.HomeEnlightenment.com for more information.

Geopathic Stress

You may have heard the term *geopathic stress* before, but you may not have realized that it is something that could be affecting you or your family daily. Geopathic stress is a term used to describe the potentially harmful effect that radiation and electromagnetic fields have on your health and well-being.

When radiation rises up through the earth and is distorted by weak electromagnetic fields (such as underground streams, mineral deposits, fault lines, and underground cavities), it's referred to as geopathic stress. There are also man-made sources of geopathic stress, including electromagnetic fields caused by electrical wiring, lighting, and appliances (including computers, TVs, some microwaves, electric clocks, and radios) and by electric generators, transformers, and power lines. Geopathic stress can also be caused by excavation, well drilling, and general construction. When natural or electromagnetic radiation is distorted, it may be harmful to living organisms because it may distort brain rhythms and weaken the immune system.

The practice of geomancy offers hope by identifying and correcting geopathic stress. Balancing the energy grid of your home or business makes it resonate with the positive, life-enhancing vibrations of the earth.

The ancient art of dowsing is often recognized as a remedy for geopathic stress. Dowsing is a type of divination and is usually employed to find a missing object, a source of water, or information about something. A dowser uses a rod, stick, or pendulum to make contact with invisible energies that can give yes or no answers.

Dennis Wheatley, author of *Principles of Dowsing,* notes that "dowsing tools act as 'indicators' when a dowsing target is found. An L-rod will swivel and a pendulum will gyrate. The body reacts to the target, and the dowsing tools respond to a dowsing reflect mechanism." Master dowser Janet Draves, a naturopath by trade who trained with the Hazel Parcels Institute, taught me to dowse energy. Janet and I have, as a team, dowsed and identified geopathic stress in homes, and we have successfully removed it. We have done this work in both of our homes, and almost everybody notes the resultant tranquil energy. We have spent endless hours together investigating geopathic stress and the energetic vibration of our homes, neighborhoods, stones, crystals, water, and even Janet herself.

The water for the well of the house where I was raised was "discovered" by master dowser Kenneth Roberts, the author of *Oliver Wiswell, Northwest Passage,* and other books, including *The Seventh Sense,* a book about dowsing. My grandmother was the book editor of the *Boston Herald,* and through her work, she became friends with Roberts. Roberts found the water vein on my family's land in New Hampshire by map dowsing. It is an interesting story and one our family has retold to our children.

I have also successfully removed geopathic stress by practicing energy healing. Energy healing uses the mind's intuitive abilities to connect to energy waves and patterns. With training, the healer removes blocks and stress. While an energy healer's technique for removing geopathic stress is different than working with the pendulum, it is no less successful.

The Human Kingdom

A wise and thoughtful Cherokee medicine priest, David Winston, told me that the Cherokee believe that humans are here on Earth, in part, as caretakers of the Great Life. Creation gave us all gifts, and the gifts are the basis for that specific species' offering back to Creation. The bee makes honey, the maple tree runs sap, and a silkworm spins silk. Our gift as humans is our large cerebral cortex, and our offering—or role—is to find our way back to the path of being truly human and to leave the earth better than we found it by using our problem-solving abilities. We can't make honey or maple sap, but we can be caretakers of the planet in a way not possible by any other species.

The Cherokee believe humans couldn't shoulder the responsibility of our cortex; it was too much. The trauma of this failure was so severe that the human spirit shattered into two pieces. The heart splintered off into one piece and the shadowy side of human nature into another piece, with the two broken parts vying for control. The result of this shattered spirit is the "John Grabs All" mentality toward the earth—the deeply broken and disharmonious relationships with ourselves, families, communities, and the Great Life.

Weaving our heart and shadow back together is very hard work, which the Cherokee call remaking yourself. Our greatest challenge, David believes, is to heal so that we may find our way back onto the path to fulfill our sacred spiritual contract and become caretakers and fully human.

Caretaking for Hope and Healing

True healing often starts on the inside—from the heart and soul—rather than from external medical intervention. The stories you read of finding hope after a tragedy and finding a fresh perspective after days, months, or even years of despair can bring renewed vitality to your own life. If you look hard enough and open your heart during a stressful time, you're bound to find glimmers of positive energy to inspire emotional, physical, and spiritual well-being.

Restoring Nature in Your Backyard

John Beal is a disabled Vietnam veteran who was given 4 months to live after a diagnosis of inoperable cancer. He survived three heart attacks and post-traumatic stress disorder from his experiences in war and experienced pain and deep spiritual suffering. John says, in a quote from *Yes!* magazine, "I went down to the stream behind my house and just cried, wondering how I'd care for my wife and four kids. . . . Then the idea came to me: If you're going to check out, so to speak, try to leave this place better than it was when you found it. I looked at this wreck of a stream (a backwater tributary of a Seattle shipping channel laced with toxic waste), filled with refrigerators, computers, old tires, torn garbage bags, broken swing sets, and stinking carpets, and all I wanted to do was clean it up."

Beal cleaned and restored the polluted stream behind his house and even the entire watershed of which it is a part. Now, 23 years later, he is alive and well and has recruited hundreds of people to help him. He's discovered that environmental restoration is restorative in itself, and it's kept him alive. He's also noticed a redemptive feeling in others who work alongside him on the river restoration. "I've seen remarkable things happen to people who connect with Mother Earth. They see a light go on. . . . When you are so overwhelmed by your depression, anxiety, or sense of illness, connecting with nature—to something larger than yourself—takes away the worry; it calms the fear." John healed and restored the earth, his body, his heart, and his home.

The transformation and healing you discover when you leave the earth better than you found it is a golden thread weaving through a shared cloth of many belief systems.

Feeling the Ground under Your Feet

The place to start connecting with yourself and the world around you is where you are right now. Accept whatever and wherever that is. The first step is to "ground"—to notice where you are and to feel your senses so you can pay attention to life. The more you feel your senses, the more you connect to nature.

You hear a lot about someone being "in their head," when you just can't turn the inside chatter off. "Did I put the clothes in the washing machine?"

Safe and Sound

MEDITATIONS FOR GROUNDING

There are a number of different meditations to help you ground. Here are two that are easy and effective. You can find other grounding meditations on the Internet. Choose the meditation that feels right to you. I like to ground at least once a day. It is important to be rooted where you are and to not reside in your mind too much.

Tree Roots and Branches Grounding Technique: An age-old grounding technique is to imagine that you are a tree. Feel where your ancient old roots are and where the new fresh roots are—deep down in the ground. Sense your root system under you, and feel how deeply you have sent the shoots down to drink up Earth's energy. Then imagine leafy branches coming off the trunk of your body and surrounding your head to drink up the light of the sun. Above and below, pull the energy of the cosmos into your body.

Asking the Earth to Come Up and Anchor You Down Technique: My favorite grounding technique is to stand with my feet slightly apart, with my hands palm down toward the ground, and to call down deep into the earth, deeper than the ocean beds, down, down, down, and ask the earth to come up for life and anchor me down into the ground. I feel the energy come up through my feet, up my legs, up to my heart, and I feel the tug of gravity make me feel centered and connected to the earth.

"What's for dinner?" "I can't forget to pick up milk."

I am sure you have experienced that sense-numbing and tedious list-making in your head—I certainly have. Many of our jobs and preoccupations keep us in our minds and don't allow us to sense our deep roots in the earth. In the book *Medicine for the Earth*, Sandra Ingerman describes grounding as a way to "distinguish truth from mental chatter."

Sometimes we become "ungrounded" when a tragedy like September 11, 2001, happens. Everyone needed to find a place where they felt safe and could regroup themselves. Making bread and homemade family dinners became paramount for many of us during that time. Trauma can also make someone avoid regrounding. An abused child may not want to be in her body, so she enters the world of the mind to avoid her feelings.

Finding your inner center can take time. Grounding helps you connect with your natural world and with yourself, and it helps you notice which things, events, and experiences influence you. If you pay attention, you realize that you feel well when you eat nourishing foods and use healing materials and less well when you don't. Paying attention gives you the information you need to be a caretaker.

The earth's gravity is the greatest healer. If you are grounded, the energetic pull of the earth clears you of stagnant low-vibration energy that obstructs light. It also helps pull pollution out of you.

Sensing the Earth in Your Home

Try to build or fill your home with as many natural materials as possible. If your hands touch a wooden railing instead of plastic, and your feet are held up by wood, bamboo, or stone instead of vinyl, you are doing much for yourself. The energy that these natural materials emit is much more suited to your well-being than the energy of synthetic materials.

Track down the chemical smells in your home, and bit by bit, replace materials that came from a chemical factory with natural materials from the earth. Change your cleaning habits and use minerals and plants instead of chemicals. Many of the same minerals and plants work wonders for repelling insects. Over time, substitute natural building materials for synthetic.

One of the most stunning natural homes I've experienced is in northern Vermont. It is a solar, full of light, off-the-grid house built with sustainably harvested poplar from the land. All the furnishings are natural fiber and wood, and the interior simply "breathes" with the air of the local environment. Even the walls are poplar—very light colored with a bare hint of sweet-smelling terpenes. No plastic or petroleum has touched the place! The energy present in this home is as uplifting as any home I've been in; it is a sanctuary for well-being.

Decorating with natural earthen materials and using natural fibers are some of the ways to enhance the natural energy of a home. The rule of thumb for clean indoor air is to build with inert natural materials.

The big wooden ceiling beams in the home I grew up in made me feel that I was in a home built of earthen materials. I used to imagine and daydream about the tree that produced such big beams. The plaster on the walls (made of pure mineral materials), the wide-plank pumpkin pine floors, the old-fashioned brick around the fireplace (made of all-natural red clay) helped unite the outdoors and the indoors in that house, and that's dramatically different from what most of us live with now. And those old drafty windows, despite our putting up storm windows every winter, ensured good airflow. Even on cold winter days, you could almost appreciate the fresh air that made its way inside the house.

Recycled, reused, and salvaged building materials, timber, and furnishings translate into living more lightly on the earth. Simple and natural elements can help ground you and bring a sense of peacefulness to a home.

The Mineral Kingdom

Stones (rocks, gems, and crystals) are all energetic, oscillating at various vibrations that can be measured. While there are many ways they are used by humans, my primary purpose of offering the information here is to introduce you to the incredible benefits stones can bring into your life—benefits that can't always be measured.

The most important benefits are for spiritual healing and as teachers of intuition. In learning to open yourself to stones, you listen to a part of yourself that's often underutilized but that is a carrier of great wisdom. That part of your mind is called the right brain and is represented by the sixth chakra or "third eye."

Stones: Stones are ancient, ageless, and timeless. Solid rock, they are rich in minerals and are, quite literally, the bedrock of our existence. From caves to Stonehenge, engagement rings to grave markers, humans have felt a sense of the mystery of stones from the beginning of time. And now, technology brings to light some of the mystery behind using them to transmit and transmute electromagnetic energy.

Minerals: Minerals are inorganic, formed from materials that were never alive. Nearly all rocks (stones, pebbles, gems, and crystals) are made up of minerals. Every mineral has a crystalline form, whether in a plant, human, animal, or rock. Of the 4,000 known minerals, just a few dozen are commonly known, such as silicates, which are one of the most common rock-forming minerals. Rocks are formed from molten lava, from mixtures of minerals, or from once-living plants and animals.

Gems: Gems are very highly prized because they are rare, brightly colored, and beautiful and often have a mystique

---

Annie's Insight

THE POWER OF METEORITES

When visiting the stone collections at the American Museum of Natural History in New York City, I was impressed at how in need of clearing the stones were! They were so tired and worn out. Many are touched by hundreds of hands a day or at least a week, and the stones were overwhelmed with all the energy they had absorbed over time. Stones can get irretrievably clogged with other energy, and many of these were. The noticeable exceptions were the meteors, whose vibrancy was so high that some of them virtually hummed. They vibrated to the touch. I had heard that meteors were self-clearing, and from my observations, I would agree.

One meteor I have had a lot of experience with is moldavite. From a meteor shower more than 15 million years ago that landed in Czechoslovakia, moldavite is a luminescent hunter green and very powerful. I was once at a workshop by Robert Simmons, author of *Moldavite: Starborn Stone of Transformation*, and he passed around a necklace made up of many stones of moldavite worth many thousands of dollars. The long necklace was the size of a Hawaiian lei. He suggested that we each put it on for a time to feel its energy. I had a case of Lyme disease at the time—with a bull's-eye rash and all—and to my astonishment, the rash began to recede while I wore the necklace. A similar necklace brought feeling back to a man's leg even though he'd had polio years and years ago as a child! Miracles of healing or not, moldavite is a powerful stone with many gifts. It is helpful to have at the computer because it seems to block the vibrations from the electromagnetic fields from your body if you place the stone between the computer and your body. The feathery moldavites are supposed to have the highest vibration. They appear feathery because they were in liquid form when they hit Earth's atmosphere and "froze" in this shape. I have a small piece—just 1 inch by ½ inch—and it cost around $30, but it has been well worth it over time. Moldavite is healing for the heart chakra, although Simmons says that moldavite clears all chakras.

of their own. The English "Crown Jewels" are stored in the Tower of London, where their beauty is on display. Legends about opals are commonplace and awe-inspiring. Some consider them to be bad luck for all but those who have it as an October birthstone. Some gems reputedly cause death or transformation that seems to hold true for generations.

Crystals: Crystals vibrate, generating an electrical charge. Their electrical and strongly magnetic behavior plays a role in healing and technology. Crystals amplify energy and are used to amplify a particular healing vibration. Some are so strong and powerful that their vibration can shift the energy in a room and even an entire house or ecosystem. "It is believed that crystals are natural purifiers of subtle energies because they absorb negative energies and transmit only those frequencies of a positive, beneficial nature," says Richard Gerber, MD, in *Vibrational Medicine.* The biocrystalline system within the body responds to the resonance of crystals, and this is called sympathetic resonant healing.

Crystals produce electrical voltage at a constancy and concentration that enables the impulse to be transmitted and programmed, which is why computer chips are powered by silicon crystals. Quartz crystals are central components of watches and clocks because their vibration is constant when stimulated by electricity. The wave of the future may bring storage of thousands of three-dimensional holographic images in crystals.

Crystals for Health and Healing

During this "New Age," rocks are often called crystals, gaining a prominence as energetic healing forces. Herbalists often share the belief that most of the herbs that you need for your own personal health will be growing nearby. If you or someone in your family needs the nutrient-rich healing properties of a specific herb—say, burdock root—soon you'll find one growing nearby. They believe the needed herb will come to help. I happen to have burdock growing in the midst of my front porch steps, and I expect it may be pointedly trying to get my attention.

I've always been touched by the notion that the earth provides for us if we only look. It conjures up ancient beliefs that the earth is the Great Mother who wants to heal and help us. Many wild plants possess what herbalists call plant signatures, or the Doctrine of Signatures, meaning that they are shaped like the human organ they are meant to help, thereby guiding us to them. Ginseng, for example, is one of the herbs used for overall human

CLEARING CRYSTALS

Tending to the crystal's needs before yours is an important step to keep your crystal humming along at its highest healing vibration. Before I understood this, I overused a crystal without soaking it in salt-water to cleanse the energy it had drawn into itself. I completely wore it out, and it has never fully recovered.

Make sure you check all your crystals now and then to ensure that you clear them when needed. This is a wonderful way to develop your intuition. Your crystals will tell you what kind of clearing they need. Trust what you hear, see, or seem to know from the crystals, even if what you hear is that no clearing is needed and that the crystals hate saltwater.

health, and it's shaped like a man. Lungwort has white spotted leaves resembling a diseased lung, which indicates to herbalists that it is a plant for pulmonary problems.

Many healers and indigenous peoples believe stones and crystals are here to heal us too and that the Doctrine of Signatures also applies to them. They believe that the right stone comes into our life when we need it. A red stone would help the blood, tiger's eye a human eye. The Renaissance physician Paracelsus first coined the term "like treats like," and this concept is used in homeopathy. Crystal healers believe that a crystal's vibration helps humans to balance trauma, emotions, and related energetic blockages. As with herbs, many energy healers believe that the crystals needed for emotional health and healing can often be found nearby, in a driveway, or near a favorite tree.

I was lucky enough to learn about using crystals as spiritual healers, and I have paid particular attention to them ever since. Crystals do seem to balance energy, a phenomenon well known to those who heal with them. In the words of Richard Gerber in *Vibrational Medicine,* "When healing energy is focused through the crystal, it is sent into the body of the patient and distributed to the areas most in need of energy balancing. There is an almost innate intelligence to this focused energy as it is always directed at the body regions where it is needed. . . . As the energies pass through the crystal, they are both amplified and directed to the part of the subtle anatomy which requires energetic reorganization and healing."

Crystals can transform the home in the same way that they heal the body: A stone doesn't need a healer's energy sent through it to be healing because it radiates energy in its own right. I was almost knocked over by the energy of a

4-foot high Shiva Lingams when I stepped in front of it at a Woodstock, New York, store. Shiva Lingams are stones formed by river water in India. It wasn't until I was 20 feet away that I stopped feeling the stone's vibration. I was repelled. My friend was drawn to it. The vibration was not in alignment and harmony with my energy at that time, but it was with my friend's. Furthermore, because she was drawn to it, I expect the stone would have been healing and balancing for her. Because of its energy, this big stone would need to be placed carefully! It is hard to imagine any room in a house that would be appropriate to handle this level of intense energy; a very big garden would be a safer location.

By placing big crystals (or everyday stones you might find on your land that are a foot high or so) in the corners of the room, you take away shadows. By taking away square corners, you make the room a circle, echoing the great stone circles of the past. Square rooms made into circles bring centering and grounding, as well as softening, to the room. The soul is often represented by the center of a circle, so when your room is a circle, it is symbolic of your soul being in the center of the circle. Being in the center of a circle offers healing to the heart center. The circle embraces you and gives you safety.

Getting Started with Crystals

Although expensive, crystals are a treat. Shopping for crystals is a lot of fun if you walk into a store and allow yourself to be led to the stone that is calling to you. I have a few favorite books that teach about different crystals. The series of books beginning with *Crystal Enlightenment* by Katrina Raphaell offers comprehensive yet very accessible guidance for understanding specific crystals; it also explains what the different sizes, shapes, and markings imply. You will learn about the intriguing demarcations in so-called Isis crystals, Record Keeper crystals, or tabular crystals, to name a few. *Love Is in the Earth* by Melody is another wonderful reference book focusing on the metaphysical properties of crystals. Lastly, I love the Crystal Deva Cards and the accompanying book by Cindy Watlington.

Crystals and Intuition

Crystals can have a profound effect on your life, and exploring crystals and their energy can be enlightening. Crystals can also be very powerful, as described by the Shiva Lingams example, so you need to take care when you select and use them. When you bring a crystal into your home, pay attention to how it feels there and make sure you move the crystal around your home until the placement feels just right. Some stones are very bright and cheery, perfect for the living room. Others are more dormant until utilized with intention; these stones can be placed in quieter places.

To get to know any new stone, I follow six steps.

1. Go outside and allow yourself to be drawn to a stone, pebble, or a rock. If you are in a store that sells crystals, open yourself to the crystals you are drawn to or to the crystal that calls your name.

2. Open your heart to the crystal. Hold it in your hand. If it is too big for your hand, put it on your lap. Put your hands around the crystal until you start to get a sense of its vibrating energy.

3. Observe simple things. Is it a happy crystal? A tense crystal? A dense crystal? Does it seem to have a low vibration or a high vibration? What do you want to know about it? Note that you might find the answers in mental pictures, from words that pop into your head, or by a sense that you know the answer.

4. Observe your reaction to the crystal. Do you want to keep it near you or clutch it to you, or do you want to set it aside?

5. Once you have decided on the crystal you want to get to know and

have purchased it, sit with it and ask it what it needs. Does it want to be soaked in saltwater overnight? Does it need a day in the sunlight? (For more information, see "Clearing Crystals" on page 114.)

6. After your crystal is clear, start getting an intuitive sense of what you want to do with it. Do you want to clutch it? Put it in your lap? Put it in a pouch and wear it around your neck? Follow your gut on this. I once had a quartz crystal and was overcome with a strong urge to put it at the base of my skull. I found a headband and placed it there (with a sheepish eye for when my daughter came home from school, so I could remove it before she saw this contraption). The crystal felt very healing in that indent at the top of my spine, and it felt right to keep it there for about 45 minutes. My self-doubt for having done this left the very next day when I read in *Science News* that quartz crystals were being used successfully to heal brain damage.

Let the crystals themselves teach you what they can do for your life and which part of your body will benefit if you hold them close.

I'd like to interject some personal wisdom about crystals: They are vibrating at a unique frequency all their own, and different crystals may affect you in different ways. Some crystals (in one case, for me, a seemingly simple garden crystal) can make you feel spacey. Others can trigger some emotional issues. One such experience I had involved a rose quartz pendant. After a few hours of wearing it near my heart chakra, my body felt wooden and strange—then I remembered to take off the crystal. Usually you adapt to any new crystal after a few days and can wear it all the time, but you must integrate each new crystal into your life with care. It doesn't mean the crystal isn't good for you if you get spacey from it—often just the contrary. It just means that you should integrate it into your life slowly.

Stones, Crystals, or Gems

In order to have a powerful stone as a helper, you don't need a crystal or a gemstone. In fact, in my experience, a rock is often even more powerful. I've dowsed the vibration of rocks, gems, crystals, and some lap-size stones I've found on my land. The stones from my yard can have a vibration almost as high as that of Stonehenge and significantly higher than diamonds.

I've had the pleasure of communicating by e-mail with English author Sue Phillips. Sharing thoughts with her and reading her book *Healing Stones* have taught me about finding healing stones

where you are. There is a crystal store in my town, and over the years, I had gravitated there every few weeks, stopping in to buy a new stone. The stones usually cost only a few dollars, and I have a lot of them by now. Whenever I thought of finding new stone energy, I went to the crystal store. I hadn't looked out of my front door at the rocks there or spent time with the pebbles brought home from ocean beaches. I thought of rocks, stones, and pebbles as so inanimate that it never occurred to me to pay

Stones can have a meditative, Zen look when they are placed aesthetically in your home. If you're drawn to a stone—whether it's a driveway stone, a round river stone, or a rock released from the earth—find a way to display it in your line of sight, so you can feel its energy.

attention to them. I ignored them just as I have the burdock root in my front steps, thinking of it as a nuisance. What lessons I have learned!

After reading about stones, I went looking for a stone on my land one cold, raw, early spring day when snow flurries were falling. I took Sue at her word that the stone for me wouldn't be one that needed to be dug up or one that disturbed the earth in any way. She doesn't believe in causing any disruption to the earth when gathering stones. Mindful of this, I was drawn to a tree that had crashed to the ground over the winter in an ice storm and was still sprawled there with its root system unearthed. I went there thinking the upheaval might have unearthed a stone. Sure enough, right where the roots had been was a quartz stone fully released from the earth and ready to be picked up. I brought it back and took the time to get to know it. I was, and still am, dazzled by this radiant, friendly, cheery stone. I have measured its vibration by dowsing using a Biometer scale, and it vibrates at 16,000 gHz, which is a very high vibration for a stone. (A gigahertz is a frequency level of 1 billion vibrations per second.) A beautiful amethyst pendant I inherited with a deep purple, clear, colored stone measures a vibration of 11,000 gHz, as do amber and diamonds. Stonehenge produces around 25,000 gHz. These gigahertz figures show the magnitude of the vibration of the stone that I found under the uprooted tree in my yard.

I found another stone near my dirt driveway. I must have passed this stone 100 or more times but never really saw it, because if I had, I would never have dismissed such a remarkable rock. This stone is weather worn into the image of a man that looks like a combination of a bear and an owl or like some sort of shamanic mask. What a face! Because I was trained to see and feel energy move during my healer training, I have watched and felt this stone use what feels like magnets pulling stagnant and low-vibration energy out of me and into itself to be neutralized.

Placing Crystals in Your Home

Welcome stones into your home and place them where you are guided. They are like butterflies of light, and they'll clear and raise the energy wherever they are placed. Here are some ideas.

❖ Introduce a new stone into your life as a marker of an event. Often people exchange or are given gems to wear when they marry. The gem honors the bond. Stones are also appropriate gifts at the birth of a baby or for a big event.

I have always noticed that people cherish the gift of a crystal. I have always been drawn to opals, and I gave myself an opal ring for my 50th birthday.

❖ Honor a place in your house with a crystal or stone. I have placed an amethyst geode on the counter near the stove in my kitchen. My kitchen is a centering place—a gathering place where I want people to feel comfortable and connected. On the counter, the amethyst shines and sparkles, welcoming all to it. A nice-size amethyst like this, about 12 inches by 8 inches, brings a very nice glow of light to a room, and the aura of its vibration surrounds it for all to enjoy.

❖ Placing stones inside your home reminds you that stones are washed by streams, heated by the sun, and tumbled by the crashing ocean waves. Let your mind travel into the earth as you wonder where they came from.

❖ Place stones here and there for the pure enjoyment of them. I have a few crystals and rocks around my bathtub, for example, and a threesome scattered on a porch railing.

❖ Sometimes putting a crystal in a dark area of your home shifts the energy to one of cheer. Try different stones in places where you don't feel fully comfortable, and see if the energy changes.

❖ Holding a stone or crystal while meditating can amplify the experience.

❖ Enjoy! Stones are helpers for you. They provide unconditional love and energy balancing, no matter what!

Remember that indoor stones and crystals need attention now and then. They may need to be soaked in saltwater overnight or placed in the sun.

Placing Stones Outdoors

What about placing a big standing stone in your yard? You and your family could sit by it when life feels to be in turmoil, and it may just pull some of the pain from you, lightening your load. I've noticed that many people have big stones as markers at the entrance to their driveways or at the corner of a garden. It often seems that the person who put it there intuitively felt the power of the rock's presence.

Cairns are giant markers made by human hands—pyramids of rough stone. A cairn would be a great way of making a structure as big as a Stonehenge standing stone, without the challenge of moving stones that are too heavy. Used as boundary markers, landmarks, or indicators, cairns traditionally have a look of mystery or a hidden story about them. Cairns have a sculptural quality about them—the result of an artistic idea linked with rocks that evokes an ancient thought or message that is just out of grasp.

Stones as Building Materials

The natural beauty of stone brings the outdoors inside the house. You can feel it immediately in houses that have stone spaces inside, such as floors, baths, fireplaces, and open stone spaces. Stone is very hard and durable and requires almost no work to maintain. Most stone is used in tile form, and the tiles are commonly about a foot square.

Stone can be slippery when used as flooring, although sandblasted stone tile has traction. It can also be a bit cold, but stone warms up nicely and stores heat when used for radiant floor heating.

Stones are also some of the most beautiful materials available. Some shimmer. Some are luminous. Others are dark and absorbent of heat, and they are not flammable. Stone caves are the oldest buildings known to man. Over the millennia, stones have been a mainstay of human shelter, and they still are. Synthetic versions of stone—cement and bricks—are seemingly sad replacements for the natural materials that are the essence of Earth.

If you use local stone, such as the bluestone quarried where I live, you can find abundant, relatively inexpensive supplies that can be gathered with no harm to the environment. But stone isn't perfect. Its disadvantages include its weight and the fact that it doesn't insulate well. Stone walls grow damp with condensation during the cold months. Using stone for countertops and flooring is simple and is without some of the inherent difficulties.

Minerals for Cleaning

Minerals are used in both industrial and homemade cleaning formulas. Minerals are very alkaline, and some, such as washing soda, are caustic, although they may not give off harmful fumes. Because they are also slightly abrasive, they make handy cleaners. My experience with minerals for cleaning is that if they are the right material for the job, they will always work if you use enough of the mineral and you allow it sufficient time to work (usually hours). Minerals are problematic in the home when there are so many in the water supply that the water is considered hard. So-called hard water often makes laundry gray faster, and it causes scale to build up around tubs, shower stalls, and sink faucets.

Baking Soda: A commonly available mineral full of cleaning attributes, baking soda is made from soda ash and is slightly alkaline (its pH is around 8.1; 7 is neutral). It neutralizes acid-based odors in water and adsorbs odors from the air. Sprinkled on a damp sponge or cloth, baking soda can be used as a gentle nonabrasive cleanser for kitchen countertops, sinks, bathtubs, ovens, and fiberglass. It will eliminate perspiration odors and even neutralize the smell of many chemicals if you add up to a cup per load to the laundry. It is a useful air freshener and a fine carpet deodorizer.

Washing Soda: A chemical neighbor of baking soda, washing soda (sodium carbonate) is much more strongly alkaline, with a pH around 11. It releases no harmful fumes and is far safer than a commercial solvent formula, but you should wear gloves when using it because it is caustic. Washing soda cuts grease, cleans petroleum oil, removes wax or lipstick, and neutralizes odors in the same way that baking soda does. Don't use it on fiberglass or aluminum or waxed floors—unless you intend to remove the wax.

The Plant Kingdom

Amy Goldman's heirloom vegetable garden in upstate New York is an archive of seeds. These seeds are ancient in their heritage, coming from roots that first drank water that came up pure from down deep in the earth and pure as no water we now know. The plants that Amy grows are lush and bountiful, and their seeds are replenishing as I write in midsummer. They stem from the ancients, and at the cellular level, they hold mysteries and healing far surpassing what humans can now grasp. Their origins go back long before their genetic survival was tinged and controlled by multinational corporations.

Amy came to grow heirloom vegetables as a natural progression of her passionate love for gardening that began when she was 18 and her deepening understanding of how important seeds are for our very survival. She began experimenting with open-pollinated, biodiverse seeds in the early 1990s and has been a card-carrying seed saver, collector, and advocate ever since. She's authored two definitive books, *The Compleat Squash: A Passionate Grower's Guide to Pumpkins, Squash, and Gourds* and *Melons for the Passionate Grower.*

Protective stones guard the garden Amy has grown from saved seed. Encircling stone walls are higher than a man in places, with slit openings to look through, giving the look of an old Arthurian castle keep, such as Tintagel Castle. The stones that look like the ruins are positioned as fences for the garden, and you instantly recognize the contemporary hand involved in its design.

This is Amy's garden and her legacy to the future. She single-handedly saves genetically diverse seed jewels from Africa, Brazil, China, Russia, and other places from around the world. She has gathered virtually every melon and squash known, and harvests them on her land, a genuine replenishment of species otherwise lost to oblivion. She works with precision, dedication, and detail, and with the eye of a scientist.

I have seen her extensive drying racks in the fall when they have overtaken her garages, and they are overflowing with squash and melons. Gourds of every imaginable shape, size, and color rival those of birds, fish, and butterflies and the glories found in art. And in Amy's words from her gorgeous and archival book *Melons for the Passionate Grower,* the melons "smell or taste like pineapple, mango, peach, and perfume!"

The Need for Genetic Diversity

Humans today rely upon just 20 varieties of plants for 90 percent of their food. Experts throughout the world think that this lack of biodiversity could provoke an agricultural calamity. The Irish potato famine, which led to the death or displacement of 2½ million people in the 1840s, is an example of what can happen when farmers rely on only a few plant species. In just the past 15 years, more than half of the varieties once available from seed catalogs have disappeared.

A seed isn't just something you spit out when you're eating fruit. It's actually the gift of life. I believe the growing crisis over the quality of our seeds and the lack of seed-saving efforts, as well as the fight over worldwide water supplies, may set the course for the future of the earth and for global discord.

To understand the impact seeds have on our lives, it's important to understand the types of seeds available today.

❖ One kind of seed, called First generation hybrids (F1 hybrids), has been hand-pollinated and is patented, often sterile, genetically identical within food types, and sold by multinational seed companies.

❖ A second kind of seed is genetically engineered. When a seed has been genetically engineered, the DNA of the plant has been changed. A cold-water fish gene could be spliced into a tomato to make the plant more resistant to frost, for example. Many individuals and organizations have spoken out against genetic engineering and have called for a halt to the technology until safety studies can be performed, but bioengineered seeds are fast contaminating the global seed supply on a wholesale level and threatening the purity of seeds everywhere.

❖ A third kind of seed is called heirloom or open-pollinated; these genetically diverse jewels have been passed from generation to generation. With heirloom seeds, there are 10,000 varieties of apples, compared with the very few F1 hybrid apple types available in most supermarkets today.

The Mayan word "gene" means "spiral of life." The genes in heirloom seeds give life to our future. Unless the 100 million backyard gardeners and organic farmers keep these seeds alive, they will disappear altogether. This is truly an instance where one person—a lone gardener in a backyard vegetable garden—can potentially make all the difference in the world.

Seeds of Change, a certified organic seed company whose mission is to help preserve biodiversity and promote sustainable agriculture, produces more than 2,000 kinds of seeds—a hundredfold increase in the number of edible plants available to most people today.

You can also purchase heirloom seeds from seed-saving organizations, such as Seed Savers Exchange and Native Seeds/SEARCH. These organizations represent a movement of several thousand backyard gardeners who are searching the countryside for endangered vegetables, fruits, and grains.

Seed Savers Exchange is a nonprofit, tax-exempt organization that is saving old-time food crops and garden plants from extinction. Kent and Diane Whealy founded the organization in 1975 after an elderly, terminally ill relative bestowed upon them two kinds of garden seeds brought from Bavaria three generations earlier. The Whealys began searching for other "heirloom varieties" (seeds passed down from generation to generation) and soon discovered a vast, little-known genetic treasure.

Seed Savers Exchange members maintain thousands of heirloom varieties, traditional Indian crops, garden varieties of the Mennonite and Amish, vegetables dropped from all seed catalogs, and outstanding foreign varieties. Each year, hundreds of members distribute and share heirloom seeds to ensure their survival. The 450-page Seed Savers Yearbook contains names and addresses of 800 members and 11,000 listings of rare vegetable and fruit varieties that they are offering to other gardeners. Seeds are obtained by writing directly to the members who are listing those varieties.

Native Seeds/SEARCH is a nonprofit seed conservation organization working to preserve the traditional native crops of the US Southwest and northwest Mexico. For centuries, Native American farmers have grown corn, squash,

Safe and Sound

SEED-SAVING TIPS

In *Melons for the Passionate Grower*, Amy Goldman shares her insight into saving seeds from heirloom melon varieties. If you're intrigued by melon varieties with names such as Minnesota Midget, Georgia Rattlesnake, Ali Baba, and Sweet Siberian, this recap will outline the basic steps for saving their seeds.

❖ In order to save pure seed, you must prevent bees from leaving traces of pollen from other varieties on the plant. The easiest way to do this is to limit yourself to growing one melon and one watermelon that you value and know to be heirlooms, rather than growing hybrids. Make sure no neighbor is growing melons within ½ mile of your garden. (Hand pollination is another option to ensure pure seed, and detailed directions are offered in the book.)

❖ There's no need to sacrifice the fruit for the seed. When you're ready to eat the melons, cut them open and retrieve the seeds at that time.

❖ Rinse seeds gently in a colander, blot extra moisture from the seeds with a paper towel, and turn the seeds out onto sturdy, absorbent paper plates.

❖ Dry the seeds at room temperature for a week or two, occasionally turning them over on the paper plate, until they can be cracked or easily broken in two.

❖ Store seeds in airtight containers in a cool, dark, dry place such as a refrigerator or freezer.

beans, and other crops under a variety of growing conditions. Native Seeds/SEARCH encourages the continued use of these plants in their native habitats. They also distribute seeds widely to home gardeners and researchers, and they support Native American farmers by offering seed free of charge. Wild relatives of cultivated crops, such as wild beans, chiles, gourds, and cotton, are included in the organization's conservation efforts. Their informative annual seed catalog lists more than 200 varieties for sale.

Without the seed-preserving work of gardeners like Amy Goldman, seed-saving organizations like Seed Savers Exchange and Native Seeds/SEARCH,

companies like Seeds of Change, and other garden caretakers around the world, whole plant species and their varieties will disappear forever.

Plants for Health and Healing

Native Americans utilized a variety of wild plants that most of us have never heard of. From agarita, alpine strawberry, American turk's cap lily, and arrow grass to white oak, wild calla, woolly milk vetch, and yellow wild indigo, their cultures included a rich diversity of native plants. Unfortunately, their knowledge has become obscure.

Herbalists agree that a diet of wild

plant foods can be a powerhouse of nutrition, producing energy from eating just small amounts of wild plants. Most herbalists are working to share with others the wisdom they glean from plants and weeds. According to the herbalist Deborah Lee, "The weed's role is to come and heal the imbalance of the soil. Clover fixes (or restores) nitrogen, for example, and burdock root—with its very deep taproot—breaks up tightly packed soil and brings nutrients up from the subsoil." Dandelions and nettles are healthful and healing weeds as long as a pesticide hasn't been sprayed on them. Herbalists use the term *simples* to describe herbs that you can utilize one species at a time (instead of combining them in complex formulas). This is a wise way to learn about herbs, and it entails getting to know one herb as a tea, for example, before moving on to another. Unless you live in the city, you will have an array of wild food within ¼ mile of your house. Be cautious, however, when selecting wild plant foods because many of the plants in your area may be polluted by lawn or farm chemicals, petroleum byproducts from engine exhaust, or other environmental hazards.

Aromatherapy

Aromatherapy has been used for thousands of years, starting in India (essential oils are mentioned in Vedic manuscripts from 3000 BC) and ancient Egypt. The term *aromatherapy*, coined in the 1920s by a French chemist, refers to the therapeutic use of essential plant oils and essences for healing, to bring energy to the whole self, and to alleviate tension, stress, fatigue, and pain. Essential oils were also valuable as antiseptics during times of plague. Very popular today in Europe, essential oils are available in many French drugstores, and pharmacists there are trained in their uses. Aromatherapy didn't become known in the United States until the late 1980s.

At the heart of aromatherapy are natural essential oils—extracts distilled from the flowers, leaves, fruit, bark, resins, and roots of plants. More than 1,000 essential oils exist, ranging from commonplace scents like peppermint and cinnamon to more exotic scents such as tea tree, patchouli, and rosewood. Essential oils are potent, often concentrated to 50 to 100 times stronger than the herbs from which they come.

Recently, I sank into a deep tub of steaming water that I had infused with a pure flower essence. The infusion of water and air was soft, subtle, and gentle. The scent merged into the vibration of the room, helping it become something sweet, uplifting, and almost otherworldly. The experience transformed my mood to one of happy tranquility. It

Infuse your bathwater with pure essential oil for a soothing, therapeutic, and healing ritual at the end of the day. (Put a few drops into an ounce of a "carrier" oil such as almond or apricot oil before adding it to your bathwater.) At the heart of aromatherapy are natural essential oils—extracts distilled from the flowers, leaves, fruit, bark, resins, and roots of plants—that provide care for the body and soul.

was healing on many levels, and it provided do-it-yourself plant spirit medicine.

The Power of Scent

Scent affects the limbic system of the brain, and the range of responses is extensive, depending on the plant's signature essence. Some believe that scent acts like a drug on the body, mind, and spirit, and in fact, most aromatherapy is used for medicinal purposes.

The essential oil of a plant is thought to be its "soul." The strong effects (relaxation, arousal, and altered con-sciousness) that scents can have on us were thought to be magical by our ancestors. Studies show that smells may give off vibrations that can be sensed even if the molecules don't reach the nose. The vibration of a scent corresponds to the infrared part of the spectrum, which is very close to the visible spectrum—it's called invisible color. Science is now reinforcing ancient empirical knowledge. Essential oil of chamomile, for example, contains azulene, an azure blue oil. Azulene is an anti-inflammatory agent, hence the effectiveness of chamomile in cases of itching or inflamed skin.

Essential oils can be used as inhalants and also used topically because they have very small molecules that penetrate the skin and find their way into the blood system. Many stimulate skin cells to heal more quickly, and others are antibacterial or antiviral—valuable natural alternatives to chemical antibiotics. Used alone, certain types of oils can cause burns or allergic reactions, so be sure to dilute them into a mild carrier oil such as almond or apricot oil before applying them to your skin. Pregnant and nursing women should always check with their doctors before using botanicals in any way.

Aromatherapy Scents

If you'd like to try aromatherapy, these are a handful of the basic scents available. Keep a journal noting how you feel when you're using the oils, and use it to guide your selections in the future.

Cinnamon: Produces feelings of homey comfort and well-being.

Jasmine: Antidepressant; sensual, soothing, relaxing, euphoric.

Lavender: Antidepressant and mood tonic; healing, relaxing, stress-relieving all-purpose oil that's perfect for soothing baths or sleep pillows.

Lemon: Antidepressant; uplifting, bright, and invigorating, and induces clarity of thought.

Neroli: Reduces stress and anxiety.

Peppermint: Mental stimulant; invigorating and revitalizing. Good for mental alertness.

Rose: Soothing, calming, and sensual, and produces feelings of euphoria.

Rose Geranium: Antidepressant, nerve tonic, and sedative; relaxing and healing to the emotions.

Rosemary: Invigorating, energy-boosting, and revitalizing. Good for memory.

Sandalwood: Soothing, relaxing, and sensual.

How to Use Aromatherapy

You can easily add aromatherapy to your self-care routine. Be sure to always buy pure essential oil from a reputable producer, and don't be afraid to inquire about the product if you're not sure.

Aromatherapy is, of course, all about the senses. Many enjoy burning candles to create a calming mood; look for 100 percent pure essential-oil aromatherapy candles made of soy, beeswax, or vegetable wax to avoid petroleum fumes, and be sure to avoid lead or metal wicks. You can also add a few drops of essential oil to the melted wax at the top of a pillar candle if it doesn't contain natural scent. Try adding a drop or two of pure essential oil to a lightbulb ring to gently diffuse scent throughout the room.

Add a few drops of essential oil mixture (see page 126) to a warm bath. You will both breathe the scent and absorb it through the skin, giving you instant psychological and physiological benefits. Add a drop or two to your favorite carrier oil and use it for massage. Place a drop or two on a tissue and inhale the scent, or simply whiff essential oil straight from the bottle. Use essential oils to create lotions and creams for skin care (and spirit care!).

Add drops of essential oils to a pot of simmering water on the stove or in a slow cooker for a gentle steam. Invest in an aromatherapy diffuser. These are generally made of unglazed terra. You fill them with oil, allowing the oil and its scent to gradually evaporate and diffuse throughout the room. (They work nicely in cars too.) And add a drop or two to your homemade potpourri; fill small bowls with the mixture and place them strategically throughout the house.

As with any natural therapy, you need to be cautious as you experiment with the benefits and results of aromatherapy and 100 percent pure essential oils. Please consult a professional if you are pregnant or nursing because some essential oils can cause miscarriage. Beware of allergic reactions if you have sensitive skin or allergies. Always consult a professional before ingesting any essential oil.

Essential oils are very strong and need to be used with care. Certain types can cause allergic reactions or environmental health problems if they are not pure. Some oils have petroleum-based solvents added, which can be very toxic. You can do an easy purity test with blotting paper to see if your oils are pure. Simply put a few sample drops of your oils on the blotting paper, which you can buy in art stores. If the blotting paper dries and there's no visible mark, the essential oil is pure; petroleum-based essential oils will leave a residue once they've evaporated.

Flower Essences

An English physician, Dr. Edward Bach, developed the concept of flower essences. The Bach flower remedies are widely available in health food stores and are recommended for spiritual challenges, such as healing addictions, aiding depression, and helping a person express their creative side. Since Dr. Bach, many others have developed flower essences. (For more resources, contact the Flower Essence Society at www.flowersociety.org.)

Flower essences work to heal energetic imbalances in the body and are taken orally as an extract. "Like homeopathic remedies, flower essences are vibrational in nature," explains Patricia Kaminski and Richard Katz in *Flower Essence Repertory*. "Flower essences are generally prepared from a sun infusion of either wildflowers or pristine garden blossoms in a bowl of water, which is further distilled and potentized, and preserved with brandy."

Consider flower essences for emotional issues in particular, such as the healing of insecurity, indecision, a sense of inadequacy, impatience, and more.

The Vital Nature of Trees

Anne Raver, writing in the *New York Times* about a landscape architect's tree plantings, notes, "To the casual eye, it is just a row of maples. But if you have grown them from young whips to venerable trees, have watched their lime-green buds open in spring, their leaves turn fiery red in fall for more than 13 years, each trunk takes on a character of its own."

I feel similarly toward the trees around my house. They are a big part of my home life. In the spring, we watch them bud with that stunning heart chakra color lime-green. In the summer, they soak up the sun and provide housing and protection to birds with their leaves, and nothing heralds in the autumn more than the changing of leaves and the smell of wood smoke.

I grew up in northern New England, with 18-inch-wide pumpkin pine floorboards and big wooden beams dividing the ceilings in all the downstairs rooms.

The wooden doors were a rich, honey-colored wood with old wrought-iron hardware, and the kitchen had hand-crafted wooden cabinets. Over the years, I noticed and identified the growth rings and markings of each piece of wood with different parts of my life.

Trees provide a wonderful array of stimulation for our senses, if we just take a minute to notice. The taste of trees can be sweeter than any other plant. Maple sap, straight from a tapped tree in the spring, is as sweet as sugar water, and when you chew on a black birch branch, it exudes a sugary birch beer and spearmintlike flavor. The smell of trees is strong, especially the smell of softer woods, such as pine, and cedar's essential oils repel bugs. Just being in a forest awakens your senses with the scents of sap, pitch, leaves, and tree trunks. Hearing trees rustle means recognizing the power of the wind, and watching trees on still or windy days is a beautiful experience in any season. There is always something interesting to observe.

Connecting with Trees

Trees were deeply sacred to the Druids. What did they know that wasn't passed down through the generations? I think trees and their energy fields are an untapped mystery and that it would be exciting to explore the possibilities.

Plant trees as windbreaks to slow down howling winter winds and reduce heating costs. Your windbreak should contain one to three staggered rows of deciduous and evergreen trees and shrubs and should stretch along the north and west sides of your property.

Connecting with trees can be easy if you keep an open mind.

Think about which tree draws you. You'll know the one for you in a flash, I expect. Go up to it and say hello. Put your arms around it, place your ear to its trunk, and listen. Listen to the sound of its energy. Hear how the energy inside the tree moves so freely and seems as if it is going somewhere? It sounds as if the tree roots draw up earth energy from deep within the ground and dissipate it into the air through their leaves and branches. Listen to the tree and ask if there is some-

thing you can do for it; open your heart to this tree, and it likely will spread its branches over your life and protect you.

I was happy when I was able to do something that helped the trees on my land. My neighbors and I worked to keep a cell phone tower from being built near our homes. The radio waves would have interfered with all the trees near my house and invaded my home. We won. I have a tree here that has become a destination—a place I go when I am in need of hope and reassurance. I often nestle stones I have found into the hollows where the roots go into the ground. The tree often wants them for a few days, and then it releases them back to me. Once I was listening to my tree, and I heard what can only be called its heartbeat. It was a deep, mellow sound. I asked my English friend, Sue Phillips, author of *The Book of Dowsing and Divining,* about this, and she said, "Yes, a tree's heartbeat comes every 7 or 8 hours."

Tree Essences

Like plant essences, tree essences can provide spiritual healing. Author Patrice Bouchardon and his wife, through their observations of trees over a long period of time, discovered nine trees that they feel provide individual qualities essential for health and well-being: birch, beech, fir, pine, hawthorn, wild rose, box, walnut, and broom. They believe that by working with these tree essences, you can heal aspects of yourself, in a way similar to how an energy healer can remove blockages or aromatherapy can influence a mood.

The Bouchardons' method of transferring tree energy to others is by soaking parts of the tree (without cutting or removing it from the tree) in an oil and water emulsion. The oil is then rubbed onto the skin. Tree oils are particularly effective to use on a chakra. Birch helps with qualities of gentleness and reconciliation, and beech helps with serenity and confidence. Tree essences are healing, and they help develop self-esteem, increase motivation, help you become free of the past, and let you see more clearly.

Trees and the Environment

Trees are considered the lungs of the planet, and selective and responsible harvesting of trees is critical. Trees give off oxygen, remove dust and gases from the atmosphere, and filter water remarkably well. A forest absorbs water and then "transpires" it back into the environment, thereby providing a critical step in preserving and purifying the earth's water. Trees play a vital role in the health of the water on the planet. The great canopy and humus floor of forests provides an ecosystem that cleanses and purifies water. "If the forests die, then the springs will dry up, the meadows will become barren . . . ," writes naturalist and water expert Viktor Schauberger (see more on water on page 199).

Much of the forest we now know on the earth will go through a major transformation in the next 50 to 100 years due to global warming, according to scientists. In the future, maple trees and others that thrive in cold northerly climates might not exist in the eastern United States; only the northern reaches of Canada may have temperatures low enough to sustain cold-climate trees. Huge change is afoot with our ecosystems because of global warming, so a tree that may be thriving now may be endangered just half a century from now—not from logging but from climate change.

Trees play a vital role in energy savings in a home because of their ability to shade the sun and provide a windbreak. Place trees on the southern side of your home to save energy; in summer, they'll shade the windows from the southerly sun with their leafy canopies, and in winter, their bare branches allow sun to stream through the windows to provide some much-needed heat. Trees can also be placed as a barrier between your house and the prevailing direction of the winds.

Conserving Trees

"Reduce the amount of newly harvested wood homes by 50 to 80 percent, and our children and grandchildren may get to experience forests that are more than the equivalent of cornfields," says Sim Van der Ryn, founder of the Ecological Design Institute, in the preface of the book *Building with Vision*.

Finding wood that has been certified as sustainably harvested is not easy. Unfortunately, there is not enough consumer demand, and the mainstream industry won't quickly respond until there's consumer interest. Fortunately, a number of states have taken the initiative and don't allow the sale of imported tropical timber.

The Internet is an excellent time-saver in the challenge of finding certified sustainably harvested wood (see page 457 for sources). Here is an overview of what to look for.

Certified Wood Products: There are a few wood certification services available that are well worth contacting and supporting. Although they are fledgling initiatives, we can hope they'll grow over time.

Rediscovered or Reclaimed Wood: This is wood that has been salvaged from landfills, fallen trees, deconstructed buildings, and demolition projects. The SmartWood Program of the Rainforest Alliance has developed the "SmartWood Rediscovered Wood Program" for certification of reused, reclaimed, recycled, and salvaged wood products.

Green Wood: This is reconstituted wood using recycled content, often from less-used species such as aspen and poplar. It is fabricated with low-toxicity, formaldehyde-free composites. "Green" particleboard is often labeled as "environmentally clean." Medium-density fiberboard can be compiled without formaldehyde.

Secondary Species: Lesser-known trees, such as sweetgum and madrone, are excellent substitutes for well-known wood types and are sometimes grown purposely to "take the pressure off" species that are stressed by over-harvesting.

What to Consider When Buying Wood

With a few exceptions, the key to buying ecologically sound wood depends on how the wood is grown and harvested. Maple that is harvested in a responsible way is not the same product as maple that hasn't been harvested ecologically! Exceptions to this rule include certain species of mahogany, which have been so overharvested that they are too rare for any of it to be harvested in a sustainable manner.

There are also a few undervalued North American species available from the Forest Stewardship Council's certified wood sources. These lesser-known species offer the same qualities and beauty of more widely available woods, but they are considered more sustainable, at least at this point in time. As alternatives to the commonly used building hardwoods (cherry, aspen, and red and white oak) whose supplies are now under pressure, look for stock of big-leaf maple, California black oak, cottonwood, hackberry, madrone, paper birch, sweetgum, sycamore, tanoak, and willow.

According to the Hardwood Council, the wood species with the highest harvests in the United States are red and white oak, consisting of 52 percent of the market; next is poplar with 11 percent of the market, followed by maple with 8 percent, ash with 5 percent, cherry with 4 percent, and alder with 3 percent. A combination of lesser-known woods such as basswood, cottonwood, gum, hackberry, pecan, walnut, and others make up the remaining 17 percent.

There are also a number of good

SHOPPING SOLUTIONS
CERTIFIED WOOD PRODUCTS

The Forest Stewardship Council represents an environmentally credible program. FSC requires third-party, independent monitoring of supplies of virgin wood materials from well-managed forests to be sold as FSC-certified. FSC considers local and regional environmental issues. FSC-certified wood products include framing lumber, interior plywood, wooden flooring, siding, trusses, engineered wood products, furniture, doors, windows, cabinets, decks, veneers, and particleboard. Visit www.fscus.org or contact the council at 1155 30th Street NW, Suite 300, Washington, DC 20007. The phone number is 202-342-0413.

STOPPING THE SILENT SPRING

Rachel Carson noted how the birds stopped singing after a pesticide spraying. I noticed, too, after the campus where I was living was heavily sprayed with herbicides to kill dandelions. The raucous early-morning bird cacophony went eerily quiet for a week or more. The silence of the birds is haunting when you know the cause.

Lawn and garden chemicals kill insects and weeds—two of the major food sources for birds. So when birds ingest insects or plants treated with pesticides, herbicides, or chemical fertilizers, they can suffer greatly and die. Talk to your neighbors about reducing or eliminating the neighborhood's pesticide burden and switching to organic gardening methods to give backyard birds a healthy haven in which to raise their young.

replacements for rare trees. Lesser-known tropical species that can be used for fine woodworking details include amapola (yellowish red), black cabbage (yellowish brown to dark reddish brown), cumaru (yellowish brown), curupay/cebil (chestnut brown with light streaks), granadillo (violet to dark red to brown), ipe (whitish), manu (light to dark olive brown), nispero (light to dark reddish brown), piquia (yellowish to light grayish brown), and santa maria (pink or yellowish pink to brick red). All of these choices are discussed in detail on the Certified Forest Products Council's Web site at www.certifiedwood.org.

It is worth noting that in Europe, wood is considered an inferior building product to masonry in terms of durability and fire resistance. The old-growth forests of Europe are gone, forcing nations to find alternatives to wood products. Are North America's far behind?

The Animal Kingdom

Scientists at the Natural Environmental Research Council Centre for Ecology and Hydrology, in Dorchester, England, warn that Earth may be on the brink of the sixth mass extinction. Their research shows that 71 percent of the butterfly species, 56 percent of birds, and 28 percent of plants have decreased in all major ecosystems since 1984 throughout England. Atmospheric nitrogen pollution (caused mainly by the burning of fossil fuels) is considered largely to blame. Other suspected influences include human activity, leaching from landfills, increased paving, toxic effluents, altered waterways, and clearing of forests. Grief for loss of species is a very real spiritual problem many of us face. I often wondered how Jane Goodall managed to cope with the tidal wave of mourning she must have felt for the slaughter of her beloved chimpanzees for bushmeat. She is one of the earth's greatest caretakers. The light of egoless love shines from her. When I heard Jane speak, her message was simple and resonated with wisdom: "I just do the very best I can every day."

Butterfly, plant, and bird numbers are all in decline. Eighty percent of most bird species die in the first year of life. We can help! You can positively impact the earth's ecosystems and wildlife by making your backyard hospitable to flora and fauna.

Create a bird-friendly backyard! Bird feeders are centers of life and activity. Deer and turkey even come to mine in the deep winter to retrieve seeds and hulls discarded or dropped by the birds. In spring and summer, just the colors of the birds brighten up my day.

It is fascinating to watch bird behavior at bird feeders. Over time, I have noticed that birds will always wait their turn to fly to the feeder. They perch on trees surrounding the feeders—often with many different species in the lineup. They wait, patiently or not, for their turn. One by one, each has its turn, and then they get a chance at the feeder

again. They somehow know when it's their turn; I've never seen two birds even come close to a collision at the feeder. And they never overstay their allotted time, which is always fleeting.

Feeding Birds through the Seasons

If you choose to have bird feeders, there are seasonal decisions and commitments you need to make for your sake and that of the birds. If you want to feed birds in the winter, you must commit yourself to the task because birds depend on specific sources of food when it's scarce and will nest near such places. If the food they have been counting on suddenly disappears, they can starve. In the winter, I fill the same two feeders every 2 days.

Keep in mind that birds may take a while to learn about your feeding station. Sometimes, it might take up to 3 weeks for them to begin to frequent your yard. During summer and spring, your feeding station will represent only a portion of their overall diet, so not feeding them for a week because you're on vacation is perfectly acceptable. Winter is a different story, however. If you're leaving in the middle of the cold season and have neighbors who are fond of birds, ask them to fill the feeders when you are gone. If you have no one to attend to the feeders, it's good to taper the food a little in advance so they have time to discover other food sources.

Spring

By the time early spring starts rolling around, a bird's natural food sources are depleted, and birds may be scrounging for berries, seeds, and plant food. The birds that have wintered over will be searching for any food they can find, and those that are migrating will find few sources of food as they pass through the area. Suet, which is a type of fat derived from beef kidneys, is eaten by 80 percent of North American species, including woodpeckers, chickadees, titmice, and orioles, and it's a good high-energy source. Water is also important for year-round residents and migrating species. The more hospitable your yard, the more likely you are to find birds nesting at your doorstep in late spring.

Special Spring Needs: Spring is a busy time for birds and backyard birders.

❖ Birds nest and lay eggs in the spring, so females require high levels of calcium right before they lay their eggs. Chicken (and other) eggshells are rich in calcium, so save them; rinse the shells, bake them at 250°F until dry, then crush them. Mix ground eggshells with corn meal, and sprinkle the mixture on a platform near the feeders.

❖ Get your feeders out pronto! You may need to add an extra feeder or two if numbers swell.

❖ Fresh water is key to a bird-friendly backyard, so keep birdbaths full, and clean out debris from ponds and water features to keep water fresh.

❖ Offer delicacies to keep birds coming back: nuts, mealworms, suet, over-ripe fruit, and peanut-butter treats.

Summer

Summer is the only time that feeding birds isn't of real benefit to the birds—although it's perfectly okay to do so. The earth becomes rich with food sources in the summer and fall. Sometimes I stop feeding my birds in mid-June because the birds devour two hanging feeders of seed in half a day! Keeping up with the job is time-consuming and expensive. I've gradually evolved to just feeding them the same amount that I do in the winter (when the birds go through those same two feeders every 2 days); this keeps the birds nearby and coming to the feeders but allows them to enjoy the plentiful banquet of seeds, berries, and plants in my yard. At temperatures above 70 degrees, sun-warmed suet can mat down a bird's feathers, which leads to problems with reduced insulation and waterproofing and, of course, a loss of feathers; try the Special Summer Suet below, and see how well it fares in warmer weather. Personally, I think that summer feeding is the most fun, though, because you can attract such a wide variety of backyard birds.

Special Summer Needs: Offer birds a little extra in the summer to keep them at your feeders.

❖ Attract insect-eating birds, such as tanagers, thrush, and warblers with a Special Summer Suet. Combine 1 cup of vegetable shortening (organic and nonhydrogenated), 4 cups of cornmeal, and 1 cup of flour. Place the suet in suet feeders, or push it into the cavities of hanging food logs, and make sure it's in a shady spot to lessen the chances of its going rancid.

❖ To attract nectar-loving birds, such as brightly colored hummingbirds, set out sections of overripe citrus fruit on a platform feeder, and watch the feast begin.

❖ Seed-eaters, such as goldfinches, chickadees, and titmice, will readily stop by tube feeders filled with niger and tray feeders offering black oil and other sunflower seeds.

❖ Summer's not summer for a bird without a plump and juicy worm! Offer protein-rich mealworms, squiggles and all, and watch bluebirds, woodpeckers, and purple martins dive into your drive-in for a feast.

❖ Keep birdbaths full, and offer the sounds of gurgling, spritzing, or babbling water with a small water feature, a dripper, or a recirculating fountain.

Fall

Many birds start to migrate in mid-August, and the demand for nourishment increases. As fall draws near, both migrant and nonmigrant birds will establish their winter feeding territory. Therefore, late summer into early fall means a return to the bird feeder routine to fortify the migrants and to reestablish your yard as a feeding ground. Though natural food sources will remain abundant for most of the season, birds will become more reliant on feeders as the weather cools. Indeed, if you're primarily interested in feeding birds during the winter, it is important to begin putting out feeders early in September. Many birds return to the same feeding grounds year after year, both for the duration of the winter and on their migrant journeys.

Special Fall Needs: Birds start to prepare for cold weather, so be sure to offer high-energy foods.

❖ Low-height feeding trays are the way to go for many ground feeders, including mourning doves; be sure to keep plenty of cracked corn because a flock of doves can devour more than you might expect.

❖ Keep the hummer feeders filled until the temperature drops to the near-freezing mark. There are always late migrants passing through.

❖ Water is still a vital need for birds, so make the effort to keep fresh water available. And be sure to regularly clean out fallen leaves from birdbaths.

❖ Hang plenty of suet feeders and fill with fresh homemade or purchased suet. And there's no need for embedded nuts, seeds, or birdseed mixes. The plain suet is what most birds are after.

❖ During this season, many species of birds will be developing their flight feathers, and they'll need rich sustenance. Oil-rich sunflower seeds and niger seeds provide ideal nourishment for migrants.

Winter

As fall turns into winter, naturally occurring food sources decrease and all but disappear eventually. Providing a continuous supply of food can significantly decrease the mortality rate of local birds. Chickadees, for example, have a higher survival rate when supplemental food from feeders is available, especially during weather extremes such as cold snaps, snow cover, and ice storms.

When feeding birds in the winter, keep in mind that dawn and dusk are the most important times to make food available—that's when birds tend to forage the most. It is important to be scrupulous about continuing to feed all winter because some birds have made your yard their feeding ground and will depend on the food you provide.

Special Winter Needs: Homemade goodies will keep winter residents flocking to your feeders.

❖ Mix suet with peanut butter and cornmeal, or add raisins, grapes, and cherries. Try your hand at homemade suet cakes: Melt 3 cups of suet, and stir in 3 cups of cornmeal and 1 cup of peanut butter. You can also mix in raisins, rolled oats, and fruit. Mold in recycled plastic suet containers or margarine tubs. You could also press the mixture into pinecones and hang them from tree branches to distribute nourishment to your feathered friends.

Bird Feeders

An ideal environment for feeding birds would include several feeders—a platform feeder, a tube feeder, a hopper feeder, a suet feeder, a peanut feeder. Hang feeders from reasonably high branches in a southern area of the yard to optimize warmth and sunlight. Or mount feeders on poles with squirrel and predator baffles; baffles range from slippery metal or aluminum domes attached to the top of a feeder to slick plastic guards mounted below the feeder.

While birds prefer nearby shrubs or cover to make a quick escape if a predator comes close, keep feeders away from dense undergrowth where large predators, such as cats, might lurk. Avoid placing feeders near large windows and buildings. Birds seem to be incapable of detecting clear or reflective glass; one study suggested that 97 million birds collide with windows each year. Hanging things like strips of cloth over windows or closing curtains during the daytime offers birds a warning and hopefully will prevent any ill-fated (and potentially fatal) encounters.

Bird feeders should be refilled every few days to keep seeds fresh and prevent unhealthy bacterial growth. Birds simply prefer fresh seed of good quality. Neglected bird feeders will do more harm than good by promoting the growth of fungi such as *Aspergillus fumigatus,* which causes respiratory infections in birds. Though feeding birds your stale bread is perfectly acceptable, try not to toss too much out into your yard or onto your platform feeder, since it will become damp and quite susceptible to growing hazardous molds.

Make sure that you clean all your bird feeders once a month. (Hummingbird feeders require even more care; see page 141.) If you enjoy feeding birds and operate more than a couple of feeders,

cleaning them on a rotating schedule will prevent your having to clean them all at once—a potentially burdensome task. Make sure that you call wildlife officials immediately if you notice that the birds in your vicinity seem sick. A concentrated congregation of birds enables avian disease to spread quite rapidly. You may see a rise in bird population around your well-maintained feeding stations, and you may occasionally stumble across a dead bird near the feeder. Bury dead birds immediately.

Keep in mind that birds won't be the only animals with their eyes on the banquet that you provide; squirrels and other creatures, such as cats, raccoons, skunks, and opossums, are in a perennial struggle with our feathered friends for their food. Though many ingenious devices have been crafted to thwart their efforts, they continue to successfully purloin seeds and suet. I have a special bird feeder that is designed to deter squirrels based on their weight. Once the squirrel steps onto the bar stand where the birds stand, the stand drops and blocks entrance to the food. Excited that I finally had a way to keep the squirrels from the food, I next saw them hanging from the top of the feeder and reaching into the food source upside down, so they didn't have to put any weight on the stand!

Choosing a feeder can be exciting— and overwhelming. The variety avail-

Offer a variety of birdseed and feeders, and you'll go a long way toward inviting wildlife into your backyard. Being a good steward means maintaining and cleaning feeders, placing them in a sheltered area within easy reach of safety from predators, and being consistent about offering seed, especially during cold spells.

able at wild bird centers, hardware stores, and department stores allows you to attract a specific species or birds indigenous to your area. There are different shapes and sizes of feeders depending on the type of food and seeds you plan to offer. Ask for advice from shop owners and knowledgeable friends, make your choice, then sit back and enjoy the increase in traffic from your feathered friends.

Platform Feeders: A platform feeder is exactly what it sounds like—an open tray of food (usually seeds) that can accommodate many birds at one time. Birds enjoy this sort of feeder because it is open and accessible. The lack of restriction encourages birds of all shapes and sizes. Screens and grates are available in order to restrict squirrels and other predators from stealing the

goodies. Scatter seed on top of the feeder, and watch hungry evening grosbeaks flock to the feast. During the summer, you may want to offer treats of overripe citrus fruits and bananas on your platform feeders.

Tube Feeders: Tube feeders are long cylinders with feeding perches and seed ports. You can fill the cylinders with several types of food at one time to encourage a variety of birds to visit. Tube feeders attract mostly small birds, such as finches, titmice, and chickadees. You can purchase a wide baffle to hang over the top of the feeder to prevent squirrels from devouring your offerings.

Hopper Feeders: Hopper feeders are the icons of the bird-feeder world. They are usually fashioned like miniature houses, with wood and Plexiglas walls that hold in the seeds. The bottom tray is wide enough for larger birds, such as doves and sparrows. Seeds are kept dry by a small roof, and gravity handles the distribution. A hopper feeder is a good first purchase for someone with a growing interest in backyard birding. They are easy to clean, hold a few days' worth of seeds, and bring in lots of birds.

Hummingbird Feeders: Hummingbirds are drawn to bright colors, so look for nectar feeders with red accents when purchasing a feeder. Begin filling hummingbird feeders in early spring in order to encourage hummers to choose your yard for their summertime habitat. A simple mixture of 1 part sugar to 4 parts water (boiled for 2 minutes) is perfect for filling nectar feeders. There's no need to add red food coloring to your mixture, though; the red components on your feeder are enough to bring in hummingbirds. Unfortunately, your delicious sugar water solution will inevitably draw unwanted visitors, such as ants, bees, and wasps, to your feeders, but you can easily deter these interlopers by putting some vegetable oil around the feeder opening.

Due to the nature of their design, hummingbird feeders tend to gather bacterial and fungal growth quite rapidly. Wash all parts of the feeders, inside and out, every few days with a mixture of 1 cup of vinegar to 1 cup of hot water. Neglecting to do so could result in dire consequences for your local hummingbird visitors—nectar that's allowed to ferment in warm, summer air can cause enlarged hummingbird livers.

Suet Feeders (and Cages): Suet feeders are heavy wire cages that hold purchased or homemade suet cakes. For the intrepid bird feeder who makes her own suet mixtures, these hanging cages work great because it's a snap to refill them—just flip up the lid and insert a new suet cake. If you prefer a more natural suet feeder, you can turn pinecones and small logs into suet feeders. Spread suet between the scales of the pinecone, or drill holes in a log and insert suet into the cavities. Suet is mostly a cold-weather food for birds because it goes rancid quickly at temperatures above 70°F. To keep predators from raiding your suet, make sure suet feeders are hung high off the ground. Suet can be a winter staple and will be easily devoured by wrens, catbirds, woodpeckers, chickadees, and sapsuckers.

Peanut Feeders: Peanut feeders are cylindrical wire cages or mesh bags that you fill with peanuts and other seeds. These feeders will attract nuthatches, chickadees, titmice, and woodpeckers. If you spend a lot of time watching birds, then this type of feeder is of special interest, since the birds often have to spend a good bit of time working to liberate their treats in tiny pieces. Be sure not to get a feeder that's too large for your usual crowd of birds, however, since peanuts that are left out can get moldy. Monitoring the average consumption will help you to prevent overfilling the feeder and wasting food.

Natural Feeders: If you're interested in an alternative natural feeder, try hanging large, hollowed-out gourds filled with seeds, like the Native Americans did. Even a hollowed-out orange half filled with seed makes a quick feeder when hung from a branch in winter.

Placing Feeders for a Variety of Visitors

Different varieties of birds prefer feeders at different heights and at various locations around your yard. It's important to site feeders in areas where birds feel safe because you want to keep steady visitors coming back and attract new species to your backyard landscape. Keep these guidelines in mind when you create your bird-feeding habitat.

Platform Feeders

Many birds forage on the ground for their daily sustenance, and there are dozens of backyard birds who look to platform feeding stations to supplement the natural seeds and foods they find in the landscape. American robins, black-capped chickadees, blue jays, brewer's blackbirds, brown-headed cowbirds, brown thrashers, bushtits, cardinals, Carolina chickadees, chipping sparrows, crows, dark-eyed juncos, European starlings, flickers, fox sparrows, and grackles are drawn to seed scattered directly on the ground and platform feeders placed just a few inches off the ground. You'll also attract house sparrows, mourning doves, red-winged blackbirds, ring-necked pheasants, rufous-sided towhees, song sparrows, tree sparrows, tufted titmice, white-crowned sparrows, white-throated sparrows, and wood thrushes with ground feeders.

In fall, remember to leave a few untidy areas to attract birds. Allow fallen leaves to blow under a sheltering hedge or around the base of a shrub. Then use this area as a ground feeder by sprinkling seeds and nuts still in their shell on top of and mixed in with the leaves.

Hanging Feeders

Hanging feeders are preferred by many birds, including the American goldfinch, black-capped chickadees, blue jays, cardinals, Carolina chickadees, cedar waxwings, the common flicker, hairy woodpeckers, house finches, mockingbirds, northern orioles, pine siskins, purple finches, red-breasted nuthatches, scrub jays, and tufted titmice. By hanging a feeder in a tree or near a large shrub, you've given a bird quick cover if trouble threatens. And if you add flower beds full of tall flowers and grasses underneath or nearby, it adds to the security.

Birds that spend most of their time in trees obviously prefer hanging feeders, but hungry birds will quickly acclimate to these same feeders when snow or ice covers other food sources. Trees can offer some shelter from winter winds, so you may find new species trying out the hanging feeders in your backyard when Old Man Winter blows in frigid air.

Pole Feeders

Pole or hopper feeders cater to birds that don't mind some company at the dinner table. You might find a black-capped chickadee, blue jay, Carolina chickadee, common flicker, downy woodpecker, or hairy woodpecker sharing a place at the feeder with a mockingbird, red-breasted nuthatch, or white-breasted nuthatch.

These feeders usually have over-hangs or roofs so birds feel protected, even when there are two or more at the feeder. When purchasing a hopper feeder, look for one with a wide tray beneath the seed storage area. Some models hold up to 10 pounds of seed,

relieving you of daily refilling tasks. The most popular seeds for birds at hopper feeders include sunflower seeds, millet, or a mixed offering.

Banquets for Birds

Birds have different nutritional needs as well as different culinary preferences. If you want birds to visit your backyard, you'll need to figure out which seeds (and plants, of course) will bring them to your banquet table. If you're just starting as a backyard bird feeder, you can purchase large bags of wild bird food, which is usually a mix of generically popular seeds. Once you lure species out of your trees and begin to identify who your visitors are, you can better target your feeding efforts.

Lower-cost seed mixes may not be as economical as you think. Many of these mixes contain fillers, such as oats, milo, rice, wheat, or peanuts, that aren't readily gobbled up by feeder birds. The easiest plan is to stick to three well-loved seeds—black oil sunflower seed, gray-striped sunflower seed, and white proso millet. You'll find the best deals at feed mills if you plan to buy in bulk; otherwise, your local wild bird store will have the freshest and highest-quality seed. Be sure to store any bulk seed purchases in a metal trash can with a tight lid (or metal pretzel or cookie tins for smaller quantities). If you find that

BASIC BIRD MIX

BIRD FEEDER'S STARTER MIX

If you're new to bird feeding or just trying to entice a few flyovers to your yard, try this starter mix to roll out the welcome mat.

50 percent sunflower seed
35 percent white proso millet
15 percent cracked corn

Combine the seed, millet, and corn in a large container. Store in a dry trash can or storage can with a tight-fitting lid. ❖

mice have gotten into your seed, your seed is infested with insects or worms, or it's damp from moisture, you might as well dispose of it because birds won't touch seed that's moldy or insect infested.

Gray-striped sunflower seed was the birdseed of choice for decades. But bird lovers have grown more savvy over the years as they realized that they could attract a wider variety of species if they offered specialty seeds. This quick rundown of the most popular bird treats will help you bring your favorite local species into your backyard.

Black Oil Sunflower Seed

Higher in calories and smaller than gray-striped sunflower seed, black oil sunflower seed can be offered in tube, hopper, or platform feeders. Or you can simply scatter it on the ground when birds have trouble finding food because of foul weather. Black oil sunflower seed entices a great number of birds, including the American goldfinch, black-capped chickadee, blue jay, bushtit, cardinal, Carolina chickadee, dark-eyed junco, house finch, mourning dove, pine siskin, purple finch, and white-breasted nuthatch.

Gray-Striped Sunflower Seed

The broad appeal of gray-striped sunflower seed will draw all sorts of birds, including chipping sparrows, common flickers, downy woodpeckers, fox sparrows, grackle, hairy woodpeckers, pine siskins, red-breasted nuthatches, scrub jays, song sparrows, tree sparrows, tufted titmice, white-breasted nuthatches, and white-crowned sparrows. These birds use their large bills to crack the tough shells for the sunflower meats inside.

White Proso Millet

You've probably seen the round, cream-colored millet seeds in seed mixes; it's a popular ingredient because most birds across the country will eat it. It's a staple of sparrows and wrens as well as buntings, doves, juncos, and starlings. And many other birds will switch to millet once the sunflower seed is gone from a feeder. If you find yourself with an abundance of pine siskins dwelling nearby, try offering them millet to attract them to your backyard. Millet is a bargain too; a 5-pound bag contains thousands and thousands of seeds.

Niger

Often called thistle seed (even though it's not from a thistle, but from a sunflower cousin), niger is a small, rice-shaped seed that attracts a big, big crowd. Hang a thistle tube feeder or a thistle sock, and you'll be amazed at how many finches, goldfinches, sparrows, juncos, and siskins crowd the feeder. Then watch below the feeder for the ground feeders eager to pick up any fallen seed.

Cracked Corn

If you're interested in catering to sparrows, doves, and quail, sprinkle cracked corn on the ground. Other cracked corn lovers include blue jays, brown-headed cowbirds, chipping sparrows, crows, European starlings, grackle, house sparrows, mourning doves, red-winged blackbirds, ring-necked pheasants, rufous-sided towhees, scrub jays, song sparrows, tree sparrows, white-crowned sparrows, white-throated sparrows, and wood thrush.

Peanuts

Peanuts are a treat, both in and out of the shell. Crows and jays (not to mention squirrels) love the challenge of shelling peanuts, while Carolina wrens, chickadees, nuthatches, titmice, and woodpeckers will readily devour shelled peanuts. Buy peanuts in bulk, but nibble one or two before you buy if you can to make sure they're fresh and not rancid. Choose either raw or roasted, but avoid salted peanuts if possible. Peanut feeders are inexpensive, so be sure to indulge in at least one in your backyard.

Suet

From suet cakes to butcher-supplied suet, you'll find that suet feeding is rewarding for beginner and experienced bird watchers. Suet is a high-calorie, low-maintenance food; just hang a wire suet feeder or smear suet on a homemade feeder to provide a high-energy treat.

Suet, with or without imbedded seeds, particularly appeals to birds such as black-capped chickadees, blue jays, Carolina chickadees, chipping sparrows, common flickers, downy woodpeckers, grackles, hairy woodpeckers, mockingbirds, northern orioles, red-bellied woodpeckers, red-winged blackbirds, scrub jays, song sparrows, tufted titmice, and white-breasted nuthatches.

cedar waxwings, Eastern phoebes, gray catbirds, mockingbirds, northern orioles, red-breasted nuthatches, and tufted titmice. Orange halves are of particular interest to orioles. Many varieties of birds enjoy dried fruit; rehydrate it in warm water until it's plump, then toss some of that outside as well.

Other Staples and Treats

Offering your birds some year-round sand particles or dried eggshells in a pan or platform feeder is a good idea. Since birds don't chew their food; they depend on their gizzard and available grit to aid in digestion. Calcium-rich grit and eggshells offer them assistance if they consume a sticky substance that they can't entirely swallow. Coarse sand or ground clamshells are perfect grit offerings. You can also crush eggshells and bake them until they're dry, then set them outside. Female birds, especially during nesting season, seek out sources of calcium. Offer grit and crushed shells in an open area, away from feeders.

If you find yourself with an abundance of overripe (but not moldy or spoiled) fruit, slice it and place it out on a platform feeder to attract American robins, brown thrashers, cardinals,

Water and Birds

Fresh, moving water is very important for birds, and providing it is a real challenge, especially in winter. Some of the best birdbaths and water bowls I have seen have a heater or a dripper to provide fresh, moving water in icy cold weather. Providing fresh water to birds in winter can be a lifesaving practice, literally.

Birdbaths, much like feeders, must be maintained carefully to prevent the development of algae and festering bacteria. Make sure to clean them every couple of days or as soon as you notice that they have been soiled by bird droppings or other debris. You can render a simple birdbath from an upside-down trash can lid (a metal one, since plastic can be too slippery for the birds) or a ceramic flowerpot saucer. However, birdbaths made to endure wintertime temperatures may include submersible thermostat-controlled heaters or other complex features designed to make thirsty birds comfortable.

Birdbaths with a constantly moving water drip can be fed from your outdoor faucet. It is important to remember that birds identify water by both sight and sound, so having a constant drip will alert them to your birdbath's presence. A simple way to do this is to poke a very small hole in the bottom of a plastic milk jug and another hole near the top for ventilation. Fill it with water and hang it on a pole a few feet above your birdbath. You'll probably need to refill it daily. If you notice that the jug is collapsing, enlarge the vent hole slightly.

Wildlife in Your Neighborhood

While one of the great daily thrills of life, especially if you live in a particularly rural area, is the opportunity to see wild animals going about their business, there is such a thing as too close. We might delight in watching squirrels jump from tree to tree and delight in noticing a family of raccoons trotting around the edge of the forest at twilight; however, the next morning when the garbage is strewn up and down the driveway, that same cuddly family finds itself at the receiving end of an angry tirade.

There are some general nuggets of wisdom to keep in mind about wildlife,

MAKE IT YOURSELF
MOTH MILK

Moths are fascinating and beautiful creatures, and you'll enjoy seeing how many species you attract. Lure moths in droves by making this moth attractant.

> 6 ounces flat beer
> 1 ounce flat cola
> ½ rotting banana
> 1 rotting peach
> 2 pounds brown sugar

In a small saucepan, mix the beer and cola. In a bowl, mash the fruit into a pulp. Heat the beer-cola mixture over low heat and add the sugar slowly until dissolved. Add the mashed fruit to the liquid mixture, mixing thoroughly. Allow moth milk to cool completely.

When there's little or no breeze, spread the mixture on tree trunks, large rocks, and fence posts located near bushes or shrubs (which the moths use as protective cover). Wait until it's fully dark, and check the locations where you put the bait; shine your flashlight near, but not directly on, the sites with the moth milk. ❖

no matter what size or shape. Don't store pet food in an easily accessible place; outdoor cat bowls, large bags of dog food, or even birdseed kept near a garage door can attract all sorts of hungry animals. To prevent raccoons from getting into the trash, use trash cans with snug lids, or weight the tops with heavy rocks or bricks. Keeping shrubbery and debris away from your home's foundation may spoil a pest's plan to make their home there. Finally, make sure to keep your chimney covered with either a heavy metal screen or a metal mesh chimney cap. This measure may prevent animals—mainly squirrels and birds—from seeking refuge and building nests in your chimney.

Encouraging Beneficial Wildlife

When you transform your backyard into a haven for wildlife, you'll find you can coexist peacefully with docile, non-destructive creatures. The easiest way to invite and encourage wildlife is to put out a bird feeder or birdbath—these lovely visitors arrive full of song and color (and devour many harmful insects during their visit as a bonus).

If you're committed to providing a safe haven for backyard wildlife, the National Wildlife Federation sponsors a Backyard Wildlife Habitat program that encourages homeowners to plan and plant their backyards with wildlife-friendly features. To date, almost 50,000 backyards have been certified! Imagine how many species have benefited from the time and care that homeowners have invested to make a haven for wildlife in their backyards.

Tending to backyard birds is easy and rewarding, and there are other creatures you may want to invite to share your space. Just a little effort on your part will go a long way to providing food, habitat, and shelter for many forms of wildlife. You can share your backyard with many creatures, including these.

Bats: Worth their weight in gold, bats not only pollinate many food plants, they are the only major predators of night-flying insects. It is estimated that a single big brown bat can eat between 3,000 and 7,000 mosquitoes per night. They also feed on other harmful pests, including cockroaches and gnats. Bats eat thousands of tons of harmful agricultural and forest pests annually. Pesticide use and loss of habitat has led to the decline of many bat populations.

You can encourage a resurgence in your neighborhood by building bat houses for them or by maintaining their ideal foraging and roosting sites. Bat-foraging sites include marshes, streams, farm ponds, beaver ponds, seasonal pools, large drainage ditches, and river drainages. Common roosting sites are hollow snags, live cavity trees, abandoned homesteads, caves, old stone chimneys, crevices in rocks, and paths where animals travel.

Butterflies and Moths: Besides being lovely, bright little creatures, an abundance of moths and butterflies in your backyard means you have living art all around. In addition to adding beauty to your landscape, butterflies help to pollinate plants.

Fireflies: Bright and blinking, fireflies are charming company on those balmy summer evenings spent sitting around the patio with friends. In order to develop your firefly population, discontinue all pesticide use on your lawn. If you're not adverse to a less rigorous lawn regimen, allow grass to grow double the length usually considered desirable, and encourage weedy areas, a habitat conducive to fireflies.

Quail: Sadly, modern farming methods are destroying the quail habitat—yet another reason that cutting back on the use of hazardous chemicals is vitally important. Unless you are lucky enough to have large, lush fields, there isn't a large amount you can do with your property to counteract these effects. If possible, encourage farmers to strip-disk their fields, which results in wide bands of crops alternating with strips of weeds and grasses. Finally, it is important to permit hedgerows to grow

once again since quail need protective cover when they tool around your yard.

To encourage any quail in your vicinity, place a mixture of cracked corn, wheat, sunflower kernels, and soybeans in a ground feeder. Quail are also ready diners of fruit, such as berries and grapes, and they eat lots of insects too. A shallow water source may go a long way toward attracting quail if you have the appropriate sheltering site.

Beneficial Pest-Killing Insects

Trying to determine which bugs you'd like to keep around versus the ones you don't want can be a bit difficult, especially for the inexperienced or squeamish. These beneficial insects feed on harmful insects and benefit the environment.

Assassin Bugs: As their name suggests, assassin bugs fancy various irritating pests, such as beetles, flies, large caterpillars, and mosquitoes.

Bald-Faced Hornets: Excellent pest predators, bald-faced hornets pounce hawklike on several types of flies.

Ground Beetles: These voracious creatures feed on soil-inhabiting pests, such as cutworms and root maggots. Some eat slug and snail eggs, and some climb trees to attack tent caterpillars.

Lacewings: Lacewings are often produced commercially and offered for sale to home gardeners to help control pests—that's how voraciously they feed on small, soft pests, such as aphids, spider mites, and thrips.

Lady Beetles: Some of the best pest fighters around, lady beetles feed on aphids, mealybugs, scale insects, and spider mites.

Parasitic Wasps: Parasitic wasps lay their eggs in a pest host, such as aphids, moths, and whiteflies, and the larvae eventually kill the host.

Praying Mantids: These lovely, bright insects prey on a variety of pests and a few harmless insects as well.

Soldier Beetles: Soldier beetles tend to feed on aphids, beetle larvae, caterpillars, and grass-hopper eggs, as well as other insects. Adult beetles feed on prey around flowerbeds, while beetle larvae

find prey in the soil and near the ground.

Syrphid Flies: Similar in appearance to bees or yellow jackets, syrphid flies lay their eggs in insect colonies; the larvae then prey on aphids, mealybugs, and other small insects in the colonies and keep pest populations low.

Tachnid Flies: Tachnid flies are great predators of various malignant caterpillars, including cutworms, codling moths, tent caterpillars, cabbage loopers, and gypsy moth larvae.

Despite their stinging nature, you may also consider encouraging bumblebees, honeybees, and other pollinating insects. Without their pollinating work, we wouldn't have apples, pears, cherries, citrus fruits, nuts, berries, coffee, melons, cucumbers, squash, or many other common foods. Allow them

Safe and Sound

DEER-RESISTANT PLANTS

Deer have a wide range of plants in their diet, and they're very adaptable to new tastes when one plant source is scarce. These plants seem to be the most resistant to hearty deer appetites, so include them in your landscape. But if a hard winter is in the making, a large deer herd may eat every plant in sight, favorite or not.

Bleeding heart (*Dicentra* spp.)
Boxwood (*Buxus* spp.)
Coneflower (*Echinacea* spp.)
Holly (*Ilex* spp.)
Iris (*Iris* spp.)
Marigold (*Tagetes* spp.)
Nasturtium (*Nasturtium* spp.)

Northern red oak (*Quercus rubra*)
Snapdragon (*Asarina* spp.)
Spruce (*Picea* spp.)
Strawflower (*Bracteantha* spp.)
Yucca (*Yucca* spp.)
Zinnia (*Zinnia* spp.)

to have space and to peacefully coexist in your backyard habitat.

Combatting Nuisance Wildlife

Just as there are some elements of the wild that you'd delight in seeing pass through your patch of heaven, there are other critters that are better left outside your lawn. But that's not a reason to resort to poisons and harmful measures. A little understanding of why the problem is occurring and some ingenious solutions will have marauding, stinging, and plant-grubbing critters heading for someone else's yard.

Deer: Rarely a day goes by that I don't see at least a few deer from my office window or while driving here in Dutchess County, New York, less than 100 miles outside of New York City, and where the deer population is very dense. Growing up in New Hampshire, however, is an interesting comparison because I hardly ever saw a deer in those vast forests. While seeing a new fawn or watching deer stroll by my window is always a captivating experience for me, having a dense deer population creates a real danger for humans because of the many car-versus-deer collisions. Deer also carry the deer tick that transmits Lyme disease, and they raid flower, landscape, and vegetable gardens to every gardener's dismay.

Deer-o-Scaping is a term coined in the book *Deer Proofing Your Yard and Garden,* by Rhonda Massingham Hart. Hart recommends that you avoid plants deer like, that you grow plants deer don't like, and that you design gardens that discourage deer.

I like the common sense of this, although it has taken most of us many years to finally just go with the flow of living with deer and skip planting their favorite meals in our planters. I've switched to marigolds and zinnias in certain areas the deer frequent, for example. There are many plants that deer tend to avoid, so planning parts of your garden around these plants would mean a giant step forward.

Scented soap, dogs, rotten eggs, human hair, blood meal, and predator feces (available from zoos) have reportedly worked as deer deterrents—but nothing seems to work everywhere all of the time. If you have a vegetable garden you want to protect, you must do the research to find a fence that will really work for your specific needs. Just any fence won't do—in most cases, the fence needs to be 8 to 10 feet high! Nearly invisible garden fences and netting are sold in areas where deer are known to ravage gardens every night.

My dogs have taught me a lot. Putting them in the kennel for a weekend was all the invitation deer needed to come and eat all the flowers in the garden! But when the dogs are home, even inside the house, the deer never venture through the yard.

Geese: If you have a lot of geese loitering in your backyard, you're probably well-acquainted with the mess they create, along with the occasionally raucous bursts of noise. To scatter them quickly, bang a drum to startle them into flight. To prevent their presence in a more long-term way, consider allowing your grass to grow long—they dislike long grass, thinking predators might be lurking there. If you're not into the unkempt look, or if you want to keep your grass shorter for fear of being overrun with ticks, spray grape soda around the area that the geese frequent. They dislike the smell.

Mice: If you discover mice infiltrating your residence, plug holes around drainpipes and small openings with steel wool or quick-drying cement (for a more permanent solution). You can plug larger openings with ¼ inch or smaller mesh hardware cloth. Unless you have blocked interior access, live-trapping probably won't work because mice will return—often within a few hours.

Moles: Notoriously difficult to eradicate, moles may not always be the enemy after all. Why? Moles eat grubs that destroy lawns. Their tunneling aerates soil, carries humus farther down, and brings subsoil near the surface, making organic plant food more readily available to your garden. Granted, if you're overrun to the extent that a summer's stroll on your once-firm lawn could break an ankle, you're probably going to want to do something about the infestation. If the moles are posing a particular threat to your garden, surround it with an L-shaped fence that is driven in at least 12 inches deep with the above-ground portion bent outward

---

MAKE IT YOURSELF
HOMEMADE RABBIT REPELLENT

Rabbits are notorious for nibbling on tender tree bark, and it could mean death for the tree. If you are unable to wrap your trees, try this easy-to-mix rabbit repellent to deter the furry critters.

7 pounds lump rosin (available from woodworking suppliers)
1 gallon grain alcohol

Dissolve the rosin in the alcohol. Apply to the tree's trunk and low branches with a paintbrush. After application, wash the paintbrush with warm, soapy water. Store the repellent in a labeled glass jar indefinitely. ❖

at a 90-degree angle for an additional 10 inches. Never, under any circumstances, use poisons or gases to eradicate moles; not only is this hazardous to animals and your lawn, but it could also affect your health and the health of your neighbors, especially when you're growing vegetables.

Mosquitoes: Planting marigolds around your yard may keep mosquitoes at bay because they seem to hate the fragrance. Standing water is a breeding ground for mosquitoes, so eliminate sources when possible, or consider purchasing floating mosquito dunks (available in garden centers and from garden catalogs), which kill larvae before they grow up to bite. These mosquito dunks are environmentally safe and contain no toxic chemicals. Put them anywhere that water lays and pools. You can break the dunks into smaller pieces for small-size pools (one dunk treats 100 square feet of water). Then, tidy up around your home and garden, making sure there aren't any containers, flowerpots, buckets, or flat surfaces that allow water to pool.

Rabbits: To deter roguish rabbits from ravishing your garden, fence the area with chicken wire 36 inches high; bury the fence several inches in the ground to thwart their tunnel-making efforts. You can also create wire protectors around individual trees with cylinders of woven or welded wire. Make

sure there are at least 6 inches between the trunk and the wire to allow room for growth. Wrap tree trunks with commercial tree wrap, wire mesh, or heavy aluminum foil as high as a rabbit can reach if standing on top of your expected snow cover.

Raccoons: Healthy raccoons rarely leave evidence of their visitation—that is, until they devise a way to open up your garbage can or discover the tasty bounty of your garden. Persistent and intelligent, these tricky creatures have both agility and strength on their side, so it might take a while to discover an effective method to weight your garbage can lids. To deter them from ravaging your garden, electric fencing is the most effective (though, unfortunately,

Gardeners know that animal pests can do as much damage as insect pests, so you may have to resort to fencing to keep moles and raccoons out of your vegetable garden. Chicken wire and hardware cloth barriers may be the solution for protecting young transplants and root crops.

elaborate) solution. Use a fence that charges in pulses, or you will pose a threat to birds; follow the manufacturer's suggestions for placement around your garden.

C-shaped chicken wire fences are also useful. The fence should be shaped like a large letter C opening outward from the garden. The bottom of the C rests on the ground to stop raccoons, rabbits, and other animals from going under the fence, and the overhanging part keeps them from climbing or jumping over. Secure the fence to the ground with U-shaped pins (fashioned from metal coat hangers), then fasten the middle of the fence to sturdy posts to provide structure and support. Leave the top of the fence floppy.

Finally, a sturdy cloth barrier might fool raccoons into thinking there's actually no garden there. Heavy muslin,

lightweight canvas, or heavy plastic at least 4 feet wide can be fastened to rope tied to posts 8 to 10 feet apart. The bottom edge should lie on the ground and be weighed with bricks or rocks.

Squirrels: So much energy and ingenuity has been dedicated to preventing squirrels from feasting on the treats we leave out for our birds. Yet, no matter how elaborate our ploys, these persistent little animals seem to always get the goods. So, rather than fight a losing battle to keep squirrels away from your bird feeders, feed them! Toss a handful of whole roasted peanuts on the ground, or give them whole cobs of dried corn or dried apples. If you absolutely need to shoo away squirrels because they're emptying your feeders *and* your wallet, invest in baffles that discourage their visits to your seed supply. Baffles that wobble are usually quite effective because

Safe and Sound
WHAT TO DO IN A WILDLIFE EMERGENCY
If you see an injured animal, what should you do? Should you pick up a bird that has just been hit by a car? What about a baby squirrel that is alone and appears abandoned? Should you feed them? Sometimes the answers to these questions aren't obvious, and in one's impulse to help, it is possible to make a situation worse for the animal and more dangerous for yourself.

If an animal is obviously injured, call a wildlife rehabilitator or a wildlife agency for information as soon as possible. Do not touch the animal unless you are advised to do so.

Sometimes baby animals are picked up under the assumption that they have been abandoned. Usually the mom or dad is nearby but out of sight, especially in the case of baby birds, so allow a few hours to go by before you give up hope that the animal parent has truly rejected the youngster. It's best to call a wildlife agency or animal expert before moving any baby from its environment.

they don't give squirrels a steady platform for climbing, but you'll need to recognize that squirrels are also quite adept at conquering new obstacles.

Wildlife-Safe Watering Holes

If you have a swimming pool, you probably know the heartbreaking feeling of discovering an ill-fated creature in your filter basket. Luckily (for the animals and for you), there are options available to prevent such mishaps. If you have a smaller pool (an aboveground or wading pool, for example), pick up a small plastic floating island at the pet store and place it in the pool. That way, if an animal happens to find his way into the pool, he has a chance of making it to safety. When you find him in the water, use your pool skimmer to scoop him out, then place him in a sheltered spot to recover. Sticks placed across very small ponds and near the water surface also help an animal that gets a little too soaked while bathing or investigating; the sticks can act like a bridge or a resting spot for overly enthusiastic bathers.

5

the kitchen

Food, family, and friends gather in the heart of the home—the kitchen. It's a place of nourishment and community. It's in the kitchen where we hope to start the day on the right foot at breakfast (teenagers, anyone?), plan dinners that are healthy and delicious, connect with family over late-night snacks, and create celebratory feasts. Most of you can recall a favorite dish from childhood or a meal that still makes your mouth water, and I can bet that you remember as many details about the kitchen as you can about the food. The kitchen is a calling card. Whether an open hearth in a humble abode or a five-burner stove in a large, modern home, the trappings become incidental when the main purpose of the room is love and caring.

Given that the kitchen is the center of our homes, it is a particularly stark indictment that food in the modern world has become a by-product of packaging, processing, manipulation, speed, and homogenization. On some deep, primal level, we know that we are missing something essential for our well-being if we regularly eat food that comes out of a box from the freezer, gets thrown in a microwave oven, and is wolfed down on the run. No wonder so many of us are flocking to farmers' markets and roadside stands. If you haven't already discovered the "Slow Food" movement, I recommend that you check it out—its goal is to revive the kitchen and table as the center of pleasure, culture, and community and to promote ecologically grown and organic foods.

Establishing a healthy kitchen—

emotionally, physically, and nutritionally—is paramount for your well-being and the well-being of your family. Healthy, real food prepared with love in an ecologically friendly and welcoming space is the first goal of living in an enlightened home. Establishing such a haven takes time, and I recommend that you proceed one step at a time if you are new to this, so you won't be overwhelmed. People tell me all the time, however, that once they start the process of "greening" their kitchen, the feeling of centering, connectedness, and interconnectedness is so satisfying that they want to continue and expand the process.

Create a Pleasing Kitchen

Little connects us to the earth as much as food, since that's where it comes from. What better image to represent a healthy home than ears of beets, blackberries, corn, melons, peaches, pumpkins, squash, string beans, and walnuts—all foods that are nutritious, colorful, fragrant, and delicious.

Ripening fruits and vegetables on kitchen counters brings nature into your home. Dried vegetables, such as red peppers on a string or garlic garlands, can bring a down-to-earth, wholesome quality into a kitchen. Potted herbs for cooking and remedies placed in kitchen windows are especially nice, as are potted plants with flowers, such as paperwhites or narcissus in the deep winter. In the fall, the sight of winter squash, apples, and onions on your counter can anchor you to the season in the blink of an eye.

How do you feel about the drinking water in your kitchen? Clean, pure water is essential. I remember when we finally got a reverse osmosis water filter in our kitchen (we have well water, so that filter was the most appropriate). The filtered water is *so* sweet, I've been drinking eight glasses of water a day ever since. Cooking with filtered water is also important, because you don't want to add any contaminants to your food. Research the best filter for your water supply (see page 211).

What kind of heat do you use for cooking? The indoor air quality of a kitchen is significantly affected by your choice of heat for cooking. Cooking with a gas stove can cause surprisingly high indoor air quality problems (see page 179).

To improve indoor air quality, install an exhaust fan in your kitchen vented to the outdoors, especially if you have a gas stove. It will also help to exhaust cooking fumes, especially those from oils that are heated past their flash point and are toxic. All of us have burned something and had to air the house out. An exhaust fan vented to the outdoors does a thorough job.

Lastly, make some sense of a hearth in your kitchen, if you can. We can't all have a wood-fired oven in a kitchen to roast a turkey or bake bread, like organic chef Alice Waters—as much as we would love such a thing. But we can do other things to anchor the space with a sense of the fire element: beeswax candles on the kitchen table, a strand of red chili peppers, or a big window to let in the sun.

We may use our senses the most in the kitchen, and I think it's vitally important to please each sense in a pure, natural, and healthy way. Think about how you can awaken your senses in one of the most important spaces in your home.

Sight: What do you see in your kitchen? How does what you see reflect what you actually want people to see? Envision the statement you want your kitchen to make, then make one change at a time to achieve your vision.

Open your eyes in the kitchen. You'll see that the color of food is always beautiful because nature's colors never clash. Put heirloom yellow, orange, and red tomatoes in a bowl, and you'll be overwhelmed by their rich tones. The earthy browns of a wild rice mix easily remind you of the importance of healthy dark soil. And there's nothing as vibrant as the greens of cukes and dill ready for the canning jar.

Flowers also bring the colors of nature into your home. A pot of heather, with its blend of greens and purples, brightens a kitchen window for months in the winter. Brighten the dull days of winter with brilliant amaryllis and orchids.

You can also enhance the colors of nature with your color choices for furnishings in the kitchen. I have purple countertops. The plum purple is the exact opposite of the hue of green I see in the wood of the cupboards. When I was choosing the color of the countertops, I picked up a purple color chip just for fun because I loved the color. Once in the kitchen, I held up the various color chips (mostly staid off-white) to see how they looked. Then I held up the purple. Wow! The color resonated perfectly with the wood! Who would ever have guessed? We decided to be brave, and we went with the purple. We've never regretted the choice. Seeing a fully ripe, lush red tomato on the purple countertop is a sight to behold. Oranges look beautiful there, too. In fact, I can't think of any fruit or vegetable that isn't enhanced by the purple backdrop.

Taste: What does the food cooked in your kitchen taste like? We all have different tastes, but whatever your food styles, make sure they please the senses! I feel all of our lives would be enriched every day if we ate real food from ancient-seed gene pools grown in nutritious soil. The flavors of food grown this way are incomparable to food grown on industrial farms using sterile seeds or seeds that are genetically modified and grown with pesticides and artificial fertilizers. Period.

Hearing: What mood does the sound in your kitchen reflect? Voices? Electronics? Nature? What sound mood do you want your kitchen to reflect? Hearing is the sense that can be underutilized in the kitchen. Try piping in music or National Public Radio (NPR), for example. My mother loves to cook dinner listening to NPR. I love to cook listening to music because my mind tends to roam free then. I love to hear the birds singing, particularly in the spring, and other sounds of nature coming through an open window. Food and meal preparation can be a solitary task for some, but if you involve family members, you have a chance for real conversation and listening.

Touch: Natural materials are always the most comforting and centering. Are the napkins paper or linen? How much plastic is used in your kitchen? Natural materials are always the best to touch. Holding an onion while you slice it, kneading bread with your hands, and washing carrots before you peel them helps food become tangible to you. The resulting meal quite literally has your touch. I've served meals—as most of us

have—where the food never touched my hands: frozen food poured out of plastic and dropped onto a pan, removed from the oven, and deposited on plates with a spatula. The more vested you are in the making of a meal, the more interested you're bound to be in its nutritional impact to nourish those you love and care about.

Washing the dishes and wiping the counters is another way we experience touch in the kitchen. Everyday tasks can keep you connected. And it's so important to use natural cleansers and dish detergents when cleaning kitchens and washing dishes so that you don't absorb artificial ingredients into your skin.

Smell: The aromas in the kitchen imbue every home with their essence. In fact, I always feel bad when I haven't really cooked in a while because the hominess of the house seems to lessen, quite literally, without the smell of simmering food on the stove or in the oven. The smell of freshly baked bread wafting through a home is a descriptive cliché for a wonderful home life, but there is real truth to it. Who doesn't want to go into a home where your senses are met with an aroma like that? I expect the scent of soup simmering in a pot is compelling at the most basic level. The "Slow Food" movement must be tapping into this gravitation to the cook pot. Slow is the antithesis of fast food and dashed-off meals and, instead, favors the sensual pleasure and long-lasting enjoyment of food prepared with time and care.

Sixth Sense: Sit in your kitchen and take it in. Does it provide what you want? Does it feel right? What more can it be than it is in order for it to be more meaningful to you? How can you improve it? While I believe that all of our senses are deprived because of the modern way we deal with food, our sixth sense is, almost by necessity, the most turned off during this era of fast, packaged food. If we listened to our sixth sense, we would be in full rebellion against the current nationwide food system and the supermarket chains that sell the food.

We'd rebel against industrial farming with its chemical processing that produces bland, less nutritious food. We'd rebel against an industry that gives growth hormones to cows to make them produce more milk, which in turn can make human cancer cells grow faster. We'd reject companies that give farmers their genetically modified seeds that require that same brand's herbicide to grow them, and then those same seeds contaminate all neighboring crops. We'd boycott the huge supermarket chains that sell only a few food commodities (such as wheat and corn), repackaged 100 ways in different boxes that add cost to the food and deprive

our world of genetic diversity and our diets of variety.

Most important, we would listen to our taste buds and to all of our senses, and we would not eat food that we know isn't good for us. We wouldn't eat refined food that lacks many of the nutrients that we require to fully metabolize the food we eat. A while back, I remember taste-testing muffins made with white flour and sugar and muffins made with whole foods. When I tasted the refined-flour and -sugar muffins, I craved more—I believe it was because the muffin was lacking nutrients to complete the nutritional spectrum my body expected. The whole foods muffin, on the other hand, was completely satisfying and left me feeling satiated.

Wholesome Food for Your Whole Self

The famous line in the poem by Gertrude Stein that goes "A rose is a rose, is a rose, is a rose . . ." just doesn't hold true anymore, not with genetically modified (GM) organisms designed by multinational corporations. A corn kernel is no longer what we may think it is. Real whole foods are a perfect nutritional substance for us; they ground and center us with their full spectrum of nutrition. Real food, prepared simply and well, is one of the goals for my kitchen.

The truer you are to real food, the truer you are to the food your body was designed to eat. One way back to a timeless connection with food is to find its roots. If you haven't ever dabbled in gardening, plant a watermelon or a sweet pea seed, tend it, then watch it grow. Or, if you don't have room or time for a garden, take your children to an organic pick-your-own farm so they can smell a tomato vine. Most of all, though, if you have a small plot of land, a small patch of grass, or a place for some potted containers, try your hand at growing a few vegetables. Deeply imprinted on my mind is the process of planting and picking produce as a child, yet that experience isn't part of my daughter's childhood, nor that of most of her friends. I wish it were, for their sakes.

When we disconnect food from its relationship with the earth, it's easy to think that food is connected to a brightly lit supermarket with all the amenities and to glitzy advertising. A dinner of frozen pizza comes out of a box—simple enough—but its roots are not there. Pizza is a meal of an abundant harvest—a harvest when the weather was just right and there was adequate rainfall and rich, nutritious soil to grow wheat, tomatoes, herbs, and green peppers. If you don't know this, then you don't know how critical the weather is to our very survival or how important rainfall is or how necessary seed protection or diversity is.

Making contact with the farms that grow our food is an important way to make choices about the food we choose to eat. If we learn enough about industrial farming to know the extent of pesticide and herbicide use and then compare this to the food produced on organic farms, we can make educated decisions about which food we choose to buy and which method we choose to support.

If we choose to eat meat and take time to remember that it came from a live animal that was raised to provide others and us with food, we will then have a stake in how the animal was cared for. Have you seen comparisons of factory farms and organic or free-range farms? Do you know how differently the animals are treated at each type of farm? The reality may surprise and shock you.

There are many people who believe that animals raised in confined, inhumane conditions impart the fear, pain, and stress of their lives to their meat or milk, and it, in turn, affects us. This makes sense to me. I buy only animal products raised on humane farms without chemicals and drugs, and it has not been hard to find local sources of organic animal products.

Real Food

Lack of time seems to be what makes it hard to shop, cook, and eat in a timeless way. I am aware of the irony of this observation, so I am really examining it and trying to clear away the clutter in my mind about food. I realize that I am frustrated with how supermarkets have transformed themselves into convenience centers, full of packaged and processed foods, with only a small supply of real, whole food despite the huge size of most stores.

I'm overwhelmed and saddened by the amount of branded, packaged food and all its packaging and how easily shoppers can be confused over ingredients in a product because they are obscured by the boxes and brands and artificial flavors. It amazes me how many different trips to different stores (from health food stores to whole foods stores to farmers' markets) I make to find the range of food I buy for my family. And I struggle with the amount of advertising for packaged food with synthetic ingredients that is targeted to children because it makes providing a healthy diet an uphill battle for parents.

WORDS TO THE WISE

FIVE BASIC RULES FOR HEALTHY FOOD SHOPPING

Put all the food you consider buying through a mental "health screen." Most of the items that fill up the average shopper's cart today won't pass my test and should be left in the store.

❖ Buy only real, whole food, and eliminate refined, processed, or genetically modified food.

❖ Buy local and seasonal food whenever it is affordable and available.

❖ Buy organically produced food whenever possible. Organic farms nourish on a number of levels by growing food without synthetic chemicals in healthy soil. They don't pollute the water system with chemicals. They provide healthy habitat for 40 percent more birds and five times more wild plants than industrial farms. Organic farms use 70 percent less nonrenewable energy, and they don't contribute to topsoil runoff. Those who work on organic farms or live nearby are not at risk from pesticide poisoning. Infertility is only one of the problems industrial farm workers are experiencing because of exposure to herbicides.

❖ Avoid additives such as artificial sweeteners, preservatives, and MSG.

❖ Buy animal products from farms that raise them humanely. American Humane protects farm animals through the Free Farmed program. Through this program, consumers can be guaranteed that the products they select are from animals that were raised and treated compassionately and humanely (www.americanhumane.org).

Thoughtful and careful food selection takes time—precious hours that are hard to fit in most people's day. Many supermarkets are so large now that just walking straight from one end to the other takes 5 minutes because of the vastness of the store and the many freestanding displays you have to navigate. I reel against the toxic supermarket buildings; the cleaning aisle alone is enough to deter most people from wanting to shop, and the fluorescent lighting and lack of windows tend to help people space out enough that they often forget what they are shopping for.

The act of cooking doesn't seem like much after all this, although our busy lives create an ever-present need for quick, simple, easy menus. It seems we spend the most time acquiring the food and planning the meals. The tiresome "what are we going to have for dinner" refrain is very old and hard for most of us.

One store where I shop caters to those of us who cook from scratch. All the whole foods are divided into sections, and there is almost no processed food available. If they offer packaged food, it's of very high quality and made with whole food ingredients. I am never overwhelmed in this wildly popular store. I come home with enough food for the week, and real meals emerge from the groceries bought.

Choose Organic Animal Products

Obviously, I'm a big advocate of buying local and organic food. And there are lots of reasons why I think you should consider buying it too.

I think buying organic animal products is particularly important. A good reason to buy organic milk is that this milk comes from cows that haven't been injected with the bovine growth hormone (rBGH) to increase milk production. While rBGH itself doesn't come through in the cow's milk, what does increase abnormally in the milk is a growth hormone that, at least one study suggests, can speed up cancer cell proliferation.

❖ Organic farms raise animals more humanely.

❖ Animal products from animals fed organic feed, rather than that with animal by-products, will help avoid animal-derived proteins, considered the cause of Mad Cow disease.

❖ According to the journal *Nature*, 50 percent of the world's antibiotic supply goes into farm animals. Organically raised animals aren't given antibiotics or growth hormones.

❖ The guidelines for organic meat are very strict, and no additional chemicals or treatments such as irradiation are allowed in the processing and preparation.

Produce from Your Neighborhood

Local, organic, seasonal produce is your best choice for the freshest, healthiest, and most environmentally friendly food for you and your family. Some studies suggest that organic produce is more nutritious than that grown on industrial farms because it's grown on soil that has been carefully enriched using manure and other natural additions and is rich in micronutrients.

To avoid pesticides, or when organic produce is too expensive or hard to find, the best substitute is that which is locally grown and seasonal. Even in midwinter, local root crop vegetables that have been stored locally are preferable to produce shipped in from foreign countries with less stringent pesticide laws or produce grown across the country, picked before it was ripe, and treated with chemical preservatives for the long trip to your local food store.

The forecast for organic produce is sunny. More than 20 million acres are being farmed organically around the world, so the chances are good that you can find nonchemical produce in your region. Some traditional farms, especially pick-your-own businesses, have reduced their chemical usage because of consumer demand.

The Environmental Working Group, a nonprofit research group based in Washington, DC, has put together a list of the foods containing the most pesticides. High-pesticide fruits and vegetables include apples, apricots, bell peppers, celery, cherries, green beans, Mexican cantaloupe, peaches, spinach, and strawberries. A study in *Consumer Reports* also includes grapes, pears, and winter squash on the list of fruits and vegetables with large amounts of pesticide residues. Try to substitute organic for each of these foods, or at the very least, scrub and peel fruit and vegetables before serving them.

Eat the Rainbow

For the greatest variety of nutrients, eat a rainbow of colors in your diet. Adults should strive for five to nine servings a day of fruits and vegetables to reduce the risk for cancer, heart disease, diabetes, obesity, hypertension, and other chronic diseases, according to the USDA.

Naturally colorful foods contain vitamins, minerals, fiber, and beneficial disease-fighting phytochemicals. Remembering to "eat the rainbow" is a great way to plan your menu. From the beta-carotene in yellowy-orange fruits and vegetables to the lutein in

Fiber can taste great, and it's easy to add to your diet in small ways. A simple sprinkling of black beans in a morning omelette adds 5 grams of fiber, not to mention iron, magnesium, and folate.

green vegetables, the powerful antioxidants in these richly colored vegetables protect healthy cells in your body.

For the red in the rainbow, eat strawberries, beets, tomatoes, and apples. For the orange, enjoy carrots, pumpkins, sweet potatoes, and yams. Yellow vegetables include corn, summer squash, and yellow beans, and they're packed with natural sun protectants. The health benefits of leafy dark green vegetables are well documented, but did you know that green vegetables also keep eyes healthy? For the blue and purple fruits and vegetables in the rainbow, enjoy blueberries, violets (they're great on salads—just make sure they're organic), red cabbage, concord grapes, and eggplant.

Choose Healthy Dry Goods

When grains are milled into white flour, they lose about 80 percent of their nutritional value. Whole grains, on the other hand, are packed with fiber and have more micronutrients, like folate, magnesium, and vitamin E, than white-flour products. There are many whole grains available at supermarkets and health food stores these days. Most whole grains have a nutlike flavor and a chewy texture, and they'll leave you feeling full when you add them to your diet. Switch to whole grain cereals and breads, and experiment with the many whole grain pastas available, made with whole wheat, amaranth, buckwheat, quinoa, and more. My best advice is to educate yourself and read labels in the store and at home. Just because a bread is dense and dark in color doesn't mean that it's healthier than white bread—many breads have added food coloring, so pay careful attention to fiber content.

Need another healthy food to jump-start your diet? Try beans—canned and dried! They're loaded with soluble fiber, long known to lower cholesterol, especially "bad" low-density lipoprotein (LDL) cholesterol. Low in fat, high in both complex carbohydrates and pro-

Safe and Sound

A COOK'S GARDEN

Eating fresh vegetables is easy when you plant a simple kitchen garden right outside the back door. An assortment of seasonal produce, herbs, and flowers in a small-space garden delivers big on healthful meals. It may take a bit of time in the spring to plan and plant your kitchen garden and a few minutes a day to tend it, but the reward of simple, wholesome food at a moment's notice is worth the effort.

You can choose to build raised garden beds (with untreated cedar planks, but never with chemically treated wood or railroad ties), or you can turn over and amend your existing soil with compost. Beds can be any size or length, but a good rule of thumb is to make beds just wide enough to reach across to the opposite side so you don't have to walk in the bed. Kitchen gardens are most successful in a sunny location, although you can have a successful garden in a somewhat shady spot, too; lettuce and spinach are good choices for dappled sunlight conditions. After harvest, add chopped leaves and additional compost to the garden to replenish nutrients.

If you're new to gardening, start out with sure-fire winners, such as heirloom tomatoes, squash, peppers, onions, garlic, dill, basil, and parsley. And it's upward from there if you can utilize a nearby fence to grow cucumbers, peas, runner beans, and melons. Plant flowers and fragrant herbs, such as lavender and sage, throughout the garden to attract butterflies and pollinating bees. Rotate crop locations from year to year to reduce pest problems.

Walking past the maturing and ripening bounty will inspire you to create healthier meals for your family and may even inspire you to treat yourself to a new healthy cookbook!

tein, and excellent sources of folate and iron, beans can help manage diabetes and may reduce the risk of cancer and heart disease. Don't think twice about whether to add beans to your everyday menus; stir them into soups, stews, chili, and casseroles, and mix them into salads, omelettes, quiches, and pasta dishes.

You probably already know that you're supposed to limit your intake of fats, and I'll add to that by saying that you should avoid hydrogenated oils altogether in your diet. Hydrogenation is a process used in mass food production that increases the saturated fat levels of oils and makes them less heart healthy. In 1990, Dutch researchers concluded that artificially hydrogenated oils and trans fats (manufactured by adding hydrogen to polyunsaturated fats to make them more solid) may raise serum cholesterol levels almost as much as saturated fats do.

Enjoy Local, Seasonal Food

Eating organically grown, fresh, local, seasonal food is the most connected and timeless approach to food, especially when you can eat produce grown from heirloom and open-pollinated seeds (see page 122).

Your city or town may have its own farmers' market, and that's one of the most common ways to find local and organic products. The USDA puts out an annual directory of farmers' markets. You can also check with the Chamber of Commerce in the towns where you shop. Ask your neighborhood markets, even large grocery chains, to carry local food products. Where I live, there are many local providers of organic meats and vegetables, and they sell their products through health food stores and more progressive grocery stores.

If you haven't discovered a CSA yet, it could be one of the most rewarding ways to support local organic farmers. CSA, or Community Supported Agriculture, is a loose term describing a group of people who get together to buy from and support a farm or garden. Usually, you pay a joining or membership fee, and the farmer uses those proceeds to support his seed purchases and his investment of time and equipment to grow food. In return for your sup-

WORDS TO THE WISE

FIBER CONTENT OF FOODS

Fiber is such an important part of the diet, yet most people get only about half of the recommended 30 grams of fiber a day. Most fruits, vegetables, whole grains, and nuts are good sources of fiber, but the amounts differ greatly depending on the type and preparation of food. Consult a reliable diet guide for a full listing of the fiber content of your favorite foods.

FOOD	SERVING SIZE	FIBER (GRAMS)
Asian pear	1 pear	10
Avocado	1 medium	8
Black beans	1 cup cooked	15
Blackberries	1 cup	8
Broccoli	1 cup raw	2
	1 cup cooked	5
Brussels sprouts	1 cup cooked	6
Cornmeal	1 cup cooked	9
Great Northern beans	1 cup cooked	12
Green snap beans	1 cup cooked	4
Lentils	1 cup cooked	16
Mango	1 medium	4
Mushrooms	1 cup raw	1
	1 cup cooked	4
Navy beans	1 cup cooked	19
Peas	1 cup cooked	9
Split peas	1 cup cooked	16
Sweet potato	1 potato cooked	4
Whole-grain wheat flour	1 cup	14

Source: USDA

Community support of a pick-your-own farm is vital to the growth of organic farming. By patronizing organic farmers, you're letting them know that you support their efforts to practice sustainability and their concern for the environment. You reap many benefits from having an organic grower nearby—from cleaner groundwater and reduced pesticide drift to a sense of welcome and a healthy, vitamin-packed harvest.

port, you receive produce and farm products throughout the growing season or year. Subscription farming is a similar way to support a local gardener or farmer in whatever way works for those involved. I've informally "signed up" as a steady customer in the spring, picked up my produce every Friday throughout the season, and paid as I went along.

Pick-your-own farms have always been popular. Your county cooperative extension office will provide you with a list of all pick-your-own farms in your area. Search out organic farms to reduce your exposure to pesticides while you're on the farm and from the food.

Naturally, you can grow your own organic food. You can't beat this! Hands down, this is the best way to connect to your environment, get exercise, eat well, save fossil fuel, and have a healthy lifestyle!

Have you ever tried foraging? Every spring, I look longingly at the green shoots popping up in the woods and along roadsides, wishing I knew more about eating cattail stalks, chickweed, nettles, wild parsnip, and burdock root. I once walked my land with an herbalist friend who identified many of these edible plants for me, but even with her help, I only really got to know the wild mustard, which I do gather in the spring. My lack of awareness of what is growing right in front of me is an example of our cultural disconnection from our surroundings—herbal lore isn't part of the mainstream lexicon. Because of this, fear creeps in: What if the plants are poisonous? Local foraging classes, given by plant experts, are the answer for safe foraging because you'll learn to do it in such a way that it is sustainable and doesn't take more than the ecosystem can withstand.

In the winter months, you can eat locally grown produce that has been frozen. Frozen foods are nutritious options because the produce is usually frozen immediately after being picked. Another nutritious option in the winter is food from local root cellars. Many local farmers have root cellars and can store produce for off-season sale. Root vegetables often stored for winter consumption include beets, cabbage, carrots, leeks, onions, parsnips, potatoes, pumpkins, sweet potatoes, turnips, and winter squash.

Eat Low on the Food Chain

Generally, the smallest creatures are at the bottom of the food chain and the biggest at the top. The bigger creatures eat the smaller ones. A worm eats a plant, a chicken eats a worm, and a human eats a chicken. It's a simple deduction that those lowest on the food chain are generally considered to be the least contaminated with persistent chemicals.

Chemicals that are persistent in the environment, such as DDT, PCBs, and many pesticides, are stored in animal fat and accumulate as they move up the food chain. The more animal fat you eat (in milk, eggs, cheese, fish, chicken, pork, and beef), the more persistent chemical contamination you will have in your body. Studies from around the world report that when humans eat more food items that are low on the food chain, the higher the chances that they will be protected from heart disease, cancer, and diabetes. Vegetarians consume the bulk of their diet from foods that are low on the food chain.

There are countless vegetarian resources available, both in cookbooks and on the Internet. Vegweb.com, vegsource.com, and care2.com provide information and recipes. If you're looking to expand your vegetarian repertoire, look for a copy of *The Moosewood Cookbook*, which is a perennial favorite of many devout vegetarians. Also, *Passionate Vegetarian*, by Crescent Dragonwood, is a large, detailed, and down-to-earth guide, which will complement the cookbook shelf of dedicated carnivores and vegetarians alike.

TECHNIQUE FOR WASHING PRODUCE

It is very important to rinse fresh produce under cold, running tap water. This will help eliminate residual pesticides and chemicals as well as bacteria and more ordinary forms of dirt. Do not use detergent. I read about this produce wash in *Total Renewal: 7 Key Steps to Resilience, Vitality and Long-Term Health*, by Frank Lipman, MD. The wash was formulated by Susan Sumner, a food scientist at Virginia Polytechnic Institute and State University. It uses white vinegar (or cider vinegar) and 3 percent hydrogen peroxide (the same as found at the drugstore).

First, put the vinegar and hydrogen peroxide in two different spray bottles. The technique is that you alternate spraying first vinegar and then hydrogen peroxide. Spray the alternating materials on the produce and the work surface; don't rinse the work surface until you're finished with the food preparation. Rinse produce thoroughly under fresh running water before slicing.

Food Safety

It might surprise you, as it did me, that of the reported cases of foodborne illness between 1990 and 2002, 20 percent were related to eating produce. The next highest causes were 12.7 percent from multi-ingredient foods, 10.6 percent from poultry, 10.3 percent from eggs, 10.2 percent from beef, 7.5 percent from seafood, 4.2 percent from pork, and 3.7 percent from dairy.

More than 250 foodborne diseases have been documented. Symptoms vary widely, but the most common are diarrhea and vomiting. Food poisoning can be caused by many different bacteria (such as *Campylobacter*, *Salmonella*, and *E. coli* O157:H7), viruses (such as caliciviruses), and parasites (such as *Giardia* and *Cyclospora*). Natural and man-made chemicals, such as mushroom toxins and heavy metals, can also

occur when food is transported halfway around the world or bought just down the road at a farm stand, from unsanitary meat packing houses, or from food that is undercooked, spoiled, or has been handled by an infected person in a restaurant.

Keeping a keen eye on your perishables, washing produce (even organic) thoroughly, and adhering strictly to safe handling guidelines will help protect you from accidentally serving up some tainted goods.

Safe Handling Guidelines

In this age of factory farming and food that travels thousands of miles to your table, adhering to food-handling precautions may be more important than ever. The cardinal rule for maintaining a clean kitchen is to keep different foods separate from each other until they are actually being prepared to avoid cross-contamination. I'd like to offer some general guidelines, which broadly address how to stay healthy.

Meat

Keep raw meat, poultry, and fish—and their juices—away from other foods. I recommend that you cut meat on a plate that can be sterilized in a dishwasher and not on a cutting board. After cutting raw meats, thoroughly wash your hands, the knife, and the plate. If you are marinating meat, don't leave it on the countertop, even for a short time. Store it in a covered glass dish in your fridge.

The most recent information indicates that there is no benefit to washing meat and poultry before cooking and that cooking meat to the appropriate temperature is the only way to ensure safety.

Resist the temptation to undercook your meat, no matter what your taste. The USDA urges you to use a food thermometer every time you cook meat. Checking the firmness and color of meat is a good way to gauge approximate doneness, but a thermometer is the only way to make sure you're cooking your food long enough to destroy harmful bacteria like E. coli.

When cooking beef, pork, or lamb roasts, insert the thermometer midway into the roast, avoiding the bone. With hamburgers, steaks, or chops, placing the probe in the thickest part will yield accurate results. Beef, pork, veal, and lamb should be cooked to 160°F for medium doneness. At 145°F, the meat will be medium rare, and at 170°F, it will be well done. It is recommended that you always cook pork to at least 160°F to prevent illnesses, such as trichinosis. Pork is considered well done at 170°F. Raw ham must be cooked to 160°F, while precooked ham is safe if heated to only 140°F.

When cooking a variety of meats together, make sure that they are all cooked to at least the necessary temperature. Insert the thermometer into the thickest portion of a sampling of all of the meats in order to be certain.

Poultry

If you're cooking chicken, turkey, or other poultry, insert the probe into the thickest part of the thigh. Ground turkey and chicken must be cooked to 165°F; when you are cooking an entire bird or thighs and wings, make sure that they are at least 170°F and well browned. A breast or roast can be cooked to 170°F. When cooking stuffing inside a turkey, make sure that the stuffing temperature reaches at least 165°F. Duck and geese must be cooked to 180°F.

Eggs

Undercooked eggs carry risks of *Salmonella*, despite the fact that millions of them are consumed daily. Laying hens that are forced to molt require more antibiotics, and their eggs have a higher incidence of *Salmonella*. If you want to be safe, make sure that the whites and the yolks are cooked until completely firm. Dishes like frittatas and quiches, which contain large quantities of eggs, must be cooked to a uniform 160°F, while leftovers and casseroles must reach 165°F.

Do not wash eggs before storing or using them. "Bloom," the natural coating on just-laid eggs that helps prevent bacteria from permeating the shell, is removed by the factory washing process and is replaced by a light coating of edible mineral oil, which restores protection. Extra handling of the eggs, such as home washing, could increase the risk of cross-contamination, especially if the shell is cracked.

Make sure not to lick the bowl of raw cake or cookie batter that was made with eggs!

Thawing Guidelines

It is preferable to thaw all your meat in the refrigerator. This is the slowest, safest method. When thawing, place meat and poultry in a large bowl to prevent juices from dripping into other foods. Also, if you've thawed more meat than you need, you can refreeze it if it's been thawing in the refrigerator. However, thawing and refreezing meat repeatedly will cause the quality to deteriorate. Use refrozen meat for stews and soups mostly.

If you're looking for a slightly faster

WORDS TO THE WISE

SLOW COOKER SAFETY

Slow cookers are a great option for those of us with busy lives who want to enjoy the irreplaceable goodness of real, home-cooked food. (Ovens are neither economical nor safe for slow-cooking.) Slow-cooking relies on both constant temperature and compressed steam to eliminate potential bacterial problems. To qualify as a slow cooker (and thereby a safe cooker), an appliance must maintain a temperature of at least 140°F. To test your slow cooker for safety, fill it with 2 quarts of water and leave it on the low setting for 8 hours. At the end of that time, immediately insert a thermometer. If the water is 185°F, then your slow cooker maintains safe and accurate temperature. If it registers above this temperature, food may burn or be overcooked; if the temperature is lower, food may be unsafe. Keep in mind that vegetables cook more quickly than meat, so you will probably want to add the meat first. Resist the temptation to sneak a peek until the food has cooked for 8 hours (or however long your meal requires). Lifting the lid may cause improper cooking or foster bacterial growth.

alternative to refrigerator thawing, submerging food in cold water will do the trick. Place it in a bowl that will allow enough water to cover the meat, and change the water every 30 minutes. You must cook the food immediately after thawing.

There is much discussion surrounding the proper way to defrost a frozen turkey. Basically, it depends on how much time you have. As with smaller cuts of meat, refrigerator defrosting is the most foolproof way to ensure both quality and safety. However, it takes a long time—between 1 and 2 days for a bird up to 12 pounds and up to 5 days if you're thawing one that's more than 20 pounds. Plus, with your refrigerator already brimming over with other Thanksgiving foods, accommodating a whole turkey may be a bit more trouble than it's worth. Considering that, it is safe to defrost your turkey in a bath of cold water, making sure to change the water every 30 minutes. Generally, if you allow about 30 minutes to the pound, you can estimate how long the process will take. Also, if you have a bird that will fit into your microwave, you can defrost it there, following the manufacturer's instructions. Be sure to transfer your turkey to the oven immediately, since defrosting in the microwave can cause parts of the bird to begin cooking.

Long-Term Food Storage

Many foods can be safely frozen for a seemingly indefinite time, but in rare instances, some frozen foods may spoil or decline in quality. How do you tell if food you've just defrosted is bad or rancid? The simplest and most obvious determinant of a food's integrity is its smell. Even frozen foods take on an unhealthy, rancid odor if they've spoiled.

Freezer burn appears as frost over the package, and it can turn foods a grayish-brown. Usually freezer-burned food is dried out and inedible. Again, meat and poultry that has endured a long tour of duty in your freezer is probably best left to stews and soups so that deterioration in the texture will be masked.

Never allow perishable groceries to sit out or stay in your car before you store them in the refrigerator. Transfer groceries to the refrigerator as soon as you get home, and travel with a cooler if you're doing errands after grocery shopping. Keep the refrigerator temperature set at 40°F to ensure that all of your perishables retain their freshness and palatability.

Store canned foods and other shelf-stable products in a cool, dry place. Never keep them above a stove, under the sink, in a damp garage or basement, or in any place exposed to temperature

DATE IT YOURSELF

With the constantly changing landscape of your cupboard, you may find yourself somewhat confused about which foods you've purchased when. As a result, you might turn hopefully to the date stamped on the bottom of the package. But how reliable are these dates? According to the USDA, these dates are not safety dates, but rather a good-faith promise of a food's safety until the specified time. Currently, there is no uniform or universally accepted system of food dating in the United States. There are no standard requirements for any food product, except for infant formula and some other baby foods, which are all regulated by the FDA. Dates found on perishables, such as meat, poultry, eggs, and dairy products, are completely unregulated and totally voluntary. Therefore, it's quite important to keep other indicators of freshness in mind, including smell, appearance, and texture. You might consider adding a quick purchase date (say, 10/05) on the label of every product you buy. You'll be surprised at how that one can of cranberry sauce or that box of wild rice gets pushed to the back of the pantry, and it's not discovered until 4 years later. Better to toss questionable and old items than take the time to prepare them.

extremes. Store high-acid canned foods such as tomatoes and other fruit up to 18 months, low-acid canned foods such as meat and vegetables, for 2 to 5 years. Canned meat and poultry will keep at its best quality if stored in a cool, clean, dry place.

Bulging, leaking, and severely dented cans or jars should be discarded immediately—they might signal *Clostridium botulinum*, the worst danger in canned goods. If a can smells foul or spurts liquid when opened, toss it. *Never* taste these foods, for ingesting even a miniscule bit of botulism toxin can be fatal.

In Case of Power Outages

If you find yourself in the midst of a power outage with a refrigerator full of groceries, keep the door closed as long as you can. If you have a lot of ice on hand, open your fridge up and quickly shove it in, making sure that it's in a container that's large enough to catch drips and prevent your innocent groceries from getting soaked. Hopefully, you'll get power back within a few hours, and everything will be salvaged (including that cherished half-pint of Ben and Jerry's). Depending on the outside temperature and the internal temperature setting, refrigerators can keep food cold for 4 to 6 hours after losing power. If frozen food still contains ice crystals or feels refrigerator-cold, you can safely refreeze it. If the power outage was long enough that food in the freezer thawed, you'll need to throw it all away. Often fire departments offer dry ice during such emergencies, and you can possibly save a freezer full of food by using some.

If you have particular foods you're concerned about salvaging, remove them from the fridge and place them in an icebox or cooler, replacing the ice regularly.

Dealing with Leftovers

Depending on the nature of your leftovers, you can be a little lenient—as long as the food was thoroughly cooked initially. Try to consume food stored in the refrigerator within 4 days, and discard any food left out at room temperature more than 2 hours. If you're serving or eating food at a summer cookout or a spot where the temperature is over 90°F, discard all food that's been left out for more than 1 hour. If the temperature is less than 90°F, refrigerate leftovers within 2 hours.

Many foods, soups and casseroles in particular, can be safely frozen for extended periods of time without much compromise to their quality. Make sure you keep them in tightly sealed containers to prevent freezer burn and deterioration. Contrary to urban legend, hot food (such as soup) can be placed directly in the refrigerator, or it can be rapidly chilled in an ice- or cold-water bath. Though it may make your fridge work a little harder, it's the best way to ensure that your leftovers are safe.

Fresh Produce

Often produce is picked before it is ripe so it's not overripe before it reaches consumers. Some foods, like avocados, kiwifruit, nectarines, peaches, pears, and plums, are best ripened on the counter, then stored in the refrigerator to preserve freshness.

For best flavor and texture, apples, bananas, citrus, mangoes, melons, papayas, persimmons, pineapple, tomatoes, watermelons, and winter squash can be stored at room temperature (although put apples in cold storage after 1 week). Cucumbers, eggplant, and peppers can be left out for 3 days; after that, refrigerate them.

Berries, cherries, figs, grapes, and all other vegetables need to be refrigerated as soon as you arrive home.

Genetically Modified Organism (GMO) Foods

The increasing prevalence of genetically modified (GM) foods in the marketplace is of great concern to many organizations and individuals. GM foods contain randomly inserted genes from foreign organisms, often including elements of bacteria and viruses and sometimes an antibiotic-resistant gene. One of the largest crops of GM food in the world, a crop of soybeans, includes three varieties of genes (one from a virus, one from a soil bacterium, and one from a petunia), and none of them have been tested or used in human foods before. Logically, the result may have unforeseen side effects, including toxic or allergenic properties. A 3-year study by the government of the United Kingdom showed two or three GM crops were harmful to wildlife. GM plants have also contaminated neighboring fields. While the European Union has made significant attempts to require strict labeling and even outlawing of these foods, many Americans are not even aware of their presence.

A simple reason to avoid GM foods is the lack of studies published about the repercussions of diets containing these foods. Why so little testing? The ability to determine the effect of a pervasive rogue element in a diet would take a large, long-term study. Since GMOs have been prevalent only for the past 15 years or so, few long-term studies on their effects on mental and emotional health have been successfully conducted. Also, there is much pressure from industry sources to abstain from testing; these interests have so far quite adeptly prevented far-reaching investigations.

Of the few studies conducted, however, one did come up with results, somewhat accidentally, according to *Seeds of Deception,* by Jeffrey M. Smith. A Dutch student fed corn to two groups of mice, with one group receiving GM corn and the other natural. Rather than a simple weight difference between the two groups of test mice, he noticed that the mice fed the GM corn were "more distressed" and "seemed less active while in their cages." Their behaviors included "running round and round in the basket, scrabbling desperately in the corner, and even frantically jumping up the sides [of the cage] . . . "

Genetically modified crops cannot be labeled as organic, according to the new rules for certified organic food.

The US crops that are most often genetically engineered are soy, cotton, canola, and corn. Other prevalently modified crops, according to *Seeds of Deception,* include zucchini and yellow squash grown in the United States, Hawaiian papaya, and some tobacco. Formerly, there were a lot of GM potatoes, and though some may remain, they are no longer actively marketed. Similarly, GM tomatoes have been pulled from the market. China still produces GM tomatoes, cucumbers, and a variety of pepper.

Seek out organic products and those specifically labeled as non-GMO or organic to avoid the potential repercussions of consuming GMO crops. For example, most soy, corn, canola, and cottonseed oils are genetically modified, though it is not difficult to find olive, sunflower, safflower, or even almond oils that have not been genetically altered. In general, for every type of GM food, there is usually a variety of organic or GM-free food available. If your local chain grocery store doesn't carry GMO-free or organic products, seek out a health food store. Most likely, you'll find an array of organic products that meet your needs.

Reducing your intake of prepared and mass-produced foods will also decrease your intake of GM foods. Aspartame (sold under the brand name NutraSweet) is genetically modified. Other common food additives, such as enzymes, flavorings, and processing agents, often contain genetically engineered bacteria and fungi. A common enzyme called rennet is used in the production of many hard cheeses, though it is not permitted in the production of cheeses labeled organic because it is a GM food. The thickener xantham gum, a substance that you will rarely find in organic foods or foods found at your local health food store, is also frequently derived from a GM source.

Recombinant Bovine Growth Hormone (rBGH)

Recombinant bovine growth hormone (rBGH) is sold to many US farmers, who inject it into their lactating cows to increase their milk production. Also, cows given rBGH are prone to frequent udder infections, requiring more anti-biotics and sometimes resulting in pus in the milk. Many US dairy farmers have discontinued its usage, and Europe and Canada have banned it outright. However, due to industry pressure, it remains available and unregulated by the FDA. Therefore, the consumer should keep an eye out to make sure that he or she enjoys only organic (and hopefully antibiotic- and growth-hormone-free) dairy products and meats.

Healthy Practices in the Kitchen

To establish clean air in your home, switch to nontoxic cleaning methods, and clean up existing residue from commercial cleaning products. You'll be glad to know that some dirt is good for you, at least some experts believe. They think that the precipitous rise in allergies and asthma may be because modern-day children have grown up in such overly pristine environments and have received so many vaccinations that they haven't developed a normal immune response to bacteria and viruses.

While it's reassuring that we don't need to clean too obsessively or our immune systems will suffer, we do need to clean to ensure that the air and our surroundings are as free of pollutants as possible.

The most important rule of thumb for cleaning is to use common sense. To begin with, it makes *no* sense to clean with chemicals that by their very nature cause dirty air! The great irony of most modern cleaning products is that while they may remove surface dirt and sometimes germs, they soil the air and surfaces with volatile organic chemicals, hydrocarbons, chlorine, and more!

Indoor Air Pollution

Often the best indicator of an underlying indoor air quality problem in a house is identifying the first thing you smell after having been away for a few days. You may not notice an odor daily because your olfactory sense tends to adapt to smells, but once you're out of the house for a few days and have "cleared" the smells of your home out of your system, you're bound to notice an unpleasant, stale, or odd smell when you arrive back home. Visitors are often more perceptive than you are, and they may inquire about a certain odor. Take the time to investigate smells; they may be benign, but they may also be a source of indoor air pollution.

Gas Stoves: While gas stoves save energy, they can cause a significant amount of indoor air pollution with high concentrations of nitrogen dioxide (NO_2). *Technology Review* (August/September 1982) tracked the amount of pollution breathed by one person during a normal day (commuting to work, living in the suburbs, cooking dinner, and relaxing), and they found that they breathed the most pollution in their kitchen when cooking with a gas stove. If you must cook with gas, make sure that your stove has an automatic pilot and that your kitchen is well ventilated to the outside.

Smoke Points of Cooking Oils: Heating cooking oils to their smoke point can cause serious indoor air pollution. One way to reduce the problem is to choose your oils carefully, and cook with oils that can handle high heat without smoking. For example, refined avocado oil can be heated to 510°F before smoking, while coconut oil will smoke when heated to just under 280°F. For more about the smoke point of cooking oils, visit the Spectrum Organics Web site at www.spectrumorganics.com, and type "Kitchen Guide" into the search engine.

Exhaust Fans: Exhaust fans help remove hydrocarbons produced while cooking and may help improve indoor air quality if they're fully vented to the outside. (And it's always a good idea to circulate fresh air into a kitchen space if you've been cooking food all day.)

Refrigerators: Most refrigerators use chlorine products as coolants, and some environmental organizations, including Greenpeace, have been calling for a ban of chlorine products in all countries. Chlorine can contaminate groundwater and cause other environmental damage; its full effect on humans isn't known, but it has been linked to cancer. Some newer coolants are being introduced for refrigerators and air conditioners, so look for these improvements when purchasing a new appliance.

Refrigerators can also be a safe harbor for mold in the home. Besides the hairy green surprises growing on leftovers on the bottom shelf, be sure to check and clean the drip pan under the refrigerator and water access areas and drains in the back of the refrigerator. I almost took the kitchen apart on a hot August day trying to find the source of a horrible mold smell, and I found it in the refrigerator drip tray. You can grow some very ugly-looking mold in there. Keep up with cleaning your refrigerator inside and out. Put yourself on the same schedule for cleaning the fridge as you do for changing your smoke alarm batteries— set four times a year as your goal!

Automatic Dishwashers: As mentioned above, chlorine is hazardous to human health, and it's disheartening to know that many automatic dishwasher detergents contain chlorine bleach. Chlorine escapes into the air whenever you open a dishwasher, especially in the middle of a cycle, and it can irritate lungs. By all means, choose a chlorine-free dishwasher detergent.

Compost: Empty your countertop compost bin at least three times a week, or you could harbor large amounts of mold. Mold can be toxic, and you'd be surprised at how many people let their compost bucket languish in their kitchen before emptying it of molding food! Daily removal of food scraps is best, but if that's not convenient, empty your indoor bin every 2 days.

Garbage Disposal: Run your disposal every day. Mold and bacteria can fester in rotting food that's trapped in the disposal. Deodorize it at least once a week by pouring 2 cups of straight distilled vinegar down the drain. If odors persist, pour 1 cup of borax down the drain, and flush it with very hot water. Repeat as necessary.

Rotting Food: Rotting food can bring mold into the kitchen. Clean out the refrigerator regularly, and check any bins where you store food at room temperature. Rotten potatoes smell about as bad as anything I know of. Potatoes and onions are often a problem because they are stored in bins, usually in dark pantries, and aren't checked often.

Cabinets Made of Pressed Wood: Are the kitchen cabinets made of particleboard or other pressed wood materials? Particleboard and pressed wood can be a source of a lot of formaldehyde outgassing, especially when the "wood" is heated because it's next to a stove, heater, or refrigerator. Formaldehyde is a strong sensitizer (meaning that you can become very sensitive to other agents in the environment if you are overexposed to formaldehyde). It's also considered a carcinogen.

Products Stored under the Kitchen Sink: Most people keep a large number of chemicals and cleaning products, even pesticides like ant traps or bug killers, under the kitchen sink or in kitchen broom closets. Opened bottles of cleaning products and cans containing pesticides can leach toxic chemicals into the air in your kitchen and throughout your home, and it's especially dangerous when food is stored nearby.

Do you clean the kitchen with standard products bought at a conventional supermarket or hardware store and that contain a label with a signal word on it that is more serious than a "Caution" (see "Understanding Cleaning Product Labels" on page 187)? One of the biggest sources of indoor air pollution is cleaning products. Many contain solvents that are toxic, neurotoxic, and long lasting in the environment.

Synthetic Air Fresheners, Perfumes, and Scents: Synthetic air fresheners only numb the nose and bring more chemicals into the home. Some air fresheners are labeled as carcinogens. Synthetic fragrances can contain dozens and dozens of synthetic chemicals that are usually derived from petroleum products and contribute to indoor air-quality problems and to sensitivity in a large number of people. One-third of the substances used in the fragrance industry are toxic, according to the National Institute of Occupational Safety.

Very strong fragrances are added to most automatic dishwashing detergents. That advertised "fresh" smell is a blend of synthetic chemicals that will add to the overall polluted indoor air quality. Good alternatives are now available from green brands, found in health food stores and in some progressive grocery stores.

Safe Pest Control in the Kitchen

Pesticides are commonly used in the kitchen to kill ants, flies, cockroaches, and more, but you can easily have an insect-free kitchen without using chemical pesticides.

Grain moths are often found in bags of flour or rice and boxes of cereal. To repel them, place a few bay leaves on pantry shelves, or tape bay leaves inside canisters or cereal boxes. Grain moths like warmth and moisture, so store grains in airtight containers and in a cool place.

According to folk wisdom, other deterrent herbs are cloves and peppercorns. Place them in the food storage area.

Most homeowners have had an ant infestation at least once. An obvious cache of food could be the culprit, but many times, it may not be obvious what they're after. As a start, track ants to their entry point, then seal up any openings or cracks. Give them a shot of soapy water and dispose of their remains in an outside trash container, and then erase their designated "pathways" by wiping with more soapy water. Tidy up all kitchen surfaces, and wash pet dishes as soon as the food is eaten. If you're still hosting ants, look for natural baits that contain boric acid.

And then there's the cockroach. Holistically, keeping your house or apartment clean is a very good start for keeping roaches away, but cleanliness alone isn't foolproof, as any tidy New York City dweller can attest. However, the best treatment *is* prevention: Do not leave food out; keep surfaces free of stickiness; and be sure to inspect bags, boxes, and any food brought into the house, because this is a likely mode of roach transportation. They like warm, moist, close quarters, so you need to be vigilant about caulking, sealing, and screening all drains, pipes, and entry

MAKE IT YOURSELF
SAFE SUGAR ANT HOTEL

I make three to six of these homemade ant hotels every spring (sugar ant season) and place a few in the kitchen and wherever else ants like to frequent. I've never had to do much more than make these ant-trap hotels to rid our house of these common spring and summer pests.

    1 cup borax
    1 cup sugar water
    4 loose wads of toilet paper
    4 shallow glass jars with screw tops

In a bowl, mix the borax and sugar water. Place a loose wad of toilet paper into each jar. Divide and pour the borax mixture into the jars, soaking the toilet paper. Fill each jar with water to within 1 inch of the top. Screw the lids on the jars, and with a hammer and nail, make four to eight holes in the lid. Place the jars where you have ants (but keep them away from children and pets).

Note: The Safe Sugar Ant Hotel will catch the workers but not the queen. A more comprehensive solution is to blend ¼ cup of confectioner's sugar and 1 tablespoon of borax. Sprinkle it in ant traffic areas. There is not enough borax with this method to kill the worker ants immediately, so they take it back to the nest, ultimately eradicating it. (If the worker ants die at the powder, cut back on the borax.)

Caution: Keep borax products away from children, pets, and wildlife. ❖

points into your home or apartment. Even a few crumbs under the stove or refrigerator is an invitation to pesky roaches, so vacuum any food storage and food prep areas regularly.

There are some methods being explored to control roaches, including bait stations that use the fungus *Metarhiziumanisopliae,* which is lethal to roaches but fine for warm-blooded animals, fish, and bees. A bait station using nematodes is also being tested.

Catnip oil is an essential oil that repels many insects, including cockroaches. Sprinkle drops of this pure essential oil on cotton balls, and place them in areas where cockroaches like to travel. Or try sprinkling boric acid, available at pharmacies, along baseboards, in cracks, and around drain pipes. Make sure to keep the boric acid away from pets and children.

Ingesting Pollution

You want to eat food that is as pure as possible, so you don't want to eat food that is contaminated with chemicals from processing, packaging, or cooking methods. Use your common sense, and think through what your food comes in contact with and if the contact could cause contamination.

Leaching Plastics

Of big concern in the kitchen is ingesting plastic that has leached into food from storage containers and packaging. Plastic by-products include endocrine disruptors, such as phthalates and bisphenol-A. Endocrine disruptors can cause reproductive health problems and infertility. They are also indicated as causing cancer, especially breast and prostate, by stimulating cells sensitive to estrogen. Phthalates have been shown to cause birth defects and damage to the liver, kidneys, lungs, and reproductive system in laboratory animals.

According to the Green Guide Institute, the plastics you want to avoid because they release chemicals include these.

❖ #3 Polyvinyl Chloride (PVC)—contains di-2-ethylhexyl phthalate (DEHP)
❖ #6 Polystyrene (PS)—may leach styrene
❖ #7 Polycarbonate—this plastic contains bisphenol-A

Plastic tends to migrate into fatty foods, especially hot fatty foods. Don't use plastic in microwaves or place plastic-wrapped food in the sun! Avoid microwavable packages and the boil-in-a-bag foods. One dead giveaway that

You *can* sanitize your cutting board without resorting to bleach. Use a scrub brush and hot soapy water to rinse away food on the surface and in the indentations, then wash the board with hydrogen peroxide alternated with white household vinegar.

plastic leaches into food is that you can taste it!

Water Filters

It is important to filter your water if you have a well or get your water from municipal sources (see page 211). Municipal water contains chlorine to kill bacteria. Chlorine is a highly corrosive substance, capable of damaging skin, eyes, and other membranes. Chlorine was listed as a hazardous air pollutant in the 1990 Clean Air Act, and exposure to it in the workplace is regulated by federal standards.

Well water often has contaminants and bacteria. Unless you have complete water tests run on your water regularly, it is prudent to have a water filter. Reverse osmosis filters are popular for homes using well water because they reduce bacteria and viruses in the water source.

Cutting Boards

It can be truly satisfying to spend an hour chopping, dicing, and slicing fresh ingredients for a meal. Cutting boards can harbor bacteria in the cracks and grooves caused by knives. Wash your cutting board with hot water, soap, and even a scrub brush to remove food and dirt particles. After washing it, sanitize your board in the dishwasher. Or, wash with 3 percent hydrogen peroxide alternated with straight white distilled household vinegar. To reduce concern about foodborne bacteria on cutting boards, my recommendation is to cut meat only on plates that can be sterilized in a hot dishwasher. If you prefer to cut meat on a wooden cutting board, always wash and sanitize it before chopping vegetables and fruit.

Coffee Filters

Minute amounts of dioxin found in coffee filters can leach into the coffee you're drinking every morning. Choose unbleached coffee filters instead; you can find them in health food stores, in natural products catalogs, and in progressive grocery stores.

Cookware

One of the components of Teflon production that is released on heating is a chemical member of the PFOA fam-ily called perfluorinated chemicals—a chemical group that *never* breaks down and has become ubiquitous in the environment.

Teflon and other nonstick surfaces can exceed temperatures at which the coating breaks apart and emits toxic particles and gases linked to hundreds, perhaps thousands, of pet bird deaths and an unknown number of human illnesses each year, according to tests commissioned by the Environmental Working Group. Take care not to overheat your Teflon cookware, or, better yet, stop using Teflon cookware, especially if it shows any signs of wear.

Acidic foods can cause cookware to leach minute traces of aluminum (a neurotoxic heavy metal) from the pan, and the metal migrates to the food and is ingested. Try anodized aluminum pans, which have a thicker coating and are less likely to leach.

Cast-iron cookware labels sometimes state that the pans are preseasoned. This refers to a wax-based coating that keeps the pan from rusting between manufacture and purchase. Avoid these because the wax may be made of petroleum products; instead buy pans where the instructions for seasoning are included, then carefully season them at home.

As a general rule, the more inert the cookware, the better. Glass is the most inert of all cookware, meaning that it doesn't leach metals or other ingredients into the food. Stainless steel is also a very good choice for cooking because it is one of the most inert metals. While it reportedly does leach small amounts of nickel, adverse health effects for nickel are not documented. Stainless steel's main drawback is that it does not conduct heat evenly, although its conductivity improves when combined with other metals, such as aluminum or copper, in a layered application. Layered cookware is called clad, which is a sandwich of aluminum or copper between two pieces of stainless steel. The inert stainless steel provides the cooking surface, while the aluminum or copper improves the heat conductivity.

Porcelain-coated cookware, also called enamel, is nonreactive and conducts heat evenly. The porcelain is usually over an iron base. Enamel cookware does have one drawback—once it is chipped, it's ruined because exposed iron can rust.

In general, look for heavy-gauge pots and pans because these spread and hold heat evenly. "Heavy weight" is not the same as "heavy gauge." Gauge measures the thickness used in the cookware's construction, not its weight. Rap the pan; if you hear a thud rather than a ping, the gauge is thick enough to cook foods evenly.

Don't use cookware in the oven unless you're sure the handles will withstand the heat. Some modern plastic handles can withstand up to 400°F ovens, but older pan handles are limited to 300°F or less. Personally, I would avoid putting any plastic, even pans with heat-tolerant handles, in the oven because of concerns about fumes given off when it's heated to high temperatures.

Kitchen Housekeeping

Over the years, I have received hundreds and hundreds of letters from readers who have thanked me for my nontoxic cleaning formulas made out of kitchen cupboard ingredients. Many commercial products made them sick with a full range of symptoms, from headaches, nausea, and dizziness to rashes, skin burns, and confusion. I remember one letter from a woman who said she was cleaning her shower stall with a tub scrub that smelled like oven cleaner, and she almost passed out into the tub because the fumes were so overpowering.

The manufacturers of chemical products and the advertising industry have, I believe, brainwashed us to disbelieve what our own bodies are telling us. We've allowed ourselves to be disconnected from our own wisdom about ourselves. What other explanation is there for our continual use of products that make us feel faint, nauseous, or give us headaches?

When cleaning and caring for your home, learn to trust and pay attention to all of your senses. Your senses rule the day and are the best guides and allies in staying on top of emerging housekeeping problems. Cleaning and maintenance routines are of real value, and the senses are wonderful indicators of what needs attention and why. Have you ever picked up a dishcloth or kitchen sponge and been unnerved by the smell? Are you surprised by the amount of dried-on food and spills in the little crevice between your counter-top and stove? Maintaining a clean kitchen space is good for your health, and in my opinion, good for your soul since you spend countless hours there.

I've written an entire book on clean-ing and done careful research on the subject, not because I like to clean (I don't!), but because I know that most people are unintentionally poisoning the indoor air of their homes with cleaning products.

Nature provides us with a plethora of cleaning materials from the plant, mineral, and animal kingdoms. There isn't one thing in the house that you can't clean successfully with just these basic ingredients. The one synthetic material I choose to use, but don't need to use, is detergent. All detergents are synthetic. Some detergents don't cause as many environmental problems (because they're more biodegradable than synthetic detergents, which are derived from petroleum products), and

UNDERSTANDING CLEANING PRODUCT LABELS

Do you get headaches, rashes, or have trouble breathing when you clean? Listen to what your body is telling you! If you don't feel well after using any cleanser, whether it's natural or not, stop using it and substitute something less problematic for you.

The majority of commercially available cleaning products contain "signal" words on their labels, such as Caution, Warning, Danger, and Poison. My guideline for buying safe cleaning products is to buy only cleaning products without any of the following words on the label.

Caution: Denotes a product that can cause injury or illness to humans when it is inhaled, swal-lowed, or absorbed through the skin.

Corrosive: The product can damage skin and mucous membranes.

Danger: Denotes a product that is corrosive or extremely flammable.

Poison: Ingesting even small amounts of this product can be fatal. Sometimes used on the label with "Danger."

Extremely Flammable: Just what you'd think—the product can catch fire.

Strong Sensitizer: Chemicals that cause hypersensitivity upon being exposed a second time.

I always buy those that are dye- and fragrance-free. Detergents are especially useful if you have hard water and have to deal with soap scum (see page 345 for more information).

For hundreds of formulas using natural materials for housekeeping, see my books *Clean and Green* and *Better Basics for the Home*.

Mineral Cleaning Agents

Baking soda, washing soda, borax, chalk, clays, and rottenstone are all good examples of minerals used for cleaning. Minerals are quite extraordinary because of the unexpected cleaning attributes that make them great substitutes for toxic solvents and chemical odor removers. Washing soda peels wax off a floor, and baking soda adsorbs odors in the air and neutralizes acid-based chemicals in water. In other words, putting a box of baking soda in the refrigerator works because it draws odors to itself, and putting a cup of baking soda in the wash will neutralize chemical odors. I've used this technique very successfully to remove the "new" smell from clothes and even pesticide residue on outdoor clothes. Borax is a good deodorizer.

We often think of minerals as hard and scratchy, but not all of them are abrasive. Some are so fine that they can even be used to polish silver. The abrasive grades can work well for polishing wood and more.

Odorless and not flammable, minerals are great for heavy-duty cleaning. They can be mixed safely with most other cleaning agents and are effective substitutes for some very toxic products.

Baking soda is a gentle nonabrasive cleaner. Not only does it neutralize odors in water and air, it's also used to formulate sprays that control fungal diseases in garden plants.

Borax does multiple duties as a natural laundry booster (making the detergent more effective), general cleaner, and disinfectant.

Washing soda is the best solvent substitute because it eats away at wax and other hard-to-remove materials, such as soot and even paint. Don't use washing soda on fiberglass, aluminum, or in places where you want to keep your wax and paint intact. You must wear gloves when using it, but it doesn't give off harmful fumes.

Plant Materials

Essential oils—essences derived from flowers, fruits, leaves, roots, and trees— are a great addition to the natural cleaning arena. All of the volatile essential oils are antibacterial. These include cinnamon, clove, eucalyptus, lavender, lemongrass, rose, rosemary, tea tree,

WORDS TO THE WISE

HOUSEHOLD PRODUCTS AND TRICLOSAN

A disinfectant showing up in consumer products is raising health and environmental concerns, according to information published by Beyond Pesticides (formerly the National Coalition against the Misuse of Pesticides). The chemical triclosan is a synthetic, broad-spectrum antimicrobial agent that, in recent years, has exploded onto the consumer market in a wide variety of antibacterial soaps, deodorants, toothpastes, cosmetics, fabrics, plastics, and other products. Studies have increasingly linked triclosan to a range of health and environmental effects, from skin irritation and allergy susceptibility to dioxin contamination and destruction of fragile aquatic ecosystems, according to Beyond Pesticides's quarterly news magazine *Pesticides and You*.

On a personal note, I've found that it is hard to buy a sponge manufactured without triclosan. I often have to go to a hardware store to find a disinfectant-free sponge. Read labels very carefully; if the label says that it kills odors or germs, it's possible that it has triclosan or another disinfectant impregnated in it.

and thyme. Many essential oils work well for repelling ticks, flies, fleas, and more. Essential oil scents offer the additional benefit of aromatherapy and are often added to potpourris, air fresheners, sachets, and linen sprays.

Vinegar is the simplest plant material (made from apples) that has a myriad of uses for the household. It's also incredibly cheap (just cents for a cup). For cleaning, use white distilled vinegar because it won't stain wood or fabrics.

Animal Materials for Cleaning

Beeswax, milk, shellac, royal jelly (from honeybees), anhydrous lanolin, and honey are all animal products that can be used in the home. Lanolin, the oil from sheep's wool, is excellent as a waterproofer for boots, and it is helpful for a nursing mother's cracked nipples.

Milk is great for skin care and for removing some stains, such as ink. Beeswax is insoluble in water and is used to add stiffness to creams and waxes, and as an emulsifier.

Energy-Saving Appliances

Though all kitchen appliances use resources like electricity and water, there are many ways to make sure that you are using them in the most energy-efficient way possible. According to government statistics, the average refrigerator manufactured in 2003 uses only 500 kilowatt-hours of electricity per year, while those manufactured in 1972 used more than 2,500. This difference is astronomical and can save you hundreds of dollars a year. Whenever possible, using newer appliances is

BEST KITCHEN CLEANSERS

The kitchen may be the most-used room in your home, and it probably accumulates grease, grime, dust, and stains on a daily basis. Try these two cleaners (each with just three ingredients) for a clean that can't be matched!

GENERAL ALL-PURPOSE CLEANER

Put this cleaner in a spray bottle for cleaning baseboards, appliances, and other places where you would normally use a commercial all-purpose cleaner. Make sure you label the bottle.

> ½ teaspoon washing soda
> ½ teaspoon liquid soap or detergent
> 2 cups hot water

Combine the washing soda and soap in a spray bottle. Pour in the hot water (it will dissolve the minerals), screw on the lid, and shake to blend completely. Spritz the all-purpose cleaner every 6 inches or so on surfaces, and repeat as necessary. Wipe off the cleanser with a soft rag as you go. For tough dirt, leave the cleanser on for a few minutes before wiping it off. Shake the bottle before using; it will keep indefinitely.

Variation: Out of washing soda? Use 2½ teaspoons of borax instead.

HOMEMADE SOFT SCRUBBER

This is one of my favorite recipes. In the kitchen, I use it on countertops and the sink. In the bathroom, it's great for bathtubs and shower stalls. Make only as much as you'll use in one cleaning session because it dries out quickly. One reader wrote to say that she added some pure vegetable glycerin to the baking soda, and the mixture stayed moist for a long time in a jar with a tight lid.

> ½ cup baking soda
> Liquid soap or detergent
> 5–10 drops pure antiseptic essential oil, such as lavender (optional)

Place the baking soda in a bowl. Slowly pour in liquid soap, stirring constantly; add liquid soap until the consistency resembles frosting. Add the essential oil, if desired. Scoop the creamy mixture onto a sponge, scrub the surface, and then rinse. ❖

the easiest way to cut overall operating costs because they are so much more efficient. If you live in the United States, buy appliances with the Energy Star label. The Energy Star program is run by the United States Department of Energy, and appliance models that are significantly more energy efficient than government standards require can be awarded an Energy Star label.

Using common sense—like making sure that you fill each laundry load and that you don't use that electricity-guzzling ancient fridge—is another fail-safe way to consume electricity efficiently.

Automatic Dishwashers

Most people think that washing dishes by hand is the conscientious way, surpassing the wasteful excess of automatic machines. However, most dishwashers use only 8 to 14 gallons of water per cycle, and when properly used, they consume less overall resources than hand washing. About 80 percent of the energy used by dishwashers is consumed while heating water before it reaches the machine.

There are various guidelines to follow in order to make sure you optimize the energy you do use while running a load of dishes.

❖ Don't use the prerinse function. Do so only if you discover that it is necessary to clean your dishes.

❖ Wait until you have a full load of dirty dishes rather than running your dishwasher every time you have a small meal.

❖ Adjust the cycle time so that you are using the shortest applicable cycle.

❖ Run your washer during off-peak hours, especially if you live in a densely populated area where there is a real energy crunch at certain times of the day.

❖ If spotting on dishes isn't a problem, you can safely eliminate the heat during the drying cycle.

Since most household hot water is at least 130°F, it sanitizes dishes, leaving a bacteria count of less than one per plate, according to a study by the University of Louisville School of Medicine. The bacteria count on hand-washed dishes in this experiment was an astronomical 390 per plate, a clear indicator of the health benefits of employing an automatic dishwasher!

Refrigerators

Your refrigerator is probably the biggest electricity-consuming appliance in your house. Even if it's running well, a 15-old-year (or older) fridge isn't cost-

Safe and Sound
DISHWASHER PROBLEM SOLVING
Forget those rinsing agents for dishwashers, and use vinegar instead if you discover a problem. That foggy white film that afflicts many glasses is the result of hard-water buildup. Soaking foggy glassware in a sinkful of vinegar and water will completely eliminate the film. And if you discover that you are getting rings on your glasses after washing them in the dishwasher, try spreading the glasses throughout the top rack, rather than grouping them together, for more efficient wash and rinse cycles.

CLEANERS FROM PLANT-BASED INGREDIENTS—REALLY!

Natural is better! When you make your own cleansers, you can easily identify the ingredients and feel good about living lightly on the earth.

MOLD CLEANER AND INHIBITOR

This spray works wonders to eradicate mold and mildew. I've used it successfully on a moldy ceiling from a leaking roof, a musty bureau, a musty rug, and a moldy shower curtain. Tea tree oil is expensive, but a little goes a long way. Unless you have frequent mold crises, this mixture can last for months. Remember to label the bottle!

> 2 teaspoons tea tree oil
> 2 cups water

Combine the ingredients in a spray bottle, shake to blend, and spray on problem areas. Do not rinse. The strong odor will dissipate in a day or so. ❖

FRAGRANT FLOOR WASH

Rid the house of stale winter smells! This is an easy and inexpensive wash to mix on a whim; it can't be stored, though, so cut the recipe back proportionally for small areas. This is a great wood floor wash, and it also works well on tile.

> ⅛ cup liquid soap or detergent
> ¼–½ cup white distilled vinegar or lemon juice
> ½ cup strong fragrant herb tea (peppermint is great because it adds antibacterial qualities)
> 1 gallon warm water

Combine ingredients in a pail or bucket. Swirl the water around until it is sudsy. Mop or sponge to clean the floor as normal, then rinse. ❖

LAVENDER ANTIBACTERIAL SPRAY

This spray is great for cabinet knobs, doorknobs, cutting boards, or any other surface that might harbor bacteria. It lasts indefinitely, so it's great to have handy during cold and flu season.

> 1 cup water
> 20 drops pure essential oil of lavender

Pour the water into a spray bottle. Add the lavender essential oil and shake to blend. Spray on the surface and let set for at least 15 minutes, or don't rinse at all. ❖

efficient to run. You'll recoup the cost of a new one in just a few years because of the energy savings you'll see from improved compressors and cooling systems in newer models.

Even if your fridge is still in its first decade, take the time to clean around the seals. After cleaning the seals, check to be sure they fit tightly; for just a few dollars, you can replace a worn or cracked seal and keep the cold air in the fridge where it belongs.

ALL-PURPOSE WINDOW WASH

A dab of dish soap with vinegar and water is the perfect cleanser. Label your spray bottle, and store it with other natural cleaners.

¼ cup white distilled vinegar
½ teaspoon liquid soap or detergent
2 cups water

Combine the ingredients in a spray bottle, and shake to blend. Spray, and then remove with a squeegee, paper towel, or newspaper. ❖

BASIC WOOD CLEANING FORMULA

This is a good formula for well-used furniture. The vinegar works wonderfully to pull dirt out of wood. It stores indefinitely in a lidded jar. This is a particularly nice formula because it doesn't leave an oily residue; the little bit of oil in the formula keeps the wood from drying out.

¼ cup white distilled vinegar
¼ cup water
½ teaspoon liquid soap or detergent
A few drops jojoba or olive oil

Combine the ingredients in a bowl. Saturate a sponge with the mixture, squeeze out the excess, and wash surfaces of tired and dirty wood. The smell of vinegar will dissipate in a few hours. Dry with a soft cloth. ❖

In my opinion, there may be some trade-offs if you decide to use a certain appliance based solely on energy use. There are health concerns to consider before choosing a gas oven (see page 425). I don't have a microwave oven, and I don't expect that I ever will. While there is little research to say that microwaves are harmful, I choose not to eat food cooked in microwaves because the internal food temperature may have destroyed the enzymes and

MAKE IT YOURSELF

BEST BASIC CREAM FOR POLISH (AND SKIN!)

This cream is a great base for a wide range of household products, from furniture polish to skin cream. The fragrant smell of beeswax is a wonderful addition. Store for 6 months or so, unless mold grows on the wax; in that case, discard the cream.

> 4 ounces oil (olive or blend of oils such as jojoba wax, almond oil, and others available in health food stores)
> 1½ ounces coconut oil or cocoa butter
> ½ ounce beeswax
> 4 ounces distilled water

Combine all oils and the beeswax in a double boiler. Melt slowly until the beeswax is completely liquefied. Remove the melted liquid, pour it into a bowl, add the water, and whip with an electric or hand mixer until creamy. ❖

---

nutritional value of food. That is enough for me to take a wait-and-see attitude toward the appliance and to follow my heart-held belief that when there is doubt, follow the Precautionary Principle, which requires proof that the product is safe (with adequate and extensive testing) before using it. I want my family to eat food with vibrantly healthy enzymes.

THE ENERGY COST OF COOKING APPLIANCES

The California Energy Commission's "Consumer Guide to Home Energy Savings" compares the energy use of seven different appliances for cooking a casserole. For the energy costs, it assumes the cost of gas is 60 cents a therm (a therm is 100,000 BTUs) and electricity is 8 cents a kWh (kilowatt-hour).

APPLIANCE	TEMPERATURE	TIME	KWH	ENERGY COST
Electric oven	350	1 hour	2.0	16 cents
Electric convection oven	325	45 minutes	1.39	11 cents
Gas oven	350	1 hour	112 therm	7 cents
Electric frying pan	420	1 hour	0.9	7 cents
Toaster oven	425	50 minutes	0.95	8 cents
Electric slow cooker	200 (Low)	7 hours	0.7	6 cents
Microwave oven	"High"	15 minutes	0.36	3 cents

ELECTROMAGNETIC FIELDS FROM BIG APPLIANCES

Do family members frequently spend time very near any major appliance in your kitchen? Or is a bed on the floor right above a refrigerator or on the other side of the wall from a big appliance? The highest concentrations of electromagnetic fields in my house, when tested by a gaussmeter, were right in front of a dishwasher when it was running. The stove and refrigerator also had high fields. Note that the high fields drop off quickly, within a few feet, so if it's possible, keep kids doing homework on your kitchen table or desk away from appliances.

6

water

The cold water from a gravity-fed spring tastes as sweet as fresh running maple tree sap. After drinking even half a glass of such vibrant water, your mouth, then your throat, then your stomach seems to sing with its sweetness. Wonder water, or so it seems. Water is liquid song. It is liquid sweetness.

Scarce and sacred now, such springs speak of a time when sweet water was far more commonplace. I remember a spring-fed watering source from my childhood, from a place in Canada where we went every summer to camp. I expect my generation is one of the last that will know this taste. I know my daughter has never tasted water so sweet, nor have my friends' children. The taste of that pure energetic sweetness was so unforgettable that it has

stayed with me ever since. It is the "alive" quality of the water as well as its flavor that are so memorable.

What is the nature of the water you drink? In which you bathe? Having enough clean, living water in our bodies and in our environment is paramount to good health. We are certainly water beings. Our cells are 75 to 90 percent water, and a fertilized human egg is about 95 percent water. Without enough water, we die. Without adequate clean water, we lose our vitality. Living water is the fountain of youth—the vibrant and energizing element that revitalizes and repairs the cells of our brains, the cells of our livers, and the cells of our hearts.

We are water beings who live on a water planet. Many experts now call water blue gold, and they believe that we are at the world's most critical juncture. How will humans collectively decide to view, conserve, and protect our water for future generations? The consensus is that the decisions we make now about water will determine the future of life on Earth.

Our Water Planet

The earth is the only known planet that has a hydrosphere with water covering its surface and contained in its atmosphere. Seventy percent of the earth is covered with water. Almost all of this is saltwater found in oceans, and it's connected all around the world. Only about 1 percent of the earth's water is fresh.

Oceans become salty from the mineral salts leached from soils and carried to them from streams. During evaporation, the water leaves the ocean but the salt remains there. Over eons, seawaters became more saline until they are as salty as they are today, and they'll become even more so. But as salty as the oceans are, they are still about 96.5 percent pure water, and the remaining 3.5 percent is made up of dissolved inorganic ingredients, such as salts that have washed there from tributaries around the world.

Earth continually recycles water. The water at the surface recirculates by leaving the earth's surface, entering the atmosphere by evaporation from the sun or by transpiration from plants, and returning to the earth by precipitation. Precipitation then seeps into the ground and becomes groundwater. Earth is an ecosystem, and we have the same amount of water now that there was at the time of the planet's creation. Water consumed today will eventually be recycled for use by future generations. The water we're drinking now has been on Earth for millions of years! If you can imagine that your great-grandchildren will drink the same glass of water that you drink, you will be inspired to take better care of it.

The Properties of Water

Water is an unusual substance. As matter, water can be liquid, gas, or solid. The structure of water causes its molecules to be attracted to one another and stick together. Water molecules are held together by hydrogen bonds, which cause water to be liquid at ambient temperature.

Water is called the universal solvent because no other naturally occurring substance can dissolve more things. (A substance is said to be dissolved if it can pass through a very fine filter.) What water can't immediately dissolve, it can physically wear away over time through abrasion. According to the *Tao*

Te Ching (written in China 2,500 years ago and the basis for Taoism), "The softest thing in the universe overcomes the hardest thing in the universe."

Water bears the imprint of its surroundings, both positive and negative, in part by pulling what it has dissolved or eroded away into itself, such as minerals, soils, organic material, and pollution. In either dissolved or suspended form, it surrounds these substances and transports them away.

Water is also considered a universal storage medium—a vessel holding the energetic vibration of all it comes in contact with. Water melds and merges with its surroundings. There are no hard edges that water can't absorb into itself, no substance that it isn't merged with.

Water washes through us. Because every one of our cells is made up of water, our cells receive the information and messages from water. For us water beings, water is the energetic carrier and pathway for our biochemistry. "In reality, we are looking at a body that is constantly renewing itself from second to second as water constantly flows through our physical being," writes William E. Marks in *The Holy Order of Water*. All life is related through water, and if water is the vessel of everything, then what it is holding becomes of paramount importance!

Water entrains that which is in its environment. (Entrainment means a melding.) Consider this: If calm, healing music is played to someone who is very agitated, slowly but surely, the agitated person calms down as his body's rhythms meld with the restful music. The person becomes in sync with the rhythm and pulls it into himself, melding with it. Can the same be said of water? If we become in sync with water, and we heal our local environments and ourselves, can we change the world bit by bit?

I believe that water can hold messages of health, healing, and vitality instead of pollution and despair. Such a concept gives me a renewed sense of hope. Have you ever wondered about the saying that the beat of a butterfly wing can be felt around the world? Maybe this idea—that water currents connect us with all life and the universe—is the reason why.

Living Water

Victor Schauberger (1885–1958) was a logger, forester, and visionary who grew up in Austria, where his father, too, was a logger by trade. Back then, loggers would float immense logs down the nearest river to the mills. Victor spent his childhood studying the river, and he watched as the logs followed its winding path. Schauberger noted that "Already from earliest childhood, it was my deepest wish to understand nature and through this to come closer to the truth I could not find at school or at church. I was repeatedly drawn to the forest where I could watch the flow of water for hours on end without getting tired or irritable." As expressed by the Chinese in the *I Ching,* Schauberger believed that water is the earth's life blood.

As a naturalist of unusual observational abilities and intuition, Schauberger concluded that water "must be allowed to follow its own course to keep its energy." He coined the term *living water* to describe water's vitality when it was allowed to follow its natural course of winding, vortexing, and spiraling. He noted that in undisturbed nature, river water flowed away from direct sunlight to be sheltered by the forests, so that it could keep a cool temperature and maintain its energy and vitality. He gained wide respect for the canal he designed that mimicked water's meandering sequences as it sent logs down Austrian mountains.

The Maori, an indigenous people of New Zealand, view water as a living thing and believe that all things have a mauri, or vital essence. The Maori traditionally look at water in three states.

1. Waiora, or "waters of life," which includes rainwater, tears, springs, holy water, and special healing water that can often rejuvenate damaged things.

2. Waimate, or "dead water," which has no life essence at all and cannot support human life or food.

3. Waikino, or "bad water," which is either a representative of a dangerous place in a river, such as a rapid or snag, or water that is polluted either physically or spiritually. The Maori believe that bad water can be changed.

Schauberger believed that the perfect, most-energized water percolated down deep into the earth, where it became steam and was then imprinted with all the energy from the crystals and minerals there. Once it returned to the surface, he felt the water was "mature and full of light." Water that follows this cycle is cleansed and purified. "[Schauberger] taught that water is a living rhythmic substance. In maturity, it gives of itself to everything needing life," writes Jeanne Manning in *The Power of Water.* Schauberger also discovered that the only container that stores water in a way that it can keep its energy is the egg shape. In particular, ancient egg-shaped vessels called amphorae, uncovered in archaeological digs, are the perfect solution.

Re-Energizing Water

Schauberger's work was continued by Theodor Schwenk (1910–1986), a Ger-

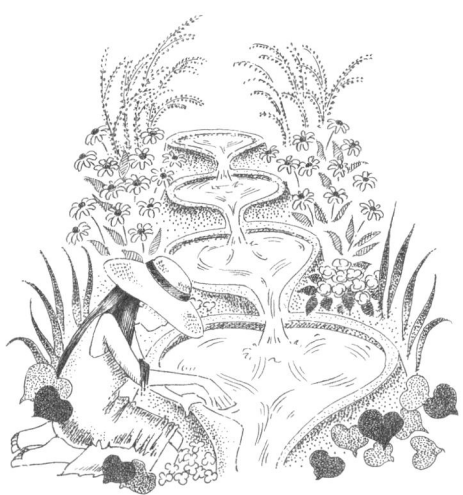

Half art and half technology, Flowform sculptures allow water to cascade in a series of figure eights, replicating the path water takes in undisturbed flows found in nature. The natural movement of the water allows for better oxygenation, and it improves the water's capacity to support life-forms. Flowforms can regenerate water's natural power and are used around the world in agricultural irrigation and sewage treatment systems.

for the sewage system at Highgrove Castle. Flowforms are also beautiful, sculptural designs, reflecting Wilkes's study of sculpture at the Royal College of Art.

The Worldwide Water Crisis

When water is allowed to stagnate and become polluted, is held for a long time in tanks, is warmed, and is not allowed to eddy, flow, and spiral, it loses its energy and becomes lackluster and lifeless. It can't self-clean if it isn't allowed to find a rhythm. Polluted water also loses its vitality.

Approximately 1.5 billion people lack safe drinking water, and 5 million deaths a year can be attributed to waterborne disease from one of the three major sources of water pollution—

man pioneer of water flow research, and later by John Wilkes. Through his applied research into the flow and rhythm of water, Wilkes invented Flowforms, a series of connected basins, where each basin is designed to cause a double vortex in a figure eight. Flowforms incorporate Schauberger's wisdom—that water needs to move in a vortex to stay clean and alive. Flowforms resuscitate "dead" water, bringing it back to life.

The vortex movement of the water provides rhythm and oxygenation and stimulates biological activity. Flowforms are now used around the world for water and sewage treatment. Prince Charles of Great Britain uses Flowforms

From Other Voices

Common sense, science, and religion inform us that it is living water that truly brings life to all things—both physiologically and spiritually. And, this water cannot be water that has been contaminated by pollution; rather it is water that is teeming with life that contains the pulse of electrical energy created by flowing vortices that imparts the life force into all things.

—William E. Marks, *The Holy Order of Water: Healing Earth's Waters and Ourselves*

municipal, industrial, and agricultural.

Water pollution experts discuss "point" and "nonpoint" sources of water contamination. "Point" sources constitute about 60 percent of the pollution found in the waterways and include discharge from specific locations, such as industrial effluent, wastewater treatment plants, and ditches. The *Exxon Valdez* oil spill is an example of a point source of pollution, as is raw sewage dumped from a cruise ship or seepage from barrels of toxic materials in Woburn, Massachusetts (reported in the book *A Civil Action*, which was subsequently made into a movie).

"Nonpoint" pollution includes pesticide runoff from agriculture, outfalls from industrial sites, toxic chemicals from urban runoff, oil drips and spills from vehicles, wastes from farms and pets (and faulty septic systems), road salt, and on and on. Crop fertilizers are also significant contributors to nonpoint water pollution. According to the Ocean Conservancy, the Mississippi River dumps 320 million tons of fertilizer nutrients and sediment into the Gulf of Mexico each year.

One example of nonpoint pollution gaining significant attention is MTBE—methyl tertiary butyl ether—a gasoline additive that makes gasoline burn more cleanly. MTBE is contaminating wells around the world. MTBE replaced lead in the late 1970s, and it has been a required additive in gasoline in states with high summer ozone pollution problems. MTBE is known to cause cancer in laboratory animals when it's inhaled in high doses.

The list of "nonpoint" pollution sources is as endless as pollution itself. Wherever there are toxic chemicals, they can end up in the water.

Ecosystem Interrupted

There is also a global water crisis that is not about polluted water. Water around the world is being diverted from its normal flows to such an extent that some believe that parts of the earth are drying up. Maude Barlow, coauthor of *Blue Gold: The Fight to Stop the Corporate Theft of the World's Water,* noted in a speech that the earth is behaving like an apple that gets brown spots when it is dehydrating. She says that there are brown spots showing up in aerial photos of China. It took me a while to understand how this could be, if, in fact, Earth has the same amount of water it has always had and will have forever. After talking to others about this, I realize that what she meant is that water is being diverted from its normal pathways by dams, concrete, roadways, and cities. Water can't flow down into the earth by way of runoff as

From Other Voices

That water bears the imprint of its surroundings is understood and accepted. That water bears the imprint of its spiritual surroundings—commonly known as Chi—and that this imprinting phenomenon is increasingly being documented, is one of the biggest developments for transforming our understanding of water and healing the environment. Masaru Emoto, a doctor of alternative medicine in Japan, has published two books full of photos of water that show its hado (Emoto's term for Chi). He has done this by freezing water and photographing the water crystals.

The earliest photos of water crystals in the books show pure water and polluted water, and these photos alone are enough to change your view of pollution forever. The pure, clean water crystallizes into stunning crystals of mesmerizing beauty. The polluted water is dark and cancerous looking. It isn't able to crystallize and stays looking like an oozing sore. Who would ever want to drink that?

But the truly awesome, mind-changing photos are of water crystals from water that has been imbued with music and crystals of water that has been imbued with love, gratitude, and even hate. It's heartening to see polluted, cancerous water transformed to beautiful crystals by love and music.

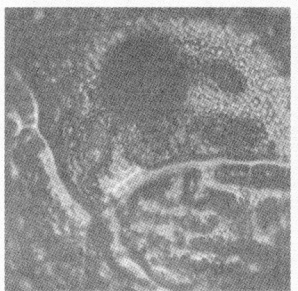 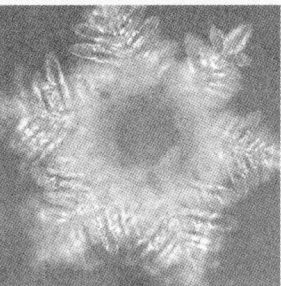 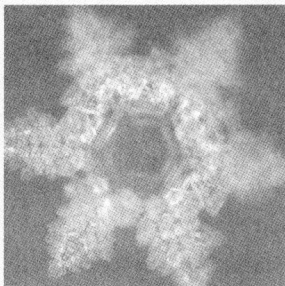

| Polluted water | Clean water | Imbued with music |

it has for millions of years. Now, the earth is dehydrating in spots from man-made obstacles. Victor Schauberger warned of vast wastelands appearing on the planet when forests disappear, and his prediction is bearing out, according to Barlow.

Interestingly, just like scientists say that rain forests are the lungs of the planet, scientists like Schauberger say that rivers are the earth's arteries. It is tree cover that maintains the rich ecosystem of soil life, and it is through healthy soil and root systems that water percolates. Ruined forests cause soil erosion and interfere with water's natural percolation into the ground.

While dams can produce massive quantities of hydroelectric power, dams can also disrupt the ecosystem because they interfere with the river's natural flow, cutting off some of its energetic vitality. When dams are built, estuaries are damaged, and fish spawning runs are destroyed. Along the entire river's length, changes occur as water temperature rises or falls, sediment and natural drainage shifts, and water is diverted. In the United States alone, there are 75,000 dams wider than 6 feet, so 75,000 small and large ecosystems have probably been altered in small ways or changed dramatically since the dams were built.

The attempt to meet energy demand drives the development of dams, often at a terrible cost. China has plans to build more than 100 dams in Yunnan Province in an attempt to satisfy energy needs. Not only will this project force nearly 1 million people off their land, but the dams will also cause significant destructive shifts in the ecosystem.

Water Wars

In India, 200 million people lack access to safe drinking water, and the situation is rapidly becoming a major catastrophe because scarce river- and groundwater is being diverted for industry and commerce. Called the privatization of the water supply, it is legal for corporations to cross borders and plunder the water supplies they find! It is also legal for a town to sell the rights to their water to corporations and then allow the corporations to charge the residents of the town exorbitant prices for it. Multinational corporations put meters on water taps. How could anybody own this

> ### From Other Voices
>
> Cultures that waste water or destroy the fragile web of the water cycle create scarcity even under conditions of abundance. Those that save every drop can create abundance out of scarcity.
>
> —Vandana Shiva, PhD, author and physicist

water? This threat to community water supplies is fast becoming what experts call the Water Wars.

Robert F. Kennedy Jr. serves as senior attorney for the Natural Resources Defense Council, chief prosecuting attorney for the Hudson Riverkeeper, and president of Waterkeeper Alliance. I heard Mr. Kennedy speak and was captivated by the power and sanctity of his message. He calls these Water Wars "Armageddon, *the* war, the last fight." Many call the privatization of water corporate hijacking. A global company, for example, is legally permitted to drill deep into the ground in an Indian neighborhood and extract excessive groundwater for its bottling plant.

Or worse, the corporation charges locals for the water they drink. In one such situation, it took 1,000 local families protesting for 20 months and bringing a suit in defiance of the state government, which supported privatization, to close a plant that was drying up their rice paddies and killing their coconut palms.

Water as a Spiritual Element

Water is the central source of our beings. It is part of every cell and fiber in us; it is our very essence. Could water be the common denominator that weaves us all (earth, animal, human, and plant) together as one? Is it the ultimate connector? It's awesome and humbling that water carries so many entrained messages, especially when we consider that there has been the same water, and the same amount of water, on the earth for millions of years. What messages are we receiving from our ancestors when we drink? And it is overwhelming to think that in the past 60 years alone, the human hand has imprinted so much pollution on the water, bringing it out of healthy balance. It is our spiritual obligation to be water's caretaker and cause it no further harm.

Meditate with Water

This wonderful water meditation and bath was created with the generous, perceptive, and experienced help of William E. Marks, the author of *The Holy Order of Water.*

❖ Fill a bathtub with water of a temperature that feels right to you. Place a glass of clean drinking water nearby in case you get thirsty. You might want to

From Other Voices

WATER PRAYER
Great wetness:
The beat of your waves is the beat of my
  breathing;
The surge of your tides is the surge of my
  heart.
My very cells pray to you; my tears, sweat,
  and blood sing your song.
Without you, I wither and die.
Teach me your secrets of ebbing and flowing,
Help me to trust in your pattern repeating.
Buoy me up, teach me to swim in you,
Help me to rest in your arms.

—Cait Johnson, in *Earth, Water, Fire, & Air*

light a beeswax or soya candle and turn off the lights. (I find turning off the bathroom lights to be an enhancement, possibly because any artificial light changes the energy of the room.)

❖ Before stepping into the filled tub, ask Water to cleanse, heal, and purify the deepest pain inside of you, whether it be physical, mental, or emotional. Your active participation in asking for healing is very important. When I ask for a healing from Water, I sense welcoming and healing love enveloping me as I step into the tub; it almost feels as if the water reaches out to take care of me.

❖ Once settled and soaking, breathe slowly and deeply. Ask for a message about your pain. Its source will usually be identified almost immediately, and more information may be provided about how to help enhance the healing, such as singing or reciting a mantra ("Om" works well). I've had some profound spiritual healing with this water meditation. For example, I've been given the insight about why some relationships affect me the way they do and how to heal the part of me that is vulnerable. Even if you don't sense a message during your bath, you will always sense and feel the healing results soon after and throughout the day. Just be a witness—in a meditative way— during the bath, so you can just "be" and receive. Let yourself feel free to go with the flow.

❖ After about 20 minutes, thank the Waters that reside within you. Also, express thanks to the waters of the tub for the healing, and then step out of the tub. Saying "thank you" for water's healing upon entering and during the bath is helpful too, because the energy of gratitude is healing in its own right and will help elevate the vibration of the water in the tub and in your body.

❖ As a variation, stir in ½ to 1 cup of Epsom salts combined with about 5 drops of your favorite natural essential oil essence (lavender and tangerine are both good choices). (See page 127 for safety guidelines for using essential oils.) Stir in the Epsom salts as you fill the tub; add the oil essence after the tub is filled and just before you enter it. For your very first healing bath, try to experience it without any additions. For future baths, you may want to experiment with salts, oils, herbs, or flower petals in the bath and soft music or rock crystals nearby. As you learn what resonates best for you, you can customize your baths to take care of your emotional and health needs.

Marks notes that the water energy for your healing can always be found within your body, but sometimes the water needs a little help being charged and activated. Thinking about this one day, I asked the water of my body to provide a healing, following much of the same process as when having this bath. I went to the well within. While not as powerful as an actual bath, I was given a meaningful healing nonetheless.

Honoring Water

Satish Kumar, the editor of the English magazine *Resurgence: An International Forum for Ecological and Spiritual Thinking*, began a weekend conference about water by having us all stand at the shoreline of a lake. We cupped our hands into the lake and then lifted the water up to our brow level. We opened our hands and let the water slowly fall back to the lake. What a powerful experience this was! It was sunset, and the falling water droplets were like jewels in the light as they fell. The sound of the water landing in the lake was a mellow waterfall sound. I felt as if I had walked out of an Arthurian legend about Avalon, honoring the sacred in a way I profoundly remembered from some other long-ago time. The meditation helped us feel water deeply in our senses and imbued water's importance in our lives.

In Tarot, the traditional Suit of Cups is the suit of water. It is receptive, a vessel, and a symbol of the deep, primordial unconscious mind and womb. Water shows us the images, or imprint, of things. Emotions, feelings, and psychic knowledge are all represented by water in the Tarot tradition. Water flows and changes, and it carries away what it cleanses.

Baptism, holy water, and other ritual uses of water are a central component of religions and spiritual beliefs. Water is the great purifier. We wash away our sins, we cleanse our wounds, and our tears bring release. As Cait Johnson notes in *Earth, Water, Fire, & Air,* "The human spirit understands water as the Great Beginning." She goes on to note that a Hopi creation myth starts, "In the beginning, the earth was nothing but water," and in the Bible's book of Genesis, you'll find "The earth was without form and void, and darkness was upon the face of the deep; and the Spirit of God was moving over the face of the waters."

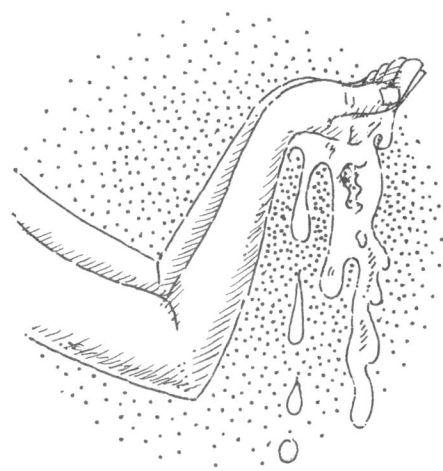

Water can be deeply spiritual and meditative. The next time you're near clean, fresh water, dip in and let the water droplets fall slowly from your hands. It's a powerful and purifying experience.

It is interesting to contemplate how central a role water has played in belief systems throughout the world, and it is a desolate thought to acknowledge how objectified it has become in modern society. A radical yet strangely down-to-earth and compelling (at least to me!) concept of water is now emerging.

Many Native American belief systems see the sun as the immediate creator. However, they believe that there is a greater power beyond the sun, a power "so big that it cannot be named." This power has no name because its greatness is beyond imagining. So, they choose to pray to the sun.

William E. Marks noted to me in an e-mail, "That which is so big that it cannot be named is the ineffable nonlinear aspect of water. Our sun is basically a collection of energy waves, energy waves that have their source from the cosmic waters that created and permeate our universe. In fact, recent science tells us that a star like our sun cannot form or survive without water. Without water, our sun would overheat and expand into its basic elements."

Water in the Home

Groundwater is the water that is beneath the surface of the ground, and it is very easily contaminated. Almost all—about 90 percent—of the world's drinking water is groundwater. In the United States, about half of the drinking water supply comes from groundwater, and rivers and river-fed lakes provide the other half.

Given runoff problems, such as agricultural chemicals, pesticides, and releases and spills, the pollution in our rivers is not encouraging. For example, in New England, because of mercury contamination, state health departments advise fishermen and residents not to eat fish caught in certain rivers. And the Environmental Protection Agency (EPA) estimates that 10 percent of wells contain pesticides.

That is just the tip of the iceberg. The toxic soup in our drinking water is much more complex than just chemicals, pesticides, and spills. Antidepressants, caffeine, birth control pills, and cleaning products are just a few of the thousands of chemicals that end up in water supplies.

Drink Water from Your Local Watershed

Want to do your part to protect water on the planet? Drink water from the watershed in which you live, leaving others' water where it belongs. Even if you live in a city such as New York and drink municipal water that is piped in from 100 miles away, it's better environmentally to consume *that* water than it is to drink bottled water shipped in from other parts of the world. It is critically important that we clean up our local watersheds and protect our municipal water from privatization so that water is available for those who live in the region. This is true around the country and around the world.

Just as we don't want a big corporation to come into our towns and cities

WORDS TO THE WISE

WHAT'S IN YOUR BACKYARD?

You can find out what contaminants may be in your drinking water by checking out your geographical location in the Environmental Protection Agency's Envirofacts Data Warehouse (www.epa.gov/enviro/index_java.html). The site has detailed information about potential areas of concern in your neighborhood, including hazardous waste producers, Superfund sites, and environmental activities that may affect air and water quality where you live.

and pull out our water and send it elsewhere, so we shouldn't allow corporations and profiteers to deprive others of their local water.

The best way to have "bottled water" without using water from another's watershed is to filter your water—whether it's municipal or well water—and take it with you in a stainless-steel thermos. (Stainless steel is inert, so there's no worry about the container leaching.)

Know the pH

Knowing the pH of your household water is important for a number of reasons. First, pH affects the taste of water. Second, pH may have an impact on the effectiveness of the laundry and personal care products you buy (for example, is a detergent better for your washing needs than a soap?). And third, having hard water may mean that you'll need to pay close attention to buildup in plumbing systems.

Often (but not always), an alkaline pH indicates hard water, whereas an acid pH indicates soft water. Most plumbing supply and some hardware stores sell pH strips for testing and determining how hard or soft your water may be.

If there are a lot of minerals in the water and it is hard (an alkaline, or high, pH), those minerals will combine with soap to form soap scum in bathtubs and on shower stalls. Detergents, on the other hand, don't bind with hard water minerals and won't form scum. If you have hard water and you use a soap instead of a detergent in your laundry, the clothes may turn gray and won't be fully clean. You can safely assume your laundry-washing product is a detergent unless it states specifically that it is a soap. Look for soap-based laundry products in a progressive grocery store or a health food store.

Lastly, if you have hard water, scale could be a problem. Scale buildup forms when minerals suspended in water cling to pipe walls, shower stalls, and other areas. This can ultimately cause a narrowing of intake and drainage pipes and can cause problems for appliances that use water. Electric hot

HEED THE MERCURY WARNING

Mercury is one of the most dangerous substances known to science. Mercury levels in the environment have risen 1.5 percent each year since 1970, largely due to pollution from coal- and oil-fired power plants and waste incinerators. When released into the environment, mercury is transformed into methylmercury. This form of mercury is extremely dangerous to humans and wildlife. It can cause neurological and developmental problems in humans. FDA data shows that around 36 percent of swordfish, 33 percent of shark, and 4 percent of large tuna samples tested from 1992 to 1998 exceeded the level of mercury that the agency considers safe.

For most adult men and women, the risk from eating mercury-contaminated fish is low, but pregnant women, women of childbearing age, and children should limit their fish consumption because high mercury levels can result in lower developmental IQs and other adverse health problems. The Environmental Protection Agency (EPA) offers three recommendations for selecting and eating fish and shellfish to reduce exposure to mercury.

1. Do not eat shark, swordfish, king mackerel, or tilefish because of their high levels of mercury.
2. Eat up to 12 ounces a week of fish and shellfish that are lower in mercury, including shrimp, canned light tuna (note that albacore—or "white" tuna—has higher levels of mercury), salmon, pollock, and catfish.
3. Check advisories about local lakes, rivers, and coastal areas before consuming fish caught by family and friends.

water heaters can be particularly troublesome because scale can build up on the heating element and short it out.

In a soft water environment, some believe that water tastes sweeter. Soaps also work more effectively, hair has more luster, and less shampoo is needed, dishes have no film after being washed, there are fewer gray clothes, and pools and home spas will require fewer chemicals.

To find out the water hardness in your area, call the local water company, public utility consumer service department, or the home economist at the cooperative extension service office.

Despite the problems with hard water, there is no proven, whole-house system that really works to soften water without side effects. Ion-exchange water softeners use salt to soften water. People with hypertension and on salt-restricted diets are often warned against using water softeners. Salt from softeners cannot be removed by wastewater treatment plants and ends up in our lakes, rivers, streams, and aquifers. Some states now ban their use because of the contamination of the wastewater stream.

Magnetic water softeners work with the use of a magnetic field that pulls minerals to it, but scientists have yet to prove their effectiveness scientifically, according to *Consumer Reports* magazine.

The Chlorine Concern

If you use municipal water, chlorine can be a problem. In the shower or the dishwasher, chlorine combines with organic matter to create harmful gases that we breathe in.

Special shower filters will remove around 90 percent of the chlorine from your water. The filters, which are made with half copper and half zinc, remove chlorine electrolytically.

Water Filtration Systems

Like the earth's surface, the human body is mostly water. Not only do we bathe in water, cook with water, and swim and play in water, we *are* water. Because we need to keep our "inner ocean" as pure as possible, the increasing stream of news about contamina-tion of the drinking water supply is disturbing. Reports of heavy metals, industrial chemicals, and pesticides seeping into drinking water, along with the offensive smell of chlorine in city water supplies, lead many to look at available home water filtration systems. It is important to learn about water filters so you can choose the appropriate kind for you.

Reverse Osmosis: Classified as a true water purifier because it reduces bacteria and viruses, a reverse osmosis (RO) filter also carries away chemicals such as lead. In RO systems, water is forced through a membrane that filters out and flushes contaminants. The purified water is collected in a storage tank. When water is pulled from the storage tank, it passes through a final carbon post filter. Most systems pro-

Safe and Sound

TEST AND FILTER, OR JUST FILTER?

Testing your water is the best way to find the right filter to suit your needs. It's especially important if you've moved to a new neighborhood or you found out something unnerving about your area's industrial or agricultural history. If your water comes from a well, you should have it checked for harmful bacteria and other contaminants at least once a year. To find a list of state-certified labs, visit the Environmental Protection Agency's Web site: www.epa.gov/safewater/labs/index.html. If you have municipally supplied water, contact your water facility for a report.

Filters run the gamut from inexpensive to costly, so you might find it helpful to do some Internet research for current information before you head out to buy. NSF-International (formerly called the National Sanitation Foundation) has a very good list of water treatment filters along with the types of contaminants they remove (www.nsf.org). Filtering your water is an important part of establishing a healthy homescape, and I believe that everybody must have a filter, no matter what the water source.

duce 5 to 15 gallons of filtered water in 24 hours. Ideal for homes with well water because they filter bacteria and viruses, RO systems are attached to the kitchen faucet and are used for drinking and cooking.

There are downsides to RO systems. They use plastic tubing, so you need to check to see if the plastic tubing in your system contains any hormone-disrupting phthalates. RO systems also waste a lot of water because they take 3 to 4 gallons of water to produce 1 gallon of filtered water. Look for an RO system with a shut-off valve so the water doesn't keep running. Also, some RO systems recycle the flushed water, which is more ecofriendly. ROs are temperature and pressure sensitive—they produce the most water when the incoming water is 77°F, less when the water temperature is 50°F. The amount of water they produce is also affected by how good the water pressure is. Hard water and iron will reduce the life of the membrane.

Carbon Filters: Affordable carbon filters remove chlorine and some toxic organic chemicals such as benzene (used in solvents), chlordane (used in pesticides), and trichloroethylene (used in degreasers and solvents). One pound of activated carbon has an approximate surface area equal to six football fields. These filters improve the flavor and the smell of the water. Many residential homes using municipal water have carbon filters on each drinking faucet to reduce chlorine. Since the chlorine in municipal water supplies is designed to kill bacteria and viruses, a carbon filter alone can be enough for those on "town water."

There are two types of carbon filter systems: adsorption and mechanical filtration. In the *adsorption* system, the contaminants stick to the carbon through weak molecular attractions. In the *mechanical filtration* system, the water passes through the filtration medium,

One of the most basic (and smartest!) things you should do if you are on municipal water is install a carbon filter on your tap. Activated carbon filters remove chlorine and other contaminants and can improve the taste and smell of your water. Be sure to change the filter regularly though; otherwise the dirt that accumulates on the filter can become a breeding ground for bacteria.

trapping larger particles. The key to successful carbon filtration is slow water flow to assure that water has as much contact with carbon as possible.

You should be aware that carbon filters aren't for every situation. They won't remove or treat bacteria and viruses. Silver-impregnated carbon filters are used to slow the growth of bacteria, but these filters release a bit of silver into the water. EPA-registered carbon filters that use silver regulate how much of it finds its way into the water. Replacing carbon filters can be expensive as well, especially if you're using them on multiple faucets. One last detail to mention: When buying a filter, block carbon is preferable to granular carbon. But if you have a lot of sand and dirt in the water, a block carbon filter will clog more easily.

Distillation: Many people are looking for a drinking water purifier that will remove everything harmful while leaving in useful minerals. No one has yet created such a product. A carbon filter removes some contaminants while leaving in the minerals, but numerous substances that you do not want in your water will pass right through. An RO system or distiller reduces most contaminants but also removes some minerals. Distillers remove 90 percent or more of bacteria, viruses, minerals, heavy metals, and synthetic chemicals.

Distillers boil water until it becomes steam, then the steam passes through a cooling coil where it returns to a liquid state. Contaminants and often heavy metals are left when water is boiled or evaporated, and they need to be disposed of as hazardous waste. Carbon filters are often included to pick up chemicals that have the same evaporation point as water.

Distillation systems aren't right for everyone though. They use energy to evaporate water, and they require extra water in the cooling cycle. Hard water residue leaves scales in the boiling tank. Make sure to choose a system made of stainless steel because it is possible that aluminum can leach from the receiver tank. Distillers also remove minerals that are necessary for good health. They can make water taste flat so that it needs oxygenation prior to consumption.

Water Pipes

Some say that the Roman Empire fell because of the lead in the water pipes. There are still lead water pipes in some very old American houses, but they are rare, thankfully. Lead is still a concern with copper water pipes though, because some water pipes were soldered with a lead-based solder. Lead-free solder has been available for many years now, but the possibility exists that lead solder was used on your pipes.

Stainless steel water pipes would be the most inert, but they are costly. PVC intake pipes should be on your "no" list because of the leaching of plastic chemicals. No matter what your water system, run your water every morning for 2 to 3 minutes before you use it to rid your pipes of any standing water.

Conserving and Caring for Water

We can work on many fronts to protect the water on our planet (and by extension, our health). Conservation is certainly one important area, and in this book, I offer water-saving tips for almost every room. I believe that living a life without synthetic chemicals is one of the most important contributions we can make to clean water. And we need to reduce our consumption of nonrecyclables. When I see plastic floating around in the ocean threatening sea life, I despair.

We are learning that caring for water may mean making comprehensive changes in our lifestyles. Water connects us all and is connected to everything. What goes down your drain? Where does it go? Does it come back to you as drinking water? Pay close attention to how your family uses and disposes of water. Do you contribute to the contaminated wastewater problem? Do you make an effort to conserve water on a daily basis?

Cutting back on water is important. When you look at the "Household Water Use" chart listing average daily water use, you can see that you can make a big improvement by installing a low-flow toilet and taking shorter showers. It is interesting to see that washing dishes uses an insignificant amount of water compared with washing clothes and taking showers. And how sad that leaks constitute a big percentage of home water use.

Gray Water

Gray water is generally defined as wastewater from washing clothes and dishes and from bathing. Many think it can be used for a number of household activities. In some states, it's illegal to install systems for collecting water that's diverted from washing machines, bathtubs, and shower stalls because such gray water can become contaminated with bacteria from these uses.

HOUSEHOLD WATER USE

Wondering what you use all that water for?

Toilet	26%
Clothes washer	22%
Shower	17%
Faucet	16%
Leaks	14%
Bath	2%
Dishwasher	1%

You can capture some perfectly clean and fresh household water just by being aware of how water is easily wasted. Keep clean buckets under sinks or in nearby cabinets. When you're waiting for the water to reach the desired temperature, use a bucket to collect the water that would otherwise go right down the drain. Use it for watering houseplants, container gardens, trees, and shrubs. Reuse the water you've used to wash and peel organic fruits and vegetables in the same manner.

However, do not reuse water containing detergents, bleach, borax, or liquid fabric softener, and do not reuse bathwater. Soap and detergent can kill plants. And it's certainly not safe to reuse water to wash or clean food and produce or to water edibles in the garden.

One way to use gray water is to pour bathwater into the toilet bowl when it's time to flush. But before trying to recycle true gray water, check your county's regulations with your local health officials. You must also check with your local government if you plan to establish a formal gray water system.

Water Savers for Yard and Garden

Why use fresh water from the tap to water landscape plants and lawns? Let's use water from the sky! Capturing rainwater has been part of many cultures historically. Under the old temple of Jerusalem is a cistern with a 2-million-gallon rainwater runoff capacity; beneath a church in Oaxaca, Mexico, is a similar cistern.

Front-loading washing machines can cut water use by almost 40 percent. And the benefits keep on coming, from causing less wear-and-tear on clothing to reducing drying time by squeezing out more water in the spin cycle. Be sure to look for the Energy Star label to select the most energy-efficient model.

How much rain does your area usually get in any given month? What do you plan to use the water for? In order to capture rainfall, you'll need to design a catchment area and storage system that meets the needs of your intended water use.

Collecting the Bounty

Where rainfall is plentiful, you'd be amazed at the large amount of rain that rolls off the roofs of your house and outbuildings. Cisterns, often made of concrete and located under a porch slab, store large amounts of water and were standard features in many farmhouses. Rainwater was directed through spouting and into cisterns for storage. Cistern water could be accessed with a hand pump or, in later years, by an electric pump and was used for watering gardens and flowerbeds. If you're lucky enough to have a cistern, by all means, use it! Your cooperative extension service agent can provide information on maintaining and using a cistern.

Have you discovered rain barrels yet? Simply direct your gutters and downspouts into a rain barrel to collect rainwater. Ideally, your rain barrel should have an overflow hose and tap. You can use this water for watering landscape plants and potted containers and watering your vegetable patch.

If you plan to use rainwater from your roof for drinking, you'll need to contact your cooperative extension service agent for advice and information about your local zoning ordinances. If you're allowed by law to collect rainwater for drinking, it will be vital to remove contaminants with a filtering system and to keep rain barrels and col-

WORDS TO THE WISE
WATER, EXPONENTIALLY

The surface where rainwater falls is called a catchment area. For every inch of rain that falls on a catchment area of 1,000 square feet, you can expect to collect approximately 600 gallons of rainwater. Ten inches of rain falling on a 1,000-square-foot catchment area will generate about 6,000 gallons of rainwater. If you have an average annual rainfall of 20 inches, you have the potential to collect 12,000 gallons of water each year.

Even if you're only slightly interested in water conservation, it's easy to see why collecting rainwater has so many benefits (not to mention, it's free!). Catchment systems range from the very simple—a rain barrel—to more elaborate systems made of galvanized metal or fiberglass. There are a number of companies nationwide that can advise and help you set up a catchment system, whether for personal or agricultural use. There's even an American Rainwater Catchment Systems Association that promotes the use of rainwater catchment systems in the United States and runs seminars to share information about new methods, techniques, and materials for collecting rainwater. Visit their Web site at www.arcsa-usa.org.

Recycle rainwater by setting up a rain barrel under a downspout. Even a light rain can add gallons to your rainwater supply; just fill a watering can from the spout on the barrel to water container gardens, window boxes, and landscape plants.

Rain, Rain, Don't Go Away

Over the past few decades, there's been a general plan to divert rain from our homes and properties. Naturally, we want to protect our home's foundation and avoid water in the basement, and we need to channel excess water from flood-prone areas, but we've often gone to extreme measures to whisk water away from where it falls.

Downspout extensions can protect your home's foundation and can direct the water where you want it. In some areas of the world, homeowners are encouraged to disconnect their downspouts. This simple act can keep rain runoff on the property instead of sending it to the sewers and, ultimately, to the rivers. In Portland, Oregon, for example, at the time of this writing, more than 38,000 homes have already disconnected, removing more than 768 million gallons of water every year from the public sewer system and keeping it instead right where it falls to provide

lection systems clean, covered, and protected.

Rain gardens are a type of filtration device that accepts runoff water from any surface and then stores the water in a permeable layer underneath a garden or under a planting zone.

SHOPPING SOLUTIONS
BUYING RAIN BARRELS

There are many models of rain barrels available, and there are helpful features for every gardener's needs, such as gutter-free designs, connecting barrels, and screen filters. Check out some of the Web sites that sell rain barrels and rain water collectors for home gardeners.

Clean Air Gardening, www.cleanairgardening.com
Gardener's Supply Company, www.gardeners.com
Rainsaver, www.rainsaverusa.com
The Green Culture, www.watersavers.com

water for home landscapes and to return it as groundwater.

Water-Saving Tips

It's up to each of us to reduce our water use, even when gardening. Rather than using an inefficient sprinkler, employ some of these techniques to put water right at the roots of the plants.

❖ You can cut water use from 20 to 50 percent using trickle irrigation. Trickle irrigation originated in the desert regions of Israel around 40 years ago, and its concept is to put water where it is most needed rather than across the whole garden or field. For the backyard, this means not wasting water on sidewalks or patios and avoiding runoff because water goes directly to the roots of needy plants. Trickle irrigation water use is measured by gallons per hour, not gallons per minute as is the case with a standard lawn sprinkler. Garden supply stores offer a number of trickle irrigation systems.

❖ Mulch your gardens to conserve water by covering soil with 2 to 3 inches of grass clippings, straw, or finely shredded wood chips to reduce the amount of water that evaporates from the soil. Mulching also blocks out the light, so weeds don't germinate as quickly.

❖ Use common sense, and avoid watering plants in the heat of the day when evaporation occurs at a faster rate. Instead, water in the early morning, and water only those plants needing it most (for example, newly planted trees, instead of well-established plants). Timers attached to hoses can automati-

Snake a soaker hose through your flowerbed, right at the roots of the plants, to provide even watering. Cover the hose with an inch or so of mulch to keep evaporation to a minimum.

cally water your garden at the times that will cause the least evaporation.

❖ To further save water, xeriscape. This concept incorporates seven basic principles that save water by combining water conservation practices with creative landscape design. These principles include planning and design, soil analysis, a lawn size that is appropriate for your needs and practical to maintain, appropriate plant selection, efficient irrigation, the use of mulches, and appropriate maintenance.

❖ Explore the wide range of hoses and hose attachments to make watering easier. Water wands, usually made of metal, screw on to the end of a hose and allow you to water directly at the soil level without having to bend down; they often feature a shut-off value at the end of the wand. Water breakers are nozzles that screw on to the end of a water wand and help to shower plants with droplets. Soaker hoses ooze water through permeable hose walls or through tiny holes along the length of the hose. Water can slowly drip from the hose right to a plant's root system, where it's most needed.

When you need to water, always look for the most efficient way to deliver water right to the landscape plants and vegetable gardens that need it most. There are many ways to reduce watering needs without sacrificing the beauty of your yard or the yield from your garden. From selecting native plants and limiting the size of your turf grass lawn to using rain barrels and drip irrigation, you can make small but effective changes to keep watering to a minimum.

7

the bathroom

Immersion in water is highly sensual, primal, and an ancient healing practice. "Wash your cares away" isn't a truism when it comes to the bath. It really does this! There is something redemptive about a bath. Long soaking in a warm bath seems to open channels of receptivity, and stresses feel as if they are literally dissolved and washed away. The experience is often meditative on a deep level.

You can transform your bathroom into a calming center. It may be the raw, naked reality of bathroom activities that draws us there when we are tired, overwhelmed, or full of care or sorrow. We have much experience letting our guard down in this room—it is one place we can really be fully ourselves. And it is a place where we guard our privacy. In the bathroom, our bodies get our full attention, and by giving the room some consideration, we can make it a place for balance, centering, healing, refreshment, relaxation, and renewal.

Design a Balanced Bathroom

How can you better include the elements earth, water, fire, and air in your bathroom? A good balance of these almost always makes a place welcoming and healing. Water is the most central element here, and it is a very big enhancement if the water you bathe or shower in is clean and pure. If you have municipal water, make sure to install a dechlorinator. Keeping the bathtub clean, too, is often all the inspiration you need to decide to indulge in a bath.

Clean, unpolluted air is also crucial to your very own healing home spa. Pure essential oils for subtle aromatherapy can gently change the air in a bathroom; not to be overused, they're wonderful when you plan to take the time for a long bath. Place plants in the room as natural air cleaners; just make sure they get enough sun and keep their soil healthy.

Beautiful, handmade soap seems to represent the earth to me. Natural earth- or mineral-toned wall or floor tiles are another centering furnishing (mine are a very pleasing turquoise and make me think of the Mediterranean Sea), as are essential oils for the bath, plants, natural fiber towels, and potpourri.

Bathing by beeswax candlelight at any time of day or night helps to acti-

Enjoy a warm stream of sunshine and privacy in the bathroom by installing top-down window treatments. Bring in more of nature by choosing natural-fiber curtains or shades.

vate "chi," according to practitioners of feng shui. Candlelight dances on the walls, window, and water of a bath, and its flame connects you with the fire element. Sometimes, I light a candle if I am having a bath at dawn because the flame is a reminder that the day is beginning outside. Natural sun and moonlight can also contribute to the fire element in the bathroom, so open your curtains wide if it doesn't intrude on your privacy. I love having a bath at sunrise or at night during a full moon.

Pleasing the Senses

Seeing is believing, or so the saying goes. Surrounding ourselves with color and nature fills us with a sense of beauty. And who knows—we may start to feel beautiful about ourselves when we're in a beautiful bathroom.

Sight: Tranquil aquamarine is a great color for the bathroom. The blue of the sky is a restful choice, too, because it is a clear and calming color. Green is a very healing color, and it contains a revitalizing quality—the energy of new life. And white, pure and pristine as it is, represents cleanliness in almost every culture. Choose a color to meet your deepest need. For more about color choices, see page 46.

Light is an important part of your bathroom. When you enter your bathroom, does the existing light enhance the space? Draw attention to the outdoor light that's entering the room by hanging sun catchers in windows and opening shades and curtains wide for natural light. If your bathroom isn't private, yet you want natural light, try using half curtains on just the bottom half of the window, so natural light comes streaming in the top.

Our bathtub had been located in a room so dark and dingy-seeming (even if it was clean) that my family and I virtually never took a bath. Renovating that room—bringing in lots of light by placing tall windows on the east and north sides to surround a deep soaking tub—transformed my life and the room. Rarely a day goes by when I don't have a bath now, and I soak looking out to the sky and the tops of trees in blizzards and blinding rainstorms and with full moons and dawn's early light. Some of my most interesting bird sightings happen when watching the sky from the tub.

Almost every bathroom has a mirror. Simple day-to-day grooming, makeup applications, shaving, and hair care are done in front of a mirror. Mirrors reflect activities that are complex and frequently stressful. Self-consciousness about our image tends to be awakened, managed, and despaired over in the bathroom more than any other room. Mirrors bring you face to face with what you look like.

Internationally known geomancy expert Ibrahim Karim, PhD, noted that when you look into a mirror with positive thoughts, *negative* thoughts are returned to you! If that's correct, I wonder if this has something to do with the fact that mirrors are a turned-around reflection? The way around this, he says, is to turn any mirror into a hexagram by covering the square corners of it with a small 45-degree triangle (masking tape is a good temporary fix). I used this technique on our mirrors (I was especially inspired because I have a teenage daughter), and I have to say that I have felt completely different about how I look ever since. Psychosomatic, maybe, but I'll take whatever I can get! And, as anyone who has a teenage daughter knows, *anything* to positively influence the effect of the mirror is worth trying!

Another welcome sight in the bath is a towel rack covered with beautiful towels and washcloths. You can tell if you have quality terry cloth towels just by looking at them: Are the threads that provide the fluff looped? If so, you have highly absorbent towels. Velour-style towels have cropped loops, but they don't snag like terry cloth loops can. Velour isn't as absorbent as terry cloth, so they won't dry you as well after a soaking bath or shower. The rule of thumb when shopping for towels and washcloths is that the more loops per

Leave the world of PVC shower curtains behind and indulge in one made of hemp or organic cotton. Most hemp is produced and processed without chemicals, and it's naturally mildew-resistant, so it wears beautifully as a shower curtain.

only as needed (keep an eye out for the growth of mildew). Hemp is a great fabric to choose for a shower curtain because it is naturally mildew-resistant. Go all the way with the concept of natural here, and hang them on hooks made of wood or metal. You can also make a great shower curtain using a natural-fiber bedspread; sometimes you see just this type of fabric used for shower curtains in department stores such as Filenes or JCPenney.

Touch: The cleansing feel of water against your skin is sensual. Water-cleansed skin is soft after oils and dirt have been washed away. Hair feels light and buoyant after washing and rinsing. Can you feel your skin drinking up water in the shower or bath or when you just wash your face?

square inch, the higher the quality of the fabric.

Even your shower curtain can have a comforting, all-natural look. Organic cotton or hemp shower curtains are the very best environmental choice for shower curtains. You can put up two—one for outside the shower stall and one for the inside. Only the inside curtain needs to be washed frequently, and then

Dry your body with the soft, welcoming luxury of a towel made of high-quality 100 percent combed cotton. Put your bare feet onto a bath mat of absorbent natural fibers. Hold a wooden brush in your hands, enjoy a few drops of pure essential oil of rose

PLASTIC SHOWER CURTAINS

Plastic shower curtains made from polyvinyl chloride (PVC) emit a complex mixture of strong plastic fumes, including compounds called phthalates, which can interfere with the healthy functioning of the body's hormones. If you must have a new plastic shower curtain, make sure to fully air it outside before hanging it in your bathroom. Lay it in the sun to speed up the off-gassing process. A better alternative is a natural cotton or hemp shower curtain; both provide an adequate barrier to water escaping to the outside of the shower.

THE PERFUME ALTERNATIVE

Many of the ingredients in synthetic perfumes are considered hazardous chemicals. Petroleum-based, synthetic perfumes are the norm, and the ingredients can be toxic to your health and the environment.

Instead, try pure essential oils! Many people who are sensitive to synthetic perfumes typically have no problems with this natural alternative.

To make your own perfume, add 1 to 20 drops of your favorite essential oil to 1 ounce of a non-greasy vegetable oil, such as grapeseed oil or jojoba (actually a liquid wax), or vegetable glycerin. Store the mixture in amber or blue glass bottles. The shelf life is indefinite. Whenever you use essential oils, avoid getting any near your eyes, and be sure to consult a doctor if you are pregnant or have health concerns. Be sure also to read labels carefully, because a few oils can cause skin reactions in sensitive individuals.

Get to know the natural brands of pure essential oils in your local markets and health food stores; these include Frontier's, Attar, and Mt. Harmony Oils.

(mixed into a carrier oil; see page 127 for details) in your tub water, and feel the steam of the hot bath before you step in. Most of all, spend time enjoying the feel of water against your skin.

The feel of water washing sweat from the brow is an age-old human experience. Cooling off with cold water on a hot day refreshes the senses, stimulates circulation, and reduces inflammation. On the next hot day, make a cup with your hands, fill it with water, and pour it on your forehead and face. Cool your body by streaming cold water on your wrists. On a cold day, warming up in a hot shower or bath is womblike and may evoke deep memories. Hot baths also stimulate the immune system.

According to naturopath Hazel Parcells, DC, ND, PhD, hot water draws toxins out of the body to the skin's sur-face, and as the water cools, it pulls toxins from the skin. Epsom salts help the detoxification process by causing you to sweat; magnesium sulfate, the ingredient in Epsom salts, is very cleansing because it is highly alkaline, it neutralizes acid-based toxins, and as an added benefit, it is a sedative for the nervous system.

A word of caution: Very hot baths can be harmful for people with high blood pressure, multiple sclerosis, or diabetes, as well as for pregnant women. Even if you don't have one of these conditions, extremely hot baths can actually dry the skin and make you feel drained, so be sure to use water that feels comfortably warm and not too hot.

You can also tingle your sense of touch underfoot. Natural fiber bath mats or rugs feel best on your bare feet after stepping out of the shower or tub.

The key to a good bath mat or rug is for it to be absorbent and skid-resistant. You'll want to wash them frequently, so make sure the ones you purchase are washable. A natural fiber *rug* with a nonslip backing is ideal, because the natural fiber absorbs more water than a synthetic fiber, and the nonslip backing feels secure on the floor. Bath *mats,* on the other hand, are made of thick cloth with no backing.

Sound: Few sounds are as calming as falling water. Filling a bath or running a shower sounds like a waterfall. After you turn off the water, the quiet is welcome. Listening to music can be nice in a bath, but just letting your mind go still—without much stimulation—can be a treat. (See "Musical Waters" for a discussion about entraining your water to the healing vibrations of music.)

Smell: Walk into your bathroom and pay attention to the scent of the room. You might smell fragrances from a wide range of personal care products, cleaning product fumes, additives in grout, and a whole host of odors from commercial products. The ideal bathroom for health and revitalization is a room with the scent of clean air. If you desire fragrances, choose natural plant essences.

Natural Beauty: The most popular spas are built and furnished with all natural materials. Bathrooms that reflect the natural world help you feel connected to the earth.

Here are some suggestions for introducing natural materials to your bathroom.

❖ Plants give a sense of fresh air, natural beauty, and herbal wisdom. They also absorb positive ions, replenishing the healthy negative ion balance. Try introducing real potted plants if you have enough light, or use dried plants such as potpourri or wreaths. You can also try using herbal sachets for the tub. Even images of flowers (especially water flowers like lily pads) on cotton shower curtains, paintings, or photos, or flowers made of silk can help connect you to nature.

❖ Line windowsills and bathtub decks with shells, pebbles, and stones you've collected from oceans, rivers, and mountain paths. Just looking at sea shells—especially a conch—opens my imagination, so I can "hear" the crashing of waves on the shore. I feel the heat of the sun and the sand on my toes.

❖ Stones and crystals can be powerful memory triggers when you see them. I like to have a few crystals around my bathtub, and sometimes I'll put one in the bathtub with me. Rose quartz is supposed to be the vibration

---

Annie's Insight

MUSICAL WATERS

Although this idea may sound a bit unusual, why not play music to your bathwater before you slip into the bathtub? I've been experimenting with imbuing my bathwater with music. Our bodies drink up water in the bath. Why not ensure that they drink up beautiful water? What is there to lose from experimenting? It may be my imagination, but I love a bath of music water. As mentioned on page 203, not only does Masaru Emoto, the author of *The Hidden Messages in Water*, believe that love changes the actual structure of water, he believes that music does the same thing. So, try playing your favorite music to the bathwater during the entire bathing process, from filling the tub to when you emerge from the water at the end. Bring along your portable CD player next time you bathe.

---

of unconditional love. Who couldn't use a little of that? *The Messages of Water* books, described on page 203, show pictures of the change in water crystals after they have been imbued with the vibration of love, and this seems to transform the structure of polluted water to beautiful crystalline shapes. Choose a rock crystal you are drawn to and place it in the tub.

❖ If you like animals and wildlife, images of these creatures in the bathroom can transport you to another place and another way of thinking. One of my bathrooms has a wooden mirror frame carved as a great blue heron standing in water. The crane symbolizes hope to me, and simply looking at it makes me feel hopeful. Perhaps you have an object or memento that connects you to the natural world.

❖ Choose a natural fiber shower curtain and natural fiber window treatments that are designed in a way that is beautiful to you.

The Joy of Washing

Washing with water is more than washing off dirt. Energy clings to you from being out in the world, and water cleans off that energy from other people and the environment. Healers wash both their bodies and their clothes every day to clear others' energy from them. Water has been used since ancient times as a purifier, so wash away your cares!

Washing your hands is the best choice for bathroom hygiene. Antiseptic soaps, just like antibiotics, may lead to the development of drug-resistant superbacteria.

There is nothing like glycerin-rich, homemade soap. It not only cleans your skin, but it also leaves it soft and moisturized. Many commercial soap

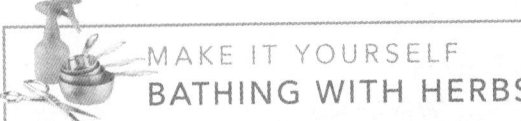

BATHING WITH HERBS

Slipping into a warm bath to start or finish your day may wash away cares, bring you peace, and soothe your body. The aroma of herbs can help impart a tranquil, meditative mood to an otherwise busy or stressful day.

HERBAL BATH BAG

The next time you're at the health food store, buy a muslin bath bag (or make your own—they're easy!) and a handful or two of different herbs, such as lavender and rose petals. Add one or the other to a bath and see how different herbs feel to you.

    ¼ cup fresh or 2 tablespoons dried herbs (try lavender buds or peppermint)
    1 muslin bath bag
    1 quart water

Add the fresh or dried herbs to the muslin bath bag, and close it snugly. Boil the water in a saucepan. Immerse the bath bag in the boiling water and simmer, covered, for 15 to 20 minutes. Let the infusion cool to lukewarm, and then add it to your bathwater along with the bath bag. ❖

BASIC BATH FIZZIES

Bath fizzies are fascinating to watch as they bubble and bloom and snap, crackle, and pop in your tub—and they're good for the skin. You can add essential oils or plant oils for extra moisturizing. Thanks to Snowdrift Farms for the basic formula and inspiration for this recipe.

    1 cup baking soda
    ½ cup citric acid (special order from your pharmacist)
    ½ cup cornstarch
    2½ tablespoons sunflower or other light oil
    ¾ tablespoon water

manufacturers remove the glycerin and use it for other processes. In my opinion, soap without glycerin is harsh and drying. Commercial soaps can also contain synthetic perfumes that pollute your bath, your bathroom, and you.

I love to make my own soap, but it is quite a project. My favorite recipe for making soap is in my book *Better Basics for the Home.* There are also a number of good soap recipes on the Internet. Making soap using commercial soap pieces and glycerin pieces isn't the same as making your own soap because you're just reblending existing soap. Making your own soap requires lye and oils. If you don't make your own soap, or if you run out of your supply, buy homemade soap from health food stores. While it may seem expensive, homemade soap lasts much longer than commercial bars that have had the glycerin removed.

Up to 10 drops essential oil (optional)

Vegetable or other natural colorant, such as blueberry or raspberry juice (shouldn't total more than a teaspoon of liquid)

¼ teaspoon borax

In a medium bowl, blend the baking soda, citric acid, and cornstarch until smooth. Set the mixture aside. In a jar, combine the sunflower oil, water, essential oil (if desired), colorant, and borax. Cover the jar tightly and shake vigorously. Drizzle the combined wet ingredients onto the reserved dry ingredients and blend thoroughly. Pack tightly into half-dollar-size molds, such as candy molds or small cookie cutters. Dry the blend overnight, then slide the fizzies out of the mold. Store them carefully in airtight containers. ❖

CUSTOMIZED BATH GEL

Bath and shower gels wash away the dead skin cells from a fading tan and leave your skin satiny smooth and moisturized. You can scent the formula with your favorite pure essential oils, or you can leave it unscented. When making the bath gel, choose an herbal shampoo made without detergents; one quite fail-safe way to identify shampoos without detergents is to read labels and find a product without versions of the phrase "sodium lauryl sulfate."

½ cup herbal shampoo

¼–¾ cup water

¾ teaspoon salt

8 drops essential oil (optional)

3 drops vitamin E (you can open liquid pills), 1 to 2 tablespoons glycerin, *or* aloe vera gel

Blend the ingredients until well mixed. Use more or less water depending on the texture desired. Use the gel in place of soap, putting a dab in your hand and washing your body; add more gel as needed. The shelf life mimics the shelf life of the herbal shampoo you've chosen. ❖

Everyday and Special Baths

A long soak in a bath of rose petals or lavender sprigs can rejuvenate you and leave your skin beautifully smooth and soft. Bathing holds a healing potential that is not just skin deep. Hydrotherapy is one of the oldest healing traditions on earth, and many believe that it's as close as you can get to the fountain of youth. Combine the benefits of water with those of natural oils, herbs, salts, and other easy-to-find ingredients to make your bathtub into a traditional spa. Your skin will drink it up.

Herbal Baths

With just a sprinkling of herbs, you can enjoy a beauty bath, a therapeutic bath using specific herbs for health conditions you have, or just a simple, relaxing, calming bath. In the words of one of my favorite herbalists, Rosemary

MAKE IT YOURSELF
DETOXIFYING SALT SOAK

Soaking in a tub of hot water with ¼ cup of salts (such as cooking sea salt or Epsom salts) relaxes muscles, draws toxins from the body, and acts as a sedative for the nervous system when the magnesium sulfate—the mineral in Epsom salts—is absorbed through the skin. In addition, it reduces swelling and is a natural emollient and exfoliant.

>   1 cup sea salt
>   2 cups baking soda
>   1 cup Epsom salts
>   1–2 tablespoons pure vegetable glycerin per bath (available from health food stores)
>   4–6 drops essential oils (rose, lavender, sandalwood and ylang ylang are good choices)

Combine the sea salt, baking soda, and Epsom salts in a bowl. Stir to blend. Pour ¼ cup or so into the bath while the tub is filling. Add 1 to 2 tablespoons glycerin to keep your skin from drying out (more for dry skin, less for oily skin) and essential oils of your choice. This mixture (minus the glycerin and essential oils) will keep indefinitely in a glass jar with a screw top. ❖

Gladstar, "Aside from your bed, your bathtub may be the most sensuously arousing place in your home, perhaps yet undiscovered." I'd suggest investing in a good book on herbal remedies, such as *Rosemary Gladstar's Family Herbal*. This book has become a favorite of mine; you never know when you will be wondering which herb to use for which condition, and this book provides a wealth of very good how-to information about a wide range of herbal remedies. Another herb book I really treasure is *Rodale's Illustrated Encyclopedia of Herbs*.

Healing Baths

Water has been used for healing since ancient times. From a spiritual healing perspective, the water element is associated with deep feelings. The secret of the healing bath, in my case anyway, is in how it opens the channels of receptivity to me and to my feelings. I become open and receptive—receptive

SHOPPING SOLUTIONS
BUY SPECIALTY OILS LOCALLY

A wide variety of specialty oils, such as grapeseed, sweet almond, avocado, apricot kernel, and jojoba wax, are common stock items in health food stores. Some brands to look for include Spectrum Naturals and Aura Cacia natural skin care oils.

to the water, receptive to the moment, and receptive to the thoughts and insights that seem to know they will be listened to in this atmosphere. The best and wisest intuitions from deep within me usually come forward.

To me, a bath is meditative, my senses are soothed, and the sound of water is primal in its appeal. My skin drinks up the hydration. It feels like a safe place to heal one's emotional and physical wounds.

Baths are great for healing and rejuvenating the physical body too. As a small example, you can reduce the swelling of sprains and bruises by adding 2 cups of Epsom salts to a warm bath and soaking until the water cools.

Bath Beads: Bath beads are really a delight—they are squishy, brightly colored balls about the size of a quarter that slowly melt in the tub, releasing scented emollient oils. I loved them as a child. My grandmother used to give them to my sisters and me, and we felt so special—like movie stars—when we used them in the tub. Sadly, bath beads are made of synthetic fragrances and colors and aren't healthy to have in a bath unless some ecofriendly manufacturer chooses to make a natural version. In the meantime, you can make a homemade version by simply adding nourishing oils and essential oils, the basic ingredients in bath beads, to your bathwater. Add ½ to 1 teaspoon of vegetable

or nut oil to the bathwater before you step into the tub (be extremely careful, though, when getting in and out of the bath because the added oils will make the tub surface very slippery).

Choose the very best oil for your skin; it will nourish and act as an emollient balm for dry skin. It is worth the money spent on three or four small bottles of pure oil to test which one works best for you. Try apricot kernel, avocado (wonderful for mature skin), jojoba (actually a liquid wax), or sweet almond oil. My skin is on its way to getting old, and apricot kernel oil feels wonderful, as does avocado oil at times, especially deep in winter. Other good bath oils include walnut, grapeseed, and sesame. In a pinch, you can use whatever pure cooking oil you might have in your kitchen cupboard, such as olive oil.

Seaweed Soak: Having a long soak in your own bathtub filled with a rich infusion of mineral-rich seaweed is, I imagine, almost as balancing, nourishing, and purifying as soaking in the Dead Sea or in hot mineral springs. Seaweed baths are one of the most divine experiences you can give yourself at home.

For my seaweed baths, I use about 3 to 4 ounces of dried seaweed (half kelp and half dulse). Kelp has very abundant amounts of calcium, potassium, iodine, iron, and magnesium, and dulse is also rich in minerals and has a very high vita-

Rich in thyroid-stimulating iodine, seaweed soaks are popular spa treatments. Fill a muslin bag or infusion ball with dried seaweed, and steep it in a pot of boiling water for ½ hour. Pour the contents of the pot into the bathtub, fill the bath with water, and soak blissfully while absorbing seaweed's nutrients.

min A content. One pound of dried seaweed becomes 10 wet pounds when it's rehydrated, so in a sense, I am giving myself a bath with about 2½ pounds of wet seaweed. I buy dried seaweed at my local health food store or online.

When using dried seaweed, fill muslin bags, large tea infusion balls, or old stockings cut off at the knee with the seaweed. (The bags are needed to keep the small pieces of seaweed from going down your drain.) Boil water in a large pot, add the seaweed, and steep for half an hour or so. Pour the entire ingredients of the pot into the bathtub, then fill the bath with water as hot as you can stand it. When using fresh seaweed, just add it to the bathtub as it is filling with very hot water, and make

sure to remove it before you open the drain at the end of your bath.

A slight gel or film from the seaweed will softly coat your body while you soak. Once it dissolves, and you don't feel it on your skin anymore, you know your bath is done, and you've absorbed the seaweed's benefits.

Seaweed baths are considered very therapeutic because of their reputation for ridding the body of toxins and because of seaweed's high vitamin and mineral content.

Skin Care

Skin care routines depend on your skin type, but there are three basic steps recommended by experts. First, clean the skin using soap and water or soapless cleansers. Second, exfoliate the skin (slough off dead skin cells) and tone it (close the pores and adjust the pH of the skin to its naturally acidic state after using an alkaline soap). Third, moisturize, hydrate, and nourish the skin.

I've included only a few skin care formulas here, and I chose these because they are tried-and-true and very simple and accessible, and they produce wonderful results. (See my book *Better Basics for the Home* for dozens of skin care formulas, from hydrating facials to creams. Included in that book is a famous, ancient Mayan skin care therapy decoded by an anthropologist. It uses harvest ingredients and works miracles on any type of skin.)

After years of researching formulas for personal care products, I am convinced that you can make more sophisticated skin care products at home than you can buy at the store. At home, you have the irreplaceable advantage of being able to use fresh, completely natural ingredients that are, by far, the most nourishing and healing for the skin.

Exfoliate and Glow

Grains and nuts make great body scrubs. Simply grind almonds or oatmeal, and combine with a few drops of oil until it is moistened. Choose an oil that feels good for your skin type. Avocado oil is great for dry, older skin, for example, and grapeseed is a good choice for oily

---

WORDS TO THE WISE

ANIMAL TESTING, ANIMAL WELFARE, AND PERSONAL CARE PRODUCTS

A grim history of cruelty to animals lies behind many personal care product ingredients. The FDA requires that each ingredient in a cosmetics product be "adequately substantiated for safety" prior to marketing or that the product carry a warning label indicating that its safety has not been determined. The FDA has established no clear criteria or standards for this testing and labeling. Cruel animal studies have often been a company's answer to the FDA's vague demand. Animals are used to test products for eye and skin irritation and are used to gather "lethal dose" data. These tests subject animals to painful and sometimes deadly procedures.

Thankfully, no new tests need to be performed if a company wishes to use an ingredient already in use in the marketplace, but companies still often test new ingredients and new formulations on animals. Ann Marie Giunti of PETA (People for the Ethical Treatment of Animals) says that "information on what's tested and how is hard to come by," because companies wish to avoid the publicity attached to animal experiments. The vague FDA requirement permits alternatives to animal testing— using computer modeling and laboratory human tissue, for example—which not only avoid cruelty to animals but can also provide more reliable data.

Concerned consumers can take the following steps to help phase out animal testing.

• If a product contains a new, innovative ingredient not commonly found in other personal care products, call the manufacturer and ask how its safety was established with the FDA.
• Buy from companies that either have pledged not to test on animals or are observing a moratorium on animal testing (lists of these companies are available at PETA's Caring Consumer Web site, www.peta.org/mall/cc.html).
• Look for third-party certifications that demonstrate that a product was brought to market without any animal testing.

Reprinted with permission from The Green Guide. See page 502 for subscription information.

skin since it is a nongreasy oil. Scoop a handful of the scrub material into your hand and massage your body gently with it, then rinse with warm water.

Another wonderful massage uses Epsom salts. Stand in the bathtub and massage handfuls of Epsom salts over your wet skin, starting with your feet and continuing up toward your face. Rinse.

Exfoliating with Fruits and Vegetables

Fruit acids are great for the skin because they loosen the glue between dead skin cells, and the cells fall away, leaving the face very smooth and soft. Alpha hydroxy acids (AHA) are found in fruits, vegetables, and other natural foods— apples, vinegar, applesauce, cider, buttermilk, yogurt, powdered fat-free milk, sour cream, blackberries, tomatoes, grapes, grape juice, wine, cream of tartar, citrus fruit (lemons, limes, grapefruit, and oranges), and sugarcane. Moisten dry ingredients with a little water before rubbing on your face.

All you need is about ½ teaspoon of liquid per face cleansing. You can squeeze the juice of one fresh lemon into a glass, for example, and refrigerate the leftovers for the rest of the week. Just dab some of the juice onto your fingers and pat on your face. Leave on for 10 minutes or so before rinsing. If you are in a rush, just cut a grape or strawberry in half (or whatever you happen to have on hand), rub it over your skin, let the juice set for a few minutes, and then rinse.

Making skin care products with AHAs is easy because you probably have most of the ingredients in the fridge or kitchen cupboards or growing in the garden.

MAKE IT YOURSELF
SEA SALT SKIN SCRUB

Use a bristle brush to apply this scrub; the brush massages your skin as it exfoliates.

  2 cups fine sea salt
  4 cups grapeseed, apricot, or almond oil
  Up to 10 drops of essential oil of choice (optional)
  Bristle brush

Combine the ingredients in a glass jar. Shake or stir to blend. Stand in the bathtub or shower stall, and wet your body. Scoop some of the salt scrub mixture onto the brush (or into your hand). Starting at your feet, massage it into your skin using a circular motion. Rinse your body thoroughly with warm water. If you have dry skin, you may want to keep some of the oil residue on your skin, or you can wash it off thoroughly. ❖

MAKE IT YOURSELF
ALPHA HYDROXY ACID SKIN CARE

Straight from the shelves of the pantry, these ingredients are always at your fingertips. You'll want to use these skin smoothers whenever you pamper yourself.

ALPHA HYDROXY ACID BLEND
This AHA formula provides a toner with malic, tartaric, glycolic, and citric acids.

¼ cup lemon juice
¼ cup apple juice
¼ cup grape juice
¼ cup cane sugar

Combine all the ingredients in a jar, and stir to blend and dissolve the sugar. Use a cotton ball to dab the mixture onto your face, then massage into your skin. Let set for 10 minutes. Rinse and pat dry. Store in the refrigerator for up to 4 days. ❖

SUGAR SCRUB FROM THE VERMONT SOAPWORKS
One day, I was speaking with Larry Pleasant, CEO of The Vermont Soapworks. He mentioned that he and his staff had spent the morning testing homemade sugar scrubs and that everyone was commenting on how incredibly soft their skin felt. Aware that sugarcane produces glycolic acid, one of the natural alpha hydroxy acids that exfoliate the skin, I was immediately curious about his recipes.

Let me warn you in advance that you'll want to use this sugar scrub on your entire body. I used the scrub on my face and returned to my desk. I tried to settle down to work, but my face felt so baby soft that my neck felt like sandpaper in comparison, so I needed to use the sugar scrub there, and on and on. If you don't have vegetable glycerin available, you can successfully substitute avocado oil.

One part white cane sugar (note that organic sucanat, a whole foods sugar, doesn't work as well for this recipe)
One part vegetable glycerin (available in health food stores)
Small amounts of aloe vera gel or vitamin C crystals
1 or 2 drops of essential oil, if desired (Larry recommends combining orange and lavender oils)

Place the sugar in a bowl, then moisten it with the vegetable glycerin. Add the remaining ingredients and mix well. Scoop some of the scrub onto your hand and massage gently onto your skin for a minute (the scrub will actually tighten onto your skin like a mask). Leave on for 3 to 4 minutes before rinsing. ❖

Avoid using these homemade peels if your skin is sunburned or you plan to go into the sun. And always take care to avoid getting skin care products in your eyes.

Skin Brushing

Dry-brushing your whole body with a natural-bristle brush is one of the best ways of detoxifying; it stimulates the

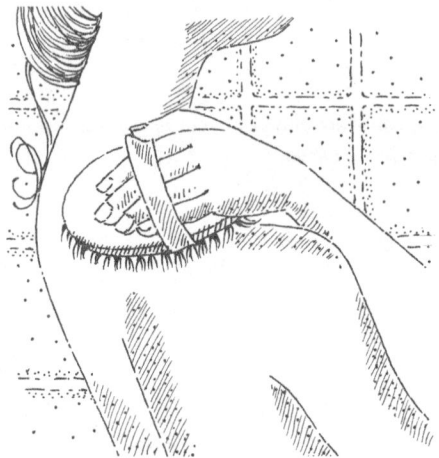

Exfoliating with a dry brush helps remove dead skin cells and stimulates the lymphatic system. Before showering or bathing, use a natural-bristle brush and long, sweeping motions to brush the skin on your arms and torso, moving up toward your heart. Then brush the soles of your feet and work up your legs to whisk away old cells.

To give yourself a natural dry-brush massage, stand in the bathtub or shower stall (to catch the dead skin cells), and starting with your fingers, move the brush in long, sweeping motions up your arms and around your torso, moving toward the center of your body at the end. Then, work up from your feet to your belly and lower back. Avoid brushing in areas where you have tender skin or a skin condition, such as varicose veins or psoriasis. After you've finished brushing, shower or bathe to cleanse the skin, then apply a soothing moisturizer.

lymphatic system, exfoliates dead skin cells, and aids circulation. Use a palm-size natural brush. You'll need a long bristle brush to reach the center of your back. Brush gently, or you may harm sensitive skin.

Aromatherapy Massage Oil

Use natural plant oils for massage—both for the base oil and for the scent. Massage therapists love coconut oil for massage because it melts on contact with the skin, leaves a protective barrier, has a slight lathering ability, and

MAKE IT YOURSELF
BASIC BODY BUTTER

You can make basic body butter with straight coconut oil (just scoop some into your hand) or by combining coconut oil and cocoa butter. Both are semisolid and can easily be blended. Cocoa butter is great for dehydrated and cracked skin.

½ cup coconut oil
¼ cup cocoa butter
Essential oil (optional)

Soften the coconut oil and cocoa butter in a double boiler over medium heat. Remove from the heat, adding a few drops of essential oil if desired. Stir to blend. ❖

An herbal steam facial opens pores, cleanses skin, and rejuvenates the spirit. Infuse the steam with therapeutic herbs, such as lavender, mint, and calendula. Drape a towel over your head, lean over the pot for about 5 minutes, and let the steam reach deep into your pores.

easily washes out of towels. Coconut oil is available in many natural food stores. You could also try vegetable or nut cooking oil. Test a few different kinds until you find one that feels great on your skin. Other oils may stain towels and are difficult to wash out, leaving towels with an odiferous scent after a while.

Mature, dry skin loves avocado oil. Grapeseed oil is less greasy and may be better for younger skin. Safflower oil is a good all-purpose solution. A variety of oils, such as organic unrefined oils from Spectrum Naturals, is available in health food stores.

Avoid mineral oil for massages and skin care because it is a refined petroleum product and provides no nutrients for the skin. Mineral oil is rated as a "suspected carcinogen" with the Department of Health and Human Services.

Steam Facials

Shut out the world for a while and breathe deeply with a relaxing and hydrating herbal steam facial. Steam opens the skin's pores while deeply cleansing and rejuvenating all the skin's layers. Using herbs in facial steams is a wonderful way to nourish your skin. All you need to make your own natural facial is a pot of water, a method of heating the

MAKE IT YOURSELF
ROSE WATER ASTRINGENT

Rose water is a wonderful toner and astringent. The scent of rose water is considered that of the higher self, and it's believed to help open one's heart to the divine.

A heaping handful of organic rose petals (dried or fresh)
1 quart of boiling water

Place the rose petals into a quart mason jar, and add boiling water to cover. Seal the jar and let it set overnight. Strain out the petals. Saturate a cotton pad with the rose water, and dab it on your face. Don't rinse unless it feels more comfortable for you to do so. Store the astringent in the refrigerator for about 6 weeks. Or, pour rose water into an ice cube tray and freeze. Just pop out the desired amount of rose water as needed. ❖

water, and a towel. Therapeutic herbs can be infused in the water so that their healing benefits will become part of the steam and reach deep into your pores.

Herbs have surprising effects on the skin. Many are emollient, softening and lubricating; others hydrate and moisturize; and most are antibacterial and anti-inflammatory. Licorice root is the number one herbal choice for steaming no matter what your skin type, because it helps open the pores, soothes, cleanses, and lubricates. Just break a piece of root into your steam pot. For dry skin, try lavender, mint, or calendula. For sensitive skin, try calendula, chamomile, or comfrey. And for oily skin, try mint, lavender, rose, or witch hazel.

A word of caution: If you have asthma or allergies to herbs, speak to your doctor before using these herbs in a steam facial. Chamomile, for example, is a member of the ragweed family.

Follow these simple directions to make your own facial steam.

1. Bring about 6 cups of water to a boil in a pot; add a handful of herbs, and simmer on low heat for up to 10 minutes. Add more water as needed.

2. Wash your face, and if you have long hair, pull it back with a hair band.

3. Remove the pot from the stove. Make a tent over your head with a towel, and lean your head over the pot of herbs. Lean into the pot only as close as is comfortable. Be cautious because steam is very hot. Steam your face for around 5 minutes.

4. Refresh your face with a washcloth dipped in cool water.

5. Close your skin's pores with an astringent, such as witch hazel, organic lemon juice, or organic apple cider vinegar.

If you are traveling, you can use the hot-towel method instead of steaming your face with herb-infused water. Saturate a towel with steaming hot water. Let it cool enough to safely touch the skin, and wrap your clean face with it. Leave it on for about 2 minutes.

Cleopatra's Milk Bath

The famed beauty Cleopatra unknowingly used the benefit of AHAs on her skin when she bathed in milk. Modern laboratories now know why milk worked such wonders for her skin: The lactic acid in milk is an alpha hydroxy acid, a natural material that helps slough off dead skin cells. Enjoy a luxurious bath by adding 2 to 4 cups of fresh milk or buttermilk to your bathwater, and soak for a good 20 minutes. You can substitute dried milk if you don't have fresh milk or buttermilk handy; just use 1 to 2 cups instead of 2 to 4 cups. *A note of caution:* Skip this bath if you are allergic to milk or are lactose intolerant.

Simple Moisturizer

One of the simplest ways to hydrate skin is found right on your windowsill. Aloe vera is a great moisturizer for skin. You can also find aloe vera gel at health food stores.

Some people are allergic to aloe vera, so test it carefully before slathering it all over your face. My skin just drinks it up, and I find it very healing and softening.

Caring for Teeth and Nails

Healthy teeth and gums are vitally important to our overall health. The bacterium that develops with periodontal disease is now viewed as a contributor to heart disease. Daily care of your teeth is really important, as is using products that ensure healthy teeth and gums but that don't add more synthetic chemicals to your body.

Shining white teeth are highly prized as a symbol of beauty in our culture, just like flashy nail polishes. You should know, though, that there could be a cost to your health from using many teeth whitening and nail products. The solvents used in both of those products can be toxic, and nail polish solvents are notorious for causing reproductive harm. Try these healthier recommendations to achieve the results you are looking for without the risk.

WORDS TO THE WISE

SYNTHETIC ALCOHOLS

Avoid personal care products that contain SD and CD alcohols because these chemicals are toxic. Look instead for alcohol-free products, or if alcohol is included, make sure it is a pure grain alcohol.

FLUORIDE AND MERCURY AMALGAM: THE PUBLIC DEBATE

The fluoridation of 60 percent of the municipal water supplies in the United States is awash in controversy. The American Dental Association claims the practice reduces cavities. The opposing viewpoints, from many European countries and many scientists, claim fluoridation—at even low levels—can be dangerous to health. Further, the fluoride added to drinking water supplies is generally derived from industrial waste silicofluorides, which are 85 times more toxic than naturally occurring calcium fluoride. Fluoride is considered more toxic than lead and almost as toxic as arsenic.

While the debate rages on, fluoride is also added to most toothpaste, many pediatricians give fluoride drops, and most dentists give children fluoride treatments. The accumulative amount of fluoride could be very high for any one child.

Until the debate resolves itself in the public forum, what are you to do? For my daughter, I followed the Precautionary Principle and a commonsense approach—I made sure her fluoride intake was low to moderate.

Another area of controversy surrounds mercury amalgams. Should you or should you not have mercury amalgam fillings removed, and should you reject them in the doctor's office? It is hard to find an answer. It's possible that removing the fillings could expose you to more mercury than would occur if you simply left the fillings intact. If you are having any health problems, especially health issues that affect your central nervous system, you might want to get some expert medical advice on the subject. One caution is to have mercury removed only by a dentist experienced with the procedure because it is very important that the amalgams are removed without releasing any more mercury into your system. Another caution is that you want to make sure that the substitute amalgam does not leach endocrine disrupters from the plasticizers.

Teeth

The most commonsense approach to caring for your teeth and gums is to eat a nutritious diet. Fruits, vegetables, herbal teas, and seaweeds are rich in vitamins and minerals. Calcium is especially important for healthy teeth and gums. Foods rich in calcium include dairy products, legumes, and greens.

Daily Care

Make sure to read the labels on any toothpaste you use. When you're brushing, you'll likely swallow some toothpaste and absorb some through your skin. I was shocked to read mainstream commercial toothpaste labels recently, something I hadn't done in many years because I buy health food store brands such as Tom's of Maine or Nature's Gate. The supermarket brands contained FD&C dyes, suspected of being neurotoxic and contributing to some symptoms of Attention Deficit Disorder, and the artificial sweetener aspartame. I would not recommend that anyone, especially children, ingest these ingredients on a daily basis. Natural brands use calorie-free herbs such as stevia for sweetening and natural flavorings, and some of the flavoring tastes great (I especially like the cinnamon-flavored toothpastes).

Cleaning Your Toothbrushes

The easiest way to clear germs from your toothbrush is to let it sit for 24 hours after the toothbrush has dried out. Why not have three toothbrushes that rotate for each member of the family? You could have a series of cups on a shelf in a bathroom cabinet labeled "Day 1, Day 2, Day 3." Every 2 weeks, soak toothbrushes overnight in straight household vinegar. Vinegar kills most germs, molds, and bacteria. Rinse brushes well.

Brushing Aftercare

Finish your oral care routine with a good mouthwash—one with antibacterial essential oils such as tea tree. A brand my dentist recommends is "The Natural Dentist." Tom's of Maine also offers a range of natural mouthwashes. Avoid mouthwash containing synthetic alcohols.

Teeth Whitening

Make a tooth-whitening paste of baking soda and 3 percent hydrogen peroxide. Dab some of the mixture on your toothbrush and brush your teeth to whiten them. Rinse well.

Nails

Nails can be beautiful without polish. Find a salon that can beautify your nails naturally, without polish.

The Natural Manicure

Do you want a real and healthy nail-beautifying manicure? Here's how it's

---

IS NAIL POLISH WORTH IT?

The fumes from the solvents in nail polish can be overwhelming and potentially harmful to the nail polish user and those in close proximity. There are no environmentally safe nail polishes on the market. Most nail polishes still contain toluene (toxic), formaldehyde (a known carcinogen), and dibutyl phthalate (DBP), a hormone disrupter.

While there are some nail polishes labeled toluene- and formaldehyde-free, there are none without petroleum solvents of some sort. Petroleum solvents are long lasting in the environment, and they are stored in body fat and passed on in breast milk. For more about DBP and for a list of DBP-free nail polishes, read the Environmental Working Group's report at www.ewg.org.

Even with knowledge about the toxicity of nail polish, many ladies will choose to use it anyway. If you can't live without it, just make sure to put it on outside and not on airplanes, trains, or other places where people around you, especially children, are unable to avoid the fumes. Always avoid applying nail polish in rooms without adequate ventilation.

done (adapted from my book *Better Basics for the Home*).

File, wash, and soak nails first: File in one direction only, and always file when your nails are dry. Wash your hands, and then soak them in warm water or a fruit acid solution (such as buttermilk or organic apple cider vinegar). Then soften, clean, and shape cuticles by applying a cold-pressed fruit or nut oil into the cuticle area near the half-moon at the base of the nail. Use the blunt end of an orangewood manicure stick to gently push the cuticles back from the nails.

Dry your hands completely. Sand and polish the top of each nail with a fine pumice-stone sand stick to remove any ridges. Do the same thing with a fine-grit block. Once the ridges are removed, smooth the top of the nail with a smoothing file and then a buffing chamois. You'll be amazed at how shiny your nails will look following these steps—almost as if you were wearing a clear polish. You can achieve a more natural, less-shiny, matte finish on your nails by using a larger-grit buffing file.

Massage your hands and nails with a moisturizing cream or lotion.

Healthy Hair

As with skin, teeth, and nails, the key to healthy hair is a nutritious diet. Hair in particular needs omega-3 oils from the diet as well as many minerals and vitamins. See my book *Better Basics for the Home* for a few dozen hair care formulas, covering everything from hair spray to acid rinse to natural dyes.

In general, use as few hair products as possible (even if you are a teenager), and make the extra effort to buy those products that are naturally scented, unscented, or scent free; there's actually a wide range of hair care products with natural scents. Remember that almost all of the formulas for hair care products are based on natural materials, even if the modern manufacturer may make it with synthetic chemicals, so it is likely that you'll find a natural alternative with some extra effort. Or, just make do. One woman I went to for a haircut wanted to use a hair wax on my hair and knew she couldn't because it was scented with chemicals. She ran to her kitchen (the salon was in her home) and came back with Crisco! It worked perfectly.

How should you choose a shampoo? Your choice is either a soap shampoo or a detergent shampoo. Most shampoos contain sodium lauryl sulfate, a synthetic chemical and pesticide. Soap and detergent shampoos are not the same, and each has advantages and disadvantages for your hair. A soap shampoo is the purest choice (next to using herbal shampoos or naturally soapy herbs, such as soap bark). However, if you have hard water, soap can cause soap scum, which will dull your hair. Soap-based shampoos will not remove all of the scalp's natural oils, and you'll need to wash your hair more frequently.

Detergent shampoos leave hair shiny. They clean oils from the scalp fully, but they can also dry out hair. Even in hard water situations, they will not leave "soap" scum on your hair. While I believe that washing your hair without a detergent is the best for your health, it isn't an easy choice to use herbal shampoos or soap shampoos because you'll need to work harder to keep your hair looking and feeling clean.

Health food stores increasingly carry brands of shampoos that use herbs and coconut oil soaps as a base. Kiss My Face, Aubrey Organics, Logona, and Real Purity are some of the brands you should try.

Hair Dyes

The purest dyes available are those made exclusively of plants and vegetables. These dyes make beautiful colors that look more natural than any commercial dye I have seen or used. The Logona brand is one line, as is Herbaltint. Both are available in health food stores and online. The drawback, of course, is having the time and patience to dye your own hair. Aveda is a salon that offers dyes with the fewest chemical additives, but the dyes themselves are not all natural.

If you use permanent hair dyes at least once a month, you should know

SODIUM LAURYL SULFATE–BASED SHAMPOOS

"If my shampoo contains sodium lauryl sulfate, am I lathering carcinogens into my scalp every time I wash my hair?" is one of the questions I am most frequently asked. Sodium lauryl sulfate is the detergent most frequently used in shampoos (and in toothpaste).

Sodium lauryl sulfate is a synthetic chemical used in consumer products that is produced in large quantities and is regulated as a pesticide. A suspected gastrointestinal or liver toxicant, sodium lauryl sulfate can be drying and harsh for the hair and may cause eye irritation, allergic reactions, and hair loss.

Sodium lauryl sulfate is not a recognized carcinogen. However, the chemical is frequently combined with TEA (triethanolamine), DEA (diethanolamine), or MEA (monoethanolamine), which can cause the formation of the carcinogenic substances nitrosamines. To be on the safe side, add antioxidant vitamins A and C to any product that contains TEA, DEA, or MEA. To help protect against nitrosamine contamination, add 1 teaspoon of vitamin C powder and ¼ teaspoon of vitamin A powder for each 8 ounces of shampoo.

about a 2001 study from researchers at the University of Southern California that analyzed the association between hair-dyeing activity and bladder cancer. The researchers note that the exposure of concern is to a family of chemicals called arylamines, an ingredient in many oxidative (permanent) hair dyes, which is a known risk factor for bladder cancer and has been found to cause cancer in experimental animals. The study found no association between semipermanent or temporary hair dyes and bladder cancer.

While the study was not a clinical cancer trial, it did make a determination of those who are at highest risk from use of permanent hair dyes.

❖ Women who have used permanent hair dyes once a month for 1 year or longer have twice the risk of bladder cancer over those who don't use dyes at all.

❖ Women who have used permanent hair dyes for 15 or more years monthly (or more frequently) have three times more risk of bladder cancer than those who do not use dye.

❖ Those who have worked as hairdressers or barbers for 10 years or more have five times the risk of bladder cancer.

Note: The United States does not require cosmetics manufacturers to file data on ingredients or report cosmetic-related injuries.

Head Lice

A woman wrote to me that a bad case of head lice inspired her to go to all sorts of toxic and nontoxic extremes to eliminate the pests. The methods she used included hormone-disrupting pesticides, gasoline, kerosene, all over-the-counter measures, olive oil, baby oil, mayonnaise, tea tree oil, pesticide bombing the home, and shaving the head and body, along with the usual recommended environmental controls. She said that most of these worked— for a while. She asked, "Do you have a solution that is not suicide?"

While this reader had been successfully killing the lice, she had been missing their eggs. The following is a successful way to rid the body of lice *and* their eggs without poisoning yourself with dangerous pesticides and hydrocarbons.

1. Buy a bar of pure olive-oil soap. Lather hair with the soap. Add a few drops of tea tree oil (and a few drops of neem oil if you have some) to the lathered hair. (Health food stores sell olive-oil soap and tea tree oil, and some carry neem. Pure neem oil is also available on the Internet.)
2. Rinse. Rewash hair with this same mixture, and do not rinse.
3. Wrap a towel around the head and wait for half an hour.
4. Comb with a nit-removing comb.

Comb all the hair, strand by strand, until all nits are removed (this takes a while).

5. Wash the hair with the olive-oil soap and rinse. Once hair is dry, check thoroughly for any missed nits. Thoroughly wash your hands.

6. To sanitize the comb, soak it in straight white vinegar. Pillows and linens can be placed in the freezer overnight. If you have a really bad infestation, spray the mattress with a mixture of 2 teaspoons of tea tree oil to 2 cups of water, and let it dry on the mattress (the smell will dissipate after a few days).

7. You can comb a lice-repellent essential oil through the hair as a preventive measure; the best choices of repellent essential oils are tea tree, neem, rosemary, lavender, eucalyptus, and rose geranium. Just add 10 drops of essential oil to 1 ounce of oil (olive oil is best, but any vegetable oil will do). Comb through the hair. Or make a tea tree oil shampoo by adding 10 drops of tea tree oil to 1 ounce of shampoo.

While it's unpleasant to discover head lice, it is important not to panic. The methods outlined above for getting rid of head lice are tried-and-true and effective! You do not need a toxic pesticide.

Cleaning the Bathroom

Studies show that the biggest source of germs in the bathroom is actually the wet drain in the sink. The Centers for Disease Control notes that sanitizing bathrooms with antibacterial cleansers won't keep you healthier and that even hospital surfaces contaminated with germs don't always cause illness. The important thing is to keep surfaces clean and dry.

Arizona researchers note that the least contaminated place in a bathroom is the toilet seat, and the most contaminated is the sink drain, according to Nicholas Bakalar, author of *Where the Germs Are*. With an 80 to 99 percent kill rate for viruses and bacteria, pouring a cup or two of straight 5 percent vinegar down your drains once or twice a week to kill germs is a good preventive measure. Or you can keep a spray bottle filled with straight 5 percent vinegar to use when needed. The smell of vinegar dissipates within a few hours.

Just like the overuse of antibiotics, common disinfectants found in household disinfectant sprays, sponges, and soaps may contribute to the creation of drug-resistant bacteria, according to researchers at Tufts New England Medical Center. Stuart Levy, MD, of the Tufts research group, notes that disinfectants aren't much different than over-the-counter antibiotics. The problem is that when a chemical kills off bacteria,

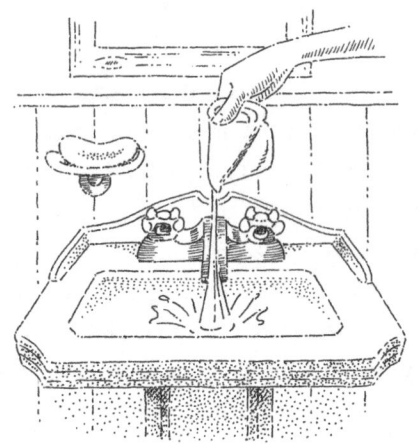

There's no need to resort to caustic measures just to clean your bathroom sink. Just turn to ordinary household vinegar—right in your kitchen cupboard. Straight 5 percent vinegar is an effective cleaner for sink drains; just pour a cupful down the drain every week to fight germs.

the bacteria grows a resistant strain that is harder to kill. This is why stronger and stronger antibiotics are needed for bacterial infections. A mirror problem is developing in the war against bacteria in the air and in the environment; stronger and stronger chemicals are needed to kill them because they are becoming resistant to the existing chemicals. The chemicals are actually making things worse. Interestingly, antibacterial essential oils do not seem to cause drug resistance.

Research at the Government Accounting Office shows that many commercial disinfectants are ineffective. Soap and water are all you need to kill germs. Many European countries have issued warning statements about products containing triclosan, a prevalent disinfectant found in household products such as sponges, hand soap, toothpaste, and disinfectants (see "Household Products and Triclosan" on page 189). According to information published by Beyond Pesticides, a study found that more than 75 percent of liquid soaps and nearly 30 percent of bar soaps contained some type of antibacterial agent such as triclosan.

The old folk recipes using herbs and essential oils to kill germs, such as those used by 14th-century doctors during the Black Plague, were based on good science. Many essential oils, like lavender and thyme, are more antiseptic than phenol, the industry's standard germ-killing ingredient.

Cleaning Tile, Tubs, and Sinks

Nonabrasive cleaners with a neutral pH, such as Homemade Soft Scrubber (see page 248), straight vinegar, and 12 percent hydrogen peroxide, are best for tiles. Avoid using soap for cleaning tiles because it can react with water and form a soap-scum film. Don't clean tiles with ammonia, either, because its high alkalinity can discolor the glaze. Try to avoid installing tiles that require sealants, and if you must use a sealant, use one that is acrylic or water-based.

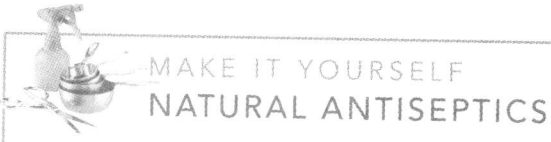

NATURAL ANTISEPTICS

Bathrooms aren't nearly as germy as you might think, but most of us still desire a bathroom that looks and smells clean. These two sprays help disinfect bathroom surfaces with just a squeeze of a bottle.

ANTISEPTIC BATHROOM SPRAY

This great antiseptic takes 6 weeks to set, but it is well worth the effort. The essential oil–based spray creates a lovely, clean scent and is great for misting areas of concern in your bathroom. It's especially effective on damp bathroom floors; just spray on the floor, wait 10 to 15 minutes, and rinse.

> Handful each of dried lavender, rosemary, sage, rue, and mint
> Large glass jar
> ½ gallon of organic apple cider vinegar

Place the herbs in the jar, and cover completely with ½ gallon of organic apple cider vinegar. Cover tightly, and let set for 6 weeks. Strain into a spray bottle. Label the bottle, and store indefinitely. ❖

LOVELY LAVENDER ANTIBACTERIAL SPRAY

You can substitute other essential oils for the lavender—cinnamon, clove, eucalyptus, orange, rosemary, and thyme are all disinfectant, antibacterial, and antifungal.

> 1 cup water
> 1 teaspoon pure essential oil of lavender

Pour the water into a spray bottle. Add the lavender essential oil and shake to blend. Spray on the surface to be disinfected, and let set for at least 15 minutes before rinsing, or don't rinse at all. Label the bottle and store indefinitely. ❖

With my easy-to-mix soft scrubber, there is no reason to use a scouring powder, but if you so choose, straight baking soda will work well! For really heavy-duty scrubbing jobs, try a bit of washing soda; this will take a lot of rinsing, and you must wear gloves because it is very alkaline.

The harder your water is, the more scale (mineral buildup) you may have. Scale often appears around faucets and shower stalls; it looks like soap scum or dried white minerals. It is very alkaline and can usually be removed easily with an acid, such as vinegar or lemon juice. For scale that's difficult to remove, soak a

CLEAR VIEW BATHROOM CLEANERS

It's easy to keep the shine in the bathroom with these cleaning recipes. All of them can be mixed up quickly with ingredients and supplies you keep in your bathroom vanity or linen closet.

HOMEMADE SOFT SCRUBBER

This creamy-like-frosting soft scrubber is my favorite homemade recipe of all time; it's such an important part of my cleaning repertoire that I've also included it in the kitchen chapter. It's taken from my first book, Clean and Green, and it's the best solution for cleaning the bathtub without synthetic fragrances and toxic chemicals. It also works well for vanity tops and shower stalls. The softly abrasive quality of the baking soda provides the grit to scrub off dirt and soap scum, yet the recipe rinses off very easily.

½ cup baking soda
Liquid soap or detergent
5–10 drops pure antiseptic essential oil such as lavender, tea tree oil, or rosemary (optional)

Cleaning bathtub tiles and shower stalls isn't a chore when you use a safe, homemade recipe that gets the job done. My creamy soft scrubber recipe takes only a minute to mix and easily cuts through soap residue.

Place the baking soda in a bowl. Slowly pour in liquid soap, stirring constantly; add liquid soap until the consistency resembles frosting. Add the essential oil, if desired. Scoop the creamy mixture onto a sponge, scrub the surface, and then rinse.

Note: If you have hard water (water with a high mineral content), choose a liquid detergent instead of a liquid soap. Most health food stores offer all-purpose liquid detergents and soaps without synthetic perfumes; sometimes the detergents and soaps are formulated with all plant-based materials. These green products are great choices because they include no synthetic perfumes and dyes, and they tend to be the most concentrated. If you are lucky enough to have soft water and can use a liquid castile soap in your soft scrubber, consider one in which peppermint has been added for extra antibacterial action. ❖

MIRROR FOG PREVENTER

Wouldn't it be nice if the mirror didn't fog up during a bath or shower? Try this effective formula for preventing fog on medicine cabinet mirrors.

washcloth in vinegar and lay it on the area overnight. Scrub off the scale in the morning. Otherwise, spray straight vinegar or fresh lemon juice right on the buildup, let it set for 5 to 10 minutes, and rinse.

Keeping faucets and fixtures clean doesn't require harsh and dangerous chemicals. If you discover mineral buildup from hard water clogging the shower nozzle, spray the holes with straight

½ teaspoon vegetable glycerin (available in health food stores)
¼ cup water
Clean cotton cloth

Combine the glycerin and water in a bowl, dab some onto a clean cotton cloth, and rub the solution onto the mirror before taking a shower or bath. ❖

MIRROR AND WINDOW CLEANER
Be sure to use a clean, pure cotton cloth to avoid getting lint on the glass. Synthetic fiber cloths will leave streaks on mirrors and glass and just don't hold water as well as cotton does.

¼ teaspoon all-purpose liquid detergent (such as Life Tree's Home Soap)
1 cup water
Lint-free, clean cotton cloth

Combine the detergent and water in a spray bottle, and shake to blend. Spray onto the mirror or window, and wipe off with a clean cotton cloth. Store labeled bottle indefinitely. ❖

TUB AND TILE CLEANER
Easy, economical, and environmentally friendly! This cleaner is terrific for weekly tub and tile maintenance.

½ cup vinegar
½ teaspoon all-purpose liquid detergent (such as Ecover's Home Soap)
2 cups very hot tap water

Combine the ingredients in a spray bottle. Shake well. Spray the mixture onto tiles and rinse with a sponge. Store the labeled bottle indefinitely. ❖

MILDEW CLEANER
Tea tree oil is the essential oil typically used to remove mildew because it is a broad-spectrum fungicide.

1 teaspoon tea tree oil
2 cups water

Combine the ingredients in a spray bottle, and spray onto the mildew. Don't rinse. The strong smell will dissipate in a day or two. Store the labeled bottle indefinitely. ❖

vinegar and don't rinse. For tough buildup, remove the nozzle or showerhead and soak it in straight vinegar. Use an old toothbrush to brush away the deposits.

Natural acids also clean faucets and fixtures nicely. Put white distilled vinegar in a spray bottle, and spray onto fixtures. Wipe down the fixtures with a clean cloth.

Cleaning the Toilet

One of the worst jobs in the house, right? It doesn't have to be. I've been cleaning our toilets this way for years, and it requires so little effort. This is my super-easy 3-step routine for getting toilets clean.

1. Pour about 1 cup of borax into the toilet and let it sit there for a few hours.
2. Using a toilet brush, scrub inside the bowl and flush.
3. Spray straight household vinegar (5 percent) onto the toilet rim, seat, and top. Scrub the rim with the toilet brush, and wipe the seat and top. Spray the toilet rim again with vinegar, and don't rinse.

Every once in a while, I will spray the toilet rim with an antibacterial essential oil, such as rosemary. Besides rosemary, you can also try tea tree oil, lavender, or other oils whose scent is pleasing to you. Just make sure the oils are pure.

Safe Pool and Spa Cleaning

For pool and spa owners, the struggle to maintain clean, clear, healthy water can be a frustrating and potentially dangerous enterprise. The myriad of strong acids, bases, chlorines, and bromines required pose potentially serious environmental and health consequences. In addition to the obvious chemical hazards associated with mixing acids and bases in water, Belgian scientists recently linked airborne chlorine by-products (trichloramine) to the dramatic surge in childhood asthma.

Ceramic Tile in the Bath

Tile is the material of choice to surround showers and baths because it is fully resistant to water damage. Tiles are also timeless solar energy collectors, and they retain and radiate heat. They are available in almost every color, design, and shape you could hope for. Because they're inert, they don't contribute to indoor air pollution, although the grouts used to install tile can contain harmful chemicals.

I love working with tile because it is a great do-it-yourself creative project that the whole family can enjoy. You can tile bathroom walls, floors, and most surfaces as well as make everything from tile hot plates to entire cooking islands with tiles.

In case you don't have experience with tile, there are several types of tiles from which to choose.

Unglazed: Available in terra cotta and many earth-toned colors, this type

HEALTHY HOMEMADE GROUT

Try this age-old tiling technique. It is easy to do, can be a really fun family project, looks beautiful, and doesn't leave a noxious odor. The additives in commercial, ready-made tile settings include quick-drying materials, petroleum, epoxy, and fungicides and can outgas for years. With this old-fashioned technique, tiles can be attached to bathtub frames, stovetops, and around sinks by setting them into a mudset, followed by a grout to fill in the gaps between the tiles. Natural iron oxide pigments are available and can be added to match tile color. Be sure to have your layout, color placement, and patterns figured out and your underboards and surfaces prepped before mixing the mudset.

MAKE A MUDSET
(50 pounds covers about 75 square feet)

> 3 parts sand
> 1 part Portland cement
> Water
> Natural earth pigment (optional)

Combine the sand and Portland cement in a plastic tub or large, clean container. Slowly add water, stirring as you go, until the texture is like thick sludge. (Garden tools make great mixers.) Add the pigment bit by bit until the desired color is achieved. Lay the mudset on the surface to be tiled, then lay tile as desired. ❖

MAKE A GROUT
Grout is the cementlike material between tiles. The ratio of Portland cement to sand ranges between 1:1 and 1:3, depending on how much space there is between tiles. If you have wider gaps, use more sand.

> Portland cement
> Sand
> Water
> Natural earth pigment

Combine the Portland cement and sand in a plastic tub or large, clean container. Slowly add water, stirring as you go, until the texture is like thick sludge. (Again, garden tools make great mixers.) Add the pigment bit by bit until the desired color is achieved. Use a grout sponge to wipe and press the grout between tiles. ❖

DAMP-CURE THE GROUT
Damp cure means simply to dampen grout to keep it from drying out too quickly and crumbling. It is so easy to do, and it enables you to avoid chemical dryers. I like to damp-cure tile by wetting my fingers and rubbing them up and down the grooves. Do this whenever you think of it over a period of about 10 days after you lay the tile. For large areas, use a spray bottle to dampen the grout. ❖

of tile has no glaze or coating. Unglazed tiles are very durable and resist dirt and traffic scuffs.

Glazed: Available in any home store, glazed tiles have a liquid glass applied to their surface. When they're fired, tiles become hard and nonporous; they're also stain- and fire-resistant, easy to clean, and don't fade in the sunlight. Shiny glazes are more easily scratched than matte glazes. Glazed tiles can be slippery but are easier to keep clean than unglazed tiles. Matte or semi-glass glazes are more slip-resistant.

Porcelain: These tiles are the most stain-resistant of all tiles.

Recycled-Content Ceramic: Made of 100 percent waste glass, these tiles are very durable and are moisture- and stain-resistant.

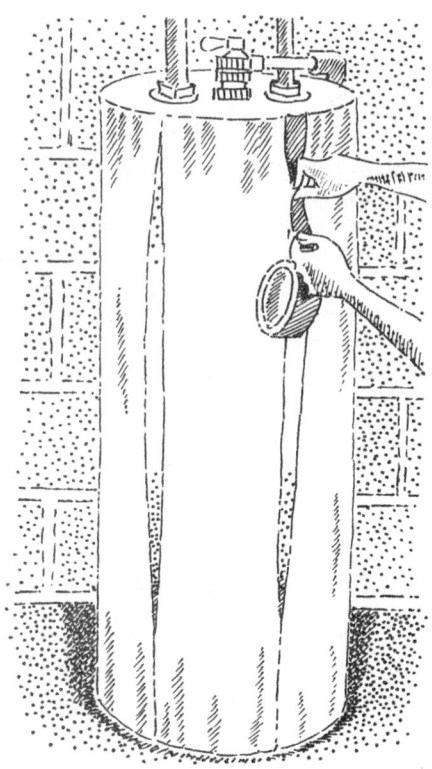

It takes only a small amount of effort to save on energy costs. Wrap your water heater with a heat-saving blanket to help keep heated water hot longer.

Conservation in the Bathroom

You may not think of a bathroom as a place to focus your conservation efforts, but you can reduce your consumption of electricity and water by making small changes. Turn off lights when not in use, and replace incandescent lightbulbs with fluorescents when you buy new bulbs. They'll last longer and save energy.

Lower the temperature of your water heater to 120°F; that's still plenty hot if you enjoy a toasty shower. Wrap the water heater with a water heater blanket, especially if it's in an unheated area. Wrap the tank and pipes for additional savings.

You'll save about 3 percent of your heating costs for every degree that you lower your thermostat during winter. During summer, you'll cut cooling costs 3 to 4 percent for every degree you raise your thermostat. How about opening a window instead of turning on a fan?

Skipping the electric hair dryer and air-drying your hair may mean a small energy savings, but think of the collective savings if everyone air-dried their hair each morning! Save water by turning off the faucet when it isn't in use, such as the minutes between wetting your toothbrush and rinsing after brushing.

Does your showerhead need to be replaced with a low-flow model to save water? Here's a quick test: Note the 1-gallon mark on the inside of a bucket. Turn on the shower, and hold the bucket under the water. Using a watch with a second hand, time how long it takes the bucket to fill to the 1-gallon mark (or 3.8 liters). If it takes less than 20 seconds to fill to the 1-gallon mark, you could save a lot of water and water-heating expense with a low-flow showerhead. Low-flow showerheads can reduce water consumption by 30 percent, yet still provide a pressurized spray.

A less-expensive solution for saving hot water is simply repairing leaks in faucets and showers. A leak of one drip per second can cost $1 per month, yet it could be repaired in a few minutes for much less than that.

Being mindful of your water use is really the first step in water conservation. Reduce water consumption by paying attention to how you use water and implementing ways to use less. In thinking through my own water use, I realized that my habit of leaving the water running when I brushed my teeth was hard to break, so I wrote a sign for myself and put it on the mirror. It took just a month or so before my habit was changed, and I could take the sign down!

Faucet Aerators

If you replace the bathroom faucet aerator with a 1-gallon-per-minute version, and the kitchen faucet aerator with a 1.5-gallons-per-minute aerator, you can probably reduce your water consumption by half, and you'll have plenty of water pressure to manage all of your tasks comfortably. You may need to have different water flow rates for bathroom

SHOPPING SOLUTIONS
AVOIDING WATER DAMAGE

In America, water damage due to faulty plumbing is the second largest expense for insurance companies. Broken washing machine hoses cost an average of $150 million each year, while frozen water pipes average more than $450 million each year. A recent item on the market is an automatic shut-off valve that monitors water flow into the house 24 hours a day. Allowing two different settings, either "Home" or "Away," the system automatically shuts off the water if it has been running continuously for a given period of time (30 minutes when "Home" and 30 seconds when "Away," for example). These are expensive (around $500), but well worth the investment. (See www.flologic.com for details.)

and kitchen faucets due to varying uses in each location. For bathroom faucets, aerators that deliver 0.5 to 1 gallon (1.9 to 3.8 liters) of water per minute may be sufficient. Kitchen faucets may require a higher flow rate of 2 to 4 gallons (7.6 to 15.1 liters) per minute if you regularly fill the sink for washing dishes. On the other hand, if you tend to let the water run when washing dishes, the lower flow rate of 0.5 to 1 gallon per minute may be more appropriate. Some aerators come with shut-off valves that allow you to stop the flow of water without affecting the temperature.

Low-Flow and Composting Toilets

Toilets manufactured before 1994 in the United States use between 5 and 7 gallons of water for every flush. Since then, federal law has mandated that the amount of water used per flush be restricted to 1.6 gallons. The first toilets made during that era received many complaints and took a few flushes to work. Since then, low-flow toilets have improved considerably, and replacing old-fashioned toilets with the low-flow variety makes great sense for the environment. Even with a low-flow toilet that uses 1.6 gallons of water per flush, the amount of water used by the average family really adds up over a day.

Composting toilets don't use any water, and the natural bacteria and fungi break down human waste, toilet paper, and even food wastes. Many systems require the addition of peat moss to aid the process. A composting toilet breaks down the wastes into "humus," which, like organic compost, doesn't smell if it is fully decomposed. Some composting toilets are single toilets, and you remove the humus from the bottom. Other systems require two separate toilets—the one that is composting is not used while household members use and fill the second one.

There are a number of advantages of composting toilets, besides their substantial environmental benefits of saving water and protecting ecosystems. Composting toilets are also the most hygienic if used properly, because when human waste is composted, all the viruses, bacteria, and toxins are destroyed by the natural bacteria that make compost. Composting toilets also don't require water, and in many states, installing a composting toilet eases the requirements for leach-field size. The downside is that the maintenance of these toilets is paramount to their success. If not properly maintained, odor problems can be very unpleasant, as would be removing the "humus" that hasn't fully composted. Another disadvantage is that most states require that the humus either be buried or hauled away by a licensed septic hauler! Almost all brands of composting toilets

SHOPPING SOLUTIONS
GOING GREEN

Green product companies such as Seventh Generation, NatraCare, and Organic Essentials offer a number of unbleached paper and sanitary products. Natural fiber towels and accessories are found at Linens and Things, Bed, Bath, and Beyond, Gaiam.com, Harmony catalog, and more.

The spa industry is really taking on the "green" concept, and this influence is making the products that are available for the bathroom increasingly compelling, spiritually uplifting, natural, and, in fact, fun. Try out some of the new "loofahs" made with sustainably harvested fibers, for example, or the natural fiber neck rests for your bath.

require a small amount of electricity, and the toilets need to be kept warm in the winter.

It isn't everybody that will be adventurous enough to consider a composting toilet, but it might be a social trend in another decade, and we might feel more comfortable with the idea in a few years. In the meantime, homeowners can replace their toilets with low-flow models. They aren't very expensive, and the benefits are well worth the investment.

Earth Conservation

Avoid buying disposable products. You can buy toothbrushes with replaceable heads and metal razors with disposable blades instead of disposable plastic razors. When you buy paper products, buy only those that aren't bleached with chlorine. Chlorine-bleached paper can contain dioxin and organochlorines—carcinogenic residues that can transfer to any food or person they come in contact with. Choose instead unbleached bathroom and facial tissue and tampons and sanitary products for the bathroom as well as unbleached paper towels, coffee filters, and napkins for the kitchen. Many health food stores and progressive grocery stores sell bathroom tissue and other paper products that have been recycled from postconsumer waste without the use of chlorine.

8

the bedroom

There is little in life as rejuvenating as a deep, peaceful night's sleep followed by waking up to fresh, clean air. I've had a few mornings recently when I awoke feeling as though I had spent the night sunken deep down in the furthest reaches of my most healing subconscious. After percolating to awareness, I felt renewed and 10 years younger.

In order to have this sort of sleep, you need to ensure that there is nothing in the bedroom to jar your senses. You should drift off to sleep without effort at night, sleep without interruption if you so choose, and on awakening, you can doze in tranquility for a while before fully coming awake (assuming a blessed reprieve from the alarm clock).

You can foster sleep like this, too—soothing, tranquil, and restorative—by making careful decisions about bedroom furnishings, building materials, and cleaning habits. Because we release poisons in our sleep (we perspire an average of 1 pint of moisture a night when we sleep), a nontoxic bedroom supports the body's natural work. I relish every minute of sleep I have in my bedroom sanctuary. You, too, can establish this regenerative environment by following a few basic steps.

Design a Blissful Bedroom

After reading a snippet about feng shui in a teen magazine, my daughter entered her bedroom with the dictum she had read in mind: Keep only what you love.

She systematically removed everything she didn't love! The result is a gem of a room—all her own and perfect in every way for her unique self.

Ask yourself: What do you love? What do you want to keep in your bedroom? What brings you a sense of calm? Which fabrics feel good to you? How do you want to decorate?

Including earth's elements in the bedroom environment enhances the space considerably. Do you like to sleep with fresh air? There is a joke in my family that my mother can't sleep unless she has a gale-force wind blowing through her bedroom. She could never sleep with closed windows. For many of us, stuffy rooms don't feel as good as rooms full of fresh air, so provide as much fresh air as you can and as the weather permits.

The earth element in the bedroom is a key component of restful sleep. I like having all natural bedding that comes from the land and not from a factory, and I want my bed to rest on a wooden floor. It makes me feel like I am grounded when I sleep. The emotional watery element of dreams and intuition has a place in the bedroom too, and dream journals help to foster a connection to this world. And fire, of course, represents passion, light, and heat. Be sure to have all four elements included in your bedroom for the most peaceful rest and restorative sleep.

Pleasing the Senses

The general premise of the bedroom is that you want as little in it as possible, and you want what you have there to be natural and clean. Renovate or paint only when you can have the windows open for enough time to fully air out the room from paint and chemical smells, and sleep elsewhere in the meantime. You'll spend one-third of your life in your bedroom, so focus your attention on making the room pleasurable.

Smell: What you *smell* when you sleep really matters. It makes the difference between rest and restlessness. Most synthetic chemicals intrude on your sleep by stimulating the central nervous system, often interrupting your rest with tension and agitation. It's better to have a tranquil sleep with soothing smells, such as fresh air from an open window or pure air from a clean, simply furnished room accented with natural materials.

Smells to avoid in the bedroom can include synthetic mattresses; carpet, paint, or stain; cleaning products such as furniture polish; clothes that have been dry-cleaned; moth balls; and anything else with a strong smell. Synthetic smells from mattresses can be subtle, but they can have a powerful impact with their blend of fire retardants, stain-resistant solvents, and pesticides.

Dry-cleaned clothes can be a serious

hazard in the bedroom. The cleaning solvents used can waft through your bedroom, exposing you to powerful neurotoxins while you sleep. My advice is to purchase natural-fiber clothing that doesn't require dry-cleaning, of course. That may not always be possible though, so switch to having your clothes wet cleaned, or hang the newly dry-cleaned clothes outside for a few days before bringing them into a bedroom closet. If you'd like to be especially vigilant, never bring dry-cleaned clothes into a bedroom; hang them, instead, in a closet far away from the sleeping areas. I personally never dry-clean anything; the solvents are terrible for the earth, for those who work in dry-cleaning establishments, and for humans and pets.

Even the natural materials in your bedroom are best if they are as inert as possible. For example, fresh pine has a smell that could interfere with restful sleep, as can a houseplant if the soil is a bit mildewed or waterlogged. Smells that interfere with a relaxing sleep may seem so commonplace that you may

not think about them, like the fragrance from a perfume bottle or the scented detergent that lingers on your sheets. It's best to wash laundry with an unscented detergent. The less you smell when you sleep, the better.

Some smells in the bedroom don't originate there. For example, fumes in the air may be a result of pesticides used elsewhere or may mean your oil burner needs tuning. Take the appropriate steps to avoid or clear away sources of pollution.

Sound: Natural noises are welcome to many of us. Going to sleep in August with the racket of crickets or waking up at dawn to the call of a wood thrush is something that's comforting to me, but it may bother you. The bird song before dawn in the summer in New York's Hudson Valley is enough to wake the dead, and many complain about it. One family I know has fans in each room so the entire family can drown out nature. "It sounds like a jet engine going through the house," the father of four noted to me. Each to their own choices! Even fans whirling or sirens and traffic

Safe and Sound
ELECTRONIC AIR CLEANERS
An electronic air filter can be helpful for serious air-quality problems. (Keep it far from the bed because of electronic smog.) Having a salt ion generator in the bedroom makes good sense to bring the positive/negative ion ratio in the air into a healthy and replenishing balance. Salt ion generators will also balance the electrostatic charges resulting from synthetic surfaces in the room.

in New York City can be harmonious if it is what you like and are used to.

I feel that you should turn off technological noise (white noise) when you go to sleep. White noise is any random noise that contains an equal amount of energy per frequency band and is generated by computers, TVs, and even white noisemakers. In simple terms, you could identify white noise as a drone or hum. Turn off the TV or the computer if either is in your bedroom. White noise can entrain your own rhythms, and that is not what you would want for deep, restful, healing sleep.

I like surrounding my sleeping environment with as much natural sound as I can manage. An indoor water fountain

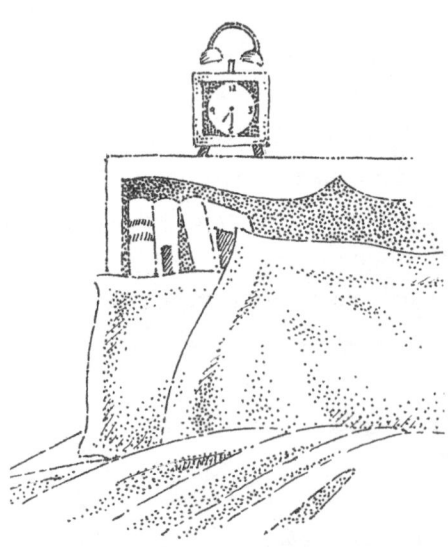

Ease gently into your morning by replacing your electronic buzzer with a more serene alarm clock. Alarms with simple chimes or nature sounds can awaken you from sleep on a stress-free note.

is one way to add harmonious, soothing, natural sounds to your nights. Water falling is a medley of tone colors and natural harmonies, and it can keep out unwelcome sounds, such as traffic and pedestrian noise. Compare that with a computer droning incessantly with no variation in tone or pitch.

The sound of your alarm clock is often the first sound you hear in the morning. I have been looking for a mellow-sounding alarm clock—something that will wake me up with crashing ocean waves or quiet music; instead, I have one that sounds as if the fire alarm is going off. A pleasant-sounding alarm clock can help start off your day with more equilibrium. A radio alarm clock that awakens me to the news is not for me simply because the news is so often sensationalist and geared toward provoking fear. That's not a way that I want to start my day.

Sight: Our natural circadian body rhythm is determined by the light of day and the dark of night. Some people have trouble sleeping because they don't receive enough natural light during the day, and consequently, their systems don't turn off at night. Others don't get enough true darkness at night to fully activate their body rhythms, an increasing problem for those who live in well-lit cities like New York.

Managing these light issues, as well as coordinating the light we receive with the sleep we need, is something most of us have to think through at some point. What parent of a young child hasn't contemplated long and hard the value of window shades when their young child wakes up with the first light of dawn? When you invest in window treatments, find a type that doesn't collect dust (like swags), and choose a simple, clean look with materials that are easily cleaned. Blinds are now made from untreated natural products, such as natural grasses, bamboo, and woods, and can be cleaned easily with a damp cloth. Natural-fiber curtains may appeal to you. Just make sure your window treatments don't have an odor. I live in the country, without streetlights or surrounding buildings, and I find that I get the sleep I need regardless of the natural light. As a result, I don't have any curtains at all because I don't need them for privacy. This minimalist approach works even for my teenage daughter.

Color is a treat for the eye, and the color of your bedroom should feel restful and conducive to harmony and quiet. The bedroom is also an intimate room, and you want it to be pleasing. Blue is often chosen for bedrooms and meditation rooms because blue's cool energy is calming, restful, peaceful, and spiritual. Blue helps inspire quiet meditation and soothes you to sleep. Color therapy with blue has been found to reduce blood pressure.

Green might be a good second choice for a bedroom color because it is naturally restful (imagine the landscape in early spring as the trees are budding). It also has a vibrancy about it, so if you go with green, make sure it is a light green. Some red touches add sensuality, but don't overdo red in the bedroom because it can be exhausting and too energizing. I recommend white ceilings because they reflect light and brighten any room.

Lighting has a few important purposes in the bedroom—for reading in bed, for finding clothes in a closet, and for giving you a sense of safety and security. I like sleeping in the deep dark, my daughter likes to have her door open and the bathroom light on to banish any images from her imagination, and my elderly mother always needs a night light to help her feel confident that she won't fall. While light for sleeping is an individual matter, be sure there is good lighting for reading in bed. Reading before sleep is a genuine pleasure, and good lighting lessens the strain on your eyes.

Touch: The amount of enjoyment we get from our skin touching the covers is determined by the sensual, soft feel of our bedding fabrics. Clean, soft, and even silky sheets are as seductive against the skin as anything man-made could ever be. Feather beds—cloudlike cushions that are placed on the mattress under the bottom sheet—are heavenly.

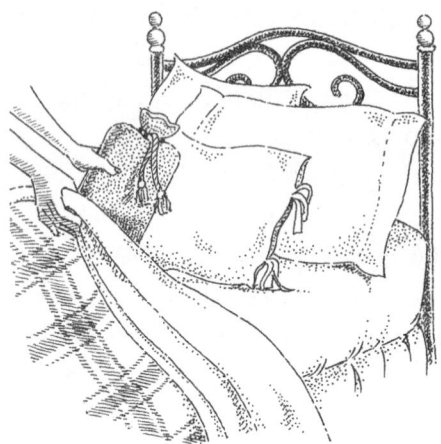

Rediscover the reason why people have been placing hot water bottles between the covers for decades! It's truly comforting to crawl in a toasty warm bed when you're chilled or when you're feeling under the weather.

The ideal bedroom temperature for deep sleep is between 55° and 68°F. During the winter, place hot water bottles in the bed before crawling under the covers to make the bed a welcoming, cozy place. My friend Pat places a hot water bottle in her kids' beds when they're sick. To me, that one small gesture shows how loving and nurturing a mother she is!

Being cool in the summer is just as important as being warm in the winter. Sleeping with moisture-absorbing sheets in the summer helps to keep you from feeling clammy from perspiration during the night. Light flax linen is a particularly cool and inviting fabric for summer, although it is expensive (try saving money by finding used linen sheets at estate sales).

How important is your choice of fabric for bedding? Very important! I recall reading about a study that compared the heart rates of those sleeping under wool versus polyester, and they reported that the heart rate is lower when sleeping under wool. On a scale from 1 to 10 (with 10 being wonderful), rate how you feel in the morning when you wake up. Keep improving your bedroom environment until you have a full 10.

Your Sixth Sense: Once you have accomplished many of the tasks required to have a nontoxic and uncluttered bedroom, take some time to sit in there and absorb how it feels. Open your intuitive mind to give you information about the room's comfort level.

❖ If you sense relationship conflict in your bedroom as a result of arguments or what have you, consider the ritual of smudging the room by burning white sage or sweet grass. For more on smudging, see page 25.

❖ Has your bedroom been occupied by previous owners or tenants? You will most likely want to clear the bedroom of their energy, given how intimate a room this is. For more about how to do this, see page 106.

❖ You might want to add a few crystals to your bedroom. Consider a rose quartz, known for bringing a vibration of unconditional love into its environs.

❖ Is your bedroom a place where you can be completely private? Can you lock your door if you desire? If not, work on ways to ensure that you can have uninterrupted time there and that no one will barge in on you. Establishing a privacy haven is important for teenagers, couples, and most anyone. We all need a place where we can be unguarded when we so desire.

Restful, Peaceful, Restorative Sleep

In the United States, nearly one-quarter of us aren't getting the amount of sleep we need to be fully alert the next day, according to the National Sleep Foundation. The deeper and more restful our sleep, the more likely we are to be full of energy, relaxed, and happy. Those with insomnia really suffer: Almost 70 percent of young adults have insomnia at least a few nights a week; almost 60 percent of the population experience insomnia no matter what their age. The National Sleep Foundation recommends that adults get 7 to 9 hours of sleep each night and adolescents 12 to 18 years old get 8½ to 9½ hours each night. Despite popular theories, the elderly do not need less sleep as they age, but they may have difficulty getting all their needed sleep at one time.

Dreams

In 1953, researchers discovered the phenomenon of REM (rapid eye movement) sleep. This led to the theory that sleep is not simply a dormant, unchanging state, but rather a complex period of activity as neurologically active as waking time, but fundamentally different. Our sleep cycles alternate between periods of quickly changing brain waves with rapid eye movement and periods of deep sleep with slow brain waves. Researchers who woke a person during a period of REM sleep found that, 70 to 90 percent of the time, they would remember their dreams. Since Freud, psychoanalysts have been very interested in the implications of dreams. However, what has been empirically proven through research is that dreaming occupies the regions of the brain associated with learning. REM sleep begins at the base of the brain and spreads to the midbrain, the thalamus, and the cerebral cortex—the areas responsible for most of our thought processes.

Sleep researchers have divided sleep into five stages; the first three are gradually deepening states of non-REM sleep, while the fourth reverses the process, lightening the sleep until REM sleep occurs. The cycle takes a total of 90 minutes; therefore, sleeping in amounts that allow this cycle to be completed leads to more restful sleep (for example, sleeping 7½ or 9 hours rather than 8 hours).

The purpose and implications of dreams have been debated for years in many cultures and will continue to be discussed for years to come. If this subject interests you, there are many books and schools of interpretation out there; find one that fits with your beliefs. You'll find other ways to encourage dreams if you keep an open mind. Try any of these three ways to help focus your attention on REM sleep and dreams.

Dream Notebooks: Keep a notebook by your bedside table if you want to remember your dreams. Write in it upon awakening, when the dream is still fresh in your mind. There are a number of good books available on dream symbolism, which might be worth keeping nearby when you want to analyze your dreams. The going wisdom about dream interpretation seems to be to determine what the symbol means to *you* because that is most likely what it means!

Dream Catchers: The traditional dream catcher has its roots in ancient amulets called spider webs and is designed to bring positive energy into a person's life. A dream catcher is made from a hoop of willow and has a

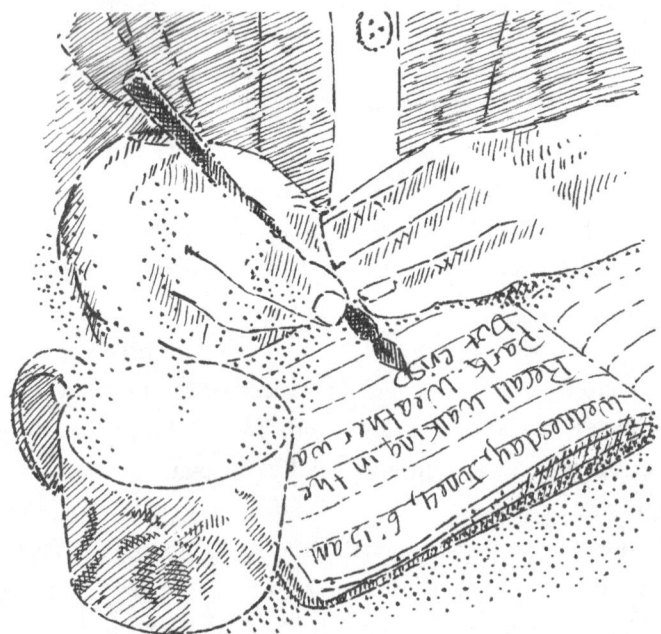

The best time to capture dreams on paper is the first few moments after you wake up, so keep a dream journal handy. Jot down key parts of the dream quickly, then look over your notebook entries from time to time to see if similar themes emerge.

mimic spider web woven over the hoop with a hole in the center; it's decorated with natural objects. Dream catchers are designed to snare bad dreams in the web; good dreams go through the hole in the center. A dream catcher hanging near a child's bed can be very comforting.

Dream Pillows: Dream pillows have been used for decades to encourage peaceful dreams and a good night's sleep. These large sachets, usually about 5 inches square, are tucked into a pillowcase along with the pillow or are placed nearby. The outer part of the dream pillow is usually made of high-

MAKE IT YOURSELF
EASY DREAM PILLOW

An absolute dream for those who find it difficult to drift off to sleep, the soothing scent of a dream pillow will ease wide-awake eyes into rest time.

Two pieces of good-quality cotton or silk, at least 6 inches square
Sewing thread and needle
Two pieces of muslin or natural fabric, at least 5 inches square
Herbs and a few drops of essential oils (see Herbal Notes below)
Pillow stuffing

With right sides of the cotton or silk squares together, sew around three sides of the pillow, about ½ inch in from the edge. Repeat for the muslin or natural fiber squares. Trim the fabric at the corners to within ¼ inch of the seams to make turning the pillows right side out easier. Turn the pillows right side out. Fill the muslin pillow with dried herbs. Don't overstuff the pillow because air circulation is necessary to waft the scent of the herbs into the air. Sprinkle just a few drops of essential oil onto the herbs. Fold in the raw edge of the muslin pillow and sew it closed. (Option: Close the seam with stick-on Velcro or snaps.) Slide the herbal pillow into the larger pillow, add pillow stuffing, fold in the raw edge, and sew it closed (or use Velcro or snaps). ❖

HERBAL NOTES
Many herbs have sedative effects and can be used in dream pillows when episodes of insomnia occur. Naturally, dream pillows work best when you make changes in your routine to promote sleepiness, calm, and relaxation. You can add herbs to your dream pillow to enhance dreams or sensuality too.

Herbs and plants for calming, sedative effect: catnip, chamomile, hops, lavender, lemon balm, passionflower, rose petals, and skullcap

Essential oils of choice for calming, sedative effect: basil, geranium, jasmine, lavender, peppermint, rose, sandalwood, and yarrow

Plants for dream recall: frankincense, mugwort, and rosemary

Herbs for good dreams: bay and thyme

Aphrodisiac herbs: catnip, passionflower, saffron, savory, southernwood, verbena, and yohimbe ❖

quality silk or cotton, and the herbs are placed in a pillow insert made of muslin or other simple-weave natural fabric.

Use dream pillows during periods of insomnia or as an occasional part of your sleep routine; it's important to balance your sleep with and without dream pillows because sleeping with fresh air is important to healing. If you are sensitive to some of the herbs in your dream pillow, you will be sub par on the days after you've slept with them. For example, valerian is a very relaxing herb for most people and is used by herbalists to treat insomnia, but it has a strong smell (some think that the smell resembles old socks), so it isn't a great choice for a subtly perfumed dream pillow! With any herb or combination of herbs, it's best to experiment to find what suits you best for a night of restful sleep.

Bed Linens for Refreshing Sleep

Clean, crisp sheets—so soft against your skin—are welcoming after a long day. You stretch and relax into a tranquil mood for sleep. The cleaner, fresher, and more natural the sheets are that you sleep on, the better. Because of the amount of perspiration given off during an 8-hour sleep, sleep under sheets that breathe and absorb moisture.

Look for untreated sheets made from organic, natural fibers. In the winter, you can cozy up in organic cotton flannel sheets. In the summer, pure linen is a wonderful luxury and becomes softer the more it is washed; linen sheets will require ironing or a toss in the dryer to keep them wrinkle free. Organic all-combed pima or percale cotton sateen sheets are less expensive but very nice choices, too, for comfortable and healthy bed linens.

Look for sheets with some heft; sheets that are too thin, even so-called active, natural fibers, won't absorb enough moisture to keep you dry. Avoid polyester sheets altogether as well as those with heavy antiwrinkling finishes. They have an electrostatic charge that attracts positive ions, which encircle you as you sleep—not the ideal environment or similar to that found in nature.

Also refrain from buying polyester sheets because they are made with petroleum-based fibers. Sheets treated with resins (no-iron finishes) should be considered toxic; washing can never eliminate the resins. I think it's ironic that these no-iron finishes are so popular—you can get that same no-iron quality by drying sheets in the dryer or on a clothesline. Combination silk/polyester sheets don't breathe, and

It is not easy to find pure fiber sheets without finishes on them. When you buy sheets, avoid those with finishes that won't wash out of the fabric. The new finishes are very tenacious—2 years and still washing, I have not yet succeeded in removing the finish from some cotton sheets we were given. I've decided to spend some time going to estate sales because I expect that is where I will find pure linen or cotton sheets. Yard sales will be a good bet too.

Natural and organic fiber bedding is easy to find and buy these days, and this is a welcome development. Here are a number of companies that offer certified organic bed linens: A Natural Home (www.anaturalhome.com), GAIAM/Harmony Catalog (www.gaiam.com), H3Environmental Corporation (www.h3environmental.com), Heart of Vermont (www.heartofvermont.com), Janice's (www.janices.com), Lifekind Products (www.lifekind.com), Under the Canopy (www.underthecanopy.com), and White Lotus Home (www.whitelotus.net). The store ABC Home in New York City carries organic bedding, and you'll also find organic bedding at a number of larger department stores.

they can make you feel clammy during warm weather. Avoid pure silk sheets, labeled "dry-clean only." Sleeping on sheets that have been dry-cleaned would be toxic because of the dry-cleaning fumes emanating from them.

Comforters, Duvets, Puffs, and Blankets

Sleeping under organic wool comforters, duvets, puffs, and blankets is deeply regenerative.

Synthetic fabrics have an electrostatic charge, and you'll sometimes get shocks when you put on a recently dried piece of synthetic clothing. When you sleep cocooned within this electrostatic charge, *positive* ions are generated and can impact your sleep. It's *negative* ions, not *positive* ions, that you want to surround you when you sleep or need

rest and recuperation because negative ions promote healing. Negative ions are found near ocean spray and in the mountains—is it any wonder we seek solace and rejuvenation at these spots?

Although organic wool comforters are expensive, with proper care, they can be passed on from generation to generation. Wool doesn't feel wet and clammy because it absorbs large amounts of moisture, such as perspiration, under warm or cool sleeping conditions. No other fiber does this as well. Wool is also naturally flame resistant. This remarkable fabric springs back into shape and bends back onto itself some 20,000 times without breaking (compared with 3,200 times for cotton).

It is important to buy comforters made of organic wool from sheep who weren't treated with pesticides or from wool-processing plants that use vegetable oils instead of petroleum. You can also make your own pure wool comforter for a fraction of the cost of ready-made ones. Just buy organic wool batting and make a comforter or duvet yourself. This is a fun project, and it would make a wonderful gift. Organic wool batting comes in a number of sizes, either packaged in precut quilt sizes or by the yard. You should be able to find bed-size batts, about 1 inch thick, for comforters and duvets. An Internet search will give you a number of sources for organic wool batting. Two great resources are www.nearseanaturals.com and www.vtorganicfiber.com.

For those allergic to wool, organic cotton comforters and blankets are the next best choice, and they are a bit cheaper than wool. Make sure to buy cotton that doesn't have a resin finish bonded to the material because you will never be able to remove it.

Down comforters are warm and long lasting and a real treat for relaxing bedrooms; see page 270 for more about down.

Comforting, Healthy Pillows

Because you sleep with your nose buried in or next to your pillow, it is most important that this part of your bedding be made of organic, untreated, natural materials that don't produce odors. I spent most of my childhood

breathing fumes from foam pillows. Most of us did. Choosing an organic cotton or wool pillow is a big improvement for your health.

Check your pillow frequently for mold. Since you perspire so much at night, your pillows can get musty if they are not aired frequently. Air pillows in the sun when you can. If you sleep on a synthetic foam pillow, or if your pillow smells of any chemicals, change as soon as possible to a natural pillow. The investment made will be rewarded by more replenishing sleep.

Choose a *soft* pillow if you sleep on your stomach, a *medium* pillow if you sleep on your back, and a *hard* pillow if

Airing out pillows in the sun will keep them fresher and cleaner and will reduce mildew, moisture, and mold. In an ideal world, mattresses and bedding should be exposed to direct sunlight once in a while, but if that's not possible, at least hang out bed linens on a hot, sunny, breezy day.

you are a side-sleeper. If your pillow is too soft, your spine won't be supported, but if it's too hard, you may not be cushioning the bones in your neck enough.

Organic Cotton and Wool Pillows

Wool pillows are particularly well suited for anyone with allergies because they are inhospitable to dust mites. They also absorb so much moisture and then naturally release it that they are naturally resistant to mold and mildew. The downside of wool pillows is that they don't hold a lot of loft. Cotton has more loft than wool, and it's softer. It's a good choice for a pillow with one caveat—cotton seeds can go rancid and can have a strong odor, so make sure to buy a cotton pillow with no seeds. For both cotton and wool, it is important to buy only organic offerings because conventionally grown and processed wool and cotton can be heavily sprayed crops. For healthy pillows, you'll be making an excellent choice if you choose organic wool and cotton.

Buckwheat

New on the sleep scene are buckwheat hull pillows. People rave about these pillows, claiming that they solve snoring problems. Some say that they have deeper sleeps and that sleeping on a buckwheat hull pillow clears their sinuses. One great thing about a buckwheat hull pillow is that the tiny organic buckwheat hulls conform to your neck. In the best hull pillows, the hulls are loosely packed so that they have room to adjust to your body and give it support where needed. Buckwheat hull pillows are slightly smaller and heavier than standard pillows. Refer to these guidelines for buying and using buckwheat hull pillows.

❖ Buy your pillow from an experienced manufacturer. Preflattened hulls are the best choice because they maintain about 93 percent of their loft; unflattened buckwheat hulls will lose loft as you use them.

❖ Make sure your buckwheat hull pillow has a zipper, so you can add or remove hulls, and make sure the hulls are encased in a cotton cover.

❖ Make sure your pillow is made of organic buckwheat hulls grown in the United States because imported hulls can be fumigated at the borders.

❖ Make sure the hulls have been cleaned prior to being placed in the pillow.

❖ Buckwheat hulls conform to your head and neck differently than other types of pillows, so it may take some repositioning to get comfortable at first.

❖ Even though the hulls make some

crackling noises, devotees claim you no longer hear that after the first night. Hang in there!

Kapok

The kapok tree is a tropical tree native to America, Africa, and the East Indies. It is fast growing, generally 45 feet to more than 100 feet tall, and it is the tallest tree in Africa. It has night-blooming flowers, which makes it highly unusual.

Like cotton, the seedpods of the kapok tree produce a silky down (sometimes called Java cotton), which is used in pillow stuffing, sleeping bags, life jackets, and upholstery. Kapok excels as a pillow stuffing because of its antibacterial qualities. It is also an "active fiber" that wicks away moisture, making it cool in summer and warm in winter.

Down and Feathers

Down feathers are the feathers that grow on the breasts and underbellies of waterfowl. The bird grows these particular feathers for warmth, so down feathers are used in comforters, pillows, and parkas. The wonders of nature are fully evident in how down keeps waterfowl warm: Just 1 ounce of down may consist of 2 million wisps of fluff. Ounce for ounce, down is three times warmer than its synthetic counterparts.

Down feathers are distinct from regular feathers grown by birds for flying and protection because they're softer. Down looks like a dandelion pod and a "soft puff," notes the Down Association of Canada.

Regular feathers, on the other hand, have a hard quill. Feathers make a harder and firmer pillow, while down pillows are softer and fluffier. Some prefer feather pillows to down pillows because they are firm, yet still flexible. Many like a combination of feathers and down for pillows because the combination is cheaper than pure down, and the result is a blend of soft and hard.

The "bounce" of down is called loft. The volume (in cubic inches) that 1 ounce of down occupies is called its fill power. The higher the fill power, the better the warmth. For example, a 700 to 800 fill power is common for lightweight, moderately priced comforters; a 550 fill power is common for less expensive comforters.

There is a range of down quality. Down from geese is the highest quality because the down feathers are larger and more insulating. Goose down is the softest, followed by duck as next softest; the hardest down is from a chicken or turkey. Eider duck down, known as eiderdown, is a highly esteemed soft down that is very warm. It can cling and compress, making it highly insulating; it also has great loft and can bounce back into shape easily. Eiderdown is hand plucked and is dark brown. The making of eiderdown causes no harm to the eider duck because the down is collected by hand from the nests. (In contrast, 90 percent of down is from the slaughterhouse.)

Syriaca Down

Sensitive individuals with allergies can have problems with down and feathers. If you or someone you are buying the bedding for is allergic to dust mites, try Insuloft goose down, which is specially cleaned to remove impurities to make it less attractive to dust mites; it's available from the natural-fiber catalog Garnet Hill (www.garnethill.com). For more about controlling dust mites, see page 275.

Mattresses for Healing, Rejuvenating Sleep

Who knew that most mattresses are chemical "wastebaskets" full of potentially health-damaging material? So concludes indoor air-quality expert Rosalind Anderson, PhD, of Anderson Laboratories, after a study of mattress emissions from some of the bestselling mattresses. Tossing and turning in a toxic bed is a miserable experience. All your nerve endings are on edge. The chemicals in bedding that are most often cited as potential sources of concern are pesticides, herbicides, fire retardants, stain-resistance solvents, various substances in synthetic fibers, and formaldehyde.

There has been a lot of media coverage lately about fire retardants used in furniture. Fire retardant compounds known as polybrominated diphenyl ethers, or PBDEs, have recently shown up in breast milk. According to the California Public Interest Research Group (CALPIRG), PBDEs have been linked to endocrine problems and may cause cancer. These compounds are very common in polyurethane foam mattresses and cushions.

Unless your mattress is pure organic wool, it probably has been treated with fire retardants. You can check with the manufacturer to find out which fire retardant has been used. Wool is naturally fire resistant and less likely to be chemically treated for this reason. And it's important to note that when you're shopping for a wool mattress, you must specify or look for an *organic* wool mattress; most sheep are regularly dipped with pesticides to control parasites, so unless it's made with organic wool, you may be exposing yourself to pesticides.

I had a goal that I worked for years and years to achieve: to end up with the mattress and bedding I now have, which is an organic wool mattress without springs, organic wool comforter and pillow, and pure cotton sheets. The combination is a heavenly cocoon that is pure and rejuvenating for sleep. The bed frame is simple and wooden. Synthetic chemicals have been completely eliminated.

It is expensive to establish a bedding sanctuary like this. If it's just not affordable for you, you can seal in some of the synthetic fumes from mattresses and pillows by using a barrier cloth encasement. Encasing mattresses and pillows will help reduce exposure to mattress and foam emissions and will protect you from small allergen particles, including dust mite and animal allergens. Barrier cloth is made of cotton that is so tightly woven (often 300 threads per inch) that it blocks fumes from passing through its weave. Look for natural, or better yet, organic, cotton barrier cloth; avoid plastic-style barrier cloths because they will outgas chemicals. You can buy cotton encasings ready made, or you can make your own by buying barrier-cloth fabric.

New mattresses from a regular mattress store would have a wide range of emissions, and using a barrier cloth to completely surround the mattress would help to limit your exposure. Don't be fooled into thinking that you can buy a used mattress to avoid outgassing.

Unfortunately, secondhand stores often fumigate mattresses (in some states, it's required by law), and many of the chemicals in mattresses are long lasting—outlasting the life of the mattress.

New or used, you should vacuum your mattress often with the flexible hose and a brush attachment. Vacuum the top and bottom and each of the four sides. Sun your mattress as often as possible too. If you have a window that lets in direct sunlight, strip the bed and let the sun shine on the mattress. Or, carry the mattress to a clean spot on a porch or deck every so often for exposure to outdoor sunlight. One of the biggest concerns with mattresses is mildew growth because we perspire so much when we sleep. Be sure your mattress isn't in a damp location and doesn't show any signs of mildew. If you plan to store a mattress, make sure it is in a dry, well-ventilated space, or the mattress will be ruined with a musty smell and mildew.

Organic Wool

Wool is an excellent choice for a mattress because it absorbs and releases water, "wicking" it off because of the oily lanolin it contains. Wool is resilient and naturally resistant to fire, dust mites, and mold. For more about the benefits of wool, see page 328.

Those who think they may be allergic to wool because it scratches them may just be reacting to the harsh detergents and finishes often used on nonorganic wool products. Test *organic* wool against your skin (assuming you aren't seriously allergic to wool) to see how it feels. I thought I was allergic to wool because I'd feel itchy wearing wool socks, sweaters, and hats. By choosing purer products, I now comfortably sleep in wool without a problem. You'll find many wool products available, and these two are worth checking into further.

"PureGrow" Wool. The California PureGrow program certifies that the sheep have been raised in an environment without chemicals, pesticides, or artificial materials. The pastures must be free of pesticides for a minimum of 2 years, and supplemental feeds must be organically based. Inoculations can contain no synthetics or hormones.

Organic Wool. According to the Organic Trade Association, "certified organic" means the item has been grown according to strict national standards that are verified by independent state or private organizations. Certification includes inspections of farm fields and processing facilities, detailed record keeping, and periodic testing of soil and water to ensure that growers and handlers are meeting the trade association's standards.

Organic Cotton

Organic cotton mattresses can be a great choice, but you need to be aware that cottonseeds become rancid and smell strong for a few months. You may have noticed this if you have lived with a new cotton futon. The seed's oils are very fragrant, and they can become rancid and bothersome as they age. It can take several months for the smell to be naturally eliminated. Fortunately, you can find some mattresses made of cotton that is 100 percent handpicked and devoid of seeds. Certified organic cotton is grown without chemical pesticides, and it is manufactured for mattresses without added chemical treatments.

However, cotton doesn't meet federal standards for fire resistance; by federal law, cotton used in mattresses must be treated with a fire retardant. In most cases, this is boric acid, or borate, a natural mineral that does not release vapors. In rare cases, you may be able to get a doctor's prescription for a fire-retardant-free mattress that you can pass on to a manufacturer if you place a custom order. Cotton/wool combination mattresses often meet federal standards without the addition of borate. So-called green cotton is not certified organic, but it is 100 percent natural and not chemically treated, dyed, or bleached.

Organic Natural Latex Mattresses

Pure latex (rubber) mattresses are the natural alternative to polyurethane foam. Latex is a milky white liquid composed of rubber particles and water; it is made into foam rubber. At first, I was very leery of these mattresses because many people are allergic to latex, and it is known as a sensitizer. When a natural latex rubber mattress is made, however, it goes through elaborate rinsing to remove the rubber protein, which is what most people react to in latex gloves and which causes sensitivity. Nonetheless, those sensitive to latex should test their reaction to this type of mattress before buying one. Make sure that the natural latex mattress is not a blend (blends are common) and that it contains nothing but pure latex. Also, be sure the latex has not been treated with drying chemicals.

People like natural latex-core mattresses because they dynamically conform to the body and offer great support. I have tried one and been impressed at how incredibly comfortable it was. Natural latex is inherently antimicrobial; it's also resistant to dust mites, mildew, and fire. It breathes and wicks away body moisture, keeping you warmer in winter and cooler in summer. A good latex mattress can last for 25 years.

Futons

Japanese futons are traditionally made from cotton batting 3 inches thick. Sleeping on one 3-inch futon feels a bit sparse, but you can combine two or more for a fuller mattress feel. Futons are available in organic cotton, organic wool, cotton/wool, and hemp. One hundred percent cotton futons are the firmest for sleeping.

Hemp is a great material for futons; hemp fiber can be grown easily without pesticides and can be sustainably harvested. Hemp is durable; it breathes and is naturally antibacterial and antifungal. Like wool, hemp is hollow at its core, so it facilitates air circulation in a futon, keeping you cool in summer and warm in winter.

When shopping for futons, you'll find both machine-quilted and hand-quilted models. Futons contain layers and layers of cotton batting, and the quilting holds the layers together. You may discover that hand-quilted futons last longer; when a futon is machine-quilted, the machine needle punctures the cotton and breaks up the batts, possibly allowing wadding to occur with use.

A drawback of most futons is that they need to be aired and sunned every few days, or they can get mildewed. If your futon is cotton, you may also notice an odor from cottonseeds (see page 273). A word of caution when shopping—

some futons have a foam core made of urethane; avoid them because there is the potential of toxic outgassing.

Bed Frame Considerations

Your bed frame should be as inert as possible. The best bet is a natural, scaled, finished wood bed frame, but that's not always realistic. At the very least, use the least toxic paints and stains on your frame, if given a choice, and don't sleep in the bed until all the smells have fully dissipated. Raw, unfinished wood can cause allergic problems for some, such as those sensitive to pine.

If you've purchased a bed with paint or stain odor, try to speed the drying time by using a dehumidifier, or seal any toxic-type odiferous stain with a sealant. Contact N.E.E.D.S. (www.needs.com) for nontoxic seal-ants. If your bed frame or bed slats are made of particleboard, you should seal it to reduce formaldehyde emissions.

Dealing with Dust Mites Effectively

Seventy percent of dust is human skin (humans shed 10 pounds of skin a year!); the other 30 percent consists of pet dander, fibers, dirt, soil, mold, bacteria, and insects. Dust mites are microscopic creatures (smaller than $\frac{1}{70}$ of an inch) that thrive on sloughed-off human and animal skin. Under the microscope, they appear as sightless, spiderlike arachnids. They breathe through their skin, and while in dormancy, they are impervious to poisons, so insecticides are worthless *even if* you choose to use them.

High concentrations of dust mite allergen are a significant risk factor for the development of allergic diseases such as asthma and rhinitis (hay fever). Eighty percent of children and young adults with asthma are sensitive to dust mites. Studies at the National Institute of Environmental Health Sciences (NIEHS) suggest that more than 45 percent of US homes have bedding with dust mite concentrations that exceed a level equated with allergic sensitization.

Where Mites Flourish

Dust mites thrive in warm, dark, moist places—temperatures of 68° to 84°F and humidity levels at 75 to 80 percent. They thrive in bedding because that is where they find their biggest meals. You can also find dust mites in dust ruffles and bed curtains (because they trap dust easily) and on feathers, furs, protein-based textiles, and other organic fibers. Polyester bedding is a well-known haven for dust mites because it traps moisture from perspiration.

Minimizing Mites

It's the feces and body parts from the dust mites that are the allergens, so simply killing the mites won't remove the allergen, although reducing populations is always a considerable help. To minimize mite populations, you need to make changes in your daily living and cleaning routines. While you may not be able to do all of these things, just implementing a few of these techniques will reduce the number of mites in the bedroom.

❖ Direct sunlight kills dust mites, so hang bedding in the sun whenever possible. (Be mindful, though, that outdoor allergens can collect on bedding hung outside.)

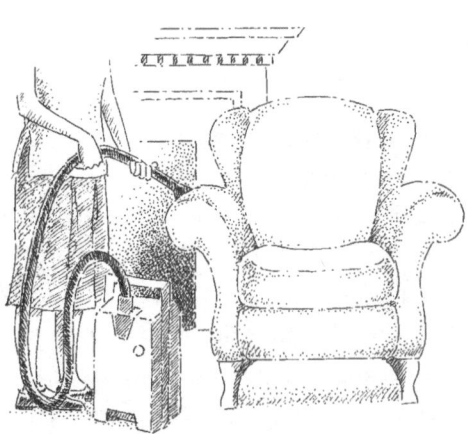

A vapor steam-cleaner's ability to eliminate dust mites offsets the purchase price if you suffer from allergies. The cleaner heats surfaces with high heat, killing mites, and is perfect for cleaning bedding that can't be laundered, such as mattresses or duvets. Since it cleans with vapor instead of saturating surfaces with water, it doesn't add to humidity concerns.

❖ Dust mites die when the humidity falls below 40 to 50 percent; use a dehumidifier if the weather is humid.

❖ Wash bed linens once a week in hot water—the water temperature should be 130°F or higher—to kill mites.

❖ Steam-cleaning carpets considerably lessens dust mite populations and deters population growth. A study in Glasgow, England, found an 87 percent drop in the concentration of dust mites per gram of dust after carpets were steam-cleaned.

❖ Vapor steam-cleaning (using a small machine that heats surfaces with dry steam) kills fungus, dust mites, bacteria, and other undesirables. This is a good way to clean bedding that you can't launder, such as mattresses. Vapor contains only 5 to 6 percent water (conversely, most steam cleaners use lots of warm water to clean), so the vapor steam doesn't contribute to a moist environment. Vapor steam deeply penetrates whatever it is cleaning, and it is great for upholstery, couches, carpets, and mattresses.

❖ The natural lanolin in wool repels dust mites—another reason to buy wool bedding.

❖ Studies at NIEHS found significant reduction of dust mites when allergen-proof covers were combined with properly laundered bedding, dry steam-cleaning, and vacuuming. Vacuuming alone didn't work as well as the combi-

MAKE IT YOURSELF
DAMP DUST MOP

Try this ecofriendly dust mop to wipe down floors, walls, ceilings, and woodwork. Use the cloth freely as a good dusting cloth too; it works well on a wide range of furniture. The acid in the vinegar will help deter dust mites and neutralize the allergens.

One part vegetable glycerin
One part vinegar
Soft, clean, dust-free cloth

Combine the glycerin and vinegar. Soak the cloth in the mixture until it has absorbed the liquid. Gently squeeze the excess moisture from the cloth, then cover a mop with the cloth. Dispose of the cloth after use. ❖

nation of vacuuming with dry steam-cleaning of carpets and upholstery.

❖ Buy a new pillow every 6 months (dust and dust mites live in pillows).

❖ Eliminate wall-to-wall carpet (especially over concrete floors because concrete generates moisture/humidity). Decorate with washable throw rugs instead.

❖ Freeze stuffed animal toys in the freezer (in a tightly closed plastic bag), and shake vigorously outside after removing them from the freezer. Or, wash stuffed toys often.

Tips for Everyday Mite Control

It almost goes without saying that keeping a bedroom clean is important for mite control. Use a HEPA vacuum in the room, and run a HEPA air filter near the bed when the room isn't occupied. Make sure the bedroom curtains or window coverings are washable. Horizontal venetian blinds can be wiped clean with a damp cloth (but they do collect a lot of dust), and if you have shades that can't easily be washed, they should be of a type that's easily vacuumed. Be sure to avoid fuzzy fabrics and bed linens and fluffy pillows; they'll attract and capture dust.

Cut the clutter. It is very hard to dust well when surfaces are covered with dust-collecting objects. Rough, raw pine and fabrics are also hard to keep free from dust. If you can't bear to get rid of certain possessions, use covered storage containers for papers, magazines, and other bric-a-brac to reduce dust-catching surfaces.

Bedbugs

A friend of mine runs an inn with her husband, and they have had a terrible infestation of bedbugs—a problem of epidemic proportions in the hotel industry, she says. The bugs were so persistent that exterminators were coming into her building every week. Coincidentally, I talked to a Tibetan doctor who wanted to know if I had any solutions for bedbug problems. Bedbugs are a terrible problem in India, where he lives much of the time. I did some research, and here's advice from *The Bug Stops Here*, by Stephen L. Tvedten.

Temperature Extremes: Bedbugs are very sensitive to heat. If you can raise the temperature of the room to 111° to 113°F for an hour or so, all stages of the bedbug will probably die. Even temperatures of 97° to 99°F will kill most of them. Or, chilling the room to between 32° and 48°F may also kill bedbugs.

Steam-Cleaning: Steam-cleaning can kill bedbugs in carpets.

Borax Spray: Spray pillows and bed linens with a mixture of ½ cup of borax to 1 gallon of water. Let dry. Wash again before using.

Castile Soap: Wash bed linens and bedding with peppermint castile soap; castile soap contains fatty acids that kill bugs. Add ⅛ cup to a laundry load.

Sprinkle Powder: Kill bedbugs by sprinkling talcum powder or diatomaceous earth on infested areas. Let set for 24 hours, then remove the powder or dust by shaking linens outside (avoid breathing in any of the powder). Launder as usual.

The Healthy Baby Nursery

It is heartbreaking for me to see well-meaning and excited new parents decorating their new baby's nursery by painting it, installing new carpeting, and buying a crib with a brand-new foam or synthetic mattress. I did some of these things when I was pregnant; I knew better, but I wanted to be "normal" (and not chemically sensitive) and provide standard things for my baby like everybody else did. I bought a new foam crib mattress, discarding it when my daughter spent her first night there after sleeping in a bassinet for a few months. That first night in her new crib, she tossed and turned all night long, exposed to the neurotoxic fumes outgassing from the foam. Fortunately for her, I knew the symptoms of central nervous system agitation, and I removed the offending fumes from her life the next day. Often, a mother-to-be paints the nursery, first exposing her baby to the fumes in utero and then from the outgassing paint when the baby sleeps in the room after birth. The nesting impulse is powerful before the birth of a baby, and I am not advocating that parents squelch this natural desire. Instead, they should be aware of chemical exposure and put their decorating efforts into nontoxic approaches (for example, non-VOC paint, natural carpet, and organic bed linens), which won't increase their baby's burden of chemical exposure. *Mothers & Others for a Livable Planet: Guide to Natural Baby Care* by Mindy Pennybacker and Aisha Ikramuddin is a good book on the subject and is full of ideas and resources.

Paint and Carpeting

Want to take the first step in ensuring a healthy nursery? Find out whether there is lead paint on the walls! Lead paint was not sold after 1978, but the walls of any home built prior to 1978 could be problematic. (See page 53 for more about lead paint.)

As cozy as carpeting may appear to be for a nursery, it can be a reservoir of dust mites, mold, mildew, and VOCs. If there is old carpeting in the nursery, pull it up and replace it with untreated hardwood floors or floors treated with a water-based, low-VOC finish. If carpet is a must for the nursery, choose completely untreated carpeting with natural latex or jute backing.

Much of today's furniture is made of pressed wood, something to avoid because of the formaldehyde in the glues that will continually outgas for the entire life of the piece. Choose real wooden furniture instead. Yard sales offer abundant supplies of simple furniture for very little cost. And what about a changing table? If it is going to be covered with any kind of plastic, the older the better, and the more used the better, as long as it is still safe and sturdy. You want the plastic to be completely outgassed before putting it in the nursery.

Toxic Crib Mattresses

In a study of six brands of crib-size waterproof mattress covers conducted by Anderson Laboratories, all were found to emit toxic fumes in various degrees, and some caused acute toxicity to the respiratory tract of male mice. Five of the mattress covers were made of polyvinyl chloride covered with cotton or polyester layers. The remaining cover was made of polyolefin. Chemical emissions included suspected carcinogens.

Crib and bassinet mattresses made of organic, natural materials are now widely available online, through catalogs, or in natural product stores. For the largest selection, go to your favorite online search engine and type "organic baby." Retailers who are likely to sell organic bedding for babies are also likely to offer safe accessories, including nontoxic toys.

If buying an organic mattress isn't feasible, enclose a standard crib mattress with a cotton barrier cloth (see page 272). Avoid plastic or polyurethane encasements. To prevent moisture from seeping onto the mattress from leaking diapers, invest in an absorbent "wool puddle pad," designed to insert between the sheet and mattress. Avoid pillows until the baby is at least 1 year old, and after that, invest in a natural fiber, organic pillow (see page 268).

Electromagnetic Fields (EMFs)

If you feel on edge when you wake up in the morning, are irritable, or have a restless night's sleep, agitation, or insomnia, consider checking into potential electromagnetic field problems in the room or elsewhere in your house.

EMFs are produced by our use of electrical power. These invisible fields and their uncertain detrimental health effects are emitted from most of our household appliances. Common sources in the bedroom include water beds, electric blankets, alarm clocks, and TVs.

Other sources include the point where electric power lines come into the house (often through the outside wall of a corner bedroom) or a refrigerator on the first floor sharing the same wall with a bed on the second floor. The most unpredictable source of EMFs is found in buildings with faulty grounding or wiring (known as askew buildings).

Reducing your exposure to EMFs is important, particularly in the bedroom. Some signs of EMF exposure include insomnia and generally restless sleeping, irritability, fatigue without being able to rest, agitation, and more. If you want to make these invisible fields visible, rent or buy a gaussmeter. EMFs in the home are measured in milligauss (mG), or thousands of gauss. A dishwasher might measure more than 100 mG if you place the gauge right at the appliance when it is running. My dishwasher registers a whopping 50 mG when it isn't running because it has an electric transformer. Opposed to this, my electric stove with two burners on the highest setting gave off 1 mG at 2 feet.

How much electromagnetic activity in the bedroom is a bad thing? Studies conducted in Sweden indicate that negative health effects may occur at levels as low as 1 to 2 mG. Most homes don't exceed this level in overall background electromagnetic radiation. However,

Electromagnetic fields are created around power lines and electrical appliances and may be linked to health problems. To reduce exposure to these invisible fields, position beds away from TVs, computers, and alarm clocks, and unplug lamps near your bed before going to sleep. You could even install a "demand switch" on bedroom circuits to cut off all electricity to the room while you sleep.

EMFs from appliances can cause localized fields well in excess of the safe minimum established by the Swedish studies.

Research in this area has been consistently contradictory. One Swedish study in 1993 found that leukemia occurred at twice the rate for children exposed to electromagnetic radiation, while another published the same year in the same country found no association. In 1979, American researchers in Denver discovered that childhood deaths from cancer occurred at twice the rate for children

living less than 150 feet from high-tension power lines. Studies are now being conducted around the world under the auspices of the World Health Organization (WHO) in hope of finding more definite answers.

Unless you have an askew building, EMFs are site specific: You cannot estimate the level in your home simply by looking for power lines or transformers outdoors. EMFs drop off very quickly (for more information, see page 370). My TV, for example, is 90 mG in the front of the screen, 20 mG at 2 feet, and 12 mG at 6.

I feel it's very important to reduce EMFs in the bedroom, and you can take small steps to provide a haven without them: Make sure your TV is at least 8 feet from the bed, and make sure your alarm clock is at least 8 feet from the bed, unless it is battery operated. Don't sleep on a water bed, because it has to be electrically heated. Avoid halogen lights or any other units that have little black transformer boxes, and unplug lamps and appliances that are near your body before going to sleep.

You can turn off the electrical current flowing to lamps and appliances when there is no demand (for instance, when you are asleep) with a "demand switch" installed on the circuit that goes to your bedroom. It automatically interrupts the flow of electric current

Safe and Sound

It's no surprise that 66 percent of Americans blame all their nighttime tossing and turning on stress, reports the Better Sleep Council. But there's a helpful, easy way to relax after a tough day.

You can quiet your mind, release muscle tension, and beat stress with a few simple stretches. In a study at Fred Hutchinson Cancer Research Center in Seattle, 86 healthy women who were having trouble sleeping needed 60 percent less sleep medication and fell asleep 30 percent faster when they stretched four times a week.

Try this soothing, 10-minute bedtime routine to stretch tight areas of the body, especially the neck, shoulders, back, and hips.

Slip into comfortable, natural-fiber exercise wear or pj's, turn on soothing music, and do each stretch at least once. Stretch only as far as comfortably possible, never to the point of discomfort or pain. To maximize the feeling of calmness, close your eyes and focus on your breathing as you do each move.

WALL ROLL-DOWN

Relaxes your lower back, shoulders, and neck. Stand with back against a wall, feet hip-width apart and about 12 inches from the wall. Inhale, pull abdominals in, and press entire back to the wall. As you exhale, roll down until only tailbone and buttocks are touching the wall. Relax neck and shoulders and let head and arms hang. Take deep, slow breaths and circle arms inward five times and then outward five times. Slowly roll up.

SHOULDER ROLL

Releases tension and relaxes your shoulders and chest. Stand with feet hip-width apart and hold a rolled bath towel down in front of you so arms are very wide apart. Inhale and lift arms overhead; as you exhale, lower them behind back. Inhale as you bring arms back up overhead, and exhale as you lower them. If shoulders feel too tight or the full movement is too challenging, only go as far as comfortably possible. Repeat five to eight times.

CAT WITH A TWIST

Relaxes back, abdominals, chest, and shoulders. Kneel with hands directly beneath shoulders and knees beneath hips. Exhale, pull belly in toward spine, round back, and drop head and tailbone

---

on a given circuit. Alternatively, you can have an electrician rewire the outlets with "flex" wiring, which enables you to turn off appliances, lamps, and other units with a hand switch.

Remove cell phones from the bedroom. Portable landline phones don't give off much of an EMF field and are far preferable. To be on the safe side, don't place even a landline phone next to the head of the bed.

Another kind of energetic electrical problem is metal interacting with electricity. If you have metal bed springs on

toward the floor, stretching like a cat. Inhale and reverse the move, arching back and lifting tailbone and head toward the ceiling. Do the sequence five times. Next, with back flat, twist and slide left arm, palm up, between right arm and right leg. Reach far enough with left hand so left shoulder, arm, and side of head rest on the floor. Hold for five to eight deep breaths, and then repeat with right arm.

UP THE WALL

Relaxes hips and back of thighs. Lie on back with buttocks as close to a wall as possible. Extend legs up on the wall, keeping feet relaxed and about hip-width apart. Using hands, gently press thighs toward the wall. Hold for five to eight breaths. Then slowly bend knees out to the sides and bring soles of feet together, sliding them down the wall as far as comfortable. The sides of feet should rest against the wall. Gently press knees and thighs toward the wall. Hold for five to eight breaths. Release.

FIGURE-4 TWIST

Relaxes hips, back, and shoulders. Lie faceup on the floor with arms out to the sides, palms up, knees bent, and feet flat on the floor. Place right ankle on left knee so legs form a shape like a number 4. Slowly let legs fall to the right as close to the floor as possible. Simultaneously turn head to the left, keeping arms and upper back relaxed and on the floor. Hold for five to eight breaths. Return to center, then lower legs to the left while turning head to the right. Hold for five to eight breaths. Return to center, switch legs, and repeat to the left and right.

LYING SIDE BEND

Relaxes hips, sides of torso, and underside of shoulders. Lie faceup on the floor with arms and legs extended so body forms an X. Grasp left wrist with right hand, and slowly pull left arm and upper body to the right. Next, cross left ankle over right so body forms a crescent. Hold for five to eight breaths and repeat to the other side.

Once you've completed your nighttime stretches, try to stay in a relaxed state and head for bed. Your breathing should already be slowed from your busy day, and you should fall into slumber free of stress.

your box frame and a halogen lamp with a transformer is located next to the bed, the springs become magnetized and interfere with the body's rhythm. Buy metal-free beds and bed frames or eliminate the halogen lamp.

Who wants to be wired and wound up in the bedroom? Nobody! Calm your central nervous system way down (and that of your family members) by removing electronic stress. The benefits of deep, peaceful, calm, and healing sleep will permeate every aspect of your life, resulting in greater well-being.

9

fire

Sunlight seems to dance sometimes; it is so bright, and everything it touches seems to shimmer. Light from the sun is life-force brilliance, fuller of the essence of life than our imagination can quite grasp. It is no wonder that native peoples around the world have worshipped the sun as the manifestation of God.

Fire is also symbolic of transformation. In nature, forest fires burn to renew the earth. Fire purifies and heals wounds by cauterizing them. Fire dries out dampness. The human heart catches fire with love. Kundalini, that primal energy that lives in the spine, is considered a fire.

As I write this, I see the brilliant yellow of a black-eyed Susan abloom in my garden, next to a purple coneflower whose roots can boost the immune sys-

tem. Both flowers have grown strong and abundant in the summer sun. The purple and yellow vibrancy is amplified by the soft green of the leaves and weeds. The trees are so alive that their leaves shimmer as the light reflects off the water droplets left from the rainy mist. The scent of fall will soon touch the air. We are coming to the end of the season when we hear the wood thrush in the woods, but the crickets are making up for their absence with a loud and steady pulse of noise. The whole neighborhood is teeming with life, and all of it is alive because of the sun. My family's evening meal is going to consist of freshly picked corn, tomatoes, vegetables for roasting, and even local peaches and blueberries, all grown in the sun of the Hudson Valley, where I live.

Where are fire and sun in our lives

now? How mysterious it feels to visit a sun- and star-worshipping site, such as sacred Stonehenge. Each giant stone is aligned so that the sun shines through it or touches it in precise ways at certain times of day or year. To this day, we don't know whom the people were who made these megalithic sun- and star-worshipping temples.

I feel uneasy on the summer solstice, the longest day of the year, and on the winter solstice, the shortest. I feel like we've lost the rituals and celebrations of these important days. I'm frustrated that I am disconnected from the sun-honoring ceremonies that would be meaningful to me—a person living in an industrialized and technological society. Both the summer solstice and the winter solstice were a part of this chapter. I originally wrote this paragraph on the summer solstice. I lit a candle as I wrote and mourned the loss of knowing what the appropriate ritual should be. When I returned to this chapter to reread and edit it a few months later, it was a few days shy of the winter solstice. It was snowing, and I was grateful for the wood stove and oil burner that keep my house warm. But more than ever, I'm disconnected from the sun, the source of all heat.

It is with new appreciation that I think of *Celebrating the Great Mother* by Cait Johnson and Maura D. Shaw, with its offering of activities to help ritualize these important earth milestones and allow us to be here in the moment. We are a society that is between times. We are dependent on an energy system that is destructive, dirty, and poisonous, yet finally, we are gearing up to discover and invent the technology we need to use the infinitely renewable and ever-present energy provided by the sun and hydrogen.

Long gone are the days of rubbing two sticks together to make a flame to burn wood for cooking food and providing heat. Gone are the days when fire was part of every home at its hearth. This shift has prompted huge evolutionary change. I often wonder if the proliferation of spas, candles, and outdoor barbecues is a result of this lack of a hearth. It's sad that the flame for modern times usually means a gas stove, an oil burner, a propane barbecue, and cigarettes.

The lack of a clean, inexpensive, completely renewable and sustainable way to produce "flame" to power our lives with electricity and heat is the cause of a huge groundswell of anxiety around the world. The day-to-day vulnerability of human beings in our time is rooted in our dependency on energy utilities for the energy we use to heat our homes, cook our food, run our cars, or turn on our lights. There is a pervasive awareness among many that our reliance on fossil and nuclear fuels is very wrong and askew. The global population is voracious for energy power.

The fears of a Y2K breakdown of the energy grid brought to the forefront how dependent industrialized societies are for the most basic necessities: access to water, heat, light, and cooking stoves. It was a relief for my family when we installed a wood stove in 1999 so that we could have heat in the midst of the deep winter if all else failed. But other than a great backup heat source for safety and spiritual sustenance, wood is not a sustainable answer for heating our homes. There are simply too many humans and too few trees.

Toxic Fire and Toxic Smoke

Outside of personal survival concerns, the deepest and darkest danger of our society's complete and unmitigated dependency on fossil fuel, nuclear, and hydroelectric energy utilities is that every one of them causes serious environmental harm. Being dependent on the energy grid, we are vulnerable to the weather (causing power loss without backup) and the vagaries of the energy industry, and the energy we are dependent on is threatening the very air we breathe.

Powering Our Lives

Currently, the majority of the world's electricity is generated by burning fossil fuels, such as coal and oil. Burning these material fuels releases a wide range of pollutants, from carbon dioxide, carbon monoxide, and nitrogen oxide to hydrogen sulfide and sulfur dioxide.

While nuclear energy is touted as cleaner than other energy choices, it can be devastatingly dangerous. Its radioactive residue has a half-life of up to thousands of years and is highly hazardous. At the present time, there is not a safe way to dispose of it. Living near a nuclear power plant is unnerving. If things go wrong, there is the potential for massive death and destruction. A power plant near me is also near New

York City—a prime terrorist target. This nuclear plant supports the light fixtures in my home and runs the heating system, but it isn't my choice. I was downwind of Three Mile Island by 100 miles when that nuclear plant malfunctioned, and we watched our potential demise (albeit depending on the wind direction), or at least the demise of healthy thyroid glands, on the evening news.

Water has provided energy for hundreds of years, from simple water wheels and belt-driven machinery to huge hydroelectric dams that span the world's largest rivers. Dams, however, have devastated entire ecosystems and societies throughout the world.

We need a new direction and new ideas. Most of all, we need hope—hope that our world "sees the light" and works feverishly to create renewable, pollutant-free, and affordable energy sources.

Emissions

The Environmental Protection Agency (EPA) reports that in 2001, electric companies contributed the largest amount of air pollution in the United States. This should be enough to make us particularly aware of our energy use and to cut back whenever and wherever possible. And, for what it is worth (and I think it is worth a lot), fossil fuel and nuclear sources of energy give no pleasure. Think about how people wax poetic about soaking up the heat of the sun or feel cozy by a hearth in deep winter. Has anyone ever been charmed or mesmerized by a nuclear power plant?

As scientists continue to understand the earth's atmosphere and the impact of increased fossil fuel emissions, the data regarding the use of these fuels gets more and more disturbing. Some try to dismiss the current increase in CO_2 levels (carbon dioxide being the most worrisome of the fossil fuel emissions) and consequent rise in the earth's temperature as just another blip on the radar of our constantly fluctuating environment. And, indeed, anyone who has tried to predict the weather understands the immense complexity of our weather system. Yet if the earth has functioned for 4.5 billion years through a constant set of checks and balances, how can our introduction of these massive emissions *not* affect the global climate? There isn't a natural check that's big enough to balance our increasing emissions.

The greatest influence on the rise of CO_2 lies in the realm of the greenhouse effect. In the words of the EPA, "The greenhouse effect is the rise in temperature that the earth experiences because gases such as CO_2 in the atmosphere trap energy from the sun. Without

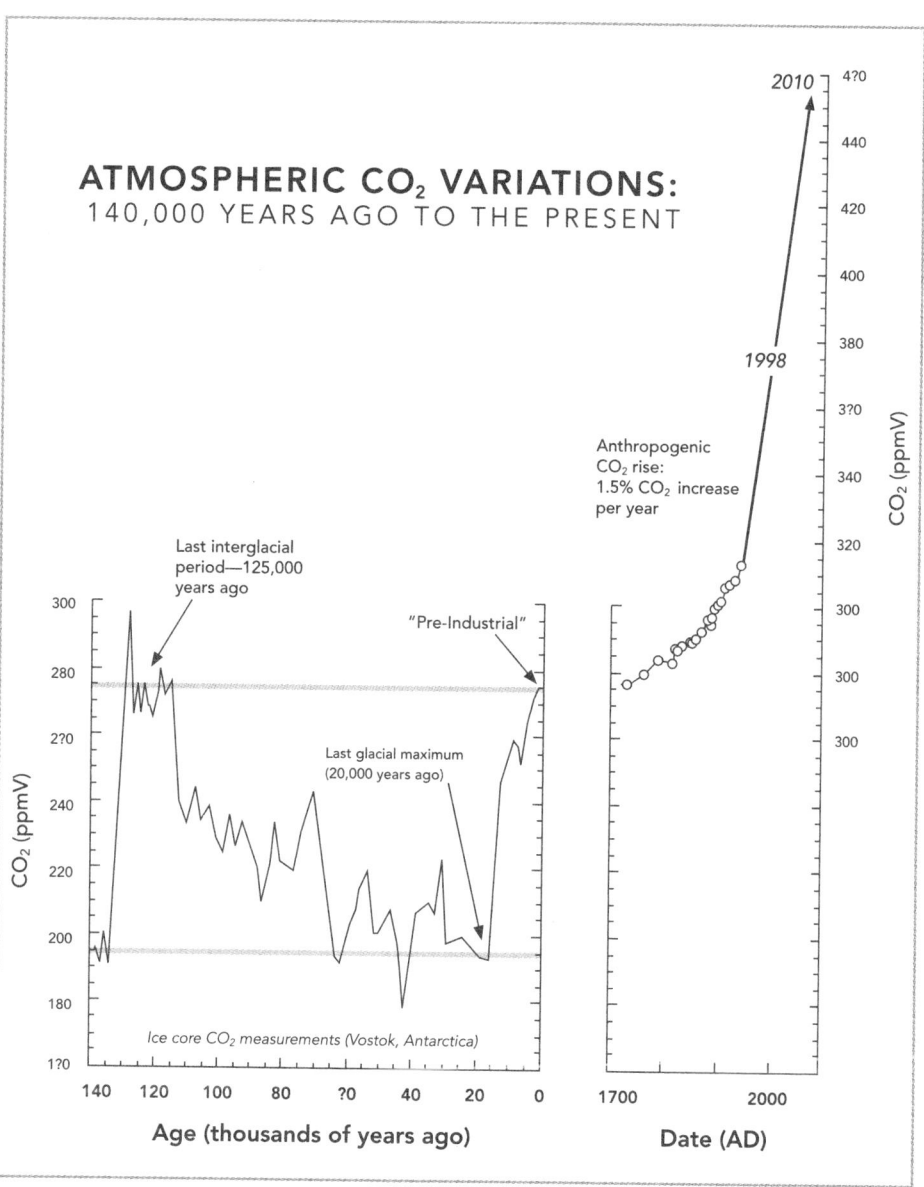

ATMOSPHERIC CO₂ VARIATIONS:
140,000 YEARS AGO TO THE PRESENT

Source: US Department of Energy

these gases, heat would escape back into space, and the earth's average temperature would be about 60°F colder." Since the Industrial Revolution, CO₂ levels have increased at a greater rate than ever before (at least as far as we can see in ice core samples dating back 140,000 years) and will continue to do so, doubling by the year 2050 if current trends persist.

Along with this increase in CO_2 (well above what our environment can process) comes an increase in temperature. As a result of rising temperatures, climatic change is greatly accelerated, leading to more water vapor in the air and potentially the release of CO_2 and CH_4 (methane) stored in thawing permafrost, leading to an increase in the greenhouse effect. We've created a vicious cycle.

Most of us are completely tied to the energy supplier in our local area by lack of affordable or easily accessible technology to go "off the power grid." As much as we would wish otherwise, every friend of mine is as tied to the energy grid as I am. Not one of us has solar panels or independent power sources. We bought ready-built homes, or we live in a city and rent an apartment, all with heating systems already installed. Financing an ecofriendly overhaul to solar is beyond our budgets.

A Smoke Screen No Longer

Fire is contradictory; it has always meant danger as much as it's meant warmth and household assistance. Fire and smoke have taken many lives. "What is that burning smell?" is a question that alerts you to potential danger in a way few other things can.

There is a very big difference between smelling and breathing the aroma of pure burning wood, burning leaves, or pure beeswax candles and breathing the smoke carried in the winds today. Toxic smoke is confusing to us on a primal level, I think, because smoke reminds us of the cook fire, the campfire, and warmth. We feel that as long as it is contained, fire is safe.

Carcinogenic and toxic smoke is a new kind of danger. *When Smoke Ran Like Water* is the story of smokestack pollution that killed or sickened half of the population of author Devra Lee Davis's hometown of Donora, Pennsylvania. When you smell toxic smoke, and it has an odor of sulfur, for example, you feel a bit like a deer caught in the headlights—confused and on edge. Or when neighbors illegally burn their trash, and you smell burning plastic, your body is violated with poison. Pregnant women and children, most especially, must be protected from toxic smoke.

Most smoke we're exposed to today is dirty and poisonous, and it destroys ecosystems. What seems like innocent burning can be hugely toxic. I grew up in Hanover, New Hampshire, and the Dartmouth students would build gigantic bonfires made out of old railroad ties. They would light them in the evenings whenever there were home football games. As children, we loved these bonfire nights, and we would run wild around the fire on the Dartmouth green. Little did we, or our parents, know that the burning railroad ties were impregnated with some of the most toxic pesticides known to man.

Firefighters are chronically exposed to a toxic blend of smoke from burning carpets, formaldehyde-based particle-board, plastic, pesticides, and petroleum. The synergistic exposure of this blend has never been studied. Exhaust smoke from diesel buses and smoke-stacks pollute our outdoor air. Indoors, the pollution in a kitchen with a gas stove is higher than in a bus station. An oil burner in need of a tune-up can gush toxic fumes into a home, causing permanent damage to a person's health.

Some communities have fought long battles for cleaner air, and we need to make sure our lawmakers know how important pollution controls are. It's a fight we'll need to wage over and over, one small victory at a time.

The Hopeful Horizon

The key to success for the environment is for the new "hydrogen economy" to be independent of fossil fuels—something many think would take a huge amount of money to accomplish. Those concerned about the possibility that fossil fuels and nuclear energy could run the hydrogen economy suggest that the money should be invested in sun

and wind energy research instead. Using the sun's energy for electricity and power in the future would give us a timeless relationship with fire in our otherwise industrial, technological culture.

Geothermal energy is in place in a handful of states, although I intuitively don't like this source of heat because it requires drilling holes deep into the earth with unknown consequences on the earth's natural energy grid. Other non–fossil fuel resources, such as wind, hydrogen, and fuel cells, are finally being considered seriously. Fuel cells can produce energy without fossil fuel combustion, and they do it much more efficiently, and fuel cell energy can be renewably derived from water or hydrogen. Development of new energy sources is a costly and lengthy process, but individuals, businesses, and governments around the world are realizing the importance of planning for tomorrow.

Fire Meditation

Watching the flames of a campfire seems to put us in a sort of trance that burns away the inconsequential and opens us up to others. As we look into the flames, we tend to have memorable conversations that matter, and we tell stories with messages and reminders about what doesn't belong in our lives.

A healer friend who practices plant spirit medicine suggested I sit by a fire to find the answer to a question I had about my life. I duly made an outdoor fire pit, and, surprising myself, I found her suggestions on how to meditate there deeply helpful. Now I try to make a fire as often as I can. Her directions couldn't have been easier: "Make a fire and ask your question to Grandfather Fire by simply sending the thought or question out. Free your mind to just 'be' as you sit there and watch the flames."

I was alone the first night that I built a meditation fire. I had spent the day fashioning the outdoor fireplace and found real tranquility in doing so. At dusk, I lit my first fire, as the wood thrush were still singing in the woods and the fireflies were lighting up the night. I sent out the life question that was on my mind—it was about this book, in fact—and I let it drift out over the fire and into the night. As the hush of dark descended and the birds went

to sleep, the fire captured my full attention. I found myself watching the flames with a mind that was still and growing ever quiet. After about 45 minutes, I found myself knowing the answer to my question. I knew it in my heart, in my blood, in my bones. I *knew*. I asked another question about a decision I needed to make, sending the pros and cons out into the fire, and I had a similar experience. In less time, maybe half an hour, I again had a deep knowing. I *knew* the choice I needed to make.

I've made meditation fires many times since, and with them have come a vast deepening of my self-awareness and a connection to who I am.

Fire in the Home

John Ott, a photobiologist, coined the term *malillumination* to describe inadequate sunlight intake. He believes that natural light is similar to a nutritional need of the body and thus is essential for good health. Others call the light from the sun a super nutrient, which supports the entire endocrine system.

When newborn babies become jaundiced, they are put under the healing light of full-spectrum lightbulbs, and with just that treatment, they recover quickly. Natural light interacts with serum bilirubin, making it nontoxic.

When children's classrooms are "day-lighted," and they have adequate exposure to the natural rays of the sun, they learn more effectively, are absent from school less, and are calmer in their behavior. When Alzheimer's disease patients are exposed to natural daylight, they sleep better. The sun's light, it turns out, is as important as any other vital nutrient. In fact, the changing light of the sun at dawn and dusk synchronizes our natural body rhythms.

It is an evolutionary wonder to me that humans living in industrialized societies get so little natural sunlight every day that we need to make a point of learning about light and lightbulbs so that we can ensure good health.

Very few of us get more than a few snatches of natural light (unimpeded by windows) here and there. Just looking at the amount of outdoor time my normal, very active extended family averages (other than in the summer) astonished and appalled me. I expect my family's exposure to light is quite typical. My college-age nieces and nephews were the only ones who fared well, and that is because they participate in outside sports year-round.

Here's a summary of my family's winter sun exposure.

❖ *My mother: 1 hour a week*. She is almost 80 and may experience 30 min-utes of natural light a few times a week when she walks outside to get her mail.

❖ *Sister #1: 1 hour a week*. She drives to work, is very busy, and gets her exercise inside on a treadmill.

❖ *Sister #2: 1 hour a week*. She, too, drives to work, is very busy, and gets her exercise inside on a treadmill. She wears UV-protective glasses.

❖ *Sister #3: 6 hours a week*. She lives in New York City, is also very busy, and walks a great deal.

❖ *My teenage daughter: 1 to 2 hours a week*. During her school lunch, it is optional for her to go outside for 10 minutes or so. In spring and summer, she spends many hours playing outdoor sports.

❖ *Me: 2 hours a week*. My time outdoors is spent walking. I, too, am very busy and spend long hours at my desk.

Judging from this sampling of my family's exposure to natural outdoor light, we are woefully undersupplied with this essential element in the winter. The analysis of my family's time outdoors is doubly ironic because we have always considered ourselves an "outdoorsy" family. We are all so busy that spending time outdoors has become a luxury we usually can't afford! This simple exercise of compiling the hours of time spent outdoors has galvanized me to change. How much time do you spend outdoors each week? Could symptoms of lacking outdoor light be an invisible epidemic?

Light and Health

There are two essential aspects of light that we need every day for good health, both physical and emotional. One is the full spectrum of the sun's light rays in its natural color balance. Most windows block this complete full spectrum. Unless you choose a full-spectrum light inside or spend time outside without glasses or sunglasses, you will be hard-pressed to receive enough full-spectrum light in your eyes to activate bodily systems.

Natural light is made up of a wide spectrum of colors; the visible spectrum is represented by the colors of the rainbow. The colors of the spectrum are also the colors of the chakras (the body's energy centers), with red being the first chakra, the center of the survival instinct at the base of the spine. Violet is the color of the crown chakra, the center of spiritual development at the top of the head.

A full spectrum of colors is healing, and some colors in the spectrum target specific problems. For example, green is the color associated with the heart chakra, and green light helps heal the heart. A combination of red and blue is often used to inspire emotional balance.

The other essential aspect of light is brightness. If the light you receive each day, artificial or natural, isn't bright enough, your body's hormones won't kick into gear to activate your circadian rhythm (see page 296). While a typical office light will provide enough light so that you can see, it is inadequate for activating the circadian rhythm.

Ultraviolet (UV) light has three wavelength designations: UVA (some-

COLOR THERAPY FOR BETTER HEALTH

COLOR	HEALS	PROMOTES
Red	Blood disorders	Vitality, creativity, better test scores in children
Orange	Lungs, kidneys	Assimilation
Yellow	Stomach, liver	Intellect
Green	Heart, hypertension	Unconditional love
Blue	Thyroid, larynx	Self-expression
Indigo	Eye diseases, vision	Psychic abilities
Violet	Mental disorders	Spirituality

Safe and Sound

SUNLIGHT FOR VITAMIN D

Forty percent of the US population is considered deficient in vitamin D. Vitamin D keeps bones strong and may help prevent some cancers. Your body (most important, your eyes) needs 15 to 20 minutes of exposure to full-spectrum sunlight *without sunscreens or UV-blocking glasses* every day in order for the skin to manufacture vitamin D.

Vitamin D isn't found naturally in most foods either (milk contains synthetic vitamin D). Other than sunlight, vitamin D supplements, cod-liver oil, and oily fish are the only ways to get vitamin D. Eyeglasses and windows also interfere with absorbing full-spectrum sunlight, so they can prevent you from meeting your vitamin D quota.

So, go out in the sun and let your skin show, but only for very short periods of time (less than 15 minutes). Avoid the sun during the hottest part of the day as well. Catch your rays in the morning or at dusk, especially if you are fair-skinned and burn easily. Just be sure to soak up a few rays every day.

---

times called near rays), UVB (also known as mid rays), and UVC (the far rays). The sun produces mostly UVA light, a moderate amount of UVB, and a small amount of UVC. The earth's ozone layer blocks most UVC light. UVA rays make up 90 to 95 percent of total UV ray exposure. UVB stimulates the production of vitamin D_3 in your skin, which is essential for the absorption of calcium in the bones.

With the thinning of the ozone layer, we are being exposed to more UVC light. UVC light is considered the most dangerous for increasing the risk of skin cancer. However, a study from 1982 indicates that moderate exposure to UVC light is safer than only a little exposure. They found that the incidence of malignant melanomas was considerably higher in office workers who worked under fluorescent lights than in people who worked in other indoor environments where some natural light was available.

Lux

The light brightness measurement is called a lux. For therapeutic reasons, you need to be exposed to light that is at least as bright as dawn or twilight (2,500 to 10,000 lux), even on cloudy days. Regular incandescent lightbulbs don't even get close, producing only 500 to 1,000 lux on your work surface, and that's not enough to glean the health requirements of light exposure. Having adequate light to see what you are doing isn't the issue; it is whether or not the light's intensity is enough to stimulate the circadian rhythm.

The Circadian Rhythm

When natural light is absorbed by the retina of the eye, electrical impulses are carried along the optic nerve to the brain and the hypothalamus, pineal gland, and pituitary gland. These impulses activate neurotransmitters that turn on many hormonal systems, including the metabolism, reproductive functions, and the internal biological clock called the circadian rhythm.

The circadian rhythm of the body is activated by light that is significantly brighter and more complex in spectrum than that which is needed for visual work. (NASA installs full-spectrum lighting in spacecraft for this reason.)

The elderly may require five times as much natural light to regulate the circadian rhythm. Some states have established lighting requirements for nursing homes for this reason. According to the Center of Design for an Aging Society and as reported at ISDesignet.com, the three key aspects for lighting design for the elderly are quantity, quality, and consistency.

Light exposure raises serotonin, which keeps you awake and alert. Serotonin is a natural hormone that reduces stress and brings feelings of calm and well-being. Conversely, melatonin levels rise in the dark, making you sleepy. Daylight suppresses the hormone melatonin, so if you don't get enough light of sufficient intensity (lux), you pro-

If you feel sluggish or irritable during the winter months, you may actually have Seasonal Affective Disorder (SAD), a form of depression that can be relieved with exposure to real or simulated sunlight. Doctors recommend early morning walks outdoors and sunlight-simulating light boxes to help relieve symptoms.

duce too much melatonin and become groggy. (If you feel tired during the day, go out and get some sun!)

Bring Light into Your Life

Sunlight therapy has been used for millennia to treat diseases such as tuberculosis, skin lesions, psoriasis, and high blood pressure. Studies indicate that those exposed to natural light experience an increased oxygen intake and a reduced heart rate. Overeating and excess body weight have also been linked in studies to a lack of full-spectrum light. Some studies point out that the absence of natural light to regulate hormonal systems triggers carbohydrate cravings.

Sunlight is often considered nature's bactericide—a natural antibiotic. The full spectrum of the sun produces wavelengths that kill numerous bacteria, molds, yeasts, and viruses. In Russia, full-spectrum lighting systems were installed in factories to help prevent worker illness, and it lowered the bacterial contamination of the air by 40 to 70 percent. Russian researchers have also found that a body's resistance to pollutants is much stronger when exposed to sunlight.

The "winter blues," or Seasonal Affective Disorder (SAD), is a particular type of depression resulting from limited exposure to natural light, usually occurring in the winter when daylight hours are short. SAD affects 10 times more people living in Alaska or northern New England than in Florida. Melatonin levels, the hormone that gets higher in the dark, are found to be very high in patients with SAD. Researchers have found that the symptoms of depression in SAD are relieved when the person is exposed to between ½ hour and 3 hours of bright, full-spectrum light. (Negative ions also give relief; see page 420.)

Children are also affected by light. They can be more hyperactive in a classroom with cool white fluorescent lighting than in rooms with full-spectrum light (some with shields to block UVC rays, allaying concern over skin cancer). A study by the Department of Education of Alberta, Canada, found that students with full-spectrum light in their classrooms learned faster, had one-third fewer absences, grew faster, and achieved higher test scores. As a result of this study, some North Carolina schools use skylights so that students can benefit from natural light.

Seek Some Sun

Many of us have been so scared of skin cancer that we don't get enough natural light to help our biological clocks function. It is important to place

Safe and Sound

SUNLIGHT CAN IMPROVE YOUR HEALTH

Sunlight is the biggest cause of visible aging, and the information you read about too much sun exposure can be unnerving—more wrinkles, age spots, and skin cancer. Yet sunlight can regulate sleep cycles and enhance your feeling of well-being. It's important to protect skin with a diet rich in fruits and vegetables, moisturizers and sunscreen, and protective clothing, yet it's also healthy to get some sun exposure. Here's why.

❖ *Vitamin D synthesis and calcium absorption:* Vitamin D balances calcium and phosphorus—minerals that are necessary for a healthy skeleton. Studies have shown that those receiving UV light absorbed 40 percent more calcium than those who were deprived of it. A winter study of veterans in a soldiers' home in Massachusetts compared calcium absorption under two lighting systems: Under full-spectrum light, calcium absorption increased 15 percent; under standard incandescent lightbulbs, absorption decreased 25 percent.

❖ *Reduces cholesterol:* According to *Liberman's Light: Medicine of the Future*, chickens exposed to full-spectrum light lived twice as long, laid more eggs, and were calmer and less aggressive; their eggs were 25 percent lower in cholesterol. As reported in the *Archives of Internal Medicine* magazine (April 26, 2004), cholesterol levels in humans are found to be higher in the winter and lower in the summer. Increase in exposure to the sun increases exposure to natural vitamin D.

❖ *Heals skin:* Sunlight is an effective treatment for psoriasis. Among other things, sunlight activates solitrol, an important skin hormone.

❖ *Increases sex drive:* Because the hormonal balance of the body is greatly affected by light, it follows that light increases the level of sex hormones. Animal studies report increased mating in captivity when the animals are provided with adequate light. (Vita-Lite, a full-spectrum light, has a balanced UV light, and it is used extensively for enhancing the mating and reproduction of indoor pets and animals.)

❖ *Helps the heart:* UV light can lower blood pressure, increase the heart's efficiency, improve electrocardiogram readings and blood profiles, and increase the level of sex hormones.

❖ *Decreases premenstrual syndrome (PMS) symptoms:* Two hours of bright, full-spectrum light each day may reduce symptoms of PMS.

the amount of UV light you really receive into perspective. Are your eyes and skin receiving 15 to 20 minutes of full-spectrum light every single day, unimpeded by windows? Most are not. This amount of UV light in the skin is necessary to synthesize vitamin D, for example. So make sure you don't block this critical amount in an overzealous attempt to block UV rays. The key is

moderation. Wisely choose the time you spend outside in the sun, avoiding noon exposure, and aiming for early morning or late afternoon's more healthful rays.

Assuming it isn't contraindicated by any medical condition, I feel that it's important to bathe in light. Bathe your eyes in natural outdoor light without any glasses for up to 20 minutes every day. It is best to do this before 10:00 a.m. or after 2:00 p.m. Soak it up—in a walk, on a deck, in a lawn chair, or at the beach. Through your eyes, light goes directly to the hypothalamus and from there to every cell in your body. *You don't need to be in the direct sun.* A porch is fine! Read the daily newspaper in the sun; look at your mail there, too. In the winter, walk somewhere that isn't icy. If you bundle in layers, the heat you generate while walking will help you stay warm. If you are disabled, infirm, or unable to get outside for whatever reason, sit by an open window for 20 minutes or so every day, if the weather permits.

Daylighting in Your Home

Daylighting is "the use of direct, diffuse, or reflected sunlight to provide full or supplemental lighting for building interiors," according to the US Department of Energy, Energy Efficiency and Renewable Energy Clearinghouse (EREC), in Merrifield, Virginia. Daylighting is very energy efficient. After all, as James Kachadorian, author of *The Passive Solar House,* notes, "The sun shines on almost every home many days throughout the year. The question is: To what extent are you utilizing the sunlight?" Through daylighting, electrical use can be reduced 60 to 70 percent during daylight hours.

While energy is saved with daylighting, it may not be enough to provide the full health benefits of sunlight unless you also assure that full-spectrum light reaches the inhabitants. Some daylighting practitioners work to reduce bright-

You need to expose your skin to sunlight in order to get adequate vitamin D, especially in winter when sunshine isn't as strong. Take a 15- to 20-minute stroll outside, and try to let your face, arms, and hands bathe in the sun's rays.

UV-TRANSMITTING OR UV-BLOCKING WINDOWS?

During the energy crunch of the 1970s, homes were insulated to the hilt and made as airtight as possible to cut down on electricity and fuel use. At the time, concerns about indoor air quality were not really on the radar screen for building consultants, and these airtight buildings became very toxic without enough of an air exchange to clear out the fumes of cleaning products or outgassing from furniture and building supplies.

In the myopic view of cutting down on energy use, as well as a panic about absorbing UV rays that could cause skin cancer, I believe that our buildings are once again becoming unhealthy. This time, the impingement to health is a result of new technology in windows that is aimed at reducing the infiltration of UV light for energy-saving reasons.

If your house has cutting-edge, energy-saving, triple-glazed moderate solar gain low-e glass, only 56 percent of the *visible* rays of the sun will be allowed through the windows, whereas, the light allowed through an old-fashioned, single-glaze, clear glass window lets in 90 percent of the visible light.

UV-transmitting eyeglasses and windows that let in natural daylight are available, but you have to really search. The truth about my current lifestyle is that for at least 9 months a year, I am woefully undersupplied in natural light every single day. I believe that my eyes need all the natural light they can get, not UV-*blocking* eyeglasses.

When choosing glasses, choose full-spectrum neutral gray. Other tinted sunglasses can block out certain colors of the light spectrum that you need for health.

---

ness and recommend glass with UV filters, coatings, or films that change tint in response to the light intensity.

If you are interested in daylighting, these are the four principles to follow:

Window Placement: Daylighting's use of windows is a science. It focuses on making sure that there is plenty of light (as a canopy of sorts) reflecting off the ceiling. It also provides filtered light, so you can look out of windows and not be overwhelmed with light that's too bright or causes glare. One principle of window placement suggests placing them high on the wall so light streams in and penetrates deeper into the room.

Brightness: Glare and bright light can be eliminated by awnings, window blinds, and other window treatments, so direct sunlight doesn't reach inside the room. Indirect lighting is provided with the canopy effect off the ceiling, and direct downlighting, such as track lighting, provides light for tasks. However, exposure to sufficient lux must be a priority. Some practitioners recommend low-transmittance glass (which transmits only small portions of the sun's light and heat) to protect from glare. I would not choose this myself because I want to have as much full-spectrum light as possible inside the building, but I would instead investigate UV-penetrating windows that shielded UVC.

Daylight Sensors: Sensors trigger a

constant, optimum light luminance for a space, and lights automatically dim or brighten to maintain that predetermined level. However, some lighting experts believe that light levels that change throughout the day are the most natural, and light without variation is not necessarily optimal.

Wall Color: Lighter colors are used on the ceiling and the tops of the walls, with darker colors below. This sort of canopy mimics the outdoors, if you think about it. You can furnish and decorate homes that feature the natural spectrum of light with either warm or cool colors. Because the light is natural, all the colors will be balanced.

Lightbulbs

The average US home has 34 light sockets! As reported in Green Seal's *Choose Green Report: Compact Fluorescent Lighting,* "If each socket is filled with a 100-watt bulb and is powered for 5 hours each day, 294 pounds of carbon dioxide (CO_2) are emitted into the atmosphere in 1 week. (One kilowatt-hour of energy emits approximately 2.5 pounds of CO_2.)"

Pay attention to the lighting use in your home from an energy perspective, and adjust wasteful use when possible. When I did this mental check in my home, I realized that I kept a full line of lightbulbs on over the mirror and sink in the bathroom every night, all night long, to light the way for my daughter if she needed it. A night-light in that room would have been more than adequate, and I have now switched to one. Changing wasteful lighting habits can also save you money. The EPA estimates that 15 to 25 percent of the annual electricity bill can be traced to lighting.

Is it best to turn lights off after leaving a room? Yes. But if you are using compact incandescent bulbs and go in and out of a specific lighted space routinely and are turning the light on and off frequently, it is best to leave the light on until you are finished in that room.

Lux and Lumens

We need enough bright light, also known as lux, to stimulate the body's biological clock. A lux of 500, commonly produced by a regular incandescent bulb, may produce sufficient light for the task at hand, but it does not necessarily have enough *lux* to help your body's circadian rhythms. This requires the 2,500 to 10,000 lux brightness provided by sunlight.

The amount of light *produced* by a lightbulb is called *lumens*. The relationship between the lumens produced and the wattage used tells you how much energy a bulb consumes. Lumens per watt (LPW) is determined by the bulb's lumens, divided by the watts. So, for example, if a compact fluorescent has a wattage of 13 and a lumens of 900, the LPW is 69.23. The law requires that the number of lumens and the wattage rating appear on the packaging of any bulb.

Full-Spectrum Lightbulbs

These lightbulbs are the most like natural daylight and are often called natural spectrum, or natural daylight spectrum light; they are available as incandescent, compact fluorescent, and fluorescent. Their color appears more blue and less pink than ordinary fluorescents and much less yellow than incandescent bulbs. Some of these full-spectrum bulbs include more UV light than ordinary fluorescents, but their manufacturers claim that after sitting in front of such a bulb for 8 hours, the amount of UV light equals around 15 minutes of comparable outdoor exposure. Because of concerns about UV exposure, some full-spectrum bulbs have a shield to block UVC rays.

Bulbs labeled as "broad-spectrum bulbs" do not have the same distribution of colors as sunlight. "Blue glass bulbs" and "daylight incandescents" have blue glass that cuts down on the excessive red and infrared, but they aren't considered therapeutic bulbs because they do not produce full-spectrum light.

Incandescent Bulbs

This standard lightbulb consumes the most energy—90 percent of which is wasted heat. Incandescent bulbs tend to be good task lights, however. They give off a yellowish-white light that's emitted

---

WORDS TO THE WISE

MERCURY AWARENESS ALERT FOR FLUORESCENTS

All fluorescents contain very small amounts of mercury in the ballasts. You may assume that incandescents are better for the environment because of the mercury in fluorescents, but most experts believe that power plant emissions of mercury to support the less energy-efficient incandescents are far greater than the mercury required to provide fluorescence to compact fluorescent lights.

When shopping for fluorescent bulbs, look for bulbs with low amounts of mercury. (These types of bulbs are often labeled as "low mercury" or have green tips.) Avoid compact fluorescents that use magnetic ballasts—they contain radioisotopes. Look for an environmental seal of approval such as Energy Star on the product to ensure a safe, ecofriendly purchase.

Be careful how you dispose of fluorescent lamps. Because of the hazardous materials in them (mercury and radioactive material), you should not toss burned-out lamps into the trash. Find out if there is a recycling program for them in your community, or dispose of them with other household hazardous wastes such as batteries, solvents, and paints at your community's designated drop-off point or during a designated day when materials will be collected with your curbside trash.

in all directions. "Reflectorized" bulbs have a coating inside them that gives better "beam control" by concentrating the light in one direction. These bulbs work well as floodlights or task lights and double the amount of directed light. Parabolic reflector bulbs produce about four times the light of a regular incandescent and are used in track lighting.

Tungsten-Halogen

These bulbs produce a long-lasting, incandescent, very bright white light, and they're quite expensive. Many prefer halogen lamps for reading because of their bright, white light. I don't recommend them because they get very, very hot and can be a serious fire hazard. Low-voltage halogens require a transformer, which in turn gives off electromagnetic fields and should be placed at least 6 feet away from where people sit.

Fluorescent

Standard fluorescent lights offer a diffuse, steady, efficient light and produce little heat, but they are not very good for task lighting. Those that use a magnetic ballast—or any light that flickers—can cause significant eyestrain and fatigue. Switch to lights with electronic ballasts to eliminate the flicker and hum of fluorescent lights (the hum alone may cause stress).

Compared with incandescents, fluorescents with comparable lumen ratings use one-fifth to one-third less electricity and last up to 20 times longer. Fluorescents are available in a wide range of color spectrums.

Compact Fluorescent Lightbulbs (CFLs)

These ecofriendly bulbs fit into regular outlets. While they are more expensive to buy than regular incandescents, they use 75 percent less energy and can save 50 to 80 percent in energy costs over the life of the bulb. Switching from incandescent to compact fluorescent bulbs can save you time as well as money in the long run. Imagine one lightbulb lasting for 11 years! These bulbs are worth the investment.

As with similar early environmental technology, the first models of CFLs were problematic, emitting a loud humming and an unnaturally bright light. Fortunately, the technology has greatly improved since the early 1990s. CFLs can now be used in most any contemporary fixture and for any lighting need. New CFLs may not work with older lighting fixtures though; future energy savings, however, may make it worthwhile to replace the old fixtures with newer versions.

According to the *Choose Green Report: Compact Fluorescent Lighting* (Green Seal, 1998), a CFL with one-third the wattage can replace an incandescent fixture and produce the same light output.

Energy Efficiency

Conservation should be the biggest priority for every household when it comes to energy use, with selecting and maintaining appliances in good condition as a close second. Conservation makes a huge impact with just small changes in your routine—if everyone in the family turns off lights when not in use, you can reduce the amount of energy used for lighting in your home by close to 50 percent.

I've seen beautiful homes with all sorts of outdoor lights shining on front doors, interesting architectural features, front gates, and dramatic landscaping, but I am discouraged when I see those lights on all night, 365 days a year. Most of the lights are unnecessary for safety, so how much energy do all those lights consume just to make a statement at 3:00 a.m.? My friend's neighbors keep floodlights shining on their

---

WORDS TO THE WISE

ENERGY-SAVING TIPS WORTH A MENTION

While lighting fixtures and lighting use can waste precious energy, other seemingly innocent appliances and household helpers can be energy hogs too. Work to reduce phantom electrical loads (equipment and appliances in "standby" mode) throughout your home. Many of these "standby" modes were designed into the equipment as time-savers so users wouldn't have to wait for internal components to warm up before use.

If you have electronic appliances with a clock that never fully turns off, such as a computer, coffeemaker, VCR, range, and microwave oven, you're consuming energy even if the equipment is not in use. Other devices that never fully turn off include anything powered by a remote control, such as a TV or sound system, and equipment that uses a "power cube" in an electrical socket, such as an answering machine or a recharging base for an electric toothbrush, cordless screwdriver, and cell phone. These "power cubes" are 60 to 80 percent inefficient in their use of electricity.

You may not be able to unplug your answering machine, but you can unplug an electric toothbrush, cell phone charger, or any other "power cube" when it's not in use. Fully unplug items, such as televisions, VCRs, sound systems, and any other appliances that have a remote control or timer clock when you plan to be away or if you don't use the equipment very often.

It may be a small change, but consider using battery-powered clocks that run on single AA rechargeable batteries instead of electric clocks.

Use less energy by lowering your water heater thermostat from 140°F to 120°F, and consider installing a timer that can automatically turn the heater off at night when you don't have a need for hot water.

---

backyard, even in winter, for hours and hours each evening; their suburban neighbors have had to upgrade nighttime window treatments just to block out the bright light to sleep. We must remember that the cost of energy isn't just what is in our monthly utility bill; there's a cost to the environment for every kilowatt-hour we use.

Always choose lighting products with the EPA's "Energy Star" mark. Check www.energystar.gov for store locators and rebate finders. Replace older fixtures because they become less efficient over time, losing 20 to 30 percent of their light output. Keep windows, fixtures, lamps, and room surfaces clean. Maintenance is vital to lighting efficiency. Light levels decrease over time because of dirt on fixtures, lamps, and room surfaces. The lightbulb will continue to draw "full power," but the light will be veiled.

Try to maximize the use of natural daylight from windows. When lighting is necessary, switch to compact fluorescent bulbs wherever possible. If you must use incandescents, select higherwatt models because they're more energy efficient than lower-watt ones.

Consider installing dimmer switches in multipurpose rooms. Occupancy or motion sensors turn lights or other equipment on when you enter (or leave) a room. The more sophisticated of these generally inexpensive devices adjust the amount of light being turned on according to how much daylight is available. Timers work for rare circumstances, such as for outdoor lighting when the lights need to come on. On the other hand, it is unlikely one would need an outdoor light on for a specific reason every single day. Think carefully before using this option so you don't use more electricity than needed.

Lighting Design

The function of a room should determine the quality and quantity of the light needed. The kitchen usually requires direct sources of light, for example, whereas the living room and bedrooms require reflected or diffused light for the mood desired. In feng shui, light helps activate the chi, so choosing how and when to use lightbulbs is important.

Ambient lighting fills the whole room's space. It's diffuse and uniform and mimics natural light. Many times, ambient light is supplied by an overhead ceiling fixture. *Task lighting* is directional; it's a direct beam of light used for a single task, such as reading, writing, and working on a kitchen cutting board. *Accent lighting* is decorative and attention grabbing. Accent lights are used to set a mood, add sparkle, and cast dramatic shadows. They're most

Want to create a friendly, inviting atmosphere and still be able to see to prepare meals? Your kitchen lighting scheme should contain three sources of light: ambient lighting to illuminate the entire space, task lighting to brighten a work area, and accent lighting to play up important features in the room.

often used to highlight artwork, fire-places, interior plantscaping, and archi-tecture. *Safety lighting* illuminates dark areas and changes in elevation. You'll often find safety lighting on the stair treads of sunken living rooms or in stairways.

You should combine subtle and strong light throughout a room. Layer bright light for task lighting (maybe two or three places in a large room) with overhead ambient light. Consider a ratio of five times the bright task lighting to one part ambient light.

Lighting designers use a variety of techniques and industry tricks to effec-tively and beautifully light a room.

❖ Use an energy-saving dimmer switch to make one light fixture per-form both ambient and task lighting roles.

❖ Flood a hall or small lobby with natural light to welcome and aid in the flow of chi.

❖ Maximize natural light by cutting back overgrown shrubs and trees.

❖ Hang mirrors so that they bounce light into dark corners.

❖ Choose light-colored paints, wallpaper, and furniture for a room that receives little natural light.

❖ Hang semitransparent drapes to diffuse sunlight rather than block it.

❖ Vary your light sources by utilizing downlights, uplights, spotlights, table lamps, floor lamps, and dimmer switches.

❖ Use candles as light alternatives when you desire a moody atmosphere, but avoid oil lamps because they require petroleum oils.

❖ Always cover bulbs with lampshades. Bare lightbulbs provide harsh light that strains the eyes.

❖ To make a small room look big, "wash" the walls with an even layer of light; these fixtures are appropriately called wall washers. Wall washers are particularly effective on light-colored paint or wallpaper.

❖ Offer some cozy spots in a large room by adding a few soft light areas.

❖ Make a narrow room seem longer by lighting the shorter walls to deemphasize the longer ones.

❖ If you have low ceilings, place uplights on the wall. If you'd like to deemphasize high ceilings, use downlighting to keep the light focused on seating areas and room features.

❖ Avoid distracting glare by paying attention to where you place reflective surfaces, such as mirrors, glass-top tables, and highly polished furniture. Reflective surfaces can brighten a room, but keep them away from reading areas and televisions to reduce glare.

Heating and Cooling

Humans feel the most comfortable in temperatures between 72° and 78°F, and if we have a fan blowing, we can be comfortable at 82°F. When using a fan, keep the air-conditioning thermostat set at 82°F. Otherwise, keep your air conditioner at the high end of comfort, around 78°F. In the winter, you can still be comfortable on the cooler side of things; set your thermostat between 68° and 72°F, and wear a sweater or keep a throw handy for times when you're relaxing and not moving around.

During the energy crunch of the 1970s, many buildings were sealed or retrofitted to become more energy efficient. This was often done without regard to the long-term consequences. This happened to my town's school when the air exchange system was sealed off! This resulted in a greatly reduced air exchange and very unhealthy indoor air.

So how much energy efficiency is advisable? When is tight too tight? The answer depends upon a number of things, including how nontoxic your home is. It is important for you to have a healthy air exchange and adequate house ventilation. Energy efficiency can go wrong, as evidenced by an e-mail I received recently from someone. This person had their house made more energy efficient only to discover that it had become too tightly sealed. As a result, mold grew around the entire roofline of the building.

If the building is made of synthetic materials and furnishings and standard cleaners are used, then a building that is too tight will be a health hazard. When you use art, craft, or building supplies, make sure to compensate with extra ventilation.

Having an energy audit of your home makes great sense. A typical home loses more than 25 percent of its

A home energy audit can determine how much energy your house consumes and how to make your home more energy efficient. It can pinpoint trouble spots, such as inadequate insulation and leaky window seals, and make recommendations on how to upgrade and make repairs for maximum energy efficiency.

heat through windows and air leaks. Some utilities offer this service for free, and many states offer financial incentives for energy-efficient improvements. Through the federal Home Performance with Energy Star program, a participating Building Performance Institute (BPI)–certified Home Performance contractor will inspect your home and provide recommendations for energy-saving measures.

BPI-certified contractors will do a blower door test with the most up-to-date technology to measure air leakage and trace airflow in the building. Armed with the results, you can then make a plan to seal air leaks, increase insulation, and solve the problems of heat loss in your home. If you choose to have the work done, the testing fee will be fully deducted from the cost of the work.

Solar Heat

If you are able to invest in a new heating system using renewable energy sources, do so! Contact your local utility to learn about rebates and incentives. Hire an expert consultant to see which technology would be best for your home. Wind, solar, geothermal, and heat pump technologies are changing and becoming more affordable all the time.

Most of us have to use our existing systems that rely on burning fossil fuels for heat. It is nonetheless important to pay special attention to protecting your health. Upgrading to sealed combustion systems would make a big difference in reducing the emissions that enter your living space. Have boilers tuned every year. Never, ever, use kerosene space heaters because, as the EPA notes, they produce combustion pollutants that can damage your health. Switch from gas to an electric stove. Make a 10-year plan to implement a heating system that is more efficient, such as solar heat.

Is your home a good candidate to retrofit for a solar energy conversion? This is the first thing you need to determine before investing in solar technology. The more direct sunlight your home receives, the more energy a solar energy system produces. Your local government can provide a wealth of information and resources about how to get started to retrofit your home to be more energy efficient and utilize renewable energy.

Sunlight provides the cleanest energy of all. It is energy that anybody can use, and it is free. In most cases, in order to tap into this energy source in a way that reduces your utility bill, you will need to invest in some technology, although it is often minimal for passive solar design. Passive solar design can reduce heating bills as much as 50 percent.

Here's how it works: The sun shines in the windows and is collected in a specially designed wall or floor that absorbs and stores heat. One type, direct gain, is a simple passive design using windows with a special glazing. Sun is absorbed by a dark surface inside the building. Another type, indirect gain, stores the contained solar energy in a special wall called a Trombe wall. Trombe walls are 8- to 16-inch-thick walls and are coated with an absorbent material. The material is covered with glass or plastic set between $\frac{3}{4}$ and 6 inches away from the masonry wall. A third type, isolated gain, is a south-facing sunroom that is heated by the sun.

The windows of your house, especially those facing south, can admit a lot of heat from the sun. Informal, natural passive solar gain can be had from something as simple as a windowsill of flowerpots, in which the soil stores the heat from the sun streaming in the windows during the day and releases the heat into the home at night. A dark, solid surface, such as a slate floor, would provide a good solar collector.

Passive solar home design must work in the reverse in the summer to keep out sunlight so the house doesn't overheat. Shade trees, awnings, and shutters can all be used to augment passive solar design. Natural ventilation can be established by adding "wing walls," installed on the windward side of the house to help natural breezes flow into the interior and increase the natural airflow.

Active solar systems use mechanical and electrical devices to utilize solar energy that has been trapped by a solar collector. The technology used includes devices such as photovoltaic cells and solar panels. Sunlight strikes these devices, and the energy generates an electrical current that is captured and stored by batteries. Called a PV system, the cells and panels are a clean power source, they're quiet and reliable, and they require little maintenance. They could be well worth the cost of from $5,000 to $15,000 for a standard-size house.

Hot Water Heaters

An average household with an electric water heater spends about one-seventh to one-quarter of its home energy costs on heating water. You can reduce your energy use by insulating hot water pipes with a high-quality pipe insulation and by insulating your water-heater storage tank with a heat blanket.

Solar water heaters can operate in almost any climate, although the colder the water, the more efficiently a solar water heater works. Solar water heaters require a solar collector in a south-facing location that receives full sun for at least a few hours each day, and they can provide up to 100 percent of your hot water requirements, although you will need to have a conventional backup system. The investment in a solar water heater will pay for itself in just a few years.

Heating with Wood

As already mentioned, using wood to heat our homes is not a practical solution to meeting the everyday energy needs of the world. In fact, it would be hugely destructive if the whole world burned wood for heating and cooking, not only because of emissions, but because it would result in the loss of forests and destruction of ecosystems around the world. However, as a backup source of warmth, having a woodstove or fireplace makes very good sense, as long as you burn sustainably harvested wood and you have upgraded your wood heating system to one that reduces wood smoke pollution into your neighborhood.

I am convinced that burning wood in a fireplace or woodstove now and then provides spiritual comfort. People wax poetic about the heat from wood, the smell of wood smoke, and the pleasure of watching the flames. Who doesn't love the comfort that comes from reading in a comfortable chair with your feet at the hearth of a nice blaze in deep winter? Does anyone ever speak this way of her oil burner? That's doubtful.

Fireplaces and Woodstoves

I have a woodstove with a glass window in the front for viewing the flames and burning logs. The red coals get so hot they look like lava. I miss the sensory stimulation of an open fireplace, especially hearing the snaps and pops of wood and the smell of wood smoke. But the meditative quality is still present with a woodstove, as is the warmth.

An efficient woodstove is healthier than a fireplace, and it provides much more heat. Many states have now devel-oped low emissions requirements for new wood-burning appliances. All woodstoves sold after July 1, 1992, should bear an EPA certification sticker. Burning wood (combustion) emits nitrogen oxides, carbon monoxide, and particulate matter, so an efficient wood-stove is important for both indoor and outdoor air quality.

Some stoves give off *radiant heat,* directly heating nearby objects. Others give off *convection heat* that circulates throughout a home. Masonry wood-stoves, which are built into the wall, reach a combustion efficiency of 90 percent.

The right size stove reduces air pol-lution, so choose carefully. If you pur-chase a woodstove that is too big, you

---

MAKE IT YOURSELF
FIREPLACE SOOT CLEANER

Washing away fireplace smoke and soot or cleaning the smoke off the glass in woodstove doors is easy and safe using washing soda (available in the laundry section of the supermarket). It's one of the best heavy-duty cleaners I know and an excellent substitute for powerful sol-vents. Washing soda can peel wax off floors, though, and it isn't recommended for aluminum, so use this cleaner only on surfaces that won't be harmed, such as unpainted wood, glass, or stone.

  ½ cup washing soda
  2 gallons warm water

Combine the washing soda and the warm water in a bucket; swirl until the washing soda is dis-solved. Wearing waterproof gloves and using a heavy-duty sponge or clean rag, wash smoke residue and soot off fireplaces or woodstove surfaces. Rinse with clean water.

Variation: For really tough jobs, make a thick washing soda paste by mixing the soda with water and then spreading the paste on the soot. Keep the paste damp by spraying it every hour or so with a spray bottle of water. Leave the paste on overnight and then rinse.

might burn a fire at a low smolder to avoid overheating. This practice wastes wood, and incomplete burning of wood causes the air pollution associated with woodstoves. Complete combustion also helps to prevent the buildup of flammable chimney deposits called creosote. A stove rated at 60,000 British Thermal Units (BTU) can heat a 2,000-square-foot home, while a stove rated at 42,000 BTU can heat a 1,300-square-foot space. (A BTU is the amount of heat needed to raise the temperature of 1 pound of water 1°F.)

Choosing and Storing Wood

When buying wood for your stove or fireplace, make sure it's from sustainably harvested trees and not from clearcut forests, and that it's seasoned (not green) wood. Seasoned wood has, ideally, had a season or two to dry after it's been harvested; properly seasoned wood should have a moisture content around 20 to 25 percent by weight. You shouldn't burn green wood that smells of sap; that's a giveaway that the wood hasn't been properly seasoned.

Make sure that any wood you plan to burn is free from pesticides or pesticide drift. Fruit trees are often sprayed with pesticides, and trees located near orchards could have been exposed to pesticide drift. You've worked very hard to keep pesticides out of your home, so

be prudent when buying or cutting wood if you aren't sure of the tree's origin or history.

Always burn hardwoods, such as maple and oak. Because they're denser, they will burn longer and won't produce creosote like softwoods, such as pine. Stack your wood away from the house, on top of boards, so as not to draw termites and to keep it off the damp ground. Wet or damp wood could produce a smoky fire.

Keeping Cool

As important as heating is to a home, cooling is just as critical, especially in climates with a hot and humid summer

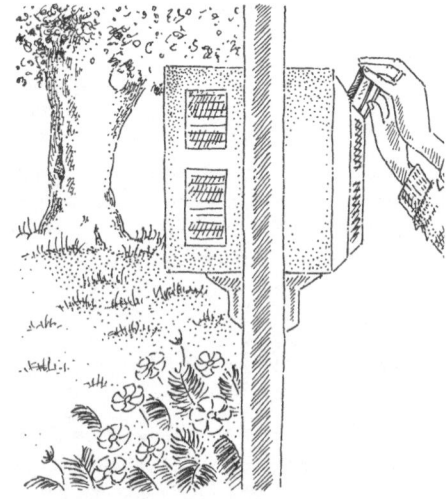

Air conditioners run most efficiently when they're in good working order. Ideally, window units should be installed out of direct sun on the eastern side of your home, and you should clean or replace the filter every 2 to 3 weeks when use is at its peak. Some filters can be vacuumed or washed in a tub of warm, soapy water, while other filters are disposable.

season. The ability to keep cool during a heat wave is a matter of life and death, as the French death toll of 15,000 people during a hot August 2003 proved. You must have a system to cool your house when experiencing unprecedented and unexpected heat.

In addition to installing or purchasing appliances that help cool and circulate air, such as air conditioners and fans, there are small ways to help keep a house cool during times of high outdoor temperatures. Lightbulbs and appliances give off heat, so try to run appliances only in the early morning or at night, and turn on as few incandescent bulbs as possible. Over the long term, try to provide shade for east and west windows by growing shade trees in the south, west, and even the east. Remember to close up the house during the day and open it at night, using fans to pull in cooler air at night when possible. When you redo your roof, invest in one that is light-colored and reflective, and install attic vents, which help release heated air.

Close south- and west-facing curtains during the day. Or consider installing awnings on the south side of the house. Use white curtains, blinds, and shades on windows that get direct sunlight, so window treatments don't absorb heat from the sun. Miniblinds can reduce solar heat gain by 40 to 50 percent. If miniblinds won't work for you, hang woven mats or bamboo shades on the *outside* of the window; you'll prevent 60 to 80 percent of the sun's heat from reaching the window.

When choosing an air-conditioning system, you'll need to consider the amount of humidity in your climate. Would you be better served with a variable or a multispeed blower that could greatly decrease humidity in your home as well as save energy? If you have an old central air–conditioning system, consider replacing it with one that has earned the EPA's Energy Star rating. Central air conditioners that have received the Energy Star rating use 25 to 40 percent less energy than conventional models. An upgraded version can save you 20 percent on your annual energy costs.

If your window air conditioner is more than 10 years old, consider upgrading to a new unit with an energy efficiency ratio (EER) above 10, making sure the unit is properly sized for the space it is covering. Many studies have revealed that most units are oversized by a whopping 50 percent. To save 5 to 10 percent on your energy costs, keep the outside part of your air-conditioning unit in the shade, placing it in a window with an eastern exposure instead of a southern exposure, if possible.

To maximize energy efficiency, thoroughly clean the dust filter at least once a month, and make sure to turn off your air conditioner if you are going to

If you have heat loss through your windows in winter, one heat-saving option is installing Window Quilts. These insulating window shades lock out winter cold and block out summer heat; they are custom-made to your window measurements for maximum energy efficiency.

be gone for more than an hour. For a bedroom unit, cool off the room and then try to turn it off before going to sleep, or use the energy-saver setting so that the unit doesn't run all night.

Energy Savings for Windows

Double-panel storm windows help a home retain heat. If you don't have such windows, use a plastic wrap seal as a temporary solution. Most varieties shrink to fit with a hair dryer and are attached to the window frame with special sticky tape. Plastic is low on the list of ecofriendly materials, but in a pinch, it's better than nothing. And make sure to use weather stripping around windows if you feel drafts.

If you've found air leaks, you are going to need to fill them in, and this is where you need to be careful not to add any unwanted pollution to your home. Caulking contains volatile organic compounds; the caulk that lasts the longest and also has the fewest additives is 100 percent silicone.

Window Quilts are an option for drafty windows, windows exposed to bitter cold winds, or climates with many frigid months. These specially designed curtains fit snuggly into the window molding and add "insulation" for cold winter nights, preventing heat from escaping. They are designed to be rolled up during the day to admit light. See page 501 for contact information.

Safe and Sound

GENERAL ELECTRICAL SAFETY

Faulty wiring accounts for 33 percent of urban electrical fires. Once a fire starts, residents have less than 4 minutes to evacuate. The appliances at the highest risk of causing electrical fires are electric stoves, televisions, clothes dryers, central heating units, radios, and stereo equipment. These guidelines will help you keep your home safe and fire free.

❖ Don't overload circuits or extension cords, and don't place extension cords in damp areas.
❖ Replace any wiring that is worn or frayed.
❖ Always buy appliances that have been tested for safety by Underwriter's Laboratory (UL).
❖ Keep all flammable materials away from appliances and heaters.
❖ Match three-prong plugs with a three-slot outlet.
❖ If any plug is hot, unplug it, and turn off any switches that are hot. Repair any lights that flicker.
❖ Don't use radios, boom boxes, or other electrical appliances near sinks, showers, or bath tubs.
❖ Don't run cords under rugs or in high-traffic areas.
❖ Don't mix water and electricity. (Basements are often damp enough to make enough "water" to cause a shock if exposed to a live wire.)
❖ Make sure your electrical system is grounded properly.
❖ Never work on any circuit unless it has been shut off.
❖ Cap outlets with a safety plug or safety cover if there are toddlers in the home.

In addition to basic electricity safety practices, it's best to consult a licensed electrician if you have any concerns about electrical safety in your home. If a plug in a certain outlet always seems hot, or a light always flickers, or you hear humming or buzzing from an outlet, lamp, or appliance, call an electrician to evaluate the situation.

10

clothes, closets, and the laundry room

Fabrics and clothing speak their own language. Linens, silks, and woolens are the stuff of novels, fantasy, heirloom legacies, and even great art. The canvases of Leonardo Da Vinci and Michelangelo were painted on stretched linen. Rustling silk is part of every movie where women wear gowns, and the drape and weave of linen evokes an elegance found in novels such as *The Great Gatsby*. Linen speaks of a lifestyle of garden parties, summer outings, and a connection with nature and temperature—an earthy warm-weather fabric with luster and texture, smelling lightly of sweet hay. Cotton is sturdy and rich with history from our everyday lives, and wool is a wonder fiber that is healing to sleep under and wear because it moderates our body temperature and heartbeat.

I can't think of anything in our lives that tells so much about our individual selves as our choice of clothing. Wrinkled or ironed, hot or cool, colorful or drab, everyday or dressy, clean or dirty, and expensive or threadbare, clothes tell of deep winter or summer seasons, financial status, daily habits, and overall demeanor. They announce if you are going to a meeting, exercise class, party, or beach. Clothing style choices can represent religious belief systems and political positions. Tartans, Eastern headdress, or kimonos may indicate your geographical location in the world.

Clothes are our second skin. They interact with our bodies and selves in ways that many of us don't recognize. They interface between our bodies and the atmosphere around us. They absorb energy and give off their own energy.

317

It is especially important that clothes, as our second skin, are in harmony with the natural elements earth, water, fire, and air. Natural fibers, harvested from plants (earth), wick moisture from us and keep us dry (water), moderate our body temperature (fire), and allow our bodies to breathe through our clothing (air). Imagine the contrast if the elements are not aligned with clothing: Synthetic fibers pollute (earth), encase us in our own perspiration (water), excessively heat us in the summer (fire), and don't allow air circulation between our bodies and the outside (air). When we're wearing synthetic clothing, the elements become hindrances and burdens; natural fiber, on the other hand, enhances us in most every way.

Pleasing the Senses

Spend a few moments sensing the feel of the fabric you are wearing against your skin. When I did this just now, I changed my clothes. I am usually very sensitive to how I feel in clothing and generally wear only natural materials. After paying attention to how I felt, I took off a fleece vest made of polyester. By really paying attention, I realized that what I had thought felt warm, sealing me in from the elements, was in fact cutting off my body's ability to breathe

out into the elements. The warmth I felt was the heat from my own body, and the synthetic fiber was sealing it in instead of moderating my body temperature naturally like an active fiber.

Barbara Brennan, an energy healer, teacher, and the author of a number of books on healing, says that natural fibers have a strongly positive effect on the energy field and that people should avoid clothes made of petroleum by-products because those can disrupt the body's normal energy flow. She says that nylon stockings strongly interfere with the energy flow up and down the legs.

Touch: Are your clothes soft or rough? Do they have a good hand? I am wearing cotton pants, and the fabric has a finish on it to keep it feeling stiff; I've washed the pants numerous times, and I haven't been able to remove the finish. Fabric finishes are a telling reflection of the societal mandate that looks are the most important virtue, even if the clothes don't feel good on your body or feel good to the touch. I'd much prefer pants that provide ventilation for my legs instead of having the fabric finish block the air.

The textile industry honors the hand when deciding if a piece of fabric or type of weave feels good. If the fabric "has a good hand," then you can expect it to drape well and have a good feel when you grasp and touch it. When I'm shopping, my hand always reaches out first to touch the fabric before holding it up to find the size and style. If it doesn't have a good hand, I move on without a second thought. My hand will tell me the source of the material—if it is naturally derived or not (and I am invariably drawn to natural fabrics, although rayon is an exception because it has a good drape and hand and feels natural because it is made of wood pulp).

Not every kind of natural fabric has a good hand. There are natural fabrics with a rough hand (such as ramie), and there are man-made fabrics that have a good hand (such as rayon). We should acknowledge our sense of touch when we pay attention to the feel of fabric and cloth. Many of us, especially in younger years, are deeply influenced by advertising and fashion, and we don't honor our own senses when we feel a PVC-based fabric and recoil when we touch it. I'm sure some of us have bought the garment anyway because it was a popular brand and a popular style—remember double-knit polyester pantsuits, blue-and-orange snorkel coats, and pleather skirts and boots? We may have ignored our senses to be in style. If we honor what we learn about the fabric's hand and origin, we learn to honor ourselves.

Smell: If your clothes smell of your laundry detergent, you should spend some time thinking about your choice of product and buy a fragrance-free version instead because that particular synthetic fragrance will be with you when you sleep and every day when you wear your clean clothes. If they have that wonderful, sweet smell of hay (like linen), and you like that smell, you are on the right track with your clothing choices. Make sure you like what you smell because it will be your second skin every time you wear that outfit.

Synthetic fabrics attract positive ions (see page 422), so the air close to you will not provide that clear, energizing, feel-good experience of negative ions.

The bioelectric nature of natural, "active" fibers makes them excellent choices for your body. The structure of the fiber, especially with an animal fleece such as wool, works to modulate temperature and control humidity. Many synthetic fibers, conversely, do none of this and in fact provide an atmosphere for static and positive ions.

Color: Bright spirits often wear black to hide the brilliant spectrum of their glowing chakras, or so a teacher of mine says. If so, could it be that everyone in New York City (where the fashion mandate is black) is a bright spirit? Probably not, but your color choices for your clothes project your personality, your self-esteem, and your well-being. It isn't hard to notice a woman who's wearing tropical colors, such as turquoise, melon, and chartreuse, in the dead of winter. Obviously, color makes her feel alive.

Your Sixth Sense: When my daughter was in nursery school, we experienced our first major battles of will, and they were over clothing. She had very determined style choices—striped leggings under shorts with a plaid skirt over the top of that, and a belt with feathers holding the whole batch up. Inexperienced as I was at motherhood, I worried what the teacher and other mothers would think, and I tried to put her in "nice" clothes. After a few days of getting my daughter to school late because we were both digging in our heels, I realized, "Oh, lucky her! She knows what she wants to wear and what she feels is beautiful!" I don't have much of a clue about that myself, given that it wasn't until I became a hippie in my teens that I had autonomy over my wardrobe. I am so disconnected from my own sense of personal style that, as a mother, I became like my mother before me—stuck in choices for clothing according to what others might think. Having given up being in charge of what my daughter wore in nursery school, I leave those decisions to her. I am now relishing how fully she's developed her sense of style as a young woman. She knows how she wants to present herself. All I can say is, "You go, girl!"

Clearing Closet Clutter

Karen Kingston, author of *Clear Your Clutter with Feng Shui,* notes that most people wear about 20 percent of their wardrobe 80 percent of the time. This is certainly true for me; I wear only a handful of outfits most seasons, and I wear them over and over again, washing and rewashing them week after week. The rest of my clothes just take up time and space.

Kingston notes that clothing clutter can make one tired and lethargic, and when it comes to clothes, I can really see why! I find myself hanging on to old sizes, clothes with memories, clothes of a potential personality that never emerged from my soul, clothes that were bought for one event, or clothes that were made of some wonderful fabric or colorful pattern that are too beautiful to give away. Kingston has a rule of thumb—if an item of clothing hasn't been worn within the past year, it is ready for the secondhand store because it isn't energetically correct for the person anyway.

Following this barometer is helpful because it will also inspire you to buy less. Before each purchase, ask yourself if this new garment will be added to your 80-percent pile. Go through your clothes and take the emotional barometer of each one. I did this with my clothes; I picked up every article, held it, and gauged its value in my life. What an interesting exercise! I found that part of the emotional barometer is the sheer sensuality of the fabric. I have clothes that I never wear but can't give up because I love their fabric.

Why You Can't Let Go

Even if you go through the 80/20 exercise, you may still need advice about what to keep. Clothes hold a lot of emotional energy, and you'll probably have to dig deep to find the reason that you can't let go of a particular garment. Are you holding onto a memory? Does the clothing reflect someone else's vision, fantasy, or style? Are you concerned about how much you spent or how much new things cost? Do you say to yourself that you might wear this sometime soon?

You'll discover other, simpler reasons for wanting to keep an item. Perhaps the fabric is lovely or the item symbolizes a buried part of your personality. I recently discovered a skirt that I rarely wear but that I really like. I also have some gorgeous silk that makes my skin color look stunningly beautiful. Pulling out this silk now and again is a great reminder of what great clothing and colors can do for a person.

Why You Should Let Go

As with any sort of clutter, clothing clutter included, when you have too much crammed into closets, drawers, and trunks, you're not appreciating or honoring the things that *do* make you feel good. There comes a day when you need to let go.

The basic rules are easy: If clothes don't fit, don't feel good, or aren't comfortable, give them away (or toss them if they're in bad shape). If you rarely wear the item or if you have something similar, clear it out. If the clothes are made of synthetic fibers and you've noticed that the fabric doesn't feel good against your skin when you wear it, pass it along to someone else. If a shirt

---

Annie's Insight

THE ENERGY OF A PREVIOUSLY WORN GARMENT

The energy of the person who previously wore a garment can sometimes be held in the fibers of the clothing, as can perfumes and other chemicals. Secondhand stores often wash clothes with disinfectants or pesticides. The way to solve all of these energy, residue, and odor problems is to soak the clothes in a full washing machine or sink of water overnight with at least 1 cup of baking soda before you launder the items. Repeat this exercise until you feel the clothes are free of scents and energy from the previous owner.

or pair of pants doesn't match something else you already own, let it go. If you're keeping something out of guilt (it was a gift or a pass-along), donate it to charity. If you aren't sure if something is still in style, it probably isn't and should be discarded.

While the 1-year rule for clothes (if you haven't worn it in a year, get rid of it) is a good one, there are circumstances when you want to keep a piece of clothing forever—or for a few more years. I made my own wedding dress, I can't throw it out, and I would never give it away. It is hard to imagine any descendant wearing the dress because the marriage ended in divorce. But the dress is as important to me as an old and treasured photo. I vividly remember choosing the fabric, covering each of the many buttons with satin, and working on the dress for months. The grass stains on the dress remind me of the reception in the garden of the house where I grew up, and I am astonished at the size of the waist. Was I ever that thin? Energetically, the dress speaks volumes to me, and it always will. And so it stays.

Try the technique that many professional organizers use: Empty your entire closet, then make it a goal to return only 50 percent of the items back to the space. The rest should be donated to a charity or friend, sold, or tossed.

Natural Fibers Equal Active Fibers

It wasn't until recently that I fully understood the astonishing range of benefits provided by natural fibers. I've known for years that wearing polyester on a hot day feels like baking in a garbage bag because the fabric doesn't breathe. I was always intuitively drawn to the feel and comfort of natural fibers, but I first got a clue about their range of benefits when a friend gave me an organic wool comforter that she no longer needed. (Organic wool hasn't been treated with pesticides.)

I already slept on an organic wool mattress (more about the wonders of that on page 272), but I had been sleeping under a cotton-covered comforter with polyester fill—a choice made solely for financial reasons. I was very grateful for the handoff because I had always wanted to sleep with totally pure, organic bedding without any synthetics surrounding my body.

Waking up the next morning after being completely cocooned in organic wool for 8 hours or so, it took a few minutes to confirm that it was me feeling so completely relaxed, at peace, and fully rested. There wasn't a tense thought or feeling in me. My body felt completely serene, and I was warm and cozy to my bone marrow. I was warm but not too warm. My body tempera-

NATURAL, ORGANIC FIBERS ARE THE BEST CHOICE

Choosing fabric made of natural, organic fiber supports environmental stewardship on every level. Organic production provides protection for workers and farming families; cares for the earth, air, and water; and protects your own health. Natural fibers can be grown and harvested sustainably, whereas man-made fibers are often made of petroleum products and nonrenewable raw materials.

The problems with man-made fibers are many; they deplete resources, they add to the chemical load on the earth, and their manufacture often increases pollution. Man-made products, such as rayon and tencel, are made of trees and wood pulp that have been cut just for the fabric (these are called virgin trees). Rayon is mostly made from spruce or pine trees. Not only are virgin tree-based fibers unsustainable, but a fabric like rayon has a huge shrinkage. Most rayon care labels advise consumers to dry-clean the garment.

The problems that synthetic fibers create for the environment and health don't stop with the particular fabric, since many may be coated with a variety of toxic finishes and may require fabric softeners and dryer sheets for static electricity. Some estimate that it takes 25,000 barrels of petroleum oil a day to manufacture synthetic fabrics, including acetate, acrylic, nylon, polyester, and many of the activewear fabrics sought by athletes.

Natural, organic fibers are best, too, because they breathe and help regulate your body moisture. Just make sure to avoid dry cleaning because you will breathe the fumes of the dry-cleaning process every time you wear the clothing.

ture was simply perfect. This experience has been repeated every morning since, and I'm convinced that natural wool fibers are the reason.

As a hands-on energy healer, I've come to look at silk in a completely different way too. I've found that silk protects me from others' energy. It is this protective component of silk that has inspired Tarot readers to practice the age-old tradition of wrapping their cards in silk scarves.

Because clothes are an important interface between our bodies and the atmosphere around us, the fabrics you choose for your clothing can either enhance or hinder the quality of your life and health. "Active" fibers (natural and preferably organic fibers) breathe, provide ventilation to the body, absorb moisture, maintain body temperature, and expand or contract with humidity. Natural fibers have a hollow structure that absorbs moisture and allows for the evaporation of humidity; they don't mildew or attract dust mites as readily as synthetic fibers.

Unlike most synthetic fibers, natural fibers do not attract positive ions; instead, they attract healthy negative ions. Clothes that don't breathe block the skin's natural bioelectric currents, and the skin develops an excess of energy called positive ions. The body works to compensate and attempt to find balance. Further, kinesiology muscle tests

SUPPORTING ORGANIC COTTON

Cotton is one of the most heavily pesticide-sprayed crops in the world, accounting for 25 percent of the world's pesticide use. Amazingly, buying a 100 percent organic cotton T-shirt saves one-third of a pound of fertilizers and pesticides, according to the Green Guide Institute. Because cotton is also found in many food products (in the form of cottonseed oil), its production has a huge impact on the planet, local environments and watersheds, and the health of human beings. Buying readily available organic cotton and supporting the organic cotton industry is an important step in reducing the chemical load on the earth.

(a standard test in alternative medicine) performed by John Ott, author and photobiologist, show loss of muscle strength when wearing some polyester clothing.

I have also found negative energetic shifts from plastic. I dowse with a pendulum for energy imprints in a manner similar to dowsing for water. Every time I dowse in a new location, I always ask the question "Can I dowse accurately here?" I am sometimes surprised at the answer.

One day, I was sitting on a wicker loveseat with plastic cushions. The answer I received was a strong "no." I thought about this for a bit, then I removed the cushions and sat directly on the wicker, and I was able to dowse again. What electrical interference was at play with those unnatural plastic cushions? Since they were powerful enough to distort my dowsing, I'd expect they are powerful enough to distort me in some subtle way that I don't even want to think about!

The Top Four Natural Fibers

I simply love cotton, linen, silk, and wool. If you haven't discovered them—and I mean *really* discovered them—I urge you to do so. Each one of these fibers has a unique role in my life that I really treasure. Cotton is the wonder cloth for everyday, warm weather wear. It softens with washing, and the clothes practically become friends because they feel so comfortable. Linen is the perfect hot weather fabric because it absorbs 20 percent or more of its weight in water. Silk is in a class by itself, and it is a wonderful choice for elegance. And wool keeps me *warm*. There is nothing like it, and I always choose it on the coldest days of the winter.

Cotton

Cotton is the soft fluff that grows on the cotton plant. It has been grown and spun into fabric since at least 3000 BC and has been one of the main fibers used for clothing in the world ever since.

Cotton fibers are hollow inside, allowing them to retain 24 to 27 times their own weight in water, and they're stronger when wet. High temperatures, like boiling or ironing, won't harm this tough fabric. That's a plus because a hot iron is often needed to smooth out wrinkles. Cotton absorbs moisture quite well, but it dries slowly. Because it breathes and provides ventilation for the body, it's a good choice for clothing.

On the negative side, cotton is vulnerable to mildew, wrinkles easily, shrinks (although most cotton made into clothing has been preshrunk), and it may also yellow in the light. Cotton fabric will weaken over time when exposed to sunlight.

Cotton has several forms. *Terry cloth* is the most absorbent cotton because of the loops in the weave. The amount of moisture absorbed depends on the length of the loops and how closely woven together they are. Closely woven long loops are more absorbent than tight, short loops. Quite white and strong, *upland cotton* comprises a full 99 percent of the cotton grown in the United States. *American pima cotton* is used for cotton thread and high-quality fabrics and is grown in Arizona, New Mexico, Southern California, and Texas. This cotton is silky, a tan-white color, and lustrous. Another long cotton staple, *Egyptian cotton*, is light brown and is used when fine, strong yarns are needed. *Asiatic cotton* is coarse and used mostly in surgical supplies.

Linen

Linen is made from the stalk of the flax plant. The word "linen" can mean cloth woven from flax (the subject of this section) *and* "linen goods," which may or may not be made of flax. "Linen goods" consist of anything you would find in a traditional linen closet—blan-

Safe and Sound

NATURALLY COLORED COTTON

Grown for centuries by indigenous peoples of Central and South America, colored cottons are now being bred specifically for cotton production and are currently available in brown, brownish red, green, and even pink and lavender tints. Using naturally colored cotton has many benefits for the environment because the color is produced without the environmental cost of synthetic dyes. Performance studies done at California Agricultural Technology Institute note that the natural cotton colors strengthen with washing—called a no-fade quality—and they have excellent light fastness (won't fade in sunlight). In addition, naturally colored cotton has a higher oxygen index than its white counterpart, so it's a good choice for upholstery because it is less flammable.

Naturally colored cottons are also resistant to many insects and diseases as well as being drought- and salt-tolerant, adding up to fewer chemicals used for its production.

kets, dish towels, sheets, tablecloths, and towels—and use for bed, bath, table, or dishes. Flax linen is one of the world's oldest natural fibers. Since most cloth was made of linen, "linen goods" literally meant all of those flax linen items.

Linen makes a great dish-drying towel because it absorbs 20 percent or more of its weight in water. Cotton dishcloths, while good enough, aren't nearly up to linen's standards. I remember many times when I have tried to dry a pot or pan with fabric less absorbent than linen and felt frustrated with the process. Cleaning up after a big dinner can use many non-linen dish towels. So now, with this kernel of reality about linen, your mind's eye can jump to people wearing linen suits in the steamy tropics, as they do in novels. You can see that linen is a wonderful summer fabric because it absorbs moisture and keeps you cool. Linen bedding also has much to offer. Because human bodies give off a pint of water a night when sleeping, the astonishing moisture absorbency of linen makes for an excellent fabric choice for pillow slips, sheets, and duvet covers.

The elegant drape and weave of linen is distinctive too. The threads of the weave vary in thickness and, when they are woven together, the resultant slubbiness adds interest to the cloth. But linen can be made into very fine

Fluffy, loopy dish towels made of synthetic fiber are no match for a linen dish-drying towel. Linen absorbs water easily, so one towel can handle a mile-high stack of plates and dinnerware.

yarns too. The fabric is earthy with luster and texture. After repeated washings, linen softens, but it wrinkles easily, and that is part of its appeal in the end. The fabric shows a bit of the wearer's immediate history, whether they have been sitting or are freshly out of the house with everything perfectly pressed. Linen tends to tell a story.

Linen is a fabric that comes to life; it is ideal for hot weather because it has excellent UV protection and amazing absorbency due to the hollow structure of the flax stalk. It is strong, beautiful, and comfortable against the skin. Linen is an "active" fiber like wool and adjusts and responds to the atmosphere (the sun and the humidity); this is one reason that it is a fabric of choice for those with skin disorders. It also sheds dirt easily. One of its few limitations is that it is vulnerable to mildew.

Linen has many more fine qualities: It is naturally resistant to bacteria, it is not damaged by moths, and it does not conduct static. Its natural wax content gives it luster, and it is lint free (and excellent for cleaning windows). Linen is the strongest of the vegetable fibers (two to three times stronger than cotton), and it can last for generations.

Linen's natural color ranges from off white to a light, earthy tan. Unbleached linen is by far the strongest. Grass-bleached linen is the most ecofriendly, and the process is least harmful to the fabric. Large bolts of linen are exposed to the sun and gradually bleached by its rays. Chemical bleaching of linen is the least desirable and usually done by boiling linen first in a lime solution, followed by hydrochloric acid—all of which weakens the yarn and causes environmental contamination.

Silk

Silk fabric is made primarily by the mulberry-fed silkworm originating in China. When the mulberry worm is fully mature, it eats enormous amounts of mulberry leaves and spins its cocoon with a continuous thread of up to 4,000 feet, which can be reeled. The cocoon's purpose is to enclose and protect the worm for its transformation into a moth. These silkworms have been cultivated in China for their silk thread since at least 2640 BC.

Silk is the strongest natural fiber. It is also the longest—one thread strand can be 1,200 to 4,000 feet long. Elastic, resilient, and somewhat wrinkle-resistant, silk fabric has an excellent hand and great drape. Because it breathes and absorbs moisture, silk is ideal for undergarments; it also resists mildew. Brightly colored or softly subdued, silk takes dyes better than any other natural fiber.

Surprisingly, silk shares some characteristics with wool—it deteriorates in sunlight, and it's an acidic material, so strong alkalis, such as ammonia, will harm the fibers. But, unlike wool, it weakens when wet, so care must be taken when it's laundered.

Raw silk is twisted into multiple sizes and types of yarns and sold on spools from which silk cloth is woven. Silk thread is gathered to make fabric after the silkworms have made their cocoons. The chrysalises are killed (stifled), usually by steam, and then the silk thread is reeled from the cocoon and blended with the thread from other cocoons (using the natural gum of the cocoon as a glue). The resulting reel of filament is called raw silk. The waste by-product of the cocoons is gathered together and made into spun silk in a process similar to the spinning of cotton or wool.

The chrysalises are killed inside the cocoon so that the moths don't break the continuous long silk filament (used for silk textile production) that makes up the cocoon. Some spun silk is made from cocoons in which the moths have broken out and emerged alive. More recent methods of silk production coerce the silkworms to spin the silk coming out of their bodies more slowly, which produces silk similar to spider silk, which is considered the strongest, toughest, most elastic thread there is. Fast-spinning and slow-spinning silkworms are developed and bred, depending on need.

There are several types of silk. *Wild silk* is created when the silkworms eat oak leaves instead of mulberry leaves. The silk thread is tan in color from the tannin in the oak leaves. Shantung, Tussah, and Pongee silk are fabrics made of wild silk. Wild African silk moths are partially domesticated for their silk. The cocoons are collected in a sustainable manner—the moths are caught in the wild and lay their eggs in the laboratory. Tussah silk is wild-crafted in India, and the fibers are pulled in continuous strands from the cocoon after the moths have emerged.

Peace silk originates in the Dominican Republic. This silk is created by allowing the moth to emerge from the cocoon after it has spun the silk, instead of being snuffed out in an intact cocoon. Unlike most silk, the Peace Silk cocoon is broken, and it is made into thread by degumming the cocoon and then spinning its thread together, instead of being reeled in very long filaments from the cocoon. The yarn made from Peace Silk is very soft and fluffy. Peace Silk is also very warm, and when made into gloves, it's reputed to provide effective pain relief for arthritis sufferers.

Wool

Wool is the fleece from sheep. The amount of wool fiber growing on the hide of a merino sheep is almost unbelievable—56,000 fibers per square inch. The fibers are called scales, and they shed water and dirt away from the sheep's body.

Wool is one of the most elastic fibers, which contributes to its incredible resiliency. It has an excellent hand and a great drape and is very strong; it can bend 20,000 times without breaking. Wool can absorb 50 percent of its

SHOPPING SOLUTIONS
WOOL TERMINOLOGY YOU SHOULD KNOW

Wool has been treasured for centuries, and many wool garments are so long lasting that they are passed down from generation to generation. Since wool is a high-priced item, it's helpful to understand wool "speak" when you're shopping at finer or specialty stores.

Boiled wool: Wool that has been washed in warm water, agitated, and dried in a dryer. The original wool fabric will shrink about 50 percent in both directions, and it will look like felt. Boiled wool is very warm, and it is often used for jackets.

Felt: Wool fibers consist of overlapping "scales" similar to that of a fish. The overlapping enables the wool to mat together to produce felt.

Harris tweed: A handwoven fabric from Scotland.

Herringbone: A twill woven with a sawtooth line.

Homespun: This wool is strong, coarse, and loosely woven.

Loden: A thick, waterproof, heavy fabric made into famous Loden coats that are characteristically green.

Merino: A fine wool made from worsted wool yarn from the merino sheep. Merino wool doesn't itch.

Tweed: Wool that is slightly felted and is sturdy with a slightly rough hand.

Wool jersey: A very soft wool that drapes beautifully. Must be preshrunk.

weight in water without dripping and 30 percent without feeling damp. It handles moisture well, it is resistant to mildew, and it helps evaporate moisture by wicking it from the body. It is a great all-season fabric because it cools as well as warms the body, depending on the need. And because it breathes, it insulates without overheating. It is considered an "active" fiber because it constantly responds to temperature and moisture change in the same manner that it did while still on the sheep. This marvelous fiber resists wear and tear, dirt, and dust mites, and it is an excellent wind barrier. Not all wool is scratchy; much of it is very soft, like merino. It is flame resistant, so much so that it is the only fiber that can legally be made into a mattress without the addition of fire retardants. And it doesn't attract a static charge.

If you handle wool garments with care, they will last for a long time. Don't expose them to sunlight because wool loses strength in sunlight. Launder wool with neutral or acidic detergent; for current and biodegradable detergents, do an online search for the keywords "neutral detergent product" or "acidic detergent product." Wool is acidic, and overly alkaline materials, such as ammonia or borax, can harm the fibers.

Natural Protein Fibers

Natural fibers come from two sources, either animals and insects or vegetables and plants. Natural protein fibers include fleece and hair-based fibers, such as wool, mohair, and cashmere. They also include silk, leather, feathers, and fur.

However, just because a fiber is natural doesn't mean it is environmentally friendly or ethical (toxic metals are used to tan leather, and there's a lack of humanity shown to animals grown for their pelts, as examples). You often have to accept a trade-off. Such is the case with buying leather shoes and purses. They last a long time, so you're not disposing of these items annually, and you're not buying replacements, which have caused natural resources to be used and exploited in the manufacturing process. But, when you buy leather products, you have to hope that they were made from slaughterhouse animals and not animals raised for their hides.

Here's another trade-off: Wool can be sheared with no harm to the sheep, and wool garments last a long time. However, the pesticides used to treat insect infestations on sheep can be very harsh and damaging. It may seem that every decision means a choice or a trade-off, and in many cases, that's true. It's always preferable to do your homework. As for natural fibers, seek out untreated, organic fabric, whether protein- or plant-based, and you'll feel good about your choice.

We each need to make our own conscious decisions about which protein fibers we will and won't wear. I buy very good, long-lasting leather shoes and pocketbooks, and I put them to exceptionally good and long use. My clogs are going into their third year, and I wear them every day except in the summer—and they are still in great shape. If I could buy well-made leather goods like those that were dyed by plant tannins, I'd choose them over conventional leather goods in a minute (for more about dyes and fabric finishes, see pages 338 and 353).

Protein fibers are wonderful for sleeping and wearing. Wool fleece– based clothing, especially, is as adaptive to the human body as you could imagine. I've come to love my wool clothing, and most wool doesn't itch. I had thought I was allergic to wool because I itched when wearing it sometimes, only to learn that higher-grade wools usually are itch free.

Fleeces are shorn from an animal, and in most cases, the shearing causes no harm. The fibers are long lasting and are easily recyclable into bedding products, clothing, home furnishings, insulation, and more. They wear so well that they often can be handed down to future generations.

The renaissance in knitting has led many women to rediscover the joy and texture of luxury fibers, such as alpaca, angora, and cashmere.

The hair yarns make incredibly luxurious products that are much sought after throughout the world. They tend to be very soft, and they can be expensive.

Alpaca

Alpaca is a long, silky, lustrous yarn from a member of the South American camel family. Stronger but softer than wool, it is a fiber that breathes and doesn't itch, and few people are allergic to the hair. Alpaca fleece lasts so long that it has been found in Peruvian ruins dating back to 1750. Alpaca fleece is produced in more than 22 colors, without needing any dyes! This broad spectrum of earth colors provides interesting ecofriendly products.

Angora

This soft, extremely light and fluffy fleece is shorn from Angora rabbits, and its cell structure makes it three times warmer than sheep's wool. Because it is warm and light, it is ideal for year-round thermal clothing. Like wool, it absorbs moisture, insulates, breathes, and regulates body temperature. There are some ethical concerns about wearing Angora because the rabbits are usually kept in cages. Check out the source of the fleece you're buying to see if the animals are housed in humane conditions.

Camel

Known commonly as camel hair, the fleece is from the soft undercoat of a camel. Like many types of fleece, it is soft, fine, warm, and light. Many of you have heard of the camel hair coat, an ideal use for camel fleece. When selecting camel hair fabric or garments, you may find that it's been graded 1 to 3; grade 1 is the softest, lightest tan hair, and grade 3 is coarsest, dark black-brown or reddish brown hair.

Cashmere

This very expensive, luxury fiber is from the Kashmir goat. The soft, downy hair of the goat is separated from longer hair, resulting in a very soft, warm fiber without bulk. Genuine cashmere is obtained by combing the goats by hand. Tibetan and Mongolian cashmere is considered the most valuable because the goats grow very long coats to survive the severe, harsh weather of the Himalayas.

Guanaco

A guanaco is a wild and domesticated relative of the llama. The wool from this animal is very soft, silky, warm, and resilient and is one of the world's most exclusive fibers; it's used for very expensive pashmina-like shawls, suits, and coats.

Leather

Leather is a catch-all term used to describe any skin or hide (from a mammal, reptile, bird, or fish) that has been tanned. The largest sources of leather are cattle and calves. Less common sources include alligators, Asian water buffalo, deer, goats, horses, sharks, sheep, snakes, and wild and domestic hogs.

Leather lasts virtually forever when it is well preserved. It has been found in Egyptian tombs and in artifacts elsewhere around the world. Older leather has a soft patina that is a much-loved attribute. No two leather pieces are identical because each piece has distinct wrinkles and scars. Leather is strong and virtually indestructible; it doesn't burn easily, and it is hard to puncture. It breathes (provides ventila-

WORDS TO THE WISE

GOOD REASONS TO AVOID LEATHER

The production of leather is one of the most polluting manufacturing processes, and many of the animals whose hides are used are treated inhumanely. Leather is often treated with solvent-based polishes that are neurotoxic to those wearing the clothing and polluting to indoor environments.

Most leather is treated with a variety of substances to create stain-resistant surfaces, tanned with chromium, and dyed with toxic aniline dyes and surface pigments. All chrome-tanned leathers are aniline-dyed. Hide markings are usually mechanically disguised, and polyurethane is often added to the surface. Soft leather has usually been heavily treated and is often called top grain.

So-called natural leather is treated less. As a result, the natural grain patterns, wrinkles, and scars aren't disguised. Natural leathers are termed "full top grain—pure leather." But leathers called natural are usually tanned with chromium and then dyed with aniline dyes, both of which cause widespread environmental problems. The term "natural" is a real misnomer in this case.

tion) and aids evaporation, so that it won't heat up or cool down. It's also a good insulator and wind barrier.

Tanning preserves leather from decay and makes it pliable. The word "tanning" is derived from the Celtic word "tannum," meaning the tannic acid found in tree bark. The original process of leather treatment used tannic acids found in plants. Before tanning, hides and skins were cured using salt or salt brine. Next the skins were cleansed of the curing salt and then soaked in a lime and enzyme mix (or sometimes man-made chemicals) to remove hairs and smooth the surface, readying it for tanning.

Today, almost all tanning is done with trivalent chromium and takes hours instead of the days required for tanning with plant-based materials. Chromium tanning is the industry choice for processing the hides of cattle, goats, lambs, pigs, and sheep, and it constitutes 90 percent of US tanning production; it comes at a very high environmental cost because chromium is a heavy metal that can contaminate the soil. Awing is an alternative method using a combination of alum and salt. Secotan is a process using dry-cleaning solvents; syntans use man-made chemicals; and other processes use formaldehyde, glutaraldehyde, and heavy oils.

Vegetable tanning is the only eco-friendly method available today. Tannin comes from the bark and wood of trees available in most parts of the world. The North American chestnut, hemlock, and oak are rich in tannin. This tanning process utilizes successively stronger tannin baths and then a finishing with natural oils. Heavy leathers and shoe sole leathers are mostly dyed with vegetable tannins to this day; you can assume other leather is chemically dyed, unless noted otherwise.

Safe and Sound

CARE AND CLEANING OF SHOES

I remember seeing cedar shoe trees in my grandfather's closet, and it wasn't until researching this book that I understood why. Cedar absorbs moisture, acid, and salt in a unique natural attribute called wicking. Leather won't crack when shoes and boots are stored on cedar shoe trees.

Sprinkle baking soda into shoes at night, and brush it out in the morning. Tannin also deodorizes shoes; you can spray the insides with tea (making sure the shoes are dark colored and won't get stained). You can remove dampness with a sprinkling of cornstarch. Let it set overnight, and brush it out in the morning.

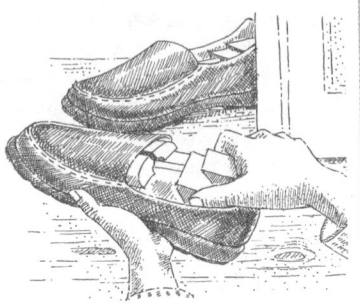

If you aren't going to wear the shoes for a week or so, you can spray the shoes with an antibacterial essential oil mixed with water (1 teaspoon to 1 cup of water in a spray bottle); there's no need to rinse them. The smell will dissipate in a few days. A good choice of essential oil is tea tree oil, a broad-spectrum antibacterial oil.

Despite the trouble with leather processing, I feel that the most resourceful way of approaching shoes is to buy a few pairs of high-quality leather shoes, and use cobblers when needed. Buying well-made shoes is important: If you weigh 150 pounds, and you walk for 1 mile, you have exerted 127,000 pounds on each foot and on each shoe. I am convinced that a few pairs of well-made, comfortable shoes will outlast a dozen cheap pairs without any contest, and you will consume much less leather (assuming you buy leather shoes).

Shoe "uppers" are still made mostly of leather due to its permeability, but 80 percent of shoe soling is currently made of synthetic material. You can find soles made of natural latex from the milk of the hevea tree and cast by hand into molds. These shoes wear wonderfully well and provide natural cushioning that absorbs up to 50 percent of the pressure to the heel caused by walking, according to information from the Arche shoe brand.

Mohair

Known and loved for its softness, this strong, resilient yarn is spun from the mohair fleece of the Angora goat (as distinct from the Angora rabbit). Mohair is very similar to wool in its characteristics, but the composition of the hair is smooth, and mohair won't mat together and shrink—also known as felting—like wool does. Mohair is also valued for its luster—the greater the luster, the greater the value.

Quivit

Quivit is the extremely long, fine hair of the musk ox. Most clothes made from quivit are warm, soft, one-of-a-kind shawls, hats, and scarves.

Rabbit

Rabbit hair is often used as a substitute for the expensive Vicuna fiber.

Vicuna

A wild, undomesticated member of the llama family that lives high in the South American Andes, vicuna is the most valuable animal fiber in the world because of its rarity; it costs hundreds of dollars a yard. Made famous by the Incas, vicuna is soft and fine and resembles raw silk. It is usually made into fine custom-made sweaters and scarves.

Yak

The yak comes from Tibet and the Qinghai and Sichuan provinces in China. It has coarse, long, dark chocolate-colored hair. The fiber is hand combed, sorted, and washed, and then it is "dehaired" to remove the longer, coarser hair. The resulting fiber is mostly the downy, soft hair. The best yak fibers are made with the smallest percentage of hair to down. The rougher yak hair is made into blankets, and the softer hair is made into knitted or woven garments.

Vegetable Fibers

Vegetable fibers include bast (phloem) fibers taken from the inner bark, or stalks, of plants and include hemp and flax (linen). Bast fibers are distinctive in that they all tend to grow well without pesticides. Seed fibers include well-

---

Annie's Insight

ETHNIC, HANDMADE FABRIC

One of the most meaningful gifts ever given to me was a handwoven tapestry made by an East Timorese woman. The women weavers from East Timor come from communities devastated by violence, and they are struggling to support themselves. All the money from the purchase of this tapestry goes directly to the woman who wove it. People use the cloth for many purposes—shawls, skirts, tablecloths, and wall hangings.

The essence of the person making such a tapestry is woven into the cloth along with the colors, yarns, and design—you can just feel it. I made the tapestry given to me into curtains for my dining room, in a place where no other curtains had ever seemed quite right. The tapestry was perfect, and I have come to treasure it. People always compliment the weaving when they come into my house. I love telling the story of its history.

known cotton. Other vegetable fibers include organic jute, kenaf, ramie, and switchgrass. Natural plant-based fabrics from agricultural by-products, such as banana, pineapple, and sisal, are increasingly available.

Hemp

Hemp is the strongest plant fiber on earth, and the earliest known use of hemp for fabric is 8000 BC. *Cannabis sativa* is the highest-quality hemp, and it is important to note that hemp fibers are derived from a specific species of Cannabis that contains only minute traces of the compound that gives its better-known sibling, marijuana, its narcotic qualities. Hemp fabric is not narcotic.

Notably, hemp produces more pulp per acre than timber. It is a sustainable choice and, because it is a very hardy plant, it requires no pesticides if grown on good soil. This very strong fabric (three times stronger than cotton) is a good choice for upholstery: It is UV resistant, naturally mold and mildew resistant, and even better than linen at handling moisture and moisture absorption. However, hemp can have a stiff drape, and it wrinkles easily. It has a slightly coarse hand, but like linen, hemp softens with repeated washings.

Jute

This stem fiber is thick and rough and is spun into carpet backing, rope, sacks, and twine. Jute is firm and durable and holds its shape. Jute usually smells of the petroleum oil used for spinning, so smell the product before you buy it because some spinning oils used are very unrefined and more like kerosene. If the jute has a strong petroleum smell, skip buying it and look for something else that won't pollute your home.

Kapok

The deciduous kapok tree is the tallest tree in Africa and grows in the tropics. It has pink, white, or yellow night-blooming flowers and lance-shaped leaves. The downy material of this plant comes from the silky pod and is sometimes called Java cotton. Kapok is used for stuffing pillows, sleeping bags, life jackets, upholstery, insulation, and more. Kapok is an alternative for those allergic to animal hair and possesses sterilizing and antibacterial qualities. It also has thermal capabilities, helping a body stay cooler in summer and warmer in winter.

Kenaf

Related to the cotton and okra plants, kenaf plants produce two fibers from their stalks—a long bast fiber from the outer bark and a short, inner fiber from the core of the stalk. Kenaf is used for rope, cording, mattresses, and some furniture.

Ramie

Ramie is a bast fiber from inner tree bark that has been made into fabrics since prehistoric times. Its high luster improves with washing, and it's the strongest of all the vegetable fibers. It absorbs more water than linen. On the downside, ramie is not very resilient and won't bounce back into shape, it wrinkles easily, and it has a bit of a rough hand. Ramie is often used to make knitted fabrics.

Natural Fibers from Agricultural By-Products

Most of us know the sturdy look and feel of a sisal doormat, but did you know that sisal fiber can be spun into a softer by-product and used for more delicate purposes? It's the same with banana fibers and coconut skins. These plant fibers offer many attributes, including antibacterial qualities and an ability to adjust to high-humidity climates (hot and arid climates, however, can be too drying for these fibers and

SHOPPING SOLUTIONS
THE SWEATSHOP STORY

Global factory sweatshops, which produce many of the brand-name clothing worn in the world, can be appalling hellholes of inhumane exploitation. Human rights violations are commonplace.

In Anita Roddick's book *Take It Personally: How to Make Conscious Choices to Change the World*, Charles Kernaghan, executive director of the National Labor Committee, says, "A leading human rights watchdog discovered a factory in Zhongshan City in 2000 where workers for Wal-Mart's contractors are forced to put in 14-hour shifts, 7 days a week, 30 days a month. They are effectively held as indentured servants in overcrowded dormitories. At the end of the month, nearly half of them owe the company money—to cover two dismal meals a day and pay deductions for talking to coworkers while sewing."

The Barred Rock Fund seeks to invest in companies that provide jobs to low-income communities and thereby helps to restore neighborhoods by providing jobs with a fair wage and with health insurance. The companies that the Barred Rock Fund invests in also provide a needed environmental alternative (as in the case of Sun & Earth cleaning supplies or supporting a diner that sells food from local farms). Brand SweatX, in the inner city of Los Angeles, is a company that the Barred Rock Fund started from scratch to provide brand-name clothing manufacturers with an alternative to sweatshops. Brand SweatX provides a fair wage and health insurance. The best news is that demand has surpassed production.

their by-products). Using agricultural by-products as part of a waste reduction goal or as part of overall earth-friendly practices means we're using resources to the fullest and making conscious decisions each time we plant and harvest.

Banana

A fiber similar to linen, banana is lightweight, elegant, and commonly used to make summer clothing. Banana fiber has been spun into fabric since the 13th century.

Coir (Coconut)

The fiber to make fabric comes from the padding *inside* the hard outer coconut shell. The fibers are hollow like some protein fibers and are very elastic, expanding and contracting with humidity. The fiber needs to have a humidity of at least 40 percent so that it won't dry out. The saturated fat of coconut is antibacterial, and so is the fiber. It is also free of static electricity. Coir is used for bags, hammocks, mats, rugs, and other home décor items.

Pineapple (Also Known as Pina)

A mainstay fabric of the Philippines, pineapple is made into lightweight clothes and household linens. It washes easily. Pineapple fiber is made from the skin of the pineapple.

Sisal

Sisal is made from pulp found inside the long, spiky leaves of the *Agave sisalana* plant. The fiber is white and is often spun together with coconut. It is strong, colorfast, flame resistant, and provides thermal insulation. Like many plant fibers, it adjusts to humidity. Sisal is commonly made into carpets, fabrics, rope, and yarns.

An Overview of Fabric Treatments

Clothing made with toxic fabric finishes such as antiwrinkle and antistain "guards" is getting more and more pervasive; as finishes are added, the clothes become stiffer. The finishes act as virtual sealants and block the flow of air through the garment, counteracting one of the major benefits—breathability—of wearing natural materials.

Fabric Treatments

No matter how many times I've washed some cotton clothing, to my frustration, the slightly stiff feel from the finish won't go away. At least the multiple washings will usually rinse away most smells. For the consumer, the most toxic part of clothing comes from fabric treatments. Chemicals that resist flames,

I'd be willing to bet that if everyone could experience the pure, clean scent of line-dried clothes, clothes dryers would be obsolete! Even if you don't have space for a full clothesline with poles, try one of the convenient fold-down outdoor models available through catalogs and online retailers.

water, moths, stains, soil, and wrinkles have been impregnated into the fabric and are often very hard to remove. Many, if not all, of these finishes are unhealthy for you and the environment, and they can substantially weaken the fabric.

Chemical treatments for clothing are notoriously neurotoxic. They are harmful to the earth's ozone layer and are developmental toxicants and endocrine disrupters. Many are persistent, chlorinated hydrocarbons showing up in women's breast milk.

Note that just because a fiber is labeled "organic," it doesn't mean that there are no finishing treatments.

Interestingly, many natural materials don't "need" chemical treatments. For example, static cling chemicals are needed only for synthetic materials, and some natural materials, such as wool, don't need flame retardants because they are naturally flame resistant.

Many fabrics could be used without wrinkle-resistant treatments too. If you shake out clothes before you put them in the dryer and remove them from the dryer promptly, you'll have few wrinkles. Hanging clothes outside on a line to dry in the sun and breeze also works successfully for keeping wrinkles out of fabric.

The truth is, you can only do the best you can in trying to avoid fabric treatments—they are everywhere and completely ubiquitous. We can only hope that as the serious environmental and health dangers of fabric treatments become more widely known (as is currently happening in the case of fire retardants), manufacturers will phase out the worst of them and work to discover safe alternatives.

Disinfectants are becoming a major contaminant of clothing. Clothes are often fumigated with disinfectants when they cross borders or if they are sold at secondhand stores. Ridding clothing of disinfectants can be very hard, but soaking the clothes overnight in 1 to 2 cups of baking soda before washing takes out a lot of the smell (repeat as necessary).

One problem with this rinsing technique is that some clothing, such as rayon, can't be washed very well without risk of shrinkage, so you have to be very careful not to agitate the clothing at all when rinsing it. In addition, this method doesn't work if the fabric is made into an elegant suit or hand-crafted garment because hand washing would be risky.

Spinning oils can also pose a pollution problem in items from third-world countries. Over the years, I've been given some wonderful ethnic clothing gifts, but I've been reluctant to wear them because the spinning oils smell so strongly of petroleum. It's almost as if the yarns have been spun with dirty car engine oil or kerosene.

What can you do to let the industry know that you aren't happy with the finishes? One idea is to speak to the manager every time you buy clothes from a catalog and suggest that the company work with manufacturers who use fewer finishes. I did this once, and I was surprised at the receptive response to the idea.

Natural Mothproofing

Insects can damage wool clothing as well as accessories made of feathers, skins, hair, and fleece. Insect damage to wool is usually due to the common or webbing clothes moth and the black carpet beetle. Keeping clothes and fabrics clean is very important. Moths and beetles do not eat clothing fibers per se; they eat food and stain residue as well as body oils and fluids from the wearer that have soiled the garment. The combined use of herbs and other techniques to repel moths can be very effective, so you don't even need to consider mothproofing pesticides.

Weavers can't take the chance of moths eating their skeins of wool, so their choices of repellent herbs really work. Weavers use herbs, such as cloves, mint, rosemary, sweet woodruff, and tansy, to repel clothing moths. You should also consider using a chest or closet made of cedar (or place cedar blocks or balls in a chest or closet) because moths are repelled by the cedar oil. Cedar chests are effective, but they must be sealed and airtight.

NATURAL MOTH REPELLENTS

Naphthalene, found in conventional mothballs, is a carcinogen. Natural moth repellents are the only safe choice, and their fragrances are effective. If you have any mothballs in your house, put them in the trash, and air anything that holds their smell in the sun as often as possible.

MOTHS-AWAY SACHETS
These sachets are lovely to tuck into sweater drawers and hang in closets; use silk fabric for a special look. You can buy bulk dried herbs at many health food stores. This recipe will fill about a dozen sachets.

    2 pieces tightly woven, natural-fiber fabric, at least 3 inches square, for each sachet
    Sewing needle and thread
    2 ounces each dried rosemary and mint
    1 ounce each dried thyme and American ginseng
    8 ounces whole cloves

With right sides of the fabric squares together, sew around three sides of the sachet, about ½ inch in from the edge. Trim the fabric at the corners to within ¼ inch of the seams to make turning the sachet right side out easier. Turn the sachet right side out. Combine the herbal ingredients in a large bowl and mix. Fill the sachet with the herbal mix. Fold in the raw edge of the sachet, and sew it closed.

Variations: Fill empty cotton tea bags for quick sachets; they're often available at health food stores. Or place the herbal mixture in a cotton bandana or handkerchief, and tie with a ribbon. You can also use any of these moth-repelling herbs: lavender, lemon, sweet woodruff, and tansy. ❖

NEEM OIL MOTH SPRAY
If you have a moth infestation, spray it with the following blend. Make sure you spot-test the garment for staining before spraying. You can try it directly on most wools, but avoid spraying it on light-colored fabrics.

    ¼ cup pure neem oil
    1 tablespoon pure, liquid castile soap
    ½ gallon warm water
    Spray bottle

Combine the oil, soap, and water and stir or shake to blend. Pour into a spray bottle and spray the moth-infested area. Do not rinse. Shelf life: indefinite. ❖

If you already have moths, neem oil may be the most effective treatment. Neem is sap from an Asian tree that is a broad-spectrum insecticide; it is particularly effective on wool moths. I've used it successfully to kill moths on an Oriental rug. To kill moths when steam-cleaning carpets, add ¼ cup of pure neem oil to the water in the steam cleaner. (Always spot-test a small patch of the rug to make sure the oil won't harm the fibers or dyes before treating the entire carpet.)

You can kill moths and carpet beetles using the freezer or the oven (just make sure extreme cold or heat won't damage the material before using these methods). Using the freezer method, wrap the fabric in aluminum foil or plastic and place it in a freezer with temperatures below 18°F for 2 weeks (if the freezer is set for 0°F, the process requires only 4 days). For the oven, wrap the fabric in aluminum foil and place it in a 120°F oven for 30 minutes.

Before packing woolens away, be sure to wash them to remove any soiling. The key to not shrinking wool while washing in water is to never twist it, agitate it, or wring it out. Add 2 teaspoons of pure neem oil per gallon of water. Water temperature should be around 100°F. Gently swirl the wool in the water, then rinse and press the water out. Wool is an acidic material, so use a mild soap or detergent with as close to a neutral or acidic pH as possible. Most of the detergents and soaps designed to clean wool or silk will usually note the pH on the label. (Any soap or detergent with a pH above 8 will harm wool.) If you're unsure about a soap's or detergent's pH, add 1 tablespoon of white distilled vinegar or lemon juice before washing. To block wool back into shape, lay it flat and shape it before drying.

Air-dry the clothing in the sun for a few hours before packing it away, and completely seal clean woolen items in aluminum foil, boxes that are sealed, and cedar chests. Airtight and cold storage in a temperature no higher than 40°F can also help repel moths.

Removing Mothball Odor

I've received a number of questions from readers who need help to remove mothball odor from baby clothes, sweaters, and other clothes stored in the pesticide. People have tried baking soda and white vinegar, and nothing seems to work.

I posed the question of how to remove mothball odor to an indoor air quality online listserve I frequent. One professional carpet cleaner observed that, for reasons nobody quite understands (although possibly because of natural ozone), placing carpets and other items outdoors in the sun for many days may remove the smell of mothballs. She claims that using commercial ozone machines inside will *not* do the trick. You might try placing the clothes outside in the sun every day (and bringing them in at night) until the smell is gone. Please note that even if the odor is removed, it doesn't mean there isn't any residual mothball chemical on the cloth.

FLAME-RETARDANT TREATMENT FOR DECORATIONS

Decorations are often nestled amidst candles or holiday lights, and they must be flame resistant. This formula may give a little added fire protection, but it's best to keep decorations away from flames or lights altogether.

7 ounces borax
3 ounces boric acid
2 quarts hot water

Dissolve and combine the borax and boric acid in the hot water. Dip or spray decorations in the solution. Safety-test small parts for flame resistance and reapply the solution if needed. Discard leftover mixture. ❖

Fabric Flammability

The Flammable Fabrics Act was enacted in 1953 by the US Department of Commerce and is enforced by the US Consumer Product Safety Commission (CPSC). The act was established in response to serious accidents involving clothing made of textiles, such as brushed rayon high-pile sweaters, that would "flash burn." Under the act, fabrics are tested and regulated for flammability. Lightweight rayons, silks, and fuzzy cotton fleece are usually the fabrics of concern.

Children's Sleepwear

Much stricter flammability standards have been established for the flammability of children's sleepwear. Children's sleepwear must self-extinguish when exposed to small, open flame. Polyester and other synthetic sleepwear must be flame resistant, so they're treated with flame-retardant chemicals. The CPSC recommends that children's pajamas be either flame resistant or snug fitting.

The natural and safest choice for children's sleepwear is snug-fitting, 100 percent cotton sleepwear because it doesn't have to be treated with flame-resistant chemicals. Pure wool sleepwear would also be exempt from mandated treatment. Avoid loose-fitting pajamas because they create air spaces that can accelerate flames; less oxygen lies beneath tight garments.

Bedding Flammability Standards

The flame retardant of choice for fabrics, clothing, electrical equipment, foam cushions, and mattresses is often brominated flame retardants. They are suspected endocrine disruptors, are bioaccumulative (will enter the breast milk and are stored in fat), and are persistent in the environment.

Your safest bet is to choose wool bedding. It is naturally flame resistant and meets or exceeds federally mandated flame-retardant standards.

Environmentally Friendly Laundry

Doing laundry has a significant environmental impact. The energy used to heat water is staggering, as is the pollution when our dirty laundry water— suds and all—goes out into the wastewater stream from our homes. When phosphates were part of virtually all laundry detergents (they have since been banned in almost all states of the United States), the resulting algae bloom choked the life out of lakes and streams. While phosphates have been phased out, your choice of detergent is still crucial because detergents differ in their biodegradability and their ingredients (some ingredients are endocrine disrupters). We must make safe laundry product choices; if we all choose environmentally safe products, the impact will be enormous.

Water is a universal solvent. If you washed fabric with nothing else but water, you would accomplish a great deal of cleaning! Water dissolves soluble salts in dirt, and soaps and detergents are designed to work with the natural solvent properties of water as well.

If I had to scrub all of my family's clothes by hand in a washtub or in a stream with sand, I would approach buying clothes in a completely different manner. I assume you would too. It's worth imagining such a thing. (I asked my teenage daughter how she would like to have to hand wash each item of her clothes every week. Her look of astonished horror at the thought spoke volumes about our culture, as did imagining having only three strong and resilient outfits to cut back on the wash load.) If this were my situation, my quantity of clothes would be gone, and I would focus almost exclusively on quality for the few clothes I did buy. I would want the fabric to be strong, resilient, attractive, and "active"— meaning natural and breathable.

Is Your Water Soft or Hard?

The hardness or softness of your water is determined by the amounts of calcium and magnesium salts that are present. Hard water has the most minerals. Hard water makes for difficult laundry problems, and it can become a problem for the appliance because of the calcium buildup.

Water hardness is expressed in grains

per gallon (gpg), parts per million (ppm), or milligrams per liter (mg/L). Soft water has fewer than 3.5 grains per gallon (50 ppm or mg/L); hard water, at the other end of the spectrum, has a mineral count of 10.6 grains per gallon (or more than 180 ppm or mg/L). See page 209 for more on water hardness.

If you'd like to soften washing machine water, you can use vinegar or lemon juice. Add a cup or less of straight white distilled household vinegar to the laundry water, and agitate for a few minutes before adding the detergent.

Detergent or Soap?

Many people are confused about the difference between soap and detergent—with good reason. Often manufacturers will call a detergent a soap when it is, in fact, a detergent. Soap used for washing laundry went out of favor in World War II, at least for much of the world. Detergents were developed during World War II when fats and vegetable oils to make soap were scarce. Petroleum oil was cheap and readily available, so oil became a mainstay for the household cleaning products industry.

When soap and minerals react in water, it leaves an insoluble film that can turn clothes a dull gray and leaves a soap-scum residue. Detergents were specifically designed not to react with the minerals in hard water that cause soap scum. For all practical purposes, detergents are the product of choice for laundry if you have hard water. Those lucky enough to have soft water can use soap flakes for laundry.

There is little doubt that soap is better for your health and the environment than detergents. Soaps are made of materials found in nature. Detergents are mostly synthetic, and they can be toxic to fish and wildlife.

Health food stores carry a number of brands of detergent that are made with renewable materials rather than petroleum-based ingredients; some manufacturers are formulating eco-friendly detergents made from natural,

If you have soft water, consider switching from liquid laundry detergent to soap flakes, which are easier on the environment.

sustainable vegetable oils. Environmentally conscious detergents often have natural essential oil fragrances and are made without dyes. Health food stores also sell liquid vegetable-oil soaps called castile soap. Add 1 ounce of castile soap to an average laundry load or follow the manufacturer's instructions.

Choose Laundry Products Wisely

Choosing the healthiest and most eco-friendly laundry detergent can be a bit overwhelming. I buy only from manufacturers I trust to protect my health and the environment. You should know that detergent formulas change quickly, and the changes are often due to the price of the raw ingredients. It is impossible to keep on top of formula changes, and most of them are proprietary anyway. If you buy from a company that you know has very high integrity for environmental quality, most likely you will make a great choice. I've observed the innovations and changes in the laundry product industry for 20 years or so, and I'll be glad to share my wisdom.

❖ Buy a brand with a proven track record of initiating product innovation to protect health and the environment; a great public relations record isn't enough.

❖ Buy fragrance-free, dye-free products.

❖ At the present time, the most biodegradable, vegetable-based detergent on the market is alkyl polyglycoside. However, you will need to contact the manufacturer to see if your brand uses this. Often labels specify only "anionic and nonionic surfactants." (A surfactant simply means the ingredient that does the washing.) This lack of disclosure is very frustrating for an environmentally conscious consumer.

❖ Many states ban phosphates in powdered detergents. Not only do phosphates cause algae bloom in lakes and streams, but they are also often contaminated with heavy metals— arsenic, in particular. Liquid laundry detergent is always phosphate free.

❖ If you use soap flakes or powdered detergent, add the soap or powdered detergent to the washing machine before the water and clothing have been added. This helps to fully dissolve the cleanser. If you want to wash the clothes with cool water, you can dissolve the soap or powdered detergent in a cup of hot water first; however, hard water combined with cool water temperature can result in some mineral residue on fabric from the powdered detergent. If you have very hard water, add ½ cup of vinegar to your rinse water to minimize mineral staining.

MAKE IT YOURSELF
LAUNDRY HELPERS

One of the keys to successfully using natural materials is using the right thing at the right time. These do-it-yourself recipes will help.

LAUNDRY DUST MITE ERADICATOR
Tea tree oil is a broad-spectrum miticide and the strongest broad-spectrum natural antiseptic known to man.

½ teaspoon tea tree oil
½ cup warm water

Mix the tea tree oil and the water and add it to the laundry rinse water to kill dust mites. Shelf life: indefinite. ❖

NATURAL STARCH
You can easily make your own starch as an alternative to synthetic fabric stiffeners.

2 teaspoons cornstarch
1 cup water
Spray bottle

Mix the cornstarch and water and fill the spray bottle. Shake to dissolve and simply spray onto clothing before ironing. Discard any leftover starch. ❖

❖ When fabric is very dirty, such as after floods or with clay and ground-in dirt, you may want to choose a powdered laundry detergent. If the laundry isn't full of soil and dirt, liquid laundry detergent is the better choice; it's less likely to leave mineral residue on the clothes if you have hard water. When washing really dirty clothes, wash whites separately (even if they're dirty, too) because they will turn gray in dirty water.

Laundry Additives

Keep whites white with oxygen bleach. Dry oxygen bleaches contain ingredients that become hydrogen peroxide, and liquid oxygen bleaches are simply hydrogen peroxide and stabilizers. These are not chlorine bleaches and are preferable for the environment because they naturally degrade into oxygen and water.

"Natural oxygen safe bleaches" are commercially available and are found primarily in the health food store marketplace. They are based on hydrogen peroxide. It's best to buy commercial nonchlorine bleaches instead of making your own version using store-bought 3 percent hydrogen peroxide. The commercial brands include oxygen bleach

Safe and Sound

A CHLORINE BLEACH ALTERNATIVE

Chlorine bleach is sodium hypochlorite, a moderately toxic chlorine salt that can bond with other chemicals to form cancer-causing organochlorines in the wastewater system. Chlorine bleach should be skipped not only for environmental reasons, but because chlorine retention can also cause yellowing of whites.

Instead, add ½ cup of lemon juice to the rinse cycle of a medium load of whites to lightly bleach the clothing. This technique is especially effective on clothes that are then hung to dry on the line in the sun.

stabilizers to help reduce the product's reactivity in the environment.

When you bleach with oxygen bleach, the hotter the water, the less time it takes for the bleach to work its magic. If the water temperature is below 130°F, you need to allow soaking time for the bleach to work.

If using liquid bleach, put a few drops directly onto an inside seam to see if there is any color change. For dry oxygen bleach, mix a teaspoon to 1 cup of hot water and test the same way.

Oxygen bleach is a good choice to remove mildew. If your clothes have visible mold or a mildew smell, soak them in oxygen bleach and hot water before washing as usual.

Keeping Whites White

Read clothing labels; some direct you to dry your clothes out of direct sunlight. On the other hand, though, storing whites in the dark can cause yellowing. A rule of thumb is that most natural fibers love the sun, and hanging them outside to dry on the line is your best bet.

Well-washed whites actually have a yellow undertone. Most commercial detergents contain fluorescent whitening agents called optical brighteners, but optical brighteners do *not* degrade in the environment. In the olden days, blueing was widely used, and it is still available in many grocery and department stores. You just mix 3 cups of baking soda with ½ teaspoon of Prussian blue, and add 1 teaspoon per load of laundry.

To brighten whites if you don't have hard water, add either ½ cup of borax or washing soda to a medium load of laundry. Both of the minerals borax and washing soda are available in the laundry section of your supermarket.

Fabric Softeners

The smell of fabric softeners is on the minds of many Americans, or so I assume from the volume of e-mail I receive on the subject. Many are frantic to get the smell out of their dryers or out of their clothes, and most want alternatives.

Fabric softeners were developed in response to the pummeling fabrics get in washing machines. After all that agitation, a fabric often needs to be "softened." A dryer can help fabric soften on its own, but if you don't use a dryer, a natural softener is helpful.

A recent study from Anderson Laboratories gives a clue as to why this particular household product has become a bee in so many people's bonnets. Their chemical analysis of the airborne emissions of five different kinds of mainstream fabric softeners revealed that the fabric softeners emitted many toxic chemicals, many of which cause acute respiratory tract irritation and inflammation.

Fabric softeners are static cling busters. They reduce static cling by coating fabric with a waxy film that fluffs up clothes and by removing the electrical charge from the detergent.

Interestingly, natural fabrics don't develop static the way synthetics do. Shake out clothes to reduce static. Fortunately, "green" fabric softeners—made of vegetable-based surfactants, salt, and natural ingredients for scent—are now on the market. If you can, switch to all-natural fabrics, such as organic cotton, a little at a time.

When I was visiting my sister Yari in New York City, my skirt kept sticking to my tights. She suggested I just sprinkle my tights with a bit of water. It worked! I felt I could leave her apartment and step out onto busy New York streets without my skirt stuck to my legs. What's easier than water?

Water Temperature for Laundry

The lower the temperature of the water, the more detergent you need. If the temperature of the water is below 60°F, no soap or detergent performs well. But don't make the water too hot. Washing heavily soiled articles with hot water can set stains. If you have heavily soiled clothes, prewash them in cool water with powdered laundry detergent, then wash them again in water that is 130°F or higher. For whites, typical dirty clothes, and diapers, use hot water (130°F or above). For man-made fibers, knits, and silks, use warm water (90°F). And for dark, bright colors that bleed, use cold water (80°F).

The rinse water can always be cold without any harmful effects on the wash load. If you rinse fabric in cold water, it will reduce wrinkling and save energy, and it won't set stains.

Dryer Tips

The Soap and Detergent Association recommends shaking out wet clothes

MAKE IT YOURSELF

LAVENDER BUNDLE

Toss this fragrant bundle into the vacuum cleaner bag or your dresser drawers.

½ cup dried lavender blossoms
Several drops lavender oil
Purchased small muslin gift or jewelry bag

Place the lavender blossoms and several drops of lavender oil in a muslin bag. Close bag tightly. Use in vacuum bags or in clothing drawers and trunks. When fragrance fades, refresh with a few drops of lavender oil.

Variation: Substitute cinnamon, cloves, lemon verbena, or rosemary herbs and essential oils for the lavender. ❖

---

before putting them in the dryer. This makes sense because it helps the clothes from being tangled up together and prevents further wrinkling. Folding clothes or hanging them on hangers as soon as the dryer has finished its cycle will also help prevent wrinkling. The heat of the dryer can age fabrics, and some recommend taking the clothes out when they are slightly damp.

Fabric Fresheners

Unless clothes are 100 percent organic, wash new clothes before you wear them. That "new" smell is a potent mixture of chemicals, such as formaldehyde and urea resins, and it should be removed. The chemicals are used to "finish" fabric for a range of purposes including stain resistance, mercerizing (a thread-strengthening process), and wrinkle protection, and sometimes for disinfecting. Many fabric finishes con-

tain volatile organic compounds, which, like formaldehyde, are often sensitizers and suspected carcinogens.

I've been successful at removing the new smell from clothing, and my method also works for low-level chemical contamination from normal household substances, such as perfume. Place the clothes in the washing machine with enough water to cover them. Sprinkle one small-size box of baking soda (or about 1 cup) into the washing machine. Soak the clothes overnight. When convenient during the soaking, agitate the machine for a few minutes. Launder as usual. Repeat until the smell disappears from the clothing.

Some imported clothes are now impregnated with long-lasting disinfectants. You can identify these clothes by their smell because the smell is very hard to remove, and the baking soda method mentioned above doesn't work. I've started asking catalog companies if their clothes are disinfected, and I don't purchase them if the clothing contains these harsh chemicals.

Waterproofing

The most natural waterproofing available on clothing is a coat of natural rubber or linseed oil. "Oil" slickers are traditionally coated with linseed oil. Many of us like to waterproof our winter boots, but all of the commercially available products (that I'm aware of, anyway) for this purpose use toxic solvents—most of them petroleum-based. A wool expert introduced me to lanolin as a safe alternative for waterproofing leather. Lanolin is the oil in sheep's wool, and it is a natural water repellent that can be removed with no harm to the sheep. It's available in phar-macies as "anhydrous lanolin." This rich, lubricating cream comes in a small tube and costs just a few dollars. Health food stores now offer liquid lanolin for cosmetic purposes at a reasonable cost.

Caring for Specific Fibers

Almost all fibers and clothing can be machine or hand washed. I haven't dry-cleaned anything in about 25 years, and nothing is worse for the wear as long as I pay attention and tend to problems (such as stains) as they happen. Some fibers need a bit more attention and require hand washing, such as wool and rayon, but once you know the rules, washing them by hand is very easy and successful.

MAKE IT YOURSELF
LAVENDER LINEN WATER

With this simple formula, you can "sweeten" your linens, and if you aren't sensitive to essential oils, you can use it to freshen rooms. Sprinkle on sheets or other linens for a fresh scent and spray on linens before you iron them.

1 teaspoon (100 drops) lavender essential oil
5–10 drops peppermint, spearmint, or rosemary essential oil (optional)
2 ounces 80+ proof vodka
Bottle with tight-fitting lid
24 ounces distilled water

Pour the essential oils and vodka into a bottle. Tighten the lid and shake until the oils are emulsified (suspended throughout). Mix with the distilled water. Shake well before each use. Pour into a shaker jar or spray bottle to use. Shelf life: indefinite. ❖

Dry Cleaning and Wet Cleaning

I recommend that you avoid dry cleaning because of the toxic chemicals used. These chemicals are extremely hazardous for the central nervous systems of the workers in dry-cleaning stores and can cause harm to the environment when they are being manufactured and disposed of. Dry-cleaning fumes can also waft throughout your home and expose all family members to these neurotoxins.

Rest assured that you can wash many clothes by hand that say "Dry Clean Only," but you need to learn some tricks. Almost all dry-cleaning establishments in the country clean with perchloroethylene, a neurotoxic chlorinated solvent that bioaccumulates in fat, is a probable carcinogen, and is a suspected endocrine disrupter—meaning it is a chemical that may confuse the body into thinking it is estrogen! I spent many hours researching the newer, so-called greener dry-cleaning approaches, and I've concluded that some are simply false "greenwashing" of toxic materials, and others are harmful to the workers. Instead of having your clothes dry-cleaned, search out a dry cleaner that does wet cleaning. Dry-cleaning establishments all over the world are adding wet washing to their services, and this is the way to go if you choose to have your better clothes professionally cleaned. Otherwise, we can take charge of getting our "Dry Clean Only" fabrics cleaned safely by learning the wet-clean process.

Through hard-earned experience (I shrank a lot of rayon outfits three sizes before I finally figured out what I was doing wrong), I've finally learned how to wet-clean fabrics such as rayon, silk, and wool. The most critical bit of information you need to know is that agitating rayon, silk, and wool causes the fabric to shrink, not just hot water. Even the agitation of the gentle cycle in a washing machine is too much for these fabrics; they need to be hand washed. Make sure to spot-test the fabric for colorfastness first.

Most fabrics and fibers can be safely hand laundered at home. Fancy, once-a-year clothes may need only airing out or direct sun, unless there's a stain or the fabric shouldn't be exposed to light. Many fuzzy and furry fibers, such as angora and cashmere, can also be washed at home. This guide will help take the mystery out of cleaning some of your most valuable clothing fibers.

Angora

Hand wash angora with warm water and pure soap. Rinse thoroughly, spin dry, then block and shape on a flat drying surface.

Cashmere

Gently hand wash cashmere and block and shape on a flat drying surface. You can iron cashmere only if you place a thick fabric or bath towel between the iron and the cashmere.

Down

When you wash down, make sure it is very clean when it is finished so that the fabric relofts. Because down is designed by nature to get wet and to dry, it can get thoroughly wet without worry. The natural oils in down repel water. Down does wonderfully when dried in the sun. Spread down clothing, comforters, and pillows outside on top of a car, deck, or sheet. Fluff occasionally. Down can be dried in the dryer on medium heat, but take it out and fluff it occasionally as it's drying. You can provide continuous fluffing of down fabric in the dryer by placing a tennis ball in the dryer. Down parkas and comforters can be scrunched up tightly for storage, and they will rebound fully if stored in the off season; it's not ideal to keep them compressed for more than a few months, though.

Leather and Suede

Wash finished, smooth leather with soap and water. Use liquid castile soap (found in health food stores) and not a detergent. Rinse with a clean, damp cloth. You can iron leather if you're careful by selecting the rayon setting on the iron and placing a heavy press cloth between the iron and the right side of the leather. Don't overheat.

The dye used on leather and suede can change over time. Some dyes simply fade and oxidize, and sometimes the leather finish is lost in dry cleaning or the dyes fade.

Protein stains, such as blood, egg, and milk, attach deeply to leather and suede and are hard to clean. Use an enzyme cleaner, but make sure to spot-test first because it can affect the dye.

There are inherent risks of having leather and suede dry-cleaned with solvents (besides exposure to the perchloroethylene outgassing from the cleaned leather). Solvent-based dry cleaning is an added problem for leathers that have been dyed using solvent-soluble dyes; much of the dye will be removed during the dry-cleaning process. Sometimes defects in the leather have been dyed by the manufacturer, and the cleaning process can expose the defect. Vivid top dyes can fade and bleed during dry cleaning. For leather and suede gloves, dry cleaning can dissolve the glue that attaches the lining to the leather. Whenever possible, it's best to just spot-clean leather and avoid washing procedures that may cause more harm than good.

To protect leather from your skin's

oils, wear a scarf around your neck when wearing a leather jacket. Store leather in an environment that isn't too hot, too cold, overly dry, or overly wet. Air circulation keeps leather from drying out, so don't store leather in plastic bags. When leather gets wet, just hang it to dry and don't heat it. Use a strong, dense sponge to raise the nap of leather after it has dried. Avoid metal hangers because the metal can leave marks on leather.

As for spot-cleaning suede, brush suede using a bristle brush, suede brush, or dry sponge. Never use a wire brush.

Linen

Most linens can be washed in the washing machine, and washing linen actually softens it. The older, more frequently washed the linen, the less it wrinkles. Make sure to wash linen separately from synthetic fibers such as polyester because the linen can pick up the "pills" that surface on synthetic fabric. Eco-friendly detergents are best because detergents with optical brighteners can cause the linen's colors to change. Plain linen can be washed at 103°F, although hand-embroidered linen should be washed separately at a cooler temperature, such as 100°F. Soaking linen in a weak hydrogen peroxide bleach solution can remove mildew. Avoid chlorine bleach on linen because it can weaken and harm the fibers.

The sun will lighten linen, and it will be wrinkle free if line-dried when damp. You can also dry linens in the dryer on a tumble dry air cycle with no heat.

Store linen on slatted shelves or on hangers for air circulation. Avoid starch on linens because it can attract silverfish. Linen is very sensitive to acids; acid materials can cause streaking and yellowing, so don't use plastic bags to store linen. Use cotton or muslin instead; you may need to make these fabric bags yourself because they are not easy to find. Avoid placing acidic, aromatic wood, such as cedar or pine, with your linens. If you wrap your linen with tissue paper to help protect it, make sure the tissue paper is acid free.

Mohair

Hand wash mohair with mild detergent. Squeeze dry by rolling in a towel (don't wring). Lay flat to dry. You can put mohair clothing in a pillowcase and place it in the dryer on gentle and low heat, if you do so cautiously.

You can steam-clean mohair with a teakettle or handheld steamer. Boil the water and then hold the kettle a few inches away from the fibers. Brush the fibers in their natural direction with a natural bristle brush after passing the steam over the garment.

Avoid storing mohair in plastic bags, and don't hang mohair on hangers because its weight can pull the fabric out of shape.

Rayon

Rayon absolutely must not be agitated at all. It is a weak fiber and shrinks easily. Hand wash rayon in a sink by gently swirling the clothes in cool water; never twist or wring out rayon. Most all-purpose detergents or a liquid castile soap will be fine to use. Even a harsh detergent won't harm rayon. Gently press out water and hang to dry.

Silk

Silk is an acidic fabric and sensitive to alkaline materials, such as baking soda, borax, and washing soda. Any harsh lye-based soap with a pH above 10 will destroy silk. Hand wash silk in a sink by gently swirling the clothes in cool water; never twist or wring silk. A mild liquid castile soap, such as Dr. Bronner's baby soap, is best for cleaning silk because it won't strip the natural oils. Shampoo—with its ability to remove body oils and neutral pH—can be a good choice for washing silk that has been stained; just a little dab is needed. Gently press water from the fabric after washing and hang silk to dry.

Spot-clean with vinegar or lemon juice, but test for color fastness first.

Wool

Wool is an acidic material. Hand wash wool in a sink by gently swirling the clothes in cool water; never twist or wring out wool. Use a mild detergent with a pH below 7 for wool, such as one from the Clean Environment Company. If necessary, spot-clean with vinegar or lemon juice, but test for color fastness first.

After washing, gently press water from the fabric. Block and shape wool before drying by laying it flat on a towel and stretching it to the correct size and shape. Wool is resilient and recovers quickly from wrinkling if you hang it. (Hanging sweaters may leave hanger marks around the shoulders, though.)

Sunlight helps wool's loft and helps repel pests; the ultraviolet rays deodorize the wool. If you need to iron woolen clothing, always use steam and avoid pressing the iron directly upon the material.

Stain Removal

Are you befuddled when you see a drop of chocolate ice cream on your new shirt? Chocolate is one of the hardest stains to clean from clothes. My friend Pat and I are always complaining that we seem to spill more food down our fronts than any other people we know. Daunted by how many of my T-shirts had stains and discouraged about how

(continued on page 358)

STAIN-REMOVAL SUPPLIES

Your laundry cabinet doesn't need to be filled with dozens of toxic products, each with a specialized purpose. Simple, natural supplies give equally terrific results when removing stains and lighten the environmental load in your home and on the planet.

SUPPLY	GOOD FOR
3 percent hydrogen peroxide	Lightening stains and an antibacterial agent on clothing
Baking soda	Abrasive cleaning
Citrus solvents	All-purpose stain removal (apply to stain before laundering)
Cornmeal	Absorbing oily and thick, messy stains
Enzymes	Protein and carbohydrate stains
Freezer	Removing gum and candle wax
Glycerin	Softening old, hardened stains
Laundry detergents	Various stains
Natural acids, such as lemon juice and vinegar	Mild bleaching and neutralizing alkaline stains and odors
Rags	Blotting up stains
Salt	Killing sweat bacteria, absorbing liquids, and abrasive cleaning
Soap	General stains
Sodium perborate	General laundry needs
Spray bottles	Dispensing cleaners
Toothbrush	Tamping stains
Washing soda	Heavy-duty stain removal
Water	Rinsing stains and fresh food drips, blood stains
White distilled vinegar	Stubborn stains, such as tea and coffee; deodorizing

COMMENTS

Should be considered a mild bleach; pretest first to check for color fading.

Can act as a mild bleach and can neutralize acid-based stains.

Do not use if you have cats in the house.

Cornmeal works well as a blotter to remove damp, oily stains when they happen; it also helps absorb moisture quickly.

Digestive enzymes work on stains just as they do in the stomach—by digesting proteins and carbohydrates. Buy pepsin/papain for protein and amylase for carbohydrate stains and buy the highest ratio of enzymes to filler. Health food stores sell enzyme products made from "natural" enzymes that have been custom-made for stain removal. Try my simple "Eat-It-Up Enzyme" paste—just grind up the enzymes and mix with enough water to make a paste to cover the stain. Discard leftover paste after use.

Helps harden gummy or melted materials; scrape material with a blunt knife or credit card edge.

Buy vegetable glycerin in health food stores.

Liquid detergents are better at normal stains; powdered are better at oil-based stains, such as lipstick and makeup.

Make sure to pretest on colored fabrics.

Cotton and linen rags are best because they absorb lots of moisture.

Helps break down greasy stains.

Use liquid, flakes, or a cake of soap; choose a pure soap without fragrances or deodorizers for stain removal. Soap can set fruit stains, so don't use it with wine, fruit, or jam stains.

This is a powdered oxygen bleach; use hot water to dissolve the powder.

Fill clean spray bottles with stain removers, such as vinegar and peroxide, then spray directly on stains. Label all bottles.

Just bounce toothbrush on stains to help lift stain particles; avoid brushing stains.

Make a paste with water and apply to stain. Leave the paste on for a few hours, keeping it damp.

A great solvent and cleaner in its own right without anything else added. Soak blood stains in cold water; use boiling water to sterilize clothing contaminated with material that could harbor bacteria or viruses. If you have very hard water, use spring or distilled water for stain removal.

An excellent natural acid for trouble stains.

much it would cost to replace them, I decided to see if I could reclaim them. Toxic, chemical spot removers aren't a good solution, even if I could use them, because the one-fix-for-all-stains approach is usually a failure. Instead, by understanding the chemistry of a few stain-removing materials, such as vinegar, baking soda, and simple digestive enzymes, you can solve most stain problems. I was able to clean up the stains on all of my T-shirts, except the one with an old chocolate stain.

Guidelines for Stain Removal

The sooner you attend to a stain, the better. But think twice before just throwing stained clothing in the laundry. The heat of the water and dryer can set many stains, so you need to analyze the stains before doing laundry. First, scrape, blot, vacuum, or otherwise remove as much of the stain as you can. Never rub in the stain. Then, identify the stain. This is important for the chemistry of stain removal because you need to use the right treatment at the right time. Once you have determined the best treatment, pretest on the fabric to make sure that the fabric won't be harmed by the treatment.

Warm or cool water is the safest for stain removal because hot water and heat can set stains.

Synthetic stain removers can harm natural fibers, such as silk and wool, and some synthetic stain removers are flammable.

Stain-Specific Cleaning

Many aerosol stain removers contain neurotoxic petroleum solvents. They will permeate your home while you are working with the stain, causing toxic indoor air pollution. There are safer alternatives.

Beer: Vinegar.

Berries: Vinegar.

Blood: Soak in cold salt water or just cold water; use a hydrogen peroxide soak for stubborn stains.

Chewing Gum: Put in freezer for a few hours; once cold, peel off gum.

Chocolate: Soak in detergent and launder. If stain remains, soak in "Eat-It-Up Enzyme" mixture (see the enzymes entry in the Stain-Removal Supplies chart on page 356). The enzymes will eat up the dairy products in the chocolate. If you still have a stain after trying enzymes, try soaking the spot in 3 percent hydrogen peroxide.

Cigarette Smoke: For yellow stains, try washing soda or sodium perborate.

Coffee and Tea: The stain in caffeine drinks is from the tannin and from milk and sugar, if that has been included. Spot-clean tannin stains with vinegar. If dairy products have left stains, soak in

"Eat-It-Up Enzymes" mixture (see page 357). For old coffee and tea stains, rub with glycerin before laundering or try sodium perborate.

Crayons and Candle Wax: Freeze the stain, remove the residue, and pull off the wax. Next, heat an iron, cover the wax stain with an absorbent cloth, and melt the wax onto the cloth.

Decals and Price Stickers: Rub with vegetable oil.

Egg: Enzymes.

Feces: Enzymes.

Fruit: Lemon juice or vinegar.

Grass: Enzymes.

Grease: Detergent; it's best to blot the stain. Sometimes olive oil can be used to remove oil, but be careful not to create a new stain. Also, try cornstarch or citrus solvent.

Grout Stains: Hydrogen peroxide.

Ice Cream: Enzymes.

Ink: Soak in milk, vinegar, or citrus solvent.

Leather Stains: Saddle soap (which is soap and polish combined).

Lipstick and Makeup: Use a few drops of oil or glycerin, being careful not to spread the oil farther than the stain. Scrape off. Pretreat with detergent, and then wash in hot water.

Medicines, Herbs (Turmeric), Chemicals: 3 percent hydrogen peroxide.

Mildew: Vinegar.

Mold: Vinegar.

Mustard: 3 percent hydrogen peroxide.

Oil: Glycerin.

Perfume and Essential Oils: Vinegar or baking soda.

Perspiration: Enzymes; soak item in salt water. Lay clothing in the sun for a few hours. Clean with shampoo (the chemistry of shampoo is designed to remove body oils).

Petroleum Oil: Washing soda.

Protein Stains: Enzymes or shampoo.

Ring around the Collar: Shampoo.

Rust: Borax paste.

Tomato Sauce: Vinegar.

Urine: Enzymes; alternating between vinegar and baking soda.

Vomit: Enzymes; alternating between vinegar and baking soda.

Wax: Freeze the stain, remove the residue, and pull off the wax. Next, heat an iron, cover the wax stain with an absorbent cloth, and melt the wax onto the cloth.

Wine: Pour boiling water from a height of 3 feet; may be more effective if you rub salt on the stain first.

the home office

In today's telecommuting world, you can make a living from a mountaintop or the beach, as long as you have a computer and Internet access. I work from home, and the people with whom I work out the minute-to-minute production details for Care2.com's online publishing are all over the country. With instant messaging, it's as if we were sitting at the same table. Sometimes I work in a snowstorm when the local roads, schools, and businesses are closed, and I can communicate in seconds to California or Texas. Although it can be isolating at times to work from home, for at least part of the week, it is an increasing option for a huge segment of the workforce.

I've worked from a home office for years as a full-time working mom. I am glad to be at home for my daughter when there is a snow day or when she is sick, but I am also driven mad sometimes by the often-blurry boundary between my work and my family life. How can you put in a good, full, office workday on the day before Thanksgiving when your child doesn't have school that day and you have a dozen family members arriving for that night's dinner and staying for a few days?

From the child's perspective, a parent working at home is comforting (there is always someone there), but the situation can also be alienating for the child when they really need attention (and parents are busy and distracted on the computer or on a conference call). It's critical to set clear office boundaries for yourself and for your family to be successful at the work-from-home option.

That said, as I write, I am looking out of my office window at white-tailed deer, goldfinches swarming my bird feeders, and flowers blooming in the garden. I do a lot of things I like to do during the time most people commute; it's a rare cherished time for myself. And I am *home*—home for my dogs, home for my family, and in my case (and hopefully yours), home in an environment that is nontoxic and healthy for me so that I can thrive.

Create a Pleasing Office

What helps you thrive? What makes you feel your best? The elements are often not fully balanced in home offices; the fire element is usually very strong, and the rest of the elements are quite weak. I had a feng shui expert come to my office, and she said, "Annie! You are burning up with fire in here!" With all the books and papers, my passion about my subject matter, and the energy needed to manage my workload, fire was consuming much of the energy. There was so little of the water element that she advised I put a fountain in the room. The air in my office is quite healthy, but even so, it has more positive ions than I would like, so I bought a salt lamp to help (see page 424). The earth element in the office becomes stronger all the time because I am always bringing rocks into the room, I have a wooden desk and furniture, and my window allows views of plants and wildlife.

WORDS TO THE WISE

CLARITY, CONCENTRATION, AND CHEMICALS

Homes and offices often contain "everyday chemicals" that are, in fact, neurotoxic and can affect your brain. These very powerful chemicals can affect your concentration, clarity, and ability to focus. The chemicals are usually petroleum-based and are solvents found in printer ink (including copiers), markers, furniture polish, synthetic scents (including synthetic aromatherapy oils and candles), and even the glue holding the wood together in some furniture.

Your reaction to the exposure may be so subtle that you don't clearly attribute it to any one thing, just a general sense that it is hard to focus. The last place you want to be exposed to neurotoxic chemicals is in your office—a place where you have to think and concentrate.

Start by removing items in the office that have a chemical smell, such as synthetic scents and inks. Choose solid wood furniture and natural accessories. Keep office supplies to a minimum, and keep your choices simple—for example, choose a graphite pencil over a scented marker with a specialized plastic grip. If your climate and weather permit, open the window as often as possible. Store office supplies, such as ink and toner cartridges, away from your work area to minimize exposure to strong chemical odors.

Sight

Most of us see a lot of electronic equipment in a home office. Between the answering machine, fax machine, printer, computer monitor and CPU, keyboard, CD player, TV, and more, there are a lot of cords. Use enough power surge protectors to handle all the plug-ins, and try to consolidate the wires as much as possible. Exposed cords are hard to keep clean, and they become obstacles to movement, impeding placement of your papers, books, and other items.

Full-Spectrum Light: Since many of us spend long hours looking into the light of a computer screen or looking at natural light through the filter of windows, we may not be getting the amount of full-spectrum light our endocrine systems need. Consider full-spectrum lighting in your office, especially if it's in the basement. I am a recent convert to full-spectrum light in the office (and my office has plenty of natural light), and I feel my eyes drinking up the light from my new desk lamp. It wasn't even $30, but what a huge difference in my overall energy and comfort! Having a full-spectrum light in your office brings with it better sleep, a reduced appetite, and an overall sense of better harmony. For a detailed explanation about the benefits of full-spectrum lighting, see page 294.

Task Lighting: Whether you enjoy full-spectrum lighting or not, the more spot-specific lighting you can manage in the office, the better. Ambient lighting, such as a light in the middle of the ceiling, isn't the best choice for this space. The eyes are naturally drawn to the bright spot, and it tires the eyes to search out the place to focus when everything is evenly lit. Halogen lamps give good spot lighting, but the transformer (black box) they require emits high electromagnetic fields (EMFs) near the box and can be a fire hazard because it gives off so much heat (see page 303).

Glare: Glare from lighting and bright sun shining in the windows takes on a special urgency in the office—if there is glare on your computer screen, you probably can't see your work. Offices with glossy and shiny surfaces have even more of a glare problem, so choose less-reflective matte surfaces (and add a desk blotter or desk calendar to break up large expanses of desk). Be sure to add task lighting or spotlights near your work area to light the specific work at hand, and adjust these lights to minimize glare. Try placing a light behind you or in front of your work. I have a light behind my right shoulder about 7 feet up from the floor. It illuminates my computer screen and my desktop without glare (although sunlight can sometimes complicate things).

Place your desk near a window with

north light. This is the beautiful light made famous by great painters such as Vermeer. Glare won't be a problem for your computer screen when lit by north light because you won't have to contend with the sun's reflections.

Adjustable window shades can also help to protect against glare. You may want to look out the window from your desk like I do but find there are times of the day in certain seasons when the sun shines directly into the room, interfering with your ability to see. I can reach the shade's pull-cords from my desk chair, making shade adjustment very easy.

Energy-Efficient Lighting: Compact fluorescent lights (CFLs), especially full-spectrum models, are a great choice for the office because they use one-quarter of the electricity of a standard incandescent. The key is to position CFLs so that they don't cause glare on your computer screen.

Upholstery Fabric: Fabric with colorful prints or stripes is nice to have on pillows, lounge chairs, or couches in a home office. This touch has made my office more inviting for other people when they visit the room. I even have a couch in there for my daughter, so she can do her homework near me or sleep when she is sick. This was a careful decision. My office is always a place where she knows she can be any time

she wants my company, but she also knows that she must be quiet there. (We do it the other way too. I take my laptop to the living room to be near her at her favorite place to do homework.)

Fish Tanks, Birds, and Pets: Fish tanks are very relaxing to observe and are meditative for the mind, like a fire in a fireplace. I find pets are also assets in an office. One of my dogs is almost always at my feet in my office. When the dogs are visiting, their presence engenders a very companionable and connected feeling. Birds can also add interest to an office, but they can be loud at times. One summer, we bird-sat for Spinach and Zebra, two parakeets that were part of my daughter's class menagerie. We kept them in my office, where they quietly passed the time, until I was on the telephone. Then, they wanted to chime in every time they heard me talk, and what a racket they made! If you work at home or spend considerable time in your home office, carefully consider which pets would make the best office companions.

Plants: Plants help connect you with nature and are another way to bring the outdoors into the office environment. Hang a few spider plants or other plants that are known to help clean indoor air (see page 77), for an added bonus.

Hearing

While working in your office, can you hear the rain or the wind? Hearing weather helps to keep you from being too disconnected from the outside world and can provide delightful background sounds. Keep your windows open whenever possible.

Have you ever noticed if the noise of the computer bothers you or puts you on edge? Entrainment (or melding) is a big issue for the office. It can happen when there is a loud hum, such as from a fan in the computer. The hum is powerful enough to entrain or become the same as your body's vibration, making you uncomfortable because your own rhythms are overpowered.

This is a constant problem for me, and I wish I could put the CPU in a soundproof unit that is vented to the outside so that its fan worked without disturbing me. (This would be a good business for somebody, by the way; I'd be a customer in the blink of an eye!) Fortunately, most of the newer computers generate a less powerful hum. Music, white noise, or other sounds can also help you to avoid entrainment to your office computer.

One healer I know recommends accepting the entrainment to the computer because fighting it is stressful, but she recommends that we fully smudge the area and ourselves with white sage after a day's work to break the entrainment (see page 25). You can also smudge your desk area at the end of every working day. If only I would remember to do so!

Music: Music is the best entrainment block that I know of, and I use it quite a bit. I have a CD player right next to my computer. Like most of us, I find that there are certain types of music I can't listen to when I work, but I have some helpful standby CDs that are almost always a support. I once managed a huge workload over many weeks by playing a very droning CD—Bob Dylan's *Time Out of Mind*—over and over and over again. The droning kept me entrained to the monotony, and I could last long hours at my desk.

White Noise: White noise is a combination of all the different frequencies of sound playing at the same time, drowning out everything else. Imagine some 20,000 tones—a white noise machine overwhelms them all so that you hear only the white noise. A portable fan approximates white noise, according to some researchers. I don't think that there is enough research about white noise machines to recommend them, though, to prevent computer entrainment.

Fountains: Rain furnishes soothing, natural rhythms, and tabletop fountains can provide equally relaxing sound. They'll even increase the negative ion balance in your office to a small degree. In most home offices, water is a barely represented element. In Tarot and other spiritual traditions, water is known as the carrier of feelings and of love. The King of Cups in traditional Tarot decks is the king of the heart. It is interesting that water is underrepresented in the office, since emotion is not integrated into most of our work worlds. Where and how can you be more heart-centered in your work? There are opportunities every day to contribute to society from a place of love. Adding the water element to your home office can start you down a fulfilling path.

One of the nicest water fountains I have seen is one where the water falls onto four or five rose quartz crystals that are each about 4 inches high. A soothing tabletop fountain can be as little as $50 (and upward, of course), and it's well worth the cost. Search for one that pleases your senses.

Smell

There is nothing more conducive to a clear head and good health than clean, fresh air! Keep alert to toxic smells in your office and eliminate them immediately. I've found that they enter the office with mail, packages, new office equipment or furnishings, and even newly printed books.

Open the window in your home office and enjoy the clean smell of sunshine and the outdoors. Tightly sealed homes often have poor indoor air quality, so refresh and replenish the air in your home by allowing for cross-ventilation and good air flow.

Ventilating your office is very important. Say you have a newly installed printer cartridge and are printing a large number of documents. Airing the room after this print job is important to remove the volatile organic chemicals (VOCs). Or after receiving a shipment of something with a strong odor, you should open the windows for some fresh air exchange.

Markers: Avoid markers containing petroleum-based solvents. Read the labels on the packages. If the product says it is flammable, then you can assume it is petroleum based. If the markers aren't labeled, then smell them. Solvents have a strong chemical odor. These are commonly used on whiteboards and in permanent markers. These markers are considered to be so neurotoxic that they can cause behavioral problems in children. Adults can easily lose concentration from exposure to them. For this reason, my town's public school is considering banning them completely from use. Water-based markers are a harmless substitute.

Plastics: Inhaling fumes from plastic is not advisable. Many plastics contain endocrine disrupters, and it isn't easy to tell which plastics in your environment could be wreaking havoc with your hormones and which ones are benign. Avoid plastic furnishings and desk accessories whenever possible, and ven-

tilate rooms after you have brought in new equipment that outgasses plastic fumes (such as a new computer) until the "new" smell is gone. This is a good time to use an air filter if you have one!

Aromatherapy: *Aromatherapy for Healing the Spirit* by Gabriel Mojay is one of the most informative resources about aromatherapy that I have found. Some of Mojay's suggestions and ideas may help with a wide range of work challenges and workplace experiences. Aromatherapy uses the vibrations of plant essences to heal, and they replace a negative vibration with one that is

WORDS TO THE WISE

PARTICLEBOARD AND FORMALDEHYDE

Currently, government regulations regarding chemicals state that formaldehyde—a gaseous by-product of the glue used in most pressed wood and particleboard products that are made into desks and bookcases—is a recognized carcinogen and suspected to be toxic to the liver and to reproductive and neurological systems. It is grouped among the top 10 percent of compounds determined to be hazardous to both ecosystems and human health by Environmental Defense, a leading national nonprofit environmental advocacy organization. Given this danger, it is astonishing that every office store sells furniture that is made almost exclusively with pressed wood and particleboard. Wooden and metal furniture are good alternatives, as long as there isn't a urethane or stain odor on the wood. You want office furniture, including bookshelves, to be as inert as possible. New or unfinished pine bookshelves aren't a great choice because the smell of the pine terpenes can take many months to fully offgas; it is best to seal in the smell with a low-VOC paint.

Formaldehyde stays in pressed wood and particleboard furniture for months, even years, because the glue containing formaldehyde is part of the structure of the "wood." Waiting for it to completely offgas will be an exercise in frustration.

When formaldehyde heats up (simply from direct sunshine warming up a desk or a bulletin board, or a heater warming your desk), it volatizes more gases into the atmosphere.

If you must use furniture that offgases formaldehyde, you can seal it in with a product made specifically for this purpose. While sealing won't totally correct the problem, it helps a lot. AFM Safecoat & Safechoice provides this sealant, and it is widely available in ecofriendly specialty stores. See page 487.

more positive. An easy way to use aromatherapy in your office is to add a few drops of essential oil to ¼ teaspoon of vegetable oil, mix, and put a drop or two on a lightbulb that is turned on. Make sure the essential oils are 100 percent pure.

❖ *Clear the air.* Ginger is a great essential oil for "clearing the air" of old thought patterns and habits. Mojay writes that he believes ginger helps with initiative, self-confidence, and accomplishment.

❖ *Relieve nervous tension.* Lavender calms the mind. Other essential oils that help calm the mind and central nervous system include neroli and bergamot. If you are under a lot of pressure or are agitated, consider chamomile, bergamot, and orange. If you are tense and exhausted, try clary sage, cypress, and lavender.

❖ *Calm your mind.* Sandalwood and frankincense calm the intellect when it is overactive. If you find yourself obsessing about a work problem, consider sandalwood. If you can't see the proverbial forest for the trees in the midst of a project, try frankincense and lemon.

❖ *Boost your confidence.* If you find you're challenged by a project and having trouble with self-confidence, consider rosemary and laurel. If your morale is low, thyme, pine, and cedarwood may help.

❖ *Gain clarity.* Clary sage helps promote clarity (is there any surprise, with that name?). Rosemary, laurel, and peppermint help a person become alert and focused.

❖ *Become empowered.* If you feel as if you aren't comfortable being assertive, try pine and thyme. If you need to be more determined, use a blend of cedarwood and ginger.

Sixth Sense

A balance of yin and yang is essential for a productive office environment. When you contemplate the yin and yang in your office, you will find that most offices have a lot more yang than yin energy. Feng shui practitioners would argue that a better balance of yin and yang makes the office run more smoothly. *Yin* office energy is found in fabrics, wooden furniture, textures, art, creativity, conceptual thinking, and a quiet atmosphere. *Yang* office energy includes electronic equipment, straight lines, reflective surfaces, aggressive business models (such as promotion and sales), deadlines, metal, and a busy atmosphere. An office with too much yin could be unproductive while an office with too much yang energy could be stressful.

If you work from home or do a great deal of work in your home office, you should *want* to spend time in there. Be sure that you have the healing and uplifting energy of negative ions in your home office. Positive ions often heavily outweigh negative ions, causing imbalance in the office. Plastics, synthetic building materials, and EMFs all attach to positive ions, and the air becomes heavy with this energy. Salt ion generators are an excellent choice for the office because they neutralize positive ions. See page 423 for more about ion balance.

Enhance Your Office Performance

Everything has a vibration uniquely its own. There are vibrations to colors, sounds, crystals, computers, and cell phones! Offices have a lot of unnatural vibrations from the deluge of electronic equipment. To help offset this, surround yourself with vibrations that are harmonious to your own body's rhythms and that enhance them—this is a secret of a healing environment. At the same time, removing, solving, neutralizing, and reducing disharmonious vibrations can be a huge boost to overall well-being. Step-by-step, you can add and remove objects, colors, crystals, and electronic equipment to improve the quality of your workday.

Color and Crystals in the Home Office

Color is a subtle but important choice in office space planning. Yogic philosophy employs your body's chakras (energy centers) as an influence.

Sky blue is the color of the throat chakra, the center of communication and creativity. Wear blue crystals or hang them near your desk to help activate these qualities. Blue crystals include aquamarine, azurite, larimar, blue fluorite, and lapis lazuli. Aquamarine and larimar are perfect for strengthening the throat chakra.

White enhances clear thinking, and it is, along with rose, the color of the eighth chakra, that of the higher self. A quartz crystal is a clear stone that can be placed in front of you when you work. White desktops are helpful for clarity too.

Yellow represents the third chakra, and it is the seat of mental energy, affirmation, integrity, willpower, and hard work. Yellow crystals that might help in these areas are citrine, amber, yellow fluorite, or tourmaline. Place a painting with lots of yellow within eyesight of your desk chair, or simply tape a strip of yellow paper to your computer.

Orange symbolizes the second chakra and can help strengthen emotions, financial power, and creativity (the throat chakra also influences creativity). Rhodochrosite, citrine, and amber are good stones for the second chakra. Something as simple as a fresh orange sitting on a countertop can help strengthen this chakra. Including a fountain in the office introduces more emotion to the room.

Wall Color

Your choice for wall color in your office is important for your well-being. White is clear and clean, and it is my preference. Some people have womblike offices with very dark-colored walls, and this is obviously their preference. I am not sure that there is any right or wrong, but it's important to know that the color of your office could influence you positively or negatively.

Cool-colored offices emanate a clear and purposeful vibration. Yellow is the one warm color that is successful in an office because it is uplifting. Yellow, the color of the third chakra, helps self-esteem and success in the world.

Dark colors in your office require a lot of artificial light to compensate. I believe that a dark red office would be so full of an energetic vibration that it would be an exhausting room to work in all day—at least for me. Red is the color of the first chakra and is focused on survival issues. With a red room, you might become overly focused on survival and less on creativity and clear thinking.

Red and orange are social colors and not so conducive to focused, solitary work. Blue, especially dark blue, is so relaxing that you might want to nap instead of work.

EMFs

Exposure to electromagnetic fields (EMFs) is a big problem in our home offices. The good news is that EMFs drop off very quickly the farther you are from the source. For example, my computer might register quite a high exposure level right at the monitor if I held a gaussmeter there for an accurate reading, but just 1 foot away, the field might drop to a negligible amount. This drop-off of EMFs is why it is so important to be at least an arm's length away from the monitor.

Distance from a monitor isn't possible with a laptop, but laptops generally emit a lower EMF frequency. If you usually use your laptop in one place, you can attach a keyboard that is separate from it, enabling you to be farther from the screen.

Place the computer's central processing unit (CPU) as far away from your desk chair as possible; place it under or beside your desk, if you can, instead of on the desk in front of you.

As mentioned previously, power cubes (often black or white boxes), which may be used to plug in your computer's sound system, your answering machine, fax machine, or halogen lamp, give off high levels of EMFs. My computer's sound speakers are plugged in with a black box—a giveaway that there is a transformer. Place them as far from your desk chair as possible. These transformers are also very wasteful of electricity (60 to 80 percent inefficient) because they're on 24 hours a day.

There are new products coming onto the market all the time that purport to reduce the EMFs you receive from electronic equipment. This developing field is new and constantly changing, so if you want information in this area, spend some time researching products on the Internet.

One of these products, the BioElectric Shield, was designed by a physicist and is a matrix of crystals that refracts electromagnetic frequencies from computers and other stressors. The shield is a circular pendant that is about 1½ inches in diameter and is designed to hang around your neck. (As background, Max von Laue won a Nobel Prize in Physics in 1914 by showing that x-rays could be reflected and redirected with a zinc-sulfide crystal, in much the same way as mirrors are used

to reflect and redirect visible light. William Bragg won the Nobel Prize in 1915 for establishing "Bragg's Law," which determines the specific crystal spacing needed to reflect and redirect any type of electromagnetic energy. Since then, scientists have used natural crystals to reflect and redirect other types of electromagnetic radiation, such as gamma rays.)

According to designers of the Bio-Electric Shield, crystals are reportedly woven into your energy field and will refract anything not compatible with your resonance, whether it's a computer, power line, microwave tower, television, cell phone, or even other people.

On a personal level, I think this shield has been very helpful for me. If you decide to use a crystal shield, be sure to follow the specific directions and guidelines for the shield you choose. Another product, called an eCrystal, reportedly "organizes" the EMFs in your vicinity to a frequency that is easier for your body to manage. You can read about these products online.

Wearing a crystal around your neck can certainly help. Just make sure to clear the crystal once a month or so by soaking it in salt water overnight or placing it in the sun for the day. A meteorite called moldavite is a good self-clearing stone—it protects the whole body. Hematite is a metallic-looking

Safe and Sound

HEALTHY OFFICE GUIDELINES

In visiting friends and family in their home offices, I've seen a few common mistakes that would detract from a healthy environment. Look over this list and see which issues you should be aware of, then make improvements for a healthier office space.

❖ Setting up an office in a basement or an attic makes the rooms feel isolated, unwelcoming, and unhealthy because they offer little ventilation or natural light. Besides, basement rooms are often musty. If there is no other space than a basement for your office, install a dehumidifier and full-spectrum lightbulbs. And have the basement tested for radon before making a decision to locate a home office there. If you must use a basement or attic as your office or work space, invest time and money in making the space pleasant and uplifting.

❖ You'll need access to clean, fresh air. Keep your computer near a window so you can enjoy fresh air when the weather is nice. If it's too cold to keep a window open, step outside for some air a few times a day. If you're working in a basement, make sure you're not working near an oil burner or other heating appliance that isn't completely ventilated to the outside. If you have an attic office in an older home, be sure to ventilate the space and allow for fresh air exchange as often as possible.

❖ It's vital to have a comfortable workstation. People often sit too close to their monitor because the table it sits on isn't deep enough to keep the monitor at least an arm's length away from the keyboard. Most home offices I have visited, except one, share this problem, and computer users are exposed to EMFs from the monitor. The one office that was properly set up belonged to someone who worked at home a few days a week. I was inspired enough by his computer setup that I copied it. He had a sliding keyboard drawer under the desk. When he pulled it out, not only did it put him at a safe distance from the monitor, but it was also at a perfect ergonomic height for his hands when sitting in a chair of normal height.

❖ Choose solid wood or metal tables and desks, instead of particleboard office furniture that out-gasses formaldehyde. Breathing formaldehyde every day is not a good idea—it's a sensitizer and a recognized carcinogen.

---

crystal that neutralizes unhealthy energy. Try wearing hematite around your neck when you work on the computer.

Surge Protectors

I have so much equipment to plug in near my desk that I have three surge suppressors. Lights, computers, and printers all need electrical current, and the pileup is usually overwhelming for the normal household outlet system. I have three power cubes plugged into the surge suppressor outlets, and they are as far from my body as possible.

It's important to use surge suppressors for your electronic equipment, especially your computer. An electrical surge, such as when electricity goes out or comes back on, can actually ruin your computer, and surge suppressors

❖ Be sure to have adequate lighting and a focused task light. There's no need to have eyestrain when a full-spectrum task light is very affordable.

❖ Even if you're short on space, think twice before shoehorning a home office into a closet with the door removed or in some other place that doesn't inspire you. Shop for a wooden armoire workstation instead—it's self-contained and takes up little space, yet it's pleasing to the eye.

❖ If you have to locate your home office in the middle of the family room, try to create some boundaries to give you full ownership of the space. If the room is large, perhaps you can build a half-wall or countertop to separate the office space without closing it in. Or buy a nice folding screen to visually screen off your workstation.

❖ If your finances permit, I feel it's very important to have a home office phone line in addition to the family line. Separating these two worlds with two different telephone lines is worth its weight in gold for peace of mind. There are many times when I am not working when I don't want a phone call to jolt me into my working world, just as there are times when I am working and need to screen calls from friends and family.

❖ Keep your office space as free from clutter as possible. Besides collecting dust, piles of clutter and paperwork can weigh down the energy of a space. If you plan to spend many hours a week in your home office, focus your energy on work, not long-forgotten papers.

If you earn your living from home, spend the time to make your work room a productive, welcoming space that meets your needs. Style a healthy haven that will make even long work hours tolerable. Keep it as free as possible of synthetic chemicals, despite the plastic computer and printer ink. Use nontoxic cleaning products. And remember to stand up, stretch, and get away from the computer at least once an hour.

will block this spike in electricity. To be safest, always turn off your computer during an electrical storm.

It is important to note that not all power strips are surge protectors—many are simply fancy extension cords. Look for a model that specifically says that it protects from power surges, and buy one that is energy efficient and has a low surge overload rating. Look for a UL-1449 rating to ensure adequate testing by Underwriters Laboratories. A label that says just "UL Listed" does not mean it has been tested. Make sure that the surge protector has a "clamping" voltage of 330 or below. (Clamping refers to the level at which the surge suppressor starts to block the surge; the lower the clamping number, the better.)

The ability of a surge suppressor to absorb a surge is called a joule rating. Look for a joule rating of at least 400; a rating of 600 is best. The surge suppressor should respond to a surge in 10 nanoseconds or less. Make sure that there is an on/off switch that allows you to shut off power to every connected component; these are ideal for saving energy. Some surge suppressors allow you to turn off some plug-ins and not others.

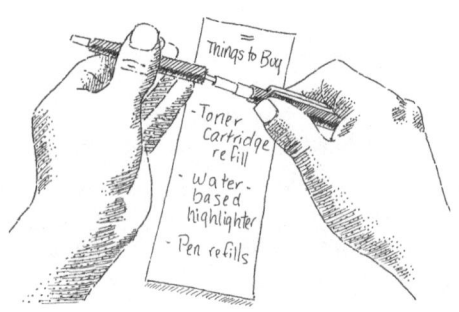

In our throwaway society, we've almost forgotten that many office supplies may have refills available. Pen refills are usually very inexpensive and can help to reduce consumption of raw materials.

Cell Phones

Cell phones are widely used, yet extensive studies on their health effects haven't been conducted. Children may be particularly at risk. Studies in Europe have documented brain damage in animals exposed to cell phone radiation. Until the research about the health effects of cell phone use and exposure to their radio waves has been studied more definitively, use a landline whenever possible in your home office.

Choosing Office Supplies

Offices that respect natural resources have a nice feel about them. You can sense it somehow. The furniture is made of natural materials, and there's very little plastic used. There might be a colorful cotton throw rug on a wooden floor, plants, and natural light. Even the smallest ecofriendly choice will improve your surroundings.

I am in a writer's group, and one night, we were all talking about practical matters, such as how we like to write, what writing utensils we use, and whether we like to write on the computer or on paper. I was impressed at how loyal each of us was to our choice of writing tool. Personal preference plays a big part in our selection of pen, paper, equipment, and even ink. Because of what I learned that night, I hesitate to give you rules for a healthy office because personal choice is really important, so I'll share some of what I know about making ecofriendly choices.

Paper

There is more paper used in the home office than anywhere else in the home. The goal of a paperless office is more within our reach all the time—one floppy disk can store the equivalent of

750 sheets of paper, and a CD-ROM can store the equivalent of more sheets of paper than you could use in a year or two. Unfortunately, most people still print hard copies, but you can try to reduce your consumption of paper by working smarter on-screen. Print out only the very final version of your work, and print only if you need a hard copy to refer to. E-mail instead of sending paper or faxes. And cut and paste small portions of what you're printing rather than printing a whole Web site page containing lots of blank pages with

SHOPPING SOLUTIONS
GREEN CHOICES IN THE OFFICE

"Green" office supplies are finally being added to the product lines in some office supply and department stores. Recycled paper is the most readily available "green" product, but you'll be able to find recycled-paper folders and report covers too. Buy refills instead of new notebooks or new pens, and look for energy-efficient equipment whenever possible.

❖ Ask for the most ecofriendly product, no matter what it is you are looking for. Not only can you end up buying the best product for the environment, but you can let the store know that environmental products are important to you.

❖ Choose ecofriendly products with caution, however. Often ecofriendly products are so labeled only because of their recycled content, when in fact the material can be quite toxic. Recycled tire products are an example of a product I would never suggest someone have in their office because the offgassing would be unhealthy. Palm rests for keyboards or mouse pads can be made of this material, for example, and I would never recommend that you buy them. Even if a product is recycled, make sure that it's the least toxic alternative available before you buy.

❖ Ask if there is an ecofriendly way of disposing of the product you are buying, if it is a printer, computer, monitor, facsimile (fax) machine, copier, or ink cartridge. And ask if the store has its own in-house recycling center so you can bring the equipment or cartridges back to the store for disposal.

❖ For electronic equipment, always ask to see its Energy Star rating, and try to choose the most energy-efficient product. For example, a battery-powered clock is a much more efficient choice than a clock that is plugged into the wall; a battery-powered clock may run for a year on a single AA rechargeable battery.

One of the fastest-growing sources of landfill trash is electronic equipment, along with its toxic soup of e-chemicals, such as lead, mercury, phosphorus, PVC plastic, and solvents, that can leach into soils and contaminate groundwater. Seek out a computer recycler in your area that can remove reusable components and recycle the plastics and metals in your equipment instead of carting your computer to the curb.

header addresses. Check to see if your printer recommends printing on the back of already-printed paper—that's two for the price of one!

Green Seal, a nonprofit organization that researches and defines ecofriendly standards for products, recommends that you choose paper that has at least 30 percent postconsumer recycled fiber content. The best paper is made from pulp that has not been processed with elemental chlorine; paper bleached with chlorine dioxide instead of elemental chlorine is a better choice.

Even though most US paper mills have switched to less problematic chlorine dioxide, the large-scale papermaking process is far from a sustainable enterprise currently. Worse, most paper is made from trees cut solely for papermaking, even though much of the paper we use can be manufactured from recycled content. According to the Green Guide Institute, the pulp and paper industry uses more trees than any other industry in the world; it's also the largest industrial consumer of water, using up to 50,000 gallons of water per ton of chlorine-bleached paper.

How can you make an impact in the paper department? First, use less paper. Second, recycle what you can. Third, shred your ecofriendly paper trash and use it as packing material or compost. And overall, shop carefully and buy ecofriendly offerings.

Tree-Free Paper: Whenever possible, avoid wood-based paper. For special reports, letters, and other specialty writing jobs, try rice, cotton, or even hemp paper. Handmade paper is a joy to use. Agri-pulp paper uses 45 percent agricultural waste, 43 percent postconsumer waste paper, and 12 percent calcium-carbonate filler. Agri-pulp paper is acid-free, chlorine-free, and effluent-free. As with most issues, there is a downside to agri-pulp paper too. Calcium carbonate must be mined from the earth; residents living in communities with calcium carbonate mines are struggling with a number of environmental issues as a result of this mining process.

Fax Paper: Choose a plain paper fax machine whenever possible, because continuous fax paper on rolls has a chemical coating. Plain paper fax machines are certainly more common now than they were 10 years ago.

Acid-Free Paper: If the project you are working on would benefit from paper that has a long life, make sure to choose acid-free paper. The benefit of acid-free paper is that it won't be damaged by dust.

Batteries

It is very important to recycle all batteries. I keep a basket on my refrigerator where I put all dead batteries. Every year or two, I contact my county to find out the next date for household hazardous waste drop-off, and I deliver them to the waste site. Batteries contain toxic heavy metals and must not be disposed of in the garbage. Investigate using rechargeable batteries too. A good detailed Web site with information about how to do this is http://store.greenbatteries.com/index.html.

Books

Many of us surround ourselves with books in our home offices—books we love to read, books we use for research, and books we love to look at for inspiration. Books are an important part of the home office. But with books come the potential problems of dust, mold, and silverfish. The safest way to diminish dust is to vacuum the page edges of books with a soft-bristled brush attachment. If your office has moisture problems or high humidity and you discover mold on books, fan out the book pages and expose them to air circulation. If a book is really damp, sprinkle its pages with cornstarch. Leave overnight and then dust the pages clean.

Silverfish bugs are flat, elongated, and about ⅓ to ¾ inch long; adults are a silvery color. They prefer 75 to 95 percent relative humidity, so you'll often find them in damp, cool places. They feed on glue, book bindings, paper, and

photographs, and they are active at night. Often, large numbers may be found in new buildings and during construction because there is a high moisture content in green lumber, and the walls were exposed to the elements.

To reduce and eliminate silverfish, lower the building's or the room's relative humidity with dehumidifiers and fans. If you find them in your books, the publication *Common Sense Pest Control* suggests that you microwave the books for 30 to 60 seconds (except for very old, valuable books). Or make a glass jar trap by wrapping the outside of an empty glass jar with masking tape, so bugs have something to grip, and then place the empty jar (without a top) near the books at night. The silverfish will crawl up the jar sides and fall in. In the morning, you can flush them down the toilet.

Computing Ergonomics

If you spend much time at your home office desk, a well-designed office chair is worth its weight in gold for your comfort. Here's how to choose one.

Look for one with a 5-star base on casters for stability. Place the chair on a carpet or a chair mat so that it doesn't slide around uncontrollably. (Just make sure that the mat isn't made of a plastic that outgasses fumes.) A swivel chair

An ergonomically designed workstation is good for your body and for your health. Your setup should be natural and comfortable; if you don't feel right when you're working, consult an ergonomics expert to design a work area that minimizes the risk of strain or repetitive motion injury.

makes working at various tasks easy; you can swivel to answer the phone or to turn another way to put in a different CD. Are you tall or short? Check the chair's dimensions. The seat should end a few inches from the back of your knee when you are seated.

Adjustable Chair

Adjustable chairs are important so that you can be properly positioned. Buy a chair that features a backrest adjustment. Your lower back should be flush against the back of the chair—there should be no space. The curve supporting your lower back shouldn't be so pronounced that your posture is awk-

ward. If you are short like I am, your back might not reach the back of the chair when you sit. You can buy individual lumbar cushions to add to your office chair if it doesn't have enough lower back support. If you've taken a long road trip, you've probably noticed that having an adjustable seat made all the difference in your comfort level. The same is true for desk chairs.

Monitor

Place the monitor 28 inches from your body. This is especially important to reduce your exposure to electromagnetic fields. The top of the screen should be at eye level. Make sure that your neck doesn't get sore when you work, and adjust your chair height or the computer height as needed to be comfortable.

Before buying your monitor, make sure you can adjust the resolutions. As a rule, larger screens have more resolution options, and they are easier on the eyes. And flat-panel monitors have less flicker. When I bought a new computer a few years ago, I felt my eyes were burning out of their sockets from the monitor glare. I darkened the monitor and found blessed relief. If I hadn't been able to do this, I would have returned the computer.

When you are working on the computer, look into the distance every 10

COMPUTER KEEPING

Computers are sensitive to temperature extremes, dust, humidity, smoke, magnets, and air pollution. Make sure the environment is as clean as possible. One friend of mine burned aromatherapy candles in his office, and the soot from the smoke ruined his computer!

Keeping computer and electronic equipment free of dust is important. Static draws dust right to it, and dust can be pulled into motors easily. Wool's natural antistatic properties make it a great material for cleaning the computer keys, monitor, and other components. Visit a local secondhand store, and buy a cheap, used wool skirt or other woolen clothing item. (Make sure you choose a soft, smooth wool.) Cut the clothing into pieces, making sure to remove buttons, snaps, and zippers. Dampen the wool slightly, and damp-clean computers, keyboards, and any other area with static electricity.

To clean dust from a monitor, use a soft flannel cloth. Every few months, you might need to clean the monitor more thoroughly, using a cotton or wool cloth with just a dab of a homemade window cleaner (see page 193). Make sure to avoid ammonia-based products.

minutes to rest your eyes and give them a workout. If you can see out a window from your desk chair, you might be more inspired to do this. Try putting a bird feeder in view or add a few pots of plants in your line of sight.

Keyboard

Don't raise the back of your keyboard, even if your keyboard has tabs in the back, because this position requires you to tilt your wrists. Not sure, though, what works best for you? There are a number of alternative keyboards on the market. Choose yours carefully. One option worth considering is a pullout, adjustable keyboard tray. It allows you to type so that your forearms are paral-lel to (level with) the ground. After buying one of these trays for myself (you can buy these to attach to your desk), I found that my hands were much less stressed.

Mouse

Your mouse may have a scrolling wheel in the middle of it, and is designed to reduce the need for moving the tool bar up and down or dragging around the cursor, which can cause repetitive stress injuries. There is a range of mouse alternatives on the market, so investigate them if you use the mouse a lot and feel that you would benefit from an ergonomic setup.

Family
Disaster
Kit

the basement

The basement is the home's closest connection to soil and rock, but it's often far from being a place of spiritual connection to the earth. Basements and crawl spaces are usually places where all the elements are stagnant, and the rooms have a walled-off feeling—they are walled off from the ground and the views and the house above. When you open the door to most basements, you tend to peer down rickety stairs into a dark concrete area of wires and cinderblock, and the air has various layers of furnace fumes and mold. The stairs down to these rooms are usually very inconvenient, either too steep or with dangerous turns, and the clutter of pipes and old furniture is enough to keep you from wanting to venture down.

Basements can also be full of old cans holding toxic pesticides, paints, and stains. The fumes waft upstairs and into the home and can be a serious health hazard. One woman I know grew up on a farm, and while visiting home, she found the basement full of old, discarded pesticide barrels that had been there for decades! Lying in bed at night on the third floor, she could smell the fumes from the pesticides through the old farmhouse's floors. Imagine the impact on generations of family members.

If you already have a basement that is a pleasure to be in, you are lucky. But if you don't, you *can* turn your basement into a place that adds to the healthy atmosphere in your home by making appropriate decisions and changes. Clearing the clutter, removing poisons, and working to balance the elements are good starting points.

Basements can also be havens of safety during emergencies. I remember venturing down into mine during a tornado warning with four third-grade girls who were visiting my daughter; I was grateful for the thick walls and sturdy structure of my basement. You can use your basement to store emergency supplies and provide shelter, and that should inspire you to tidy up and improve the space, even in small ways.

The four natural elements—water, air, fire, and earth—are usually very present in the basement or crawl space and are usually in an unhealthy state. Even so-called finished basements can have a frustrating, never-ending battle against moisture, heating system odors, and lack of sunlight. Bringing the elements into balance in the basement and joining forces with them can sometimes be all that is needed to bring health to a home.

Pleasing the Senses

For most of us, we don't need to transform our basements or crawl spaces to places where we can spend a lot of time, but making them healthy makes a big difference because the air percolates up into the house. Many children spend some time in the basement at some point in their lives because of the extra

space it may afford for setting up a large dollhouse, kicking around a spongy soccer ball, or helping out at a workbench. More than we care to think about, children may spend their time in the basement with oil burner fumes contaminating the air they are breathing. Thankfully, the time has come when heating systems are vented to the outside in new construction.

Sight

Cluttered basements are a quagmire of stuck chi (or energy). Though it is time-consuming, clearing out the old and broken computers, long-forgotten board games, and rusting bicycles is worth a lot in releasing the past and living in the present. Make arrangements for household and hazardous waste pickups, reuse things that are in good shape, and dispose of or donate items you no longer can use or have space for, such as outdated electronic equipment, hand-me-down furniture, workshop tools, or storage clutter.

Bringing in more light will help create a more pleasing basement (and will help discourage mold because mold thrives in the dark). If you can't put in new windows, try putting in a few full-spectrum lightbulbs; consider putting them on a timer so that they stay on for about 12 hours a day.

Hearing

Tuning your ear for unusual sounds from your furnace or the water pipes is a good safety net to let you know if a system is malfunctioning. (Of course, carbon monoxide escaping from your furnace doesn't have a sound, so you'll need to install a carbon monoxide alarm.) Noises from the heating, ventilation, air-conditioning, and plumbing systems of your house and basement can alert you to signs of parts wear-and-tear or needed repairs.

Smell

Mold and furnace fumes can cause big indoor air-quality problems in a basement. (Pesticides and asphalt-based wall and floor sealants are also cause for concern. The petroleum fumes from sealants can contaminate a home for years.) You can easily increase air circulation in a basement by opening a few windows to reduce mold and heater fumes. It is difficult to establish good air circulation in an unheated basement or during winter weather. Contact a building contractor for advice about adequate ventilation.

Sixth Sense

If I think about my own basement, I know that there would need to be a big overhaul to make the space a place I would like to be. I'd need to clear out clutter, find ways to infuse the place with light and air, and more!

I did one intuitive thing for my basement. After really thinking about basements and the fact that they are the actual interface between a home and the earth, I felt like I wanted to enhance the connection. Because I live in a house and not outdoors, I want to increase my sense of being connected to the earth. I found a small stone on my land that really spoke to me. I took it down to the center of my basement, and I placed it on the floor there, where it felt right.

Mold

Mold announces itself with an earthy, musty smell. Your nose is the best indicator of a mold problem. If you smell mold, track it down. Moldy houses have a damp and heavy energy, and you can lighten the atmosphere of the home by correcting moisture problems.

You might be surprised to learn that many people who are allergic to mold have "cerebral" reactions to it, such as depression and lack of concentration. Many people may not be able to connect their depression to chronic exposure to mold (such as having a damp basement or living over a crawl space), but it shouldn't be overlooked as a cause. I know others who have arthritic symptoms when overexposed to mold or who suffer from chronic respiratory problems or asthma.

Molds release volatile organic compounds (called MVOCs to denote their microbial origin). Although rare, mold mycotoxins can further complicate autoimmune diseases and asthma.

Mold Prevention

Mold needs water and food to grow; it won't grow on dry material. Damp wood, paper, carpet, textiles, and plastics all provide "nutrients" for mold growth. Sometimes the "nutrient" can be skin oils from items you have handled and stored in a damp location. Mold produces spores that reproduce and thrive in temperatures ranging from 40° to 130°F.

Some mold problems are temporary and occur only during a very rainy summer, for example. But if mold grows on furniture and belongings during this time, the mold lingers; you'll need to remove moldy possessions and dry out a moldy location to stop the spread of mold spores. You may need to have an expert examine your basement and recommend water-drainage solutions. Choose a solution that will be long term or permanent, such as B-Dry (see page 483).

A variety of factors can contribute to mold growth in a home or basement, and it's important to know that a combination of factors, instead of just a single cause, could be at work. Once you identify what's causing mold, it's vital that you do whatever you can to eliminate it.

Relative Humidity: As houses cool down, relative humidity increases. For example, if a house has an unheated basement, the basement is colder than the air above it (which is heated). The interface between the cold basement and the warm upstairs is a spot of high relative humidity and a place where mold can grow. A basement's carpet is often damp for the same reason, as are carpets on the cold floor over a crawl space. The higher the contrast in temperature, the higher the relative humidity due to the contrast. Relative humidity increases near water centers in a home, such as indoor swimming pools, large fish tanks, and fountains.

Be on the lookout for mold when a house is left unheated for a season (vacation homes, for example) or in areas where the heat is turned off at night (such as spare bedrooms). High relative humidity can encourage mold growth in mattresses, bedding, and upholstery. A dehumidifier can be your first line of defense with relative humidity.

Condensation: The higher the relative humidity, the higher the tempera-

HUMIDITY GAUGE

Consider using a hygrometer to monitor humidity levels so that air maintains a healthy 30 to 55 percent humidity. If the levels of moisture in your basement are too high, you'll see condensation on windows or mold growth, and you'll probably smell a damp, musty odor. Install a dehumidifier and improve ventilation to reduce the humidity.

Monitor the basement humidity with a moisture meter or hygrometer, then take action to lower the humidity when it reaches a level of concern.

ture at which condensation takes place. For example, the wall cavities can grow mold when the cavity is between a warm moist wall and a cold wall. Plumbing condensation can happen around uninsulated cold water plumbing lines. You'll need to install a dehumidifier, improve air circulation and ventilation in the space, and insulate plumbing lines.

Other Sources of Water: Roof leaks can easily cause mold, so it's important to keep your roof in good repair and to immediately address suspected leaks. Inadequate flashing around chimneys and exhaust pipes and on roofs and porches can cause water damage. If basement walls or floors are moist or damp, water may be forcing its way through porous or leaky foundation walls, joints, and floors. Investigate the source of the moisture, then work quickly to improve drainage around the

foundation, add gutter extensions to channel away rainwater, apply water-based sealers, or install a sump pump; or contact a building contractor who specializes in basements for advice and solutions.

Black Mold: Black mold (*Strachybotrys*) is greenish-black and thrives in high cellulose content, such as paper or fiberboard. It is found in only 2 to 3 percent of homes and requires constant moisture. Call for professional help if you suspect black mold.

Mold Cleanup

Mold cleanup is often beyond the capabilities of a homeowner. Call for professional help if there is anything more than a small mold problem or if a small mold problem returns after an initial cleanup. Cleaning up mold can be dangerous if you're not properly protected, and dead mold can cause allergic reactions.

Unfortunately, your finances may dictate how far you can go in fixing a moisture problem. Redoing the roof is not cheap, nor is a drainage overhaul for the basement. Be sure to do your homework, talk to a few contractors, and invest in the best remediation plan you can afford; you don't want perma-nent damage to your home, nor do you want chronic health problems.

Large Mold Problems: Consulting with a mold expert is the very best deci-sion if you have a large mold problem. Be sure to throw out moldy materials that can't be salvaged, such as carpets, drywall, insulation, and ceiling tiles. Painting over mold won't kill it, nor will it eliminate it. Solve the mold prob-

---

MAKE IT YOURSELF
FAVORITE MOLD HELPERS

Having a few natural mold-killing sprays and tricks up your sleeve is invaluable for any home-owner. I hugely value my Melaleuca Mold Spray formula, and while I use it only a few times a year at most, when I do, I really need it.

MELALEUCA MOLD SPRAY

Australian tea tree oil, an essential oil from the Melaleuca tree, is a broad-spectrum fungicide that is often used medicinally. I've used it to kill small patches of mold on musty furniture, mold grow-ing on the ceiling from a leaky roof, and other transient mold problems. (Note, though, that the underlying mold source had been identified and dealt with before I used this spray to clear away the mold residue.) Always investigate and rectify the conditions under which you find mold before removing the spores.

    1 teaspoon tea tree oil
    1 cup water
    Spray bottle
    Unscented detergent for cleanup

Combine the tea tree oil and water in a spray bottle and shake to blend. Spray directly on the mold or the musty material. Don't rinse. After a few days, remove the dead mold stains, if there are any, by washing the surface with an unscented detergent and drying thoroughly with a towel.

Note: Even though most people tolerate the smell of tea tree oil, it is very strong, and you might not like it. The smell will dissipate after a few days. If you or others who live in the house are sensitive to this smell or to essential oils, try the vinegar, borax, or grapefruit seed extract recipes instead. ❖

VINEGAR VANISH

Studies have shown that a straight 5 percent solution of vinegar kills 82 percent of mold spores.

    White distilled 5 percent household vinegar
    Spray bottle (optional)
    Unscented detergent for cleanup

lem first. Don't turn on your HVAC (heating, ventilation, and air-conditioning system) if you think it is contaminated with mold. Central vacuums are often vented to the outside and can remove mold, as do HEPA vacuums that collect small particulates.

Wet Basements: There are many innovative solutions for solving wet basement problems, even if your house is like mine—on the downside of a hill on a ledge with a never-ending flow of water entering the foundation. In my instance, we were able to solve the flood problem by using the B-Dry system (see page 483); the contractor dug trenches into the floor and wall using jackhammers, and the trenches channel water away properly. We have had a dry basement ever since.

Spray or pour straight vinegar onto the mold area. Don't rinse. The smell will dissipate in about a day. After a few days, remove the dead mold stains, if there are any, by washing the surface with an unscented detergent and drying thoroughly with a towel. ❖

BROAD SWEEP WITH BORAX
More of a deodorizer than a fungicide, the high pH of borax reduces mold spores and is worth using in some situations where the tea tree spray isn't practical (for example, the smell would be too overwhelming due to the size of the space needing treatment—like a large cement wall in the basement). Wash plaster walls, cement walls, and any other big surface with this strong borax solution to reduce mold.

> 1 cup borax
> 1 quart water hot enough to dissolve the borax

Wearing gloves and using a sponge, scrub the walls with this borax solution. Let dry without rinsing, and then brush off the borax. ❖

GRAPEFRUIT SEED EXTRACT
Grapefruit seed extract is antibacterial, antifungal, and more expensive than vinegar or borax by far, but it has no odor, is widely tolerated, and works successfully to kill mold.

> 25 drops grapefruit seed extract
> 1 cup water
> Spray bottle
> Unscented detergent or soap for cleanup

Combine the grapefruit seed extract and water in a spray bottle, and spray on the mold. Don't rinse. After a few days, scrub off the dead mold by washing the surface with an unscented detergent or soap and water and drying thoroughly with a towel. ❖

Avoid sealing your basement with petroleum-based sealants because the unhealthy fumes will stay in the house for years and years. There are less toxic sealants that are not made of petroleum. Consider dehumidifying the basement during the summers. Clean roof gutters every year, and insulate cold pipes so they don't sweat.

A number of people recommend placing bags of zeolite or lime around the basement to absorb odors. If you have a water problem, these small fixes won't hold up, so I wouldn't bother. All your efforts should be focused on removing the water seepage and moisture.

Dehumidifiers: Dehumidifiers remove moisture from the air by pulling air over cooling coils. The moisture, in turn, condenses to liquid water, and it collects in the bucket attached to the machine. While dehumidifiers reduce humidity, they do not cool, although heat without humidity feels much cooler. A 20- by 30-foot basement room would need a 40-pint dehumidifier to manage and reduce the humidity.

Small Mold Cleanup: Scrub small amounts of mold with a mixture of water and unscented detergent (¼ cup of detergent to 1 gallon of water), and then dry with a clean rag. Speed up the drying process with fans. Make sure that anybody with mold allergies is out of the area. Experts also recommend vacuuming surfaces first with a HEPA filter. The Environmental Protection Agency (EPA) recommends wearing long gloves, goggles (so mold spores don't get into your eyes), and an N-95 respirator, available at many hardware stores and Internet sources. I like to scrub mold with "green" pads if the surface can handle them and won't be scratched; they're available in most supermarkets.

Air and Sun: Sunlight kills mold, and the ultraviolet spectrum and the bright high-vibration light of sun do wonders for moldy pillows, mildewed books, and more. I often put pillows on the car hood on a bright sunny day— the car hood keeps the pillows perfectly dry and off the ground. Cross ventilation and air circulation are also very important to help reduce mold.

Infestations

Cohabitating peacefully with a few mice and insects is, unfortunately, of increasing concern because of the new infectious diseases they can carry. Getting bitten by a mosquito just isn't the same as it used to be, not with West Nile–like viruses, for example; and sweet country mice now may carry the deadly Hanta virus, even in Maine, far from New Mexico, where the most cases have been found. So with this increase in danger comes an increased need to pay attention when you have the beginnings of any kind of insect or rodent infestation. You need to eradicate the problem right from the start. It is crucial, however, to not poison yourself and your family at the same time. Besides being health hazards, rodents and insects can also cause structural damage to your home, of course—another reason to be vigilant.

Mice

Studies at Johns Hopkins Medical Center have shown that rodent dander and droppings are one of the leading causes of asthma in children. The common house mouse is a real problem for many of us, and I am happy to say that I've successfully gotten rid of significant mice problems twice, using different methods each time. The mice always seem to come in the fall as the weather gets cool, and they look for someplace warm. One pair of mice can produce as many as 90 offspring a year, so you want to take measures to prevent the mice from getting into the house in the first place. Follow these pointers to head off the pitter-patter of little mice feet.

❖ Turn off the lights in the basement on a bright day, assuming you don't have many windows, and see where the light filters through. (If you have windows, close the shades.) A mouse can squeeze through a hole smaller than a dime. Experts recommend sealing off these entranceways with copper mesh because the mice can't chew it and applying caulk all around the mesh (choose 100 percent silicone caulk or a nontoxic caulk from AFM Safecoat & Safechoice; see page 487). Make sure you take these steps in the summer before the cold weather arrives.

❖ Stack piles of wood away from the house and off the ground because mice use woodpiles for shelter.

❖ Get tight-fitting lidded bins for storing bird and dog food. Make sure to remove dog food and water at night, when mice are actively searching for food sources.

❖ Keep trash in lidded containers.

❖ Seal holes where pipes poke out from the wall (around pipes for hot-water baseboard heat and plumbing pipes under the sink).

Getting rid of mice without poisoning or killing them is very hard, but I have learned how. We've used every trick in the book, including two Havahart traps (from which we collect and drop live mice off miles from our house every morning) to essential oils of mint (mice hate mint) and lemongrass, and ultrasonic devices. Even though they can be pesky, I can't bring myself to kill the

Removing the food source for mice (and ants) is one way to prevent an infestation. Try to pick up food bowls after your pet has finished eating, and clean and put away food bowls overnight.

mice, so I have been determined to find alternative means to get rid of them.

I have used essential oils quite successfully to keep mice out of specific areas (but it doesn't solve the overall problem because the mice go elsewhere). I find that the base note essential oils (clary sage, lemon, fir needle, balsam fir, and rosemary) are the most effective for repelling mice; peppermint is also considered effective. The oils are expensive, and the smells are strong, which are definite downsides of this technique, but the scents are very helpful.

To use essential oils as mice repellents, sprinkle about 10 drops of the essential oil onto cotton balls, and place them in infested areas. The essential oil of peppermint can be very invigorating. Refresh the cotton balls with fresh essential oils every 3 days or so.

Spiders

If mice aren't tops on your creepy list, then spiders probably get the prize. Spiders, unless they're poisonous, won't harm you and will help you with other potential pests. You should never need to use chemical pesticides to control spiders. If you suspect activity, take a flashlight at night and look around, but generally taking a broom or vacuum to any areas of activity and homes will disrupt them enough that they will move out. Outside, use a hose to clear away spiders that are living on or near the house.

Most spiders are small and inconspicuous arthropods that are harmless to humans. They are considered beneficial because they can keep insect popu-

SHOPPING SOLUTIONS
FRESH CAB AND PEST A CATOR FOR MICE

The two solutions for mouse control that have worked for me long term are products—one is an herbal blend called Fresh Cab and the other is a gadget that you plug into your electrical outlets called a Pest A Cator.

Fresh Cab is made of essential oils and spices mixed into corncob chips. This blend of scents (including base note essential oils) has been proven effective in chasing away mice, flies, moths, and mosquitoes. These pouches are designed to be put in camper cabs and cabins, under hoods, and in trunks. If you can tolerate the strong smell of the essential oils, you can use Fresh Cab in the main part of your house; I used Fresh Cab pouches in the basement and had good results. For Fresh Cab odor-absorbing products, contact Crane Creek Gardens at www.earth-kind.com or 800-583-2921.

Pest A Cators plug into outlets in your house and send a pulse throughout the house on the building's wiring, driving mice out of the walls, floors, and ceilings, and eventually out of their nests, into the house, and then away. This worked like a charm for me—eventually. At first, all the mice came out of the walls, and the situation was alarming. I went back to the store to take advantage of my money-back guarantee, and the employees urged me to give the Pest A Cator products another week (it had already been 3 weeks). I agreed, and they were right. Virtually all of the mice left the house within the following week. Apparently the mice leave their nests in the walls and confusedly run around in the house before abandoning the domain altogether. One Pest A Cator works for 2,000 square feet, but I was desperate enough that I purchased one for every floor—the basement, the first floor, and the second floor—even though the house is 2,500 square feet. For more information on Pest A Cator products, contact Global Instruments at www.global-instruments.com or 800-338-5028.

lations in check. Only two groups, recluse spiders and black widow spiders, are considered poisonous to humans, unless you're allergic. Recluse spiders inhabit many southern and midwestern states and live in human habitats. They are 1 to 1½ inches long, and their color ranges from orange-yellow to dark brown. The distinctive "violin" shape near the head, with the scroll pointing down the neck to the back, is a conspicuous marking. Black widow spiders generally live outside and around houses. They are typically jet black, and on the underside of their abdomen are two reddish triangles that may form an hourglass shape. Adult black widow spiders average ½ inch long. Other spiders will bite, but most adults and children will have only a minor reaction.

To get rid of spiders, get rid of their food—insects. Seal your home with caulk, screening, and weather stripping to keep spiders from entering. Where possible, wash off outside areas, particularly under roof eaves, with a garden hose. Clean up window wells and leaf litter in the fall to remove spider habitat. In general, spiders build webs in areas with air circulation or drafts, so you're likely to find spiders in cracks and holes. If you have a container you suspect of housing poisonous spiders, simply freeze it for 48 hours.

Ants and Termites

The first step to ridding your house of an insect infestation is to figure out what you've got. If you're handy with an insect identification book, catch one of the suspect insects (or find a dead one) and try to identify it. Or contact a local entomologist or cooperative extension office for assistance.

The differences between ants and termites are pretty easy to see, especially with an insect guide handy. Ants have small, constricted waists and wings of unequal length, with the front pair longer than the hind pair. Their antennae are bent at right angles midshaft. Termite bodies are not narrowed at the middle; their wings are of equal length; and their antennae are rather straight with beadlike segments.

By following a few simple guidelines, most pest infestations can be avoided. First, seal all of the little holes that insects could use as entryways. Use caulk (choose 100 percent silicone caulk or a nontoxic caulk from AFM Safecoat & Safechoice; see page 487) and seal around baseboards, cupboards, pipes, doors, windows, electrical outlets, and anyplace where pests could get inside. If you need to close up large holes or cracks, use #20 screening first and then caulk the openings.

Be sure to keep everything dry. Insects love moist places, often needing moisture as much as food, so replace any decaying or moldy wood (especially if you live in an area that has termites!), fix leaky pipes or drains, don't leave dishes to soak overnight, don't leave wet rags and sponges out to dry, and insulate pipes where condensation forms.

Make sure that the soil around your foundation slopes away from the house to direct unwanted moisture—and pests—away. Keep a cushion of space around your house that is bare of foliage. Don't stack wood against the house, and keep landscape plants at least 2 feet away from the house. Trim any branches that touch the house, and consider removing large trees or stumps that might have decaying roots touching your foundation.

Take away an insect's hiding places, including piles of newspaper and magazines and stacks of clutter, and bring light to corners and areas where pests would build nests and webs.

Ants

There are more than 12,000 species of ant, so the most important step is to find out what kind of ant you have. Most ants are harmless and cause more annoyance than anything. Carpenter ants and termites, on the other hand,

MAKE IT YOURSELF
LONG-TERM ANT CONTROL BAIT

Clean these bait containers and freshen up the bait solution every few days; it will take a few weeks until the worker ants have carried enough of the solution back to the nest to kill the colony.

    1 teaspoon boric acid
    6 tablespoons sugar
    2 cups water
    Cotton balls
    Small plastic tubs with lids

Dissolve the boric acid and sugar in the water, and be sure all the boric acid crystals are dissolved. Soak cotton balls in the bait solution. Punch holes in the lids of the tubs so ants can get inside. Put the soaked balls in the tubs, and cover with the lids. Place these bait containers wherever you see ants.

Note: After a few weeks, reduce the boric acid to ½ teaspoon in the recipe and keep the containers in place until the ants are gone. ❖

can cause significant structural damage, so you'll need to deal with them more vigorously.

To destroy common ants once they've established themselves, you need to follow the trail and find the nest. If the nest is outside, pour a full kettle of boiling water down the hole. If the ants are inside, there are a couple of techniques that may be effective. The first is vacuuming up the nest. Start by locating the nest. You will most likely find the nest near heat and moisture, such as around water heaters, sinks, toilets, and bathtubs. Then, you can get rid of the nest by using a vacuum with a HEPA filter, putting a little cornstarch in the vacuum bag to asphyxiate the ants.

I've successfully rid the house of ants by washing the floor with a strong concentration detergent and citrus solvent (available in health food stores). The citrus repels ants, but you shouldn't use it if you have cats. There are essential oils that repel ants, too, including mint oil and orange oil; pine oil is often successful for fire ants. (Note that many people are sensitive to essential oils, so test in a small area first; pregnant women should discuss the use of essential oils with their doctors.)

Carpenter Ants

Carpenter ants burrow in wood to make their nest, and they usually seek out decaying, moist, or soft wood, especially along a foundation wall. They will usually leave piles of frass at the openings to their nests and will make rustling noises in the walls; the frass is usually composed of wood bits, soil, food, and dead ants. They are larger than general sugar ants, usually measuring between ¼ and ½ inch long, and they can have wings. If carpenter ants choose to burrow into your home, they can cause serious damage.

One of the best resources for all-around advice and real hands-on help about eliminating carpenter ants is Beyond Pesticides (BP). In BP's literature, they report that carpenter ants survive only in a very narrow temperature range, and specialists can eliminate carpenter ants by "baking them out." Another option is BoraCare, a product recommended by BP as the least-toxic approach to killing carpenter ants; it needs to be applied by a licensed exterminator.

If you think you have carpenter ants, determine if they are still active and then try to determine how extensive their range is. Since carpenter ants are very sensitive to temperature, tenting the house (surrounding and sealing it with tarps) and heating it (or freezing it with liquid nitrogen) could solve your problem. Call around until you find a pesticide applicator that will use innovative, nontoxic controls. (Don't let them do anything but nontoxic controls!) You could also ask your local exterminator if he's trained in the use of BoraCare.

One of my friends discovered a rather large infestation of carpenter ants, and she called many exterminators until she found one willing to work with a borax-based solution. When the exterminator came to investigate the situation, he told her that he had looked into alternative solutions since their phone call and had found a low-toxicity spray that was being used in Europe where pesticides regulations are more stringent. Out of concern for her young daughter (whose bedroom was just above the infestation), the environment, and her chemical-free lifestyle, my friend still insisted on the even-less-toxic borax spray treatment (along with removal of all infested wood in the area). "So far, so good," she reports, and she feels comfortable with her decision. In my opinion, she made the correct choice because I believe there is no compromise when it comes to pesticides; you must always choose the course of no harm to humans and pets.

Termites

Termites are not as scary as you might think because they work slowly, so you have time to assess the damage and find the best way to get rid of them. (They

can be beneficial in some circumstances because they play a huge part in the natural world by "recycling" dead material.) If you suspect that you already have termites, confirm it with an inspection by a professional (make sure that you are not also agreeing to treatment by agreeing to the inspection). There are also specially trained dogs that are able to sniff out and hear termite activity. Or bring a sample termite or two to your county extension office or an entomologist for identification.

If you have a termite infestation, you'll need to determine which type of termite you have—either drywood, dampwood, or subterranean. Drywood termites are the most difficult to detect because they live entirely inside the wood; signs that you're dealing with a drywood termite infestation are fallen wings, fecal pellets, and wood that sounds hollow. Dampwood termites can be found around damp or damaged wood; you'll notice holes or tunnels in the wood. You may also notice swarms after rainfall. Subterranean termites live in the ground and swarm in the spring during their reproduction stage. They forage for wood in the ground or for wood in contact with the ground; you may notice mud tubes in the soil or aboveground as a sign of infestation.

Controlling termites may be as much prevention as treatment. When building, make sure that there are 12 inches of clean concrete foundation between the soil and structural wood. Steel termite shields can be built directly into the building structure. These shields keep termites from entering the building between the foundation and masonry walls; discuss this option with your builder. Sand barriers are sometimes put around the foundation of a house. Sand with certain size particles (1/16 inch) is used to physically block termite entry into structures. Since termites burrow using their mouths, these large sand particles are too big for their mouths, and they can't move them.

Once you discover termites, you have a few options, although most are not ideal from an environmental or health standpoint. Heat treatment will work on drywood and dampwood termites provided that they are aboveground. If the temperature of the termites' home can be brought above 100°F, they will die. (This is best done by a professional.) By tenting the house and blowing hot air through the infested areas with propane heaters, the temperature is brought up to 130°F for 35 minutes and is 90 to 99 percent effective in killing termites. The temperature is not high enough to damage your house or building; however, it can negatively affect electronic equipment and other belongings, so keep that in mind before choosing this option. Most

exterminators will advise you that this method is only for major infestations because of the cost involved.

Cold treatment is also effective, although not on dampwood termites and not on subterranean termites if they are currently aboveground. With cold treatment, a hole is drilled in the wall, and liquid nitrogen is poured in, lowering the temperature sufficiently to kill termites. This method is reported to be 95 to 99 percent effective, and it's good for inaccessible places.

A technique for eliminating drywood termites is the Electrogun (this will not work for dampwood or subterranean termites). The Electrogun uses high-frequency, high-voltage, low-amperage electrical current to zap termites, and it can be 95 percent effective if used properly. However, it is ineffective near metal, concrete, or the ground because these will divert the current.

The most common method for dealing with subterranean termites is finding their colonies outside and digging them up. They use mud tunnels to move between their homes and their wood source and to protect them from predators. If you can open up these tunnels, often predators (such as ants) will destroy the termite colony.

Nematodes are microscopic parasites that also prey on termites. Nematodes carry bacteria that is lethal to termites; if they are injected (in water) near a termite infestation, they will quickly spread throughout the colony. If this is not effective after a month (effectiveness has been rated between 50 and 95 percent), you may need to try a different method.

Invisible Dangers

Better safe than sorry when it comes to the killers carbon monoxide, radon, and asbestos. Carbon monoxide and radon are invisible and odorless gases, and asbestos is a dust/mineral. All three can be found in homes. Combustion appliances can cause carbon monoxide, the ground on which the house is built can cause radon, and asbestos is found in many applications around the home such as in tiles and insulation. Fortunately, there has been enough concern about these three dangers that there are straightforward tests to determine if they are a problem for your home and remediation approaches if you do find a potential problem.

Carbon Monoxide

Protecting yourself and your family from carbon monoxide is critical. High levels of carbon monoxide can kill a person in a matter of minutes, according to the EPA. Unborn babies are particularly susceptible. Like radon, you can't see or smell carbon monoxide. Carbon monoxide isn't naturally occurring but rather the result of faulty or badly vented fuel combustion.

Carbon monoxide poisoning can occur from fumes generated by these sources.

❖ Any fuel-burning appliance that is not vented properly and not maintained in good condition, including water heaters.

❖ Cars idling in an attached or even semiclosed garage.

❖ Charcoal grills used indoors. Never burn charcoal or fuel-burning camping equipment inside, whether it's in a living room, garage, RV, or tent.

❖ Unvented gas or kerosene space heaters.

❖ Gasoline-powered engines, such as those for chainsaws and generators.

❖ Gas ovens or dryers used to heat your house (never do this).

❖ Flues of fireplaces that are closed when wood is burning, and woodstoves that don't meet EPA emission standards.

❖ Gas stoves that do not have an exhaust fan vented to the outdoors.

❖ Flameless catalytic chemical heaters.

❖ A leak, even a small one, in your car's exhaust system (have your exhaust system checked every year).

❖ Slow-moving traffic. In this case, open your vehicle's window.

❖ Fumes entering the vehicle if the back window is open while you are driving because you are carrying cargo, such as a lawn mower or furniture.

Carbon monoxide poisoning deaths happen more frequently than anybody would like. My town reeled from the news that a popular family with five children would have died in a few more minutes, according to the fire department, if their carbon monoxide alarm hadn't warned them of the high levels of carbon monoxide in their home. Their gas-run generator had kicked on during the night due to a power outage, and its fumes were sucked into the soffits of the garage and quickly spread throughout the house. Symptoms of carbon monoxide poisoning are headache, dizziness, feeling faint, nausea, and mental confusion. It's vital to get

out of the building immediately if you suspect there's a problem.

I am particularly in tune with the dangers of gas and chemical poisonings because I was poisoned by a gas leak in a restaurant where I worked. Eighty people were sent to the hospital due to the leak. The specificity of poisoning symptoms is important when it comes to diagnosing a leak. Those of us exposed to the gas in the restaurant didn't experience nausea, a common carbon monoxide poisoning symptom, so the fumes were from something else. Carbon monoxide or not, most of us became very ill with chronic and debilitating symptoms, so I'm a strong advocate for safety and knowledge when it comes to use and ventilation of dangerous gases.

If you purchase a carbon monoxide tester or alarm, be sure to select a

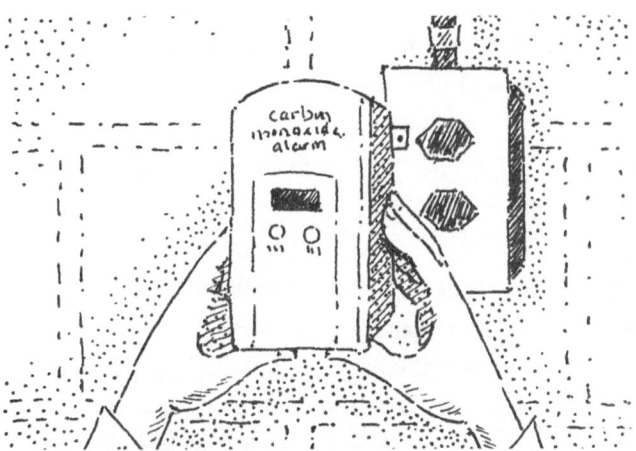

Carbon monoxide is odorless, tasteless, and invisible and results from the incomplete combustion of fossil fuels used for heat and energy. Installing carbon monoxide detectors is your best defense; place detectors in living and sleeping areas and in your utility room or basement.

model that has an audible alarm rather than one that just lights up or has a visible reading. Many carbon monoxide deaths occur at night while families sleep because the fumes incapacitate them.

Radon

Just like carbon monoxide, you can't see or smell radon. It is a natural radioactive gas that comes from the soil, and according to the EPA, it is the second leading cause of lung cancer (after smoking) in the United States. Most rocks and soils contain uranium, and when it breaks down, it becomes radon gas. Elevated radon gas collects in one out of five homes in the United States, according to state surveys. There are two ways that radon seeps into buildings: It can seep in from the soil surrounding the basement or crawl space, usually through cracks and openings. The most common way radon enters buildings is by being sucked in when the air pressure of the house is lower than that of the soil underneath it.

Radon Hot Spots

Radon pollution poses more of a problem in some geographical locations than in others. The EPA has developed maps designated into zones of concern in each state in the country. You can find what zone you live in at www.epa. gov/iaq/whereyoulive.html.

From this site, I was able to link through to my state, my county, and my town. I found out that 15 percent of the homes in my town have radon levels higher than the EPA's recommended maximum of 4.0 pCi/L.

Understanding the Radon Numbers

Radon is measured in pico-Curies per liter (pCi/L). This is the rate of the

---

ASBESTOS WATCH

Asbestos is a collective term for fibrous silicate minerals, and it is a carcinogen. Asbestos has been used extensively over many decades in more than 3,000 industrial and home applications, including vinyl floor tiles, textured paints, pipe and duct insulation, and house insulation. Homes built between 1930 and 1978 are the most likely to contain asbestos insulation around pipes and ducts and between walls. In the basement, the most likely place to find asbestos is in pipe insulation, and this type of asbestos can become airborne. Airborne asbestos fibers are very dangerous for your lungs. Some types of asbestos, such as the kind found in house siding, have a harder time becoming airborne and might be better left untouched. If you suspect that you have asbestos in your home, contact a professional. Never try to correct the problem yourself.

radioactive decay of radon. One pCi is one-trillionth of a Curie, or roughly 2.22 disintegrations per minute. If the number given to you as a result of a radon test exceeds 4.0 pCi/L, the source of the high radon level in your home needs to be identified and remediated.

The average indoor radon level is about 1.3 pCi/L. Outdoors, about 0.4 pCi/L is found in the average air sample taken. My inclination is to have the lowest exposure to pollutants as possible, so even if your test results are within acceptable levels given by the EPA, you might still want to take some corrective measures to reduce the amounts found.

How to Test Your Home for Radon

You can have your home professionally tested for radon (check with your state radon office for recommendations), or you can buy easy, inexpensive radon testing kits at any hardware store. There are two types of tests—the short-term tests, which take just a few minutes of your time to set up, but stay in the house for 2 to 90 days, and long-term tests, which also take just a few minutes to put into place, but stay in the house for more than 90 days. The EPA recommends using long-term tests for the best indication of average radon exposure.

Correcting a Radon Problem

Any time you move into a different home, you should test the radon level. Otherwise, the EPA suggests checking annually, or at least biannually, to make sure a problem doesn't develop. Radon gas is an easily correctable environmental contaminant.

Radon-resistant features can be built into new homes, and there are builders specially trained in correcting radon problems. Contact your state radon office for names of state-certified radon contractors in your area, as well as a copy of the EPA's "Consumer's Guide to Radon Reduction."

A builder trained in radon remediation can take steps to solve your radon problems. Measures to reduce radon include sealing cracks in floors and walls, establishing a barrier with gravel or aggregate between the ground and the slab or flooring system, and installing a passive radon abatement system to avoid the vacuum effect found in most houses by creating a pressure barrier of a gas-tight venting pipe from the gravel level to the roof.

Disaster Preparedness

During the Y2K scare and after September 11, 2001, in the United States, many of us became more aware of our preparedness, or lack thereof, for serious emergencies. Have you thought about where you would get water, food, or heat if you lost electricity for an extensive period of time? It's difficult to think about the possibility of war on our soil, widespread epidemics, or long-term loss of power, but most of us will deal with weather extremes, such as ice storms, tornadoes, and hurricanes and the minor and major inconveniences that go along with these storms.

No matter what the cause of the disaster, it takes just a small amount of forethought, planning, and effort to bring some peace of mind in times of hardship. Most important for survival is water, followed by food and first-aid supplies. Put together a disaster preparedness plan for your family, and discuss possible scenarios with family members old enough to understand. Then stock up on necessary supplies, and store them in a safe, dry, and accessible place. And let's hope that none of us ever has to reach for these supplies.

Water Supplies

During an emergency, each person will need about 1 gallon of water per day. A 3-day supply of water per person seems adequate for normal emergencies; you could probably stretch those 3 gallons per person to a week if necessary. Remember to store enough water for your pets too.

If a week of emergency water were necessary, I'd rather know how to purify water and search for fresh supplies within walking distance than to store that much bottled water in my basement. However, the US Department of Agriculture recommends a 14-day supply of fresh water for each family member in the case of a nuclear attack. (Water-purification techniques won't work for nuclear fallout.) Most groundwater will be protected during and after a nuclear explosion. Any water in a pressure tank, hot-water heater, and interior plumbing is also safe from fallout.

Shatterproof Water Storage: The easiest way to stock up is to buy gallons of bottled water. Store water in plastic containers, such as soft drink bottles. (Yes, in an emergency, plastic is okay!) New, thoroughly cleaned, heavy-duty, plastic containers with tight-fitting lids are shatterproof and lighter than glass. Five-gallon plastic containers full of water weigh 40 pounds, a weight most people can carry for short distances. Look for plastic containers with the Department of Transportation rating of DOT #34. This rating means the container passed a special burst test. Water that is bacteria free when it's stored in thoroughly clean containers will remain safe for several years.

Don't use unlined metal containers for water storage. Cans without a spe-

MAKE IT YOURSELF
EMERGENCY WATER TREATMENT AT HOME

Having a few bottles of regular household bleach at home makes sense because it can ensure safe water, if all that is available to you is possibly contaminated with bacteria. (This is one of the rare times I feel that buying household bleach is thoroughly justified!) In case of emergency, follow the directions on the product label or those outlined below.

BLEACH WATER TREATMENT METHOD
The flavor of the bleach is not delicious, so if you want to add flavor, you can do so, but do it after the water and bleach have set for the required time for the bleach to be effective.

> 1 gallon clear water
> 8 drops 5.25 to 6 percent sodium hypochlorite (household bleach without anything else added)
> *OR*
> 1 gallon cloudy water
> 16 drops 5.25 to 6 percent sodium hypochlorite (household bleach without anything else added)

Add the drops to the water, mix thoroughly, and let stand for 30 minutes.

Caution: Be sure that sodium hypochlorite is the only active ingredient in bleach used for water treatment. ❖

IODINE STERILIZATION METHOD
Water treated with iodine can taste a bit better than that treated with bleach.

> 1 gallon clear water
> 12 drops 2 percent iodine
> *OR*
> 1 gallon cloudy water
> 24 drops 2 percent iodine

Add the drops to room-temperature water. Wait for 30 minutes if the water is clear; wait an hour if the water is cloudy. ❖

---

cial coating of enamel or plastic on the inside tend to impart an unpleasant taste to water, especially after lengthy storage. And water can make metal containers rust.

Emergency Sources of Water: There are a surprising number of unexpected sources of water in a home. Check out the plumbing system, plumbing fixtures, appliances, toilet tanks (*not*

bowls), hot water tanks, indoor pools, canned fruit juices, and rain. Rainwater can be used without treatment.

Three Ways to Make Water Safe: In general, water can be contaminated by disease-causing bacteria, viruses, protozoa, and other organisms that can cause serious disease. There are three ways in which water can be made potable: boiling, filtering, and treating.

Boiling is relatively quick, and it is the most effective method for killing all harmful bacteria. The downside is that it requires having a reliable heat source, and in an emergency, there is no guarantee that you will have a means to boil water. Boiling will not eliminate chemical contamination either.

As soon as water reaches the boiling point (212°F), it will have killed all of the harmful bacteria. To be safe, keep the water at a rolling boil for 3 minutes. The 10-minute recommended time is overkill and an inefficient use of energy.

Filters are the easiest way to treat water. They are fast, and they do not impart an unpleasant flavor to the water. A wide variety of water filters is available at sporting goods and camping stores. The downside of filtering systems is that they are expensive and need cleaning.

When buying a "camping" filter, look for one with the smallest possible pore size (to catch as much harmful bacteria as possible) and one that is easy to clean. Confirm that the filtering system itself doesn't add any unwanted chemicals to the water. Ask for advice at a reputable camping goods store when buying a filter.

Chemical-disinfecting treatment of water is performed with bleach, iodine, or brand-name products. This method of treatment is inexpensive, the supplies do not take up much space, and it is effective in purifying water. But there are downsides to treating water—it is time-consuming, success can be dependent upon water temperature, the water generally tastes bad afterward, and the treatment can have negative side effects.

There are a number of iodine-based, commercial brands of water treatment available in drug stores and sporting goods outfitters. Once the water is disinfected with iodine, the water will stay disinfected for about a week. Iodine is temperature sensitive, so if the water is warm or cold, it will take 2 to 3 hours to be fully effective. At room temperature, it will take about ½ hour for iodine to be effective. Iodine should not be used by pregnant or nursing women or anyone with thyroid difficulty.

Tincture of iodine (2 percent—most likely what you have in your medicine cabinet) can be used, but it is less effective than commercial iodine treatments. Iodine is effective against giardia but often it is not effective against cryptosporidium. It takes 2 to 3 hours to kill amoebas. Water treated with iodine will smell and taste like iodine. If it does not, then it has not been properly treated, or the iodine is no longer effective due to heat or age. Iodine is generally considered only an emergency treatment.

There are pills that will get rid of the iodine flavor *after* the water has been treated. Other flavorings (Gatorade powders, for example) can be used, but only after the water is fully disinfected; otherwise, they will neutralize the iodine or bleach.

Bleach (sodium hypochlorite) can be used for water treatment, but it is less effective than iodine; be sure to wait at least ½ hour before drinking the water. There are also commercial chlorine-based treatments (consisting of chlorine dioxide) available at sporting goods stores. They are easy to use and actually remove some bad flavors from the water; they are less effective than filtration, though.

In Case of Nuclear Accident or Attack

You might want to store potassium iodide in your home, especially if you live within a few hundred miles of a nuclear power plant. You can buy potassium iodide pills at your local pharmacy. It floods the thyroid, blocking absorption of radioactive iodine into the gland. Manufacturers claim that potassium iodide will prevent 99 percent of the thyroid damage caused by a nuclear reactor accident or fallout from a nuclear weapon. Follow the manufacturer's directions for dosage

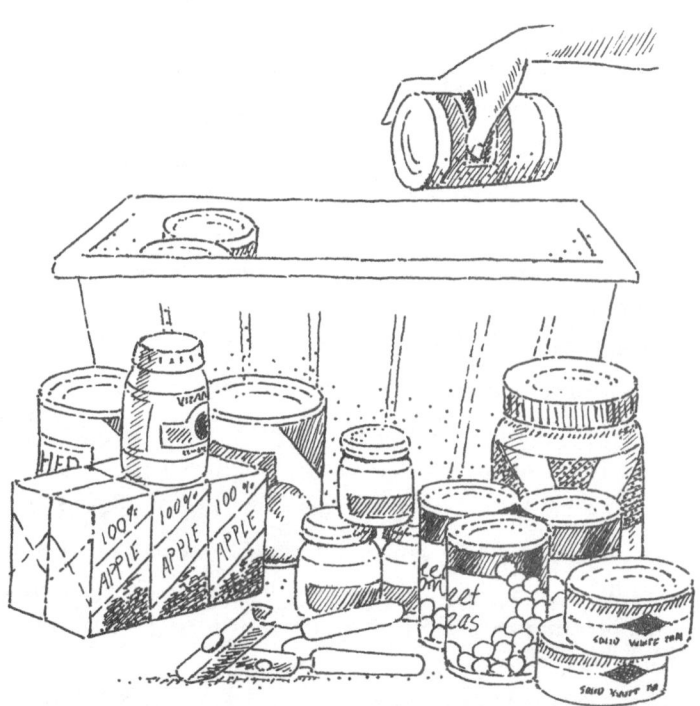

Being prepared for a disaster means keeping a 3-day supply of food and water for each family member on hand at all times. Choose items that don't require cooking and that have a long shelf life, then store supplies in an air-tight container away from heat and moisture.

WORDS TO THE WISE

CARING FOR PETS DURING EMERGENCIES

Red Cross shelters do not accept pets. Prearrange care for your pets, so if there's an emergency, you know where to take them. For more information and ideas on how to evacuate pets, contact the Humane Society of the United States, Disaster Services, 2100 L Street NW, Washington, DC 20037, or visit their Web site at www.hsus.org.

and use, and take them only if directed to do so by your local emergency management officials.

Disaster Supplies Kit

Find a few hours in your week, and head out shopping with a "disaster supplies" list in hand to stock up on necessities should an emergency take place. Relief agencies suggest that you store at least a 3-day supply of pantry staples and nonperishable food. Select foods that require no refrigeration, no preparation or cooking, and little or no water. Canned vegetables, fruits, and meats; peanut butter; baby food (if needed); and canned and bottled juices are great choices.

You should also assemble a first-aid kit for your home and one for each car.

Improvisation is the key to success here; if you don't have a bandage, then clean rags, clothing, or almost anything will work. Infection is always a concern! Also, pick up a reputable first-aid guide and read it—you'll be very glad that you know what you are doing, even moderately!

Keep items in airtight plastic bags. Change your stored water supply every 6 months so it stays fresh, and replace your stored food every 6 months. Rethink your kit and family needs at least once a year, and replace batteries, update clothes, and add items as necessary.

To get copies of American Red Cross Community Disaster Education materials, contact your local Red Cross chapter, or visit their Web site at www.red cross.org.

DISASTER SUPPLIES

These basic supplies should be stored year-round in an accessible place in case of emergency or natural disaster. Involve the whole family in shopping for, packing, and storing supplies so they can feel confident about finding and using these items when the need arises. Be sure to keep track of food and first aid expiration dates, and rotate new items into your stock every year or so.

CLOTHING

Include at least one complete change of clothes and footwear per person, and periodically update sizes.

- ❏ Change of clothes
- ❏ Undergarments
- ❏ Rain gear
- ❏ Blankets or sleeping bags
- ❏ Space Blanket (available at any camping goods store)
- ❏ Hat and gloves, thermal underwear, and coats for cold weather

EMERGENCY FOOD AND WATER

Store at least a 3-day supply of nonperishable foods that require no preparation or cooking. Water should be stored in clear plastic containers.

- ❏ Water (one gallon per person, per day)
- ❏ Nonperishable, high-energy foods
- ❏ Ready-to-eat canned meats, soups, fruits, and vegetables
- ❏ Peanut butter
- ❏ Cereal bars
- ❏ Canned juices
- ❏ Multivitamins
- ❏ Food for infants, elderly persons, and persons on special diets
- ❏ Comfort and snack foods

FIRST AID

Assemble a first-aid kit for your home and for your car.

- ❏ Two pairs of latex or other sterile gloves (if you are allergic to latex)
- ❏ Sterile dressings to stop bleeding
- ❏ Cleansing agent, soap, and antibiotic towelettes to disinfect
- ❏ Antibiotic ointment to prevent infection
- ❏ Burn ointment to prevent infection
- ❏ Adhesive bandages in a variety of sizes
- ❏ Eye-wash solution to flush the eyes or as general decontaminant
- ❏ Thermometer
- ❏ Prescription medications you take every day such as insulin, heart medicine, and asthma inhalers (periodically rotate stored medicines to account for expiration dates)
- ❏ Prescribed medical supplies, such as glucose- and blood-pressure-monitoring equipment
- ❏ Printed first-aid guidelines

MEDICAL SUPPLIES

Store medical supplies in a moistureproof container that's sturdy and easy to carry.

- ❏ Scissors
- ❏ Tweezers
- ❏ Tube of lubricant
- ❏ Potassium iodide (in case of a nuclear accident)
- ❏ Pain reliever
- ❏ Antidiarrhea medication
- ❏ Antacid
- ❏ Syrup of Ipecac (use to induce vomiting if advised by a poison control center)
- ❏ Laxative
- ❏ Activated charcoal (For use in some poisoning cases and only if advised by a poison control center or qualified persons. Activated charcoal in powder form is available at pharmacies. There are serious contraindications, so administer only on expert advice.)

SANITATION

A little comfort goes a long way during an emergency, so stock up on toiletries and bathroom supplies.

- ❏ Toilet paper and towelettes
- ❏ Soap and liquid detergent
- ❏ Feminine supplies
- ❏ Daily personal hygiene items (toothpaste, toothbrush, shampoo, and deodorant)

TOOLS AND SUPPLIES

Keep these items handy for emergencies. It's best to pack these things in a duffel bag with other disaster supplies.

- ❏ Cell phone
- ❏ Hand-held can opener
- ❏ Utility knife
- ❏ Battery-operated radio and extra batteries
- ❏ Mess kits, or paper cups, plates, and plastic utensils
- ❏ Flashlight and extra batteries
- ❏ Matches in a waterproof container
- ❏ Paper and pencils
- ❏ Whistle
- ❏ Cash, traveler's checks, and change
- ❏ Compass

Adapted from the "Family Disaster Plan," developed by the Federal Emergency Management Agency and the American Red Cross.

13

air

Air is the centerpiece of existence on earth and the fuel of human life. Without air entering our lungs, we would die in 7 minutes. The earth's atmosphere feeds our heart with every breath we take. Air oxygenates our blood. Breathing in the air of our natural environment fully integrates us as beings on this planet. Air is invisible, yet essential. It is air that makes the earth habitable for us.

Weather is carried by air. Meteorologists often speak of air temperature, air pressure, and air humidity. Pollution is carried by air too. The smoke from coal-fired plants in the Midwest is carried to the East Coast, causing acid rain and mercury contamination of lakes and rivers.

The memories of our lives relate in some way to air. Remind yourself of a summer night and its balmy heat. The aromas of the day still hang in the air when we think about freshly cut grass, the fragrant whiff of a rose, and the sweet earthy smell of silk from an ear of corn. All this is brought on air, including the cooling breeze that comes in as night descends.

Air is a mixture of nitrogen, oxygen, carbon dioxide, water, and some other gases and elements (such as dust particles). Oxygen is a critical component for the lives of animals and humans. Ozone, helium, and hydrogen are found higher in the stratosphere.

The air close to the earth and the layers of air surrounding the earth are called the earth's atmosphere. There are four layers. The *troposphere* layer reaches as high as 18 kilometers above the earth at the equator and 8 kilometers at the

Antarctic, averaging about 11 kilometers in height. The temperature drops 1°F for each kilometer away from the earth. The *stratosphere* begins where the troposphere stops, and it reaches more than 50 kilometers from the earth's surface. Solar radiation creates ozone from oxygen in this layer. The *mesosphere* layer is from about 50 to 90 kilometers above the earth's surface. The fourth layer is the *thermosphere,* the layer closest to the sun, and it is made up of very hot air above 1,000°C and thin air of very low density. Solar activity affects the temperature of the thermosphere, spiking even higher temperatures during solar flares.

We hear so much, both good and bad, about ozone that we should set the record straight. Stratospheric ozone is good ozone because it shields the earth from the sun's rays. Most of the media reports focus on holes developing in the ozone layer; when a hole opens up (due to the release of man-made chemicals), harmful UVA rays can pass down to the earth and cause damage to life, such as increasing the rate of skin cancer in humans. Ozone-depleting refrigerants used in cars and refrigerators are being regulated by the government, and the more-damaging refrigerants are being removed from the market.

Tropospheric ozone, on the other hand, is bad ozone. This type of ozone is produced on hot, sunny days when the sun's rays react with pollution, such as exhaust fumes and emissions from power plants, industrial boilers, chemical plants, and other sources. Tropospheric ozone is in the layer of air that we breathe, and it's very damaging because it can destroy living tissue, forests, and even rubber and other materials. People of all ages are more susceptible to the damaging effects of ground-level ozone when they're active outdoors because ozone can penetrate more deeply into the lungs. Ozone-related problems are often seen in people with respiratory diseases, limited lung function, and asthmatics. You can reduce your risk of lung damage on high-ozone days by limiting your exertion when you're outdoors.

Air as a Spiritual Element

In spiritual symbolism, air represents consciousness—the power of the mind. Air and thought are both invisible, yet they are very powerful. The air element also represents freedom, like the free flight of a bird. Feathers are often used in ceremonies to represent the air element and as a spiritual element symbolizing freedom.

AIR QUALITY INDEX FOR OZONE

The Air Quality Index, or AQI, is a scale used by the Environmental Protection Agency to report actual levels of ozone and other common pollutants in the air. The higher the index value number, the greater the health concern.

INDEX VALUE	LEVEL OF HEALTH CONCERN	CAUTIONS
0–50	Good	None
51–100	Moderate	Unusually sensitive people should consider limiting prolonged outdoor exertion
101–150	Unhealthy for sensitive groups	Active children and adults and people with respiratory diseases (such as asthma) should reduce prolonged outdoor exertion
151–200	Unhealthy	Active children and adults and people with respiratory disease, such as asthma, should avoid prolonged outdoor exertion; everyone else, especially children, should limit prolonged outdoor exertion
201–300	Very unhealthy	Active children and adults and people with respiratory disease, such as asthma, should avoid all outdoor exertion; everyone else, especially children, should limit outdoor activity
301–500	Hazardous	Everyone should avoid all outdoor activity

Source: EPA

Sacred Smoke

Nearly every culture on earth has burned dried plant material to invoke spiritual connection. Smoke rises on air, and most people conceive of spirits as being somehow higher up. The act of burning sacred smoke as a plea for help, as an intercession to a deity, or as an offering to the sacred is an ancient one. Indigenous people around the world have used pipe ceremonies (where they smoke sacred plant medicine) as a way of uniting heaven, earth, and man. As long as there have been people to pray, they have sent their prayer smoke up to the place of the Most High.

Burning sacred plant medicine, in a pipe, incense, or by fire, releases its aroma, which many believe holds the energy of the earth, sun, rain, moonlight, stars, and soil. Any use of plants with conscious intention (and good intent) can become a sacred ceremony. One way to do this is to make a small fire using the plant material in a heatproof bowl or ashtray. Favorite herbs for sacred smoke include sage, lavender, sweet grass, thyme, cinnamon, frankincense or myrrh (both resins), and clove.

Air and Spiritual Healing

Our lungs breathe in air, and the oxygenated blood goes to our hearts. From there, air goes deep inside to our deepest essence. It is to this deepest essence that the great Buddhist breathing meditation Vipassana goes. Vipassana was rediscovered by Gautama Buddha more than 2,500 years ago. In a Vipassana meditation, a person focuses on the breath, paying attention to it as it goes in and out of your body. While the mind presents thoughts and distractions, you keep coming back to focus

on the breath. Gautama Buddha felt that this meditation would cure all ills.

There are a number of meditations that focus on the breath, from cultures all over the world. One of my favorite ones is Native American, described in *Prayers and Meditations of the Quero Apache,* by Maria Yraceburu.

Breathing meditations help you move your personality—with all its shoulds and oughts and directives—out of the way so that, for once, you can just be.

From Other Voices

AIR PRAYER

Air, sometimes I forget to look up, and the
    view is so small:
cracked sidewalk, feet plodding.
Then you push a button; an umbrella inside
    me
bursts open, is blown inside out.
Leaves scurry up and down your clear
    highways
and thoughts with black feathers rise
    cawing, a stream of thick smoke.
Today I opened my mouth, and out flew
    your song. There were wings
on every syllable.
Air, your hands stretch me open and
    squeeze me shut:
I'm your accordion, you play me with every
    breath.
Air of unbearable spaciousness,
    open me wider still.
I would be your apprentice, learn to ride
    on those rafts of wind, send me thoughts
    spiraling up to your place beyond
    words where every breath is a blessing,
    every breath is a song.

—Cait Johnson, in *Earth, Water, Fire, & Air*

Sound Healing

Sound is made up of vibrations in the air. Our senses respond to vibrations, and there is a law of physics that makes a vibration want to start being harmonious with vibrations around it and to be in synchronicity with them. This phenomenon is called entrainment. In sound healing, the dissonant chord is gradually influenced by the harmonious chord, and the disharmony changes to harmony over time.

The assumption behind healing with sound is that disease is inharmonious with and not the same frequency as good health. Everything in the universe has a specific vibration, from an ant to a vibrantly healthy heart. In other words, the frequency of a healthy heart wouldn't be the same as the frequency of an unhealthy heart, but you can bring health to the heart by bringing it sound that is harmonious and in balance with a heart that is in healthy vibration. Through entrainment, the disease gives over to health.

Initial research into the transformative power of art and music took place in the late 1950s when Alfred Tomatis, MD, investigated the effects of playing Mozart's works for children with communication and speech disorders. He found that certain musical frequencies aid in the stimulation of developing language centers and improve coordination. The theory, the Mozart Effect,

refers to the use of music and art to enhance a variety of skills that include memory, awareness, development of learning strategies, and creativity. The Mozart Effect originally referred to the specific works of Mozart, but it has since broadened to include all the transformational powers of music and art in health, education, and well-being. The Mozart Effect also refers to the actual reduction of anxiety or depression and attention deficit disorder (ADD) symptoms.

Though controversial, by 1990, the Mozart Effect experiments had become so established that there were hundreds of centers across the globe employing Mozart's music, particularly symphonies and concertos, to help children with dyslexia, speech disorders, and autism. During the past decade, ongoing experiments investigated the music's effect on spatial intelligence and epilepsy.

Mozart's violin concertos—with their high frequencies, wonderful harmonies, and intriguing melodies—may be the most intellectually enriching music ever written. His music possesses an elegant organization that avoids excesses of emotion, entering the consciousness in subtly powerful ways. Even while still in utero, we are aware of the high frequencies with which his concertos are rife.

As seems more and more to be the case, modern science has recently come to appreciate ancient wisdom regarding

Used for many centuries by the Aborigines, an enchanting instrument called the didgeridoo is now used by people around the world to practice sound healing and meditation. Made from branches hollowed out by termites, the didgeridoo produces low-frequency sound and vibration you can see and hear.

sound. Dr. Tomatis, who was instrumental in researching the effect of listening to the music of Mozart, found that the potent high frequencies, called harmonics or overtones, that appeal to the human brain are integral components of the sacred sounds of many cultures.

Harmonics and Toning

The use of sacred sound for healing has been around as long as there have been humans. Australian Aboriginal traditions incorporated sacred sounds created by the didgeridoo, a long, hollowed-out tree limb, which creates a sound akin to a low moan. The sound produced by this instrument is rife with harmonics, and its use for healing is being rediscovered in modern times. Various shamanic and mystical traditions, such as Native American spirituality, Tibetan Buddhism, and Mongolian Shamanism have utilized sacred drumming and the use of harmonics. The Tibetan singing bowls are famous examples of sound used to heal. The Greeks and Pythagoras also employed sound for healing.

Harmonics work by employing vowel sounds, which are a cornerstone of most chanting practices. From Hindu mantras to Sufi and Kabbalistic practices to even the "Aaaaaaaamen" of Christianity, something about this form of "toning" transcends language and culture and provokes powerful resonance in the physical body. Ohm (Aum) is considered to be the mother tone, one that contains the frequency of all other sounds. By manipulating overtones or singing at least two simultaneous notes, chanters hope to invoke various energies and also help in healing the chakras (energy centers).

If our various energy centers and organs are vibrating at unharmonious frequencies, we can become encumbered by disease. By using sound and pin-

From Other Voices

WHAT IS SOUND HEALING?

Cultures around the world use sound to attune, invoke, and transform consciousness. Sound is a powerful tool because it is vibrational in nature, and we are vibrational beings, says Zacciah Blackburn, a sound healer trained in classical healing and shamanic traditions and sacred sound cultures. Indeed, the most modern science shows us that all life is vibrational in nature. This is in line with the age-old mystical thoughts of most cultures, which often allude to the vibrational nature of Creation.

There is an inherent potency to the very nature of sound itself, as it is part of the creative matrix of the universe. Whether spoken, sung, or voiced through an instrument, sounds can move us into ecstatic states of rapture or through deep states of despair.

Sound healing is the intentional use of sound to create an environment that becomes a catalyst for healing in the physical, mental, emotional, or spiritual aspects of our being. To become "healed," simply means to become "whole," says Blackburn, director of education for the New England Sound Healing Research Institute and cofounder of the World Sound Healing Organization. Sound healing can assist us in understanding our highest potential as human beings and in finding our way back to wholeness and well-being. Modern medicine is rapidly investigating and finding that music and sound therapies have an incredible potency of activating neuropeptides in our body, which generate homeostasis, or well-being, as well as heightening alpha and theta brain activity, which leads to greater states of relaxation and deeper insight in consciousness.

Understanding the nature of sound and clarifying one's intentional use of it create a powerful matrix for healing, whether it is through an instrument or voice. By surrendering to the highest vibrational nature of our essence, a practitioner can become a conduit for peace, healing, change, or growth and can assist others in that vibrational attunement. Modern sound therapies might include ecstatic or sacred chanting; the use of intuitive or "guided" music; bathing in the purifying tones of quartz or Tibetan metal "singing" bowls; utilizing the specific vibration of tuning forks to attune the body's energy "meridians"; assisting us in "toning" the deep-seated guilt, pain, suffering, fear, abandonment, or anger we have held in our bodies since an early trauma; or aligning with the highest reaches of the cosmos and channeling those energies through our voice and body with specific guided meditations.

No matter what techniques are used, sound is the current carrying unconditional love and grace from the subtle to physical dense realms of the universe. By attuning to and sounding these sound currents and coupling them with our own clear potential and intention, we amplify their force (or voice) and open to and carry aspects of the sanctity of creation into our being, into our environment, into the earth, and into the consciousness of others.

pointing the elements of the body that are out of sync with the rest of the body, we can project the appropriate frequency at the offending part and return it to a state of good health. The fundamental goals of most of today's innovative sound therapies are to create balance and alignment in the physical body, in the chakras, or in the etheric fields.

We use sound to keep our bodies healthy and aligned. Just think of music's role for teenagers. Their music seems to help them become part of the social network around them and to contribute to their being able to move out into society.

Chakra Healing

I first really understood how we hold emotions in our bodies while doing yoga. Every time I came to a certain pose, I would well up with grief for my father, who had died a number of years before. It was always one pose and one place where I hit the well of pain I was carrying about his death. That experience was my first introduction to chakras and how they hold on to the vibrations of emotions that haven't been fully processed.

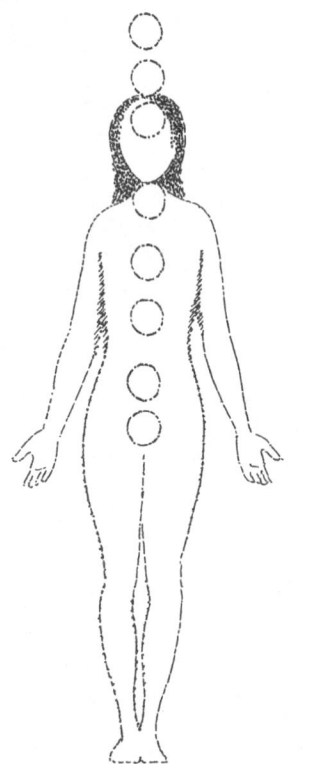

With their beginnings in Eastern thought, chakras are swirling energy centers located along the spine and connected to breath, movement, thought, and physical and mental well-being.

Chakras are swirling energy centers (of sound and vibration) and are found throughout the body along the line of the spine. Chakras are an interface between the life force energy of the universe and our inner spiritual and physical worlds. Chakras absorb and drink up this energy, sometimes known as prana, and then distribute it throughout our bodies. They are also the filing cabinets of all of the emotions that we haven't healed.

Spiritual healing of the chakras is a treasure worth cultivating for your life because it will open it to new horizons. Yoga is one wonderful way of releasing old emotional pain from chakras. Establishing a place to practice yoga or a similar type of spirituality in your home will benefit you and help you heal. It was yoga, in fact, that helped me to put my first conscious foot on the path of spiritual energy healing. There are many avenues to spirituality; find one that resonates with you.

The Chakras

Getting to know your chakras and what they hold is a potent doorway to spiritual healing. When life events "push your buttons," take note of where you feel the stress in your body. For example, if you are criticized, do you feel emotionally punched in the stomach (third chakra)? When you identify the chakra under stress, ask your Higher Self to send it healing, and ask for insight about your emotional wound.

All color is a vibration, and each chakra has a color of a particular vibration associated with it. You could almost determine the colors intuitively—the root, or first, chakra is red and earthy, and the seventh crown, or chakra, the connection to the divine, is a regal purple.

❖ **First Chakra:** Located at the base of the spine, the first chakra is associated with group consciousness, community, and the community's laws, which ensure the safety and continuance of their people.

Color: Red

❖ **Second Chakra:** An inch below the belly button, this chakra is about one-on-one relationships, personal power, power over others (and powerlessness in one-on-one relationships), and sexual and financial power.

Color: Orange

❖ **Third Chakra:** At the solar plexus, this golden orb of a chakra is connected to issues surrounding self-esteem, self-worth, fear, intimidation, and personal power in the world. It is also a chakra of endurance, and it is connected to the adrenal glands.

Color: Yellow

❖ **Fourth Chakra:** The heart chakra is located under the breastbone, and it is the seat of love, unconditional love, the love of the world, and forgiveness (and their opposites, such as grief and loneliness).

Color: Green

❖ **Fifth Chakra:** The throat chakra is about personal will, self-discipline, communication, and creativity.

Colors: Blue and sky blue

❖ **Sixth Chakra:** The brow chakra, also known as the third eye, is the center of intuition, the power of the mind, seeing the truth, and spiritual clairvoyance.

Color: Indigo

❖ **Seventh Chakra:** At the crown of the head, this chakra is about spiritual faith and service to the Divine.

Colors: Purple and violet

❖ **Eighth Chakra:** This chakra, the Higher Self, is about 8 inches above the top of the head and is the place of the soul's connection to the human personality.

Color: White

Sound and the Chakras

Just as each chakra has a color related to it by virtue of a similar vibration, each chakra has sound connected to its vibration as well. Singing the simple song "Doe a Deer" will tell you the right pitch for each chakra: Doe is the sound of the root chakra; ray, the second; and on up to the seventh chakra.

Provide Your Chakras with Colors from Nature

Color is also vibration. We can provide deep and healing color therapy to our chakras by looking at the natural world around us. I've done a number of different kinds of color therapy. My chakras drink in their color the most deeply when my eyes are looking at a fully alive color found in nature, such as the vibrant green of spring for the heart chakra or sky blue for the throat chakra.

Here is the method I use to give my chakras color therapy:

Start with your Higher Self, the eighth chakra found about 8 inches above your head, and then one by one, move down to the lower seven chakras when you are ready (see chakra diagram on page 416). Using words (unspoken or aloud), open one chakra at a time, and allow it to drink in the color. I find that I know when the chakra really needs the color because my eyes really lock onto an object of a particular color, such as a yellow tulip. I also find that my concentration dims when I've had enough of the color—an indication that I can move on to the next chakra.

❖ White to the Higher Self (eighth) chakra: Look at a white cloud or a white stone, such as quartz. Imagine complete purity, while bringing your awareness to the place 8 inches above your head where the Higher Self resides.

❖ Violet or purple to the crown (seventh) chakra: Look at a ripe plum, an amethyst, or a purple flower, such as an iris. If there is no natural purple around you, imagine light filtering through purple stained glass into your chakra, or imagine another image you prefer. Keep imagining or looking at the color until you feel your chakra has gotten what it needs.

❖ Indigo or cobalt to the brow (sixth) chakra: I like to imagine the night sky right before dawn, a sky full of stars, for the indigo for this chakra. Looking at or imagining stones, such as sapphires, lapis lazuli, and azurite, also works. Holding and gazing at a stone at the same time is perfect because you can also absorb the energy of the stone. Looking at and eating blueberries also helps you drink in and absorb blue internally.

❖ Sky blue to the throat (fifth) chakra: The throat chakra color is best described as aquamarine. Imagine your throat chakra filling completely up with the blue sky. Let the chakra drink in as much of the sky as it needs. Stones to hold include aquamarine, turquoise, Larimar, and blue tourmaline.

❖ Leaf green to the heart (fourth)

chakra: Where I live, early May is vibrantly alive with budding green leaves. The entire landscape is bursting forth with various hues of bright green. When working with the heart chakra, I just drink in the landscape. In the deep winter, you can look at a potted plant or imagine new green foliage instead. Or look at (and then eat!) an unpeeled Granny Smith apple!

❖ Yellow sun to the solar plexus (third) chakra: Imagine the bright yellow sun in your solar plexus, its energy radiating out from a yellow center, clearing and healing as it goes. Or you can look at yellow flowers, such as a yellow tulip or lily, or a banana. Stones to hold and look at that are infused with a lot of third-chakra yellow include yellow tourmaline, celestite, kunzite, garnet, topaz, sapphire, and rhodonite. Amber also carries yellow, although I like to use the more rust-colored ambers for my second chakra.

❖ Orange to the navel (second) chakra: I like to imagine dried tree sap or warm honey-colored wood found on the inside of tree bark for the color of this chakra. Petrified wood with dark orange works nicely too. A pumpkin is a perfect vegetable for an orange meditation, as are the stones orange calcite and carnelian. Daylilies and poppies are great flowers to have growing nearby in the summer months. In the winter, a few bright, healthy oranges will provide plenty of orange and more—the orange color on that fruit is so alive that it seems to sing.

❖ Red to the base of the spine (first) chakra: The red dirt in the American Southwest comes to mind for me when my mind casts around for a red from nature, so I can imagine that for the first chakra. The red on a robin or a red apple or a tomato also brings energy to the first chakra.

Air in the Home

A comfortable room temperature is considered to be between 66.2° and 73.4°F (19° to 23°C). Most people rely on heating and air-conditioning systems to maintain these temperatures, but there are also many supplemental techniques to help reduce the need for heat and air conditioning, such as whole-house fans, awnings to reduce sun penetration, and adding sealants and caulk to drafty areas.

Ideal humidity for a home is somewhere around 40 percent (with underfloor heating, the humidity should be at 55 percent). A dehumidifier can be used to reduce humidity. Increasing humidity can sometimes be a big challenge in the winter, when heating systems dry out the air. I've seen simple to elaborate setups to increase humidity in the air—from humidifiers installed on heating systems to open pans of water set right on heaters to evaporate into the air.

How does your home receive fresh air? The required amount of fresh air in a given space is at least 8 liters (or 488 cubic inches) per second per person, and in areas of heavy smoking, 25 liters (or 1,526 cubic inches) is required. This translates into the fact that in a period of an hour, the total air supply should change at least four to six times! It is hard to reach this in the winter with the windows closed, especially if you live in an airtight home. Most of us need to crack a window to maintain this amount of fresh air, or we need to install an air-to-air exchanger.

Nature's Natural High—Negative Ions

Air contains billions of electrically charged particles—or ions—that are formed when energy acts upon a molecule, such as CO_2, oxygen, water, or nitrogen. These electrical charges in the air can affect our moods, energy, and health. Negative ions actually feel good; too many positive ions make us feel bad. Ions act upon our capacity to absorb and utilize oxygen and therefore cause powerful effects on our lives and well-being.

A hit of pure oxygen is said to bring about a euphoric feeling because of the straight oxygen electrical charges. Breathing negative ions produces a similar result; when negative ions are present in significant enough concentration, your mood, energy, and overall health can be improved. In fact, some research suggests that high levels of negative ions encourage a myriad of positive mental health side effects. These include increased levels of serotonin, an alleviation of symptoms of seasonal affective disorder (SAD), higher self-esteem, improved overall cognitive functioning, improved memory, and increased levels of relaxation.

Ions are biologically active, stimulating the production of the powerful chemical serotonin. According to Albert Krueger, MD, a microbiologist and experimental pathologist at the University of California, Berkeley, serotonin causes profound neural, glandular, and digestive effects throughout the body. Ions also decrease hormone levels, which is a benefit.

Increase the Negative and Reduce the Positive—Ions, That Is

The ideal ratio of negative to positive ions is about 2,000 negative to 1,000 positive ions per cubic centimeter. This ratio is found at the seashore, where waves crashing on the shore release thousands of negative ions. The higher the negative to positive ion ratio, the better. What you *don't* want is what you find in really polluted environments, such as the ion count in Los Angeles. During rush hour, the negative ion count is fewer than 100 per cubic centimeter! Unfortunately, many indoor environments also have fewer than 100 negative ions per cubic centimeter.

Negative Ions: The beneficial effects of negative ions were first discovered in 1932 by C. W. Hansell, PhD, at RCA Laboratories. Apparently, Dr. Hansell took note of the erratic mood swings of a coworker who was stationed beside an electrostatic generator. He observed his behaviors and discovered that his colleague was ebullient when the machine produced negative ions and despondent when it generated positive ones.

Dr. Hansell's observations proved to be the foundation for much further research into the nature of ions and their effects on mood. Originally, negative ions were found to speed recovery in burn and asthma patients. Later, they were discovered to profoundly affect serotonin levels in the bloodstream, stabilize alpha (relaxed) brainwave rhythms, and positively impact our reactions to sensory stimuli. The greater level of alertness found in those in higher negative ion concentrations has

been found to translate into improved abilities to learn.

Dr. Krueger found that an astonishingly small quantity of negative ions could kill bacteria and quickly take them out of the air so that they were less likely to infect people. Negative ionization of the air is mandatory in many European and Russian hospitals for this reason.

The positive benefits of negative ions are innumerable; an abundance of them makes one alert, refreshed, and exhilarated in the way of a crisp, cool day in October or like being on a mountaintop. They provide relief of illnesses and allergies, they elevate moods, heighten alertness even after a long day, help to tranquilize patients in severe pain, and help an ordinary, healthy individual feel just plain wonderful. In order to receive the benefits of negative ions, you must breathe them through your nose. If you breathe through your mouth, you won't benefit!

Positive Ions: Ever feel sort of lifeless and tired from sitting in the same stale room for too long, even if you've gotten enough sleep? Maybe the room you are in has a disproportionate excess of positive ions. Stale air, besides the obvious stuffy, dry feel, can cause headaches, eye sting, vague malaise, and tiredness. Why? Simply, the lack of oxygen in the air exhausts the body as it attempts to derive its requirements out of a depleted source. Long-term exposure to such environments also affects moods and can cause hypertension, anxiety, headaches, and decreased mental functioning. Additionally, hyperthyroid response, depression, vasoconstriction, and increased respiration rate may be linked to environments replete with positive ions.

Beyond simple irritation, overexposure to positive ions can cause rather debilitating effects. This includes (but is in no way limited to) an alteration of the central nervous system and, through it, the peripheral organs. Fortunately, Dr. Krueger cautions that "the biological (nonclinical) effects produced by atmospheric ions are not dramatic; on the contrary, they tend to be limited in degree."

Ions Indoors

In the words of William Rea, MD, founder of the Environmental Health Center in Dallas, "Houses don't breathe like they used to." Most modern buildings have impermeable walls that cannot breathe or admit negative ions as a result of using plastic, glass, and concrete rather than porous materials, such as brick and stone. Modern, synthetic materials are well known for their susceptibility to electrostatic charges. More and more synthetic building materials are being used all the time.

These aspects of a home can increase positive ions, and you should work to correct, modify, or change these features.

❖ Vinyl siding has replaced wood on many buildings, which is unfortunate because many plastics bring with them positive static charges. In a typical interior, the negative ion count may be depleted to fewer than 100 per cubic centimeter.

❖ Synthetic clothing and furniture coverings absorb positive ions, as do the metal ducts covering heating and air-conditioning outlets.

❖ Tightly sealed windows trap stale, ion-depleted air, so take care to ensure and restore good air circulation.

❖ Air-conditioning vents that are improperly grounded are usually positively charged. If you are in the market for an air conditioner, make sure to look for ion-control air conditioners.

❖ Ductwork bringing air in from outside should not contain sharp edges or right-angled bends because these cause friction that knocks off electrons. This will leave the positively charged atoms to make their way into your home's air.

❖ Though energy efficiency is important, it has significantly lengthened air-recycling periods, thereby worsening positive ion ratios.

❖ Every wiring circuit induces an

electric and magnetic field of ions around it. Current-carrying wires, monitors, photocopiers, printers, scanners, shredders, electric coffee makers, fax machines and phones, and all electronic equipment in both home and office significantly deplete negative ions. You should consider keeping most of your electrical appliances separate from your more comfortable, inhabitable living spaces.

Balancing Ions inside the Home

With this overwhelming profusion of commonplace synthetic substances throwing the healthy ion count ratio out of whack, what can you do to keep those precious negative ions in healthy abundance? The most important thing is to use natural, permeable building materials. This isn't always feasible, of course, especially if you rent or don't plan on remodeling. If you can't control your environment, try to have your surroundings be as inert as possible with few synthetic smells, and do as little as possible to change the environment by avoiding synthetic materials (such as commercial furniture polish and other cleaning agents, paints, and furnishings).

Ionizers are also invaluable tools and are employed at hospitals to improve the quality of air and to decrease airborne infections. Clive Begg and colleagues at the University of Leeds first demonstrated that air ionizers (which emit negative ions) can comprehensively disinfect hospital wards, reducing infection to zero. The staff at St. James Hospital in Leeds was so astonished and impressed that they asked the researchers to leave the equipment with them after the yearlong trial.

Why do ionizers work? Ionizers disperse negatively or positively charged ions into the air; these ions attach to particles in the air, such as dust or pollen. The dust or pollen particles attach to other surfaces, such as furniture and walls, and can be cleaned away.

If you're considering an ionizer, it's important to realize that there is some minor inconvenience caused by these devices. Effective ionization will deposit dust on the surfaces close to the ionizer. There is no way to prevent this and still have a good negative charge in your air. Though the dust collection on the walls is an annoyance, it is evidence of all of the particulate that you are not breathing. A word of caution, however: Some brands of ionizers emit levels of ozone that can be harmful for people who suffer from heart, lung, or respiratory illnesses. (For a list of ionizer brands tested, see *Consumer Reports*, May 2005.)

More portable solutions include adding water fountains, salt lamps, and pure beeswax candles into your home.

Determine which areas have an abundance of positive ion generators (such as appliances), and use these lovely decorative elements to help balance these out. Ion meters are expensive ($600 plus), but may be worth considering, particularly if you can't root out problem areas or you live in an environment prone to imbalances.

Salt lamps, which resemble glowing stones when illuminated, are another way to help balance out the ion ratio in problematic areas of your home. They can easily be placed near televisions and computers, around smokers, in offices with air conditioning, in meditation rooms, and anywhere else you want to restore or preserve the natural air quality. Salt lamps have a hollowed-out crystal where a bulb can be inserted. Nonilluminated salt lamps still work as mini ionizers, and when they are illuminated and warm, they emit an even higher number of negative ions.

Salt lamps emit negative ions because the salt and water from the air combine to create negative ions. A series of scientific studies have demonstrated that salt lamps can increase the negative ion count by up to 300 percent.

I have a salt lamp in my office. I put the salt lamp near my computer for the first few weeks (I was within 3 feet of it), and I found that I was very tired at the end of the day, which surprised me. Then it dawned on me that I was too close to the lamp, and I was absorbing all those positive ions being drawn to it. I moved the lamp to the other side of the room, and I have felt great in the room ever since.

Indoor Air Quality

I'm a person who doesn't breathe very openly and fully. I think the reason is because the air that's available is so often toxic. I find myself holding my breath when I am traveling in cities or in places with an especially high toxic overload, such as the mall. I've been on an unerring quest for clean air for years, in fact. I come to life in fresh, clean air. Who wouldn't? And after being poisoned, it was amazing how fast I became well in a house with clean air.

Unfortunately, most indoor air quality (IAQ) is truly unhealthy. This is particularly unfortunate because, in the United States, people spend about 90 percent of their time indoors. The Environmental Protection Agency (EPA) has noted that IAQ can be 10 times more polluted than the air outside, and the agency considers IAQ the nation's top pollution problem.

Many factors contribute to the breathability of indoor air, including ventilation, the relative draftiness of your home, your appliances, the number of candles you burn, and synthetic pollutants. By rejecting polluting products and paying attention to the pathways of air in your home, you can increase your indoor air quality and make a healthy living environment for yourself and your family.

Eliminate Combustion Appliances

Vented and unvented gas and kerosene heaters emit significant quantities of toxic fumes. Avoiding these is one of the most important things you can do to improve IAQ. A recent Australian study demonstrated that the presence of a gas stove in the household caused a threefold increase of asthma and a twofold increase in respiratory symptoms.

Reduce Candle Use

Candles (not including pure beeswax) and incense compromise IAQ, due to the significant quantities of carbon particles that they produce. Of course, carbon or soot production varies with candle type, with scented candles emitting consistently higher levels. The highest level of carbon emissions occurs when candles are extinguished. Some metal wicks contain lead and should be avoided altogether.

Black deposits on indoor surfaces and appliances, on wall surfaces near ceilings, on and near electrical outlets, and outside stud areas are called candle ghosting. The most significant ghosting is usually from aromatherapy candles. Unfortunately, the more black soot that collects, the more you are breathing.

Install Air Filters

Have you heard of heat recovery ventilation units (HRVs)? They're ideal for tight, energy-efficient homes. Heat is captured from the exhausted airstream and then the heat is filtered and given back to the incoming air. With this system, there is little energy penalty in exchange for good air quality. HRVs can recover up to 85 percent of the heat in the outgoing airstream and typically contain filters that keep particulates, such as pollen and dust, from entering your home.

High Efficiency Particulate Arresting (HEPA) filters can remove 99.9 percent of microparticulates from the air that goes through the filter. HEPA filters can be used in furnaces, air cleaners, and vacuum cleaners.

Choose a vacuum cleaner equipped with a HEPA filter. The filters help to relieve allergens like pet dander and dust mites. Unlike regular vacuum bags, where fine particles may pass through a filter and escape into the air through the exhaust, vacuums with HEPA filters employ microfiltration capabilities, using a bag with smaller pores or a second, electrostatic filter in addition to the standard motor filter. If you have a model without a HEPA filter, it may still be useful; many performed as well as vacuums with HEPA filters in *Consumer Reports* magazine emissions tests, because the amount of dust emitted depends as much on the design of the entire machine as on its filter.

Ventilate!

No matter where you live, keeping the air in your home fresh and temperate might seem a constant struggle. Living in upstate New York, I love those first glorious spring days after winter when I find myself throwing the windows open whenever possible. You can almost taste the difference in the quality of the air; everything suddenly seems more vital than you could possibly have imagined after having been in closed-up rooms all winter. Ventilation is by far one of the most important aspects of keeping an environment healthy.

Furnaces, water heaters, clothes dryers, and bathroom and kitchen exhaust fans expel air from the house, making it easier to depressurize an airtight or sealed house. Air pressure within a house is a complex issue that's important to address, especially if you have gas- or oil-burning appliances. Differences in air pressure in the home can be a hazard because pollutants can be sucked from high-pressure areas to low-pressure areas in the home through something as small as a leaky light-switch hole. You want to ensure there are no "backdrafts," or loss of the "chimney effect," which could suck dangerous fumes, such as carbon monoxide, into the home. Ask a professional to perform a Combustion Safety Test.

Exhaust-only ventilation means that you have only one fan in place, designed to draw air out of the home. One of the few benefits of a leaky house is that this sort of ventilation is often sufficient. Otherwise, you will need to extract the stale air from your home and draw in new air at the same time.

An attached garage is the single most significant contributor to poor IAQ because the fumes from the car enter the house. In order to help prevent some of the pollutants from entering your home, make sure not to let cars idle inside the garage. An exhaust fan installed in the garage is a great idea; install it on the wall opposite the door into the house.

Managing Your Home's Seasonal Ventilation

The first thing to do when considering ventilation solutions is to learn how air flows naturally through your home.

Then find ways to improve the ventilation in as many natural ways as possible.

In the summer, trees and shrubs can shade windows and allow fewer hot rays of sunshine into your living area, but you want to maintain a clear path for airflow both inside and outside your windows, so make sure not to have trees and shrubs fully blocking windows. Whenever possible, take advantage of cool night air, and draw cooler air into your home by natural or mechanical methods first thing in the morning.

Experts consider it best to close your windows, doors, and window coverings in the morning before your home starts to heat up. As the day's heat wears on, you may find it so stuffy that you need to open the window for air exchange.

Even on cool nights in spring and fall, keep the windows open and snuggle under a blanket just to keep air circulating through your home.

Natural ventilation works best in climates with cool summers or cool nights and regular breezes. In warmer climates, natural ventilation can't circulate enough air through a home to provide sufficient cooling at night to remove the day's heat. Mechanical ventilation can provide continuously moving air that will keep your home cooler, day and night, with circulating fans, whole-house fans, and evaporative coolers.

If you're using air-conditioning, keep the temperature between 66° and 73°F (the higher, the better). Turn it off completely if you'll be gone for more than a few hours. Make sure that there is air movement; studies have shown

Unhealthy air needs to be vented, especially in a garage where carbon monoxide fumes, pollutants, and out-gassing fumes from paints and chemicals can quickly build up to toxic levels. Install a garage vent fan on the wall farthest from the door to the house, so it pulls noxious air out of the garage to the outdoors.

that changing air movements are preferable to constant conditions. These "random gusts" tend to make people seem happier, healthier, and more alert.

Balanced ventilation is a more comprehensive form of regulating your home's airflow. This might include kitchen and bathroom exhaust fans in combination with a fresh air intake joined to your furnace's air circulation system. Some newer systems can vary temperature and ventilation. This form of ventilation is useful in newer houses, where more attention has been paid to ensuring that they are not terribly drafty.

Use windows and doors for cross-ventilation. Inlets and outlets located directly opposite each other—for example, two windows—cool only those areas in between the two or those areas in the direct path of the airflow. You'll cool more of your home if you force the air to take a longer path between the inlet and outlet. Use small window openings for the inlets and larger openings for the outlets. This increases air speed and improves the cooling effect. Air from cooler, shaded outdoor areas provides the best intake air. Experiment with different patterns of window venting to move fresh outside air through all the living areas of your home.

Solar heat travels in through the roof and radiates into the attic. Attic ventilation reduces attic temperature 10° to 25°F and slows the transfer of heat into the living space. Contact an expert in ventilation to make sure you are doing as much as you can to make your attic as well ventilated as possible.

Circulating Fans

Fans create a wind chill effect and can make hot air seem cooler, just because of the movement of air. Circulating fans most often used for home cooling include ceiling fans, table fans, floor fans, window fans, and fans mounted to poles or walls.

Ceiling Fans

Wind makes hot air much more tolerable, and a ceiling fan can make you feel significantly cooler. If you use air-conditioning, a ceiling fan will allow you to raise the thermostat setting about 4°F with no reduction in comfort. In temperate climates or during moderately hot weather, ceiling fans may allow you to avoid using your air conditioner altogether.

Consult a ventilation expert about installing ceiling fans in your home. As a rule of thumb, larger ceiling fans can move more air than smaller fans. A 36- or 44-inch-diameter fan will cool rooms up to 225 square feet, while fans that are 52 inches or more should be installed in larger rooms. Multiple fans work best in rooms longer than 18 feet. Small- and medium-size fans will provide efficient cooling in a 4- to 6-foot-diameter area, while larger fans are effective up to 10 feet.

Make sure you choose a fan that operates quietly and smoothly. Check the noise rating, and if possible, listen to your fan in operation before you buy it.

Window Fans

Window fans are one of the lowest-cost cooling systems available. They should be installed on the downwind side of the house facing out. They work most efficiently when doors are open and a window is open in each room of the house to let air flow through.

If the wind direction changes frequently in your area, use reversible-type window fans, so you can either pull air into the home or push air out, depending on which way the wind is blowing. Experiment with positioning the fans in different windows to see which arrangement gives the best cooling effect.

In a larger house, consider installing a window fan that blows air in through a lower-level window in a cool area and another window fan that blows air out through a higher-level window in the hotter area.

Always be cautious with larger exhaust fans. If there isn't sufficient ventilation, the fans can pull combustion products (for example, carbon monoxide from furnaces or water heaters) into your living space.

Whole-House Fans

If you're looking for a more economical solution but the same cooling ability as central air-conditioning, whole-house fans are a good option. An average whole-house fan uses $\frac{1}{10}$ the electricity of an air-conditioning unit. A whole-house fan can substitute for an air conditioner much of the year in most climates. Whole-house fans combine with ceiling and portable fans to provide acceptable summer comfort for many families, even in hot weather. Whole-house fans must be mounted in a hallway ceiling on the top floor of the house.

The whole-house fan pulls air in from open windows and exhausts it through the attic and roof. It provides good attic ventilation in addition to whole-house ventilation. You regulate cooling by simply closing windows in the unoccupied area and opening windows wide in occupied areas. Many people cool the bedrooms at night and the living space during the daytime. Whole-house fans should provide houses with 30 to 60 air changes per hour (check with a professional to determine what is appropriate for your home). The air-change rate you choose depends on your climate and how much you will depend on the whole-house fan for cooling. A whole-house fan should be installed by a professional.

Ions Outdoors

Abundances of positive ions in outdoor environments often take the form of hot, dry winds. In Switzerland, the blowing of the Fohn brings with it unfavorable social conditions, such as increased hospital admissions and sky-rocketing suicide and crime rates. According to experts, this is due to a high positive to negative ion ratio.

Some places enjoy the benefits of a bounty of negative ions. A home near the ocean or downwind of a waterfall will have an abundance of negative ions in the air. Crystalline salt, abundant in places situated near the sea, acts as a natural air ionizer. At Yosemite Falls, the negative ion count is more than 100,000.

There are usually 1,000 to 2,000 ions per cubic centimeter of indoor air; usually, these are balanced between positive and negative, with slightly more positive ions than negative ones. Generally, outdoor air has many more ions, generally 3,000 to more than 5,000 per cubic centimeter. Fresh country air is chock full of negative ions, with between 2,000 and 4,000 per cubic centimeter. Because trees and plants absorb carbon dioxide and other pollutants that create positive ions, these forested, undeveloped places tend to have abundant quantities of negative ions.

But other unspoiled outdoor environments may be riddled with over-abundances of positive ions. For instance, a home downwind of a desert will be affected by surges of positive ions when the winds blow. Also, positive ions increase dramatically before a storm (but negative ions surge in the midst of the storm, which is why you sometimes feel wonderful during a big storm).

Perhaps you've heard of or seen the phenomenon of wild turkeys gobbling like crazy in the woods before high winds, despite lacking any obvious indicators to suggest such weather might be coming. This occurs because they can sense when the barometer falls. Ants, which will block tunnels from impending rain, also possess this intuition. How are these things obvious to these creatures? They can detect an abundance of positive ions, the same ions that cause soaring rates of illness and irritability in humans. Famous examples of this natural phenomenon are the hot, dry, seasonal winds such as the Alpine Fohn and the Rocky Mountain Chinook. During the peak of these winds, complaints of joint pain, illness, and irritability all spike. Also, there is a significant jump in the crime rate, which all but evaporates with the passing of the winds.

Full Moon Stress and the Ions Connection

The moon's cycle is tied strongly to the overall balance of ions in the atmosphere. According to *Sick Buildings and Healthy Homes* by Coghill Research Laboratories, a full moon exerts an influence on the ionosphere and pushes this delicate mantle slightly out of balance, bringing more positive ions to the earth's surface. The ionosphere's positive ions mix with those more negatively charged at the earth's surface, which results in some changes to our bloodstream.

Our blood cells are normally negatively charged, as are the walls of our arteries and veins. This ensures an easy flow because the charges are similar. However, during the full moon, when the ion ratio turns to more positive ionization, it results in a "stickier" flow of blood, which results in poorer oxygenation and an increase in stress. This constantly shifting balance is relevant not only to humans but also to our gardens. Planting during the waxing phase aids new growth or new development.

Various natural phenomena generate ions, including cosmic rays, radioactive elements in the soil, ultraviolet radiation, the friction generated when high winds blow sand or dust, and rain. Many plants, most notably pines and asparagus ferns, have negative ions pouring off their leaves and are great to have around because the negative ions will make you feel great.

Modern Cities and Polluted Homes

The pollution found in cities produces a large excess of positive ions. Car exhausts, industrial fumes, tire dust, cigarette smoke, and cooking and heating fumes either neutralize or positively charge negative ions.

Steel and concrete buildings absorb the charges of negative ions, though all buildings, regardless of construction, act as ionic magnets, since ions tend to congregate around sharper points. This is clearly demonstrated in pyramidal structures, where ions accumulate at the point.

Wisdom of the Ancient Structures

In contrast to the ionic misery provoked by many modern cities, most ancient structures were constructed in ways that promote healthy abundances of negative ions. Obviously, though wise in many ways, our antique forefathers probably had no idea of this bonus implicit in the construction of their structures. However, some of the awesome majesty and exhilaration that one must have felt when stepping into a newly completed pyramid may have been the result of a bloodstream saturated with negative ions!

Pyramidal structures draw large concentrations of negative ions toward the apex. The Great Pyramid of Giza, set precisely on the earth's north-south axis, with its shimmering sides of exceptionally polished limestone, provided an almost entirely negative ion atmosphere in its interior chamber. Since stones radiate heat, crystalline stones exposed to direct sunlight excite and release electrons. Therefore, when heated up, structures such as Stonehenge in England, the great pyramids of Egypt, and sites at Newgranges are generators of negative ions.

I was recently in Vermont and was struck once again at how great I feel there. The air has a quality that makes me feel alive and happy. I suspect that this exuberant feeling is caused by powerful negative ions coming off the mountains and the many brooks. There are few cars and factories.

Seek out wonderful-feeling air whenever you can and recognize how positively it affects you. It seems to me that when we find value in clean air, we will work to protect it.

Wind Energy

Wind energy can be generated by both individual consumers and large companies. In fact, it won't be long before ranches in the Midwest will be making more money from the wind power they generate than from the beef they raise. These ranches generate energy with large windmills—or turbines—which turn in the wind and power electricity generators. It is estimated that more than 20 percent of the total electricity used in the United States could be generated by 16,000 square miles of wind farms. And the land required by these wind farms, primarily open space with occasional access roads and compact windmills, could still be utilized mainly as farmland.

There are numerous benefits to increased use of wind energy. A single coal-fired plant will generate over 8,500 tons of CO_2 each year. Wind energy, on the other hand, produces no residual greenhouse gases. Replacing fossil-fuel sources with wind energy eliminates as much CO_2 as a 500-acre forest would eliminate.

Wind energy is clean; it provides almost zero disruption to the natural environment. It's also cost efficient. As more wind plants are built, costs continue to decline and are more viable each year. Wind energy also provides long-term stability for the farmers and ranchers who maintain them and place them on their land.

Wind energy is free and renewable and releases no dangerous emissions, but turbines need to be constructed where wind speed is dependable and consistent, limiting its usage in some areas. In the United States and abroad, wind power is the fastest-growing source of energy and is seen as a viable alternative to burning fossil fuels.

You Can Have Wind Energy

Depending on your location, you might not be afforded the luxury of purchasing wind energy, or you may not live in a locale with enough wind to make the installation of your own system worthwhile. But, small wind energy systems are available for the homeowner. They can be connected to your power grid and will reduce your consumption of utility-supplied electricity. In the event that your turbine does not provide enough energy to power your home, your utility company can supply what you need. If you find yourself with an excess of energy, you can sell it to the utility company—a process that happens automatically.

If you live in a remote area or are simply intrigued by the idea of providing your own energy, stand-alone systems are another option, and, if they're large enough, they can even power small communities.

While there is no way around the fact that personal wind energy systems require a significant financial investment, the decreased energy costs (which can extend over a lifetime) may make it a worthwhile endeavor.

Is Your Site Right?

Personal wind energy setups aren't for everyone. Certain requirements, beyond the sheer cost, must be in place for it to be feasible. In order to have a stand-alone wind energy system, you need to live in an area with annual wind speeds of at least 9 miles per hour. You must also make sure that you have a backup energy system, due to the intermittent quality of wind.

If you are interested in a grid-connected system, you need to live in an area with average wind speeds of at least 10 miles per hour. In order to determine this, you can either do some research or look into measuring your wind speed for a year. Record wind speed with a recording anemometer (they cost between $500 and $1,500 a year). Be sure to take your readings at "hub height," which is the top of the

Safe and Sound

Wind technology isn't as new as you might think. Europeans have been using windmills since the 1500s, and Americans adopted them in the late 1800s to pump water and provide power before the advent of cheap electricity. Despite America's brief love affair with wind technology in the 1980s, windmills again took a backseat for a decade when they seemed incapable of supplying the vast amounts of energy that this burgeoning country required.

Some of the first wind farms were erected on the West Coast, but the technology was plagued with development problems—generators frequently broke and occasionally caught fire, and blades were short and cracked easily. Nearby residents protested the view and the noise coming from wind farms. The first windmills had a devastating impact on bird populations who liked to perch on the high towers, giving opponents a rallying cry against the "ecofriendly" wind farms.

Newer wind technologies have greatly lessened the bird problem. Wind propellers are much higher (often at a height of 200 feet, much higher than perching height), and the redesigned longer blades are easier to see when they spin. Before siting a wind farm, scientists conduct extensive bird population studies to assess the impact a wind farm may have.

America has many locales suitable for wind farms, from eastern Montana and the Dakotas through Nebraska and Kansas and into Texas. For many farmers, wind has become a new cash crop and a way to save the family farm. Farmers can lease thousands of acres across the country for wind farms. Since windmills actually take up such little space, 97 percent of the land is left free for crops and grazing.

tower where you will install your turbine. The windier your area, the more power you will generate.

When considering a wind energy system, it's very important to review product literature from many manufacturers to find one that best serves your needs. The American Wind Energy Association provides useful information concerning many aspects of wind energy on their Web site at www.awea.org.

which combines elements of solar power and wind to work with the changing elements. If you find that you live in an area where wind speeds are low in the summer, though the sun is shining in abundance, using both wind and photovoltaic technologies will likely provide you power when you need it. It may also eliminate the need to fall back onto a utility company as you would in a grid-connected system.

Hybrid Wind Systems

Another option for home renewable-energy systems is a hybrid wind system,

14

a community
of resources

My stepfather, Reese, taught me a lot about caring for a home; he was a conservationist at heart, I think, and he also valued good craftsmanship. He always bought high-quality goods that he hoped would last more than a lifetime if well cared for, and he took good care of *everything*—down to keeping nails dry in baby food jars in the garage. Our tools—saws, car-washing equipment, garden hoes, hammers, vacuum cleaners—will last for generations if we care as well for them. Reese also grew up in the Great Depression and learned from that time not to be a spendthrift or wasteful. If something broke, you figured out how to fix it. I admired him, and his careful buying habits of high-quality products combined with the loving care of his purchases inspired me. He was principled, and although he could afford to throw broken things away, he chose to lovingly maintain them.

Juxtaposing Reese's care of his belongings with the lifestyle of the 21st century seems hard at first because our current lifestyles are so fast and highstrung. Imagine taking an entire Saturday, like he did, to fix or polish things or to research and buy the very best pitchfork. More likely, we'd rush to the mall to pick up a new light fixture (having already thrown out the broken one) and a few other things, and on our way home, stop at the garden shop to buy the cheapest pitchfork that happened to be on sale. We'd come home from the mall frazzled and quickly become irritated with the impossible plastic encasement around the light fixture. We'd finally hack open the container with a knife and scissors only to realize that we need to call the electrician anyway. (I expect I don't need to mention that, of course, the electrician could have fixed the light fixture to begin with.)

Because I couldn't afford to buy really good products, I often justified not approaching my "belongings" like Reese did. But I also think that the word "resourceful" has had a bad rap, deterring people from such a lifestyle. I expect it was Madison Avenue's advertising that may have instilled the image of the resourceful homemaker as dowdy, old-fashioned, and wearing sturdy, serviceable, unattractive shoes.

But the times are once again "a changin'," and this time around, we need to look at our buying habits in relation to our planet and our health. I often think of an environmental rule that a friend lives by: "Buy only what you need, not what you want." I'd add to buy only what is healthy for you and your family and forgo the rest.

This list contains the categories of companies I've included in A Community of Resources. Take some time to read through the entire listing of companies too; I'm sure you'll find many manufacturers, products, and organizations that can help you on your path toward home enlightenment.

Category Listings for Quick Reference

Government Organizations

Air
Emergency
Energy
Health

National Programs
Solid Waste
Water

Nonprofit Organizations

Air
Art Supplies
Bedding
Clothing
Disaster Relief
Energy
Farming
Fibers
General Environment and Nature

Pets
Pest Control
Recycling
Toxics Information
Water
Wildlife
Window Shades/Quilts
Wood

Products

Air Purifiers and Ionizers

Alternative Toilets and Graywater
  Recycling

Architecture

Aromatherapy and Essential Oils

Backyard Play Equipment

Bath Linens

Bedding

Beer, Wine, Chocolate, and Coffee

Blessing Herbs

Buckwheat Pillows

Candles

Carbon Monoxide Detectors

Carpets—Natural

Chime Alarm Clocks

Cleaning Supplies—Natural

Clothing—Organic

Compasses

Cooking Oils

Crafts: Children

Crystals and Stones

Dehumidifiers

Diapers

Disaster Preparedness Kits

Doorknockers

Doormats

Dream Catchers

Dream Pillows

Dried Herbs, Cones, and Botanicals

Flooring

Flower Essences

Flowers—Freshly Cut Organic

Furniture

Gardening Supplies

Gravity Water Filters

Heirloom and Organic Seeds

Home Test Kits

Hygrometers

Insect Repellent (Personal)

Ion-Control Air Conditioners

Lanolin

Lightbulbs and Light Products

Lunar Calendars

Magnetic Water Filter Systems

Menstrual Products

Mineral-Based Cleaning Products

Mold Prevention

Mold Removal

Natural Wreaths

Neem Oil

Odor-Absorbing Products

Office Paper

Office Supplies

Organic Silk

Outdoor Fire Pits and Fireplace
  Accessories

Outdoor Furniture—Natural

Paint

Paint—Wood Finishes

Paper Products

Personal Care

Pest Control

Pesticide and Pollution Information
  Sources

Pet Care

Plant Room Deodorizers

Plastic Lumber

Rain Barrels

Rodent Control

Salt Lamps

Shower Filters/Dechlorinators

Solar Energy Products

Solar Garden/Path Lights

Solar Radios

Testing Kits

Tile

Ventilation Units—Heat Recovery

Washing Machines/Dryers

Water Filters

Water Fountains

Water Purification Tablets

Water-Saving Fixtures

Wind Energy Systems—Residential

Windows—Energy Efficient

Window Shades/Quilts

Recommended Magazines and Newsletters

Trade Organizations

Miscellaneous

Solar

Stone

Tiles

Toxics

Wood

Government Organizations

Air

Energy Efficiency and Renewable
   Energy
Mail Stop EE-1
Department of Energy
Washington, DC 20585
202-586-9220
www.eere.energy.gov

Along with information on numerous
renewable energy resources, the EERE
provides extensive facts, figures,
charts, publications, etc., on wind
energy for home use.

Environmental Protection Agency
Indoor Environments Division
Ariel Rios Building
1200 Pennsylvania Avenue NW
Mailcode 6609J
Washington, DC 20460
202-272-0167
www.epa.gov

The Indoor Environments Division
deals with radon, mold, and all other
aspects of indoor air quality, from dis-
semination of research to solutions.

Indoor Air Quality Information
  Clearinghouse
PO Box 37133
Washington, DC 20013-7133
800-438-4318
www.epa.gov/iaq/iaqxline.html

Set up by the EPA, this is an extensive
source of information about all facets
of indoor air quality.

Emergency

Federal Emergency Management
  Agency (FEMA)
500 C Street SW
Washington, DC 20472
202-566-1600
www.fema.gov

FEMA is an independent agency of the
federal government with a mission to
reduce loss of life and property and
protect infrastructure from all types of
hazards.

Energy

Energy Star
US Environmental Protection Agency
ENERGY STAR Programs Hotline and
  Distribution (MS-6202J)
1200 Pennsylvania Avenue NW
Washington, DC 20460
888-782-7937
www.energystar.gov

Energy Star provides lists of Energy
Star–qualified products, including
appliances and windows, as well as
information on its energy-efficient
homes program.

National Renewable Energy Laboratory
1617 Cole Boulevard
Golden, CO 80401
303-275-3000
www.nrel.gov

The NREL is the research and development arm of the government for
renewable energy and related technologies.

United States Fire Administration
Office of Fire Management Programs
16825 South Seton Avenue
Emmitsburg, MD 21727
301-447-1000
www.usfa.fema.gov

As an entity of the Department of
Homeland Security and the Federal
Emergency Management Agency, the
mission of the USFA is to reduce life and
economic losses due to fire and related
emergencies, through leadership, advocacy, coordination, and support.

US Department of Energy
1000 Independence Avenue SW
Washington, DC 20585
800-342-5363
www.doe.gov

The Department of Energy promotes the use of environmentally sound energy sources. Through research, technology development, science, and education, it creates the energy policies for the United States.

Health

Office of Prevention, Pesticides, and
    Toxic Substances
US Environmental Protection Agency
Ariel Rios Building
1200 Pennsylvania Avenue NW
Washington, DC 20460
www.epa.gov/pesticides

The Office of Pesticide Programs protects public health and the environment from the risks posed by pesticides and promotes safer means of pest control.

United Nations Environment
    Programme
United Nations Avenue, Gigiri
PO Box 30552, 00100
Nairobi, Kenya
www.unep.org

UNEP was established to provide leadership and encourage partnership in caring for the environment by inspiring, informing, and enabling nations and peoples to improve their quality of life without compromising that of future generations.

World Health Organization (WHO)
525 23rd Street NW
Washington, DC 20037
202-974-3000
www.who.int

WHO is a specialized agency of the United Nations that was established with an objective of the attainment by all peoples of the highest possible level of health.

National Programs

Bureau of Land Management
1849 C Street,
Room 406-LS
Washington, DC 20240
202-452-5125
www.blm.gov

The Bureau of Land Management is a government organization with a vast scope of responsibilities. Conservation, education, wild horse and wild burro adoption, archeological digs, and cleanup of abandoned, hazardous mines are just a small part of what the BLM does.

National Institute of Environmental
    Health Sciences (NIEHS)
PO Box 12233
Research Triangle Park, NC 27709
919-541-3345
www.niehs.nih.gov

NIEHS is a government organization dealing with environmentally related causes of health issues. The organization works toward prevention via research, education, and outreach. There are numerous publications available, including those with the NIEHS's latest work on electromagnetic fields (EMFs).

National Park Service
1849 C Street NW
Washington, DC 20240
202-208-6843
www.nps.gov

The National Park Service preserves, protects, maintains, and educates the public about the hundreds of national parks, national preserves, and national monuments across the country.

Natural Resources Conservation Service
Attn: Conservation Communications
    Staff
PO Box 2890
Washington, DC 20013
202-720-6297
www.nrcs.usda.gov

The NRCS works with consumers, policymakers, farmers, and others to preserve, conserve, and maintain our natural resources. They have numerous programs in conservation, politics, wildlife management, etc.

US Geological Survey
888-275-8747
www.usgs.gov

The USGS is a scientific source for educational information on the earth and its natural resources and physical phenomenon as well as a research body for investigating how to make the most of those resources.

US Naval Observatory
Astronomical Applications Department
3450 Massachusetts Avenue NW
Washington, DC 20392-5420
202-762-1438
www.usno.navy.mil

The USNO is the government's scientific resource for all things astronomical, from moon phases to precise time around the globe.

World Health Organization (WHO)
525 23rd Street NW
Washington, DC 20037
202-974-3000
www.who.int/peh-emf/en

The World Health Organization is a UN organization dedicated to investigating and educating people about world health issues. There is an extensive body of work available on electromagnetic fields (EMFs).

Solid Waste

Environmental Protection Agency
  (EPA)
Ariel Rios Building
1200 Pennsylvania Avenue NW
Washington, DC 20460
www.epa.gov

The EPA is the government agency
that deals with all facets of maintaining and improving the environment.
Among the vast informational
resources available through the EPA is
a great deal of gardening information,
from the use of safer pesticides to
choosing lawn mowers.

Environmental Protection Agency
  (EPA)
Office of Solid Waste (5305W)
1200 Pennsylvania Avenue NW
Washington, DC 20460
www.epa.gov/osw

The Office of Solid Waste (OSW) regulates all the waste under the Resource
Conservation and Recovery Act. The
EPA's map shows the states that have
universal waste regulations; they link
to the regulations for each state.

US Department of Agriculture
1400 Independence Avenue SW
Washington, DC 20250
202-720-3631
www.usda.gov

The USDA is involved with research,
education, aid, and more for farmers
and ranchers. It also maintains the US
National Arboretum.

Water

Environmental Protection Agency
  (EPA)
Office of Water (4101M)
1200 Pennsylvania Avenue NW
Washington, DC 20460
www.epa.gov/water

The EPA's Office of Water seeks to provide clean drinking water for Americans, increase watershed areas and
improve the quality of these watersheds, and reduce water pollution
while educating the public on conservation, pollution, etc.

National Oceanic and Atmospheric
  Administration/Great Lakes Environmental Research Laboratory
  (NOAA/GLERL)
2205 Commonwealth Boulevard
Ann Arbor, MI 48105-2945
734-741-2235
www.glerl.noaa.gov

GLERL provides federal research on
the Great Lakes. It works to develop
policies and regulations and conducts
ongoing research.

National Oceanic Data Center
    (NODC)
NOAA/NESDIS/E/OC
SSMC3 4th Floor
1315 East-West Highway
Silver Spring, MD 20910-3282
301-713-3277
www.nodc.noaa.gov

NODC is a scientific, educational
government organization for oceanic
research. It provides education and
information about oceanic data
around the world.

USDA, NRCS (National Resources
    Conservation Service)
USDA, NRCS, Conservation
    Communications Staff
PO Box 2890
Washington, DC 20013
202-720-3210
www.nrcs.usda.gov

The NRCS provides assistance to communities in building dams and maintaining and rehabilitating watershed
areas.

USGS, Water Resources of the United
    States
US Geological Survey
http://water.usgs.gov

USGS Water Resources provides maps,
scientific facts, learning tools for edu-
cators, and publications about water
use, water quality, water resource programs, etc. Additionally, it acts as a
clearinghouse for state water information.

Nonprofit Organizations

Air

American Indoor Air Quality Council
PO Box 11599
Glendale, AZ 85318-1599
800-942-0832
www.indoor-air-quality.org

This council provides education, training, and networking within the indoor
air-quality industry.

American Lung Association
61 Broadway
6th Floor
New York, NY 10006
212-315-8700
www.lungusa.org

The American Lung Association provides complete information on lung
diseases, research, education, policy,
and lawmaking to maximize and protect indoor air quality.

Asthma and Allergy Foundation of
America (AAFA)
1233 20th Street NW
Suite 402
Washington, DC 20036
202-466-7643
www.aafa.org

The AAFA engages in education,
research, support, law regulation, and
policy changes to improve indoor air
quality and help asthma and allergy
sufferers.

Environmental Defense
257 Park Avenue S
New York, NY 10010
212-505-2100
www.environmentaldefense.org/home.
cfm

Environmental Defense is a leading
national nonprofit environmental
advocacy organization dedicated to
protecting the environmental rights of
all people.

Indoor Air Quality Association, Inc.
12339 Carroll Avenue
Rockville, MD 20852
301-231-8388
www.iaqa.org

The IAQA is a nonprofit, multidisci-
plined organization dedicated to promoting the exchange of indoor

environmental information, through
education and research, for the safety
and well-being of the general public.

National Safety Council
1121 Spring Lake Drive
Itasca, IL 60143
800-767-7236
www.radonfixit.org

The NSC has an extensive radon
awareness program, working with the
EPA to increase awareness and help
homeowners to remedy homes with
excessive radon.

Organic Consumers Association
6101 Cliff Estate Road
Little Marais, MN 55614
218-226-4164
www.organicconsumers.org

OCA is a grassroots nonprofit organization that promotes food safety,
organic farming, and sustainable agriculture practices in the United States
and internationally. They provide consumers with factual information to
make informed food choices. They
have more than 500,000 names in
their database, including subscribers,
volunteers, and supporters, and 1,800
cooperating retail co-ops, natural food
stores, CSAs, and farmers' markets.

Art Supplies

The Art & Creative Materials Institute,
  Inc. (ACMI)
PO Box 479
Hanson, MA 02341-0479
781-293-4100
www.acminet.org

ACMI is considered a leading author-
ity on art and craft materials and
works to provide the public with nontoxic art and craft materials. They are
dedicated to providing leadership,
guidance, and education to individuals, organizations, and society in general to achieve greater participation in
art- and craft-related activities.

Bedding

Better Sleep Council
501 Wythe Street
Alexandria, VA 22314-1917
www.bettersleep.org

The Better Sleep Council is a nonprofit
organization working to educate the
public about sleep habits and healthy
sleep environments.

International Institute for Bau-Biologie
  and Ecology (IBE)
PO Box 387
Clearwater, FL 33757
727-461-4371
www.buildingbiology.net

The International Institute for Bau-
Biologie and Ecology is a nonprofit
organization whose purpose is to
educate people on how to make their
homes and offices healthier and
more attractive, using a holistic
approach that encompasses a variety
of methods.

Wool Traditions
HC78 Box 10731
Ranchos De Taos, NM 87557
800-665-9786
www.wooltraditions.org

Wool Traditions is a nonprofit center
dedicated to building and maintaining
the local wool trade through sustainable agriculture. They seek to educate
people about and support the cultural
traditions of the indigenous people of
that area—the Hispanic, Pueblo, and
Dine (Navajo).

Clothing

American Sheep Industry Association
9785 Maroon Circle
Suite 360
Centennial, CO 80112
303-771-3500
www.sheepusa.org

The American Wool Council division
of the ASI works to both educate consumers, growers, and manufacturers of

wool and wool products and to promote and improve the marketing of wool and wool products.

Clean Clothes Campaign
www.cleanclothes.org

Clean Clothes Campaign is a socially and environmentally conscious watchdog organization that monitors and works to improve working conditions in clothing manufacturing companies.

Mama DOC
5806 North Vancouver Avenue
Portland, OR 97217
503-286-4149
www.mamadoc.org

Mama DOC is a nonprofit organization that is trying to raise enough money from various ecological development projects and donations to allow a group of indigenous people of the Dominican Republic to buy their land from the government and preserve their unique way of life.

Mohair Council of America
233 West Twohig
PO Box 5337
San Angelo, TX 76902
800-583-3161
www.mohairusa.com

The Mohair Council of America is a nonprofit organization that assists mohair growers and promotes and markets mohair.

Under the Canopy
1141 South Rogers Circle
Suite 7
Boca Raton, FL 33487
888-226-6799
www.underthecanopy.com

Under the Canopy's mission is to make a positive impact on the future of the planet, creating a product line that utilizes the earth's resources in an ecofriendly, sustainable manner.

Wool Traditions
HC78 Box 10731
Ranchos De Taos, NM 87557
800-665-9786
www.wooltraditions.org

Wool Traditions is a nonprofit center dedicated to building and maintaining the local wool trade through sustainable agriculture. They seek to educate people about and support the cultural traditions of the indigenous people of that area—the Hispanic, Pueblo, and Dine (Navajo).

Disaster Relief

American Red Cross Disaster Services
2025 E Street NW
Washington, DC 20006
202-303-4498
www.redcross.org/services/disaster

American Red Cross Disaster Services
focuses on meeting people's immediate
emergency disaster-caused needs.
Their Web site has information on
how to prepare for and cope with a
variety of disasters.

Humane Society of the United States
    Disaster Services Program
www.hsus.org/ace/18730

The HSUS Disaster Services Program
has online information on how to protect animals from disaster and prepare
for your animals' needs in case of a
disaster.

Energy

American Solar Energy Society (ASES)
2400 Central Avenue
Suite G-1
Boulder, CO 80301
303-443-3130
www.ases.org

The American Solar Energy Society is
a nongovernmental branch of the
International Solar Energy Society. It
serves to expand and promote the use
of solar energy, to provide information, and to educate through confer-
ences and literature. Additionally,
ASES has created the Solar Action Network.

Energy Federation Incorporated
40 Washington Street
Suite 200
Westborough, MA 01581-1013
508-870-2277
www.efi.org

Energy Federation promotes the use of
energy-conserving products and
makes these products available to consumers and businesses.

Public Citizen's Critical Mass Energy
    Project
1600 20th Street NW
Washington, DC 20009
202-588-1000
www.citizen.org/cmep

Public Citizen's Critical Mass Energy
Project is dedicated to creating policies that will protect against the dangers of nuclear power and developing
and supporting environmentally
sound energy use.

Renewable Energy Policy Project &
   CREST (Center for Renewable
   Energy & Sustainable Technology)
1612 K Street NW
Suite 202
Washington, DC 20006
202-293-2898
www.crest.org

The Center for Renewable Energy &
Sustainable Technology is a nonprofit
organization dedicated to the
increased use of renewable energy,
specializing in the development of
renewable energy policies and distribution of information.

Farming

Ecological Farming Association
406 Main Street
Suite 313
Watsonville, CA 95076
831-763-2111
www.eco-farm.org

The Ecological Farming Association is
a nonprofit organization that educates
people all over the world about organic
farming and sustainable agriculture.

Heifer Project International
PO Box 8058
Little Rock, AR 72203
800-422-0474
www.heifer.org

This organization uses donations to
provide animals and training to poor
families in communities around the
world. By providing families with the
means to raise food, the organization
helps communities develop income
sources to improve standards of living.
The Heifer Project also trains farmers
in these communities, teaching them
sustainable agriculture techniques.

Organic Consumers Association
6101 Cliff Estate Road
Little Marais, MN 55614
218-226-4164
www.organicconsumers.org

This nonprofit organization is dedicated to promoting sustainable agriculture, ending the use of genetically
modified food crops, working with the
environment, and increasing organic
agriculture.

Fibers

Hohenstein Institute
Schloss Hohenstein
D 74357 Boennigheim
Germany
+49 7143/271-0
www.hohenstein.de/englisch/kurz2.htm

The Hohenstein Institute is a research
center for textiles. They do consulting
and testing for harmful substances in
textiles.

North American Industrial Hemp
   Council
PO Box 259329
Madison, WI 53725-9329
www.naihc.org

The North American Industrial Hemp
Council is a nonprofit organization
dedicated to increasing the use of
industrial hemp through education,
research, and development. It seeks to
educate consumers and the industry at
large on the many uses and advantages
of industrial hemp.

Organic Fiber Council
PO Box 547
Greenfield, MA 01302
413-774-7511
www.ota.com

The Organic Fiber Council is the
organic fiber voice of the Organic
Trade Association. The OFC educates
consumers and suppliers on many
aspects of the organic fiber trade, dealing with cotton, wool, and other
organic fibers.

United Nations Development Fund for
   Women (UNIFEM)
304 East 45th Street
15th Floor
New York, NY 10017
www.unifem.org
212-906-6400

UNIFEM is an international nonprofit
organization that assists and supports
women's rights, improves their economic standards, and achieves equal
rights. The women weavers of East
Timor are one of many groups aided
by UNIFEM.

General Environment and Nature

American Bamboo Society
750 Krumkill Road
Albany, NY 12203-5976
www.bamboo.org

The American Bamboo Society is dedicated to the preservation and propagation of bamboo species; it provides
research support and education about
bamboo.

International Wildlife Rehabilitation
   Council (IWRC)
PO Box 8187
San Jose, CA 95155
408-271-2685
www.iwrc-online.org

The International Wildlife Rehabilitation Council provides training and
certification for wildlife rehabilitators.

National Fire Protection Association
1 Batterymarch Park
Quincy, MA 02169-7471
617-770-3000
www.nfpa.org

The National Fire Protection Association is an international nonprofit organization and clearinghouse of fire prevention information. Additionally, the organization works to establish fire codes and to educate and train in all aspects of fire prevention.

Natural Resources Defense Council
40 West 20th Street
New York, NY 10011
212-727-2700
www.nrdc.org

The Natural Resources Defense Council is a worldwide environmental action organization involved in both action and policymaking on issues as far-reaching as sustainability, global economic fairness, nuclear monitoring, water and coastal protection, environmental health issues, and more.

Nature Conservancy
4245 North Fairfax Drive
Suite 100
Arlington, VA 22203-1606
703-841-5300
www.nature.org

The Nature Conservancy's mission is to preserve the plants, animals, and natural communities that represent the diversity of life on earth by protecting the lands and waters they need to survive.

Sierra Club
85 Second Street
2nd Floor
San Francisco, CA 94105
415-977-5500
www.sierraclub.org

The Sierra Club works both locally and nationally to observe, educate about, and lobby for environmental and political issues, including clean water programs, wildlands preservation, and an end to commercial logging.

Pest Control

Beyond Pesticides
701 E Street SE, #200
Washington, DC 20003
202-543-5450
www.beyondpesticides.org

Beyond Pesticides works with allies in protecting public health and the environment to lead the transition to a world free of toxic pesticides.

Bio-Integral Resource Center (BIRC)
PO Box 7414
Berkeley, CA 94707
510-524-2567
www.birc.org

The Bio-Integral Resource Center (BIRC) specializes in finding nontoxic and least-toxic integrated pest management (IPM) solutions to urban and agricultural pest problems.

Neem Foundation
www.neemfoundation.org

The Neem Foundation is the center of all neem movements around the world and is supported by leading scientists and environmentalists who are involved in neem-related research.

Northwest Coalition for Alternatives
   to Pesticides
PO Box 1393
Eugene, OR 97440-1393
541-344-5044
www.pesticide.org

The Northwest Coalition for Alternatives to Pesticides works to protect people and the environment by advancing healthy solutions to pest problems.

Pets

The American Society for the Prevention of Cruelty to Animals (ASPCA)
424 East 92nd Street
New York, NY 10128-6804
212-876-7700
www.aspca.org

The American Society for the Prevention of Cruelty to Animals works to provide effective means for the prevention of cruelty to animals throughout the United States. They offer national programs in humane education, public awareness, government advocacy, shelter support, and animal medical services and placement.

Recycling

National Recycling Coalition, Inc.
   (NRC)
1325 G Street NW
Suite 1025
Washington, DC 20005
202-347-0450
www.nrc-recycle.org

The National Recycling Coalition represents the diverse interests that are dedicated to maximizing recycling to achieve the benefits of resource conservation, solid waste reduction, environmental protection, energy conservation, and social and economic development.

Toxics Information

Environmental Working Group
1436 U Street NW
Suite 100
Washington, DC 20009
202-667-6982
www.ewg.org

Arsenic testing kits are available from
the Environmental Working Group,
which is a team of scientists, engi-
neers, policy experts, lawyers, and
computer programmers who pore over
government data, legal documents, scientific studies, and laboratory tests to
expose threats to your health and the
environment and to find solutions.

Healthy Building Network
927 15th Street NW
4th Floor
Washington, DC 20005
202-898-1610
www.healthybuilding.net

The Healthy Building Network focuses
on ways in which careful selection of
building materials can reduce environmental health threats of toxic chemical
emissions.

International Programme on Chemical
    Safety (IPCS INCHEM)
www.inchem.org

Through IPCS INCHEM, one can
access internationally peer-reviewed
information on chemicals commonly
used throughout the world.

International Toxicity Estimates for
    Risk Database (ITER)
2300 Montana Avenue
Suite 409
Cincinnati, OH 45211
513-542-7475
www.tera.org/iter

The International Toxicity Estimates
for Risk Database is a free Internet
database of human health risk values
for more than 600 chemicals of environmental concern from several organizations worldwide.

Scorecard
Environmental Defense
1875 Connecticut Avenue NW
Suite 600
Washington, DC 20009
800-684-3322
www.scorecard.org

Scorecard is a resource for information
about pollution problems and toxic
chemicals. They offer information
about the pollution problems by
community.

Toxicology Excellence for Risk
    Assessment (TERA)
2300 Montana Avenue
Suite 409
Cincinnati, OH 45211
513-542-7475
www.tera.org

Toxicology Excellence for Risk Assessment (TERA) is a nonprofit corporation dedicated to the best use of
toxicity data for risk assessment.
TERA maintains the ITER chemical
database.

Water

American Rivers
1025 Vermont Avenue NW
Suite 720
Washington, DC 20005
202-347-7550
www.amrivers.org

American Rivers is a nonprofit organization dedicated to the conservation of
America's rivers through education,
awareness, and practical hands-on
work on both the national and grassroots levels.

American Water Resources Association
4 West Federal Street
PO Box 1626
Middleburg, VA 20118-1626
540-687-8390
www.awra.org

The American Water Resources
Association is a nonprofit association
exploring water resources and their
management, through research, community involvement, and education.

American Water Works Association
    (AWWA)
6666 West Quincy Avenue
Denver, CO 80235
800-926-7337
www.awwa.org

The American Water Works Association is a nonprofit organization dedicated to improving the quality and
supply of drinking water. AWWA is
actively involved in ongoing research
and technology development as well
as water-conservation education for
the individual consumer.

National Ground Water Association
    (NGWA)
601 Dempsey Road
Westerville, OH 43081
800-551-7379
www.ngwa.org

The National Ground Water Association is a nonprofit organization dedicated to the protection of ground
water resources through education,
research, and political action.

NSF International, The Public Health
and Safety Company
PO Box 130140
789 North Dixboro Road
Ann Arbor, MI 48113-0140
800-673-6275
www.nsf.org

The National Sanitation Foundation
develops national standards for public
health and safety, providing consumer
information on topics such as rainwater collection, water treatment,
and more.

Oceana
2501 M Street NW
Suite 300
Washington, DC 20037-1311
800-862-3260
www.oceana.org

Oceana is an international nonprofit
organization dedicated to saving the
world's oceans through education,
political and legal action, science, and
research.

Wildlife

National Wildlife Federation
11100 Wildlife Center Drive
Reston, VA 20190-5362
800-822-9919
www.nwf.org

The National Wildlife Federation is a
charitable organization actively
involved in conservation and education. They are dedicated to protecting
wildlife and wildlands through practical and political action.

World Wildlife Fund
1250 24th Street NW
Washington, DC 20037-1175
202-293-4800
www.panda.org

The World Wildlife Fund is an international organization with a six-prong
conservation program (global warming, sustainable forestry practices,
water conservation, endangered
species, threatened species, and toxic
environment issues). The WWF
researches, educates about, lobbies for,
and helps create worldwide policy for
conservation of the earth.

Window Shades/Quilts

Sustainable Village
717 Poplar Avenue
Boulder, CO 80304
888-317-1600
www.thesustainablevillage.com

Sustainable Village carries a line of
low-e window films and heat/UV ray
blocking shades. They work in developing countries to provide renewable
energy solutions. Note: Access to their
products may be limited to those in
developing countries.

Wood

American Bamboo Society
750 Krumkill Road
Albany, NY 12203-5976
www.bamboo.org

The American Bamboo Society is dedicated to the preservation and propagation of bamboo species; it provides research support and education about bamboo.

Forest Stewardship Council—US
1155 30th Street NW
Suite 300
Washington, DC 20007
202-342-0413
www.fscus.org

The Forest Stewardship Council—US certifies forest products so that the wood they have certified has been harvested in a way that protects biological diversity and is conservation-conscious. Additionally, this body certifies that the land used for harvesting has been obtained in a way that respects the rights of indigenous people.

SmartWood
The Rainforest Alliance
665 Broadway
Suite 500
New York, NY 10012
888-693-2784
www.smartwood.org

SmartWood is a certification program for forest products. It is a part of the nonprofit Rainforest Alliance and certifies that wood has been harvested using sustainable forestry practices that work to protect biodiversity.

Products

Air Purifiers and Ionizers

Aller Air Industries
888-852-8247
www.allerair.com

A wide selection of air purifiers utilizing both HEPA and mass-activated carbon bed filters in many styles and sizes.

AllOrganic
591 Ulalena Loop
Haiku, HI 96708
877-864-4793
www.ionizers.org

Air ionizers and air purifiers.

Aprilaire
608-257-8801
www.aprilaire.com

A large array of indoor air-quality products, including several air cleaners. Dealer locations are available via phone or Web site.

Bionaire
The Holmes Group, Inc.
32B Spur Drive
El Paso, TX 79906
800-788-5350
www.bionaire.com

Air purifiers, air cleaners, and a range
of air filters.

Gaiam, Inc.
360 Interlocken Boulevard
Suite 300
Broomfield, CO 80021
877-989-6321
www.gaiam.com

Air purifiers and air filters as well as a
car ionizer.

Green Home
850 24th Avenue
San Francisco, CA 94121
877-282-6400
www.greenhome.com

Air purifiers and air ionizers.

Lifekind Products, Inc.
PO Box 1774
Grass Valley, CA 95945
800-284-4983
www.lifekind.com

Air purifiers and a variety of HEPA air
filters.

Alternative Toilets and Graywater Recycling

Architerra Enterprises, Inc.
0186 SCR 1400 BRR
Silverthorne, CO 80498
800-563-9720
www.thenaturalhome.com

Graywater recycling systems and
composting toilets for residential use;
also plans and consultations for new
homes and retrofitting projects.

Clivus Multrum, Inc.
15 Union Street
Lawrence, MA 01840
800-425-4887
www.clivusmultrum.com

Natural, sustainable solutions for the
conservation of water and soil through
the development and distribution of
composting toilets and graywater systems.

Envirolet
Sancor Industries
Canadian Distribution Centre
140-30 Milner Avenue
Toronto, ON MIS 3R3
Canada
800-387-5126
www.envirolet.com

Variety of composting toilets.

Architecture

Ecological Design Institute
PO Box 989
Sausalito, CA 94966
415-332-5806
www.ecodesign.org

EDI and Van der Ryn Architects create innovative design solutions that link nature, culture, and technology.

Aromatherapy and Essential Oils

Amrita Aromatherapy
1900 West Stone Avenue
Fairfield, IA 52556
800-410-9651
www.amrita.net

Essential oils, some organically grown, some wildcrafted, some ethically harvested.

AromaLand
1326 Rufina Circle
Santa Fe, NM 87507
800-933-5267
www.aromaland.com

Essential oils, some of which are organic or wildcrafted.

Camden-Grey Essential Oils
3591 Northwest 82nd Avenue
Miami, FL 33122
305-500-9630
www.essentialoil.net

Organic essential oils, herbs, etc.

Essential Aura Aromatics
3070 B Barons Road
Nanaimo, BC V9T 4B5
Canada
250-758-9464
www.essentialaura.com

Organic essential oils; actively involved in eco-agriculture and supports responsible farming and education.

Frontier Natural Products Co-op
PO Box 299
3021 78th Street
Norway, IA 52318
800-669-3275
www.frontiercoop.com

Wide variety of natural and organic products. They sell the Aura Cacia line of essential oils, which includes organic essential oils.

Greenfeet.com
1360 East 1st Avenue
Chico, CA 95926
888-562-8873
www.greenfeet.com

Aromatherapy products, such as essential oils, carrier oils, and diffusers, and other natural products.

Merz Apothecary
4716 North Lincoln Avenue
Chicago, IL 60625
800-252-0275
www.smallflower.com

Natural products include essential oils, carrier oils, diffusers, and candles for aromatherapy.

Nature's Gift Aromatherapy Products
314 Old Hickory Boulevard East
Madison, TN 37115
615-612-4270
www.naturesgift.com

Supplier of pure essential oils, most organically grown or ethically wildcrafted. Purity tests are currently available on many of their products.

Stony Mountain Botanicals
155 North Water Street
Loudonville, OH 44842
888-994-4857
www.wildroots.com

Organic essential oils, herbs, and supplements.

Vermont Soapworks
616 Exchange Street
Middlebury, VT 05753
866-SOAP-4U2 (762-7482)
www.vermontsoap.com

Vermont Soap Organics was created to produce healthy, nontoxic alternatives to the often irritating chemical and detergent bases used today. They make very special bar soaps, liquid soaps, bath and shower gels, nontoxic cleaners, and more.

Young Living Essential Oils
Thanksgiving Point Business Park
3125 Executive Parkway
Lehi, UT 84043
800-371-2928
www.youngliving.us

Cultivates, distills, and sells organically grown essential oils; actively involved in research and education regarding the benefits of essential oils.

Backyard Play Equipment

Burke
PO Box 549
Fond du Lac, WI 54936
920-921-9220
www.bciburke.com

Backyard play equipment made from 95 percent recycled materials.

CedarWorks
799 Commercial Street
PO Box 990
Rockport, ME 04856
800-462-3327
www.cedarworks.com

Swing sets made from chemical-free
and splinter-free white cedar.

ChildLife
800-467-9464
www.childlife.com

Play equipment is made from nonarse-
nate, non–chemically treated wood.

Bath Linens

EcoChoices
PO Box 1491
Glendora, CA 91740
626-969-3707
www.ecochoices.com

Natural home products, including
organic cotton towels and hemp
shower curtains.

Heart of Vermont
PO Box 612
131 South Main Street
Barre, VT 05641
800-639-4123
www.heartofvermont.com

Organic bedding and linens; furniture,
mattresses, etc.

Lifekind Products, Inc.
PO Box 1774
Grass Valley, CA 95945
800-284-4983
www.lifekind.com

Provides information and products to
help reduce daily exposures to unnecessary and hazardous chemicals.

Native Organic Cotton
180 Standard Street
El Segundo, CA 90245
800-766-7454
www.nativeorganic.com

Organic home furnishings manufactured from the raw cotton fiber to the
finished item.

Rawganique.com
9000 Rayelyn Lane
Denman Island, BC V0R 1T0
Canada
877-729-4367
www.rawganique.com

Full line of organic hemp products for
the home, including hemp shower
curtains, towels, bath mats, soaps, and
scrubbing cloths.

Bedding

ABC Home
888 Broadway
New York, NY 10003
212-473-3000
www.abchome.com

ABC Home carries an extensive line of organic bedding.

Abundant Earth
762 West Park Avenue
Port Townsend, WA 98368
888-513-2784
www.abundantearth.com

Hemp and flax throws, buckwheat pillows, and assorted organic bed linens.

Allergy Buyers Club
486 Totten Pond Road
Waltham, MA 02451
888-236-7231
www.allergybuyersclub.com

Bedroom furniture with nontoxic lacquers and sealants; also wool, down, and silk pillows and comforters, allergy-free bed linens, and comforters and pillows made with Syriaca down.

American Sheep Industry Association
9785 Maroon Circle
Suite 360
Centennial, CO 80112
303-771-3500
www.sheepusa.org

Educates consumers, growers, and manufacturers of wool and wool products and promotes and improves the marketing of wool and wool products.

A Natural Home
PO Box 21
Fredericktown, OH 43019
740-694-HOME (694-4663)
www.anaturalhome.com

A Natural Home is a family-run company that works with the Amish to manufacture organic cotton innerspring and 100 percent natural latex mattresses.

Coyuchi, Inc.
PO Box 845
Point Reyes Station, CA 94956
888-418-8847
www.coyuchi.com

Organic sheets, duvet covers, blankets, and baby bedding. The cotton used meets the standards of the International Federation of Organic Agriculture Movements.

EcoChoices
PO Box 1491
Glendora, CA 91740
626-969-3707
www.ecochoices.com

Environmentally sound products for the home, such as custom-ordered chemical-free mattresses made with organic cotton and wool, natural latex, and sustainable wood frames. They have bedding in organic cotton and Pure Grow Wool—wool that is raised and harvested with no bleach, formaldehyde, or dyes and is cruelty free.

Gaiam, Inc.
360 Interlocken Boulevard
Suite 300
Broomfield, CO 80021
877-989-6321
www.gaiam.com

Products designed to create a healthy, holistic lifestyle; product line includes a wide range of organic and allergy-control bedding.

Garnet Hill, Inc.
231 Main Street
Franconia, NH 03580
800-870-3513
www.garnethill.com

Natural fiber products, including bedding.

Heart of Vermont
PO Box 612
131 South Main Street
Barre, VT 05641
800-639-4123
www.heartofvermont.com

Organic cotton and wool bedding, including mattresses, sheets, blankets, pillows, comforters, futons, and pajamas; some organic baby bedding.

H3Environmental Corporation
12439 Magnolia Boulevard
Box #263
Valley Village, CA 91607
818-766-1787
www.h3environmental.com

The H3 Environmental Corporation seeks to provide its clients with the highest-quality products and services so that they may create healthy, nurturing homes, an improved quality of life, and a respectful, harmonious relationship with nature.

Lifekind Products, Inc.
PO Box 1774
Grass Valley, CA 95945
800-284-4983
www.lifekind.com

Natural and organic mattresses and bedding, including natural rubber mattresses, organic wool and cotton linens and mattresses, and organic baby bedding.

Nirvana Safe Haven
3441 Golden Rain Road
Suite 3
Walnut Creek, CA 94595
800-968-9355
www.nontoxic.com

Organic cotton and wool mattresses, futons, and adjustable beds as well as chemical-free furniture and organic bed linens and pillows.

Organic Cotton Alternatives
3120 Central Avenue SE
Albuquerque, NM 87106
888-645-4452
www.organiccottonalts.com

Organic cotton bedding, including mattresses and sheets; organic wool, buckwheat, and kapok pillows; organic baby bedding; also wooden bed frames that can be ordered without an oil finish for those who have chemical sensitivities.

Rawganique.com
9000 Rayelyn Lane
Denman Island, BC VOR 1TO
Canada
877-729-4367
www.rawganique.com

Hemp futons and a variety of organic bedding.

Shepherd's Dream
140 South 11th Street
Montague, CA 96064
800-966-5540
www.shepherdsdream.com

Wool mattresses, mattress toppers, comforters, and pillows.

White Lotus Home
191 Hamilton Street
New Brunswick, NJ 08901
877-HAND MADE (426-3623)
www.whitelotus.net

White Lotus manufactures futons with a company mission devoted to taking care of their customers, their employees, and the planet.

Beer, Wine, Chocolate, and Coffee

Avalon Organic Coffees
Victor Allen's Coffee, LLC
1101 Moasis Drive
Little Chute, WI 54140
800-394-5282
www.victorallen.com

Organic, shade-grown, fair-trade coffees.

Butte Creek Brewing Company
945 West 2nd Street
Chico, CA 95928
530-894-7906
www.buttecreek.com

Organic beers and ales.

Café Habitat, Inc.
7 Old South Street
Northampton, MA 01060
413-586-1045

Organic, shade-grown, fair-trade coffees.

Chartrand Imports
PO Box 1319
Rockland, ME 04841
800-473-7307
www.chartrandimports.com

Wines that are certified organically
grown by an independent third party;
offer several wines that are made with
no added sulfur as well as a full line of
organic, low-sulfite wines.

Dagoba Organic Chocolate Company
1105 Benson Way
Ashland, OR 99520
800-393-6075
www.dagobachocolate.com

Organic chocolate.

Dean's Beans
50 Moore Avenue
Orange, MA 01364
800-325-3008
www.deansbeans.com

Organic, fair-trade coffees.

Equal Exchange, Inc.
50 United Drive
West Bridgewater, MA 02379
774-776-7400
www.equalexchange.com

Equal Exchange is the oldest and
largest for-profit fair trade company in
the United States, offering gourmet
coffee, tea, sugar, cocoa, and chocolate
bars.

Frontier Natural Products Co-Op
PO Box 299
3021 78th Street
Norway, IA 52318
800-669-3275
www.frontiercoop.com

Organic teas, herbs, spices, and
kitchen accessories.

Green & Black's
2 Valentine Place
London, England SE1 8QH
401-683-3323
www.greenandblacks.com

Organic, shade-grown, fair-trade
chocolates.

Green Mountain Coffee Roasters, Inc.
33 Coffee Lane
Waterbury, VT 05676
888-TRY-GMCR (879-4627)
www.greenmountaincoffee.com

A socially responsible company that
roasts high-quality coffees, including
organic coffees, from around the
world.

Ithaca Fine Chocolates
125 Heights Court
Ithaca, NY 14850
607-257-7954
www.ithacafinechocolates.com

Organic chocolate; percentage of proceeds go to art programs for children.

Organic Coffee Company
1933 Davis Street
Suite 308
San Leandro, CA 94577
888-829-8886
www.organiccoffeecompany.com

All Organic Coffee Company coffees
are grown without pesticides, herbicides, or chemical fertilizers.

Organic Wine Company
888-326-9463
www.ecowine.com

Sells wines that are organic and made
with no sulfate and no spray.

Organic Wine Press
175 2nd Street
Bandon, OR 97411
541-347-3326
www.organicwinepress.com

Wines that are organic or no-spray,
and wines that have no sulfites added.

Wolavers
Otter Creek Brewing
793 Exchange Street
Middlebury, VT 05753
800-473-0727
www.wolavers.com

Organic ales, beers, and stout.

Blessing Herbs

Houseblessings.com
4507 Cory Place
Las Vegas, NV 89107
www.houseblessings.com

Houseblessings.com carries a house-
blessing kit, garden-blessing kit, and
an office-blessing kit.

Buckwheat Pillows

Lang Co/Makura Pillows
12882 Joy Street
Suite K
Garden Grove, CA 92840-6321
800-777-5264
www.makura.com

Buckwheat hull pillows in several
sizes and shapes.

Northern Naturals
Box 1182 Main Street
Middletown Springs, VT 05757
888-293-3985
www.northernnaturals.com

Organic buckwheat hull pillows in
organic cotton covers.

Candles

Abundant Earth
762 West Park Avenue
Port Townsend, WA 98368
888-513-2784
www.abundantearth.com

Vegetable wax, beeswax, and aromatherapy candles.

Blossomland Supply
999 West Front Street
Buchanan, MI 49107
269-695-2310
www.blossomland.com

Beeswax candles as well as bulk
beeswax and other candle-making
supplies.

Bluecorn Naturals
PO Box 122
Rico, CO 81332
888-350-4929
www.beeswaxcandles.com

Pure beeswax, soy wax, palm wax, and
vegetable wax candles.

Colonial Soap and Candle Factory
150 Route 193
Deblois, ME 04622
207-638-2073
www.soapcandlefactory.com

Soy candles, some scented with
organic essential oils.

Dakota Prairie Products
208 Dakota Avenue S
Huron, SD 57350
605-353-7694

Aromatherapy soy wax candles and
herbal hemp oil soaps.

Da Mater Unlimited
404-636-0029
www.damaterunlimited.com

Organic beeswax candles in a variety
of unique shapes and sizes.

Ditto Candles
256 Private Road 8571
Winnsboro, TX 75494
800-346-7221
www.dittocandles.com

Soy wax candles in many scents.

Greenfeet.com
1360 East 1st Avenue
Chico, CA 95926
888-562-8873
www.greenfeet.com

Beeswax and vegetable wax candles.

Tao Arts
PO Box 578248
Chicago, IL 60657
877-826-2787
www.taoarts.com

Organic beeswax candles.

Carbon Monoxide Detectors

First Alert
800-323-9005
www.firstalert.com

Home safety devices including a line
of carbon monoxide detectors.

Kidde Safety
1394 South Third Street
Mebane, NC 27302
www.kiddeus.com

Carbon monoxide detectors including
the Kidde Nighthawk.

Positive Energy Conservation Products
The Green Builders Catalog
PO Box 7568
Boulder, CO 80306
800-488-4340
www.positive-energy.com

The latest in Green Building technology. Their catalog includes carbon
monoxide monitors and alarms.

Carpets—Natural

Earth Weave Carpet Mills, Inc.
PO Box 6120
Dalton, GA 30722
706-278-8200
www.earthweave.com

Manufactures and promotes renewable
resource floor coverings.

Fibrework Corporation
1729 Research Drive
Louisville, KY 40299
800-843-0063
www.fibreworks.com

Sells natural fiber floor and wall
coverings.

Nature's Carpet
1428 West 7th Avenue
Vancouver, BC V6H 1C1
Canada
800-667-5001
www.naturescarpet.com

100 percent natural, biodegradable,
and ultra-low-toxicity floor coverings
for health and comfort.

Chime Alarm Clocks

Now & Zen, Inc.
1638 Pearl Street
Boulder, CA 80302
800-779-6383
www.now-zen.com

Progressive chime alarm clocks and digital clocks.

Cleaning Supplies—Natural

The Clean Environment Company
8609 "I" Street
Omaha, NE 68127
800-266-2353
www.cleanenvironmentco.com

An extensive line of ecofriendly cleaning products.

Dr. Bronner's Magic Soaps
PO Box 28
Escondido, CA 92033
760-743-2211
www.drbronner.com

Pure castile and plant oil–based liquid and bar soaps with a wide range of uses. Some of these soaps are now organic.

Earth Essentials, Inc.
PO Box 40339
Santa Barbara, CA 93140
800-347-5211
www.goturtle.com

Life Tree line of highly concentrated, natural, and biodegradable cleaners.

Earth Friendly Products (Ecos)
44 Green Bay Road
Winnetka, IL 60093
800-335-3267
www.ecos.com

Nontoxic, plant-based cleaners.

Ecover, Inc.
PO Box 911058
Commerce, CA 90091-1058
800-449-4925
www.ecover.com

Natural, nontoxic, biodegradable cleaning products.

Seventh Generation
212 Battery Street
Suite A
Burlington, VT 05401-5281
800-456-1191
www.seventhgeneration.com

Extensive line of nontoxic, environmentally safe cleaning products.

Sun & Earth
125 Noble Street
Norristown, PA 19401
800-298-7861
www.sunandearth.com

Natural, nontoxic cleaners made from citrus and coconut oils.

Clothing—Organic

A Happy Planet
209 Kearney Street
San Francisco, CA 94108
888-424-2779
www.ahappyplanet.com

Organic cotton shirts, sweatshirts,
sweatpants, and undergarments for
children and adults.

Birkenstock
PO Box 6140
Novato, CA 94948
www.birkenstock.com

Sandals and shoes manufactured in an
energy-efficient factory with practices
that include recycling the water used
in production and using water-based
glues.

Ecolution
PO Box 697
Santa Cruz, CA 95061
800-973-4367

Hemp shoes, boots, and bags.

Eileen Fisher
www.eileenfisher.com

Beautiful fabrics are an essential element of Eileen Fisher clothing. The
fabrics are resilient and easy to care
for, and they travel well.

Feeling Goods
5511 Keybridge Drive
Boise, ID 83703
877-349-2102
www.organic-clothing.com

Clothing for women and men in
organic cotton, hemp and hemp/silk
blends, merino wool, and alpaca.

Grass Roots Natural Goods
13 South Linn Street
Suite 9
Iowa City, IA 52240
www.grassrootsnaturalgoods.com

Hemp shoes as well as an extensive
line of women's and men's clothing in
hemp, hemp blends, and organic cotton; also a limited line of baby clothing in organic cotton.

Indigenous Designs
975 Corporate Center Parkway #110
Santa Rosa, CA 95407
707-571-7811
www.indigenousdesigns.com

Clothing for women and men using
organic cotton, wool, alpaca, and natural dyes and produced by workers'
cooperatives and following fair-trade
principles.

Maggie's Functional Organics
306 West Cross Street
Ypsilanti, MI 48197
800-609-8593
www.organicclothes.com

Socks, shirts, and camisoles as well as accessories made from wool, hemp, linen, and organic cotton. Maggie's actively supports fair labor practices and sustainable farming techniques, and products come, in part, from international workers' cooperatives.

Patagonia
8550 White Fir Street
PO Box 32050
Reno, NV 89523-2050
800-638-6464
www.patagonia.com

Sportwear for adults and children, made from organic cotton, wool, and "Synchilla," a fleece made from recycled soda bottles. Original member of the Fair Labor Association, committed to environmental and social action.

Splaff Flopps
PO Box 7604
San Diego, CA 92167-0604
619-221-9199
www.splaff.com

Stylish sandals made from recycled tires, used bike inner tubes, and hemp. Durable and 100 percent recycled sandals that will stand the test of time.

Thirteen Mile Lamb and Wool
   Company
13000 Springhill Road
Belgrade, MT 59714
406-388-4945
www.lambandwool.com

Organic wool hats, sweaters, and scarves.

Under the Canopy
1141 South Rogers Circle
Suite 7
Boca Raton, FL 33487
888-226-6799
www.underthecanopy.com

"Eco-Fashion" line of clothing for children, women, and men, made from innovative organic fibers and fiber blends, such as organic denim, organic cotton blended with angora and organic fibers made from soy and bamboo. Clothing is produced under fair labor practices and without chemicals.

Compasses

Brunton
620 East Monroe Avenue
Riverton, WY 82501
307-856-6559
www.brunton.com

A 100-year-old company that carries a wide selection of compasses.

Silva
Johnson Outdoors
555 Main Street
Racine, WI 53403
800-572-8822
www.silvacompass.com

Variety of compasses at locations throughout the United States.

Cooking Oils

Spectrum Organic Products
5341 Old Redwood Highway
Suite 400
Petaluma, CA 94954
www.spectrumorganics.com

Spectrum Naturals commits itself to working with talented, dedicated people to create the best cooking oil products possible and using processes that are gentle to both the planet and our bodies.

Crafts: Children

A Child's Dream Come True
PO Box 163
Sandpoint, ID 83864
800-359-2906
www.achildsdream.com

Natural crafts, toys, and more.

All Natural Kid Specialty Toy Store
877-314-5437

Products for kids that are made from natural materials; organic stuffed animals and beeswax craft products for kids.

EcoBaby Organics
7550 Miramar Road
Suite 650
San Diego, CA 92126
800-596-7450
www.ecobaby.com

Organic and natural toys, bedding, and clothing.

Green Home
850 24th Avenue
San Francisco, CA 94121
877-282-6400
www.greenhome.com

Natural and sustainable art supplies, such as recycled construction paper; also other ecofriendly toys for kids.

Hugg-A-Planet
7A Morse Drive
Essex Junction, VT 05452
802-878-8900
www.huggaplanet.com

Organic cotton stuffed animals.

NaturalPlay.com
124½ South Main Street
Viroqua, WI 54665
608-637-3989
www.naturalplay.com

Toys that encourage interaction with
nature and the world.

Crystals and Stones

Colorado Gem & Mineral Company
PO Box 424
Tempe, AZ 85280
480-966-6626
www.coloradogem.com

Supplier of crystals and gemstones.

Heaven & Earth, LLC
PO Box 249
965 Route 14 S
East Montpelier, VT 05651
802-476-4775
www.HeavenAndEarthJewelry.com

Extensive catalog of crystals.

Dehumidifiers

Nirvana Safe Haven
3441 Golden Rain Road
Suite 3
Walnut Creek, CA 94595
800-968-9355
www.nontoxic.com

Dehumidifiers and other products that
help create nontoxic and natural
homes and workplaces.

Diapers

Ecobaby Organics
7550 Miramar Road, #650
San Diego, CA 92126
800-596-7450
www.ecobaby.com

Organic diapers, baby clothes, baby
bedding, and more.

Gladrags
PO Box 12648
Portland, OR 97212
800-799-4523
www.gladrags.com

Organic cotton diapers.

Seventh Generation
212 Battery Street
Suite A
Burlington, VT 05401
800-456-1191
www.seventhgeneration.com

Chlorine-free diapers and wipes, plus
a variety of other natural home-care
products.

Disaster Preparedness Kits

American Red Cross
www.redcrossshop.org

Disaster preparedness kits.

Doorknockers

Natural Spaces Store
6401 Macadam Avenue
Portland, OR 97201
877-877-4929
www.naturalspaces.com

Products made from only recycled or natural and sustainable materials; also, doorbells and doorknockers that are made from recycled military hardware.

Dream Catchers

Korczak's Heritage, Inc.
Crazy Horse Memorial
Avenue of the Chiefs
Crazy Horse, SD 57730-9506
605-673-4681
www.korczaksheritage.com

Native American–made arts and crafts items, including dream catchers.

Pueblodirect.com
PO Box 66236
Albuquerque, NM 87193
866-922-8578
www.pueblodirect.com

Native American art, often purchased directly from the Native American artist, including dream catchers.

Dream Pillows

Blessed Maine Herb Farm
257 Chapman Ridge
Athens, ME 04912
207-654-2879
www.blessedmaineherbs.com

Herbs and herbal products, including handcrafted herb-filled dream pillows.

Global Exchange
2017 Mission Street #303
San Francisco, CA 94110
415-255-7296
www.globalexchange.org

Wide range of products made by Native artisans, following fair-trade practices, including Native-made dream pillows by Native Scents.

Dried Herbs, Cones, and Botanicals

Attar Herbs & Spices
21 Playground Road
New Ipswich, NH 03071
603-878-1780
www.attarherbs.com

Attar Herbs & Spices carries an extensive line of botanical products.

Dried Flowers 'R' Us
1761 Goodrich Avenue
Winter Park, FL 32789
888-527-5778
www.driedflowersrus.com

Dried and preserved flowers, ferns,
and foliages.

Greenwood Organics, Inc.
3571 Twin Elm Road
(RR # 2—Richmond)
Ottawa, ON K0A 2Z0
Canada
866-256-8813
www.greenwoodorganics.com

Dried organic herbs and botanicals.

Flooring

Duro-Design Cork and Bamboo
    Flooring
2866 Daniel-Johnson Boulevard
Laval, QC H7P 5Z7
Canada
888-528-8518
www.duro-design.com

Bamboo and cork flooring.

EcoPlanet/EcoChoices
PO Box 1491
Glendora, CA 91740
626-969-3717
www.ecochoices.com

Cork flooring and cork wall tiles as
well as other earth-friendly products
for the home.

Eco-Products
3655 Frontier Avenue
Boulder, CO 80301
303-449-1876
www.ecoproducts.com

Building and office products including
natural flooring, such as natural
linoleum, cork, wool, recycled content, marble, slate, and bamboo.

EcoTimber
1611 Fourth Street
San Rafael, CA 94901
415-258-8454
www.ecotimber.com

Certified ecologically sound hardwood
flooring as well as bamboo and palm
flooring.

The Environmental Home Center
4121 1st Avenue S
Seattle, WA 98134
800-281-9785
www.environmentalhomecenter.com

Green building supplies, including
EcoTimber flooring, salvaged and
reclaimed wood flooring, as well as
cork, bamboo, and natural linoleum.

Hoboken Floors
70 Demarest Drive
Wayne, NJ 07470
800-222-1068
www.hobokenfloors.com

Large variety of flooring, including bamboo, ceramic tile, and hardwood; several locations throughout the Northeast.

Natural Cork
1710 North Leg Court
Augusta, GA 30909
800-404-2675
www.naturalcork.com

Supplier of natural cork flooring and cork wall tiles.

Natural Home
PO Box 1677
Sebastopol, CA 95473
707-571-1229
www.naturalhomeproducts.com

Cork and sustainably harvested hardwood flooring.

Flower Essences

Bach Flower Essences
www.bachflower.com

The original flower essences. Essences, books, and consultations are available through the Web site; Bach remedies are available in most health food stores.

Flower Essence Society
PO Box 459
Nevada City, CA 95959
800-736-9222
www.flowersociety.org

The Flower Essence Society (FES) is an international membership organization of health practitioners, researchers, students, and others interested in deepening knowledge of flower essence therapy. They offer flower essences, books, and publications; also provide training to flower essence practitioners and conduct ongoing research.

Garden of One
60 Thunder Hill Road
Rensselaerville, NY 12147
518-797-3373
www.gardenofone.com

Vibrational essences using plants and crystals in an environmentally conscious and ecologically sound facility.

Flowers— Freshly Cut Organic

Organic Bouquet
242 Redwood Highway
Mill Valley, CA 94941
877-899-2468
www.organicbouquet.com

National distributor of organic cut flowers and fresh organic fruit.

Furniture

Gaiam, Inc.
360 Interlocken Boulevard
Suite 300
Broomfield, CO 80021
877-989-6321
www.gaiam.com

Furniture made from natural and
sustainable materials.

Green Culture
32 Rancho Circle
Lake Forest, CA 92630
877-204-7336
www.eco-furniture.com

Products made from recycled materials, ecologically harvested timber, and
other earth-friendly ingredients.

Green Home
850 24th Avenue
San Francisco, CA 94121
877-282-6400
www.greenhome.com

Sustainable and ecologically sound
furnishings and home accessories.

The Wooden Duck
2919 Seventh Street
Berkeley, CA 94710
510-848-3575
www.thewoodenduck.com

Recycled wood furniture from around
the world.

Gardening Supplies

Abundant Earth
762 West Park Avenue
Port Townsend, WA 98368
888-513-2784
www.abundantearth.com

Composting equipment, houses for
bats, bees, and ladybugs.

Extremely Green Gardening Company
PO Box 2021
Abington, MA 02351
781-878-5397
www.extremelygreen.com

Organic fertilizer, organic lawn care
products, organic soil care, and gardening tools.

Gardener's Supply Company
128 Intervale Road
Burlington, VT 05401
888-833-1412
www.gardeners.com

Outdoor living products, including
organic pest solution (liquid pest control), ladybug hibernation houses, and
mosquito rings.

March Biological
800-328-9140
www.marchbiological.com

Environmentally sound pest control
products and accessories such as bat
houses, mosquito dunks, and sound
lures for mosquito control.

Planet Natural
1612 Gold Avenue
Bozeman, MT 59715
800-289-6656
www.planetnatural.com

Organic gardening supplies, composts
and composting supplies, grow lights,
beneficial insects, natural animal
repellents, and more.

Real Goods/Gaiam, Inc.
360 Interlocken Boulevard
Suite 300
Broomfield, CO 80021-3440
800-762-7325
www.realgoods.com

Outdoor living products including
mulching mowers, mosquito-repelling
devices, an environmentally sound de-
icer, composters, graywater systems,
and rain barrels, buckets made from
recycled tires, and more. A division of
Gaiam.

Gravity Water Filters

Lifekind Products, Inc.
PO Box 1774
Grass Valley, CA 95945
800-284-4983
www.lifekind.com

Gravity water filter system that utilizes
ceramic and carbon filters.

Heirloom and Organic Seeds

Heirloom Seeds
PO Box 245
West Elizabeth, PA 15088-0245
412-384-0852
www.heirloomseeds.com

Heirloom and organic seeds as well as
soil-testing kits, organic fertilizers, and
all-natural deer repellent.

Planet Natural
1612 Gold Avenue
Bozeman, MT 59715
800-289-6656
www.planetnatural.com

Heirloom seeds.

Seed Savers Exchange
3076 North Winn Road
Decorah, IA 52101
563-382-5990
www.seedsavers.org

A nonprofit organization that saves and shares the heirloom seeds of our garden heritage, forming a living legacy that can be passed down through generations.

Seeds of Change
888-762-4240
www.seedsofchange.com

Seeds of Change is a certified organic seed company whose mission is to help preserve biodiversity and promote sustainable agriculture. It specializes in organic seeds, some heirloom seeds, and organic seedlings; also sells composters, beneficial insects, and more; provides extensive information, and publishes an informational newsletter.

Seeds Trust
PO Box 596
Cornville, AZ 86325
928-649-3315
www.seedstrust.com

Teaches seed-saving techniques and is dedicated to sustainable agriculture and increasing agricultural diversity; also sells organic, heirloom, and native seeds.

Home Test Kits

Frandon Lead Alert Kit
Pace Environs, Inc.
120 West Beaver Creek Road
Unit 16
Richmond Hill, ON L4B 1L2
Canada
800-359-9000

Tests are available for determining lead levels in soil, paint, dust, ceramics, utensils, and water.

HybriVet Systems, Inc.
17 Erie Drive
Natick, MA 01760
800-262-LEAD (262-5323)
www.leadcheck.com

Develops, manufactures, and sells self-administered test kits, such as Lead-Test Swabs, to detect lead and other heavy metals in the environment.

Lead Inspector Kit
Michigan Ceramic Supplies, Inc.
4048 Seventh Street
PO Box 342
Wyandotte, MI 48192
800-860-2332

Lead inspector kits.

Hygrometers

The Weather Store
146 Main Street
Sandwich, MA 02563
800-646-1203
www.theweatherstore.com

Weather instruments including hygrometers, barometers, thermometers, and anemometers.

Insect Repellent (Personal)

Bite-Blocker
Homs, LLC
PO Box 724
Clayton, NC 27520
888-270-5721
www.biteblocker.com

All-natural, no-DEET insect repellent.

Burt's Bees
PO Box 13489
Durham, NC 27709
www.burtsbees.com

Variety of beeswax and herbal personal care products, including an all-natural herbal insect repellent.

Buzz Away
Quantum
PO Box 2791
Eugene, OR 97402
800-448-1448
www.quantumhealth.com

Quantum is an herbalist-owned and managed company that ensures the production of the highest-quality tinctures and salves. Their products are used and preferred by health professionals, both alternative and mainstream, in clinical settings in the United States and around the world. They sell all-natural, DEET-free insect repellent, made in several formulas, including a sun-blocking formulation.

Ion-Control Air Conditioners

Sharp Electronics Corporation
Sharp Plaza
Mahwah, NJ 07430-2135
201-529-8200
www.sharpusa.com

Air conditioners that utilize air purification technology through the release of positive and negative ions.

Lanolin

CedarVale Natural Health
866-758-1012
www.cedarvale.net

Oils, herbs, and other personal care products; they offer anhydrous lanolin in 8-ounce, 1-pound, 5-pound, or 20-pound sizes. Lanolin is used in a natural boot waterproofing formula.

Lightbulbs and Light Products

Buylighting.com/SPEEC, Inc.
1436 East Cliff Road
Burnsville, MN 55337
888-990-9933
www.buylighting.com

Natural lighting products including sodium bulbs, full-spectrum bulbs in a range of sizes and shapes, grow lights, etc.

Energy Federation, Inc.
40 Washington Street
Suite 2000
Westborough, MA 01581-1013
800-876-0660
www.efi.org

Promotes the use of energy-conserving products and sells to consumers and businesses.

Environmental Lighting Concepts
PO Box 172425
Tampa, FL 33672-0425
800-842-8848
www.ottlite.com

Natural light supplements in the form of natural lightbulbs in a variety of sizes and shapes; natural light lamps and light boxes.

Green Seal's Choose Green Report on
   Compact Fluorescent Lighting
1001 Connecticut Avenue NW
Suite 827
Washington, DC 20036
202-872-6400
www.greenseal.org/recommenda-
   tions.htm

Green Seal is an independent, non-profit organization that strives to achieve a healthier and cleaner environment by identifying and promoting products and services that cause less toxic pollution and waste, conserve resources and habitats, and minimize global warming and ozone depletion.

Sundance Solar
PO Box 10
2 East Main Street
Warner, NH 03278
603-456-2020
www.sundancesolar.com

Solar energy products, rechargeable batteries, battery chargers, solar battery chargers, solar panels, educational kits, and solar gifts.

True Sun
1803 Hamilton Place
Steubenville, OH 43952
877-878-3786
www.truesun.com

Light products, including sunshine simulators, dawn/dusk simulators, light boxes, and full-spectrum incandescent and fluorescent bulbs.

Verilux
Research Park
9 Viaduct Road
Stamford, CT 06907
800-786-6850
www.verilux.net

Natural and full-spectrum bulbs, sunshine simulators, and lamps.

Lunar Calendars

Celestial Products, Inc.
PO Box 801
Middleburg, VA 20118-0801
800-235-3783
www.celestialproducts.com

Lunar calendars, star charts, and more.

Magnetic Water Filter Systems

AquaDoc.com
3514 Smith Avenue
Biggs, CA 95917
800-929-7638
www.aquadoc.com

Water treatment systems including magnetic filters.

Raindance Water Systems
PO Box 2312
Ramona, CA 92065
877-788-8387
www.magneticwatersystems.com

Magnetic water filters and whole-house water treatment systems.

Menstrual Products

Gladrags
Keepers! Inc.
PO Box 12648
Portland, OR 97212
800-799-4523
www.gladrags.com

Gladrags makes reusable organic cotton pads, liners, and holders.

Lunapads International
207 West 6th Avenue
Vancouver, BC V5Y 1K7
Canada
888-590-2299
www.lunapads.com

Organic cotton unbleached tampons, cotton fleece reusable pads, and a variety of other menstrual products.

Natracare
14901 East Hampden Avenue
Suite 190
Aurora, CO 80014
303-617-3476
www.natracare.com

All-natural choice in menstrual products made from certified organic cotton without the use of synthetics, additives, or chlorine bleaches.

Mineral-Based Cleaning Products

Crane Creek Gardens
EARTH-KIND, Inc.
17 3rd Avenue SE
Stanley, ND 58784
701-628-1310
www.cranecreekgardens.com

Provider of Fresh Cab odor-absorbing products.

The Dial Corporation
877-733-5845
www.thedialstore.com

Boraxois is a unique blend of borax and powdered soap manufactured by Dial Corporation and is widely available in grocery stores.

Nature's Odor & Germ Control, Inc.
1521 North Jantzen Avenue, #135
Portland, OR 97217-8100
888-884-6367
www.nogc.com

Odor removing/odor neutralizing products that use zeolite.

Orange Glo International
800-781-7529
www.greatcleaners.com

Sells Oxi-Clean, an oxygen bleach product that contains sodium percarbonate as well as soda ash.

Mold Prevention

B-Dry Waterproofing Systems, Inc.
888-879-0088
www.bdry.com

Waterproofing business with offices located in several states; provides complete basement waterproofing.

Eco-Wares, Inc.
866-874-8070
www.eco-wares.com

Environmentally safe residential, commercial, and industrial building and maintenance supplies.

Mold Removal

Nature's Odor & Germ Control, Inc.
1521 North Jantzen Avenue, #135
Portland, OR 97217-8100
888-884-6367
www.nogc.com

Nontoxic, odorless products designed to naturally kill mold and mildew.

Natural Wreaths

Four Gates
26910 North 144th Street
Department WS
Scottsdale, AZ 85262
888-232-7414
www.fourgates.com

Four Gates sells natural wreaths and sconces, along with other products that promote health and wellness.

Neem Oil

Aurora Silk
5806 North Vancouver Avenue
Portland, OR 97217
503-286-4149
www.aurorasilk.com

Aurora Silk, producers of peace silk, also sells organic neem oil. This company works with natives of the Dominican Republic in economic development projects.

Golden Harvest Organics
404 North Impala Drive
Fort Collins, CO 80521
970-224-4679

Golden Harvest carries neem oil as well as heirloom seeds, beneficial insects, and natural insect repellents.

Odor-Absorbing Products

Crane Creek Gardens
EARTH-KIND, Inc.
17 Third Avenue SE
Stanley, ND 58784
800-583-2921
www.cranecreekgardens.com

Crane Creek Gardens sells all-natural odor-absorbing and scented products, such as the Fresh Cab and Prairie Air pouches

Office Paper

Ecopaper.com
PO Box 3458
Ventura, CA 93006
805-652-1787
www.ecopaper.com

Ecopaper carries recycled paper and paper from natural materials (coffee, banana fiber, etc.)

Living Tree Paper Company
1430 Willamette Street
Suite 367
Eugene, OR 97401
800-309-2974
www.livingtreepaper.com

Living Tree carries writing papers made from nonwood fibers and post-consumer waste.

Office Supplies

Eco-Products, Inc.
3655 Frontier Avenue
Boulder, CO 80304
303-449-1876
www.ecoproducts.com

Eco-Products carries recycled office supplies.

Organic Silk

Aurora Silk (Peace Silk)
5806 North Vancouver Avenue
Portland, OR 97217
503-286-4149
www.aurorasilk.com

Aurora Silk sells organic, sustainable, cruelty-free silk yarns.

Outdoor Fire Pits and Fireplace Accessories

Country Flame
900 George Street
Marshfield, MO 65706
417-859-0990
www.countryflame.com

Country Flame sells a variety of wood and pellet stove inserts as well as corn-burning stoves.

FireplacesNow.com
4577 Lyman Drive
Hilliard, OH 43026
877-669-4669
www.fireplacesnow.com

Fireplaces Now is a source for fireplaces, stoves, and fireplace inserts, produced by a variety of manufacturers.

Fire Science, Inc.
2153 Niagara Falls Boulevard
Amherst, NY 14228
716-568-2224
www.fire-science.com

Fire Science carries an extensive collection of outdoor fire pits and chimneys, fire pit kettles, etc.

Patio Accessories Unlimited
1136-1146 Stratford Avenue
Stratford, CT 06615
800-667-8721
www.kitchenandpatio.com

Patio Accessories Unlimited is a source of portable fire pits and fire rings.

Outdoor Furniture—
Natural

Abundant Earth
762 West Park Avenue
Port Townsend, WA 98368
888-513-2784
www.abundantearth.com

Abundant Earth offers a variety of
environmentally sensitive products,
including outdoor furnishings made
from recycled plastic.

Atlantic Adirondack Chair &
    Furniture Company
2257 Vista Parkway #23
West Palm Beach, FL 33411
866-869-8122
www.atlantic-adirondack.com

This company sells a full line of
Adirondack-style furniture from 100
percent post-consumer, high-density
polyethylene resins, and outdoor
wood furniture made from sustainably
harvested wood.

Communitymade.com
200 Tanager Lane NW
Floyd, Virginia 24091
www.communitymade.com

Communitymade.com is an online
store that sells products handcrafted
by intentional communities (small
communities of persons pursuing

common interests and sharing basic
resources) throughout the United
States. Among the many items they
sell on the Web site are all-natural
hemp hammocks.

Furniture Yard
888-346-8307
www.furnitureyard.com

Furnitureyard.com sells wooden outdoor furniture—tables, chairs,
loungers, etc.—made from eucalyptus
grown and harvested on Forest Stewardship Council–approved plantations.

Gardener's Supply Company
888-833-1412
www.gardeners.com

Gardener's Supply Company sells an
extensive array of outdoor living
products, including a small selection
of furniture made from sustainably
harvested wood.

Green Culture
32 Rancho Circle
Lake Forest, CA 92630
877-204-7336
www.eco-furniture.com

Eco-Furniture.com offers products
made from recycled materials, ecologically harvested timber, and other
earth-friendly ingredients.

MoonWeavers
PO Box 191
Monticello, KY 42633
606-348-1764
www.rainbowhammocks.com

MoonWeavers hammocks are handmade by members of Wimmin's Land
Trust, an intentional community dedicated to sustainable ecoliving.

The Open Room
370 Walnut Avenue
Ketchum, ID 83340
208-622-0222
www.openroomfurniture.com

The Open Room sells a broad range of
outdoor furniture from several designers in sustainably, responsibly harvested
jarrah wood, cedar, wicker, and more.

Rawganique.com
9000 Rayelyn Lane
Denman Island, BC V0R 1T0
Canada
877-729-4367
www.rawganique.com

Rawganique.com offers a wide variety
of products made from sustainable and
natural fibers. They sell a 100 percent
hemp hammock for two.

Wicker Woman
1250 Highway 25
Angora, MN 55703
218-666-6189
www.wickerwoman.com

Wicker Woman offers resources and
information on wicker furniture
repair.

Paint

AFM Safecoat & Safechoice
800-239-0321
www.afmsafecoat.com

AFM provides a complete range of
chemically responsible building and
maintenance products.

Bio Paints
4096 Highway 6401/Hanwell Road
Fredericton, NB E3B 4Y9
Canada
506-366-3529
www.biopaints.com

Bio Paints sells natural paint and coating products for walls, floors, furniture, windows, doors, and other
surfaces.

Eco-House Inc. Natural Products
PO Box 220, Station A
Fredericton, NB E3B 4Y9
Canada
877-326-4687
www.eco-house.com

Eco-House carries a wide variety of
solvent-free, silicate wall paint.

The Old Fashioned Milk Paint
    Company, Inc.
436 Main Street
Groton, MA 01450
866-350-6455
www.milkpaint.com

The Old Fashioned Milk Paint
Company creates authentic milk paint
in a variety of colors.

Paint—Wood Finishes

AFM SafeCoat & SafeChoice
800-239-0321
www.afmsafecoat.com

AFM provides a complete range of
chemically responsible building and
maintenance products.

Auro USA Natural Products
1340-G Industrial Avenue
Petaluma, CA 94952
888-302-9352
www.aurousa.com

Auro carries natural exterior and interior paints and finishes for a variety of
surfaces, including wood.

Tried & True Wood Finishes
14 Prospect Street
Trumansburg, NY 14886
607-387-9280
www.triedandtruewoodfinish.com

Tried & True carries environmentally
safe, solvent-free wood finishes made
from polymerized linseed oil.

Paper Products

Seventh Generation
212 Battery Street
Suite A
Burlington, VT 05401
800-456-1191
www.seventhgeneration.com

Seventh Generation manufactures a
wide range of home-care products
including 100 percent recycled fiber
bathroom and facial tissues, which are
not chlorine-bleached. They provide
consumer education and support community and environmental nonprofit
organizations.

Personal Care

Aubrey Organics
4419 North Manhattan Avenue
Tampa, FL 33614
800-282-7394
www.aubrey-organics.com

Aubrey Organics creates and sells natural and organic hair and skin care products, including makeup and perfume.

Avalon Natural Products
1105 Industrial Avenue
Petaluma, CA 94952
800-227-5120
www.avalonnaturalproducts.com

Avalon Natural Products manufactures and sells six brand names of natural personal and beauty care products including deodorants, bath products, and skin and lip balm.

French Transit, LTD
398 Beach Road
Burlingame, CA 94010
800-829-7625
www.thecrystal.com

French Transit sells crystal rock deodorant in several forms, including a liquid roll-on.

Janice's
30 Arbor Street South
Hartford, CT 06106
1-800-526-4237
www.janices.com

Janice's products provide comfort and relief to scores of people who suffer from sensitivities, allergies, and dermatological problems.

JASON Natural Cosmetics
3515 Eastham Drive
Culver City, CA 90232
877-527-6601
www.jason-natural.com

JASON sells botanically based personal care products that contain no petrolatum, mineral oils, or environmentally hazardous ingredients. JASON products are not animal-tested, and several products contain ingredients that are certified organic.

Kiss My Face
PO Box 224
144 Main Street
Gardiner, NY 12525
800-262-5477
www.kissmyface.com

Kiss My Face is a line of natural personal care products, including skin and hair care items, made with natural botanicals and limited chemical ingredients. Some products contain organic ingredients.

NatraCare
14901 East Hampden Avenue
Suite 190
Aurora, CO 80014
303-617-3495
www.natracare.com

NatraCare is committed to offering organic and natural solutions for personal health care that leave a soft footprint on the earth.

Nature's Gate
Levlad, Inc.
601 22nd Street
San Francisco, CA 94107
866-972-6879

Nature's Gate is a company dedicated to developing personal care products based upon botanical remedies.

NEEDS, Inc.
800-634-1380
www.needs.com

NEEDS is an information and product warehouse, supplying a variety of brands of natural health and personal care items.

Organic Essentials
www.organicessentials.com

The mission of Organic Essentials is to expand organic agriculture by building the world's leading brand of high quality, certified organic cotton personal care products.

Real Purity, Inc.
PO Box 2858
Crossville, TN 38557
800-253-1694
www.realpurity.com

Real Purity offers a full line of all-natural hair, skin, body care, and cosmetic products for the entire family.

Tom's of Maine
Consumer Dialogue Department
302 Lafayette Center
Kennebunk, ME 04043
800-367-8667
www.tomsofmaine.com

Tom's of Maine makes and sells toothpastes and mouthwashes, deodorants and antiperspirants, and hair care products as well as herbal supplements made from naturally derived ingredients. Products are not tested on animals. Packaging is environmentally sound, and the company donates 10 percent of its profits to charity.

Weleda, Inc.
1 Closter Road
Palisades, NY 10964
800-265-2615
www.weleda.com

Weleda makes and sells a wide range of natural personal care products, using organic and wild-crafted ingredients. Weleda also carries a line of homeopathic remedies.

Pest Control

Eartheasy
PO Box 531
Parksville, BC V9P 2G6
Canada
www.eartheasy.com

Eartheasy offers information, activities, and ideas to help live more simply, efficiently, and with less impact on the environment. They have devoted an entire section of their Web site to natural pest control.

Etex Limited
3200 Polaris Avenue
Suite 9
Las Vegas, NV 89102
702-364-5911
www.etex-ltd.com/index.html

Electrogun is a technique for eliminating dry wood termites.

Gardens Alive!
5100 Schenley Place
Lawrenceburg, IN 47025
513-354-1483
www.gardensalive.com

Gardens Alive! is one of the country's leading mail-order companies dedicated to the biological control of garden pests and the distribution of environmentally responsible products that work. They sell a variety of natural pest controls, including Neem-Away Insect Spray.

Havahart Traps
800-800-1819
www.havahart.com

By offering bird feeders, live animal cage traps, dog crates, dog doors, pet electronics, stray cat rescue kits, and rabbit homes, Havahart covers a wide spectrum that truly is caring control for pets and wildlife.

Natural Pest Controls
8864 Little Creek Drive
Orangevale, CA 95662
916-726-0855
www.natpestco.com

Natural Pest Controls sells beneficial insects, ladybugs, praying mantis eggs, fish, and bacteria as natural ways to control pests in the garden.

Peaceful Valley Farm and
    Garden Supply
PO Box 2209
125 Clydesdale Court
Grass Valley, CA 95945
888-784-1722
www.groworganic.com

Peaceful Valley Farm Supply offers supplies for organic gardening and farming. They have many natural and nontoxic methods for pest control available.

Pest A Cator
Global Instruments
819 Industrial Drive
Trenton, MO 64683
800-338-5028
www.global-instruments.com/what.htm

Pest A Cator sells a device to repel rodents without chemicals, exterminators, or traps.

Real Goods
360 Interlocken Boulevard
Suite 300
Broomfield, CO 80021-3440
800-762-7325
www.realgoods.com

Real Goods has products to control pests without the use of poisons or inhumane devices.

Seabright Laboratories
4026 Harlan Street
Emeryville, CA 94608-3604
800-284-7363
www.seabrightlabs.com

Seabright Laboratories designs and manufactures high-quality insect traps, insect trapping adhesive, roach control systems, and humane mouse-traps.

Victor Pest
800-800-1819
www.victorpest.com

Victor Pest has a variety of products that are low in toxicity or nontoxic for controlling pests of all kinds.

Pesticide and Pollution Information Sources

Extension Toxicology Network
5123 Comstock Hall
Cornell University
Ithaca, NY 14853
607-255-1866
pmep.cce.cornell.edu/profiles/extoxnet

EXTOXNET is a pesticide information project of cooperative extension offices of Cornell University, Michigan State University, Oregon State University, and University of California at Davis. EXTOXNET provides pesticide information profiles for those who want to know about the potential effects of pesticides.

National Pesticide Information Center
800-858-7378
npic.orst.edu/index.html

The National Pesticide Information Center (NPIC) serves as a source of objective, science-based pesticide information on a wide range of pesticide-related topics. A toll-free telephone service provides pesticide information to callers in the continental United States, Puerto Rico, and the Virgin Islands.

Pet Care

All the Best Pet Care
8050 Lake City Way
Seattle, WA 98115
206-254-0199
www.allthebestpetcare.com

All the Best Pet Care sells all-natural pet foods from a variety of manufacturers.

Biocontrol Network
5116 Williamsburg Road
Brentwood, TN 37027
800-441-2847
www.biconet.com

Biocontrol Network promotes products and methods that use natural, nontoxic ingredients for animal care.

Havahart Traps
800-800-1819
www.havahart.com

By offering bird feeders, live animal cage traps, dog crates, dog doors, pet electronics, stray cat rescue kits, and rabbit homes, Havahart covers a wide spectrum that truly is caring control for pets and wildlife.

Natural Animal Health Products
7000 US 1 North Street
Augustine, FL 32095
800-274-7387
www.naturalanimal.com

Natural Animal Health Products offers products that are effective, environmentally sound, and based on herbal and earthly wisdom. They supply herbal flea powders, herbal shampoos, pet supplements, and homeopathic remedies, among other items.

NaturesPet.com
23 Ackerman Avenue
Elmwood Park, NJ 07407
201-796-0627
www.naturespet.com

NaturesPet.com provides natural and holistic pet care products.

Solid Gold Health Products
    for Pets, Inc.
900 Vernon Way, #101
El Cajon, CA 92020
800-364-4863
www.solidgoldhealth.com

Solid Gold has a variety of natural, holistic pet products that include food, supplements, and health and coat care products.

Plant Room Deodorizers

Earth Friendly Products
44 Green Bay Road
Winnetka, IL 60093
800-335-3267
www.ecos.com

Earth Friendly Products produces
Uni-Fresh, a nontoxic air freshener.

Ecco Bella
50 Church Street
Suite 108
Montclair, NJ 07042
877-696-2220
www.eccobella.com

Ecco Bella produces Ecco Mists, air
fresheners made only with essential
oils, water, and emulsifiers.

Kokopelli's Green Market
PO Box 353
20 Farr Way
Brandon, VT 05733
802-247-4100
www.kokogm.com

Kokopelli's Green Market sells a broad
range of natural home products
including the following natural room
air fresheners: Ecco Mist; Air Scense;
Uni-Fresh.

Plastic Lumber

Ecologic, Inc.
921 Sherwood Drive
Lake Bluff, IL 60044
800-899-8004
www.ecoloft.com

Ecologic designs and manufactures
products from recycled materials.
They have an entire line of outdoor
furniture made from recycled plastic.

Green Culture
32 Rancho Circle
Lake Forest, CA 92630
877-204-7336
www.eco-furniture.com

Green Culture offers a variety of plastic lumber outdoor furniture as well
as other products made from recycled
materials, ecologically harvested
timber, and other earth-friendly
ingredients.

Renew Resources
780 Birchmount Road #1
Toronto, ON M1K 5H4
Canada
800-439-5028
www.renewresources.com

Renew Resources manufactures and
sells products that are made from recycled materials. They have a line of
Commingled Plastic Lumber that is
manufactured from recycled plastic.

Rain Barrels

Clean Air Gardening, LC
5802 Penrose Avenue
Dallas, TX 75206
214-370-0530
www.cleanairgardening.com

This is an online source for rain barrels in different sizes, styles, and materials, with or without pumps.

Gardener's Supply Company
128 Intervale Road
Burlington, VT 05401
888-833-1412
www.gardeners.com

An extensive gardening catalog and online resource that includes assorted rain barrels and rain barrel components.

The Green Culture-Watersavers.com
32 Rancho Circle
Lake Forest, CA 92630
877-204-7336
www.watersavers.com

The Green Culture's Watersavers.com Web site is dedicated to the conservation of water through water filters, shower filters, rain barrels, water heaters, and other ecofriendly products.

Rodent Control

Havahart
69 North Locust Street
Lititz, PA 17543-1714
800-800-1819
www.havahart.com

Havahart traps feature a variety of sizes and styles to catch many different wild animals.

Kness Manufacturing Company, Inc.
2053 Highway 5 South
PO Box 70
Albia, IA 52531
800-247-5062
www.kness.com

Kness has a line of tested products for catching all kinds of pests from ants to rats.

Pest A Cator
Global Instruments
819 Industrial Drive
Trenton, MO 64683
800-338-5028
www.globalinstruments.com/what.htm

Pest A Cator sells a device to repel rodents without chemicals, exterminators, or traps.

Salt Lamps

American BlueGreen, LLC
179 Capital Lane
Roseburg, OR 97470
877-224-4872
www.americanbluegreen.com

American BlueGreen sells salt lamps in two sizes.

ArtPol
508-615-6604
www.art-pol.net

ArtPol sells an extensive line of salt lamps in a variety of sizes, shapes, and styles.

Shower Filters/ Dechlorinators

Custom Pure
1514 Northeast 179th Street
Seattle, WA 98155
206-363-0039
www.custompure.com

Custom Pure designs and manufactures water filtration and water treatment systems. Products include water treatment filters and shower dechlorinators.

Green Home
850 24th Avenue
San Francisco, CA 94121
877-282-6400
www.greenhome.com

Green Home is an online source for a variety of green-living products, including a line of shower filters. Additionally, Green Home sells low-flow faucet heads and aerators and hemp shower curtains.

Solar Energy Products

Energy Outfitters, LTD
543 Northeast E Street
Grants Pass, OR 97526
800-467-6527
www.energyoutfitters.com

Energy Outfitters carries a wide range of solar energy products for the home.

Gaiam, Inc.
360 Interlocken Boulevard
Suite 300
Broomfield, CO 80021
877-989-6321
www.gaiam.com

Gaiam has an extensive selection of solar energy products, from lighting to water heaters and more.

Solar Direct
5919 21st Street E
Bradenton, FL 34203
800-333-9276
www.solardirect.com

Solar Direct specializes in solar water heating and solar electric technology.

Solar Garden/Path Lights

Brendagan Enterprises, LLC
PO Box 516301
Dallas, TX 75251
www.4mypatio.com

This is a good source for an extensive variety of solar path and landscape lights from the simple to the ornate.

Plow & Hearth
PO Box 6000
Madison, VA 22727
800-494-7544
www.plowhearth.com

Plow & Hearth sells a wide selection of home products, including a small collection of solar path lights.

Solar Radios

The Green Store
71 Main Street
Belfort, ME 04915
207-338-4045
www.greenstore.com

The Green Store specializes in green living products for the home.

Testing Kits

Abundant Earth
762 West Park Avenue
Port Townsend, WA 98368
888-513-2784
www.abundantearth.com

Abundant Earth offers lead, mold, and water test kits, along with providing other environmentally sensitive products and services.

Black Mountain Stores
1721 North Texas Avenue
Odessa, TX 79761-1226
800-760-7942
www.katadyn.net

Black Mountain Stores carry a full line of a variety of home testing kits.

Tile

American Tile Supply
2839 Merrell Road
Dallas, TX 75229
972-243-2377
www.americantilesupply.com

American Tile Supply sells a wide variety of stone and tile flooring options.

Ventilation Units—Heat Recovery

Air Mechanical, Inc.
16411 Aberdeen Street NE
Ham Lake, MN 55304
763-434-7747
www.airmechanicalinc.com

Air Mechanical sells Venmar heat recovery ventilation units.

Thermal Associates
21 Thomson Avenue
Glens Falls, NY 12801
800-654-8263
www.thermalassociates.com

Thermal Associates sells Venmar/vanEE heat recovery ventilation units.

Washing Machines/Dryers

Asko North America
AM Appliance Group
PO Box 851805
Richardson, TX 75085-1805
800-898-1879
www.askousa.com

Asko manufactures a variety of stainless steel energy- and water-efficient washing machines and dryers that meet or exceed Energy Star standards.

Maytag Customer Service
240 Edwards Street
Cleveland, TN 37311
800-688-9900
www.maytag.com

Maytag manufactures the Neptune line, washing machines and dryers that are energy efficient, meet Energy Star standards, and are water-conserving.

Miele, Inc.
9 Independence Way
Princeton, NJ 08540
800-843-7231
www.miele.com

Miele washing machines have low water consumption and meet Energy Star standards. Some washing machines have special, extra-water cycles for those who are highly sensitive to detergents and need deeper rinsing.

Water Filters

Brita Products Company
PO Box 24305
Oakland, CA 94623-9981
800-242-7482
www.brita.com

Brita carries a line of faucet-filtering devices and water-filtering pitchers using carbon filters and ion-exchangers.

Culligan International
One Culligan Parkway
Northbrook, IL 60062-6209
847-205-5979
www.culligan.com

Culligan sells drinking water filtration systems, shower filters, and whole-house water treatment systems.

Gaiam, Inc.
360 Interlocken Boulevard
Suite 300
Broomfield, CO 80021
877-989-6321
www.gaiam.com

Gaiam sells a variety of products designed to create a healthy, holistic lifestyle. Their product line includes several brands of titanium silicate/carbon block water filters; ceramic and carbon water filtering crocks; reverse osmosis systems; and faucet filters.

Polar Bear Water Group
PO Box 113
#1 Main Street
Pickardville, AB T0G 1W0
Canada
800-363-7845
www.polarbearwater.com

Polar Bear is known for their stainless steel appliances for water distillation and purification.

Pur
800-787-5463
www.purwater.com

Pur has an extensive line of faucet filters, water pitcher filters, and whole-house water treatment systems utilizing activated carbon filters.

Water Fountains

Gaiam, Inc.
360 Interlocken Boulevard
Suite 300
Broomfield, CO 80021
877-989-6321
www.gaiam.com

Gaiam sells a variety of meditative water fountains made from copper and natural river stones.

Water Purification Tablets

Eastern Mountain Sports
1 Vose Farm Road
Peterborough, NH 03458
888-463-6367
www.ems.com

Eastern Mountain Sports sells a variety of water purification tablets and drops.

Water-Saving Fixtures

American Standard
PO Box 6820
1 Centennial Plaza
Piscataway, NJ 08855-6820
800-442-1902
www.americanstandard-us.com

American Standard produces a wide variety of bathroom and kitchen fixtures. They carry a full line of low-consumption toilets.

Kohler
800-456-4537
www.us.kohler.com

Kohler manufactures a variety of bathroom fixtures, among them water-saving, low-flow toilets, showerheads, and faucets.

Lifekind Products, Inc.
PO Box 1774
Grass Valley, CA 95945
800-284-4983
www.lifekind.com

Lifekind has an extensive line of ecologically sound products for the home, including shower dechlorinators, organic bath towels, and organic shower curtains.

Wind Energy Systems—Residential

American Wind Energy Association
1101 14th Street NW
12th Floor
Washington, DC 20005
202-383-2500
www.awea.org

The American Wind Energy Association provides useful information concerning many aspects of wind energy.

Bergey Wind Power Company
2001 Priestly Avenue
Norman, OK 73069
405-364-4212
www.bergey.com

Bergey manufactures and sells wind energy systems for home and farm use.

Daystar Energy Systems, Inc.
Five Cliffordale Park
Rochester, NY 14609
585-377-1155
www.daystarenergysystems.com

Daystar sells a number of renewable energy systems for homes, including small wind turbines.

Solar Wind Works
PO Box 2511
Truckee, CA 96160
877-682-4503
www.solarwindworks.com

Solar Wind Works is a distributor of wind turbines for on- and off-grid customers.

Windows—Energy Efficient

Andersen Corporation
100 Fourth Avenue N
Bayport, MN 55003-1096
651-264-5150
www.andersenwindows.com

Andersen is a well-known name in windows, with dealers located throughout the country. They sell glazed and low-e windows.

Do-It-Yourself Sun Control
800-836-8478
www.do-it-yourself-windowtinting.com

A source of window tints, window tinting tools, and window films for the do-it-yourselfer.

Gaiam, Inc.
360 Interlocken Boulevard
Suite 300
Broomfield, CO 80021
877-989-6321
www.gaiam.com

Gaiam carries natural daylighting products, low-e window films, and reflective insulation.

Hurd Windows
575 South Whelen Avenue
Medford, WI 54451
800-223-4873
www.hurd.com

Hurd manufactures and sells insulating and low-e glass windows. Dealers are located around the country.

Window Shades/Quilts

1WindowQuilts.com
4 Laurette Drive
Essex Junction, VT 05452
877-966-3678
www.1windowquilts.com

1WindowQuilts.com sells insulating, high-value window quilts in several colors and styles.

Solar Components Corporation
121 Valley Street
Manchester, NH 03103
603-668-8186
www.solar-components.com

Solar Components makes and sells window quilts and window shades.

Recommended Magazines and Newsletters

Body + Soul
20 West 43rd Street, 25th Floor
New York, NY 10036
212-827-8000
www.marthastewart.com

A holistic approach to living—one
that recognizes the interdependence
between physical and spiritual health,
relationships, and the environment.

Breathe
Breathe Media, Inc.
141 Fifth Avenue
New York, NY 10010
www.breathemag.com

Breathe is a unique new magazine that
understands the desire to go deeper
and to find meaning and balance while
living in a material world.

The Green Guide
Prince Street Station
PO Box 567
New York, NY 10012
212-598-4910 (voicemail)

The Green Guide and www.thegreen
guide.com are published by the Green
Guide Institute, an independent media
service designed to provide new, informational, and educational material to
consumers and others. The mission of
the Green Guide Institute is to offer
the most objective, responsible, and
accurate environmental and health
information in print or on the Web.
Subscribe at www.thegreenguide.com
to receive bimonthly issues, free
Pocket Guides, product reports, and
more than $350 worth of coupons.

Interiors & Sources
840 US Highway One
Suite 330
North Palm Beach, FL 33408
561-627-3393
www.ISDesignet.com

Interiors & Sources magazine is dedicated to people; it recognizes the
designers, firms, and organizations
that are making significant contributions to the profession as well as
working toward promoting the value
of design services in the creation of
healthy, functional, and aesthetically
pleasing environments.

Mother Earth News
1503 Southwest 42nd Street
Topeka, KS 66609-1265
www.motherearthnews.com

Mother Earth News serves readers who
have a passion for living more satisfying, self-reliant, and sustainable lives.

Mother Jones
222 Sutter Street
6th Floor
San Francisco, CA 94108
(415) 321-1700
www.motherjones.com

Mother Jones is an independent non-profit whose roots lie in a commitment to social justice implemented through first-rate investigative reporting.

Natural Home & Garden
201 East Fourth Street
Loveland, Colorado 80537
(800) 272-2193
www.naturalhomemagazine.com

Natural Home & Garden offers today's health-conscious, environmentally concerned homeowners the information they need to practice earth-inspired living.

O at Home
Harpo Productions, Inc.
110 North Carpenter Street
Chicago, IL 60607
(312) 633-1000
www.oprah.com

O at Home magazine is written for real people with real design needs and challenges.

Ode
PO Box 2402
3000 CK Rotterdam
The Netherlands
Tel: + 31 (0) 10 4360995
www.odemagazine.com

Ode brings you inspiration and hope with meaningful stories of people, culture, environment, integral science and health, forward-looking politics, and responsible business.

OnEarth
Natural Resources Defense Council
40 West 20th Street
New York, NY 10011
(212) 727-2700
www.nrdc.org/onearth/

OnEarth, NRDC's award-winning environmental magazine, explores politics, nature, wildlife, science, the threats to our planet, and the solutions that promise to heal and protect it.

Real Simple
Time/Life Building
Rockefeller Center
New York, NY 10020
www.realsimple.com

Real Simple helps its readers do what they need to do so they have more time to enjoy what they want to do.

Resurgence
Ford House, Hartland
Bideford, Devon, EX39 6EE, UK
Tel: +44 (0) 1237 441293
www.resurgence.org

Resurgence features positive ideas about the theory and practice of good living: permaculture, community-supported agriculture, local economics, ecological building, sacred architecture, art in the environment, small schools, and deep ecology.

Sierra
85 Second Street
2nd Floor
San Francisco, CA 94105
(415) 977-5500
www.sierraclub.org

Sierra is a bimonthly national magazine publishing writing, photography, and art about the natural world.

Spirituality and Health
74 Trinity Place
New York, NY 10006-2088
(212) 602-0705
www.spiritualityhealth.com

Spirituality and Health strives to address spiritual questions from diverse viewpoints, drawing on the world's wisdom traditions as well as science, psychology, sociology, and medicine.

Utne
1624 Harmon Place
Suite 330
Minneapolis, MN 55403
612-338-5040
www.utne.com

Utne magazine reprints the best articles from more than 2,000 alternative media sources bringing the latest ideas and trends emerging into culture.

What Is Enlightenment?
PO Box 2360
Lenox, MA 01240
(413) 637-6000
www.wie.org

What Is Enlightenment? is a spiritual, cultural, philosophical, and otherwise category-busting magazine committed to bringing a new perspective to politics, business, science, the arts, and the environment.

Trade Organizations

Miscellaneous

CMA (Cookware Manufacturers Association)
PO Box 531335
Birmingham, AL 35253-1335
205-823-3448
www.cookware.org

CMA is a nonprofit trade organization dedicated to continuously researching and discovering new technology for cookware and promoting its use.

Epsom Salt Industry Council
www.epsomsaltcouncil.org

The Epsom Salt Industry Council is a group of Epsom salt manufacturers who provide information to and education for the public on the uses of Epsom salts.

Hemp Industries Association
PO Box 1080
Occidental, CA 95465
707-874-3648
www.hempindustries.org

The Hemp Industries Association supports the hemp industry through educating the public, developing new uses for hemp, and encouraging the use of environmentally sound farming methods.

New Hope Natural Media
Natural Food Merchandizer
1401 Pearl Street
Boulder, CO 80302
303-939-8440
www.newhope.com

The definitive publication about the natural products industry.

Organic Trade Association
PO Box 547
Greenfield, MA 01302
413-774-7511
www.ota.com

The Organic Trade Association encourages and supports the organic industry in North America. Numerous organic resources are represented, among them the organic cotton growers.

Solar

Solar Energy Industries Association
805 15th Street NW
Suite 510
Washington, DC 20005
202-682-0556
www.seia.org

SEIA is a trade organization for all facets of the solar energy industry, with the goal of increasing the use of solar technologies.

Stone

Marble Institute of America
28901 Clemens Road
Suite 100
Westlake, OH 44145
440-250-9222
www.marble-institute.com

The Marble Institute provides information regarding the use of natural stone and standards in the industry. Among its goals are the education of consumers and industry workers and the promotion of the use of natural stone building materials.

Tiles

Terrazzo Tile and Marble Association
    of Canada
163 Buttermill Avenue
Unit 8
Concord, ON L4K 3X8
Canada
800-201-8599
www.ttmac.com

The Terrazzo Tile and Marble Association provides information and resources within the tile, marble, and stone industry and works to promote the use of these natural materials in building.

Toxics

North American Hazardous Materials
    Management Association
    (NAHMMA)
8826 Santa Fe Drive
Suite 208
Overland Park, KS 66212
913-381-4458
www.nahmma.org

The NAHMMA is a professional organization that is dedicated to pollution prevention and the reduction of hazardous constituents entering the waste stream from households, small businesses, and other entities.

Wood

Hardwood Manufacturers Association
American Hardwood Information
    Center
400 Penn Center Boulevard
Suite 530
Pittsburgh, PA 15235
800-373-9663
www.hardwoodinfo.com

The American Hardwood Information Center provides extensive information on hardwoods and hardwood resources.

in gratitude

Margot Schupf called me when she accepted her new job at Rodale as executive editor of *Organic Style* books and suggested that I write this book—a complete compendium of how to live in a natural, ecofriendly way at home. My reaction was that I would love to do so, even if I was terrified and humbled by the responsibility. I am grateful for her vision.

Rodale's Karen Bolesta has been a thoughtful, engaged, wonderfully straightforward, and committed editor for *Home Enlightenment*. She, too, has believed in this book from the beginning. I am so grateful for this and for how doggedly she has slogged through such a very long manuscript.

My thanks also go to my agent, Lisa Ross of The Spieler Agency, for her advocacy, laser-beam-like insights, and tenacity, and to Randy Paynter and Marlin Miller, CEO and COO respectively of Care2.com, for their flexibility and their support of my taking a sabbatical to write the book.

Many people helped me with practical writing matters, from researching to proofing. My gratitude goes to Ashling Kelly, my nephew David Keck, Jodi Marcus, and Jessica Puglisi and to Judy Rubenstein for her valuable editing help. Gratitude also goes to Rachel Pollack for her *The Shining Tribe Tarot* deck; it often helped me find my way.

Last, I'd like to express my gratitude to my friends and family, who kept me from being overwhelmed with the demands of the project. In particular, I'd like to thank friends Kate DeChard, Amy Goldman, Cait Johnson, Pat Beecher, Roie Lattimer, Judith Asphar, Deb Walker, and my former husband, Daniel Berthold. My three sisters, Kathy Gibbons, Carolyn Keck, and Yari Bond, and my mother, Nancy Prosser, always sent me their love. Thank you! And to my daughter, Lily—well, she got through another book project of mine, and I'd like to thank her for her patience and open heart.

literary and
photography sources

The "Earth Prayer," "Water Prayer," "Fire Prayer," and "Air Prayer" are excerpted from *Earth, Water, Fire & Air: Essential Ways of Connecting to Spirit*, © 2003 by Cait Johnson (Woodstock, VT: SkyLight Paths Publishing). $19.95 + $3.75 s/h. Order by mail or call 800-962-4544 or online at www.skylightpaths.com. Permission granted by SkyLight Paths Publishing, PO Box 237, Woodstock, VT 05091.

The carrot photos on page 4 are used with permission from Cilla Sturt.

"Why Reuse Beats Recycling" on page 39 is adapted from *Choose to Reuse: An Encyclopedia of Services, Products, Programs, & Charitable Organizations That Foster Reuse* by Nikki and David Goldbeck © 1995 and used with permission from Ceres Press.

"The Energy Cost of Cooking Appliances" on page 194 is adapted from information published by the California Energy Commission and is used with permission.

The photographs of water crystals on page 203 are used with permission and are featured in *Messages from Water* by Masaru Emoto (HADO Kyoikusha Co., Ltd., 1999; www.hado.com); copyright is held by I.H.M. General Institute.

The water meditation on page 205 is used with permission from William E. Marks.

The information in "Animal Testing, Animal Welfare, and Personal Care Products" on page 233 is reprinted with permission from *The Green Guide*. Subscribe at www.thegreenguide.com to receive bimonthly issues, plus free Pocket Guides, product reports, and more than $350 worth of coupons.

"What Is Sound Healing" on page 415 is used with permission of Zacciah Blackburn, The Center of Light, PO Box 389, Ascutney, VT, 05039, 802-674-9585; for more information, visit www.thecenteroflight.net and www.worldsoundhealing.org, or e-mail info@sunreed.com.

We have made every effort to credit sources and contributors in the text; we would be pleased to make appropriate changes and add additional credits for future editions of the book.

index

Boldface page references indicate illustrations.
Underscored references indicate boxed text.

F